OUTRAGEOUS FORTUNE

OUTRAGEOUS FORTUNE

The Tragedy of Leopold III
of the Belgians
1901–1941

ROGER KEYES

Secker & Warburg
London

First published in England 1984 by
Martin Secker & Warburg Limited
54 Poland Street, London W1V 3DF

Copyright © Roger Keyes 1984

British Library Cataloguing in Publication Data

Keyes, Roger
Outrageous fortune.
1. Leopold III, King of the Belgians.
2. Belgium—Kings and rulers—Biography
I. Title
949.3'042'0924   DH687

ISBN 0-436-23320-7

Photoset in Great Britain by
Rowland Phototypesetting Limited, Bury St Edmunds, Suffolk
and printed by St Edmundsbury Press
Bury St Edmunds, Suffolk

To my father, Admiral of the Fleet Lord Keyes of Zee-brugge and Dover, whose constant concern, to the end of his life, was that the facts chronicled in this biography should be fully revealed.

'He loved chivalrie, trouthe and honour, fredom and cur-teisie. . . He was a verray, parfit gentil knyght.'

Geoffrey Chaucer,
The Canterbury Tales

'The love of one's neighbours, the sense of duty, truth and justice, if applied to daily life, would spare mankind count-less sufferings, troubles and anxieties . . . The solution of the problems which oppress the world can only be found in the practice of Charity between individuals and between nations.'

LEOPOLD III, 1936

Contents

List of Illustrations, Maps
and Documents

Between pages 144 and 145

Between pages 304 and 305

Documents

Introduction

When King Leopold III died on September 25th 1983 my sorrow was all the more profound because my biography, of which this is the first volume, had not yet been published. He had been looking forward to its appearance, and I to the pleasure of handing him the first copy. Sadly he had decided not to read the complete manuscript I sent him for his comments, because he did not want there to be any suggestion that he might have influenced me. In the initial stages of its compilation, however, the King co-operated unstintingly – as did his wife, Princess Lilian – throughout my three weeks' stay at Laeken in 1953, by answering my innumerable questions with the utmost frankness, and giving me his personal recollections of every stage of his life.

The warmth of the King's reception on this and all the occasions on which I have met him, and his bestowal of this unique privilege, was because I was the son of a man of whom he said 'No man ever had a better friend.' Like his father, Albert I, the King had a great affection and admiration for Admiral Keyes, as he had for them. Indeed, the three men were alike in many ways. They all shared the same high principles and the qualities of dauntless courage and tenacity of purpose, combined with humility and gentleness of manner. And all three possessed the gift of inspiring the fervent devotion of their followers.

On my father's death in December 1945, I inherited not only his diaries and papers covering King Leopold's brave conduct and loyal co-operation with the Allies in May 1940, which he had witnessed, but his determination to put the record straight with regard to this most unjustly maligned monarch. My father's initial attempts to nail the 'great lie' by which, on May 28th 1940, the French Premier, Paul Reynaud, turned the much praised King and his army into the reviled scapegoats for the defeat of France – and of the British Army – were frustrated by Winston Churchill's government. But as described at the conclusion of this volume, in June 1941, despite the Cabinet's attempts to muzzle him, the Admiral's libel action against the *Daily Mirror* achieved a complete vindication of the King in the world press, under headlines such as 'Leopold was a hero'. But since memories are short and mud sticks, many of the lies which were spawned as a result of Reynaud's character assassination of the King are still in circulation.

Hence the need, which I have tried to fulfil, for a full-scale exposure of the truth about the late King, based on the irrefutable documentary evidence and testimony of all those involved. Since I embarked on this project after my retirement from the Royal Navy in 1949, I have spent all the time I could spare from my other commitments, gradually building up the mass of comprehensive source material, in addition to my father's archives (some of it secret and hitherto unpublished), on which this biography is based. In compiling it over the years I have received help, advice and encouragement from so many people that lack of space prevents me from naming them all.

Firstly, my warm thanks are due to my wife and family for their unfailing help and support from start to finish. I must also express my gratitude to the following people for their co-operation in the early stages of my work. To Tom Lindsay for his help in drafting the original manuscript; to Major Claude Knight, formerly head of the Belgian Section of SOE, for his reminiscences; to Professor Cammaerts for providing much information and source material; to Sir Basil Liddell Hart for doing likewise in even greater measure and, above all, to Brigadier George Davy for recounting his experiences as head of the British Liaison Mission at King Leopold's GHQ, and allowing me to quote from his reports and unpublished memoirs. During the same period I received invaluable help from a number of distinguished Belgians, including Professor Pirenne, Vicomte Gatien du Parc, Comte Willy de Grunne, Colonel Hubert Rombauts, Colonel Bill Grisar and Commandant Georges Cuissart de Grelle. To Jean Vanwelkenhuyzen, whom I first met in those early days and who later became head of the *Centre de Recherches et d'Etudes Historiques de la Seconde Guerre Mondiale*, I owe a special debt of gratitude for his friendly co-operation over the years. I am also grateful to M. Verhaeghe of Belgian Radio and Television, for furnishing me with the results of his deep historical research into the Royal Question.

For their co-operation in more recent years I am indebted to Ronald Lewin, who helped to reduce my over-long manuscript to manageable proportions, and to Dr Brian Bond, Dr Noble Frankland and Professor John Rogister, who read it and made suggestions for its improvement, as well as providing me with valuable information. For doing me this same favour I am most grateful to Colonel Baron Philippe van Caubergh, to Mrs Marjory Taylor and Mrs Barbara Emerson, the author of a recent biography of Leopold II, who lives in Belgium. Mrs Emerson's advice and co-operation in the last few years, and during my visits to that country, are particularly appreciated.

Above all, my thanks are due to my publishers, and especially to the late David Farrer for espousing my cause and taking me under his wing. I must also thank Peter Grose for his cheerful encouragement; Peter Leek and Helen Owen for their meticulous editorial work on my manuscript, and David Charles of Kirkham Studios, for producing such excellent maps so expeditiously.

Finally, grateful acknowledgement is made to the authors and publishers of all the books, articles and letters quoted in the text.

KEYES
West Farleigh
April 1984

CHAPTER ONE

The Cockpit of Europe

'Belgium opens to us Germany's door. We can debouch on the lower Rhine when convenient. We turn all German fortresses and stretch our hand to Holland, Hanover etc. . . . the Belgian Army once conquered, adds another 100,000 men to our effectives.'

Napoleon III, 1866

To be born the son of a famous and universally respected father can prove a *damnosa hereditas*. An outstanding parent's qualities may fail to be transmitted to the next generation. But what if a son possessing those qualities faithfully follows his father's example, steadily trains himself to be a worthy heir, then finds himself arraigned before the bar of history as false to his father's memory, a traitor in his country's time of need, a man preferring self-interest to patriotism, faint of heart and feeble of will? What if these accusations are promoted or endorsed by statesmen and soldiers, countrymen and allies? And what if they are untrue? Here are the elements of tragedy – and of the fate of King Leopold III of the Belgians.

Leopold's father never expected to be King. The younger son of a younger son, Albert was sixteen when in 1891 the death of his elder brother Baudouin unexpectedly made him heir to his formidable old uncle, Leopold II. At the age of twenty-five Albert married the Duchess Elisabeth of Bavaria, and for the next nine years their home was the Hôtel d'Assche, a spacious but unpretentious house in the Quartier Léopold of Brussels. It was here that on November 3rd 1901 the future King Leopold III was born, joined in 1903 by a brother, Charles, and after three years by a sister, Marie-José (later to marry Umberto, Crown Prince and, briefly, King of Italy).

Because of the reasonable assumption that Prince Baudouin and his descendants were destined to rule Belgium, Albert's early education was less comprehensive than he would have wished. But Leopold was now in the direct line of succession, and the consequence was a complete plan for his education, intimidating by modern standards and imposed with Victorian strictness.

The children's upbringing was simple and austere, with regular hours and a plain diet. Although a strict parent, insisting on punctuality and physical fitness, Albert was gentle, kind and considerate, while his serious

mien was relieved by a wry sense of humour. Relations between Leopold
and his father were regulated by a certain formality, but they were closer
than was usual in that period, with a strong bond of affection between
them. Indeed, Leopold's devoted admiration for his father was to be a
determining influence on his future thoughts and actions.

An early photograph recalls the brisk walks to which Albert was
addicted when he was unable to follow his favourite pastime of rock
climbing – walks during which the tall, long-legged father pressed ahead
at a steady four miles an hour, while the diminutive Leopold had to spring
to keep level. Still, he kept abreast. And there was nothing repressive
about this spartan regime. Leopold was part of a happy and close-knit
family – and he was particularly close to Albert, because he was able to
come up to his father's expectations, unlike his younger brother Charles,
who was a disappointment to his parents and whose tantrums and rages
gave advance warning of subsequent instability. As Leopold matured and
was taken more and more into his father's confidence, Albert would
express his anxieties about his 'difficult' younger son.

Unlike Leopold II, whose autocratic manner and irregular private life
had estranged him from his subjects, Albert practised a democratic way
of life, and lived as an irreproachable paterfamilias. The society life
of Brussels was of little interest to Albert or Elisabeth and their guests
rarely included any of its members. Their home was, however, fre-
quented by some of the best minds and most cultivated people in the
Western world. Thanks to Albert's thirst for knowledge and penchant for
gathering to him men and women engaged in such fields as politics,
economics, mathematics, science, engineering and exploration, the
atmosphere in which Leopold grew up and by which his own interests
were stimulated was one of civilized enthusiasm for the worlds of thought
and action. As to the realm of culture, Elisabeth, with her devotion to
music and the arts, was his guide. Her circle included men and women
from the world of music, the theatre, art, poetry, architecture, literature,
medicine and even journalism.

The family spent their summer holidays in the simple coastal villages of
Brittany or at the modest Belgian seaside town of La Panne, where they
owned an old-fashioned red-brick villa. Here Leopold learned to swim,
fish, sail and ride, and under his father's guidance he soon became a keen
and proficient mountain climber, and later an expert skier. Father and
son would go off to the Ardennes or Alps, whenever they could spare the
time, to pursue these two passions. When rock climbing the King and his
heir would be roped together, with Leopold, when he reached strong
young manhood, taking the lead.

In 1909, when Leopold had just passed his eighth birthday, the old King
died and his father succeeded as Albert I. Leopold became the Duke of
Brabant, the traditional title of the Crown Prince. The family now had to

move to the vast Château of Laeken, the Belgian equivalent of Windsor
Castle. Situated on the outskirts of Brussels and surrounded by beautiful
gardens and a spacious, wooded park, Laeken was for the children a vast
playground with its 350 acres and enormous glasshouses ablaze with
exotic plants and flowers from the Congo.

When Albert came to the throne his popularity with the Belgian people
was not based upon the dynamic qualities he was soon to reveal, but upon
the solid domestic virtues of a happy family life – beloved of the Belgians,
but notably absent from the Palace in the days of his predecessor. But
they had underestimated his qualities, for Albert was high-principled and
strong-willed. The politicians may have wanted a rubber-stamp king, but
pliability was quite foreign to Albert's character. The Socialists, who had
circulated scandalous leaflets at Leopold II's funeral, demonstrated with
shouts of 'Vive la République' at Albert's accession. Yet the burning
sincerity and firmness of his speech from the throne made a profound
impression on them. Indeed, Albert got on so well with the Socialists that
one of their leaders said that if there was ever a republic in Belgium he
would choose Albert as President.

Like his predecessors, the most important problems with which Albert
had to deal were those of internal harmony, foreign relations and
defence. Above all, he took an uncompromising stand on Belgium's
status of neutrality which had been guaranteed by the five Great Powers,
Britain, France, Prussia, Austria and Russia, at the outset of the reign
of his grandfather, the founder of the dynasty. Since these were the
issues with which Leopold was principally concerned during his years
on the throne, some of the key events in Belgium's brief history, which
were to provide precedents and guidelines for him, must now be described.

Until 1830 Belgium had neither a corporate history nor a national
identity. For centuries she has been a battlefield and a prize of victory,
dominated successively by foreign powers – Spain, Austria, France,
Holland and Germany. The armies of Marlborough and Turenne, Wel-
lington and Napoleon constantly trampled back and forth across Belgium's territory. Hardly a place-name on her map now fails to recall some
great battle of the past: Ramillies, Oudenarde, and Waterloo, besides
those which revive memories of the 1914–18 War, such as Passchendaele,
Ypres, Mons, Zeebrugge and the Yser. Indeed, no country of modern
Europe has had a more storm-ridden history.

After Napoleon's defeat, the Congress of Vienna handed over all the
provinces of the Spanish Netherlands to Holland, but in 1830 the Catholic
South rebelled. The London Conference held by Britain, France, Russia,
Austria and Prussia created a new country, Belgium, from the dissident
areas which rejected the rule of the Calvinist North. In order to stabilize a
region which, because of its geographical situation and the needs of

military strategy, offered a standing temptation to an aggressor, the articles of this convention, formally confirmed in 1839, declared that the Five Powers 'guaranteed the perpetual neutrality, integrity and inviolability of Belgian territory' and stated that 'Belgium will be bound to observe this neutrality towards all other states'. Thus a principle was established which was of crucial significance for Albert and Leopold, since it was this status of neutrality which Germany, France and Great Britain each found inconvenient and planned to violate before both the First and Second World Wars.

On July 21st 1831, Queen Victoria's revered uncle, Prince Leopold of Saxe-Coburg, was sworn in as the first King of the Belgians. Earlier that year the Belgian National Congress had decided on a constitutional monarchy, as opposed to a republic, by 152 votes to 13. Only a tiny minority of revolutionaries supported a republic, for the moderates had reminded the Assembly that a state so insecure both internally and externally needed stable institutions. The presidency of a republic, necessarily held by a Walloon or a Fleming, by a man of one political creed or another, could only be another element of instability, whereas a king, above party strife and racial rivalries, would be a strong and unifying influence.

Prince Leopold, backed by Great Britain, had been chosen by the Belgian National Congress as their King – wisely, for he was regarded as the ablest Prince of that period and was related to most of the ruling families of Europe. He had married the Prince Regent's daughter Charlotte, the Princess Royal, who died in childbirth eighteen months later. He was made a British subject, a Field Marshal and a Privy Councillor. Had his wife and son not died so tragically, he would have been the Consort of the Queen and the father of the future King of England.

The liberal constitution thus established in Belgium remains largely unchanged to this day. Unlike the British, the Belgian Sovereign has important political powers and duties. The King, besides holding the formal presidency of the Cabinet, is not only expected to give his Ministers guidance, but is entitled to initiate policy himself. Besides giving assent to Acts of Parliament like a British monarch, he can also issue decrees which are constitutionally valid provided they bear the counter-signature of a single Minister, although he would only sign if his Cabinet colleagues were in agreement. When Leopold came to the throne, therefore, he was undertaking not just the conventional sinecures of monarchy but an active and responsible role.

The issue of 'ministerial signatures' was to become a recurrent theme amid the discord of 1940. Although the King need not attend routine Cabinet meetings, as President du Conseil des Ministres he and not his Prime Minister is the effective head of the Government. Thus in Belgium 'Minister of the Crown' retains a direct, practical meaning which it has lost in Britain.* The Belgian Sovereign's position in times of crisis or controversy can therefore be lonely and exposed. This Leopold was to discover when he came to the throne and he would also learn the full meaning of another provision in the original Constitution which distinguishes the Belgian Monarchs from their British equivalents. Under Article 68 not only is the King Commander-in-Chief of the Armed Forces, but he actively commands them in the field when his country is at war. This duty of personal leadership is implicit in the oath of accession, whereby the King swears 'to maintain the national independence and the integrity of the territory'. In fulfilment of that pledge Albert and Leopold remained in active command of the Belgian Army throughout hostilities in two World Wars.

The great powers and responsibilities which these articles of the Constitution impose upon the Kings of the Belgians have on many occasions proved of immense value to the State, but they have also more than once proved dangerous to their persons and have threatened the stability of the Monarchy. In such times of crisis or war, men of ill-will have been able to exploit or misinterpret the King's powers and position under the Constitution for their own ends. A succession of able kings combined with the accidents of history have managed to preserve the Belgian Crown. Leopold, however, was destined to pay dearly for this exposure to responsibility for the course of events.

Unfortunately the *Blitzkrieg* of 1940 was merely the last of a series of threats to and assaults on Belgium's neutrality by the Great Powers who had jointly guaranteed it in 1830. In 1866, shortly after Leopold II came to the throne, the Emperor Napoleon III made a secret arrangement with Bismarck which gave France a free hand to annex Belgium by armed force. The Emperor accordingly ordered his General Staff to prepare plans for the invasion of that country. 'Belgium opens to us Germany's door,' he wrote to his War Minister. 'We can debouch on the Lower Rhine when convenient. We turn all German fortresses and stretch our hand to Holland, Hanover etc. . . . the Belgian Army once conquered, adds another 100,000 men to our effectives. If we lose the opportunity, when shall we find another?'

Prussia and Great Britain, however, blocked this project and the latter's influence was partly instrumental in saving Belgium from invasion when the Franco-Prussian War broke out in 1870, although fortunately on that occasion neither of the belligerents considered such an incursion necessary for their strategic plans. But after the war by a supreme irony Bismarck, in fear that a French *revanche* would send her armies over the

* The British Sovereign's position was similar until George I's accession, when his lack of interest in politics and poor command of English gave scope for the gradual development of a Prime Minister, who subsequently inherited or usurped much of the Crown's political power.

Meuse, begged Leopold II to build those very forts commanding the river-crossings which in 1914 and 1940 were to play so important a part in delaying the Germans' advance. Leopold II immediately seized this opportunity to urge his government to make the suggested increases in Belgium's defences. In a letter to his Prime Minister he wrote 'We must prevent any foreign army from crossing Belgian territory without striking a blow. Not to do so would be to commit suicide. We should once more become the battlefield of France and Germany . . . we must act without further loss of time.'

Before, during and after the Great War Albert faced many of the problems which would later haunt Leopold – not capitulation, it is true, or captivity, or extreme defamation, but a whole spectrum of political and military issues which presaged his son's experience. Before both World Wars not only Germany but also Britain and France planned to violate their guarantees of Belgium's independence and invade her territory. The official *British Documents* published in 1932 reveal that a note appended to a Foreign Office memorandum in November 1908 stated that if Belgian neutrality were to be violated by France, it was 'doubtful if Russia or Britain would lift a finger to defend it'. And during the Agadir crisis of 1911 Britain intended to land troops on the Belgian coast without prior invitation if war broke out. When the British Military Attaché later admitted as much to the Belgian Chief of Staff and asked what Belgium's reaction would be to such a landing, the latter replied *'Nous vous recevrions à coups de canon.'*

In 1912 Joffre formulated a plan to forestall a German attack by moving troops through Belgium irrespective of Albert's agreement – although Britain's reminder that she would be called upon to defend Belgium's neutrality if France were to violate it, caused him to desist. Yet none of these threats to Belgium's integrity was as enormous in its implications as the Schlieffen Plan, the grandiose scheme developed in 1904 by Kaiser William II's Chief of Staff, to bring France to her knees by a rapid surprise attack through Belgium, before her slow-moving Russian allies could mobilize and deploy. But for the plan to succeed there were two other prerequisites. Firstly, that the Belgians would allow the massive thrust of the German right wing through their territory unhindered in order to outflank the frontier defences of France and, it was hoped, reach Paris within a matter of weeks. Secondly, it was essential that the British should not intervene – or if they did, should arrive too late and with too little to prevent France from being crushed.

Like Hitler, the Kaiser worked by threats and bribes. When the aged Leopold II visited him later that year to sound him out on these aggressive plans, which had – perhaps deliberately – been 'leaked', the Emperor declared: 'In the formidable struggle which will take place, Germany is certain of victory, but this time you will be obliged to choose. You will be with us or against us. If you are with us I shall give you the provinces France took from you . . . I will re-create for you the Duchy of Burgundy.' The Kaiser held out a dazzling vision of a 'Greater Belgium', including French Flanders, Artois and the French Ardennes. The old King was so aghast that he wore his Prussian Dragoon Guards helmet back to front during the carriage drive to the railway station. But on his return to Belgium he immediately renewed his campaign to persuade his government and people – although with little success – to strengthen Belgium's army and her defences 'so that we may be able to defend ourselves, and thus, in conformity with our international obligations, make the passage as onerous as possible for whoever should try it'[1] – the theme that was to become a precedent for his successors.

Ten years later the Kaiser was no more effective in persuading Albert to connive in destroying his country's integrity and independence. This time he confined himself to threats, telling the King at Potsdam on November 6th 1913 that war with France was 'inevitable and soon' and getting his generals to demonstrate by their boasts that it was 'imperative for the weak to side with the strong'. Albert's reaction to this attempt to intimidate him was the same as that of his uncle – to press forward with the strengthening of his country's defences.

Under constant pressure from one or other of the Powers to take some step which would commit Belgium to a breach of her neutral status, King Albert resisted successfully up to the very moment of the German invasion in 1914. It had long been appreciated in Belgium that the invader would seize on any pretext to justify his action and that a move by one side would immediately provoke an armed incursion by the other. If Belgium had entered into any prior agreement with France and Britain in regard to their troops crossing her frontiers before or after a German attack, she would have been held guilty of having broken the treaties by which her inviolability was guaranteed and Germany would have been given all the justification she needed to launch her invasion. A strict observance of the treaties had preserved Belgium's security for over eighty years and Albert was determined not to compromise his country's integrity by leaning towards one side or the other – whatever he thought of the relative merits of their respective causes.

Ironically, as in World War II, the opposing Powers assumed that neutrality was merely a screen behind which the Belgian Sovereign would be prepared to join the side most likely to gain the upper hand rather than a binding article of faith. Moreover, the French suspected that the Belgians were in league with the Germans and vice versa, in this as well as the later conflict. In both World Wars, however, the Belgian Kings were equally scrupulous in honouring the pacts guaranteeing their country's inviolability and gave neither belligerent any excuse for breaking them. That distinguished Belgian patriot and Anglophile Professor Emile

Cammaerts stresses the essential difference between the Belgian and Anglo-French attitudes: 'The most enthusiastic admirers of King Albert in Great Britain and France looked upon him as the champion of their cause against the Central Powers. It never occurred to them that if Belgium had sided deliberately with the Allies she would have been as much in the wrong as if she had allowed the German armies to cross her territory in order to fall upon the French.'[2] Leopold learned this lesson as a boy, for on the outbreak of war Albert mobilized his small army and made it clear that he would fight if any foreign army entered his country's territory uninvited – but only then.

Soldiers, politicians and civilians who wondered in the days of Hitler why Leopold similarly rejected all attempts to draw Belgium into a military commitment which would involve her in hostilities before she was actually attacked, forgot the star by which he steered. It requires an act of intense and sympathetic imagination to measure what it meant for father and son, as Sovereigns of their little country, to expose it to an overwhelming onslaught by the same aggressor twice in a lifetime – and to do so by choice. Apart from the devastation of their country and the slaughter of their civilian and military subjects, an inevitable enemy occupation meant sufferings for the Belgian people only too harshly expressed in the atrocities of 1914–18 and the Nazi subjugation after 1940. Each could have taken the pragmatic view that their defence forces were so outmatched as to make resistance hopeless and, accepting the loss of face, allowed the German armies to cross their territory unhindered. Both chose to make the immense sacrifice inherent in resisting, in the hope that right would prevail in the end.

The German 'Note' received by Albert on August 2nd 1914 claimed that the French were about to march through Belgian territory against Germany and 'that it was essential for her self-defence' that her armies should enter Belgium to parry that attack. It went on to declare that if Belgium 'maintained an attitude of friendly neutrality' towards Germany she would 'guarantee the possessions and independence of the Belgian Kingdom in full . . . and pay an indemnity for any damage done by German troops, on the conclusion of peace'. If, on the other hand, Belgium should oppose the German troops, she would be treated as an enemy. The Note, which gave the Belgians twelve hours to decide whether or not to grant the right of passage to the German armies, concluded with the pious hope that Belgium would do so and thus 'strengthen the friendly ties which bind the two neighbouring States'. The reaction of the King and his government was uncompromising. In rejecting this cynical proposition Albert reiterated that Belgium would resist any invasion from whatever direction it came. Despite the decisive tone of this response, the German High Command remained convinced that the ill-equipped Belgian Army of only 117,000 field troops would make no attempt to resist the overwhelming onslaught of their armies – or that at worst it would put up only a token resistance.

In launching their invasion of Belgium in this expectation and on the assumption that Great Britain would not be drawn into the war, the German military planners had fatally miscalculated – for Albert, by waiting until his country's territory had actually been violated before invoking the military help of her French and British guarantors and then fiercely resisting the invader, won an incalculable moral victory. His scrupulous adherence to the terms of the Great Powers' treaties of guarantee, which Germany had so flagrantly violated, showed Germany up in the eyes of the world as an unmitigated aggressor – a factor which was, in the words of Sir Basil Liddell Hart, 'decisive in hardening British opinion to the point of intervention'.[3]

Up to this point the policy of the British Government and the desire of the people had been to keep out of the war in Europe. Not only was the British Empire brought into the war, but the Allies were given an immeasurable ideological propaganda advantage. They could now represent what was really a war between the Great Powers for the hegemony of Europe as a crusade for the liberation of a small and innocent country – and proceeded to do so with great effect. Moreover, the determined but unsupported resistance of the Belgian Army, in addition to putting a fatal brake on the Schlieffen Plan, gave the unprepared Allied armies time to mobilize and deploy.

The Germans were so taken aback by the resistance of the Belgians, which had crystallized world opinion against them and jeopardized their war-winning plan, that they sent an almost apologetic Note to King Albert on August 9th, praising the brave defenders of Liège and offering the restoration of Belgium's independence if the German armies were allowed to pass through her territory, now that Belgium had 'upheld her honour by heroic resistance against vastly superior numbers', and 'to spare her further horrors of war'. But the King and his Ministers firmly rejected this proposal. The Germans retaliated by bringing up their new 'secret weapon', enormous siege guns to pulverize first the Belgian fortifications covering the Meuse and later those at Antwerp, and by intensifying their reign of terror against the civilian population.

To avenge the Belgian Army's stubborn resistance which was wrecking their plans for a rapid victory over France, the Germans embarked upon a deliberate campaign of mass executions, arson and pillage. Towns, villages and farms were razed to the ground – the worst example being the sacking and burning of the ancient city of Louvain, renowned for its churches, its university and its irreplaceable library. This was just a foretaste of the harshness of the German military government which was imposed on the luckless Belgians under General von Bissing.

Despite massive and sustained attacks, which reduced them to rubble,

the Liège forts did not succumb until August 16th. Moreover, the task of
overcoming the mainly obsolete fortifications at Namur absorbed six
German divisions and five hundred guns for five days. The resistance of
the Belgian Army 'seriously weakened the German right wing,' wrote
Liddell Hart, 'when it fell upon and sought to overwhelm the Allied left
wing in the critical battles of Charleroi and Mons'. And after the war the
French General Baratier recalled that 'the German deployment was
retarded by fifteen days . . . an extremely important delay, since speed
was a primary condition for the success of their operations'.[4]

Meanwhile, Albert was persistently urged by the Allies and his own
government to go to England or to follow them to the distant sanctuary of
Le Havre, to which his Ministers had fled. But just as his son would do
twenty-six years later, Albert rejected all these importunities and firmly
declared that he would never abandon his army and his people – come
what may. Albert had expected that the Allied armies would hurry to his
aid while his troops and fortresses held up the enemy's great offensive,
but instead the French concentrated their armies along their eastern
frontier with Germany, while the British Expeditionary Force of only
four divisions was sent not to Flanders, but to support the French left
wing, fifty miles from the Belgian front. Thus Belgium was left by the
Allies to bear the brunt of the German mass attack alone.

After two weeks of desperate fighting Albert learned that German
forces half-a-million strong were bearing down on his positions and, since
the Allies would not provide him with any support, he decided – despite
strong criticisms from the French High Command – to wheel his army
back to the great entrenched camp covering Antwerp rather than respond
to their demands that he should retire southward to join their left wing.
Colonel Adalbert, of the French liaison mission at Albert's *Grand
Quartier Général*, protested with particular emotion and violence – accusing the King of 'abandoning his allies'. But the withdrawal of the Belgian
Army to this fortified line behind the Escaut and the Lys was of immeasurable benefit to the Allied cause, as they would later concede, for it
now constituted a serious threat to the exposed German right flank.
Furthermore, the series of counter-attacks which Albert then launched
on his own initiative greatly eased the pressure on the French and British
armies at Mons and along the River Sambre.

King Albert's 'aggressive defence of Antwerp' – as Liddell Hart described it – 'resulted in a serious detachment of German strength and a
chronic irritation to German nerves', while the last of his unsolicited
counter-attacks, which coincided with the critical day in the Battle of the
Marne, 'had all the incalculable psychological effect of menacing news at
a moment of crisis. The German retreat gathered momentum and spread.
With it turned the tide of the war.' Moreover, the need to 'contain' the
Belgian Army in the fortress of Antwerp deprived von Kluck's armies,

locked in that crucial battle, of fourteen desperately needed divisions. As General Baratier sums up: 'Without the presence of the British Army, without the heroic resistance of the Belgians . . . the French would have been numerically inferior . . . If these [German] forces had been available there would have been no victory on the Marne. *We must never forget.*'

It was only after more than two months of fighting by the Belgian Army that small-scale Allied reinforcements, including Winston Churchill's Naval contingent, were sent to support them in beleaguered Antwerp. Unfortunately only the King and Churchill – then First Lord of the Admiralty – appreciated the strategic importance to the Allies of holding the Channel coast and ports on the enemy's vulnerable right flank. Despite their urgings these reinforcements were too meagre and too late to enable Albert to hold on to the fortress of Antwerp and thus retain the vital ports of Ostend and Zeebrugge in Allied hands. After holding out for three weeks of merciless bombardment by hundreds of heavy guns, Albert was therefore compelled on October 8th to abandon this formidable bastion and obstacle to the enemy's advance. 'The attitude of the King and Queen through those tense and tragic days was magnificent,' wrote Churchill. 'The impression of the grave, calm Soldier-King presiding at Council, sustaining his troops and Commanders, preserving an unconquerable majesty amid the ruin of his Kingdom, will never pass from my mind.'

The retirement down the coast of the battered remnants of King Albert's army was greatly hampered by the million and a half pitiful refugees who encumbered the restricted coastal area in appalling conditions of starvation and distress. The situation looked black indeed to Albert, but having ignored his government's entreaties to join them in their flight into exile, he rejected the Allied leaders' pleas to hand his army over to one of his generals and allow it to be withdrawn to France and merged with those of the Allies. Instead, the King rallied his exhausted troops to win the epic battle of the Yser and so preserved inviolate for the remainder of the war twenty square miles of Belgian soil behind the flooded waterline of that river. By so doing he was responsible for the retention of at least the French Channel ports in the Allies' hands, and for anchoring their left flank firmly on the coast.

General Brécard – the head of the French liaison mission at the King's headquarters, who had earlier complained about his stubbornness in retiring on Antwerp rather than towards France – wrote that his army, 'which had already suffered such severe losses, and has been separated from the Allies, still defends with the utmost energy this last corner of Belgian territory . . . The King is alone . . . with the Queen, facing his responsibilities. Both are sustained by their deep patriotism and sense of duty towards their people. What an example and what a lesson!'[5] And

General Azan, the chief historian of the French General Staff, which had at first been so critical of King Albert, gave this answer to the question of what would have happened to the Allied line if the Belgian Army had failed to halt the German onslaught on the Yser: 'It would have been outflanked and the Allies would have been cut off from the sea . . . In refusing to give the order to retire in spite of the critical situation, he showed an admirable firmness . . . In his relations with the Allies he was calm, thoughtful, well-balanced . . . and the strategic course he followed exerted a decisive influence on the outcome of the war. He closed the gateway in the North to the German invasion and with troops which had reached the very end of their endurance, kept it closed until assistance arrived.'[6]

These undoubted achievements of the Belgian Army and its leader formed an impressive precedent for his son when, a generation later, he faced the same challenges from the same aggressor – and the same appeals from his own side to abandon his army and his country.

CHAPTER TWO

Heir Apparent

'My son is prepared.'   King Albert, in 1934

On August 4th 1914 Prince Leopold, not yet thirteen, was taken by his mother to the joint session of Parliament where he heard his father, in general's uniform, deliver his stirring speech in which he declared that as King he would never betray his constitutional oath. For a time after King Albert had taken his place at the head of the Army the Royal family remained at Laeken, but as the Germans advanced they were compelled to retreat with the Government to Antwerp. Later in the month, however, when the Zeppelins began their bombing, it seemed prudent to send the two young Princes and their sister to England escorted by their mother. The family's friends Lord and Lady Curzon had offered them the hospitality of their country house, Hackwood, and here the children remained in the care of their English governess, Miss Hammersley.

The Queen herself soon returned to her place by Albert's side in beleaguered Antwerp and, after the Belgian line had been stabilized behind the Yser, the King and Queen established themselves in their modest seaside villa at La Panne, where they remained for the rest of the war. During the first winter of the war Leopold stayed with his parents in La Panne and accompanied his mother on her visits to hospitals and relief centres. But he was not content with these occasional visits to the last strip of free Belgium territory or with civilian errands of mercy. He asked his father insistently that he should be allowed to serve as a soldier. It was surprising enough that King Albert should have responded to the spirit of his son by allowing him to 'join up' when so young, but to put the Heir to the Throne in the ranks was quite unprecedented.

On April 5th 1915 the 12th Regiment of the Line was drawn up on the beach at La Panne and the King presented to them the diminutive Heir Apparent, dressed in the blue uniform of a Belgian private soldier suitably cut down to size. The King explained that his son had claimed the privilege of wearing their uniform and that he would be proud to serve in a regiment with such a distinguished record. 'Princes,' he proclaimed, 'must be brought up early in the school of duty.' Then the regiment marched past, Leopold taking his place in the third platoon of the fourth company of the first battalion.

Back at the Royal villa the King instructed the regiment's Colonel that Leopold must undergo the same training as the rest, sharing the duties and fatigues of his comrades. 'Make him dig trenches,' he said, 'so that he may know what it is like to have blistered hands.' Every morning, therefore, Leopold had to fill fifty sandbags to reinforce the parapets. He undertook, in fact, the whole regular course of training for the infantry recruit – physical exercises, lessons in handling arms and grenade-throwing, drill and the maintenance of equipment. Of course a boy prince could never be truly the equal of a private soldier, but Leopold never forgot what he learned at close quarters about the attitude of the ordinary man and the sympathy for the underdog that he invariably showed was a product of his life in the ranks.

On May 4th Leopold insisted upon being taken into the front line. On one occasion he manned an advance post within pistol shot of the enemy. On another he was in a dugout when a heavy shell exploded a few yards away. As the smoke cleared, the young Prince was seen collecting hot splinters as souvenirs. Not surprisingly, he was taken to the heart of his company, which had the nickname '*les Incas*' (a corruption of *un-quatre*, the fourth company) and he was soon known as 'the last of the Incas'.

There now began one of the most extraordinary phases of Leopold's life. After the first six months of his service with the Army, Lord Curzon persuaded King Albert to send Leopold to Eton. Dr Lyttleton, the headmaster, came over to La Panne for an interview with the King, who told him that in no circumstances did he wish his son to adopt the habits of rich young Englishmen, 'who spend money freely and who make their sports their only ambition'. History does not record the headmaster's reply, but Leopold duly went to Samuel Gurney Lubbock's House at the beginning of the winter 'half' ('term' in Etonian language) in 1915. For the next four years he led a life of curious contrasts – alternating between school in England and vacations spent with his regiment, with a few days at home. Such an existence would tax the adaptability of any boy, but Leopold responded wholeheartedly and good-humouredly – and flourished. His 'holidays' were naturally the envy of his schoolfellows.

Leopold's memories of Eton are affectionate and happy, though he recalls that his first half was hard for him, as a foreigner, before he became completely fluent in English. Leopold was fortunate in having S. G. Lubbock as his House Tutor. A revered figure in the Eton hierarchy, Lubbock was a man of remarkable qualities, to whom Leopold was devoted and considered he owes much. They remained lifelong friends.

When in 1956 Leopold paid his first post-war visit to Great Britain (to receive the freedom of the town of Enniskillen on behalf of the famous regiment of which he was Colonel-in-Chief) he had a reunion with Lubbock, then aged eighty-three, in the author's house. Both men were deeply moved, and this meeting led to Lubbock and groups of Leopold's contemporaries from his House visiting Laeken Palace later that year and on subsequent occasions. The following year Leopold flew to London for a second time, to attend the annual reunion of the boys of Lubbock's House which was always held on the eve of the Eton and Harrow cricket match.

From the numerous letters the author and his father received from Leopold's school fellows and from Lubbock and others who knew him well in those days, as well as discussions with some of them, a picture emerges of the affection, sympathy and admiration they maintained for him throughout all his adversities. Lubbock's feelings were aptly summed up in a letter he wrote to the author in 1953: 'Of course from the very first neither I nor anyone, boy or master, who knew him at Eton believed the lies that were told about him; we all knew that he was incapable of anything false or dishonourable . . .' Since one of the charges laid against Leopold during and after 1940 was that he had treacherously abandoned his English allies, it should be remembered how Eton brought England into the very core of his being. To the author, indeed, he once remarked that it was at Eton that he made his 'best friends in life', adding that he deeply regretted that circumstances had prevented him from sending his own three sons to Eton.

Leopold became a fag to Lord Kingsborough and was treated exactly like the other boys – or possibly worse – in accordance with tradition. But by the second half he had made many friends and began to enjoy himself. The fag masters were strict, but not unkind. Lubbock always kept a friendly eye on him and was full of tact and sensibility, never forcing. After his reunion with Lubbock in 1956 Leopold told the author 'I really loved that man; he was like a second father to me; he showed me the way.' When the Court was at Windsor, Leopold would occasionally be asked to lunch by King George V and Queen Mary. The King would do his rather intimidating best to make his young guest feel at ease, though not hesitating to reprove him if his boots were insufficiently polished.

At Eton Leopold was soon accepted on equal terms. In a letter to the author his life-long friend Oliver Thynne wrote: 'Eton in those days, and Lubbock's House in particular, was acclimatized to royalty, and Prince Henry (the Duke of Gloucester) and Prince Leopold were able to live the lives of perfectly normal Etonians. Leopold became Anglicized (or Etonianized) amazingly easily. At all stages of his four years at Eton he was always completely "one of us" and, I would say, universally popular. He was quite a brilliant player of the Eton Field Game and was for his last year a member of the House Library' (equivalent to being a prefect in other schools). Thynne adds that 'Leopold as an Etonian acquired a truly English sense of humour. He was in fact a wonderful companion, and it was always the greatest fun to do anything with him.' Another friend, Bill Snagge, put it this way: 'After looking round, Leopold soon made friends

– without any effort – and I should think no enemies. He knew his own mind, and was very thorough in his pursuit of things that interested him, such as engineering. He was great fun and enjoyed the lighter side of school life.' If this side of Leopold's character is emphasized it is because a legend grew up, after he was falsely accused of treachery in 1940, that he was 'completely devoid of a sense of humour' – as a stiff-necked British diplomat, who had only met him on formal occasions, wrote in *The Times*.

Another of Leopold's contemporaries at Eton, Denis Brinton, wrote to a friend years later: 'He struck me then as having great strength of character – a person who would stick to a course of action once he had made up his mind . . . although there was quite a handful of Belgians in the school, during those odd years of the First World War, Leopold was the only one who seriously competed with the rest of us and carved out a place for himself on his own merits.'

Leopold's former fag, Peter Hesketh, described to the author the scenes of jubilation which took place at Eton on Victory Day, 1918, and the great send-off that Leopold was given as he left to resume his private soldier's uniform and take his place in the triumphant Victory parades through Belgium's liberated cities. Among those who were sad at Leopold's departure was the 'Dame' of Lubbock's House, Miss George, who wept copiously as she helped Leopold to pack.* As Bill Snagge recalled: 'Some of us were a bit anxious that we should be losing one of our best players in the House Football Ties which began that month. Leopold said he'd be back for them at all costs, *and he was*.'

While Leopold was learning to understand and to love England and also the realities of war as an infantryman, his father was facing those realities as King and Commander-in-Chief, in a fashion which had a marked influence on Leopold's subsequent conduct. King Albert had decided that he would in no circumstances desert his country and people – and that while such forces as were left to him were able to fight and be supplied he would continue to defend his country's territory and maintain his army's place on the extreme left wing of the Allied line. Albert was uncompromising about the constitutional duties he had sworn to fulfil: 'to maintain the integrity of the Country' and to command the armed forces in time of war. He had rejected and would continue to reject the many pressing invitations to come to England, or to follow his government into exile at Le Havre. These were siren voices to which his son would one day also have to close his ears.

---

* When Leopold was married in 1926, he insisted that Miss George should have one of the best seats in the Cathedral and greeted her warmly – putting his arm round her shoulder and kissing her. The international press was mystified by this dowdy old lady who was addressed so respectfully as 'Ma'am' by Prince Leopold and the Duke of Gloucester, assuming that she must be royalty. The rumour spread that she was a relative of King George, travelling incognito.

For the rest of the war Albert firmly maintained his sovereignty over that part of his kingdom which remained free and the command of the army which defended it. Nevertheless, there was to be constant denigration and criticism from the *émigré* Belgian politicians in their safe haven in France. But any hopes they may have entertained of undermining the King's position were shattered in the tide of victory, for Albert was the first to be greeted by the liberated Belgian people, who swept away the absentee political leaders and replaced them with others who enjoyed the King's and their own confidence.

The inside story of King Albert's relationships with the Government and Parliament, as well as his Allies, during the Great War was not revealed until 1953 with the publication of his private diaries.[7] In his review of their English translation written for *The Listener* in 1955 Liddell Hart observed:

Its main significance now lies in the way it indirectly shows that King Leopold was the faithful disciple and pupil of King Albert, sharing his father's thoughts and closely following the precepts that his father had indicated. It is an irony of history that the son suffered violent criticism in consequence and lost his throne, while the father remains universally a cherished figure whose reputation has never been affected by the storm that broke over the son who so loyally sought to carry out his father's teaching . . .

The diaries reveal that throughout the war King Albert was concerned to keep Belgium from becoming a satellite of her powerful partners, France and Britain, and from too close association with their aims, which he considered dangerous to future peace and the stability of Europe . . . . It becomes evident, too, that he had more trouble with his Ministers and was subject to more pressure from his allies than ever appeared on the surface. Moreover it is very clear that he had a wide regard for humanity's interests, combined with a far more realistic grasp of the military factors than was shown by the Allied military leaders.

From 1915 onward many passages reveal his foresight about the length of the struggle and the futility of bludgeoning offensives, as well as his acute sense of the conditions necessary for success. He never shared the optimistic illusions of Joffre, Foch and Haig. That sense of reality made him more anxious that no opportunity should be missed of restoring peace on a reasonable and negotiated basis. He was the one leader in Europe who showed a grasp of grand strategy – which conducts war with regard to the state of peace that will follow.

Although Albert greatly disliked the part, he was forced by circumstances and Allied propaganda into the role of a legendary hero fighting courageously in a completely united cause. He was almost deified as the symbol of 'Right defying Might', and it was made to appear to the world that he had wholly subordinated his country's interests to those of the Allies. This was far from being the case; but in the First as in the Second World War, as Leopold discovered, it was an immeasurable propaganda and psychological advantage for the British and French Governments to be able to maintain that Belgian interests and aims were identical to theirs, and that they were fighting as much for poor little Belgium's sake as for their own. In fact, King Albert repeatedly affirmed that Belgium's position and war aims were entirely different from those of her allies, though this was never publicly proclaimed at the time because of the subservient attitude of the Belgian Government-in-exile towards France and Britain. Indeed, Albert's feelings about 'countries like Belgium' are clearly defined in two of his diary entries for November 1915:

> November 3rd: . . . dragged into war despite themselves, against their will, they have everything to lose in being chained to an indestructible Empire like that of Great Britain. When all is said and done they receive blows which are not aimed at them . . .

> November 10th: Belgium must be no one's vassal, neither England's nor France's. She was neutral before the war. The mass of the people do not want to be tied up with any of their neighbours.

This was an attitude with which Lord Curzon agreed, for he once remarked to King Albert: 'I am a supporter of Belgian neutrality, because I can see no other solution. The choice lies between neutrality or alliances – but alliances with whom? For the alliance of a small nation with a Great Power is never anything but vassalage.' Once Belgium was invaded, Albert could only preserve the territorial integrity of his country in a minimal sense. But, as he saw it, there was another integrity to be maintained – the avoidance of vassalage. If Belgium's vital interests appeared to diverge from those of the *Entente* then he must declare and stand by them.

An example of such a divergence occurred when the German Government put out peace feelers towards the end of 1916. Both King Albert and King George V* recommended the serious consideration of this German approach, but the British and French Governments' reaction was a brusque rejection, coupled with a demand that the Belgians should merely countersign their reply. But as Albert declared to his Ministers: 'We cannot make our reply identical to that of the Great Powers. The Belgian point of view is not the same . . .'

Although Albert's views remained unheeded by the Allies, he continued to deplore their refusal to consider any possibility of a negotiated peace and persistence with the dogma of 'unconditional surrender', which he considered would prolong the bloodshed and devastation, but ensure

---

* As Harold Nicolson writes in *King George V*: 'The King was afraid that Mr Lloyd George with his impulsive vehemence might reject the German overture in terms of such violence as to strengthen the militants in Berlin and alienate moderate opinion in the United States.'

neither the permanent destruction of the enemy nor a subsequent lasting peace – a view shared by many wise men in both World Wars. As late as July 1918 he declared to Lloyd George, in words very similar to those used to the latter by George V, that 'the vast extent of the Allied Governments' war aims, and their violent language, have brought support to the German military party, and have hindered the effective action of the moderates . . .' Thus while Leopold was commuting between Eton and the Belgian front line, the *Roi Chevalier* was laying down principles of action which would have a critical significance for his son when he became King and Commander-in-Chief: solidarity with Belgium's friends, but not a solidarity unqualified by reason, justice and the highest interest of his kingdom.

As the war ran on, the Belgian politicians in France, remote from the battlefront, continued to bicker and recriminate. Things came to a head in 1916 when the Prime Minister, Comte de Broqueville, reported to the King that certain members of the refugee Government in France were accusing him of taking a line different from their own. Albert noted in his diary: 'In Le Havre they went as far as speaking of treason on my part . . .' and wrote in reply to de Broqueville: 'That it is a dangerous game to play. The Monarch . . . has his own responsibility in time of war and will be held responsible for the country's misfortunes.' This was an ominous portent, though it would not be King Albert but his son who would be blamed for his country's misfortunes since the father was able to retain his hold over a part of his kingdom and to return to his capital as the victorious champion of his martyred people – thus silencing all those malicious and ungrateful tongues, and making his position unassailable. His son, on the other hand, having been equally loyal to his allies and having fought no less courageously at their side and for his country's integrity and honour, would be deprived of both these advantages – and would suffer accordingly.

In the last year of the war there began a friendship between the Belgian Royal family and Roger Keyes, which was to be cemented by shared experiences in both World Wars and would have a profound effect on Leopold's life. Shortly after taking over command of the Dover Patrol, which he was to make so famous, on New Year's Day 1918, Vice Admiral Keyes met King Albert and Queen Elisabeth, and formed a deep admiration and respect for them and, as he grew to man's estate, for Leopold. Keyes was soon admitted to a close personal friendship which is shown by the affectionate tone of the many letters which he subsequently received from them. There was a good deal of VIP traffic passing through Dover and the Admiral would make one of his destroyers available to carry members of the Belgian Royal family back and forth across the Straits. Prince Leopold was at Eton, Prince Charles a naval cadet at Dartmouth, the Princess Marie-José at an English girls' school. They would all be made welcome at Fleet House in Dover and the Admiral would see them safely to their destinations.

Queen Elisabeth happened to be passing through Dover on April 24th 1918 – the day following the famous St George's Day Zeebrugge Raid, which Lloyd George described as 'the one naval exploit of the war that moved and still moves the imagination of the Nation', adding that 'Sir Roger Keyes, who directed the attack, had the unmistakable Nelson touch', while Winston Churchill declared that 'It may well rank as the finest feat of arms in the Great War and certainly an episode unsurpassed in the history of the Royal Navy.'* The Queen had lunch with the Admiral and his wife and met a number of the officers who had taken part in this classic exploit, being given a first-hand account of the action.

King Albert was one of the first to write congratulating Keyes and to 'pay a tribute of respect and admiration' to the officers and men engaged in what he called 'the most daring action of the whole war'. A few days after the Raid, Sir Roger – as he had then become – was entertained to an informal lunch party at La Panne by Albert and Elisabeth. 'After lunch,' the Admiral wrote in his diary, 'the King took me out to the sand dunes opposite the villa, and very shyly gave me the Star of a Grand Officer of the Order of Leopold, and said very nice things about our exploit.' A year later, when funds were being raised for the memorial to the Dover Patrol, King Albert sent Keyes his personal cheque for £1,000, the accompanying letter being signed: 'Your very affectionate Albert' – a demonstration that the two men were by now close friends.

For the rest of the war Admiral Keyes was in close touch with the King and Queen of the Belgians, while the numerous warships and Royal Naval Air Service bombers, fighters and reconnaissance planes under his command actively supported the Belgian Army in its vital role of anchoring the extreme left wing of the Allied front on the Channel Coast.† On one occasion the Admiral and the Royal couple shared a dangerous adventure which might have had fatal consequences. On October 17th 1918, when it was learned that the Germans were withdrawing from Ostend – the first Belgian town to be evacuated – the King and Queen prevailed upon Keyes to take them there in the destroyer HMS *Termagant* and to land them after dark in a small boat, from which they climbed up a slippery iron ladder on to the quay. The incredulous inhabitants gave their 'liberators' a tumultuous welcome, but while they were celebrating in champagne with the Burgomaster and the Council, the Germans started shelling the town and the party was compelled to

---

* See Appendices I and II.
† Naval aircraft and warships of the Dover Patrol, including monitors carrying fifteen inch guns, constantly bombarded the Germans facing the Belgian Army, and when the latter went over to the offensive, Naval planes parachuted supplies to its advanced units – for the first time in history.

return to the *Termagant*. As the King and Queen were in a hurry to get back to La Panne, they and the Admiral transferred to a tiny Coastal Motor Boat and set off at forty knots. Unfortunately the craft lost its escort and broke down in mid-Channel, and it was some hours before the party was rescued. In after years Keyes would remember with horror the risks they ran that night. But the King and Queen had greatly enjoyed themselves and overwhelmed him with thanks for their 'wonderful experience'.

A few days later King Albert insisted that the Admiral should join him on his triumphal ride into Bruges at the head of his army. Keyes rode immediately behind the King, the Queen and Crown Prince Leopold – steel-helmeted and wearing his private soldier's uniform. And after the Armistice had been signed, there was a state entry into Brussels when all four rode close together again, accompanied by Prince Albert, the future King George VI. Admiral Keyes' 'Belgian Diary' describes the scene as they rode through the capital amid the cheering populace and the jubilant pealing of bells:

> The densely crowded streets were all lined with the veteran troops, little children were allowed to sit at their feet, and a ceaseless roar of cheers accompanied us from Laeken to the House of Representatives, where we dismounted and the King addressed his Parliament, making a particularly generous reference to the services of the British Navy and the force under my command . . .

Against a background of suffering and ruin the whole population was paying a heartfelt tribute to their King, who for four years had been the symbol of their defiance and of their hopes. The retreating Germans had left behind them a hideously devastated country, denuded of livestock and with an almost worthless currency. They had destroyed all Belgium's communications – roads, railways, telephones and most of her factories. From King Albert's discussions with leading figures who had remained in Belgium during the occupation and representatives of the *émigré* Le Havre government it soon became clear that the latter was completely discredited in the eyes of the liberated population and the Prime Minister accordingly resigned. The King therefore appointed a non-political figure, Delacroix, to head an all-party Government of National Union, which obtained a vote of confidence a few days later, when King Albert presented himself to Parliament to account for his four years of stewardship.

The bright hopes with which the post-war period began were soon exchanged for the disillusionment and wrangling of the Peace Conference which opened in Paris in January 1919. The Allies' spontaneous 'Declaration of Sainte Adresse' in 1916, which had guaranteed Belgium a place at the Conference table, was virtually ignored. The Conference divided the twenty-seven Allied states into those which 'had given everything, their soil, their blood, their treasure to the common cause' and those with 'restricted interests'. Illogically Belgium was placed in the latter category, as one of the twenty-three nations such as Siam and Cuba which had made few if any sacrifices. The result was that Belgium's representatives were – as Emile Cammaerts put it – 'kept in the ante-chamber of the Conference and were scarcely allowed to state their case'.

King Albert was shocked by the lack of gratitude and consideration shown by the Allies, whose praises and promises had been heaped upon Belgium when she 'held the pass' for them at the outset of the Great War and whose courage and suffering had supplied them with their principal propaganda weapon. He decided, therefore, to make a direct personal appeal to the Big Three – Wilson for the USA, Lloyd George for Great Britain and Clemenceau for France. Speaking of this successful intervention, which enabled the tremendous task of reconstruction upon which the country's whole future life depended to go forward, Albert recalled: 'It was a hard fight. At one moment, I was told, rather sharply, that Belgium wished to impose excessive sacrifices upon the Allies. I could not help replying: "These sacrifices are the consequence of the Belgians' faithfulness to their promises. I ask you to keep yours." '

After the war the friendship between the Belgian Royal family and that of Sir Roger Keyes was maintained with regular correspondence and several exchanged visits, both official and private. The Admiral would invariably be attached to King Albert or to British Royalty on Anglo-Belgian occasions. It was on one of these, the Belgian State visit to London in 1921, that Albert remarked during a walk in Hyde Park that in his view Winston Churchill had initiated the two strategic master-strokes of the war – the landing of the Naval Division at Antwerp and the plan to force the Dardanelles with warships alone in 1915. He had always been grateful to Churchill for this reinforcement of the Belgian Army at Antwerp, which had helped it to delay the Germans' advance and to remain on Belgian soil behind the Yser. The Dardanelles operation, the King considered, had been a brilliant strategic concept and had it not been frustrated[a] it might have broken the deadlock on the Western Front, saved Russia, shortened the war considerably, and spared the British the costly Gallipoli, Mesopotamia and Palestine campaigns.

Keyes was an old friend and admirer of Winston Churchill and when he asked Albert if he would like to say all this to him in person, the King readily agreed. Knowing that Churchill was playing polo at Roehampton that afternoon, Keyes drove Albert down there and as he recalled in his diary: 'I brought Churchill over to the King – hot and dusty as he was – and the King, in his slow deliberate way, said all those nice things, which must have been very gratifying to Churchill as he was still much condemned and criticized for both episodes.'

This encounter might well have proved to be of great consequence. It was a notable feature of Churchill as Prime Minister that with his prehensile memory and his passionate sense of loyalty he went out of his way to advance the sons of those who had supported him in the past, particularly during his military youth and his periods in the political wilderness. He always felt a savage contempt for the critics of Antwerp and the Dardanelles campaign and reciprocal warmth towards those who recognized their merits. And yet, in his unfathomable way, he withheld from King Albert's son that generosity of spirit which the father displayed during this chance meeting.

The return of peace – just before Leopold's seventeenth birthday – meant a farewell to the 12th Regiment of the Line for him, but when the liberated citizens of Liège gave a tumultuous welcome to their own Regiment, there still marched with them in his blue private's uniform the youngest soldier of the Belgian Army, Prince Leopold, the Heir to the Throne. In September of the following year Leopold accompanied his parents on their official visit to the United States, returning to Eton for a month in November. He left finally, with many regrets, at Christmas time in 1919.

To fit the Heir Apparent for his role, King Albert now began to train his son in what he called 'the difficult business of Kingship'. In 1920, therefore, Leopold's studies were widened under four distinguished Belgians. His best subjects at Eton had been geography, mathematics and science. Now under the tutelage of Jacques Pirenne, son of the great historian Henri Pirenne, he studied history and the important question of relating immediate political issues to historical perspectives. Law, political economy, and the Constitution were taught by two Cabinet Ministers, George Theunis and Henri Jaspar, while a more personal influence was exercised by his tutor in philosophy, the Primate, Cardinal Merciers, who had fearlessly defended the Belgians' spiritual freedom under the German occupation. And of all Leopold's princely duties one of the most imperative was to master the Flemish language, for Belgium is a divided society, split by differences of language, by religion and fragmented by political schisms.

After 1918 King Albert struggled hard to create a *Union Sacrée* which might unite the Flemings and Walloons, but the past was too powerful. A new Party with right-wing tendencies disinterred all the old demands of Flemish regionalism, while Walloon separatists stepped up their extremism on the far-left of the political spectrum. Such bitter rivalries would continue to disrupt the life and unity of the Kingdom into and beyond Leopold's reign.

On November 20th 1920, shortly after his nineteenth birthday, Leopold entered the *Ecole Militaire* – the equivalent of Britain's Sandhurst. He worked hard in this spartan environment and took a leading part in sports, especially swimming, football and riding. In 1922 he passed out near the top of his class with the rank of *sous-lieutenant* and was appointed, in accordance with tradition, to the 1st Grenadier Regiment. Characteristically, soon after he had been gazetted, he paid a personal visit to his old regiment at Liège.

The pattern of the Heir to the Throne's future was soon established. Although the high position for which he was being prepared involved heavy responsibilities and duties Leopold was determined to remain a person while performing efficiently and conscientiously as a Prince. Now that he had a good grounding in all subjects considered to be necessary for the Heir Apparent, Leopold was able to develop his interest in exploration, science, archaeology, botany, natural history, and all those intellectual horizons which beckoned him.

There now began the most enjoyable and rewarding period of the young Prince's life, for while he was still understudying his father and becoming more and more his trusted confidant and helper, he was able to embark on a series of official and private overseas voyages which would constantly extend his experience and intellectual range. As an insatiable explorer with a vital interest in remote parts of the world, Leopold acquired a vast store of knowledge on innumerable subjects – showing a particular aptitude for scientific research.

A fuller description of the many fascinating and rewarding journeys embarked upon by Leopold before and after World War II will appear in the second part of this biography. But among the fruits of the thirty-one such voyages made by him are a remarkable collection of photographs; eight documentary films; four books written and four sponsored, plus the collections of a vast number of specimens of flora and fauna, including live animals, which he presented to museums and zoos. If he had done nothing else, his achievements as an explorer, collector, author, film-producer, scientific innovator, and colonial reformer would alone constitute a record of which any man would be proud.

During the first of Leopold's journeys, which took him to Egypt, the Sudan and the frontiers of Ethiopia, he had a unique experience. Among her many interests Queen Elisabeth was an ardent Egyptologist. The news of Howard Carter's discovery of the tomb of Tutankhamun, therefore, brought her swiftly to Luxor, accompanied by Leopold. Lord Carnarvon held back the opening for twenty-four hours to enable them to arrive and so it was that Leopold was present at the moment on November 26th 1922 of which Carnarvon wrote 'Surely never before in the whole history of excavation had such an amazing sight been seen as the light of our torch revealed to us.'

At Luxor the Queen and her son met the English Colonel Watson Pasha, an erect, wiry little man with a toothbrush moustache, and a cane under his arm, who had been on Kitchener's staff. They soon struck up a friendship, and as a result Leopold was allowed to go off on an adventurous and enjoyable two months' tour with the Colonel. For the first time in his life he was a person, not a prince, even though Watson's careful chaperonage became a joke as Leopold started to spread his wings. In his own words, he 'began to live'. They went first to Khartoum and then, via the Blue Nile, to what was still Abyssinia. During their journey Leopold shot his first crocodile, but he preferred to do his big game hunting with a camera rather than a gun.

In 1925 Leopold embarked upon an exhaustive tour of the Congo, during which he criss-crossed the territory of Belgium's vast and prosperous colony for seven months and studied its every aspect. The programme for the Crown Prince's voyage of discovery had been carefully worked out in advance by King Albert and his advisers and its purpose was serious* – to report back his detailed findings to the Second Colonial Congress which was to be held the following year. Upon his return in January 1926, therefore, Leopold delivered an address to the Congress in the chamber of the Senate.

In a forthright and lucid survey the Prince described and paid tribute to his countrymen's achievements in developing Belgium's prosperous overseas possessions and proclaimed his faith in their future. But he did not hesitate to deal frankly and forcefully with the other side of the coin. The fashion in which the Congo had been administered during the reign of its founder, Leopold II,† had been oppressive and, although Albert had introduced widespread reforms after visiting the Congo, his son found further improvements urgently needed. During his tour Leopold sought out and questioned the humblest of his father's African subjects and studied their conditions of housing, work, health and medical care. In his speech he therefore advocated a whole series of progressive measures to improve those standards and to protect the native labourers from exploitation. Although Leopold's speech was widely acclaimed, his home truths were resented by certain vested interests and his recommendations undoubtedly caused the first stirrings of a groundswell of antipathy in big business circles which would harm him in his subsequent years of adversity.

However, an event later in the year was universally welcomed. The Crown Prince was now twenty-four, popular, handsome, charming and modest – a singularly eligible Royal bachelor. In the autumn Leopold and his mother, using the incognito of 'de Rethy', visited Stockholm and there he met Princess Astrid, the third daughter of Prince Charles and Princess Ingeborg of Sweden. Leopold could not speak Swedish, nor Astrid

---

* As a diversion from his gruelling itinerary Leopold, who was now an expert mountaineer, climbed the 11,000-foot-high volcano of Chalinagongo.

† Surprisingly, Leopold II, having developed the Congo and presented his country with this immense source of wealth, never visited it.

French, so they conversed in English and what could have been a dynastic contrivance became a love-match which captured the popular imagination. Astrid confided to a friend that 'I do not believe that there is any man in the world who better deserves to be loved', while Leopold wrote to his former Eton Housemaster, S. G. Lubbock, in glowing terms about his bride-to-be. On November 10th 1926, six days after a civil ceremony in Stockholm, the couple were married by Cardinal Mercier in the Cathedral of Saint Michel et Gudule, amid scenes of pomp and splendour. The marriage was the occasion for general rejoicing and as the bridal carriage made its way through streets lined with cheering crowds, Leopold's classmates from the *Ecole Militaire* detached the horses and dragged it in triumph to the Palace.

There followed seven idyllic years of happy married life based on the Château of Stuyvenberg, opposite Laeken. It was here that their three children were born – Princess Josephine-Charlotte on October 11th 1927 and, on September 7th 1930, the future heir to the throne, Prince Baudouin. The youngest was born four years later – a few months after Leopold's accession – and named Albert, after the grandfather he was never to see.

During this period Leopold worked hard at understudying his father – helping him with documents and reports and representing him at innumerable functions – usually accompanied by Princess Astrid. The home life of the young couple was quiet and simple. Leopold, like all his family, was a great reader with a wide and varied taste. He was also an able mechanic and a keen motorist – thus when Astrid and he had a day or two free from official engagements, they would go off by car on golfing, fishing, swimming, mountaineering or skiing trips. In Astrid, Leopold now had a companion, not only in his official and family life, but also to share in the excitement and adventures of his overseas journeys.

The first of such tours made by the young couple began in November 1928 and lasted for seven months. Leopold's visits to the Far East had the triple aim of gratifying his love for exploring remote places, collecting specimens for the Natural History Museum in Brussels and studying the scientific methods of agriculture and colonial system evolved by the Dutch, so that they could be emulated in the less advanced Belgian Colony. First the couple went right across Sumatra and Java and traversed Bali on foot from north to south. After visiting Borneo and the Moluccas they then made the hazardous journey into the Vogelkop area of New Guinea. In Java, where the main research stations and plantations were concentrated, Leopold acquired a wealth of knowledge from the Dutch and established a happy relationship with them, which resulted in many subsequent exchanges of specimens and information. Leopold recorded everything he had learned in detailed reports with recommendations, which could have been of immense benefit to the Congo, had they been adopted. But sadly, the Belgian colonials largely ignored the information he had so assiduously obtained for them, while the Dutch derived considerable benefit from the reports and samples the Prince sent them, in exchange, from the Congo. However, one positive result for his country of the Prince's voyages was the establishment of the *Institut National pour l'Etude Agronomique du Congo Belge.*

In 1932, before setting out on another long journey to the Far East, the young Prince and his wife lunched in Paris with the Minister for Colonies, Paul Reynaud, to request facilities for the study of French colonial methods. (This was the first and only time he met the man who was to precipitate the ruin of his life.) After visiting Singapore, traversing Malaya and staying with the King of Siam in Bangkok, they made the long wild journey by rail, road, horse, foot and canoe to Luang Prabang – the 'Kingdom of a thousand Elephants' – and then on to Hanoi. From Tonkin they were taken up to the border country to meet the French Foreign Legion by General Billotte, who also, in 1940, was to have an impact on Leopold's fortunes.

After visiting Hong Kong, the couple crossed to the Philippines, where the Governor, Theodore Roosevelt, lent them his yacht, in which they cruised through that fabulous chain of islands. After revisiting Bali, Java and Surabaya, the Prince ventured alone up the Banto River right into the heart of Borneo, the trip being considered too arduous for women. They then sailed home, with the results of the scientific side of the expedition, including many rare specimens for the Natural History Museum in Brussels.

In 1933 the Prince, again accompanied by his wife, paid his second official visit to the Congo – this time on a special mission for the Colonial Ministry. After a three month tour they returned home by air and Leopold rendered his report direct to the Senate. Once again his speech was marked by frankness and a series of uncompromising conclusions – causing further stirrings of antagonism towards him amongst those who believed that their profits would be affected by his proposed reforms.

After reporting that over-exploitation of the mines and other industrial projects had unbalanced the economy, the Prince made detailed proposals for the scientific development of agriculture and the increased prosperity of the Colony. And once again he pressed for sweeping measures to improve the moral and material welfare of the native population. The sensibly progressive tone of his address won favourable comment abroad as well as in Belgium. One British Governor thought so highly of Leopold's report that he advised the Colonial Office to send a copy of it to all their officials. Later that year the Prince was invited to deliver a lecture to the African Society in London and at the banquet in his honour the toast was proposed by the Prince of Wales. Finally his vigorous and humane colonial policy was embodied in Belgian law by the decree of December 5th 1933.

Although this was a happy and fruitful period for Leopold, for King Albert it was one of intense anxiety and disappointment. He was to reign for fifteen years after the Armistice, but they were years in which crisis followed crisis. The King had to intervene repeatedly to calm public opinion, to fortify successive governments and prevent them from falling – all the same problems and dilemmas that would confront Leopold after his succession. As early as 1921 Albert had declared: 'Unless we return to some form of equilibrium, disarmament will be impossible.' In 1928 the King strongly supported the Catholic Government in its fight, against the Socialists' opposition, to secure a period of eight months' compulsory military service and successfully pressed for the total reorganization of Belgium's defences, to be completed in 1931. Since the international situation continued to deteriorate, he was determined to make his country as strong as possible in her own right – a policy which was bequeathed to and actively pursued by his son.

After the short-lived boom of the early 1920s, Belgium found herself sliding into a financial crisis which in 1926 brought about the fall of the Government. But Albert was able to form a Government of National Unity with special powers, and by bringing in the brilliant economist Emile Francqui to direct the national finances, solved the crisis. Albert's concern at this time was much evident in his letters to Sir Roger Keyes. The worldwide economic slump of 1929 hit Belgium hard and she was suffering from workers' strikes and left-wing demonstrations against the Monarchy. Her political and ethnic unity – always precarious – was being undermined by the intrigues of politicians, intensified by the growing strength of the Left. At times Albert even discussed with Leopold the idea of abdication.

To get away from all this the King would retire to the Ardennes for a day's climbing, and so it was that one afternoon in February 1934 he was last seen alive, walking towards the Roche du Bon Dieu on the Meuse near Namur. He only intended to exercise himself in preparation for a climbing holiday with Leopold at Cortina d'Ampezzo, for which he was making plans. He had gone alone because none of his usual climbing companions was available for one reason or another, and when he failed to return to the rendezvous with his manservant the latter became alarmed. There was a hectic search in the darkness. After midnight he was found, spread-eagled on his back with a deep head wound. The peak is not a difficult climb, but it appeared that a rock which he had grasped had given way.*

Leopold returned post-haste with Astrid from Switzerland, where they

---

* Sensational stories were nevertheless published in the press – particularly in Britain – suggesting the King had been assassinated or even that he had commited suicide.

had been skiing. Four days later, through dense mourning crowds, Leopold followed his father's coffin to its last resting place at Laeken. Beside him in the funeral procession walked the Prince of Wales, with Admiral of the Fleet Sir Roger Keyes in attendance. Only a few days before, King Albert had written to this old and trusted friend: 'I am in full health and the prime of life.' It was a life that was well summed up by Sir Basil Liddell Hart:

> King Albert was the first world hero of the war, and in contrast to others his fame was not dimmed nor his stature diminished by the depressing course of that prolonged struggle. He is enshrined in the memory not only of his own people but of the allied peoples, as the model type of a warrior-king, combining dauntless courage with gracious chivalry.

The whole world mourned the untimely death of a great King. The *Roi Chevalier* of the Great War could no longer guide and lead the country he had loved and served so well. The Heir Apparent must accept his own destiny, but, as Albert had said only a few months before: 'My son is prepared.'

CHAPTER THREE

A Difficult Legacy

'Je me donne tout entier à la Belgique.'　　　　　King Leopold III

For Belgium her new King's accession was a joyful event, though muted by the recent tragedy of his father's death. The country's admiration and affection for King Albert had been profound, but the young heir with his attractive wife and children brought a touch of romance to the throne and a new sense of the future. But as Leopold made his preparations at Laeken for the accession ceremony on February 23rd 1934, his heart was heavy with grief for it was not long since he had accompanied the body of his much-loved father to the family tomb. And as for the reign that lay ahead, he was aware of the looming difficulties and dangers through which it would be his duty to guide his people.

As if symbolically, a week-long fog lifted and the Royal procession moved off from the Palace under a clear blue sky, with Leopold on horseback in the uniform of a Lieutenant-General at its head. As they approached Brussels the trumpets sounded, there was a salute of guns, and at the city's limits stood the Burgomaster to welcome the young King. Crowds packed the avenues, the squares, the crossroads, acclaiming their new leader, while flowers showered down from the upper windows. Leopold's gestures of response showed that he was deeply moved by his people's fervour, but the effect of his grave demeanour was lightened by the natural warmth of Queen Astrid and the fair-haired young Prince and Princess, as they smiled and waved from their open carriage in answer to the continuous cheering.

Meanwhile, in the great chamber of the Palace of the Nation the members of the Government and both Houses of Parliament were assembled to hear their new King swear the Oath of Accession. Round the purple canopied throne, surmounted by the Royal crown, was gathered a glittering array of foreign Royalty (including the Prince of Wales, attended by Sir Roger Keyes, representing King George V), ambassadors and dignatories of State, Church and Army. As the slim and youthful-looking King advanced to a fanfare of trumpets, the Communists (one of whom, Lahaut, weaves in and out of Leopold's story) were heard to shout *'Vive la République!'*, but their interruption was drowned by a storm of cheers, as the assembly rose to its feet to acclaim their new

King. Standing before the throne, his right arm extended, Leopold swore 'to observe the Constitution and the laws of the Belgian people, to maintain the independence of the Nation and the integrity of its territory'. He then delivered his accession speech in French and for the first time in Belgian history repeated the address word for word in Flemish, thus emphasizing at the outset the unifying purpose of his reign and that he was indeed the King of all the Belgians.

In swearing to abide by the Constitution, the King declared that he was thus creating a reciprocal pact of confidence between Sovereign and people. He reminded them of the dangers which confronted them and vowed to protect their liberty and the integrity of the country. 'An indivisible and independent Belgium,' he said, 'is an historic necessity for the European balance of power.' He spoke of his father's dedication to the wartime army, in whose ranks he too had been numbered, and promised to his soldiers an absolute devotion. After touching on such topics as the Colonies, social improvements, industry, etc., and promising the whole-hearted assistance of the Queen, the King declared '*Je me donne tout entier à la Belgique.*'

One observer recalls that the assembly was so moved by Leopold's obvious sincerity that his closing words were drowned in a burst of acclamation which 'reached the heights', whilst dignatories waved their plumed hats in the air, and that, amongst others, some Socialist Ministers 'wept with joy'.[8] After their ceremonial drive back to the Royal Palace, cheered all the way by the enthusiastic populace, the Royal couple were repeatedly called to the balcony to be acclaimed by the surging crowds outside. This memorable and triumphal day ended with Leopold lifting his three-year-old heir, Prince Baudouin, high in the air for the people to see.

Like his father, the new Sovereign had a strong Christian faith and a high sense of duty and service. Modest and quietly spoken, in his dealings with people in all walks of life he was gentle, considerate and courteous. But beneath this almost shy exterior lay great strength of character and determination. He would always listen carefully to advice, and scrupulously weigh the conflicting issues of a problem, but once he had made up his mind about the right course to adopt, he was not to be deflected. Not only did Leopold have in his father a notable example of enlightened monarchy to follow; his accession to the Belgian throne in the troubled nineteen-thirties exposed him to a range of problems that would have tested even the most experienced ruler.

The essential loneliness and vulnerability of his country was fully evident to Leopold when, like his predecessors, he publicly dedicated himself to the service of his people. Most of the problems which King Albert had found so distressing during the last years of his life worsened considerably during the first years of his son's reign. Nazi Germany –

emboldened by British appeasement and French apathy – grew more and more menacing, while Belgium itself was in a dire state. Unemployment figures were rising and a grave budget deficit was imminent. The world depression threatened her with financial ruin and the country was deeply divided and politically unstable. There were strong independence movements in both Flanders and Wallonia. If he were to fulfil his promise to his country, the King would have to solve many intractable problems, internal as well as external, but at least he occupied a position of great personal strength.

As we have seen, the Belgian Constitution of 1831 gives the King powers, both political and military, exceeding the modest right of the British monarchy, as Walter Bagehot puts it, 'to be consulted, to encourage and to warn'. But paradoxically, the very strength of the King's personal position was a weakness. He was the one solid element in the midst of flux. Belgium's parliamentary system, riddled by party faction and intrigue, is inherently unstable. If the Sovereign himself exercises his right and duty to guide and control he risks being assailed from all sides by the dissatisfied. As Leopold himself once said to the author, it was his fate *d'attraper les coups*. Yet the need for a Head of State above the party conflict is vividly illustrated by the fact that between February 1934 and May 1940 there were no less than twelve ministerial crises, four Cabinet reshuffles and six different Prime Ministers. But for the King's vigilance this record might well have been worse; for, as in his father's reign, it was only by the often forceful intervention of the Sovereign that Cabinets were formed or reconciled – or dissuaded from resigning on trivial issues.

In Belgium no single party commands sufficient strength, as in Great Britain or the USA, to form an effective government. The electoral system is governed by proportional representation, with one member for every 40,000 voters, voting being compulsory. The largest group was the Catholic Party (it changed its name to the Social Christian Party in 1945), whose strength was usually greater than that of the Socialist and Communist parties combined. Thus the Liberal Party, itself too small and weak to form a government, was able to tip the balance one way or the other. The task of the King in finding a politician who at a given moment could form an administration under these conditions was far from easy. Short-lived coalitions were the norm, and 'wheeling and dealing' the prevailing practice. Only the Monarch could provide stability: only he, indeed, could stand *au-dessus de la mêlée*, representing neither this political party nor that, neither Flanders nor Wallonia, but Belgium.

The Kings of the Belgians have always had to contend with a far less well-behaved Parliament than the British House of Commons. The whole atmosphere is much more emotional and excitable, with constant clashes of party interest, language and temperament. Moreover, the standards of Belgian parliamentary life were low – politics being regarded by many as a well-paid career with substantial perquisites and opportunities for material gain. But subservience to the 'doctrine' of the political party's ruling caucus was mandatory, any divergence being fatal to the career of the dissident. Indeed, the discipline in the parties was so strict and effective in holding Deputies to the party line that issues were almost invariably judged from that narrow viewpoint, rather than from that of the national interest. Of all the eighteen changes of government which took place during the inter-war years not one fell as a direct result of a vote in Parliament – all being due to party manoeuvres and intrigues behind the scenes. That contemptuous phrase of the French, *espèce de député*, would have been equally relevant in Brussels.

The roots of the political situation facing Leopold in 1934 lay deep. For the factions of Belgian political life there are historic as well as contemporary reasons. The country was born of strife. The Left of the Belgian political spectrum is deep-dyed in the colours of the French *Commune*. The Communists, the Trotskyites, the Walloon Separatists and the Socialists are all fundamentally Republican, anti-Monarchist and anti-clerical, although not all Socialists other than members of the strong Marxist contingent would openly admit to the Republicanism which is enshrined in their party's constitution. Indeed the Socialists, who are mainly Walloons, have always regarded themselves as the heirs to the French revolutionaries and wrote their dedication to the 'Republican Principle' into the constitution of their party, when they founded it in 1885. They would always seize every opportunity to attack the Crown and the Monarchy. In December 1909, for example, the Council of the Socialist Party published a manifesto which included the following:

> Between Socialism and Monarchy there is no possible reconciliation, and when official Belgium prepares itself to acclaim Albert I . . . a loud clamour of hope and defiance will rise from all the workers' hearts: *Vive la République Sociale!*

It is true that a few of the Socialist leaders, including Emile Vandervelde, came to admire and respect King Albert, but even they recognized him only as 'the first citizen' of the Country and not as its King. The party's Republican and anti-Monarchist sentiments remained undiminished, however, and Vandervelde was reproached, after King Albert's death, by the Socialist rank and file, with, as he himself put it, 'the betrayal of our Republican principles in becoming one of . . . the King's Ministers'. Vandervelde extended his support to King Albert's son, but, as will be seen, other Socialist leaders would always seize on any pretext to fan the smouldering fires of anti-Monarchist sentiment favoured by the majority of their followers.

Although not inherently anti-Monarchist, the Liberals – or 'Liberal-Left', as they prefer to describe themselves – like the Socialists, are bitterly opposed to the strongly Royalist Catholic, or Social Christian Party, as it is now called. This anti-clericalism was particularly strong amongst the Liberals grouped round the powerful Grand Orient Free-mason caucus, which controlled the party with its secret directives and, as will be seen, was capable of changing its entire voting sentiment over-night. Utterly unlike British Freemasonry, this particular sect is highly political, anti-Church, materialist and secretive. Liberals are to be found in the French-speaking and Jewish communities and among the wealthy and professional classes, particularly lawyers, throughout Belgium, but mainly in Brussels and the Walloon towns.

Socialist and Liberal-Left hostility towards the Church is mainly due to the great political strength of the Catholic community. Belgians tend to be either Catholic or anti-Catholic – there is very little 'no-man's-land' in between. There is complete liberty of worship, but there are very few Protestants in Belgium. The influence of the Church is stronger in the Flemish than in the Walloon provinces, but Catholicism is woven into the very fabric of everyday life, and its strength was increased during and after the two World Wars, as a result of the firm and dignified attitude of resistance it maintained towards the invader throughout those conflicts. Following in the footsteps of Cardinal Mercier, Primate in World War I, Cardinal Van Roey was a similar pillar of moral strength throughout the last war. Documents have been published revealing the paper war he conducted with the German Governor-General and the occupation authorities, whom he refused ever to meet. By the end of the war, 528 priests had been arrested by the Germans, 33 had been shot or had died in concentration camps and 135 were still imprisoned.

The Catholic or Social Christian Party embraces most of the aristoc-racy, the military hierarchy and those large sections of the middle and working classes who are fundamentally for God, King and Country, with their belief in the solid virtues of regular chuch-going, hard work and high standards of family life. Consequently Belgian trades union members are by no means all supporters of the left-wing parties – indeed they are almost equally divided between the Christian (and solidly Royalist) unions and those of the Left, which are controlled by the Communists and Socialists. Moreover, members of the left-wing unions are not necessarily opposed to the Monarchy or their Sovereign, despite the Republicanism which is inherent in the parties of the Left – as was shown by the *Consultation Populaire* of 1950, when a large number of Socialists and the majority of Liberals voted for Leopold's return from his enforced exile. But cutting right across all political, religious and class barriers was the antipathy and rivalry between Fleming and Walloon, already ancient in 1830 and still unresolved.

This permanant racial problem was latent in every Belgian political crisis of Leopold's reign. The Flemings, being of Dutch origin, closely resemble them both in their language and customs. Numerically they are stronger than the French-speaking Walloons, probably in a proportion as high as 3 to 2. As the language of the Belgian Government, society, law-courts and universities had always been French, the Flemish were at a political and cultural disadvantage throughout the nineteenth century. However, the Flemings learned French easily and considered it the more fashionable language, while very few Walloons ever took the trouble to learn Flemish. So the Flemings gradually won their battle for equality of treatment, and were no longer debarred by linguistic limitations from the universities or from exercising the liberal professions.

During both World Wars the Germans tried to encourage the revival of extreme Flemish nationalism. This produced an equally noisy minority of Walloons who, in the post-war years, made greatly exaggerated allegations of collaboration with the Germans by the Flemings. Racial antagonism also found expression in the growth of extreme separatist movements before, during and after World War II – those of the Walloons being far to the Left and those of the Flemish Nationalists politically right-wing. In this unpropitious climate Belgium was fortunate in having a Constitution which requires the Sovereign to play a positive and unifying part in the government of the country, and a King with the dedication and strength of purpose to fulfil this task. This was generally recognized at the time – even by those who, after the surrender of the Belgian Army, would criticize Leopold for the way he exercised those rights and powers.

The Prime Minister whom Leopold inherited from his father was the Comte de Broqueville, an experienced statesman of the old school, who had long enjoyed King Albert's confidence. He lacked, however, the iron hand necessary for the control of a government which contained no personality competent to cope with an economic crisis. For four months de Broqueville pursued a half-hearted policy of deflation: then, discouraged by the lack of support in Parliament, he tendered his resignation.

This was the King's first experience of dealing with a change of ministry. Despite all his efforts, the governments that were formed fell in quick succession, while the economic situation went from bad to worse. Finally in March 1935, to save his country from ruin, Leopold had to assert his constitutional powers to the full by calling in, from outside Parliament, the brilliant Princeton-trained economist and Governor of the National Bank, Paul Van Zeeland, to form a government. This man-of-the-centre was able to form the relatively stable National Government consisting of Catholics, Liberals and Socialists, which was to remain in power until October 1937 – with immediate beneficial effect on the stability and economy of the country. With Leopold's full support, Van Zeeland introduced sweeping economic reforms which, within eighteen months, had halved unemployment and increased exports by one third. The King was widely praised for having taken positive action to halt the slide and put the country back on its feet.

On becoming King, Leopold changed the style of his personal living little. He and Queen Astrid still lived with their young family – now increased to three by the birth of Prince Albert in September 1934 – at the pleasant, unostentatious Château de Stuyvenberg. Here he was able to relax, confide his problems to his wife and play with their children, a husband and father enjoying the privacy of his home. But this happy married existence was soon to be cruelly ended. In the summer of 1935, Queen Astrid was killed while motoring with the King in Switzerland. Returning from a climbing holiday in the Dolomites they had paused for a few days at their villa on Lake Lucerne. On the morning of August 29th they had set out on another climbing expedition in two cars, Leopold driving the first, with his wife at his side and the chauffeur in the rear seat. The road along which they approached the little village of Kussnacht was good, but narrow and winding and with a stone kerb a few inches high. The Queen diverted her husband's attention by asking him a question about the map she was studying, and in that split second the wheel of the car jumped the kerb. The King lost control. Below the road was a meadow with apple trees, leading down to a lake. One of the trees was close to the kerb and the King's last memory was of the tree looming in front of him. They were both hurled out of the car. Leopold recovered consciousness to find his head cradled in the lap of an unknown woman who helped him to where Astrid was lying. He heard the doctor who was taking her pulse say 'She is dead.' For a moment he was incredulous, then he saw that his wife was wounded as his father had been. Her head was cruelly gashed. He himself had been run over, and he had broken several ribs. Covered with blood, he was assisted by the doctor to a car and noticed a photographer point a camera at him and an angry bystander knock it out of the man's hand.

Five days later, after the funeral service at the Cathedral of Sainte-Gudule in Brussels, the Queen was buried at Laeken. Against doctor's orders, the King followed the coffin for four miles on foot, a lonely limping figure, his arm in a sling and head bandaged; he was still weak and shocked from the accident. This sudden bereavement, following on the loss of his father eighteen months before, tested Leopold's fortitude to the utmost. Sensitive by nature and deeply dependent on the affections and intimacies of family life, he now faced his royal responsibilities alone. Drawn more closely than ever to his motherless children, the young Sovereign braved it all in the spirit of Lord Weir of Hermiston in Stevenson's novel: 'On he went up the great bare staircase of his duty.'

Leopold's temperament, his intense concern for the welfare of his country and people, and now the tragedy of his wife's death, combined to shape his public image into something different from his true *persona*.

That warm, civilized, humorous and humane being, the Leopold known to his family and friends, seemed to be gradually overlaid by a mask – a carapace of austerity, reserve, withdrawal. The 'leaden cope of responsibility' pressed on his shoulders. He was admired, respected: he aroused warm sentiments of sympathy and devotion, but for years after his wife's death he seemed like a man apart. Astrid had brought serenity and an intense happiness into his private world; her love and companionship had smoothed the young King's path. She had shared the passion for sport and the open air which he inherited from his father, and together they had travelled the globe.

When Leopold brought home from Switzerland the body of the Queen, his train, with drawn blinds, was met at the frontier by the principal parliamentary figures of Belgium. Among others, he received in his compartment the Socialist Paul Henri Spaak, who was then Minister of Transport, Posts and Telegraphs. Spaak remained alone with the King and somehow contrived to say exactly the right thing – for which, indeed, he had a great gift. Both Spaak and Leopold were deeply moved and from this meeting Spaak gained the Monarch's personal friendship and trust. Thus there entered into the arena the chameleon figure of a man who, more than any other, was to play in Leopold's life the part of a genial Judas.* For those who are conscious only of Spaak's post-war reputation, this might seem a harsh judgment.

The pioneer of Western European Union, who set Belgium on the course which made her the home of NATO and the centre of the Common Market, seems strangely cast in the role of a Judas. But Spaak is only explicable in terms of his own inner contradictions. Count Capelle, Leopold's Private Secretary, recalls how Spaak moved from the extreme-left to the centre-right of the political spectrum 'less from conviction than for tactical motives' and 'engineered compromises which gave him the reputation of being a frequent turncoat . . . His own boldness often causes him surprise, if not actual alarm, for he is a sensitive creature, with the hands of a woman.'[9]

Paul Henri Spaak was born in a fashionable Brussels suburb in 1899. His father, Paul, was a successful playwright and became a director of the 'Monnaie', the Brussels Royal Opera House. His mother was the daughter of Paul Janson and sister of Paul Emile Janson, both eminent Liberal leaders. In 1921 she herself became a member of the Senate. One of Spaak's brothers, Claude, was a playwright and the other, Charles, a film producer whose daughter Catherine Spaak became a film star. With this background it is surprising that Spaak, after qualifying as a barrister in 1932, should have entered politics as a far-left Republican Socialist Deputy – a cloth-capped revolutionary anti-militarist. Spaak was 'delight-

* On January 14th 1918 Field Marshal Haig wrote from France to his wife about the War Minister, Lord Derby: 'I hear he is called in London "genial Judas!" '

ed to lead rioting mobs', as H. D. Ziman, a British Foreign Correspondent who got to know him well, recalls, adding 'One Conservative newspaper used to show me the "anti-Spaak grille" they had installed after he and his friends smashed their windows in 1934.'[10]

It was during this period of violent revolutionary action that Spaak began to develop, in close concert with his friend and mentor Henri De Man, the concept of an authoritarian form of Socialism. De Man describes in his autobiography, *Cavalier Seul*, how he and Spaak, having lost faith in the parliamentary system, developed 'authoritarian . . . principles in clearcut opposition to the traditional conceptions of social democracy . . .' 'Socialism,' De Man continues, 'should break with the bourgeois and liberal conception of a democratic state and demand what Paul Henri Spaak and I called an authoritarian democracy . . .'[11]

De Man's development of the authoritarian ideas which he and Spaak had formulated would enable him to switch effortlessly to the Nazis' brand of Socialism, after they had devastated and occupied Belgium in May 1940. Indeed he would then dissolve the Belgian Socialist Party, of which he was the President, and persuade the bulk of its leaders and members to join the National Socialist movement, which he formed to replace it and dedicated to collaborating with Hitler's New Order in Europe. In the proclamation to his new party's members which followed, De Man declared that the German occupation forces should not be resisted and that 'the collapse of the parliamentary regime . . . far from being a disaster . . . is a blessing for the working class'.

Whether or not Spaak would have remained in step with De Man along the National Socialist road he took after the Belgian capitulation, as did so many other Belgian Socialists, will never be known, as he was deprived of the opportunity to do so. Indeed his plan – and that of his Cabinet colleagues who, like him, fled to France – to come to terms with the Germans and return to enemy-occupied Belgium in the summer of 1940 was frustrated by Leopold, as Spaak would frankly admit in a television interview twenty-eight years later. He would then declare: 'We were saved by the King's refusal to listen to us.'* But by the nineteen-sixties Spaak had mellowed considerably, having become, after a bewildering series of volte-faces, an eminent European statesman, a wealthy capitalist and company director.†

The first of Spaak's many volte-faces was made in 1935, at the height of his extreme left-wing activity. In February 1934, as a Deputy, Spaak had refused to vote for the two Chambers' loyal address to the King, because he was a Republican. In November he scorned the idea of Socialists

* See Appendix IX, for Spaak's 'recantation'.
† Spaak's sojourn on one board of directors came to an abrupt end in 1970, when he was 'extracted' – according to the *Sunday Times* of July 23rd 1972 – 'by an appalled family friend' from the fraudulent *Real Estate Fund of America* before it crashed, and its founder, Jerome Hoffman, began a jail sentence in America.

joining Cabinets containing capitalists – demanding instead a Popular Front with the Communists – but within three months he had joined a predominantly bourgeois coalition government, commenting that 'poachers make the best gamekeepers', and later under the King's patronage he went on to hold successively the posts of Foreign Minister and Prime Minister.

The street agitator who became an ardent Royalist and the King's trusted friend and right-hand man would betray him – and yet, beyond all reason, retain his Sovereign's quizzical affection. Indeed an amused tolerance remained when their relationship had passed through all its phases – after Spaak had held ministerial office under the King and ceaselessly praised him in the nineteen-thirties; denounced him in 1940; praised him again to the world from 1941 to 1944; made his peace, and quickly turned coat again in 1945; led riotous mobs against the Palace on his Sovereign's return to Belgium in 1950; and finally, four years before his death in 1972, publicly recanted in a television interview. 'Men cannot help their characters,' King Leopold once said to the author. 'If I were to meet him somewhere, I would still hold out my hand to him, for we have been such friends in the past and have been through so much together. He is fat and jolly and likes all the good things in life. He can always see the funny side of things. We would sit down together, and in no time he would be making me laugh – probably with some outrageous story about one of his colleagues. I can forgive him anything for that.'*

Spaak was ambivalent: a man, as one contemporary described him, of 'successive sincerities'. 'By looking at this weathercock,' writes the French author, Fabre-Luce, 'one can always tell which way the wind of Europe is blowing.'[12] The feminine streak in his character, which enabled him to respond with an instinctive delicacy when he met the bereaved King, enfeebled him when he came under pressure. He was a born opportunist, but the opportunities he grasped were always for the easier way out. In the nineteen-thirties Leopold saw in Spaak, who was only two years older than the King, a young, promising, sympathetic, quick-minded politician on whose qualities he thought he could rely, and there is no doubt that Spaak gave him solid support and basked without reluctance in his favour. But it was a fair-weather friendship, and when the pressure was on Leopold himself and his army was facing defeat in May 1940, Spaak turned against him with the same speed and facility that enabled him, in October of that year in London, to adopt as his slogan '*Je suis pour le Roi!*' Eloquent, broad of vision, but too easily seduced by self-interest, this man of many facets was at once more attractive and a

* When Spaak was Foreign Minister in the nineteen-fifties he received a telephone call from Sir George Labouchère, the British Ambassador, who began '*Ici Labouchère,*' to which he replied '*Bon. Envoyez-moi deux kilos de boeuf.*' On another occasion Spaak remarked 'I am often told that I look like Winston Churchill and speak English like Charles Boyer, but I wish it was the other way round.'

more colourful personality than Hubert Pierlot, who would, with Spaak, desert the King on the battlefield and share the odium for what was to follow.

Pierlot emerged from the political merry-go-round of Leopold's peace-time reign as the Prime Minister in office when the Germans invaded, from which position, after many vicissitudes, he became head of the Belgian 'Government-in-exile' in London. Here was Spaak's exact oppo-site, a man who trod narrow paths towards.fixed ends. There was nothing flexible, visionary or sensitive about Pierlot. A contemporary, Professor Georges Henri Dumont, describes him thus: 'Pierlot is timid, cold and lacks self-confidence. He has a rather narrow outlook on life, having travelled hardly at all either in time or space. He does not know foreign statesmen; he hardly knows those of his own country. Any situation that is at all out of the ordinary appals the Doctor of Law, who is more familiar with legal text-books than with realities . . .' Spaak might have said of himself, like Walt Whitman, 'Do I contradict myself? Very well then I contradict myself, (I am large, I contain multitudes).' But Pierlot had the self-consistency of the small-minded. He was at sea in the maelstrom of the nineteen-thirties and forties. As a Prime Minister in peacetime he was colourless and indecisive: one politician who had been summoned to see him said that after an interview of three-quarters of an hour he still did not know why he had been asked to call. In his memoirs, the ebullient and volatile Spaak describes Pierlot as 'serious to the point of severity, honest to a fault, a tireless worker, fervent Christian [Spaak was not a believer], patriot and model of civic, professional and family virtue'.[13] His failings, according to Spaak, were an exaggerated love of detail, a lack of human warmth, and rigidity of thought. When the Germans invaded, Pierlot's very rigidity prevented him from reading correctly a situation beyond his comprehension. Such, however, were the men on whom Leopold had to depend.

In the negotiations following the resignation of Van Zeeland in November 1937 the King showed great tact, patience and statesmanship. He charged – amongst others – both Pierlot and Spaak with forming a government, but neither was able to do so. After calling on two other Socialist leaders, Henri De Man and the veteran Emile Vandervelde without success, the King adopted Vandervelde's recommendation, which was made 'not in a spirit of warm conviction, but because it was the lesser evil', and summoned Spaak to the Palace. In his memoirs, Count Capelle caught the atmosphere at the Belgian Parliament brilliantly in his description of Spaak's first attempt to form a ministry:

During these consultations, the lobbies of the Chamber took on the appearance of an Eastern Market. Ministerial portfolios were up for sale, and there were plenty of bidders. M. Spaak was eyed as though he was a nabob. Charming smiles welcomed him on every side. He himself took soundings either directly or through intermediaries. But one had the impression that he was singeing his wings.

After this attempt had failed, the King charged the Liberal leader, Paul Emile Janson (Spaak's uncle), to negotiate with the party leaders and recommend a solution to the deadlock, but he was unsuccessful and the deadlock continued.

Once more the King summoned leaders of the three major parties to the Palace, and stressed the gravity of the situation. The political parties, he said, were putting themselves in the place of Parliament, the only body entitled to grant or refuse confidence to new ministries. The parties claimed to want national union, but blocked every attempt to bring it about. He then pointed out that only a coalition of the three major parties was possible, and urged the politicians to cease their back-stage intrigues, which were preventing potential Prime Ministers from forming Ministries. On November 23rd Janson succeeded in drawing up a list of Ministers (with Spaak as Foreign Minister) acceptable to the majority. The King, and the King alone, had brought the country safely out of a deadlock which had lasted for thirty days.

But all was not well with the Belgian parliamentary system. At the first audience granted to his new Prime Minister, the King warned him against the increasing tendency to issue press statements after Cabinet meetings. Too often these press statements spoke of Cabinet 'decisions', as though the Cabinet were of itself capable of taking decisive action without the formal approval of the Sovereign. No conclusion reached by the Cabinet could be more than a 'proposal' until it was countersigned by the King. When, after six months, Janson's Government fell as the result of financial problems, the King decided that only by rapid and decisive action could another long and demoralizing crisis be avoided. Spaak had learned his lesson from the 'Eastern Market' fiasco; and when the King charged him with forming a government, he conducted his negotiations from his office and created a record by presenting an agreed list of Ministers to the King within twenty-four hours.

Throughout Spaak's premiership crises continued one after the other, the recurrent theme being the Socialist party's treatment of the Prime Minister and the other Socialist members of the Government as their nominees rather than as Ministers of the Crown – and Spaak's threats to resign, rather than come into conflict with his party. Ironically, having survived a whole series of major political and international crises, Spaak fell from power in February 1939 over a trival domestic issue known as *L'affaire Martens*.

This affair was a significant example of the quicksands of Belgian politics and also of the way that circumstances forced the King to rule as well as reign. A group of Flemish extremists had long sought to circumvent a regulation whereby those who had 'collaborated' during the German occupation of 1914–18 were debarred from public positions. Their chance came when nominations were required for membership of the Royal Flemish Academy of Medicine. The relevant Minister, Merlot, was a Walloon, and too easily accepted the inclusion in the list of a certain Dr Martens, whose name was tainted by his activities during the First World War. Although Merlot suggested to the Prime Minister that the King should be warned of the significance of Dr Martens' name, Spaak replied 'Don't worry – it's not worth bothering about.' Moreover, the list of names was marked 'After discussion in the Cabinet', although it later emerged that three Ministers had not been consulted. But worst of all, the contents of the decree were published before it was presented for signature. The King was therefore obliged to sign the decree to avoid showing dissension between himself and his government. Ugly scenes in Parliament followed, and when groups of ex-servicemen demonstrated in the streets Spaak was set upon and roughly handled.

The King moved swiftly. On February 2nd 1939 he summoned a Cabinet meeting at the Palace.

> You are my Ministers and my colleagues. My words are addressed to you only. A Cabinet meeting is the only opportunity I have of speaking my mind with absolute frankness . . . Ministries have by now become a miniature edition of Parliament, in which all shades of political differences have to be represented and adjusted, and so they have become more and more transitory and difficult to form . . . Ministers are becoming the mouthpieces of their parties: Governments split and resign without being overthrown in Parliament.
>
> All semblance of responsibility is lost. We are facing a crisis of authority, of disorder, of confusion, sometimes of demagogy, and this at a moment when dangers are mounting and the country's situation demands the greatest stability of government, the highest economic endeavour, and manifest evidence of order and discipline in public life. Gentlemen, the fault does not lie with our institutions; the fault lies in the shortcomings of those who are entrusted with governing the nation.

Moreover, the King pointed out, he was often presented with decrees for signature, the contents of which had been published or leaked before submission. The Martens affair was an example. 'These indiscretions cannot be tolerated. Such practices do not allow the Head of State to fulfil his constitutional function. He is no longer protected by his Ministers – on the contrary, it is he who protects them.'

Even the King could not protect Spaak. The Liberal Ministers told the Premier that they would resign if Martens' appointment were not cancelled, and a week later the Government fell. There was a futile attempt to form a national coalition, and when at the King's request Pierlot achieved a Catholic-Socialist combination it survived in office for only five days. With great reluctance, in view of the perilous international situation, the King decreed the dissolution of Parliament. When he wrote to Pierlot deploring the need for an appeal to the country, he hammered home his previous comments on ministerial irregularities. 'If the principles of our national charter are forgotten, the Head of State cannot carry out his functions, and the Crown is most improperly made a target for criticism, although the Ministers alone should bear before Parliament the responsibility for Acts signed as the King . . .'

The election took place on April 2nd. On the same day Martens withdrew his name from the list of Academicians. But though Pierlot emerged as leader of the largest party, ten days' bickering in which the Socialists made difficulties as to the terms in which they would support the Government followed, during which he failed to form an administration. Again the King intervened, by calling a meeting of party leaders and appealing to them to place country before faction. The situation was extremely grave, he declared, because 'instead of attending to principles and ideas, the parties waste their time in discussing the exact grading of influences and in satisfying party requirements'. After denouncing the political and personal interests which were threatening to bring the whole machinery of government to a halt, he concluded:

Of all the reforms which must be achieved, the most important is that of the mentality of the men in power – of the Ministers, that is to say. Without this reform, which needs no legislation, all others will be vain and impossible . . . You must reach agreement.

There was little or no response to this appeal. First the Socialists and then the Liberals expressed their dissatisfaction with the posts they were offered, and it was not until April 17th that a list was presented to the King. Five hours later a meeting of the Socialist Party Congress voted by a large majority not to support the Pierlot Government – and all the Socialist Ministers were obliged to resign immediately. Pierlot carried on with a Catholic-Liberal coalition until, with the outbreak of war at the beginning of September, the Socialists rejoined him in a National Government.

If a certain sense of tedium is evoked by the record of these shufflings in the corridors of Belgian politics, to recall them is nevertheless necessary. Even this summary account vividly illustrates how the King, torn between his private misery and deep concern for his country's safety, was driven to intervene, to upbraid, to exercise Royal authority. Yet what was the alternative? Apathy? In Belgium's earlier time of trial he knew that his father had spoken out against the politicians in what he believed to be the best interests of the nation. During the nineteen-thirties the menace of the Führer was even greater than that of the Kaiser. 'If a house be divided against itself, that house cannot stand.' His duty, as he saw it, was to establish responsibility in central government. If his methods sometimes seemed forceful, it was mainly because of the strain of trying to be a statesman with few wise, disinterested or dependable men at his side. Although Leopold's firm leadership was accepted and applauded at the time, all this would later be brought up as 'evidence' that he had imposed a personal and autocratic rule on an unwilling Parliament and people.

Ironically it was Hubert Pierlot who would refute at least some of these charges when they were levelled at Leopold after the war. In his memoirs Pierlot wrote: 'It must not be concluded . . . that there was any ill-feeling between the King and his Ministers; on the contrary all the Ministers were deeply attached to the King. The prestige of the King and the Royal institution was very great in Belgium. The members of the Government came, probably more than others, under its radiance . . .'[14]

But the difficulty in any attempt to give an objective account of King Leopold's life is that the animosities of wartime and the virulence of post-war years have distorted the record. As the story unfolds, it is essential to carry in mind Thucydides' reflection on the party strife in Greek cities during the Peloponnesian war: 'Words had to change their ordinary meaning and to take what was now given to them. Reckless audacity came to be considered the courage of a loyal ally; prudent hesitation, specious cowardice; moderation was held to be a cloak for unmanliness; ability to see all sides of a question inaptness to act on any . . .' So, in Leopold's case decisiveness was to be translated into autocracy, impartiality into bias, patriotism into self-interest.

Such was the uncertain climate of Belgian politics amid which the King strove to protect his country against the growing menace of Nazi Germany. As a coda to this chapter, therefore, it is relevant to recall that only a fortnight before the *Blitzkrieg* was launched, Leopold was faced with a final flutter of irresponsibility. In the last days of April 1940 a wrangle broke out over the Government's proposals for linguistic reform and when on April 25th the Liberals refused to accept the educational budget, Pierlot threw in his hand. Leopold was adamant. 'This,' he said in refusing to accept Pierlot's resignation, 'is not the time to provoke a ministerial crisis on internal and domestic matters.' Thus it was thanks to the King that when the *Blitzkrieg* struck on May 10th, Belgium still had a government in office headed, ironically, by Pierlot and Spaak – the men who would play a leading part in the events which caused Leopold to lose his throne.

CHAPTER FOUR

The Tightrope

'The whole world and especially the small nations today turn their
eyes towards England. If England will act now she can lead Europe
. . . it is your last chance. If you do not stop Germany now, all is
over. France cannot guarantee Czechoslovakia any more because
that will become geographically impossible. If you do not maintain
the Treaty of Locarno all that will remain to you is to await
rearmament by Germany against which France can do nothing . . .
If you do not stop Germany by force today, war is inevitable, even
if you make a temporary friendship with Germany.'
                    Pierre Etienne Flandin, the French Foreign Minister,
                                            in London, March 1936

As we have seen, the kingdom Leopold inherited was looked upon by the
Great Powers of Europe as a strategic instrument, rather than an
independent sovereign country. Indeed, in the world of *Machtpolitik*
Belgium's role was that of a convenient battleground or passageway for
her more powerful neighbours.

When Leopold came to the throne, Hitler had been Chancellor of Nazi
Germany for a year and already his programme of clandestine rearmament was well advanced. Suppose *Mein Kampf* were true? Suppose he
were to march? Belgium was no Switzerland, secure behind mountain
passes; she was the cockpit of Europe. Chill winds were blowing and
Belgium seemed exposed to every gust. This was the climate in which the
King and his Ministers had to forge a new policy for Belgium. Leopold
had to walk a tightrope over a whirlpool.

Albert and Leopold had watched with profound dismay the disintegration of Europe from 1919 onwards and the rise of forces which threatened
to take ruthless advantage of the weakness and disharmony of the former
Allies. Indeed, next to German rearmament and the timidity shown by
Britain and France in facing up to Hitler, a cardinal factor in Belgium's
change of policy was the continual disagreement between these two
countries on every possible subject. In particular, the French deeply
resented Britain's policy of encouraging the recovery and rearmament of
Germany and of persistently trying to weaken France's defensive capacity. A month after his accession, therefore, the King asked five of his
Ministers to meet him at Laeken and discussed with them the problems of
foreign policy and national defence. All agreed that Belgium should act as

the honest broker between Britain and France, without committing herself to an alliance with either, and that she should strengthen her defences so as to give pause to any would-be aggressor.

As Europe began to emerge from the economic depression, hopes for continuing peace had been set on the League of Nations, with its theory of Collective Security, and on the Locarno Pact, which had been initiated by Gustav Stresemann, the German Foreign Minister, and signed in 1925. Under this treaty the inviolability of the German-Belgian and the German-French frontiers had been guaranteed by those countries and also by Britain and Italy. The five signatories had pledged themselves to keep the peace and to unite against any member which might break the pact. All five Locarno nations also undertook to maintain the demilitarization of the German Rhineland on the eastern frontiers of Belgium and France, the stretch of territory on both banks of the Rhine in which Germany had been forbidden to maintain troops or fortifications under the terms of the Treaty of Versailles. The demilitarized zone was the chief safeguard for Belgium and France against a renewal of German aggression, and both countries had accepted the setting up of this protective barrier as compensation for deferring to their allies' wishes in regard to other provisions which affected their national security.

Belgium had thus been induced to abandon her pre-war status of guaranteed neutrality – and France to drop Marshal Foch's demand that her frontier should extend to the west bank of the Rhine. (When Foch learned that the Versailles Peace Treaty left German territory virtually intact, he commented prophetically 'This is not Peace. It is an Armistice for twenty years.') The demilitarized zone was of even greater importance to Belgium, for, as her Premier Van Zeeland was to observe after it had been violated by Hitler: 'In proportion to the forces of the various countries, Belgium had the longest and most exposed common frontier with Germany.'

In signing the Locarno Pact, on the basis that her territorial integrity would be protected by the demilitarized zone, Belgium had exchanged her guaranteed status for that of a guarantor, for, although a much smaller nation than the other four, she was committed to rendering military assistance to whichever of the co-signatory powers became the victim of unprovoked aggression from another. Thus Belgium, Britain and Italy were pledged to defend either France or Germany if one launched an unprovoked attack on the other. Winston Churchill's view about Locarno was that 'while France remained armed and Germany disarmed, Germany could not attack her; and that on the other hand France would never attack Germany if that automatically involved Britain becoming Germany's ally . . . I was therefore always equally opposed to the disarmament of France and to the rearmament of Germany, because of the much greater danger this immediately brought on

Great Britain.'[15] So long as Germany remained relatively disarmed, with the Rhineland demilitarized, and while France and Britain retained their superiority in arms and their will to fight to fulfil their Locarno obligations, Belgium had little to fear.

Shortly after Hitler came to power, however, there began a chain of events which was to remove these safeguards and place Belgium in such a state of peril that the King and his Ministers were compelled to reorientate their foreign and military policies. In July 1933 Nazi Germany walked out of the Disarmament Conference, after the French had demurred at her categorical demand for the removal of all restrictions on her right to rearm. Hitler had been emboldened by the support he had received from certain quarters in Britain. *The Times*, for example, had spoken of 'the timely redress of inequality' and the Socialist *New Statesman* of 'the unqualified recognition of the principle of the equality of States'. In pursuance of this theme Britain put pressure on the French Government, which then coaxed the Germans back to the conference. This was hailed by the Left as 'a victory for peace'.

The Socialist Prime Minister of the British coalition Government, Ramsay MacDonald, now produced the 'MacDonald Plan', which, in the words of Winston Churchill, involved 'asking France to halve her army while Germany doubles hers'. It also stipulated that France should destroy all her heavy weapons. In a parliamentary debate Churchill sternly denounced this plan to weaken France and strengthen Germany, at a time when that country was showing 'a tumultuous insurgence of ferocity and war spirit . . .'

In October 1933, however, the British Government, having induced France to conform, submitted the MacDonald Plan to the Disarmament Conference. But Hitler, who was pressing forward relentlessly with his clandestine rearmament programme, spurned the Allies' quixotic offer and contemptuously withdrew Germany not only from the Disarmament Conference, but also from the League of Nations. And yet, undeterred by these rebuffs and danger-signs, Ramsay MacDonald, supported by Stanley Baldwin, continued to press for the disarmament of France well into 1934. After a speech in which Churchill forecast that Germany would soon possess a powerful air force and called for the strengthening of the RAF, Baldwin commented: 'The support Mr Winston Churchill received came only from a very small group of Members.'* Unfortunately, this was to remain true right up to 1939.

In the summer of 1934 Hitler consolidated his position by having about 6,000 divergents shot in cold blood. 'This massacre,' wrote Churchill,

---

* One of Churchill's closest associates and supporters was Admiral of the Fleet Sir Roger Keyes, who had entered Parliament in 1931 as MP for Portsmouth North to campaign for the strengthening of the armed forces of the Crown – and in particular the Royal Navy and its Air Arm – in order to safeguard the country against war.

'showed that the new Master of Germany would stop at nothing and that conditions in Germany bore no relation to those in a civilized State. A dictatorship based on terror and reeking with blood had confronted the world. Anti-Semitism was ferocious and brazen, and the concentration-camp system was already in full operation . . .' However, all this had little effect on the minds of the MacDonald-Baldwin Government, who continued to behave as though 'the German Chancellor' was the most reasonable of statesmen.

The British Socialists and Liberals remained even less affected by these grisly signs and portents. Both parties continued to demand unilateral disarmament and to vote against the Government's always-inadequate Defence Estimates – denouncing anyone who differed from them as 'sabre-rattlers' or 'warmongers'. In the year that Hitler came to power, Professor C. E. M. Joad, who later became a radio celebrity on the BBC Brains Trust, having inspired the members of the Oxford Union to pass the resolution that 'This House refuses to fight for King and country', urged the Universities' Congress in Cambridge: 'In the event that your country is invaded: Disobey all orders. If a general strike were declared . . . If the Civil Servants refused to obey orders, it would be impossible for any enemy power to overrun the country.'

Sir Stafford Cripps, who became the post-war Labour Chancellor of the Exchequer, went even further in urging the Armed Forces not to fight and the workers to refuse to work in such circumstances, but to welcome the invaders as brothers, while the leader of the Labour Party, George Lansbury, insisted that all nations must 'disarm to the level of Germany, as a preliminary to total disarmament'.

When in July 1934 the Baldwin Government made some inadequate proposals to strengthen the weak and obsolete Royal Air Force, the Labour Party, supported by the Liberals, moved a vote of censure against them. Flaying those who would thus jeopardize the security of the kingdom, Winston Churchill warned: 'Let us remember this: our weakness does not only involve ourselves; our weakness involves also the stability of Europe.' But Clement Attlee, on behalf of the Labour opposition, declared: 'We deny the need for increased armaments . . . We deny the proposition that an increased British Air Force will make for the peace of the world, and we reject altogether the claim to parity' (with the *Luftwaffe*). A few days later, George Hall (later a Viscount and Labour's First Lord of the Admiralty) said: '. . . it is madness to assume that more and bigger armaments are required to preserve peace, to give security, and to deter aggression . . . We will vote against the Service Estimates at every stage.' In the same debate the Liberal leader, Sir Archibald Sinclair, declared: 'We on these Benches will feel bound by speech and vote to do all in our power to deflect the Government's policy from its present dangerous and wasteful course.' A year later, after the country had learned that Germany had already caught up with Britain in the air, Clement Attlee was still adhering to this theme: 'Our policy is not one of seeking security through rearmament, but through disarmament.'

On March 4th 1935 the British Government published a White Paper which commented meekly on the 'anxieties' caused by German rearmament. The Belgians, and indeed the whole world, witnessed with amazement the hysterical outcry from the Left in Britain against this inoffensive document. The National Peace Council described it as 'the most incredible document that has ever been published by a government'. The Liberal and Socialist press were beside themselves. The *News Chronicle* wrote that the consequences of the White Paper would be 'a catastrophic increase of Germany's suspicions and fear of encirclement. We hope that the British Government will not spare any efforts . . . to assuage the anger which is aroused in Germany.' The *Daily Herald* (the official organ of the Labour Party) wrote: 'The White Book is not only an insult to Germany, it is also the rejection of the entire system of Collective Security . . . Germany is repeatedly accused of "breaking the treaty", of "aggravating the situation", and of "bringing about a situation which imperils the peace" . . . Let us hope that the effects will not be catastrophic . . . But let the world understand . . . that this is not the voice of the English people.' The incredulous glee evinced in Nazi circles by these outbursts in their support was only equalled by the disillusionment of the small nations who concluded that Britain, whom they had respected for so long, had fallen from her high estate.

Leopold viewed these manifestations with sadness and as the dire events they helped to engender began to unfold, became increasingly convinced that while the danger of another European war was mounting, the ability and willingness of Belgium's guarantors to uphold their Locarno guarantees of her security were vanishing. Following a discussion with his Ministers, therefore, it was decided that enquiries should be made to find out precisely what help Belgium could expect from France and Britain in the event of a German invasion. Accordingly, the Chief of the Belgian Staff, General Cumont, was sent to Paris for confidential military Staff talks and was instructed to approach the British General Staff for the same purpose. But the British Military Attaché in Brussels reported that his government was opposed to such Staff talks and regretted its former statement that 'Britain's frontiers were on the Rhine'.

As the British Official Historian, Major Ellis, explains, Britain spurned the Belgian request for Staff talks 'lest the fact that such conversations were being held should give Hitler an excuse for counter-measures'.[16] The British attitude to the French was the same and it was not until March 1939, six months before war broke out, that the British reluctantly agreed to Staff talks between the two High Commands. 'Such Staff conversations,' Major Ellis continues, 'are apt to imply a military alliance and involve definite military commitments, and at that time the British Government (and their military advisers) were unwilling to proceed so far while the policy of appeasement was being pursued.'* After the British rebuff General Cumont's terms of reference were restricted to Paris and from then on secret exchanges of military information took place between the Belgian and French General Staffs, as described in Chapter 10.

The first of a whole series of fatal blows to European peace and security fell in 1935. In March Hitler tore up the military clauses of the Treaty of Versailles and announced the official constitution of the *Luftwaffe* (it had been formed in secret eight years previously and rapidly expanded with the help of Russia)† and a week later the introduction of universal military service and an increase in the size of the Army to thirty-six divisions. France immediately called for an emergency meeting of the League of Nations Council, but Britain did no more than make 'a solemn protest'.

This was a clear signal for Hitler that his policy of rearmament was unlikely to encounter any serious opposition from Britain. Indeed the Führer was actually receiving encouragement in that direction from the British Government, for even as they joined France and other countries in condemning Hitler's violation of the *military* clauses of the Treaty of Versailles at the League of Nations, they were actually inviting him to break the *naval* clauses of that same treaty. When Hitler's brazen action was proclaimed, it was assumed that Sir John Simon and Anthony Eden would cancel their projected trip to Berlin, in the face of such an insult, but they duly presented themselves to the Führer. It was in the course of their discussions that Ribbentrop was invited to secret talks in London to negotiate the disastrous Anglo-German Naval Treaty of June 18th 1935.

Although the details of this treaty were kept secret, the British Government had – in breach of at least six international agreements – not only sanctioned the building by Germany of a powerful modern fleet, but had approved the construction of submarines, which had been banned by the Treaty of Versailles, up to the same number as the Royal Navy possessed. William L. Shirer, a leading American correspondent in Berlin at the time, noted in his diary: 'The Wilhelmstrasse quite elated. Germany gets a U-boat tonnage equal to Britain's. Why the British have agreed to this is beyond me. German submarines almost beat them in the last war, and may do in the next.'[17]

* In 1951 Sir Alexander Cadogan wrote to Lord Templewood: '. . . of our top military, naval and air people whom I questioned on the subject, I don't think I found one who did not think that "appeasement" was right.' Quoted in *The Diaries of Sir Alexander Cadogan*.
† In spite of the loudly proclaimed ideological differences between the two authoritarian systems, the Russians had been training German military pilots in secret since 1927, in exchange for the supply of aircraft and expertise. A Junkers factory was even set up near Moscow.

France and Italy protested furiously, for, despite the fact that they were Britain's Allies and co-signatories of the Versailles, Locarno and Stresa Treaties and major maritime powers, they had neither been informed nor consulted. The League of Nations had likewise been ignored. The advantages to Hitler were incalculable. Great Britain had shown the world she was prepared to condone and even incite treaty-breaking and to encourage German rearmament. Moreover, Mussolini was led to believe that the United Kingdom would not take too seriously the similar flouting of the Covenant of the League of Nations which his projected invasion of Abyssinia would involve.

Indeed, when the Duce acted on this assumption and struck – on October 3rd 1935 – Britain, after leading 50 out of the 54 members of the League Council to condemn Italy for her violation of the Covenant and calling for 'collective resistance to all acts of unprovoked aggression', headed the retreat from imposing oil sanctions – the only action short of armed intervention that could have been effective – when Mussolini warned that oil sanctions would mean war. The League's half-hearted gestures did not stop Mussolini from conquering Abyssinia, but they did alienate Italy from her traditional friend, Great Britain, and drive her into the alliance with Germany that Hitler had specified in *Mein Kampf* was necessary for his plans for world domination.

Thus the Rome-Berlin axis was born (it was joined by Japan in November 1936, when the Anti-Comintern Pact was signed), enabling the Führer to proceed along his predetermined deadly course. Mussolini had hitherto protected Austria's independence, but now Italy – one of Britain's principal Allies in the First World War – was in the enemy camp. The whole balance of power was now loaded against the democratic nations, and the small and weak countries of the world realized that it would be madness to look towards Britain or France for help against an aggressor. Furthermore, the League of Nations had shown itself to be completely impotent.

A new and critical factor, not only for Leopold and Belgian policy, but for the future of world peace, now emerged. On March 7th 1936 Hitler staked his whole future by reoccupying the demilitarized zone of the Rhineland. This was a flagrant violation not only of the Versailles Treaty, which had been imposed on Germany, but also of the Locarno Pact, which she had actually promoted and signed voluntarily in 1925.

Hitler's generals and his circle were almost unanimous in their opposition to the move, as their weak token force of only three battalions was vastly outmatched by the one hundred divisions which could be put into the field against them by the French. Indeed General Jodl testified at the Nuremberg Trials that the French covering force alone 'could have blown us to pieces' and that Hitler had ordered the invaders to beat a hasty retreat back over the Rhine if the French Army made the slightest countermove or gesture.

Hitler later admitted that if the French Army had marched into the Rhineland, or merely threatened to do so, the resulting fiasco would have ended his career. Indeed, he declared 'A retreat on our part would have spelled collapse', while Dr Schmidt, his interpreter, records that he often heard his master say: 'The forty-eight hours after the march into the Rhineland were the most nerve-racking in my life. If the French had marched in, we would have had to withdraw with our tails between our legs . . .'[18] But as the publication of the French State documents revealed in 1964,[19] their generals had no stomach for military action to chase out Hitler's handful of regiments which were parading about in the forbidden zone behind blaring brass bands, without armoured vehicles and not even equipped for battle.

At a meeting with General Gamelin and the other military leaders on March 9th, Premier Sarraut and his Foreign Minister, Flandin, urged that police action was all that was needed to put the puny German force to flight. But the generals prevaricated, claiming that such action would provoke a cataclysmic general war, with a rain of bombs on the Allies' cities, and grotesquely exaggerating the strength of the German land and air forces. Although Sarraut and Flandin continued to call for positive action, they received little support from the majority of their colleagues in the caretaker government, who were distracted by the imminent general election and discouraged by the defeatism of the military leaders and, above all, by the active dissuasion of the British Government. France, Britain, Italy and Belgium were fully entitled – if not obliged – to take military action, under the terms of the Treaty of Versailles and as signatories of the Locarno Pact. Moreover, France had the enormous preponderance of military power which would have ensured its success even without the support of her Locarno allies. In fact the Belgian Government, having cancelled army leave, was the only one of the Locarno nations to offer France immediate military assistance, although Russia, Poland, Czechoslovakia, Jugoslavia and Rumania all spontaneously made the same promise of military and moral support.

That notable absentee from the volunteers, the British Army, was then almost non-existent; but it was moral rather than military backing the French Ministers sought from the British. Instead, they were met with wordy procrastination and opposition to any action by France and Belgium to drive the tiny German force out of the protective strip on which their security so crucially depended. The British islanders did not feel at all menaced by the seizure and remilitarization of the Rhineland by a potential invader of Belgium and France – and were firmly resolved to accept Hitler's coup as a *fait accompli*.

On hearing of the coup, Anthony Eden, Britain's newly-appointed

Foreign Secretary, immediately insisted 'very strenuously' to the Quai d'Orsay that France should not take any military measures, 'before prior consultation with the British Government'. The Prime Minister, Stanley Baldwin, 'said little, as was his wont on foreign affairs,' wrote Eden. 'He was clear in his mind that there would be no support in Britain for any military action by the French. I could only agree.'[20] Eden accordingly advised the Cabinet that 'military action by France against Germany should be discouraged' and that 'we must resist any attempt to apply financial and economic sanctions'.

Eden then announced in the House of Commons 'There is happily no reason to believe that Germany's present action implies a threat of hostilities' – adding that the Government would examine Hitler's new peace proposals 'seriously and objectively' and concluding 'If we want peace, it is our manifest duty to rebuild.' This was an echo of that morning's leader in *The Times*, whose policy of abject appeasement of Nazi Germany was so actively pursued throughout this period.* It was headed 'A chance to rebuild'. This attitude was shared by the majority of the British newspapers, with Labour's *Daily Herald* well to the fore. Many expressed their belief in the sincerity of Hitler's 'Peace proposals' and welcomed his tongue-in-cheek offer to rejoin the League of Nations as 'a guarantee of peace'. The British public could not understand what all the fuss was about, and there was even considerable sympathy for the Germans. Lord Lothian's unfortunate, but much-repeated *mot* 'After all, they are only going into their own back yard' expressed the common reaction of press and public. At the meeting of the League Council which France and Belgium called, von Ribbentrop declared that the Locarno Pact no longer existed, having been broken by France when she formed the Franco-Soviet military alliance, which he described as being 'directed exclusively against Germany'. Eden nevertheless continued to negotiate with him for a 'new Locarno', as though nothing had happened.

On March 11th Flandin flew to London and made a great personal effort to gain British support for positive action against the Germans. But he received damping responses to his exhortations from both Baldwin and Chamberlain, then Chancellor of the Exchequer. After these meetings Flandin returned sadly to France, convinced that in view of the active opposition by the British to any positive action being taken he would have to adopt a policy of compromise towards an increasingly aggressive Nazi Germany.

At the meeting of the four remaining Locarno members (excluding Germany) called by Belgium and France and held in Paris on March 10th,

* 'I do my utmost, night after night', wrote Geoffrey Dawson, the editor of *The Times*, on May 23rd 1937 to one of his foreign correspondents, 'to keep out of the paper anything that might hurt their [the Germans'] susceptibilities. I can really think of nothing that has been printed now for many months past to which they could possibly take exception . . .' John Evelyn Wrench, *Geoffrey Dawson and Our Times*.

Eden continued to procrastinate in order to gain time for inaction. But
Paul Van Zeeland, the Belgian Prime Minister, greatly impressed his
hearers by the eloquence with which he presented his country's case and
attempted to bridge the gulf between the French and British positions.
His theme was 'If you march, Belgium will march with you, and if you
cannot agree I will do my utmost to help you reach agreement.' In moving
terms he underlined the alarm that had been caused in Belgium by the
coup and reminded his listeners that, like France, his country was now
directly menaced by Hitler's seizure of the protective zone. He therefore
called upon the signatories of the Locarno Pact to fulfil their obligations
and take immediate action, but unhappily all his efforts were unavailing.

All that emerged from this meeting, and those of the Locarno nations
and of the League Council which followed in London, was a 'joint
declaration' asserting belief in Collective Security and in the League of
Nations; reaffirming the Locarno obligations; authorizing military Staff
talks; inviting Germany to appear at the Hague Court; and asking her to
stop sending troops into the Rhineland. General Henry Pownall's* diary
entry for March 30th reveals that he regarded 'the projected Staff
conversations with the French and Belgians to which HMG have committed us . . . as more of a political gesture to please the French than as of any
practical value', adding that 'Germany won't believe that they were in
fact confined to banalities and will fear and suspect much more . . .'[22]

The practical result of the joint declaration and of the Staff talks –
which petered out after the two-day session in London, never to be
resumed – was precisely nothing. As far as Belgium was concerned, she
was still committed to rendering military assistance to France if that
country were to suffer an unprovoked attack by Germany, for an
'arrangement' was hurriedly cobbled together on March 19th to replace
the Locarno obligations. This was a temporary expedient to cover the
period in which Anthony Eden pursued his misguided attempts to coax
Germany and Italy back into the fold and negotiate a 'new Locarno' with
the two dictatorships. Under the terms of this provisory agreement
Britain and France renewed their guarantees of military assistance to
Belgium for the duration of those negotiations – in return for the renewal
of her reciprocal undertakings to assist them in the event of their suffering
unprovoked aggression.

The Belgians were left to face the fact that the French and British
Governments had allowed Hitler to get away with his coup and the
Locarno front to collapse. The detrainment points for the German Army
had been advanced by a hundred miles and in future Belgium's security
would be constantly threatened by the presence of German troops on her

---

* Pownall, who figures later as Chief of Staff to the British Expeditionary Force in France
and Belgium, was at that time a member of the Secretariat of the Committee of Imperial
Defence.

border. The Belgians were appalled by France's timidity and the evidence that Britain would restrain her if she showed any signs of taking firm action against the totalitarian powers. If the French Army would not march into the undefended Rhineland, what hope was there of her doing so when that zone was heavily fortified?

The building of the Siegfried Line was now pressed forward, while the German Army, Navy and Air Force were rapidly expanded, equipped and trained on a vast scale in preparation for fresh acts of aggression. The *Luftwaffe*, having overtaken the Royal Air Force in 1935, steadily increased its lead. The German war factories worked flat out, night and day. While the standing of Britain and France was now much diminished in the eyes of the world, Hitler's power and prestige was greatly enhanced by the success of his coup. It confirmed his hold over the Reich and greatly weakened the influence of those who had hitherto tried to restrain his megalomania – particularly that of the generals, who were the only group which had the power to overthrow him.

During this same period France was progressively weakened militarily, economically and socially under the *Front Populaire* Government of Socialists and Communists headed by Léon Blum, which came to power shortly after the Rhineland coup. As Winston Churchill put it 'A great nation was rotted from within, before it was assaulted from without.' In Britain only Churchill and his circle of like-minded men, including Sir Roger Keyes, appreciated how disastrous it would be if Hitler was allowed to get away with his gamble. Indeed Churchill's was one of the few voices which cried out forcefully against inaction. 'Surely it is worth making a supreme effort,' he wrote on April 3rd, 'to control the hideous drift of events and arrest calamity upon the threshold?' And in Parliament he declared 'The violation of the Rhineland is serious because of the menace to which it exposes Holland, Belgium and France . . .' But when Churchill called for a secret session of Parliament, it was turned down on the grounds that it would cause needless alarm.

In July, however, Churchill persuaded the Prime Minister, Stanley Baldwin, to receive a deputation of leading political and military figures, to lay before him and his Defence advisers the facts which led them to believe that the Kingdom was in danger, and to urge that its defences should be strengthened without delay. (The Labour and Liberal leaders, Clement Attlee and Sir Archibald Sinclair, though invited, declined to attend.) This distinguished body was headed by Neville Chamberlain's brother, Sir Austen, and included Admiral of the Fleet Sir Roger Keyes and Marshal of the Royal Air Force Viscount Trenchard. Churchill's opening address concluded with the words:

We are facing the greatest danger and emergency in our history . . . we must lay aside every impediment in raising our own strength . . . we must increase the development of our air power in priority over every other consideration . . . if we delay too long in repairing our defences we may be forbidden by superior power to complete the process . . .

Unfortunately Neville Chamberlain, who was shortly to succeed Baldwin as Prime Minister and replace the latter's passive form of appeasement with his own active version of that policy, did not attend to hear the deputation's powerful warnings.

It must of course be remembered that all the tardy and half-hearted steps taken to strengthen Britain's almost non-existent defences by the Baldwin and Chamberlain administrations – including the 'symbolic' introduction of conscription in 1939 (to appease the French) and the attempt to rearm after Munich – were persistently denounced and opposed by Labour, trade union and Liberal leaders and their followers in Parliament, the press and the country.

In November 1936 – the month in which Japan joined Germany and Italy in signing the Anti-Comintern Pact – Stanley Baldwin made the second of his famous 'confessions' in Parliament. In May 1935 he had admitted that he had been 'completely wrong' about the relative strengths of the RAF and the *Luftwaffe*. Now he explained why he had shrunk from attempting to rally his countrymen with the cry that 'Germany was rearming and that we must rearm' – and admitted that he could not 'think of anything that would have made the loss of the election from my point of view more certain'.

Once again Major Ellis, the Official Historian, finds apt words to describe the disastrous course on which the British Government was now set: 'To the last minute the British people's desire to keep the peace and the Government's knowledge that we were in no condition for war were joined in a policy of appeasement to which the Government clung obstinately, hoping against hope to reach agreement with Hitler . . .'

In sharp contrast was the vigorous policy of rearmament in defence of Belgium's integrity and independence on which Leopold and his Ministers now combined to rally and unite their countrymen.

CHAPTER FIVE

The Policy of Armed Independence

'The increasing tension resulting from the actions of Germany,
Italy and Russia presaged a great ideological war. With a dangerous neighbour to the East, Collective Security an illusion, Locarno
disavowed, and France bound to a distrusted ally, the Belgian
people felt that the bases of their foreign policy needed drastic
change. On October 14th 1936 their young King gave them the
direction they sought.'

J. K. Miller, *Belgian Foreign Policy
Between Two Wars*

In King Leopold's career there are three climaxes – his decision to
capitulate in 1940, his abdication in 1950 and the moment in 1936 when he
expounded a new policy for Belgium. This was the concept of 'armed
independence' – a principle whose subtle but profound difference from
'neutrality' still continues to confuse his critics.

The Belgians had always been uneasy bedfellows with the Locarno
Great Powers, for the reciprocal clauses of that pact required their small
country to give military aid to France or Germany – whichever was to
suffer an unprovoked attack from the other. Ever since the end of the
Great War, a large part of Belgian public opinion had been mistrustful of
French intentions and, in spite of Locarno, feared another Franco-
German war. That mistrust was not unjustified, for French generals and
politicians of all shades of opinion had made it abundantly clear that they
regarded Belgium as a vassal and her territory as a convenient battleground, which France would have the right to enter uninvited in any war
with Germany.

But the whole attitude of France towards Belgium between the wars
can be pinpointed in an indiscretion committed by Marshal Pétain. In
December 1933 the Belgian Ambassador in Paris reported to King Albert
that he had had a long conversation with Pétain in which the Marshal had
expressed his conviction that Hitler's Germany would one day attack
France. The Ambassador pointed out that Belgium had reserved the right
to decide whether or not the Franco-Belgian military agreement should
come into force. '*We* shall be fighting *you*,' was Pétain's retort.

One of the calumnies that were propagated after the capitulation of the
Belgian Army, and which persists to this day, was that King Leopold had
'refused to allow the French to extend the Maginot Line to the sea'. The

fact is that as soon as the Maginot Line proper was completed the Belgian Government, on the initiative first of King Albert and then of King Leopold, made repeated *démarches* to the French Government in attempts to persuade them to prolong their great military obstacle along the Belgian frontier, from Sedan to Dunkirk.* But they were unsuccessful for, as the post-war *Commission d'Information* stated:

> . . . the absence of fortifications on France's northern frontier was an incitement to Germany to invade Belgium in order to reach that frontier. These appeals failed, for Marshal Pétain and the majority of the Supreme Council of War remained in favour of a war of movement to be developed through Belgium.

The Belgian representations were renewed again and again, and later there were conversations on the subject with Daladier, Gamelin and the President of the Army Commission of the French Senate. In November 1936 a Belgian communiqué, published in agreement with the Quai d'Orsay and the French Ministry of War, stated:

> In 1932 Baron de Gaiffier d'Hestroy, then Belgian Ambassador in Paris, had been instructed by his Government to make known in French official quarters that Belgium would be glad to see France fortify her northern frontier and thus bring to the defence of our territory, against any possible attack from the East, considerable material as well as moral support.

Apart from the fact that there was nothing either Albert or Leopold could do to prevent the French from building an extension of the Maginot Line on their own northern frontier, they were naturally most anxious that France should do so, and thereby greatly lessen the danger of a German attack through Belgium. It was ironical that after the French had suffered the consequences of their failure to extend their fortified line to the sea, the Belgians – and in particular their King – should have been blamed for this fatal omission. Interlinked with the Maginot Line problem were the difficulties King Albert's government had experienced in securing the huge funds required to complete the work which began on their own powerful system of fortifications along the Albert Canal in May 1930. While the Socialists and Communists inevitably opposed these appropriations, on the grounds that the money ought to be spent on social rather than national security, the Flemings for once joined them in opposition, for different reasons. These were spelt out by one of their leaders, Senator Lindekens: 'Flanders does not want to be sacrificed for France . . . Let France fortify its northern boundary – then Germany will leave Belgium alone.'

* See Appendix VIII.

As Germany began to rearm and France to look around for new allies, mistrust of both those countries had grown in all sections of the Belgian population. When, in May 1935, France added pacts with Czechoslovakia and Communist Russia – a regime most Belgians detested as much as they did the Nazis – to her existing pact with Poland, there was clearly a danger that France might get involved in hostilities with Germany under these commitments – and call in Belgium, which would thereby become involved in a conflict which was none of her business. That danger was even greater in the aftermath of Hitler's Rhineland coup, for despite the disintegration of the Locarno Alliance, Belgium remained committed – under the temporary Agreement of March 19th 1936 – to giving military assistance to France and Britain in the event of an unprovoked German attack – a danger which was not mitigated in Belgian eyes by the provisory guarantees they had been given by the two Powers which had so recently and submissively shrunk from fulfilling their Locarno obligations.

The rapidly worsening international situation made it imperative that Belgium's military defences should be increased to the maximum and that she should free herself from entanglements with other countries which might involve her in a war and whose weakness and timidity had destroyed their credibility as allies and guarantors. The Government had in fact been subjected to increasing pressure from public opinion since the spring of 1935, when Hitler had proclaimed the formation of a vast conscript armed force, to divest Belgium of her dangerous external commitments. But while many Belgians recognized the urgent need for rearmament, few were prepared to support measures to increase Belgium's armed forces while she was still treaty-bound to deploy them to assist the military operations of France and Britain. The Government therefore could only hope to get the men and money which were essential for Belgium's own security by assuring Parliament that the Army would be used only for the defence of the realm. This was demonstrated in February 1936, when a Military Law designed to increase Belgium's defensive capacity and the period of military service, which had been initiated by the King and presented to Parliament by the Government, failed to pass, due to lack of support from the Flemish as well as the Socialist parties.

Belgium's need for military preparedness and independence had become inseparable – and the only way in which her different racial and political factions could be united and persuaded to make the sacrifices essential for her security was for her government to persuade Britain and France to release Belgium from her reciprocal commitments to them and to recognize her status of 'armed independence'. As the King and his principal Ministers conferred on the problem, all were agreed that by pursuing a more forcefully-backed version of the policy of his predecessors, the Government would not only be safeguarding her own territorial integrity, but also making the maximum possible contribution to the security of France and to the preservation of peace in Europe. They believed that a more powerfully defended, united and independent Belgium would be a considerable deterrent factor in another Franco-German confrontation, for a belligerent would thereby be forced to attack his opponent across the heavily-fortified terrain on the Franco-German border. Alternatively, if he chose to enter Belgium by force of arms – to use her territory as a passageway or battleground – he would be met with strong resistance and world opinion would be aroused against him, as in 1914.

As it turned out, these deterrents very nearly worked – and might well have dissuaded Hitler from launching his *Blitzkrieg* in 1940, had they been conjoined with such other deterrents as a well-armed and prepared France and Britain – for the decision was Hitler's alone and he made it against the advice of a formidable body of opinion. His opponents included almost all his generals from the Commander-in-Chief down and even Franco and Mussolini warned Hitler against violating Belgium's neutrality and thus repeating the crime the Kaiser's Germany had committed in 1914.

In the six months following the Rhineland coup it became increasingly clear to the King and his principal Ministers that Anthony Eden's futile efforts to negotiate a new Locarno Pact with the Nazi and Fascist powers would shortly lapse into oblivion; that Europe was hardening into two opposing camps; that Collective Security was a chimera and that the League of Nations was dying, if not dead. The first indication to the outside world of the change that was taking place in the Belgian Government's strategic thinking came in July 1936, when Spaak delivered an address to the Foreign Press Union in which he declared 'I want only one thing, a policy exclusively and wholly Belgian.' However, little notice was taken of it abroad, or of a speech in a similar vein by the Prime Minister, Van Zeeland, in September, in which he said that the Government was trying to avoid becoming entangled in wars between other countries, by means of a strong defence system and by freeing herself from external commitments.

This was in fact what was going on behind the scenes, for there was much diplomatic activity on the part of the Belgian Foreign Ministry in order to gain acceptance for the new policy of 'armed independence' in London and Paris. In July the Belgian Government's wishes were put privately to the British. In reply Mr (later Sir) Orme Sargent of the Foreign Office said that Britain would welcome such a policy, but he felt sure that the French would not, for at the back of their minds they had always thought of using Belgium as a battleground. Belgium's new policy received British approval in their Note of September 17th 1936, which stated that in the event of a new treaty being negotiated to replace

Locarno, reciprocal guarantees would be demanded of all the signatories – except Belgium.

In thanking Great Britain the Belgians asked for her help in overcoming the difficulties they were experiencing in securing similar acceptance from the French. To this end the Belgian emissaries had pointed out to René Massigli at the Quai d'Orsay that France had everything to gain from the new Belgian policy – for a strong and united Belgium would provide a formidable rampart against German aggression. The real reason for the initial lack of French support, as predicted by Orme Sargent, was the traditional one – they wanted to use Belgian territory to launch an attack on Germany (or resist one from that country) in the event that hostilities resulted from their treaty obligations to their Eastern allies. France had realized too late her mistake in allowing Germany to reoccupy and fortify the Rhineland, for now she could only succour those allies by crossing Belgian territory. But as Spaak reminded the French Foreign Minister, Yvon Delbos, to allow the passage of troops under Article 16 of the League Covenant was not obligatory and he strongly contested the right of France to use Belgium as a battlefield in a war with Germany.

The dangers of Belgium's situation and the need for the new policy were more apparent to Leopold and some of his Ministers than to large sections of his people. Not all the Ministers and Members of Parliament were convinced of the need for increased security and independence, despite Spaak's eloquent warnings of Belgium's vulnerability. Indeed Spaak's own Socialist Party, which derived most of its strength from Wallonia, was displeased by his 'independence' speech in July, which they interpreted as anti-French. Moreover, the Belgian Socialists, like their British comrades, were committed to disarmament and traditionally opposed to military expenditure and conscription. The General Council of his party considered it to be an attack on the principles of the League of Nations and of Collective Security, and demanded an explanation of his statements. Spaak retorted that since the veteran Socialist leader Emile Vandervelde had publicly declared that the League was a failure, a new policy was clearly necessary. Nevertheless, Vandervelde still clung to his party's line on armaments, as he explained to the King's secretary, Comte Capelle, at the time: '*Après cinquante ans de lutte antimilitariste, je ne pourrais voter la prolongation du temps de service. Je ne veux pas me désolidariser de mes camarades . . .*'

The Liberals and Catholics, to whom Van Zeeland had particularly addressed his speech in favour of the new policy, were deeply worried by the 'Bolshevik menace' – which they considered to be inherent in the military alliance between a strife-torn France under a Socialist and Communist controlled regime and Soviet Russia – and those two countries' support for and supply of arms to the Republican side in the Spanish

Civil War. It was a situation in which a strong clear lead was required. This was now provided by the King.

As a constitutional monarch, Leopold could not 'go to the country' direct (as Stanley Baldwin could have done) to arouse his countrymen to the danger that foreign aggression could lead to war, and the need for rearmament in order to avert it. But as President of the Council of Ministers, the King could put the facts squarely to the members of his government, who were drawn from the three major political parties, and urge them to enlighten their followers on the situation and rally their support for the measures which were so essential for national security and the maintenance of peace. In particular Leopold wanted to ensure that the long-delayed Military Law was passed with the least possible delay. The situation was so crucial that the King summoned the full assembly of the Government on October 14th 1936. 'He opened the proceedings,' writes J. K. Miller, 'with a speech which so well expressed the desires, fears and hopes of his subjects, that it became the official statement of Belgian foreign policy, accepted as such both at home and abroad.'[24]

'In swearing their constitutional oath,' the King began, 'the Belgian Sovereigns bind themselves to maintaining the integrity and independence of their country. Like my predecessors, I intend to keep this solemn promise. That is why it has been my wish to preside at this Council, which is to draw up measures to be submitted to Parliament in order to provide Belgium with a military status suited to the present circumstances. For more than a year, the Government has been considering how we can strengthen our present military position.' The King then went on to give the reasons why this was necessary. After referring to the rearmament of Germany, Italy and Russia, he said, with singular prescience:

> There has been such a vast change in methods of warfare as a result of technical progress, particularly in aviation and mechanization, that the initial operations of an armed conflict can now be of such force, speed, and magnitude as to be particularly alarming to small countries like Belgium.

The King then declared that the reoccupation of the Rhineland had brought the launching points for a possible German invasion right up to Belgium's borders, and that international security had been shaken to its foundations by the breaking of pacts – even freely-signed pacts – and the failure of the League of Nations to prevent or punish such violations. In reference to the Spanish Civil War, which had been raging since July, the King warned of the danger that a major war 'could result from the intervention of states with different political and social systems in the internal conflicts of other states'.

Leopold reminded his audience that the need for Belgian rearmament 'to meet external risks' had been manifest since the spring of 1935 (when

Hitler had proclaimed his creation of a vast military machine) and that he had given his Royal assent in November of that year to the defence programme which had been worked out in conjunction with his General Staff. He then traced the slow progress of the comprehensive Military Law which had been developed from that programme – without, however, receiving the necessary support in the Chamber – and stressed that its main proposals (the formation of a permanent covering force, purchases of material, anti-aircraft defences, fortifications, and the call-up systems) called for an immediate decision. Above all, it was essential that the new Militia Act should be passed before December 1st, since the call-up of the 1937 class began on that date. 'In view of the dangerous international situation,' the King continued, 'the Nation would not countenance any delay on the part of the Government in submitting the necessary proposals to Parliament.' He then came to one of the main objects of his speech – and called upon those present to explain the whole problem, which he then summed up, to the public.[b]

The King concluded his address by expressing his confidence that the Government would solve the military problem in a united and patriotic spirit, thus giving the feeling of security in the face of outside events which was so essential for the welfare of the Nation. 'You will thus prove to the Country that the chief preoccupation of the National Coalition Government is to place the higher interests of Belgium above everything else.'

What Leopold was affirming was not a policy of unresisting neutrality, but a promise that if Belgium's defences could be put in order she would fight back immediately against any aggressor. At the same time she was not prepared to be dragged into a war as a result of pacts with other countries whose weakness and unreliability as allies and guarantors had been so clearly demonstrated. His forceful and lucid declaration made a profound impression and the assembly was unanimous in acclaiming it.

The results of the King's confidential address to his Ministers were remarkable and far-reaching. All the members of the Government and very shortly afterwards the whole country, including all the political parties except the Communists, closed ranks behind the King and the new policy. This was demonstrated a fortnight later, on December 2nd, when the Military Law was passed by the largest majorities ever accorded to the Government on a Defence Bill. (The vote in the Chamber was 137 to 43, with 8 abstentions – and that in the Senate 122 to 19, with 6 abstentions.) But there are deeper considerations. The policy which Leopold defined was the only one which could have brought together the parties of Left and Right, as well as the Walloons and Flemings – and it made viable the call-up of young men, the vast expenditure on rearmament and the strengthening of its fortifications which his country undertook after 1936. Moreover, the effectiveness of his measures was amply demonstrated by subsequent events. As they contemplated the invasion of the Low

Countries and France, the German General Staff – and Hitler in particular – were deterred from launching the *Blitzkrieg* by the knowledge that Belgium had the means to fight back and that she would be a very hard nut to crack. (It is recorded in Hitler's *Table Talk*, for example, that he believed that it would cost him 'a million men' to penetrate Belgium's defences.) And when the *Blitzkrieg* did occur, the prolonged resistance of the Belgian Army until nearly two days after the start of the Dunkirk evacuation enabled the indispensable nucleus of the British Army to escape by sea – a crucial contribution to the Allies' eventual victory which could not have been made without the King's initiatives, which gave such a great impulse to Belgian rearmament.

Yet the King had to accept the consequences of taking the initiative, for when his speech was published it was seized upon by his detractors (mainly in France, but after the Belgian Army's capitulation, more generally) who claimed that it unilaterally repudiated Belgium's 'alliance' with France and Britain and characterized it as an autocratic personal policy favourable to Germany foisted upon a reluctant people by a pro-Fascist King. As must now be clear, this was untrue in every respect. The King's words did not even imply any such repudiation, nor had there ever been an alliance between the three countries. Indeed the whole object of his speech was to ensure that the people of this parliamentary democracy were informed of the dangers to their security, so that they might decide by their votes to strengthen their homeland's defences against the threat of German aggression. Moreover, the publication of the speech at the request of all the members of the three-party coalition set the seal of the Belgian Government's complete approval on its contents.

The King had always said that Cabinet meetings were the only occasions on which he felt free to speak his mind with complete frankness. His words had, therefore, been phrased for his government's ears alone and not for the general public at home and abroad. It was only on his Ministers' particular insistence that the immediate publication of the speech would be in the general interest and 'a powerful means of enlightening the public and getting them to vote for the Military Laws' that the King gave his permission for this to be done. Ironically Emile Vandervelde, the pacifist and lifetime opponent of conscription who had declared to Comte Capelle on the eve of the speech that he could never support rearmament measures, was the first to make this request and to thank the King for taking the initiative. He also promised the full support of the Socialist Party for the policy of armed independence and this was duly ratified by the party. Moreover, when praising the King for his championship of this policy in Parliament eighteen months later, Spaak referred to: 'A speech which was unanimously approved by the Ministers and published with the full assent of them all – a speech of which the guiding ideas have time after time been most warmly applauded in Parliament.' To prolonged applause Spaak then declared:

> It is therefore as absurd as it is improper to suggest, as has been suggested in certain organs of the press and in certain other quarters, that there is such a thing as the King's personal policy in opposition to that of the Nation. The much simpler and happier truth is that at a difficult moment the King, with the permanent interests of our country in mind, was able to express the will of the immense majority in appropriate words.

The Belgian press also enthusiastically applauded Leopold's speech, only the Communists abstaining. *Le Peuple*, the official organ of the Socialist Party, observed on October 17th:

> In speaking as he did, the King has used a strictly constitutional method. He has in no way departed from the prerogatives conferred upon him by our Laws . . . The suggestions contained in the Royal speech are dominated by a wholly proper anxiety to keep Belgium out of any international complications . . . This desire is shared by the whole population; it is in tune with the deepest feeling of all Belgian citizens.

On October 16th the Liberal *Dernière Heure* stated:

> The King and the Government have exercised their responsibilities most wisely . . . The warning came from a high quarter, from the representative of a dynasty which has made a glorious contribution to the greatness of Belgium, from a King whose every word and whose every action, since his accession, have shown that he honourably intended to follow the noble traditions of his House.

Le Soir, the influential independent evening paper, declared on the same day:

> The King was acting in his double role as Head of the Army and Head of State, most deeply concerned to ensure the peace and security of Belgium. This is indeed a field in which all citizens have the imperative duty to rally closely around their Sovereign . . . . It is what has been called an exclusively and wholly Belgian policy.

However, as far as the reactions of the outside world were concerned, Spaak's Foreign Ministry failed lamentably to prepare public and governmental opinion abroad for the King's speech by explaining its meaning, implications and the circumstances in which it was made. Moreover, they were slow – and accordingly unsuccessful – in correcting the misapprehensions which arose, particularly in France. It therefore became necessary for Spaak to do a lot of explaining both at home and abroad,

through Belgium's diplomatic representatives and by personal appear-
ances before Parliament, in which he stressed:

1 That the Government did not intend to return to neutrality (a word, he
  pointed out, that did not even appear in the speech).
2 That the Government would observe all its obligations as a member of the
  League of Nations.
3 That a speech could not dissolve solemn international agreements and that
  the provisional understanding reached in London on March 19th was still
  binding, while negotiations continued for a new pact.
4 That in any such pact Belgium would promise only 'to defend ourselves
  against any invader and not allow others to use us as a passageway'.

Meanwhile, French press reaction to the King's speech bordered on the
hysterical, with one newspaper actually comparing Leopold to Hitler in
terms of bad faith. 'Belgium Deserts Us', ran one headline while another
newspaper described France's attitude as 'indignation among some,
distress among others, but stupefaction among all'. The parrot cry of
'*Nous sommes trahis*' was immediately raised, as it would be again in 1940
(and had been in 1870 and 1914). The French press had taken little notice
when the Belgian Foreign Minister and Premier publicly expounded this
same policy of armed independence earlier in the year. But when
Leopold spoke in the same sense, it was immediately seized upon as a
Royal proclamation unilaterally repudiating Belgium's 'alliance' with
France and Britain.

The reaction of the French Cabinet was more realistic, for they had
long been engaged in discussions with Belgian diplomats and statesmen
on Belgium's desire for independent status, and saw that there was
nothing new in the King's speech. Although the Senate Committee on
Foreign Affairs hastily passed a motion regretting 'the unilateral denunciation of the Locarno Pact', the Foreign Minister, Yvon Delbos, acknowledged next day that the King's speech had not repudiated any
alliances or broken with the League of Nations, nor altered Belgium's
current relationship with France in any way. But in the exchanges which
continued between Paris and Brussels France behaved as though the
Locarno Pact were still alive and well – despite the fact that two of its
principal signatories, Germany and Italy, had deserted it, and the
foundation on which it had been built, the demilitarized Rhineland, had
disappeared. The French, moreover, continued to quibble over innumerable technical points and to harp on their claim to right of passage for their
army through Belgium.

In contrast, the response to Leopold's speech from the press and
Government in Britain was sympathetic. The British attitude was made
abundantly clear in a series of public statements, including the renewal by
the Foreign Office of the promises that Britain had already made to

guarantee Belgium – without any reciprocal commitment from her other than that she would resist if attacked by an aggressor. And Anthony Eden, the Foreign Secretary, publicly declared that Britain's armaments would never be used for aggressive purposes, but solely for the defence of the United Kingdom, the Commonwealth, France and Belgium, 'in the event of unprovoked aggression'.

On November 26th Van Zeeland visited London and at a banquet given in his honour he was praised by Eden and assured once again of Britain's warm friendship for Belgium and resolve to support her through thick and thin:

> Allow me to say once more that the independence and integrity of Belgium constitute a vital interest for our country and that Belgium can count on our assistance if she were ever to be the victim of unprovoked aggression. I say this very deliberately for I know that it represents the will of the British people, and to state it clearly is to serve the cause of peace.

The next day Sir Esmond Ovey, the British Ambassador in Brussels, told Comte Capelle: 'The new political orientation of Belgium contributes in a vitally important manner to ensuring the peace of Europe . . . We cannot be sufficiently grateful to His Majesty for the lead he has given.' Four months later, on March 11th 1937, after a private discussion with the King, Ovey reported to Eden that Leopold was 'unbudgeable on his general line, but entirely pro-English. He is determined to save his country from another war and wants to be free of any entanglements which might give any country an excuse to attack or pass through Belgium.'[25]

Although, as the Foreign Office documents reveal, Anthony Eden's personal attitude towards the Belgians and their new policy was cynical, and his marginal comments on such documents often facetious, there is no reason to doubt the genuineness of his public pronouncements in its favour, for, as can be seen from the Cabinet Papers, this was the British Government's considered policy, and it was based on pure self-interest. On December 3rd 1937, for example, the Chiefs of Staff submitted to the Cabinet a 'Most Secret Memorandum' entitled: 'A Comparison of the Strength of Great Britain With Certain Other Nations As At January 1938.' In their pragmatic endorsement of the policy King Leopold had expounded, they stated:

> Belgium's attitude is always purely defensive. The recent statement of her policy indicates a desire to keep clear of commitments and guarantees, and to preserve her neutrality in a war in the West of Europe. At the same time Belgium is engaged in putting her defences in order; the completion of this will increase her chances of remaining neutral, an attitude which, from the military point of view, is to the advantage of France and ourselves.[26]

The next move came from Berlin and was more effective in bringing France into line than all the efforts of Belgium and Britain had been. On December 22nd 1936 the German Ambassador in Brussels let it be known that Germany was willing to guarantee Belgium and dropped a hint that an approach from Brussels would not be unwelcome. The Belgians replied rather coldly that should other countries besides Britain and France wish to provide guarantees there would be no objection, but Belgium would not ask for any.

On January 30th 1937 Hitler made a major speech in the Reichstag, in the course of which he mentioned Belgium and Holland and his readiness 'to guarantee these two States as neutral and inviolable regions for all time'. These overtures were received with very mixed feelings in Belgium and the Government did no more than politely take note of them, but in France they were helpful to the Belgian cause. Indeed, on March 6th the Quai d'Orsay informed Belgium's Ambassador that France would no longer oppose her wishes to be freed from her reciprocal obligations under the temporary arrangement of March 19th 1936. Shortly afterwards the Germans and Italians, after many months of delay, put forward totally unacceptable terms on which they were prepared to participate in the proposed new Locarno Pact and it at last became clear to France and Britain that all their hopes for such an Agreement with the Nazi and Fascist dictatorships were dead, and that Belgium could be kept waiting no longer.

. In the series of high-level discussions which were then held in London and Brussels to work out the terms of the pact between the three democratic countries, Leopold acted as Belgium's 'unofficial representative' and was able to smooth the path of the negotiations to their successful conclusion. This was the Franco-British Declaration of April 24th 1937, an unqualified acceptance of the policy which, after their King's initiative, his government had adopted the previous October. In order to give the Declaration the force of a treaty, it was formally registered as such by Britain and France at the League of Nations. After taking note of this policy, the Declaration continued:

> . . . the Government of the United Kingdom and the Government of the French Republic declare that they consider Belgium to be now released from all obligations towards them resulting from either the Treaty of Locarno or the arrangement drawn up in London on March 19, 1936, and that they maintain in respect of Belgium the undertakings of assistance which they entered into towards her under the above-mentioned instruments.

This was a remarkable achievement for Leopold and for Spaak. Belgium's hands were now free, while she still retained the guarantees of Franco-British support in the event of a German attack. And in theory no such attack should have occurred, for in October Hitler also gave the pledge that he had promised. On the 13th he declared that the German Government would in no circumstances impair Belgium's 'inviolability and integrity, except, of course, in the event of Belgium's taking part in a military action directed against Germany'.

For the King the Franco-British Declaration was of immense personal significance. No subsequent pact was made between Belgium, Great Britain and France, nor any emendation which altered the Allies' solemn promises to protect her inviolability and uphold her independence. Yet Britain and France not only planned to invade Belgium before Germany attacked her, but after the capitulation of her army in May 1940 the French Premier, Paul Reynaud – and following his lead the British – falsely accused Leopold of betraying France and Britain and surrendering his army without forewarning them. Much was also made of the claim that the French and British had gallantly answered 'an anguished appeal' from Belgium, had rushed to her 'rescue' – and that the King had on his personal initiative renounced Belgium's 'alliance' with France in his speech of October 14th 1936.

But there had never been such an alliance, and when Germany attacked Belgium on May 10th 1940, and France and Britain marched their armies into that country, they did no more than fulfil the promises in their 1937 Declaration. And at the same time they made the strategic move they believed to be in their own best interests – and which they had long since decided to make by armed force, if Belgium declined to invite them in. Moreover, by invoking France and Britain's assistance when the *Blitzkrieg* struck, Belgium merely took up an offer which had been made freely three years previously – and by fiercely resisting the invader, instead of submitting in the face of overwhelming force, as did the Danes and the British Channel Islanders, they honoured the pledges they had given the Allies.

Since Paul Reynaud was the originator of these slanders it is not surprising that throughout all his self-exculpatory writings, including the 1,200 pages of the two volumes of his oddly-named memoirs *La France a sauvé l'Europe* and the 1,000 pages of his '*entièrement rénovée*' work *Au coeur de la mêlée*, he continuously harps on the theme that Leopold 'repudiated the Alliance' between France and Belgium and that this was the root cause of the military disasters which befell France in 1940. To take but one example:

> At the personal intervention of the King, the Belgian Government decided, on October 14th 1936, to break off the Alliance and the Military Agreement which linked Belgium and France . . . From the moment of her return to neutrality Belgium was no longer to call upon the French Army in the event of diplomatic tension.[27]

But, as we have seen, Leopold's speech in no way altered Belgium's relationship with France and the temporary 'arrangement' of March 19th 1936, which was not an alliance, was dissolved by mutual consent a year later. Similarly, the 'Military Agreement' to which Reynaud refers had been terminated by the joint Declaration of March 6th 1936, seven months before Leopold's 'armed independence' speech was made. Moreover, there had never been any agreement that Belgium should call in the French Army 'in the event of diplomatic tension'. Belgium had signed this Military Agreement, which was not an alliance either, in September 1920, to ensure technical co-operation with France during their joint occupation of the Rhineland. But it had become obsolete when they withdrew in 1930 and their mutual obligations had been redefined at Locarno. The position in which Belgium stood in relation to her neighbours, just before she was attacked by the Germans in May 1940, was neatly summed up by Spaak as follows:

> The failure of the League of Nations after the Abyssinian affair and the inability to enforce the Locarno Pact, after the reoccupation of the Rhineland, induced the Goverment, under the King's guidance, to look in other directions for the security of the Country. At the same time the urgent need to reinforce the Army and to obtain from Parliament and the Country the necessary effort and sacrifices, compelled the Government to emphasize the strictly peaceful and defensive character of its policy.
>
> Such a concept was only workable by remaining absolutely independent, outside any alliance with our powerful neighbours, whose foreign policies raised visible dangers of war. All the successive governments did everything possible to reinforce the policy . . . History will prove that their perseverance and loyalty in carrying out this policy of independence rallied almost the entire Nation, on the eve of war . . .
>
> Conscious, however, of the impossibility of defending herself alone in the event of aggression against her, Belgium accepted the guarantees of France, Britain and Germany in 1937 . . . But it should be underlined . . . that the Belgian Government has always maintained that . . . their Declarations did not bind Belgium, and the guarantees that were given could only be implemented at the express request of Belgium . . .
>
> It should be emphasized that during the whole of this period, no divergence on views on the essential elements of our foreign policy disturbed the relations between the King and the Government.

When Leopold visited England in March 1937 his object was not only to ease the negotiations which led up to the Franco-British Declaration, but also to make contact with influential personalities in order to explain his country's new policy and the reasons why it had been adopted. In particular, the King wished to set at rest the fears which were being expressed in some quarters that Belgium was drawing away from her traditional friendship with Britain. He was most anxious to preserve and nurture the ties between Belgium and the country he loved best, next to his own. Like his father, Leopold had always admired Winston Churchill, who shared their views about the need for a resolute and well-armed stand against the aggressors. Albert and Leopold – like many others abroad – had been impressed by Churchill's attempts to rally the British people to face up to the danger of Nazi aggression. Although Churchill was out of office, the King was anxious to meet the great opponent of the pacifism and appeasement which were leading Britain to disaster and which had imposed upon Belgium her policy of armed independence, hoping that he might be able to explain to him privately the reasons for that policy.

As the King remarked to the author in 1950: 'We would have had no hesitation in placing ourselves under your wing, if Britain had had a firm policy and determined leadership by a man like Winston Churchill. But unfortunately the appeasers were in power, and your country seemed to have fallen from its leading position in the world.' Unfortunately, also, the meeting between them – Leopold's only conversation with Churchill – proved fruitless.

Since the news of a private interview with Churchill would certainly have leaked out, the Belgian Ambassador, Baron de Cartier de Marchienne, gave a dinner party to which Churchill was invited along with Eden, Simon, and Hore-Belisha. After dinner the Baron manoeuvred Churchill and the King to a sofa in a quiet corner. However, Churchill plunged into an animated account of his great days with the Naval Brigade at Antwerp in 1914 and it was impossible for Leopold to bring him back to the present or to make any impression on the man who was to play so fatal a part in his future. As the King said to the author after his abdication: 'This was a great pity. He might otherwise have been kinder to me later, and more understanding.'

Leopold's meeting with Churchill coincided with a major setback for an organization whose name has been associated, quite wrongly, with the Belgian Sovereign. This was the self-styled Rexist Party led by Léon Degrelle. After 1940, those who tried to elevate criticism of the King's 'personal government' into a charge of Fascist sympathies found it easy to link him with this group. But Rexism had nothing to do with earthly kings, since Degrelle had derived the name from *Christus Rex* and called first his publishing company and then a weekly magazine *Rex*. When he formed his political party in 1936, he gave it the same name. Like the Nazis, Degrelle's para-Fascist movement profited from fear – widespread in bourgeois Belgium – of Communism. In May 1936 the party gained its first twenty-one seats in the Belgian Chamber and thereafter seemed to be making dangerous headway, though its fortunes were soon to change.

One of the causes of the rapid loss of popularity of Degrelle and his party was, as J. K. Miller contends, 'King Leopold's active leadership of his people'. This author then describes how the King's address to his Ministers 'was welcomed by many of his subjects, who forthwith abandoned Degrelle and returned to their traditional party allegiance'.[28] A few days later, on October 25th, Degrelle called a monster Rexist rally designed to overthrow the Prime Minister, Van Zeeland. But instead of the 250,000 who were expected to demonstrate, only about 5,000 appeared on the streets – many purely out of curiosity. Shortly afterwards Leopold struck a powerful blow at Degrelle and his movement, in a speech accusing them of sabotaging their country.

Van Zeeland had formed his second Ministry in June. The success of the Communists, who won nine seats in the May election, alarmed the Belgian public and might well have benefited Degrelle, but for four factors. The first was the King's public condemnation of the Rexists; the second was the disclosure that Degrelle had secretly visited Hitler; the third was the strength of the reconstituted Catholic Party; and the fourth was a trenchant denunciation of the movement by the Primate, Cardinal Van Roey. In a formal statement he declared 'Rexism is a danger to the country' and rebuked any Catholic who voted for Degrelle or even cast a blank ballot in the forthcoming by-election. Thus when Degrelle stood for election to the Chamber in April 1937, all the three main political parties joined in persuading Van Zeeland to contest the seat and Degrelle was defeated by a majority of four to one. This humiliation was the *coup de grâce*, though Rexism stumbled on and Degrelle himself survived to play his part as a leading collaborator during the German occupation.

In October 1937 Leopold went to Paris for the dedication by the French Government of a memorial to his father. He was received with great popular demonstrations of enthusiasm and his speech was loudly applauded both by the listening crowd and in the French press. Eschewing the customary empty phrases, the King seized the opportunity to explain and justify his country's policy. The response of the French was generous. Many compared the young King with his father, and one journalist wrote that 'Belgium, free, independent and sole mistress of her own destiny, remains true to her friendship with France.' But the impression created by Leopold's frankness and sincerity faded all too soon. Before long the French sky was to become ever darker with clouds of malice and mistrust, of jealousy and calumny, against Belgium and against her King.

In November, the State visit the King, accompanied by Spaak, paid to London was an outstanding personal success. A *Times* leader on November 18th declared: 'King Leopold has been welcomed in London with a warmth which must have convinced him of the deep sympathy felt in this country for him personally and for his country. An exceptional cordiality has marked the high traditional ceremonies of his reception . . .' In replying to King George's toast at the State Banquet, King Leopold affirmed his belief that though the smaller powers might lack military

strength, they could bring to bear a great moral force. Less committed to
power politics, they could at least utter the small quiet voice of sanity. He
went on to plead that the British Empire should take the lead in solving
the economic difficulties 'which lie at the root of the international
problems which beset the world'.

CHAPTER SIX

The Slippery Slope

'Everyone writes to me, since I occasionally say what I think about
peace by appeasement at any price. Personally I think we are going
down a slippery slope from one surrender to the next – accepting
one insult after another, provided we can get peace.'

Sir Roger Keyes, MP, in a letter to one
of his daughters, in December 1938

In June 1938 Joseph E. Davies took over as the new American Ambassador in Brussels and during his tenure of office, which ended in January
1940, had many long talks covering both internal and foreign problems
with the King – from which, he writes, 'I always came away with the moral
intensity of his character'.

In the King of the Belgians I found a man whose marked characteristics were a
magnificent and athletic physique, great seriousness of demeanor, unusual
modesty, and a personality which indicated a quiet, resolute strength, and
serious moral purpose. He was a hard worker; took all of his duties with the
greatest of earnestness; was a clean-living man, whose reputation was above
suspicion. His government was his all-absorbing business. He was not only the
titular head, he was the actual leader of his government. Outside of his work
and his family, his absorbing interest was mountain-climbing. He kept himself
physically fit and always looked in the pink of condition. In my judgment he was
an exceptionally able, serious and strong man . . .[29]

Throughout these years of crisis, the King was constantly concerned
with the care of his motherless children. In 1937 Josephine-Charlotte,
pretty and vivacious, was ten, Baudouin seven and Albert three. Their
studies were supervised by the admirable Vicomte Gatien du Parc, who
had been educated in Britain and spoke the language like an Englishman.
Summers were spent in the same modest villa on the coast at La Panne in
which King Albert and his family had spent their holidays and had passed
the grim years of the Great War. In those summer months of the late
nineteen-thirties Leopold's children played on the wide sands, as carefree
as he had been in the years before the 1914 conflict.

Meanwhile, as the world moved inexorably towards war, the King
warned of the perils ahead and rallied his fellow-countrymen to unite.
Leopold had always upheld the workers' interests and was a popular

figure on his frequent tours around the country, being welcomed by cheering crowds wherever he went. To one such group of factory workers he declared in July 1939: 'With arms at the ready we intend to remain masters in our own house.'

The response from all sections of the population to the King's drive to strengthen Belgium's defences was remarkable. Even the Socialists and their trade unions (unlike their British counterparts, who opposed Britain's half-hearted attempts to rearm, even after Munich) lent it their enthusiastic support and accepted the sacrifices and tax burdens the rearmament programme necessarily involved. Although the soldiers' pay and the allowances to their families were relatively small, the cost of Belgium's defence effort was crushing in comparison to her resources. By September 1939 no less than 24 per cent of her total budget was devoted to maintaining her armed forces in a state of readiness and to strengthening her defences. At the beginning of 1940, Belgium's daily expenditure on military preparedness amounted to 24.5 million francs her ordinary budget being 12 thousand million francs per annum. The estimated budget deficit for 1940 was 7,408,000,000 francs.

Because of her small size, Belgium has never been and never could be a modern military power of the first rank. When one weighs all the adverse factors which hampered the King and his Chief of Staff, it is a remarkable proof of their energy and determination that by September 1939 Belgium, with a population of only eight millions – less than that of London – had 650,000 men under arms (compared with the 152,000 troops Britain managed to deploy in France that winter), over half Belgium's men between twenty and forty years of age being in her armed forces. The order for general mobilization on May 10th 1940 brought the strength of the Belgian Army up to 900,000 compared to the 237,300 field troops by then in the British Expeditionary Force.

The military policy followed by the British Government in this same period was very different to that of Belgium – indeed, as Michael Howard recalls in *The Continental Commitment*, it declined from limited liability to 'no liability at all' as a result of government policy in Chamberlain's appeasement era. The Field Force was accordingly reorganized in February 1938 with only three divisions, 'equipped for an Eastern theatre' and at an even lower state of readiness for war. The British Army had long been starved of funds and even in the so-called rearmament programme it came a long way behind the Royal Air Force and Royal Navy, whose shares were meagre enough, in comparison to those of the German Armed Forces.

Five months before Munich, in April 1938, General Ironside stated: 'Never again shall we contemplate a Force for a foreign country. Our contribution is to be the Navy and the RAF.' But the state of the RAF was such that the Chief of the Air Staff wrote in that same month: 'We are in no position to resist any demands by Germany, and if we attempt to do so I believe we should be defeated by a knock-out blow.'

As to Britain's foreign policy, Neville Chamberlain had by now virtually taken control; and when Anthony Eden resigned as Foreign Secretary, he replaced him with the worthy but compliant and colourless Lord Halifax. But as the diaries of Sir Alexander Cadogan alarmingly reveal, it was Cadogan, as Permanent Under Secretary of State at the Foreign Office, who implemented Chamberlain and Halifax's fatal policies of appeasing the dictators, by the ruthless exercise of the extraordinary powers he was accorded. Cadogan's diary entry for February 15th is a typical example of the thinking which dominated British foreign policy throughout this disastrous pre-war period. 'Was summoned early to the FO as there was a flap about Austria. Personally, I almost wish Germany would swallow Austria and get it over. She is probably going to do so anyhow – anyhow we can't stop her. What's all the fuss about? . . . I shouldn't mind if Austria were *gleichgeschaltet*.'[30] The policies of firmness which Cadogan decried – and which incurred the contemptuous comments on their proponents that pervade his diaries – are exemplified by a minute written by Sir Robert Vansittart on March 4th: 'I submit very earnestly that we are incurring an enormous responsibility in not speaking to Hitler a great deal more firmly and explicitly than we have done . . . if not checked . . . he may carry himself and everyone else into disaster.' But unfortunately Vansittart's warnings were to remain unheeded by the members of the Government to which he was the Chief Diplomatic Adviser. From now on it would be Cadogan's views and decisions which would prevail, as Chamberlain and Halifax pursued their disastrous course of successive surrenders to threats of totalitarian power.

A few days later Hitler invaded and absorbed Austria into the Third Reich. Here was yet another object lesson, not only for the King, Government and people of Belgium, but for all the other small nations whose existence might hamper the development of the aggressive plans Hitler had so clearly set out in *Mein Kampf*. Yet Cadogan wrote in a Foreign Office document: 'It is all very disturbing and humiliating, but if we have made up our minds to accept the *fait accompli* (as in Abyssinia) it seems to me we don't improve matters by accepting it with bad grace.' With this policy, he records, the Foreign Secretary, Halifax, agreed.

Now that Czechoslovakia was surrounded on three sides by the Germans it was quite obvious that she was next on the list. Cadogan's diary entry for March 16th records that the British Government's Foreign Policy Committee was 'unanimous that Czechoslovakia is not worth the bones of a single British Grenadier'; and comments 'and they're quite right too'.[31]

In September 1938 the Sudeten crisis came to a head. On June 18th, in his directive to Keitel for the assault on Europe's 'model democracy',

Hitler had written: 'I will decide to take action against Czechoslovakia only if I am firmly convinced, as in the case of the demilitarized zone and the entry into Austria, that France will not march, and that therefore England will not intervene.' But if Hitler had any lingering doubts, these were dispelled when Chamberlain flew on his own initiative to Berchtesgaden – and a few days later to Godesberg, bearing the full acceptance of all Germany's territorial demands in Czechoslovakia, which he and the Czechs' long-standing ally and guarantor, France, had just imposed on them by threatening to leave them to their fate. But Hitler had in the meantime uprated his demands and rejected Chamberlain's submissive offering in favour of a *diktat* which stipulated that unless the whole of the Sudeten territories, which included the Czechs' strongly fortified mountain defence line, were ceded to Germany by 2 pm on the 28th, the German Army would be launched against that nation. Cadogan thus describes the scene in Whitehall on the following day (the 24th): 'P.M. [Chamberlain] made his report for us . . . he was quite calmly for total surrender . . . H [Halifax] . . . completely and quite happily défaitist-pacifist . . .'

Later that day Chamberlain told his Cabinet colleagues that he thought he had 'established some degree of personal influence over Herr Hitler' who, he felt confident, 'would not go back on his word', and that the Führer trusted him, and was willing to work with him. On the evening of the 27th Chamberlain made the pathetic broadcast in which he declared:

> How horrible, fantastic, incredible it is that we should be digging trenches and trying on gas-masks here because of a quarrel in a faraway country between people of whom we know nothing . . . we cannot in all circumstances undertake to involve the whole British Empire in war simply on her account. If we have to fight, it must be on larger issues than that . . .

Unfortunately for mankind the Prime Minister's defeatist words lifted Hitler's spirits, which had been much cast down by the bad news that had been accumulating throughout that 'Black Wednesday'. Indeed, as his interpreter Dr Schmidt told the author and also records in his memoirs, his master was evidently shrinking from 'the extreme step'[32] (the time limit for his Godesberg ultimatum ran out at 2 pm next day). Hitler had seen that his people were opposed to war,[c] and his military leaders had convinced him that Germany would suffer a catastrophic defeat if an attempt were made to invade Czechoslovakia.

Hitler therefore knew that if he ordered the Army to attack Czechoslovakia, this aggression would lead to France honouring her guarantees of military assistance to her ally. Testifying at Nuremberg, General Jodl stated that it was 'militarily impossible' for Germany's 'five fighting divisions and seven reserve divisions in the western fortifications, which were nothing but a large construction site, to hold out against 100 French divisions', while Field Marshal von Manstein declared at the same trials:

If a war had broken out, neither our western border nor our Polish frontier could have been effectively defended by us, and there is no doubt whatsoever that had Czechoslovakia defended herself, we would have been held back by her fortifications, for we did not have the means to break through.

Hitler, by now in 'a highly nervous state',* was confronted with the alternatives of suffering military defeats on three fronts if he ordered the attack, or a fatal loss of face if he climbed down and failed to do so. Then at 8 pm on the 27th came Chamberlain's submissive broadcast, providing Hitler with just the opportunity he needed to extricate himself from this agonizing dilemma. He therefore concocted a cunningly worded letter to Chamberlain, full of false promises, and designed to play on his pacific inclinations and dupe him into a bloodless surrender. Chamberlain received this apparent olive branch by telegraph at 10.30 that evening – and clutched at it. Despite all Hitler's broken promises, Chamberlain immediately telegraphed back assuring him that he could get 'all essentials without war and without delay' and eagerly offering to visit him for the third time.

At the Munich Conference of September 29th 1938 the Czech representatives were not even admitted to hear the death sentence passed on their country by their enemies and erstwhile friends. As Chamberlain and Daladier left his presence, the Führer turned to Ribbentrop and said 'It's terrible. I always have to deal with nonentities.' A few days later, in a speech at Saarbrucken, he exclaimed 'We will no longer tolerate the tutelage of governesses.' The month of extreme tension ended with a great number of people (including many Germans) wildly rejoicing when Chamberlain, on his return to London, assured the world that he had secured 'peace with honour' and 'peace for our time', as he brandished the piece of paper he had persuaded Hitler to sign.

Although the more percipient throughout threatened Europe and the world deplored the betrayal of the Czechs by France and Britain, very few people in Britain shared Winston Churchill's view, which he expressed vehemently in Parliament, against a storm of hostility, that Munich had been 'a total and unmitigated defeat'. And only about forty Conservative MPs (including Sir Roger Keyes) abstained when the House of Commons approved the Government's policy, 'by which war was averted in the recent crisis'.

One reason that has been advanced for the two Prime Ministers' abject surrender to Hitler's bluff was their fear that London and Paris would be razed to the ground by massive air attacks. But the *Luftwaffe*, like the

* William L. Shirer saw Hitler a few days earlier and thus described him, adding: 'He seemed to have a peculiar tic . . . . He had ugly, black patches under his eyes. He seemed to be, as I noted in my diary that evening, on the edge of a nervous breakdown.' *The Rise and Fall of the Third Reich*.

German Army, was concentrated against Czechoslovakia and their bombers and fighters then had too short a range to be capable of serious action in the West. For these reasons General Felmy reported to Göring that without a German occupation of Belgium, Holland and northern France no air war could be waged against Britain.

It was also argued that Munich gave Britain and France nearly a year to remedy their deficiencies in armaments – and in particular air power. But Churchill was right when he wrote: 'The year's breathing space said to be "gained" by Munich left Britain and France in a much worse position compared to Hitler's Germany than they had been at the Munich crisis.'

As a coda to Munich it is worth recalling General Keitel's reply when asked by the Czech representatives at the Nuremberg Trials: 'Would the Reich have attacked Czechoslovakia in 1938 if the Western Powers had stood by Prague?' Keitel's answer was: 'Certainly not. We were not strong enough militarily. The object of Munich was to keep Russia out of Europe, to gain time, and to complete Germany's rearmament.' But what neither Hitler, Jodl nor Keitel knew on September 27th was that nearly all the other German generals from Brauchitsch, the Commander-in-Chief, down were aware of or actually engaged in a plot by the powerful anti-Nazi underground to eliminate Hitler and his regime by a large-scale military and police operation the *following day.**

The relevance to this biography of the activities of these dedicated opponents of Hitler is that Leopold's attitudes and decisions – and a number of subsequent happenings – were influenced by his secret contacts with certain leaders of this resistance organization. Their chronicle, moreover, reveals how the course of history might have been changed for the better, if only the British and French leaders had heeded their advice – as did Leopold, Churchill and other far-sighted men – that the only way to deal with Hitler was to follow resolute policies towards him, and thus assist their plans to overthrow him and his evil regime.

The German resistance movement permeated the whole hierarchy: the armed forces, the police, the foreign ministry, important areas of the civil population, including the churches, universities and even the Secret Service (the *Abwehr*). The leader of the *Putsch* which came so near to liquidating Hitler and the Nazi regime in September 1938 was General Franz Halder, the Chief of the Army General Staff. The plan was to seize Hitler and his henchmen as soon as he issued the order to attack Czechoslovakia – the ultimatum for which expired on the 28th – and so

---

* The facts concerning the anti-Hitler movement are still little known, although the transcripts of the Nuremburg trials and the testimony of the few members who survived the Gestapo's purge in 1944 are now available. See *The Conspiracy against Hitler in the Twilight War* by Harold Deutsch, and *The History of the German Resistance* by Peter Hoffman.

prevent him from plunging Germany into a ruinous war. 'The population of Berlin,' wrote William L. Shirer, 'scared to death that Hitler was about to bring on a war, would have – so far as this writer could at first hand judge them – spontaneously backed the coup.'[33]

The military planning of the coup was under the control of Colonel Hans Oster, whose outstanding services to Belgium and the other threatened democracies in repeatedly warning them of Hitler's aggressive plans, at the risk of his life, are described later. Captain Friedrich Heinz, the commander of the task force which was to take over the Reich Chancellery, was ordered to arrest Hitler, but he and Oster decided that the Führer and the other Nazi leaders would in fact be killed 'while resisting arrest' or 'while trying to escape'.

Halder had a formidable armed force poised ready to strike, including an army corps, a crack infantry division and General Höpner's 6th Panzer Division. Ironically, two of Hitler's most dedicated opponents, Generals Beck and von Hammerstein, who had no intention of attacking Czechoslovakia, commanded the First and Fourth Armies, which were drawn up facing her frontier. The two senior police chiefs in Berlin were also in the plot and ready to deploy a large force of armed police. Other participants included Admiral Canaris, head of the *Abwehr*, Ernst von Weizsäcker, the head of the Foreign Ministry, and his confidant Carl Goerdeler, all of whom figure in Leopold's story.

At the height of the Sudeten crisis Halder gave orders for the coup to be launched on September 28th, the day on which the Führer's Godesberg ultimatum expired at 2 pm. But, as Halder described at Nuremberg in 1946, he had to cancel the operation at noon on that day, when he was on the point of giving General Witzleben the final order to execute it, because 'the news came through that the British Prime Minister had agreed to come to Hitler for further talks . . . and the entire basis for the action was thus taken away'.

To this testimony one of the conspirators added at Nuremberg: 'The impossible had happened. Chamberlain and Daladier were flying to Munich. Our revolt was done for . . . Chamberlain saved Hitler.' Such a favourable moment for the overthrow of the Nazi tyranny was never to occur again, although a number of abortive attempts were made on Hitler's life,* culminating in that by Count von Stauffenberg on July 20th 1944, which resulted in almost all Hitler's underground opponents being tortured and killed by the Gestapo.

King Leopold and his milieu had in fact been in close touch since 1937 with important members of the German underground movement and

---

* The opposition's attempt to blow up the aircraft in which Hitler was returning from the Russian front in 1942 failed by a hair's breadth to eliminate the Führer, because the extreme cold at high altitude inhibited the firing mechanism of the British-made bomb with which the plotters had been supplied by Admiral Canaris' *Abwehr*.

continuously received invaluable information, including numerous specific warnings about Hitler's aggressive intentions. One of the most interesting sources of such a warning was General von Falkenhausen – interesting because he became Military Governor of Belgium during the occupation and exercised a notable clemency, for which he suffered at the hands of the SS. Moreover, von Falkenhausen had at one time been the opposition's choice as Head of State in the non-Nazi Germany which they were striving to achieve.* These 'good Germans' were men of considerable influence with access to a vast range of intelligence, acting at the risk of torture and their lives. Their readiness to inform and warn the Belgians and their confident relationship with the King, therefore, hardly support accusations that he was pro-Hitler.

Thanks to those contacts with the German dissidents in high places, many of whom were devout Roman Catholics or Protestants and who were all Hitler's enemies, the King was able to base his actions not only on an informed estimate of the dictator's intentions, but also on an accurate appreciation of his personal insecurity. Knowing the flaws and stresses of the Nazi state, Leopold realized that the apparently monolithic strength of Germany was a delusion, that there were many within the Reich itself who were prepared to rebel against Hitler and that given time the menace of Nazi Germany might be dissolved through internal explosion. During the whole crisis-ridden period up to May 1940 an effort to gain time was therefore a fundamental element in Leopold's policy.

It might be argued that time was also the chief object of the Chamberlain administration. But the difference was that, whereas Leopold gave serious and sympathetic attention to the approaches of the German dissidents, responded to their anti-Hitler initiatives and acted on the vital information they gave him, Chamberlain regarded them as traitors to their country and stood disdainfully aloof. The contrast is particularly marked in the case of Carl Goerdeler, whose personal relationship with Leopold forms an important part of the King's story. Goerdeler, a devout Christian and ex-Mayor of Leipzig, was the leading civilian member of the anti-Hitler movement.

In Belgium the base betrayal at Munich by Britain and France of a small democratic nation which had depended upon them for its protection from Nazi aggression added yet another stroke underlining the wisdom of the Belgian policy of well-armed independence. A few days later in the Chamber, Spaak once again made himself the spokesman of the homage which the whole country was rendering to their Sovereign for his championship of that policy:

* Evidence given by Colonel Goethals (the Belgian Military Attaché in Berlin up to May 1940) at von Falkenhausen's trial.

Our hearts are united around the King, to whom – I shall never tire of saying it – we owe so much; the King, in whom all those who have approached him during these last days have clearly recognised the high values, the calm courage, the ardent love of his Country, and the loyalty to his pledged word which, in August 1914, made Albert the First the centre of our resistance.

In the negotiations preceding the Franco-British Declaration Anthony Eden had been friendly and helpful, but Leopold's confidence in Britain's good faith and intentions might have been less strong had he known that the British were still prepared to use Belgium as a pawn in the game of appeasement. As Neville Chamberlain told Flandin during the Rhineland crisis in 1936, he would gladly give away a colony if peace could thereby be secured. On November 26th 1937 he wrote to his sister that the Germans 'want Togoland and the Kameruns . . . but they do not insist upon Tanganyika, if they can be given some more reasonable territory on the West Coast, possibly to be carved out of the Belgian Congo and Angola.'[34]

On March 3rd the following year in an interview with Hitler, Ribbentrop and Göring immediately before the German invasion of Austria, Sir Nevile Henderson, the British Ambassador in Berlin, made an offer on these lines in an attempt to 'buy off' the German leaders. This he asked them to treat as absolutely confidential and not to reveal it to the Belgian, Portuguese, or French Governments. The bribe consisted of a share in a redistributed pool of African colonies belonging to those nations, plus large tracts of Northern Rhodesia – an area 'about the size of the Congo Basin'. 'When Henderson concluded his rather lengthy exposition,' writes Dr Schmidt, 'Hitler showed not the slightest interest, saying there was no hurry at all about the colonial question.'[35] The scene is graphically described by Chamberlain's biographer: 'Vainly Henderson pointed to the globe in Hitler's study, spread visions of a German share in a rearranged, philanthropic Congo Basin . . .'[36]

The full facts about the British Government's offer of Danegeld to Germany, devised towards the end of Anthony Eden's regime as Foreign Secretary in 1938, only emerged after the war, when Russia published the archives of the German Foreign Ministry, which they had captured. In July 1943 Sir George Gater wrote to Sir Alexander Cadogan about the 'embarrassment' that would occur if these documents were published. 'Out of fear of Germany,' he wrote, 'we were prepared to hand over large tracts of Colonial Empire without consulting the wishes of the inhabitants . . .' But Churchill minuted: 'I think it is a pity that Mr Eden's name should be mixed up directly with this policy of appeasement . . . There is no need to hurry about the publication of this book.' In March 1944 Eden, then Foreign Secretary once again, announced that 'the most important documents in the Foreign Office archives between 1919 and 1939' were to be made public – but those covering the colonial appeasement proposals were placed right at the end of the long series of volumes that were to be published.

As Europe slid towards Armageddon, Leopold had small grounds for optimism – and they would have been smaller still if he had known facts like these, or the full truth about Britain's lack of military resources and preparation, or the rot behind the façade of French power.

After Munich, Neville Chamberlain – who believed that he had won Hitler's respect and friendship – turned his thoughts to a reconciliation with Mussolini. Accordingly, he and Lord Halifax journeyed to Italy and presented themselves to the Duce on January 11th 1939. But this ill-judged initiative caused Great Britain and her government to sink even lower in the estimation of the Axis leaders, as Ciano's diary humiliatingly reveals:

> How far apart we are from these people! 'These men,' said Mussolini, 'are not made of the same stuff as Francis Drake and the other magnificent adventurers who created the Empire . . .' The British do not want to fight. They try to draw back as slowly as possible, but they do not want to fight . . . Our conversations with the British have ended. Nothing was accomplished. I have telephoned to Ribbentrop saying that it was a fiasco, absolutely innocuous . . .

A fortnight later Ciano wrote:

> Lord Perth has submitted for our approval the outlines of a speech that Chamberlain will make in the House of Commons, in order that we may suggest changes if necessary. The Duce approved it, and commented: 'I believe this is the first time that the head of the British Government has submitted to a foreign government the outlines of one of his speeches. It is a bad sign for them.[37]

On March 15th, emboldened by the supine policies of Britain and France, Hitler marched his armies into Prague and placed the whole of Czecho-slovakia under his rule. Speaking that day in the House of Commons, Chamberlain 'bitterly regretted' Hitler's latest conquest, but declared that, since the state whose independence and frontiers Britain had guaranteed had been put at an end by internal disruption, 'His Majesty's Government cannot accordingly hold themselves bound by this obligation.' Hitler had now brought under his control 6,750,000 Austrians and 14,000,000 Czechs, including the thirty-five divisions of their Army and the personnel of their Air Force as well as all their aircraft, tanks, guns and equipment, backed by the mighty Skoda armaments industry.

In the same month Hitler denounced the Statute of Danzig and occupied the Port of Memel in Lithuania. Three weeks later he tore up the Anglo-German Naval Treaty and the German-Polish Non-Aggression Pact. Meanwhile Mussolini, not to be outdone, chose Good

Friday, April 7th, to invade Albania; while in the Far East Japan, now allied with Germany and Italy, was attacking China.

The dilemma in which Belgium now found herself is summed up by Winston Churchill in *The Second World War* – sympathetically, in marked contrast to most of his other writings and utterances about that country and her leaders:

The Belgian leaders saw with worried eyes the internal weakness of France and the vacillating pacifism of Britain . . . Great allowance must be made for the fearful problems of a small State in such a plight.[38]

Of course, if British and French policy during the five years preceding the war had been of a manly and resolute character . . . Belgium might have adhered to her old allies and allowed a common front to be formed . . . When we recall the aloofness of the United States; Mr Ramsay MacDonald's campaign for the disarmament of France; the repeated rebuffs and humiliations which we had accepted in the various German breaches of the Disarmament Clauses of the Treaty; our submission to the German violation of the Rhineland; our acquiescence in the absorption of Austria; our pact at Munich and acceptance of the German occupation of Prague – when we recall all this, no man in Britain or France who in those years was responsible for public action has a right to blame Belgium.[39]

CHAPTER SEVEN

The Knife's Edge

'I feel I must thank the King publicly for the magnificent efforts he
has made for several years to spare our country the horrors of war
(Lively applause); for the wise counsel he has always given to the
various Governments which have succeeded one another in power;
for the strength of mind with which he performs his very heavy
task; for the example he has always set those with whom he comes
in contact, an example which compels respect, admiration, and
affection.'

Paul Henri Spaak, speaking in
the Chamber in December 1939

On August 23rd 1939 the cause of peace was finally shattered by the
signing in Moscow of the Nazi-Soviet Pact, by which Stalin agreed, in
effect, to leave Poland to the tender mercies of Hitler's armies, and share
the spoils of that country with him. Only a fortnight before, an Anglo-
French delegation consisting of unknown officials and Service officers had
arrived in Moscow to continue with the unenthusiastic conversations to
which Chamberlain had reluctantly agreed in June. These talks were a
complete fiasco, for even before they ended, Ribbentrop and Molotov
were putting the finishing touches to their non-aggression pact and secret
treaty of alliance, while Stalin toasted the Führer's health in another part
of Moscow. Meanwhile, Chamberlain pursued his frantic policy of one-
sided alliances with far-distant small nations: Rumania, Greece and
Turkey each being successively 'guaranteed', despite the fact that Britain
was militarily incapable of aiding any of those countries.

To Leopold the significance for Belgium of the two dictators' unnatural
act was unmistakable. When Germany marched in 1914 the armies of
Russia threatened her rear. Now, by this Machiavellian switch of policy,
the risk of a major war on two fronts was deferred and Germany had
immensely enlarged her freedom to attack in the West. Moreover, she
was now assured of all the essential prerequisites for a major offensive –
including the vast supplies of oil and petrol necessary to sustain it.* But the
King had no knowledge of the secret protocols, the contents of which
were only revealed after the war, when the German archives were
captured. Under their terms Hitler gave Stalin a free hand in the eastern
Baltic and in Bessarabia, which Russia had lost to Rumania in 1919.

---

* Russia delivered more than a million tons of oil to the Germans in the first year of the war.

85

Finland, Estonia, Latvia and Lithuania were recognized as being within the Soviet 'sphere of influence' and were, accordingly, in due course invaded by the Red Army. But most sinister of all, the secret protocols laid down the precise line by which the two despots' next victim, Poland, was to be partitioned between them. Thus was sealed the 'unholy alliance' between the Nazi and Communist dictatorships, which was the immediate prelude to war.

The day after the signing of the Nazi-Soviet Alliance, Hitler called a conference of his generals to brief them for the impending assault on Poland. Before the showdown with the West, he explained, it was necessary to 'test the military machine' – and Poland was the obvious testing ground. After expressing his confidence that the French and British (he described the latter as 'little worms – I saw them at Munich') would be unable to help Poland, Hitler concluded 'My only fear is that at the last minute some *Schweinhund* will make a proposal for mediation.' These fears were very real for, if such an appeal were made and he were to ignore it, his frequently repeated assertions that it was the Western Powers alone who by their encirclement of Germany were forcing war on her would be disproved to his people.

It was much to Hitler's annoyance, therefore, when the King of the Belgians came to the microphone on the very next day, to broadcast to the world a moving appeal for peace and reason from the Conference of Neutral Countries, which he had hurriedly convened in Brussels following the announcement of the Nazi-Soviet Pact. Speaking in the names of Queen Wilhemina, the Grand Duchess of Luxembourg, the President of Finland and the Kings of Norway, Sweden and Denmark, and in his own name, 'each of us acting with the agreement of our own Governments', Leopold declared that their object was:

> To establish a new Great Power, of a kind unknown to history. It is not the result of conquest, nor does it represent any material, military, or economic force, since the parts of which it is composed are scattered and isolated. But it can constitute a great moral and spiritual Power, capable of arousing world opinion. Through the union of the small States – for a peaceful purpose, as no one can doubt – this new Great Power, consisting of more than 100,000,000 citizens, is of considerable weight in the peaceful scale.
>
> We express the hope that other Heads of States will join with us in demonstrating the same concern for the peace and security of their peoples. Tomorrow, hundreds of millions of men will be of one mind with us to stop the race towards war. Let those in whose hands lies the fate of the world respond to these feelings, and accomplish the wish, which they have so often uttered, to find a peaceful solution to the difficulties which divide them . . .
>
> War psychosis is invading our homes and public opinion, although aware of the unimaginable catastrophe that a conflagration would bring upon humanity as a whole, is surrendering more and more to the idea that we are being

inevitably driven towards it. We must fight against so fatal a resignation . . . It is true that all States have not the same interests. But are there any interests which cannot be more easily reconciled before than after a war? Let the conscience of the world awáke! The worse can still be avoided, but time is short . . .

Hitler was furious. This appeal for peace and common sense, with which the Pope and the British and French Governments immediately associated thémselves, was embarrassing and inhibiting for him, because it impeded the momentum of his propaganda. Here – on the eve of his Polish campaign – was the very peace proposal he feared would be made. If the broadcast did not deter Hitler, it did at least focus attention on his total lack of principle.

Now., two days after the announcement of the Nazi-Soviet Pact, having thrown away every chance of stopping Hitler, Chamberlain – the 'little worm' of the Führer's gibe – turned, and by giving Poland a cast-iron guarantee* which Britain had no means to implement not only made a German assault upon Poland virtually certain, but ensured that Britain would be plunged into war under the most unfavourable conditions it was possible to contrive. On this same day, Hitler declared that his 'patience was exhausted' and that the annexation of Danzig was imminent.

On August 26th Leopold, after consultation with his Ministers, ordered Phase A, the preliminary stage of Belgian mobilization. Later that day the German Ambassador asked for an audience with the King and read him a message from his government reaffirming the German guarantee of August 13th 1937. Similar notes were presented by the British and French Ambassadors on the 27th and 28th respectively. After ordering Phase B of his country's mobilization, on the 28th, Leopold joined with Queen Wilhelmina in suggesting that they should jointly offer their good offices in seeking a peaceful settlement to the governments of Britain, France, Germany, Italy and Poland.

Replying to this offer, London threw the responsibility upon Berlin and Warsaw – and the Germans, while 'cordially recognizing the efforts of the two Sovereigns to maintain peace', nevertheless carefully kept all reference to it out of their newspapers. France demanded, rather plaintively, whether even this most generous inspiration could heal so wide a breach.

While the German armies stood poised to invade Poland across three frontiers and Britain and France prepared for war, Hitler hesitated. On August 28th, however, he was told by an informant that Sir Samuel Hoare had been advising his colleagues that, even if Germany did invade Poland, Britain need not involve herself but, having declared war on Germany, could remain inactive until Poland was defeated and then

* On March 31st 1939 Chamberlain had given an assurance in the House of Commons that the British Government would lend Poland 'all support in their power' in the event of her résisting an attack, but on August 25th a full Treaty of Alliance between the two Nations was signed.

make peace. Certainly other 'doves' such as Lord Halifax and his Under Secretary, R. A. Butler, were described as 'working like beavers for a second Munich' throughout this anxious period. Indeed, Halifax continued to make telephone calls to the European capitals seeking a compromise solution even after bombs started falling on Warsaw.

In Berlin Hitler soon convinced himself, but not all his reluctant henchmen, that Britain would not fight for Poland. This impression was reinforced by Sir Nevile Henderson, the British Ambassador, who openly urged that Britain and France should force Poland (as in the case of Czechoslovakia) to give in to the German demands and so avert war. Accordingly, when at dawn on September 1st – without a declaration of war and after heavily bombing the Polish airfields – Hitler unleashed the *Blitzkrieg* on Poland, Leopold immediately ordered Phase C of Belgium's mobilization.

When the British Cabinet met thirty-six hours later, neither Britain nor France had made a move of any kind in support of their Eastern ally. There were furious scenes in Parliament that evening when Chamberlain, instead of announcing the ultimatum on which the Cabinet had agreed, continued to temporize – the French Government having failed to agree to follow suit. It was only under pressure that Chamberlain was induced to have Britain's ultimatum presented to Germany at 9 am next day – followed by a declaration of war two hours later – by which time the German invasion of Poland was already in its third day. After an agonizing delay – for Britain – of six hours, the French Government reluctantly declared war.

Within ten days the Polish army – nearly two million strong – had been shattered by the *Luftwaffe* and the mechanized spearheads of the German Army, working closely together as a team. Russia then invaded from the East to reap the fruits of her bargain with the Nazis and, after Soviet and German troops had joined hands at Brest Litovsk on September 18th, Poland was submerged in the West by the *Wehrmacht* and in the East by the Red Army, as the Nazi and Communist dictatorships divided her territory and spoils between them. Since the Polish Government had fled, there was no one left to negotiate an armistice with the German conquerers. Even before the *Wehrmacht* withdrew, Himmler's political police moved in and the most atrocious reign of terror began. Under Hans Frank, the bestial Governor-General, the policy worked out by Hitler, Himmler and Heydrich to destroy Poland as a nation was put into operation. This involved the extermination of the Polish aristocracy, intelligentsia, clergy and military, in order to render the Poles a leaderless subject race. The Jews were to be confined in ghettos and gradually liquidated, while the country was systematically looted and exploited for the benefit of Germany.

There was now every indication of a complete alliance between the

Germans and Russians, but the British Government turned a blind eye to the fact – and to the equally dreadful atrocities which the Soviet occupation forces and NKVD were perpetrating in Poland. Indeed, Britain continued to strive for amicable relations with the Russians. The Belgians and the other neutrals who had counted on Britain and France to protect them against aggression witnessed with dismay the complete failure of those Powers to take any military, naval or air action in support of Poland – for whom they had gone to war – or to condemn the Russians for combining with the Germans in the brutal enslavement of her people.

A fourth small nation had now been wiped from the map of Europe – only this time Hitler had been abetted by the USSR, which had for so long posed as the champion of oppressed peoples. But worse was to come, for Stalin now moved rapidly and ruthlessly to exploit the 'spheres of influence' the Führer had ceded to him and proceeded to extinguish the liberty of another three neutral nations – Estonia, Latvia and Lithuania. Yet this aggression by the Soviets passed almost unremarked in the rest of the world. Thanks to the deal with the Nazis, Russia had, at little cost to herself, greatly strengthened her position and acquired the whole of the eastern coastline of the Baltic Sea.

On the outbreak of war on September 3rd, Leopold immediately took up his post as Commander-in-Chief of the armed forces in accordance with the Constitution, and on that same fateful day the Government issued a formal Declaration of Neutrality. There were those abroad who believed that this was the result of a *politique personelle* on Leopold's part, and even that this purpose was to play Hitler's game. In *Assignment to Catastrophe* General Sir Edward Spears describes how in August 1939 he and Churchill paid a visit to France to General Georges. 'Fears concerning what the King of the Belgians would do in case of war were apparent in what Georges told us of the French plans. Leopold was reputed to be much under German influence. He apparently intended standing alone, holding the Western Allies at arm's length, relying on his coolness towards them to obtain German indulgence.'[40]

In contrast to such misconceived and suspicious views, the observations made about Leopold's policies by the American Ambassador, Joseph F. Davies, are refreshingly objective:

> The keystone of his entire foreign policy was the maintenance of Belgian neutrality . . . It was his deep conviction that this policy not only served Belgium best, but also protected the peace of Europe . . . Immediately following the invasion of Poland, Belgium was subjected to very great pressure from both sides to swerve it from this strict neutrality . . . Against that pressure from either side he stood like a rock. It took great courage and steadfastness. In this position he was charged with being pro-Ally and also with being pro-

German. As a matter of truth and fact, he was neither – he was wholly, utterly and completely pro-Belgian.*

The pressures from the Allies were of course to force Belgium out of her neutrality and into their camp. One of the pressures from the German side, as Davies explains, was her unsuccessful attempt 'to coerce Belgium into resisting the British blockade.ᵈ It was the German position that the blockade was an attack on Belgium's sovereignty and it was intimated from Berlin that unless Belgium would protect her sovereignty in this situation Germany would have to come in and do it for her.'[41]

What French malice and British blindness overlooked were two simple, fundamental facts. The posture of 'armed independence' was the most militant that Leopold could legitimately adopt under the Great Powers' guarantees, whose validity was specifically renewed in the Notes which Belgium received from Germany, Britain and France at the end of August. In exactly similar terms the latter two countries stated that 'if Belgium adopts an attitude of neutrality' they would be 'resolute and determined to respect this neutrality fully' and guaranteed that they would fulfil the undertakings of military assistance which they had pledged in April 1937 and which, they declared, 'naturally retain their full effect' in the event of the breaching of Belgium's neutrality by another Power.

At the very outset of the war, therefore, the unanimous policy of the King and his coalition government was entirely accepted and endorsed in formal terms by their future allies. Nevertheless, in the coming months the French and British would do their utmost to induce Belgium to renege on her policy of armed independence and bitterly criticized the King and his government for refusing to bow to their will in this regard.

In any case, the thesis that Belgium's policy was personal to the King ignores the fact that at the outbreak of war and right through to the German invasion in May 1940 it was enthusiastically ratified by the Belgian Parliament and people. It is impossible to over-emphasize Leopold's achievement in uniting a country which was sectionalized by so many internal differences, racial, social, political and religious. The Belgium that mobilized with devoted unanimity in 1939 was a solid combination, to a degree that would have seemed surprising when Leopold came to the throne. While it is true that he and his principal Ministers evolved the policy of armed independence, it is equally true that this rallied his democratic countrymen to make a defence effort which far exceeded that of France and Britain in proportion to their populations and resources.

* Compare with Sir Harold Nicolson's comments on the attitude of King George V at the beginning of World War I: 'King George was neither pro-French, pro-Russian nor pro-German: he was undeviatingly pro-British.' *King George V.*

That Belgium would fight if attacked was, moreover, made abundantly clear to all. The British and French understood, whatever the cynics might say. And the Germans knew. On October 30th Leopold ordered his ADC and principal Military Adviser, General Van Overstraeten, to summon the German Military Attaché in Brussels to advise him formally of the reasons for the large-scale defensive build-up which Belgium had undertaken in the East and to give him this warning: 'I wish to draw your attention to Belgian public opinion . . . If German troops should ever enter Belgian territory, the whole nation would rise against you.'[42] This was a direct confirmation to Hitler of the promise the King had made three days earlier in a radio broadcast to the United States. After referring to the deeds of the Belgian Army under his father in the previous war he continued: 'If we were attacked – and I pray God this may not happen – in violation of the solemn and definite undertakings that were given us in 1937, and were renewed at the outset of the present war, we would not hesitate to fight with the same conviction, but with forces ten times stronger, and again, the whole country would be behind the Army . . .'*

By early October the bulk of the German armies which had conquered Poland at such lightning speed had flowed back to the Western Front and were taking up their positions facing Belgium and Luxembourg in readiness for *Fall Gelb* (Plan Yellow), the great offensive in the West. Since the original versions of that plan were, according to Hitler's directive, limited to 'gaining the Channel coast' and no invasion of Holland except for the crossing of the Maastricht Appendix† was planned, von Bock's Army Group B, comprising forty-three divisions, including nine Panzer and four motorized divisions, was amassed opposite the border – ready to strike straight through the heart of Belgium. Behind this formidable shock force stood the OKH Reserve of nine divisions, including one Panzer and two motorized divisions, with another ten infantry divisions in general reserve.

Fresh from the kill in Poland, like the Panzers they had supported with such devastating effect, and ready to play the same part in the *Blitzkrieg* against the West, were two 'Airfleets' – Felmy's *Luftflotte* 2 and Sperrle's *Luftflotte* 3, comprising about 3,700 aircraft. On von Bock's left facing the Luxembourg frontier was von Rundstedt's Army Group A, comprising twenty-two divisions without armour, with the role of crossing the Meuse on both sides of Namur in order to give von Bock's powerful thrust through central Belgium flanking protection against possible French attacks from the south-west. Since the Germans had no intention of

* See Appendix III.
† The narrow strip of Dutch territory between Belgium and Germany on the east bank of the Maas (the Dutch name for the Meuse), north-west of Aachen, which was to be crossed by the German forces attacking Belgium north of Liège.

attacking the Maginot Line, von Leeb's Army Group C, which faced it, consisted of only eighteen divisions of over-age foot soldiers, whose role was purely defensive, except for feinting operations designed to hold the French forces in their positions and prevent them from being used as reinforcements elsewhere.

Behind Belgium's 250-mile-long eastern frontier, ready to defend her soil against the Germans' overwhelming array of mechanized and aerial might, stood the twenty-two divisions of her Army and her tiny Air Force. In France, ranged along Belgium's western frontier (approximately the same length), were four French armies, the four divisions of the British Expeditionary Force on a twenty-five mile front between Halluin and Maulde being interposed between Giraud's Seventh Army on the extreme left of the line and Blanchard's First Army on the BEF's right. The ill-fated Ninth and Second French Armies under Corap and Huntziger covered the rest of the frontier as far as Montmedy, where the Maginot Line proper began.

Throughout October and November *Fall Gelb* was constantly amended by Hitler and his generals, who were unanimous in their opposition to the attack in the West. But the basic plan and objectives remained the same. A rapid and powerful thrust was to be launched straight through central Belgium to the Channel coast, spearheaded by nine of von Bock's Panzer and four motorized divisions, and supported by virtually the whole of the *Luftwaffe*. Although Hitler had temporarily eliminated the prospect of a two-front war by his pact with Stalin, he did not expect that he would be able to destroy the French Army at one blow. His thoughts were concentrated on 'getting at' Britain, which he regarded as 'the principal enemy' and, as the minutes of the OKW conference on September 27th record, 'The Führer does not intend to repeat the Schlieffen plan,* but to attack . . . through Belgium and Luxembourg under the strong protection of the southern Flank, and to gain the Channel coast.' On October 28th, therefore, Hitler directed that an attack with armour north of Liège should aim at 'the Belgian fortress', while a Panzer concentration south of that town should break through in a westerly direction and destroy the Anglo-French armies in the North. Hitler's stated object of conquering Belgium and as much as possible of Northern France with their coastlines was to secure bases for air and sea warfare against England, while at the same time forming a protective zone in front of the Ruhr.

On October 5th Hitler entered shattered Warsaw and on the following day, flushed with victory, launched his 'peace offensive'. In his Reichstag speech, which was broadcast to the world, the Führer extended to the Allies his concept of an olive branch: 'At no time and in no place have I

---

* Schlieffen's plan was also for a massive and rapid thrust through Belgium, but his object was different: the complete destruction of the French Army by a southward encircling movement.

ever acted contrary to British interests.' This was followed by some magnanimous references to the French and his declaration that there was no reason to continue the war. Poland was no more, so why fight about it? After proposing an international peace conference 'before millions of men are sent senselessly to their deaths . . .' and reminding his audience that in war there are no victors but only losers, the Führer concluded 'Let those who consider war to be the better solution reject my outstretched hand.' Although there were those in high places, including Ministers in Britain as well as France who were inclined to engage in peace negotiations with Hitler, the French Premier, Daladier, promptly and firmly rejected Hitler's *démarche*. Meanwhile the British Foreign Office temporized, while Hitler's proposals were 'subjected to careful examination'. On October 12th, however, Chamberlain declared 'We must persevere in our duty to the end.' This reply was denounced as 'insolent' by Goebbels' deputy, Otto Dietrich, who then announced – truthfully, for once – that Hitler had summoned his principal military leaders to prepare for 'war in earnest'.

Great consternation was caused among the German military hierarchy, for Hitler had assured them before launching the attack on Poland that this would not lead to war with Britain and France. Now, after it had had that result, he was telling them that if the Allies refused to respond to his peace offer, he would launch an immediate attack on France through Belgium and Holland, thus escalating the conflict into another full-scale World War. The Army leaders – and even Göring, who dreaded this prospect and wanted a peaceful settlement with the Allies – were horrified by Hitler's project. Moreover, they believed that the attack in the West would not be decisive in beating the Allies but would result in a long war which Germany could not win. Almost all therefore strove to deter, overthrow and some even to assassinate the Führer, in order to prevent him from staking their country's future on what they regarded as a suicidal gamble.*

While the generals tried to talk Hitler out of his bellicose plans, Göring continued to seek a negotiated peace by putting out 'feelers' to the British through his Swedish connections. But Hitler brushed aside his generals' objections and issued, on October 9th, his 'Directive No. 6 for the Conduct of the War'. This began: 'If it should become apparent in the near future that England and . . . France are not willing to put an end to the war, I am determined to take active and aggressive steps without much delay . . .' A powerful armoured attack through Belgium and Holland was to be prepared for launching at the earliest possible moment. In an attached memorandum designed to convert the reluctant generals, Hitler contended that Germany's limited food and raw material supplies would

* See *The Conspiracy Against Hitler*, by Harold Deutsch.

jeopardize the waging of a long war and stressed that possession of the Belgian and French Channel coast would therefore enormously strengthen Germany's position.

'Belgium and Holland', the memorandum continued, 'are dependent upon the West in the highest degree' and Britain and France could compel them to 'give up their neutrality . . .' Those two neutral countries also constituted 'a protective zone in front of the Ruhr', but England and France would seize on the first opportunity to occupy them the better to strike at that vital industrial zone. Earlier he had told his generals that 'the Belgians will call the French to come to their aid . . . we must therefore forestall this with a decisive operation . . .'

While virtually all the German generals were opposed to Hitler's plans to attack in the West, it was General von Leeb (the commander of Army Group C), a Bavarian and a regular church-going Catholic, who argued the most strongly against the violation of the Low Countries' neutrality, on the grounds of morality and conscience. As soon as von Leeb heard of Hitler's plans, he prepared a 'Memorandum on the Prospects and Effects of an Attack on France and England in Violation of the Neutrality of Holland, Belgium and Luxembourg', dated October 11th 1939. 'Even the first prerequisite for a quick success, operational surprise, does not exist,' Leeb argued, 'even now . . . Belgium is bringing up sizeable reinforcements in the direction of Liège . . .' After advancing various military arguments against the offensive, and questioning Hitler's contention that time was not on Germany's side, Leeb turned to 'political repercussions':

> Such an attack would provide England and France immediately with one thing they haven't had up to now, i.e. a forceful propaganda slogan . . . Any violation of Belgium's neutrality is bound to drive that country into the arms of France. France and Belgium will then have one common foe: Germany, which for the second time within twenty-five years assaults neutral Belgium! Germany, whose government solemnly vouched for and promised the preservation of and respect for this neutrality only a few weeks ago!

Before the end of October Halder, the Chief of Staff, von Bock and von Rundstedt had all demonstrated their agreement with von Leeb by issuing memoranda of their own, opposing Hitler's planned offensive. On October 14th Brauchitsch, the Commander-in-Chief, and Halder held a lengthy conference on the 'overall situation'. They considered three courses of action: Hitler's plan of attack, von Leeb's policy of a 'waiting attitude', and thirdly the overthrow of Hitler. Although they concluded, as Halder records, that 'none of these three possibilities offers any prospect of decisive success', he and Brauchitsch decided 'to promote every possibility to make peace'. Efforts were therefore made by the Commander-in-Chief to get various generals to 'talk the Führer out of his plan', as he tried to do himself. But Hitler rejected their pleas, declaring 'the British will be ready to talk only after a beating. We must get at them as quickly as possible.'

At the end of October both von Leeb and von Rundstedt wrote letters to their Commander-in-Chief, reiterating all the reasons why the offensive should not be launched. Von Rundstedt urged the policy of forcing Britain and France to take the offensive on land, which would put the onus of violating Belgian neutrality upon them: 'Our prospects are better if we meet the enemy moving into Belgium against the will of the Belgians, in a mobile engagement,' thus 'imposing on the French an attack which would strain their passive attitude towards the war'. After visiting the front, Brauchitsch made a last desperate effort to deter Hitler, on the pretext that the Army was not ready and the weather unfavourable. But in doing so he overstated his case and Hitler gave vent to an explosion of rage which put an end to his open opposition.

One of the most unlikely military leaders to speak out and act against Hitler was Colonel-General Walter von Reichenau, who reappears later in this chronicle as the Commander-in-Chief of the Sixth Army and King Leopold's captor when he surrendered with his army in May 1940. Admiral Canaris had been touring the military command centres in the West in his secret opposition role, to inform senior officers of the Nazi bestialities in Poland; to urge them to resist Hitler's plans and to gain support for his overthrow. Canaris was astounded to find that von Reichenau, who was not a member of the opposition, had protested to the Führer directly about the unspeakable atrocities Himmler's henchmen were perpetrating in Poland and denounced the projected violation of the Low Countries' neutrality as 'veritably criminal'. This brave stand infuriated Hitler and lost von Reichenau the supreme command of the *Wehrmacht*, for which he was in line, a few weeks later. And when, on November 6th, Hitler overruled all his generals' objections and ordered that *Fall Gelb* must be implemented on November 12th, von Reichenau took the even bolder step of informing the underground leader, Carl Goerdeler, and asking him to warn the British of the imminent attack through central Belgium. Von Reichenau's hope was that visible preparations by the Belgians and the Allies would cause the German High Command to recognize that they had lost the element of surprise and cancel the offensive.

'In support of Reichenau's logic,' writes Harold Deutsch, 'it may be noted that two months later an advanced state of Belgian, and to a much lesser extent, Dutch alert did play a major part in the postponement of offensive plans.' Von Reichenau's urgent warning was duly received in Britain via a chain of opposition agents and pro-Allied individuals. But, since he was not a member of the anti-Nazi opposition he did not know that its members – including Goerdeler and Oster – had for some time been engaged in secret communication with Leopold and others in the

West with a view to alerting them and initiating similar moves to frustrate
Hitler's invasion plans, or that his own warning had only served to
confirm those which the German underground had already given to
Hitler's intended victims. At the same time Baron von Weizsäcker, the
State Secretary at the German Foreign Ministry and a leading member of
the opposition, conceived a plan which Harold Deutsch describes as
'nothing less than a campaign to persuade the Belgian King to make an
offer of mediation that Hitler might find difficult to refuse'.[43]

As *Fall Gelb* gathered strength, von Weizsäcker had become anxious.
His department was a nest of opposition activity and he was working
closely with his fellow dissidents in the Foreign Ministry, as well as those
in the civilian sector, the *Wehrmacht* and the *Abwehr*, to frustrate Hitler's
plans. Von Weizsäcker had been at pains to plant members of the
opposition as ambassadors in all the key capitals. Now in October he used
his friend Goerdeler to convey an oral message to the German Ambassador in Brussels, von Bülow Schwante, to suggest that he might be able to
initiate a peace move by the King of the Belgians and the Queen of the
Netherlands. The Ambassador immediately paid a flying visit to The
Hague to brief his colleague, Count Zech, to make an approach to the
Dutch Queen and Government to this end. On his return, von Bülow
Schwante invited Comte Capelle (the King's principal Secretary) to
dinner and, after expressing his anxieties about the fate of Belgium once a
large-scale military offensive was launched in the West, hinted strongly
that another peace *démarche* on the part of the King might well avert or at
least postpone such a catastrophe. When Capelle reported to the King,
the latter invited von Bülow Schwante to visit him secretly, and the
German Ambassador was smuggled into Laeken Palace through a
back gate, to see the King in his study early next day. There he
repeated his warnings about the impending attack and his hints about a
démarche to avert it. As part of the plan to deter Hitler from launching
the *Blitzkrieg* on Belgium, von Bülow then sent a strongly worded
message to von Weizsäcker's Foreign Ministry (for the Führer's consumption) warning him that Leopold knew the German attack was about to be
launched and that the Belgian Army was standing ready to resist it.

Later that day the King received a more explicit warning giving the
precise date of the attack, from another section of the opposition. The
key figure in this group was Colonel Oster, now head of the Central
Division of the *Abwehr*, under Admiral Canaris. At constant risk to his
life Oster was feeding accurate reports about German military plans* to

---

* The fact that these plans were frequently changed had an unfortunate consequence. The
chief of Major Sas's department at The Hague grew sceptical. When Sas sent him an
advance warning of the date of the German invasion of Norway he fatally disregarded the
intelligence and failed to inform the British, French, Norwegians or Danes. He was again
unimpressed when Sas warned him of the imminence of the *Blitzkrieg* a few hours before it
was launched on May 10th 1940.

his friend Major Sas, the Dutch assistant Military Attaché in Berlin, who in turn passed them to Colonel Goethals, the Belgian Attaché. Goethals would then inform Van Overstraeten, and he the King. On November 6th Oster learned that the code-word had been issued for the assault in the West to be launched on the 12th. He immediately alerted Sas who passed his warning to the Dutch and the Belgians. Thanks to Oster, by late October Leopold already knew that the Germans had massed about seventy divisions, including a number of Panzer divisions, opposite the Belgian front and that Hitler had established his personal headquarters at Godesberg, only thirty-five miles from the Belgian frontier. The Belgian Army was therefore already on the alert when the news of an imminent attack was received from von Bülow Schwante and Oster.

After telephoning Queen Wilhelmina and consulting with his Cabinet, King Leopold sped off by car to The Hague, accompanied by his Foreign Minister Spaak and Van Overstraeten, to prepare concerted action with the Queen along the lines suggested by the German opposition's secret *démarche*. As a result, a joint telegram was sent next day from Wilhelmina and Leopold to the German, French and British governments, which contained the following passage: 'We, as sovereigns of two neutral states . . . are anxious to put forward by all means at our disposal . . . suggestions . . . with a view to discovering means for reaching a mutual understanding . . . which will be in the interests not only of our two peoples but of the entire world.' The two Monarchs' peace move was discussed with and approved by the Kings of Denmark and Sweden, the President of Finland and Pope Pius XII before being sent.

When the joint message arrived in Berlin in the early evening of November 7th, it fell to Erich Kordt,[e] a leading member of the opposition, to deliver the document to the Reich Chancellery, where he found Hitler preparing to depart for Munich, to attend the annual commemoration of the Beer Cellar Putsch of 1923. The Führer was much vexed, and instructed Kordt to 'tell the Dutch and Belgians that I am on a journey and cannot be reached'. (It was very nearly his last, for a bomb exploded in the *Burgerbräu* next day, a few minutes after he left, killing seven and wounding sixty-three of the Nazi 'old comrades'.)[f] 'The Dutch-Belgian *démarche* had indeed come inopportunely for the tyrant,' writes Harold Deutsch, 'threatening to wreck his propaganda plans. He had just given orders for the putting together of data tailored to show that the Belgians had always taken a pro-French position, and had instructed the compilers to "give their imaginations free reign". Straightway to invade the would-be mediators would be even more of a political liability than an attack on those countries already represented. Hitler must have left Berlin in a thoroughly disgruntled mood.'[45]

Hitler immediately ordered Otto Dietrich, Goebbels' deputy, to play down the peace appeal in the press. The reactions of the Allies were also cool – their attitude being well expressed in *L'Illustration*: 'London and Paris are in search of the alliance, rather than of the mediation of the neutral countries.' As Harold Deutsch points out: 'The negative response of London and Paris to the proffer of good offices were announced first, enabling Hitler to pose before the German public as having been prepared to give a more favourable answer, if theirs had been so.'[46]

The French and British did not appreciate – and it is still not generally realized – that the arrival of the peace message at the Reich Chancellery was a major factor in Hitler's mind when he called off the attack in the West on that very same day. At 6.00 pm Hitler postponed 'A Day' and ordered the moving forward of troops to be halted. Thereafter followed a series of cancellations and postponements, all ordered by Hitler on the basis of the 'meteorological situation' – although, as Telford Taylor observes in *The March of Conquest*, 'there is much to suggest that Hitler was not averse to using the "meteorological situation" as a face-saving device . . .'[47] Von Hassell noted in his diary shortly afterwards that 'Göring also was still against it, but could not make up his mind to resist, instead he confined himself to a certain sabotage of the plan on the pretext of bad weather . . .'

After describing the part he and his Foreign Ministry network played in this secret initiative, von Weizsäcker writes: 'I welcomed any delay, for my only idea was for peace.'[48] In postponing the planned offensive he, King Leopold and Queen Wilhelmina can certainly take much credit – for, as General Westphal records in *The German Army in the West*, 'in the end Hitler only withdrew his order to attack on November 12th when it became apparent that the enemy had obtained knowledge of it'. Von Hassell's diary entry of November 16th is also pertinent:

> I am beginning to believe that the invasion of Belgium and Holland has been given up. For weeks the foreign press has been full of reports about the fear of the Belgians and Dutch and their extreme preparations. The step taken by King Leopold and Queen Wilhelmina was the result of this anxiety and has made matters more difficult for Hitler. The opposition of our military men is also a factor.[49]

And Telford Taylor writes: 'Hitler may well have decided that this episode both threatened the hoped-for surprise element of the planned attack and weakened the basis for charging that Belgium and Holland were not truly neutral, and would consent to a Franco-British march-in.'[50]

Leopold's midnight dash to The Hague and the immediate offer of Royal mediation were instantly effective because they destroyed Hitler's carefully prepared justification for an attack. The proclamations to the Belgian and Dutch people which had been drafted on the Führer's orders declared that French forces were about to enter Belgium. He had prepared the ground by informing the Belgian Government on August 26th 'that Germany will in no circumstances impair the inviolability and integrity of Belgium and will at all times respect Belgian territory subject to Belgium remaining neutral and tolerating no violation on the part of a third power'. After the two Sovereigns' offer of mediation Hitler could scarcely persist in a pretence that the French were about to march. Moreover, his generals were strongly opposed to an offensive, particularly so late in the year – since it was evident that the Low Countries had been alerted, a German invasion would now lack any element of surprise, so the attack was called off.

It is instructive to consider the details of an action by which Hitler was indisputably thwarted, and because of which the ill-prepared and ill-equipped Anglo-French forces were saved from the *débâcle* which would certainly have followed, had the Germans launched their overwhelming Panzer and aerial *Blitzkrieg* upon them. What emerges is that Leopold was able to counter the Führer so effectively because of information which came to him by various routes through the main sections of the German opposition – the *Wehrmacht*, the Foreign Ministry, the *Abwehr* and the civilians headed by Goerdeler. The readiness of these dissidents to risk their lives by informing and warning the King of the Belgians is a tribute to the integrity of Leopold's policies and the trust which anti-Nazi Germans of high character were prepared to place in him.

CHAPTER EIGHT

La Drôle de Guerre

'What might have happened if the Germans had attacked before
the winter makes me shudder to think.'

Field Marshal Lord Alanbrooke

'In that case we haven't an earthly chance.'

General Lord Gort, on hearing
that the Germans had ten Panzer divisions on the Western Front.

One of the allegations which were made against King Leopold after the capitulation of the Belgian Army was that Belgium's policy of independence prevented the Allies coming to the aid of Poland. Indeed, Winston Churchill actually claimed in a speech in the House of Commons on June 4th 1940 that but for this policy the Allies might have 'saved Poland'. But he contradicted his own claim when he wrote in his memoirs: 'Once Hitler had disposed of Poland, he would be far more powerful on the ground and in the air than the British and French combined. There could therefore be no question of a French offensive against Germany.' As to the British, Churchill declared in 1943 'we entered the war ill-prepared and almost unarmed', and later wrote in his memoirs that 'the British Expeditionary Force was no more than a symbolic contribution. It was able to deploy two divisions by the first and two more by the second week in October.'

It would appear that there were some in France who shared this delusion about Belgium's policy. On September 1st the Commander-in-Chief, Gamelin, wrote to his Prime Minister, Daladier: 'The present attitude of Belgium is playing entirely into German hands' and he argued that only through Belgium could France bring rapid and effective aid to Poland. But in reality Gamelin's policy was purely defensive. And how could it be otherwise, in view of the immense superiority of the German ground and air forces – and the fact that it would take several months to call up France's largely immobile conscript army? In the meantime Poland was conquered by the *Blitzkrieg* in eighteen days. As early as March 28th 1939 the British Chiefs of Staff, who disliked the guarantee to Poland, concluded that '. . . neither Great Britain nor France could afford Poland and Roumania direct support by sea, on land or in the air to help them to resist a German invasion.'

At the meeting of the French Council of the War convened on August 23rd 1939, the day the Nazi-Soviet Pact was announced, Gamelin's dominating idea was to gain time. His great hope was that the two-million-strong Polish Army would resist fiercely, thus absorbing the main German forces and preventing them from turning on the French before the following spring. Although in theory the Allies were going to war to defend Poland, they were in fact counting on Poland to protect France. There was no talk at this meeting of France or Britain taking any offensive action against Germany, other than the blockade and anti-U-boat warfare. Consequently, at the very first meeting of the Allies' Supreme War Council at Abbeville at the end of September Gamelin made it clear that he had no intention of throwing his armies against the German defences and would confine his activities to patrol activity in no man's land. Daladier and the Allied Service Chiefs all endorsed this policy, as did Neville Chamberlain, who declared that 'time was on the side of the Allies'.* 'Manifestly,' writes Benoist-Méchin, 'our General Staff had only strictly defensive plans . . . everything pointed to our General Staff not departing from a policy of prudent circumspection.'[51]

During the first winter of the war, therefore, the Allies merely assembled their forces, drew them up along the French frontier and waited. Waited while Germany conquered Poland, divided that country and the spoils with Russia, and moved her armies westwards to concentrate for an attack on the West through Belgium. In this '*drôle de guerre*', or 'phoney war', all initiative was handed to the enemy. World opinion, which did not appreciate the pitiful weakness of Allied arms, was puzzled at the complete inaction. In France there were strong defeatist and subversive elements amongst the population – with the Left, taking its cue from Moscow, denouncing the war as capitalist and imperialist. 'The people and the army alike had been completely demoralized by the Blum Popular Front and rotted by Communist propaganda,' writes General Fuller.[52] This 'subversive propaganda' was directly financed by the German Government from a headquarters in Paris, according to John de Courcy, who describes how 'the mischievous influence and persistent intrigue' of the considerable number of Communist and Leftist deputies in the Chamber 'played a deadly part in the subsequent collapse'.† 'The Third Republic,' de Courcy continues, 'was plunged into a series of disputes and strikes from which it never recovered – at a time when the

---

* Almost incredibly, in view of the Germans' rapid and shattering defeat of the Polish Army and the inferiority of the Allied ground and air forces, Winston Churchill (the First Lord of the Admiralty) and General Ironside (the CIGS) expressed the view that it would be 'a good thing' if the Germans were to launch their *Blitzkrieg* in the West at an early date.

† In March 1940 the French Minister of the Interior, Albert Sarraut, declared in the Senate: 'Communist and Nazi propaganda must not be separated. It is German planes that are dropping Communist tracts over France, and the Communist radio is in Germany . . . This enemy propaganda is exploiting the miseries, the sufferings of the war . . .'

highest possible industrial output was necessary for the very life of France
. . . French opinion could be summed up in the word defence, and the
psychological reactions when no one attacked them were highly
dangerous . . .'[53]

While the French relapsed into a trance-like state of apathy and a kind
of Maginot malaise overtook them, the British remained blithely confident and unheeding of what lay in store for them – an attitude expressed
in such popular songs as 'We're going to hang out the washing on the
Siegfried Line' and good-natured references to Hitler as 'Old Nasty'.

On the Franco-German front all was quiet. 'The French did not shoot,'
writes Gordon Waterfield, 'because, as they said of the Germans, "*Ils ne
sont pas méchants*"' and "if we fire they will fire back".'[54] William L.
Shirer saw German children playing in full sight of French soldiers,
German soldiers punting a football and frolicking about, and trains on
both sides of the Rhine: 'Not a shot was fired. Not a single airplane could
be seen in the skies.'[55] While from the German side von Weizsäcker
recalls: 'It was a strange feeling in the front line not far from Trier to hear
no shot fired, but to see with the naked eye the French soldiers calmly
moving about without bothering to take cover.'[56] According to John de
Courcy, 'the Germans frequently took absolutely no notice of French
patrols and the French on many occasions reciprocated by ignoring
German reconnaissances. The Germans did everything possible to give
troops in the Maginot Line the impression that the whole business was a
farce. The French Army was getting bored and irritable. A feeling of
frustration was giving place to one of futility.'

The German propaganda campaign found ready acceptance among
many sections of the French community. The Reich had no quarrel with
or claims against France, it ran, the British imperialists had caused the
war by giving Poland a blank cheque and had then dragged France into
the war against her will. 'What are we fighting for?' was the constantly
repeated theme. It is now, alas, a platitude that the French were
incapable of fighting, being neither morally nor materially equipped to
wage the new form of high-speed warfare devised by the Germans, in
which thousands of tanks, aircraft and skilfully trained men were co-
ordinated with ruthless efficiency in powerful highly mobile shock-forces.
Neither the British nor the French had learned the appropriate lessons
from the Germans' brilliantly successful execution of the aerial and
Panzer *Blitzkrieg* in Poland. Indeed, as more than one military expert had
pointed out, the only way a nation could hope to defend itself against the
Blitzkrieg was to create and deploy a similar integrated force of tanks and
planes itself, but this France and Britain had fatally neglected to do.

Leopold was one of the few in the West to diagnose the problem. In his
1936 'armed independence' speech he had declared that new methods of
warfare allowed 'the early operations of any armed conflict to be con-

ducted with a power, rapidity and extent which are particularly alarming
to any country of limited territory such as Belgium'. (Another was Sir
Roger Keyes, who wrote in 1939: 'Modern war will be prosecuted at
terrific speed, many vital decisions will have to be made from hour to
hour . . .')[57] Nevertheless, the King's efforts to incorporate tanks in his
army were frustrated by the veto of the Belgian Socialist Party, which
played straight into the hands of the Germans – who, recognizing that the
only real defence against their Panzer thrusts was a dynamic defence in
depth supported by tanks, protested violently that they were an offensive
weapon which had no place in the army of a neutral country. Unfortunately, the ideas of such proponents of mechanized warfare in the West as
de Gaulle, Liddell Hart and Martell were spurned or ignored in France
and Britain (where the tank was invented), but adopted and developed
with devastating effect by Heinz Guderian, Erwin Rommel and the other
Panzer leaders in Germany. As a result, Britain as well as France was
'naked in terms of modern warfare', as one military expert put it.

It was Leopold's appreciation of the speed of modern warfare which led
him and his General Staff to make a military decision in September 1939
which was of crucial significance to Belgium and her allies. Until then the
main disposition of the Army was along the Albert Canal from Antwerp
to Liège and from there followed the Meuse to Namur. This line, with its
continuous water obstacle, was very strong, for under the stimulus of
Albert and Leopold enormous sums had been spent on strengthening and
supplementing the existing field works and fortifications behind it. At the
confluence of the Meuse and the Albert Canal a range of modern fortifications comparable to the Maginot Line was built, including the huge
and powerful bastion of Eben-Emael, in order to command the crossing
points. All the old fortifications covering Antwerp, Liège and Namur were
reinforced and modernized, while the three great forts of Neufchâteau,
Battice and Pépinster were constructed to complete the system.*

But in the era of the *Blitzkrieg* this line, powerful though it was, could
now only be considered as a delaying position. Indeed as Belgium's main
defence line it had four serious drawbacks. Firstly, it was lacking in depth.
Secondly, it was so far from the French frontier that aid could not be expected to arrive before it was penetrated by a German attack. Thirdly, it
was too extended for even the fully mobilized Belgian Army to defend by
itself. Fourthly, being semi-elliptical, it was dangerously exposed to flank
attacks. Accordingly, on the initiative of the King construction was pressed
forward in great secrecy of a new fortified front, known as 'the K-W Line'
– so named because it ran through Koningshoyckt, Malines, Louvain
and Wavre, thus linking the fortified towns of Antwerp and Namur.

To establish his country's main defence position on the K-W Line

---

* See map on p. 470.

required great courage and faith on the part of the King. The choice of a front which ran only ten miles to the east of Brussels meant the inevitable sacrifice of over half of his Kingdom, and the exposure of the capital and most of the chief towns – Antwerp, Malines, Louvain, Gembloux and Namur – to destruction or occupation. But if Germany dishonoured her guarantee and attacked, he and his government believed that the promises made by Britain and France in 1937 could be trusted. On that basis, the construction of the K-W Line made military sense. On March 28th 1940 the Ministry of National Defence reported as follows:

> A formidable steel barrier divides the interior of the country and forms a practically impassable barrier to attacks by tanks. The wall of steel constructed ˙by our untrained builders is at present 70 km long. It represents a weight of over 30,000 tons; 34,000 tons of steel framework, 1,000 tons of steel cables, 150 tons of camouflage colouring, and about 600 tons of various other materials. Thus, 35,000 tons of steel have been put in position in open country, across fields, woods and marshes, floods, rivers and railways.
>
> Every difficulty has been overcome – gradients, mud, water. Neither rain nor snow nor cold have stopped the work for one moment. In temperatures as low as minus 16°, when the cold was so intense that the heavy pieces of steel stuck to the hands of the men, they doggedly continued to raise this formidable barrier across our fields and woods. From November 1st to December 31st, during the rainiest season, when the winter was already very severe, our soldiers raised a steel wall 30 km long in a sea of mud, in water and in the cold.

It was to this new main defensive position that the Anglo-French armies would advance in May 1940, behind the cover provided by the Belgian Army as it resisted the enemy's assault on its first line of defence along the Albert Canal and the Meuse.

Thanks to the rearmament drive initiated by the King in 1936, by the outbreak of the war Belgium had not only greatly strengthened her fixed defences, but had raised an army of no less than 650,000 men, more than four times the number deployed by the British in France that winter. When the *Blitzkrieg* was launched in May 1940, Belgium raised their number to 900,000 – compared to the 237,000 field troops by then in the British Expeditionary Force. (As these extra 250,000 Belgian conscripts could not be fully trained, most were sent to France for this purpose.) Excluding these trainees, the strength of the army raised by Leopold when the Germans attacked was nearly three times that of the BEF and five times that of the army which King Albert deployed in 1914. In contrast, as the American statesman Henry Stimson pointed out, the United States (with a population of 137 million) had only 185,000 men in her regular army in early 1940, adding that it was 'nowhere near as well-trained as the Belgian Army'. Taking another yardstick, a similar call-up to that of Belgium by Britain would have produced 4,800,000 men under arms – a proportion of the population which was never reached by her or any other belligerent nation in the two World Wars.

There were of course handicaps in raising such a large Belgian Army, for it was found impossible to provide sufficient regular officers and non-commissioned officers to lead, train and organize all the conscripts into effective fighting units. Moreover, heavy and specialized equipment, including the larger anti-tank and anti-aircraft guns, were hard to acquire while Germany and the Allies were rearming. Belgium's light armament industry, however, provided all the smaller weapons, such as their excellent 47 mm anti-tank gun, that were needed and even supplied the British and French. The Belgian Air Force was equipped with British aircraft, but as Britain's own requirements increased the Belgians were unable to secure the modern planes they needed. Since only nine Hurricanes were supplied, Belgium ordered forty Brewster Buffaloes from the United States, but unfortunately these were not delivered in time to be used in action.

It was therefore greatly to the credit of Belgium that in September 1939 in terms of divisions in the field she had twenty-two, while France had fifty and the BEF only two divisions – another two followed in October – without armour. After the conquest of Poland, Germany placed a hundred divisions, including ten Panzer and six mechanized divisions, on the Belgian and Dutch frontier alone. In a reference to these relative strengths, a well-known American commentator was later to declare: 'If, *mutatis mutandis*, France and England had made, by the eve of the war, a military effort equal to that of Belgium, the outcome of the battles of Belgium and France would probably have been very different.'

As for France, Paul Reynaud, who was her Prime Minister when the *Blitzkrieg* struck in May 1940, wrote that 'we entered the war without armoured corps, without bomber aircraft, without an air striking force, without a general staff for national defence, without an organization for the High Command, without an armaments ministry, and it was not until after four months of war that a start was made in creating armoured divisions in France.'[58] General Weygand's criticisms were no less scathing: 'France rushed headlong into war without having the material with which to wage it – neither tanks, nor anti-tank guns, nor aircraft, nor anti-aircraft defence, and lacking a solid Western Front.[g] No military preparations. No diplomatic preparations. It was criminal to have declared war on September 3rd in such conditions. It is unbelievable that the responsible head of the French Army at that time did not tell the Government that the state of the Army made fighting impossible.'[59]

'And where were the British anyway, having regard to our tiny contribution . . . ?' asked Churchill in his memoirs – a question he had answered in January 1940, when he wrote to Admiral Sir Dudley Pound, the First Sea Lord: 'Our Army is insignificant and our aviation is terribly inferior to that of the Germans.' Moreover, as the Official Historian, Major Ellis, recalls: 'In 1939 the Anglo-French Staffs still worked by the dim light of 1914–1918 . . . the first object of the French was the defence of the Maginot Line. The British, for their part, knowing that it was proposed at this date to contribute so small a British force, could but accept the French soldiers' view as to the course which land operations on the Continent should take.'[60]

Despite all Churchill's urgings, Britain had failed to take advantage of the so-called 'period of grace' after Munich and her industries were still far from being on a war footing – her arms production being much hampered by the opposition of the Socialist and Liberal parties, the apathy of the labour force and the non-cooperation of the trade unions. Even Britain's declaration of war had not woken her up. Indeed, the number of troops with GHQ and in the main fighting force of the BEF had risen to only 237,300 by May 1940, with another 156,846 men 'with little or no military training' in the rear areas, preparing bases and installations. Many of these troops were unarmed and some had no uniforms. They included three recently arrived, but incomplete Territorial divisions which were similarly ill-equipped and untrained – 'to be used largely for labour duties'.[61]

As Gort's *Despatches* and the *Official History* reveal, the diminutive BEF suffered from grave deficiencies in almost every type of equipment, vehicles and weapon, including anti-tank and anti-aircraft guns and from shortages of ammunition of all kinds. And such equipment and weapons as the BEF possessed were mostly out of date and inferior to those of the Germans. This was particularly marked in the case of anti-aircraft guns and communications equipment, wireless sets being obsolete, ineffective and very few in number. As for armoured forces, Gort had under his command by May 1940 only a small number of what Lord Alanbrooke later described as those 'ridiculous light-tanks' (they were so thin-skinned as to be deathtraps), a few armoured cars which were all 'obsolete' and a hundred 'I' (infantry) tanks, which although heavily armoured could move only at foot-pace. Only twenty-three of these were fit for action against enemy tanks, being armed with a two-pounder gun; all the rest had machine guns only. In his memoirs Montgomery summed up the state of the BEF as follows:

> In September 1939, the British Army was totally unfit to fight a first-class war on the Continent of Europe . . . In the years preceding the outbreak of war, no large-scale exercises with troops had been held in England for some time. Indeed the Regular Army was unfit to take part in a realistic exercise. The Field Army had an inadequate signals system, no administrative backing, and no organization for High Command; all these had to be improvised on mobilization . . .
> Much of the transport of my division consisted of civilian vans and lorries

from the towns of England; they were in bad repair and when my division moved from the ports up to its concentration area near the French frontier, the countryside of France was strewn with broken-down vehicles.

It must be said to our shame that we sent our Army into that most modern war with weapons and equipment which were quite inadequate, and we had only ourselves to blame for the disasters which early overtook us in the field when fighting began in 1940.[62]

No wonder Alanbrooke observed: 'What might have happened if the Germans had attacked before the winter makes me shudder to think.'[63] Even the unimaginative Gort shared these apprehensions, and when he learned that the Germans had ten Panzer divisions on the Western Front, remarked to his ADC, Lord Munster: 'In that case, we haven't an earthly chance.'[64] Indeed, both to have attacked or to have been attacked would have been catastrophic for the Allies during those unreal opening months of the war – with the certainty of a more definitive defeat for Great Britain than she suffered in May 1940, in view of the even greater deficiencies and unpreparedness of her army and the RAF (which was twenty squadrons short of the fighting strength it possessed in July 1940, when 'the Few' barely staved off defeat) and the incomplete state of the radar stations round her coasts.

The crucial factor in warfare was now air power – as had been demonstrated in Poland, but not properly appreciated by the Western Powers. As was proved later, the side that had mastery of the air was a certain winner on land and in sea battles. But the French Air Force was small, poorly trained, low in morale and largely equipped with obsolete aircraft,* for which there was a shortage of spares and vital equipment. Indeed, as Robert Jackson recalls, 'the French Bomber Force was totally ill-equipped to wage modern warfare.'[65] After being shown the *Luftwaffe* by Hermann Göring in 1938, General Vuillemin, the Chief of the French Air Staff, observed to François-Poncet, the French Ambassador in Berlin: 'If war breaks out . . . there will not be a French plane left in a fortnight.'

As for the Royal Air Force, its strength was far below that of the *Luftwaffe* and it was also behind in providing modern aircraft and equipment. Indeed the RAF only started replacing its biplane fighters in 1938 and had but twenty-six squadrons of monoplane fighters (mainly Hurricanes) in September 1939. Moreover, the fatal handicap from which Britain's military and naval operations would suffer was the fact that the RAF – unlike the *Luftwaffe*, which was formed in secret by Army personnel and trained to operate in the closest concert with the ground forces – was jealous of its independent status and was neither motivated,

---

* France possessed only 549 fighters, of which 131 were classed as *anciens*, only 186 bombers, of which 175 were *anciens*, and 377 reconnaissance aircraft, of which all but sixty-one were *anciens*, when war broke out.

trained nor equipped for such closely integrated operation with the other Services. Furthermore, the Air Ministry's policy was that the principal function of the RAF was home defence and strategic bombing – and, as Major Ellis, the Official Historian, put it: 'Neither role required provision for air participation in large-scale land operations or for the dispatch of large mobile air forces overseas.' Furthermore, French fears of provoking reprisals by the *Luftwaffe* were so great that the BEF's small Air Component and Advanced Air Striking Force were only allowed facilities on French airfields on the understanding that their aircraft would not bomb German targets from these bases. Thus for the duration of the *'drôle de guerre'* neither the British nor the French Air Force was allowed to carry out offensive operations against Germany. The RAF therefore had to confine itself to 'bombing' Germany with leaflets at night.

It is against this perspective that King Leopold's attitude must be weighed. As Winston Churchill observes in *The Second World War*, it is quite clear that Belgium's policy would have been very different had Britain and France been strongly armed and resolute. The King's faith in Britain's ultimate survival never wavered; but in the short term it was only too obvious that the advantages lay with Germany, and he was not prepared to sacrifice his country until compelled to do so by invasion. Then he would fight. In the meantime he would resist all attempts to coerce Belgium out of her neutrality, but would continue to strengthen her armed forces and defences to the maximum. At the same time he could only hope that France and Britain would avail themselves of the precious time which this strong deterrence to Germany's invasion plans gave the Allies, to make similar rearmament efforts themselves.

The King and his advisers were not blind. They had observed Anglo-French impotence over the Rhineland, Czechoslovakia, Austria – as well as Abyssinia and Albania – and now Poland, for whom they had gone to war. They had a shrewd estimate of the Allies' military weakness, unpreparedness and deficiencies. Why should Belgium flout the pacts with her guarantors and prematurely bring down on her head a devastating assault, making her once again the cockpit of Europe, when the outcome was so predictably calamitous and while there was still a chance that the Germans would not strike?

Yet behind the scenes an event occurred which was itself a prelude to disaster – the acceptance of 'Plan D'. In spite of the inferiority of the Allies' ground and air forces, by November Gamelin had decided that if the Germans invaded Belgium, the Franco-British armies in the North would instantly move forward into Belgium and up to the K-W Line. Under this plan the French Second and Ninth Armies on the right would hold the line on the Meuse from Montmedy to Namur; the French First Army from Namur to Wavre; the British the seventeen-mile front from

Wavre to Louvain in the centre; and the Belgians, after holding up the enemy in their advanced positions along the frontier, would side-step back to the forty-mile sector between Louvain and Antwerp on the left of the Allied line. In addition the French Seventh Army, comprising virtually all France's mobile formations, was to make a dash forward on the far left flank to secure the southern shores of the Scheldt and make contact with Dutch forces. By this manoeuvre, which General Bilotte later described to Leopold as *'une geste morale'* to encourage the Dutch, Gamelin would deprive himself of his only 'mass of manoeuvre' and central reserve, which had hitherto been allocated to the Rheims area – with fatal consequences, when the German attack was finally launched in May 1940.

What were Gamelin's motives for this forward move – a forward gallop on the part of the French Seventh Army, which was certainly not bred of his usual caution? When it had been mooted earlier, the British Chiefs of Staff had considered it to be 'unsound', declaring that unless plans could be 'concerted with the Belgians for the occupation of this line in sufficient time before the Germans advance . . . we are strongly of the opinion that the German advance should be met in prepared positions on the French frontier. In this case it would of course be necessary to bomb Belgian and Dutch towns and railway centres used or occupied by German troops.' But Gamelin spelt out his reasons for moving into Belgium with revealing frankness in the report he was ordered to make by Daladier on May 16th 1940, following the rout of the French armies on the Meuse. In it he wrote:

For strategic reasons it was of the greatest importance to try to merge the twenty Belgian divisions into the Allied disposition – the equivalent of which could not be attained on our own soil, due to a decreasing birth-rate.

To go into Belgium would also carry the conflict out of our northern industrial provinces, integrate the British effort more closely in the common cause, and hold off the enemy threat from Paris.

Initially I had decided on a policy of awaiting the enemy on our own fortified line, prolonged along the Scheldt in the event of a German invasion of Holland and Belgium.

In view of the development of the forces at my disposal and what I knew of the Belgians' intention to offer preliminary resistance on the line of the Albert Canal and the Meuse, I decided in agreement with the British High Command to move our front forward to the Meuse-Dinant-Namur-Louvain-Antwerp line.

On November 17th 1939, Gamelin's 'Plan D' was approved in Paris by the Supreme War Council, both the British and French Prime Ministers speaking in its favour. It had already been discussed and endorsed in London, with the agreement of Ironside (the CIGS), Lord Gort and his

Chief of Staff, Henry Pownall. 'In sum,' writes Brian Bond, 'none of the British military experts spoke out against a project which was subsequently thought to have contributed largely to the *débâcle* in May 1940.'[66]

There is no doubt that the British as well as the French were over-confident at this early stage of the war. Both armies were equipped and organized on 1918 lines – except that the British had replaced the horse with the ramshackle motor transport described by Montgomery – and neither had assimilated the lessons of the Polish campaign. They were relying on the great strength of the Maginot Line and of Belgium's strong and well-manned fortifications to make a successful repetition of the *Blitzkrieg* in the West impossible. But they had both overlooked the key factor of air power and had failed to foresee how the *Luftwaffe* would not only secure complete mastery of the air and closely support the ground forces, but also land shock-troops by glider and parachute behind their opponents' lines to seize their strong-points and bridges. Neither the French nor the British Air Force was trained or equipped to co-ordinate their activities with the military or support them in this way, and airborne troops had not even been envisaged on the Allied side.

As for the Belgians, they had great faith in the sturdy spirit of their citizens' army and the formidable defences they had built up at such cost on the Meuse, the Albert Canal and along the K-W Line. Indeed Van Overstraeten told Sir Roger Keyes in November 1939 that a German invasion would be decisively defeated. But neither he nor the King had any conception of how impotent the Allies' Air Forces would prove to be in protecting the Belgians from the massive assaults of the *Luftwaffe* and the *Wehrmacht*.

Yet the confidence of the Belgian people was not unjustified, for their King had persuaded them to accept the heavy burden of strengthening their country's defences and to fight back if attacked – thus creating a formidable deterrent to a German invasion. This was a remarkable act of will both on Leopold's part and on the part of his people – for if Belgium were attacked, the whole country would once again be in danger of being overrun and devastated. Memories of the German invasion in 1914 and the dreadful effects of enemy occupation and repression, poverty, starvation and isolation were still bitter, which explains why the Belgians in the nineteen-thirties were so determined not to become involved in other peoples' wars – and only to fight in self-defence.

CHAPTER NINE

The King's Secret Initiative

'Formal Staff conversations are terribly liable to lead to unwanted complications – e.g. leakages (once politicians get into it), all sorts of misunderstanding, commitments real or implied or suggested by an interested party. It is odd that our politicians do not read their history books and note the recriminations that have gone on over the Staff conversations of 1912.'

General Sir Henry Pownall's diaries

One of the most delicate problems which the King had to face in his dual capacity as Commander-in-Chief and Head of State was how to tie in Belgium's military preparations with the plans of the Allies. It revolved round the issue of Staff talks. Because the King's attitude and actions in this connection have been greatly misrepresented and he has frequently been accused of having vetoed all such talks on account of pro-German inclinations, it is necessary to examine the facts in some detail. In particular, attention must be focused on the secret links with the French General Staff which Leopold established in 1936, personally strengthened with Gamelin on the outbreak of war in September 1939, and also those with the British Government, War Office and Air Ministry which he initiated through Sir Roger Keyes in October of that year.

By the end of 1938 Britain and France were beginning to think in terms of drawing Belgium out of her neutrality and into the Allied camp. France in particular had long cast covetous eyes on Belgium's potential army of twenty-two divisions, on her powerful fortifications and on her territory. But it was the British Government which acted first. In January 1939 it completely reversed its policy in regard to the 1937 Franco-British guarantee to protect Belgium's neutrality. Despite the rejection by the British Chiefs of Staff of her original request for Staff talks, their persistent objections to military conversations with France and their declaration exactly a year before that Belgium's rearmament drive and her independence were 'to the advantage of France and ourselves', Great Britain initiated a series of manoeuvres designed to embroil Belgium in such military exchanges, in flagrant violation of her neutrality.

These efforts by the British – and later the French – to destroy Belgium's neutral status were pursued right up to Germany's invasion of Belgium on May 10th 1940. The first move was made on January 29th

1939 when the British Ambassador in Brussels, Sir Robert Clive, handed the Belgian Government a long memorandum proposing Staff talks on the grounds that Germany was about to launch an attack in the West. But the Belgians replied that the memorandum's arguments were not backed by a single precise fact, nor did they agree with Belgian intelligence. Moreover, if such talks were held, the fact would inevitably leak out, and entail the ruin of Belgium's policy of independence, which was, of course, exactly what Sir Robert was trying to achieve.

On April 25th and June 13th Francis Aveling, the Counsellor of the British Embassy in Brussels, made further pressing *démarches* in an endeavour to win Belgium over to the idea of military agreements. He pointed out the difficulties involved in coming to Belgium's aid if no preparations were made in advance. But the Belgians declared that they had for the last fifteen years provided the French General Staff with all the necessary information concerning her defence organization, her resources, the capacity of her roads and railways etc. In exchange, however, Belgium had received only the vaguest information – and little indication of the forces which would be sent to aid her, if she were attacked. But Aveling predicted that Belgium would be involved in the forthcoming conflict, and that her policy of independence could not survive it.

The Belgians replied that this was a possibility, not a certainty. Holland and Switzerland had escaped the war of 1914–18. Why could Belgium not be given the same chance? In joining the Allies Belgium would immediately become a battleground, with all the ravages which would ensue. Was it not in the interests of the Allies to avoid this eventuality in view of their state of military unpreparedness, which had already caused the Munich surrender? In the event of Germany respecting Belgian territory, France and Britain would be able to shelter behind France's powerful frontier defences. If, however, Germany invaded Belgium in order to get at France, then Belgium would join the Allies, as in 1914, but with an army very much larger and better equipped. She would at the same time have the benefit of moral force awakened by unjust aggression. The Belgians would then fight with unanimous spirit, which would not be the case if they were dragged into the war for interests which were foreign to them.

The Belgians even drew Aveling's attention to a book by the French general Chauvineau in which Belgian neutrality was considered to be a trump card in the Allied hand and pointed out that this was also the belief of a number of important officials at the *Quai d'Orsay*. The best way of avoiding war, they argued, was for France and Britain to rearm as fast as possible on the greatest possible scale. But all these arguments were in vain, for France and Britain were now set on trying to draw the Belgians into their Alliance in order to help redress the balance of military resources and manpower. So great was the Allied pressure on Belgium for military agreements that the Prime Minister, Pierlot, felt it necessary in June 1939 to make a statement to calm public opinion.

From the outbreak of war in September 1939 onwards the Allies applied ever-increasing pressure on Belgium to agree to hold official Staff talks, but fortunately she did not yield to these demands, for to have done so would have presented Hitler with a perfect justification for withdrawing his guarantee and invading her territory. Even Major Ellis, the British Official Historian, concedes: '. . . such an abandonment of Belgian neutrality as would have been signified by Staff conversations might well have had other results which can now only be a subject of speculation.'[67] But speculation is not difficult. All the early versions of *Fall Gelb*, the German plan of attack in the West, which were so nearly put into effect on numerous occasions during the winter of 1939–40, were for von Bock's vast Panzer and air armada to smash through central Belgium to seize the Channel coast and ports. (The completely changed, final version of *Fall Gelb* which surprised and routed the French on the Meuse in May 1940 was only adopted after the plans for the earlier version were captured by the Belgians in January of that year.)

If therefore Belgium and the Allies had put themselves in the wrong in the eyes of the world by holding official Staff talks in breach of her neutrality and their guarantees to maintain it, Hitler would undoubtedly have seized the opportunity to unleash the *Blitzkrieg* on Belgium at a time when the deficiencies of French and British ground and air forces were even more shocking than they were in May 1940. Had Hitler ordered them to attack, von Bock's forty-three battle-hardened divisions, including ten Panzer divisions (comprising about 2,500 tanks) and supported by over 3,500 planes, could hardly have failed to lance through central Belgium, rout both the French and the minute British Expeditionary Force, and reach the Channel coast in a matter of days. Generals Gort and Brooke were being realistic when they voiced their fears about the calamitous consequences of such an assault. And Major Ellis is correct in remarking of Belgium that 'the course she took may even have been to our ultimate advantage, in that while we lost in efficiency through the absence of joint planning, we gained time, so long as Hitler respected Belgian neutrality, in which to strengthen our own forces and complete our own plans'.[68] *Fall Gelb* in the winter of 1939–40 could scarcely have ended with the escape of the BEF via Dunkirk, however gallantly the Belgian, British and French forces in the North, gravely deficient in armour and aircraft, had fought. The consequences could only have been catastrophic – for had Great Britain thus been deprived of the whole nucleus of her army, she would have had little alternative but to bargain for a compromise peace, leaving Hitler in control of Europe and free to concentrate overwhelming force against Russia.

The dangers of provoking such an attack were plain to the King and it is a grave injustice that his endorsement of his government's refusal to permit *official* Staff talks should have been used as grounds for condemnation, particularly by the British. For not only did the King initiate *secret* military exchanges with the Allies, but there is copious evidence that up to March 1939 the British persistently refused to hold Staff talks with the French, because they distrusted France and feared that this would provoke Hitler. Yet Leopold – whose country, unlike the United Kingdom, was on Germany's doorstep and the potential victim of immediate devastation – has been widely condemned for sharing his own government's similar desire not to give the Germans a pretext for attacking Belgium.

A pertinent reference to Britain's double standards regarding Staff talks can be found in the *Official History*, which observes:

> . . . before Belgium had declared her neutrality, she had asked for Staff conversations, but we had drawn back lest the fact that such conversations were being held should give Hitler an excuse for counter-measures. And when, later in that year, Belgium declared her neutrality, the British Chiefs of Staff argued that an effective Belgian neutrality would be greatly to an advantage and should not deliberately be rendered impossible . . . Yet when war became imminent three years later, both Britain and France pressed Belgium to join in Staff conversations . . .[69]

Brian Bond, too, pin-points the illogicality of the British case:

> It is hard to escape the conclusion that although the General Staff foresaw the unpleasant probability of having to fight on the Continent, they viewed the prospect of co-operating with the French with little enthusiasm. Their attitude was also inconsistent, in that while they claimed that interchange of information through military attachés was adequate to co-ordinate arrangements with France, they later protested vehemently when confined to similar contacts with neutral Belgium.[70]

But the reason for British opposition to Staff talks which General Pownall gave in his diary (he was then Director of Military Operations) was that the French 'want to get us nicely committed and tied by the leg – not merely militarily, but politically as well'.[71] When in 1939 the British at last agreed to attend Staff conferences in France, as Brian Bond observes, they 'showed a reluctant acceptance of the Continental commitment after years of appeasement . . .'[72]

Sir John Slessor, the Air Representative on the Joint Planning Committee in 1938, has criticized the Chiefs of Staff for opposing Staff talks with the French lest they should provoke the hostility of the Germans. But even the valorous Lord Gort, who was CIGS from 1937 to 1939, opposed such talks for this reason during the Munich crisis in 1938. In consequence, the two Powers remained almost completely ignorant of each other's war plans throughout this most critical period.

As far as Belgium and Britain were concerned, the Official Historian declares 'only the fact that no Staff conversations took place needs to be recorded'.[73] This dismissive conclusion is unsatisfactory. It misleads by omission and is implicitly unjust to the King and his government, since it fails to analyse the catastrophic consequences which would have followed for both Belgium and the Allies had they allowed open Staff talks to be held after the outbreak of war, and takes no account of the clandestine supply of military information to France and Britain for which Leopold was responsible.

Despite the abrogation of the 1920 Franco-Belgian military agreements in March 1936 and Belgium's conviction after the Rhineland fiasco that the support of the French Army could not be relied upon in the event of a German attack, the Belgian General Staff remained in a 'close and cordial' relationship with the French High Command throughout that summer. 'Indeed,' writes Brian Bond, 'very detailed plans were agreed upon to enable the French Army to advance right up to the Albert Canal in response to a German attack.'

After the adoption of Belgium's policy of armed independence in October 1936, however, all open contacts between the Belgian and French General Staffs and Defence Ministers were broken off in order not to compromise Belgium's neutrality. But behind the scenes, on the King's initiative, the Belgians set up a strictly secret exchange of military information through the French Military Attaché in Brussels. By this means the Belgians passed to the French General Staff, as Bond records, 'information on nearly every aspect of Belgian defence policy – troop movements, communication, fixed defences, air reconnaissance arrangements, etc.'[74] In exchange for all this valuable intelligence Gamelin passed back only meagre information, although he did let the Belgians have details of a new French concentration plan in 1937.

The secret exchanges of military information between Belgium and France continued up to the outbreak of war in September 1939, when they were reinforced by the more direct link which Leopold then set up with Generalissimo Gamelin. As Gamelin wrote in his memoirs, *Servir*: 'The King of the Belgians as the C-in-C of the Army, and his General Staff expressed the desire to be *en rapport* with no one but me, to ensure that their relations with the Allies should remain completely secret.'

Gamelin confirms without qualification in *Servir* that he was 'entirely satisfied' with the flow of information which he received from the King. He also appears never to have disclosed the existence of this confidential traffic to anyone until after the war – which explains the British and French Governments' apparent ignorance of the fact that the Belgians had provided all the military information for which the French C-in-C and his Staff asked.

Neither the King nor Van Overstraeten had much of an opinion of the French Military Attaché in Brussels, who was regarded as a 'drawing-room' type. At Leopold's request, therefore, Gamelin appointed Lieutenant-Colonel Hautcoeur to act as his liaison officer in maintaining secret contact. Hautcoeur was a trusted friend of Van Overstraeten and had been a star pupil of his at the Belgian *Ecole de Guerre*. But while Gamelin himself communicated in writing with the King and his Staff, Leopold – believing that the smaller the number of people who shared a secret the better – ensured that transactions on the Belgian side were never committed to paper. A very full record of these secret exchanges can, however, be found in *Les Relations Militaires Franco-Belges*.[75]

The appointment of Van Overstraeten's protégé, Hautcoeur, was fruitful and sensible. But the British were less subtle, for instead of seeking to initiate similar secret talks, they still persisted with their demands for official Staff talks, thus creating an *impasse* which Leopold now proceeded to resolve.

All his previous record makes it indisputably clear that Leopold was pro-British by choice, instinct and experience. As Brian Bond observes: 'King Leopold and his advisers made no secret of the fact that before and during the period of hostilities they preferred to lean on British rather than French assistance.'[76] The secret exchanges with the French were satisfactory, but though – for the reasons explained above – the King was at one with his government in opposing official Staff talks, he felt a profound need for some less obvious form of Anglo-Belgian military contact. Such liaison had to be strictly secret and wholly unsuspected by the Germans. He therefore decided to approach the man his father had always told him he could rely on in Britain, Sir Roger Keyes, whom Leopold himself had known since his boyhood. It was an additional advantage that the Admiral of the Fleet was known to have visited Laeken on precious occasions in a private capacity and so was less likely to attract attention if he returned there.

As an intermediary between himself and the Admiral the King chose Dr Walter Johannes Stein, an Austrian by birth but a naturalized British subject. A musician and friend of Queen Elisabeth, the Doctor was trusted by Leopold and his circumstances seemed to provide excellent cover for his delicate mission. After a detailed briefing by the King, Dr Stein left Belgium to make his first approach to the Admiral on October 3rd 1939.

At 9 pm the following evening Stein telephoned Keyes at his London home in St Leonard's Terrace, Chelsea, told him that he had an important message from King Leopold and asked to see him immediately. Considerably surprised, Keyes agreed and half an hour later the doctor arrived at his house. Stein told him, the Admiral's diary records:

> HM wished him to tell me that he had been asked to agree to Staff talks between our two armies. He had had to refuse, as he had to safeguard his loyalty to Belgium's neutrality. It would compromise him with his government and give Germany an excuse for declaring that Belgium had broken her neutrality, if any such talks took place. Brussels was full of spies and it would soon become known. He appreciated, however, that the situation was exceedingly dangerous – Germany might well try to force a way through Belgium, in which case it would be disastrous to any sort of combined effort on the part of Great Britain and Belgium if no arrangements had been made beforehand.

Keyes gathered from Stein, as he wrote in the memorandum which he prepared for the Cabinet on October 12th 1939, that the King 'wanted my advice as to how he could personally and secretly learn what the British Army was prepared to do in the event of German aggression. He could then arrange for the Belgian Army to co-operate as far as possible.' The King wanted Keyes, as he recorded in his diary, to confer 'with a representative of the British Government, quite privately' and to transmit any proposals or plan of action back to himself.

The Admiral's reaction was that this was a matter for the Cabinet. After listening to Stein, therefore, he telephoned the Admiralty and was put through to the First Sea Lord, Sir Dudley Pound, whom he asked to inform the First Lord, Winston Churchill, that he had an urgent message from Belgium to communicate to him. Pound quickly rang back, asking Keyes to come with the emissary to Churchill's room at the Admiralty.

Keyes hurried with Stein through the black-out to Whitehall. There Stein repeated his message, after which Churchill, impressed, tried to get in touch with General Ironside, the CIGS, but found he had gone to bed. Then, in answer to Stein, Churchill stressed that it was vitally important that Staff talks should be held as soon as possible, if Great Britain were to help Belgium effectively in the event of a sudden German attack. He said that as the British Army was then entrenching behind the Franco-Belgian frontier, it would be impossible for it to advance eastwards to the aid of the Belgians in the early stages of the war unless certain vital preparations had been made. Stein offered to convey any British proposals to the King in Brussels and bring back his answer. Churchill was non-committal, and the meeting broke up to be re-convened at ten next morning.

Churchill understandably wished to be assured of the *bona fides* of Stein and, as they were parting, asked Keyes if he could vouch for him. The Admiral answered that he could not, but showed Churchill a letter that contained a 'charming message' from Leopold. It ought to be easy for MI5 to check up on him, Keyes added, as he was a naturalized British subject. Next morning, around the octagonal table in the First Lord's room, Churchill, Pound and Keyes were joined by General Ironside and the Chief of the Air Staff, Sir Cyril Newall. Keyes reviewed the situation and Stein was then invited in and questioned. When the Doctor left, Ironside and Newall proposed that, as an alien of uncertain background, he ought to be thoroughly investigated before the British became involved. Keyes noted that they thought 'he was just a Viennese Jew, and we had better find out all about him before committing ourselves'.

Later MI5, having made a preliminary check on Stein, professed itself satisfied. Moreover, the Doctor had produced letters which showed that he was on close terms with King Leopold. It was therefore decided at Cabinet level that he should return to Belgium that night with a message from Keyes to the King, accompanied – as a final security precaution – by an officer of MI5, Captain Liddell. Before leaving, Stein, accompanied by Keyes, was taken by Churchill to Downing Street to see the Prime Minister, Neville Chamberlain. The Premier received them in the Cabinet Room, heard the arrangements and gave his approval.

Dr Stein and Captain Liddell reached Brussels late on Friday night, the 6th. Unfortunately, the King was at Le Zoute for the weekend and was not available. Stein managed, however, to get in touch with Queen Elisabeth, who that evening drove the Doctor alone in her small car to Laeken. She took him into the Palace by a side door and in his presence telephoned the King on a private line, which she assured him was secret. The Queen was careful not to mention names, merely telling Leopold that 'Stone' and a man who had accompanied him from England were most anxious to see him. The King, assuming that Stein's companion was Admiral Keyes, invited them to come to Laeken on Monday morning. On Monday, on his return to Laeken, the King was disappointed to learn from his mother that the Doctor's companion was not Keyes, for he had sent the Admiral a message through Baron de Cartier de Marchienne, the Belgian Ambassador in London, that he was 'very anxious' that Keyes should come to see him in Brussels as soon as possible. But unfortunately the King's invitation had only reached the Admiral after Stein and Liddell had left London.

In his memorandum to the Cabinet Keyes described how the King then telephoned Stein and 'speaking in English and speaking cryptically, told him that he was not to come to Laeken, but to come *alone* to the Palace in Brussels'. Stein was met outside by the King's servant, who conducted him stealthily through the back regions to Leopold 'without being seen by any Court official'. In the diary entry he made after hearing Stein's report of his secret meeting with the King in Brussels, the Admiral noted:

He told me how anxious and disturbed King Leopold was . . . that Stein should have been put in contact with the Prime Minister and Churchill. He had only wanted him to deal with me. He said the King was very alarmed at the thought of infringing his neutrality . . . but had sent me the warmest messages of thanks . . . He told Stein that his father, King Albert, had had great faith in me and he knew that I would help if I could.

In his official memorandum Keyes wrote:

The King was exceedingly kind to Stein, but was evidently much perturbed that he should have gone further than his instructions, which were apparently limited to an interview with me. (That of course was my responsibility) . . . Stein was evidently put in a very awkward position by my action in taking him so far, and the King begged him to keep out of political and military questions in future . . . In order to show that Stein was trusted by him and to regularize his position, the King wrote to the Belgian Ambassador, Baron de Cartier, asking him to give Stein a letter of recommendation to show that he had confidence in him, but that he was only concerned with economics and not political or military matters.

Stein informed Keyes, as he recorded in his memorandum, that the King – who 'hoped that I would come over and see him' – had even spoken of cancelling the whole project, but that he was 'nevertheless still anxious to hear from me privately and confidentially what can be done to facilitate the co-operation of the British and Belgian Armies . . .'
Despite the limitations he had put on Dr Stein's mission, the King had discussed the military situation with Stein, as the Admiral records:

Stein gave the King an outline of the British plan, as explained by the First Lord and Prime Minister.
There was no question of infringing Belgian neutrality, but if the Germans crossed the frontier, or indeed the Dutch frontier, the British Army would be prepared to advance to the line of the Scheldt, provided only that this could be done with celerity and by pre-arrangement, before there was any question of German mechanized columns crossing the Albert Canal and entering the open country between the Scheldt and the French frontier. Otherwise the British Army could not move out of the strongly entrenched position it now occupied, to engage the Germans under such disadvantageous conditions. British offensive action would be confined in the first instance to air attack on the German forces which had invaded Belgian.
Stein tells me that the King was very indignant that the British General Staff had apparently not given the Belgian Army credit for being able to withstand a German attack at the outset. The whole Belgian Army was mobilized and they had several strong defensive lines between the Scheldt and the German frontier.
The British General Staff must surely know the position of the Belgian lines and their strength, and he was confident that the Belgian Army would hold up a German offensive until British reinforcements arrived. He hoped that the British would be prepared to advance a good deal further than the line of the

Scheldt.* The King declared: 'This time Belgium is well prepared, the Army is in good heart and well equipped.'

The King told Stein that he was constantly pressed by the French to do things which would infringe Belgian neutrality, and he found their pertinacity very trying. He told him, however, that he had confidence in the Prime Minister's [Chamberlain's] good faith.

Dr Stein arrived back in London on the 11th. That afternoon, in response to a telephone call from Winston Churchill, Sir Roger went to the House of Commons to join the Doctor and Churchill in a conference with the Prime Minister. Stein had brought a letter from the King, but this was the one he (or rather his Secretary, Comte Capelle) had written to the Belgian Ambassador, restricting Stein's mandate to the discussion of economic matters. After making his position clear and declaring that Leopold wished to see Admiral Keyes as soon as possible, Stein left to deliver the King's letter to Baron de Cartier. The meeting ended with the Prime Minister and Churchill giving their approval for the Admiral to accept the King's invitation to go to Brussels.

The anxiety which Leopold had expressed to see Keyes and discuss in secret 'co-operation between the British and Belgian Armies' was under-standable. The immediate situation looked very threatening for the Belgians. Many German divisions were reported to be on the move to the West from conquered Poland, where the campaign had ended a fortnight earlier. Despite numerous reassurances from Berlin, the King and his General Staff faced the possibility that the Germans might strike west-wards at any time, carving through Belgium as they had done in 1914.

The Cabinet and the War Office were as anxious for Anglo-Belgian liaison as was Leopold. To them the King's invitation to Keyes to act as his special intermediary, open Staff talks being ruled out, was most welcome and solved an outstanding difficulty. And as their envoy-extraordinary the Admiral of the Fleet was ideal – a man of courage and decision, respected and trusted in the highest quarters and a close personal friend of Churchill's.

Before Keyes left for Belgium, Dr Stein visited him at St Leonard's Terrace and gave him a full report on his meeting with the King in Brussels. As a result the Admiral wrote his memorandum to the Cabinet, in which he suggested: 'I think that a personal message from the Prime Minister to say that HM Government would carefully refrain from any action which might prejudice Belgian neutrality, coupled with an assur-ance that Great Britain would go at once to Belgium's aid in the event of German aggression, would be much appreciated by the King.'

* Leopold had, of course, no idea how tiny, ill-equipped and under-trained was the BEF, nor how incapable of operating in the face of Germany's overwhelming mastery of the air the French and British Air Forces would prove to be.

CHAPTER TEN

The Admiral's Mission

'The King agreed to any British officer, from the C-in-C downwards, being taken anywhere in plain clothes by Colonel Blake, to
see for himself the whole terrain. The Embassy must, however,
arrange that they were provided with passports which would satisfy
the Gendarmerie and the Civil Authorities. No objection would be
raised by any Military Authority . . .'

Sir Roger Keyes' diary

On October 17th 1939 Admiral Keyes left London for Brussels on the first
of his secret missions to the King of the Belgians. That evening he wrote
to his wife from the British Embassy in Brussels to ask her to tell inquirers
that he was away on 'some Naval business'. Next morning he was warmly
received by the King at Laeken Palace. The two had last met in the
happier days of the previous June, when Sir Roger had dined at Laeken
with the King and his mother. Now there was little time for pleasantries.
In a two-hour interview the King repeated the gist of what he had told Dr
Stein, emphasizing that he was most anxious to keep Belgium neutral and
out of the war, and therefore wished to do nothing that would alter his
country's non-alignment. He reiterated that if official Staff talks took
place, Germany would inevitably find out. The King also pointed out that
Belgium was strongly armed and that the line of the Albert Canal was a
powerful one, which would hold until the British troops advanced. He felt
sure that the British knew a good deal about the Belgian positions, as the
French and the Germans had this information. Indeed he was surprised to
hear that the British had no spies in Belgium.

Sir Roger then put the British position as he had discussed it in London
with General Ironside. Britain, he said, had guaranteed Belgian independence and it was not reasonable to expect Britain to come headlong to
the help of the Belgians without proper previous arrangements. When he
outlined the information which the British ought to possess, the King
expressed his surprise that they did not possess it already. He had
naturally assumed that the British were obtaining the information he was
giving to France about the Belgian dispositions, which was not in fact the
case. (The King and Van Overstraeten had also, in 1938, shown Captain
Liddell Hart 'every detail' of their defence system, as described later.)
The Admiral asked what would happen if Dutch neutrality were

infringed. This was a political matter, replied the King. Later he inti-
mated that in this event Belgium would probably be brought in too. The
Belgians, he continued, would be able to hold out for at least twenty-four
hours on the Albert Canal and for an equal period on a line farther back.
Surely, he urged, this would provide enough time for the British to come
to their help? The conversation then came back to the subject of the
Belgians secretly providing the British with military information and
Keyes suggested that this could easily be done without the knowledge of
the French or Germans – for example through liaison between General
Van Overstraeten and Colonel Blake, the British Military Attaché in
Brussels. The King approved the idea, and Sir Roger told him he thought
Blake (temporarily in London) would be available shortly.

Returning to London early on the 21st, Sir Roger went straight to
inform the Cabinet and the Prime Minister. Later he saw Ironside at the
War Office. He reported that King Leopold, while persisting in his
request for information about British plans, was still opposed to formal
Staff talks. The Prime Minister conceded, as Keyes wrote to the King on
October 24th, 'that if Your Majesty agreed to Staff talks and Germany
seized on that as a pretext for invading Belgium, it would make your
position impossibly difficult'. General Ironside expressed his concern that
the BEF, in leaving its strong positions on the Franco-Belgian border,
might be jeopardized by lack of information about the military preparations, defences and dispositions in Belgium, which he felt the Belgian
General Staff should provide. But he was considerably cheered when Sir
Roger told him of Leopold's agreement to a secret liaison channel being
established between the British Military Attaché and Van Overstraeten.
He asked Keyes to tell the King that he gave his word of honour that any
information thus obtained would be treated as absolutely secret, would
not pass through diplomatic channels, and – since it was a question of
co-operation between the British and Belgian Armies – would not be
passed on to the French. The General at once sent for Colonel Blake, who
was then in the War Office, and in Keyes' presence ordered Blake to pass
directly to him any confidential information he obtained.

When Leopold learned from the memorandum which accompanied
Keyes' letter of October 24th that Ironside welcomed the proposal and
promised that all information would be treated as secret, he immediately
authorized these arrangements and agreed, 'in compliance with my
request', as Keyes recorded in his diary:

> to any British officer, from the C-in-C downwards, being taken anywhere in
> plain clothes by Colonel Blake, to see for himself the whole terrain. The
> Embassy must, however, arrange that they were provided with passports which
> would satisfy the Gendarmerie and the Civil Authorities. No objection would
> be raised by any Military Authority . . .

The King's secret concessions were indeed justified, for on October 19th Hitler had announced to his Commander-in-Chief and Chief of the General Staff that *Fall Gelb* was to be launched on November 12th. During the first week in November the French and British armies were, in fact, standing by to dash into Belgium – though General Alan Brooke (later Lord Alanbrooke) noted in his diary that 'the whole plan of the advance was fantastic and could only have resulted in disaster'.[77] Disaster was averted, as described above, but its menace nevertheless persisted, and would undoubtedly have supervened if Leopold had given Hitler the pretext he needed to unleash his *Blitzkrieg*, by agreeing to formal Staff talks or, an even greater danger, allowing the Allied armies to enter Belgium.

During Sir Roger Keyes' first visit the King had hinted, on October 18th, that his country would indeed consider herself to be attacked if the Germans invaded Holland, but he had then undertaken no firm commitment. The British Cabinet was therefore anxious to ascertain Belgium's precise intentions. Again Keyes was called in as a secret envoy between the Cabinet and the King. On November 12th, after a summons from Winston Churchill and a briefing interview, the Admiral left London incognito for Brussels. A destroyer Flotilla Leader was placed at his disposal for the Channel crossing and the following evening the Admiral dined alone with Queen Elisabeth at her house in the park at Laeken. She had recently been visiting Belgium's eastern defences and gave Keyes an encouraging report on the state of the country's fortifications. Van Overstraeten, she said, had her complete confidence: he was pro-Ally and the outstanding figure in the Belgian Army. Leopold, the Queen Mother continued, had the same determined character as his father, but it is interesting that she should have referred at this stage to his unpopularity in France – a reflection of the anti-Belgian attitude of the French which had existed since the 1914 War and would shortly intensify.

Early next day Keyes was received by the King at Laeken. They at once discussed the matter of Belgium's reaction to a German attack on Holland. The King declared that as a constitutional monarch he could only express the views of his government, whose members were against any announcement which might provoke Hitler. But, he added, he was also Commander-in-Chief of the Army – and if Belgium were attacked, he would lead his troops against the Germans with the full support of his government and people. As for Holland, the Dutch had not asked the Belgians to come to their aid if they were attacked and the Belgians did not wish to be asked. The limitations of the Dutch Army were such that the Belgians would be called upon to operate against the Germans in areas which were not at all suitable; and such operations would prejudice the defence of Belgium. Nevertheless, if Holland were invaded it was probable that the Belgians would call into their own country the forces of

France and Britain. General Van Overstraeten had in fact submitted a paper to the King on August 12th 1939, a fortnight before hostilities began, to the effect that if Holland alone were invaded, Belgium should consider herself attacked. Later General Denis (the Belgian Defence Minister) and Spaak (the Foreign Minister) so informed the French.

From the point of view of the Admiral's mission, therefore, the results of his first interview were not positive. Keyes did, however, gain an interesting new insight into the King's attitude towards the Germans – good and bad. The King told him that a certain Dr Gebhardt (subsequently hanged for war crimes), who had successfully treated him after a skiing accident, had recently paid him a visit. Unknown to the King, the doctor was a friend of Himmler's. Gebhardt had been through the Polish campaign and described in vivid terms how the *Luftwaffe* and the Panzers had shattered Polish resistance and overrun the country in a matter of days. The King told Sir Roger that he was well aware of the purpose of the visit – to impress him with the power of the *Blitzkrieg* and the futility of small nations attempting to resist such an assault. But the King had left Gebhardt in no doubt that Belgium would resist to the death any attempt by Germany to pass through her territory. Keyes heard (though not from the King) that Gebhardt had emerged from his audience with the King looking crestfallen and had immediately returned to Germany.

Next day, November 15th, the Admiral had another long discussion with the King, who reiterated his thesis that if war did come to the West, it would be a very terrible one and it was therefore of cardinal importance to gain time – time during which, as he had learned from his secret sources in Germany, there was a strong possibility that Hitler and his regime would be overthrown, to be replaced by a government run by the decent anti-Nazi Germans with whom he was in touch. Leopold did not then know that the *démarche* he and Queen Wilhelmina had made on November 7th had helped to frustrate Hitler's plan to launch the *Blitzkrieg* on the 12th, but the world was still reverberating from the Beer Cellar bomb explosion which had so nearly eliminated the Führer and from the kidnapping of two British intelligence agents at Venlo on the 8th, which Nazi propaganda was linking together.

Like Churchill, Leopold believed that 'jaw-jaw' was preferable to 'war-war' and, while he was inflexibly determined to resist a German invasion if it came, he felt that no stone should be left unturned in trying to avert such a catastrophe. He was therefore ready to try, through his secret channels with the German opposition, to explore the possibilities of a peaceful settlement. But the King assured the Admiral that if such feelers were made he would be at pains to avoid giving the impression that it was with the authority of the British Government. Such an approach would probably be fruitless, but if any reasonable proposals did come from Germany he hoped that the British Government would at least consider them. Sir Roger replied that he feared the Germans would be unlikely to propose any terms which would be acceptable to the Allies.

Among the anti-Nazi dissidents with whom Leopold was in personal contact was the head of the civilian sector of the underground, Carl Goerdeler. There is a valuable note in the diary of another distinguished member, Ulrich von Hassell, an ex-ambassador who, like Goerdeler, was arrested, tortured and executed after the failure of the plot to assassinate Hitler in July 1944. Goerdeler, von Hassell noted, had had a further secret talk with the King, 'who again assured him that definite opportunities for peace existed and that he was ready to be of assistance. But not with our present regime.'[78] This entry, made on March 11th 1940, well indicates Lepold's close relations with the anti-Hitler front and the basis on which he was ready to hold talks.

But any remaining hopes the King might have had of British support for secret negotiations with the Germans were dashed by a note he received from Sir Roger Keyes on November 20th. After his meetings with Leopold in Brussels, Keyes had returned to London on the 17th and reported immediately to the War Office. Next day he attended a Cabinet meeting and had an interview with Neville Chamberlain, at which he explained King Leopold's views. Chamberlain, who regarded the German anti-Nazi opposition as traitors and provocateurs, made it clear to Sir Roger that Britain could have no part whatsoever in secret approaches to or negotiations with Germans of any kind. Keyes accordingly drafted a short report to this effect for the King and despatched it with a sympathetic personal note which ended: 'I declared my belief that King Albert would have done exactly the same as you have done, remembering his obligations as a Constitutional Monarch, and expressed my confidence that Your Majesty would behave as fearlessly as King Albert would have done, should the occasion arise.'

Meanwhile, on November 15th Ironside had had second thoughts about secret Anglo-Belgian military liaison and wrote a confidential letter to Sir Roger explaining that as the BEF was subordinate to the French High Command, it could only act under orders from the French Commander-in-Chief. Therefore the British could not make separate plans with the Belgians for the deployment of the BEF in Belgium, but must conform to French plans. At this point Ironside's letter revealed that he was ignorant of the secret exchanges which had long been going on between the Belgian and French High Commands and that this link had been strengthened two months earlier, for he wrote that it was essential for the Belgians to approach the French first regarding possible Anglo-French military action in Belgium. As far as he knew, the General continued, no approach had been made by either the French or the Belgian General Staff to this end and it was impossible to make firm plans for future joint operations unless the British, French and Belgian General

Staffs engaged in 'free and frank discussions'. But Ironside seems to have gathered an inkling of this Franco-Belgian co-operation, for in his own hand he added this postscript:

> Our first conversations were started because the Belgians refused to deal with the French, but now the Belgians seem to be coming into line with the French. All your efforts, therefore, should be developed towards getting the Belgians to deal openly with the French. Many thanks for all you have done. We now have several useful reports from the Military Attaché (Colonel Blake) and Gort knows what he has to face.

Ironside's letter revealed the alarmingly unsatisfactory state of Anglo-French military liaison after ten weeks of war. Despite all the Franco-Belgian exchanges the French were not passing on to the British the vital information they were receiving from Brussels,* while Ironside was merely reiterating to Keyes the old diehard theory that there was no substitute for official Staff talks. But the Admiral did not realize that this constant harping on the need for formal Staff talks with the Allies was not primarily designed to obtain Belgium's military secrets, but more as part of a deliberate policy to force or manoeuvre her out of her independence and into the Franco-British camp for the sake of her army, her fortifications and her territory. But in their anxiety to compromise Belgium's neutrality the Allies had blinded themselves to the fact that if they thus provided Hitler with a pretext and provocation for launching his *Blitzkrieg* at this time of their extreme weakness in land and air forces, the consequence would be as catastrophic for them as it would be for Belgium.

Yet, contrary to the picture presented by most writers, the King's ostensibly neutral stance had not prevented him from maintaining a considerable secret flow of military information to the French and now, thanks to Sir Roger's liaison, he had made similar arrangements with the British. The authors of Gort's *Despatches* were talking nonsense when they wrote that 'the French authorities were never in a position to obtain reliable and accurate details of the plans of the Belgian General Staff in the event of an invasion by Germany'. Even the most cursory reading of the memoirs of Gamelin and Van Overstraeten and *Les Relations Militaires Franco-Belges* demonstrates the opposite.

There are many specific instances. On March 28th 1939, for example, General Laurent, the French Military Attaché in Brussels, sent a long letter to the *Deuxième Bureau* (the Intelligence Department) at the

---

* Lieutenant-Colonel George Davy, who later took charge of the British Military Mission to the Belgian High Command, wrote in a report on his service as GSO 1 of the British Mission at Gamelin's Headquarters at Vincennes that the French 'were a bit cagey' about their plans and dispositions, and only uncovered their wall maps showing them 'when they got to know us'.

Ministry of Defence in Paris summarizing a conversation with Van Overstraeten. This surveyed in detail the question of keeping Brussels an open city, defence of the Louvain area and of the Meuse, liaison with the Dutch Army, defence of the Albert Canal, etc. A month earlier, on February 21st, Laurent had filed a similar letter describing with minute precision Belgian troop dispositions for the defence of the Meuse bridges and the Ardennes. At the same time Hautcoeur pursued his fruitful liaison. On March 7th he conveyed to Van Overstraeten Gamelin's ideas for Belgian anti-tank defences between Louvain and Namur; and on March 16th he reported to the General on a long and detailed discussion with Gamelin of Belgian preparations ('*Le Généralissime est enchanté des progrès rapides réalisés entre Wavre et Namur . . .*').

As late as March 26th 1940 a British Foreign Office paper naïvely commented that 'Franco-Belgian contacts are suspected, but we have no official knowledge of their nature and scope'. In fact, Gamelin was deliberately keeping the British in ignorance of the fruits of his secret liaison with King Leopold – and of much other military information which they should have had. On the other hand, the French showed themselves to be infinitely more flexible in their handling of the intelligence problem posed by Belgian independence. Instead of pounding away, like the British, with demands for official Staff talks, they took full advantage of Hautcoeur's privileged position and got on with the job.

In contrast, the General Staff of the BEF and the War Office were singularly lacking in subtlety, imagination and enterprise in matters of secret military liaison. It was of course useless to expect anything so delicate as the confidential *rapport* between King Leopold and Generalissimo Gamelin to emerge from the British military Establishment. Both Lord Gort, the C-in-C, BEF, and Sir Edmund Ironside, the CIGS, were wholly devoid of subtlety. Indeed, in one of his waspish diary entries Sir Alexander Cadogan describes the latter as 'so stupid as to be impervious to anything', while General Spears depicts Gort as 'not a very clever man', who struck the French as 'a friendly and jovial battalion commander . . . willing and anxious to please, and do everything he was told.'[79] Hore-Belisha, the Secretary of State for War, revealed the basis on which he had selected Gort as C-in-C of the BEF on the outbreak of war, when he said that this appointment ought to go down well with the public, because he was 'a VC and a Viscount'. Although Gort's Chief of Staff, Henry Pownall, was not lacking in intelligence, he revealed himself in his diaries, which were published in 1972, as arrogant, intolerant and bigoted, with an almost obsessional antipathy and contempt for foreigners – and for the Belgians and their King in particular. It was as though Pownall had redirected towards them that strong vein of anti-Semitism which emerges both in his diary and in other accounts of the hounding from office of Hore-Belisha[h] – in which, ironically, he and Gort played leading parts. 'The picture of personal rivalries and intrigues among brass-hats,' writes Max (now Lord) Beloff, 'as much as among "frocks" is not a pretty one. The War Office with the lid off – not a pretty sight . . .'[80]

One of the first examples of the two generals' attitude to liaison with the Belgians is to be found in Gort's *Despatches*, which refer to the BEF's move into Belgium as 'carried out at a time when every moment was of value, over roads not previously reconnoitred' – the implication being that this was prevented by King Leopold's policy. The *Official History* of the campaign and Pownall's diaries give an equally misleading impression. Although the former records that some British officers in plain clothes visited the K-W Line and Pownall noted on April 1st 1940 'we've smuggled two officers over with fancy passports to reconnoitre it', all these accounts fail to mention that the British were availing themselves of the facility secretly offered by the King (through Sir Roger Keyes) to allow British officers 'from the Commander-in-Chief downwards' to enter Belgium in civilian clothes to inspect every feature of the country's defences – and that they enjoyed the full co-operation of the Belgian authorities. If Gort and Pownall neglected to take full advantage of this facility and reconnoitre thoroughly the territory on which their forces were going to operate, they had no one but themselves to blame. But it is on record – although not in the *Official History* nor in Gort's *Despatches* nor any other official account – that an extremely thorough reconnaissance of the positions to be occupied by the BEF was in fact carried out on the initiative of General Dill – by a British general. The account which follows clearly shows that the British Commander-in-Chief and his Chief of Staff could have obtained every scrap of information that was needed, had they made the necessary effort.

In March 1940 Major-General Davidson, who was then Commander of the artillery in I Corps, was told by his Corps Commander, General Dill, that he 'had been selected for a very "hush-hush" mission to Belgium in mufti, to carry out a reconnaissance of the terrain and of the Belgian defences on our I Corps front on the River Dyle and of the area around Brussels'. He was also told to contact General Alan Brooke, the Commander of II Corps, in case he could provide any information useful to him. After sundry cloak and dagger preparations he reached Brussels and spent three days in a detailed examination of the defensive potential of the Dyle position and of all areas suitable for gun positions and observation posts. 'This proved of great use later,' wrote Davidson, 'by the end I knew every inch of the terrain – different defences, roads, lakes, forests and a complete artillery layout.'

After the war Davidson sent his notes to Colonel Blake, who replied that some years after the war 'I ran into a gunner officer who had been a Battery Commander in I Corps in the advance into Belgium in 1940. He said that what had astonished him was that on arrival at his rendezvous

everything had already been "pin-pointed" – gun positions, OPs, etc. – and he had thus been able to shoot up the Germans most effectively . . .'*
It seems astonishing that Gort and Pownall did not take more advantage of the King's offer and arrange further fruitful reconnaissances like this of Davidson's. But instead, the British military hierarchy never stopped complaining about the alleged non-cooperation of King Leopold and his General Staff and gave the Belgians no credit or thanks for providing them with these facilities for secret reconnaissance and liaison. The Foreign Office document previously mentioned does, however, reveal that Van Overstraeten replied in detail to a questionnaire which was submitted to him in secret by the British and even handed over (to Sir Roger Keyes) aerial photographs of the Albert Canal defences, bridges etc. These were to assist the RAF with their targeting and Van Overstraeten was in this case thanked by the Chief of the Air Staff for this valuable assistance.

In 1938 Captain Liddell Hart (then adviser to Hore-Belisha and Military Correspondent to *The Times*) on the invitation of King Leopold and General Van Overstraeten, with whom he had been in touch since 1927, was shown by them every detail of the Belgian defence system. In his *Memoirs* Liddell Hart writes:

> I found my Belgian hosts remarkably frank not only in giving me details of their forces and defences but in discussing their prospective plans to meet a German attack. So I found it hard to believe the vehement complaints of the British and French political and military chiefs after the 1940 defeat in the West, that their planning had been badly handicapped by lack of information about the Belgian defences and plans. It seemed more likely to be an excuse for the miscarriage of their own advance into Belgium. I have reason to know, apart from my own experience, that the information was made available privately to some British representatives – however averse the Belgians may have been to official Staff conversations from fear of French security leaks and the danger that word of such talks might reach the Germans. Yet the British *Official History* of the 1939–40 Campaign, produced nearly ten years after the war, repeats the complaint that the Belgian High Command 'were unwilling to supply information as to their own plan of defence'. It was one more example of the difference between official history and the truth of history.

Reflecting on his observations during this visit, Liddell Hart squarely refutes the accusations that the King and Van Overstraeten were 'pro-German' although he concedes that they might have been 'suspicious of French designs to turn Belgium into a satellite of France . . .' 'In this respect,' writes Liddell Hart, 'Leopold and Van Overstraeten faithfully

---

* For a full account of this reconnaissance, see Major-General F. H. M. Davidson, 'My mission to Belgium, 1940', in the *Journal of the Royal United Service Institute*, December 1969.

followed the precepts inculcated by King Albert . . . It is an irony of history that the son should have suffered such sweeping criticism, and eventually the loss of his throne, by closely and loyally trying to carry out the teachings of his father, so universally admired as the heroic symbol of 1914 resistance to Germany.'[81]

Unfortunately, Van Overstraeten was intolerant and contemptuous in his attitude towards many with whom he came in contact, particularly politicians. They in turn detested him, believing him to be a bad influence on Leopold and a buffer between themselves and the King. Before, during and after the May battles, therefore, his abrasive personality caused friction, mistrust and misunderstandings.

In a small country like Belgium the number of highly skilled officers at the apex of the military hierarchy is inevitably limited and, as the King told the author after the war, Van Overstraeten was the best choice available as his principal Military Adviser. In many ways, indeed, he seemed ideal. Neat, dapper, astute, incisive, with a soldierly carriage, he had been an aide-de-camp to King Albert since 1917. Moreover, he was Belgium's leading strategist as well as a former head of the *Ecole de Guerre*. His manner was usually polite, even punctilious, but there were times when he was outspoken to the point of incivility. The recollections of British commanders who had dealings with him during the battles – Lord Alanbrooke, for example – vividly demonstrate how he did Leopold's cause a disservice in the eyes of his allies. This was even more the case where the French were involved. Since Van Overstraeten was the King's representative and mouthpiece, these abrasive attitudes, which led his critics to suggest – quite falsely – that he was pro-German, inevitably meant that some of the distaste and suspicion he aroused was transferred to his Sovereign.

Another irony was that in March 1940 Leopold supplied the French with a crucial item of intelligence – which, if only Gamelin had heeded it, might have changed the whole course of the military campaign. Thanks to Colonel Oster and his other secret sources of enemy intelligence, the King became convinced that the Germans would make their main armoured thrust through the Ardennes and across the Meuse between Givet and Longwy, which is exactly where the Germans would in fact make their successful breakthrough to the Channel coast in May 1940. Leopold immediately forwarded this warning with full supporting evidence to Gamelin via General Delvoie, the Belgian Military Attaché in Paris. The reply was a brush-off: 'Carefully established ever since peacetime, perfectly adopted to the terrain, guarded with an ever-increasing depth of echelons, covered and supported since mobilization, the fortifications which defend French territory are in a position to receive the shock of the enemy in all its parts.' The French were in fact guarding this area with a thin screen of elderly low-grade troops of General Corap's 9th

Army, through which von Rundstedt's Panzers would slice like a knife through butter. Unfortunately, as the *Official History* observes, 'the possibility of an attack through the Ardennes having once been ruled out by the French, no further thought seems to have been given to it or to its possible consequences'.[82] But, as Spaak was later to remark about the King, 'with a perspicacity which today appears to be rather horrible, he foretold the military developments which were to take place'.

CHAPTER ELEVEN

Blind Chance

'Balloon expected to go up tomorrow.'
The British Military Attaché,
telephoning London from Laeken Palace on January 13th 1940

On January 15th 1940, right in the middle of the major invasion crisis described below, there was another change of American Ambassador in Brussels. Like his predecessor, Joseph Davies, who had been so impressed by Leopold's rock-like steadiness at the outbreak of war, the newcomer John Cudahy soon came to admire the young King.

After the first of his many meetings with Leopold, Cudahy noted: 'He looked a soldier, a tall, handsome figure with well-set shoulders and the ruddy, clear skin of an athlete . . . I was struck by his extreme simplicity, approaching shyness . . . His eyes were shadowed by lack of sleep. Nevertheless, he refused to despair.'* The two men discussed the 'harsh and unfair' criticisms by the French, and the pressure they and the British were applying to Belgium to coerce her into abandoning her neutral status, which they had pledged themselves to protect. The Ambassador's article brings out strongly the King's hope – based on his knowledge of the strong opposition in high places inside Germany to Hitler and his aggressive plans – that 'something might happen to avert the blow'. Cudahy noted Leopold's determination to avoid provoking such an attack and that he felt that 'every day the struggle was kept off Belgian soil was a day gained for the cause of peace, and in the future there was always hope'.

Cudahy observes that Leopold was calm, despite 'the strain under which he suffered'. The exhausted state in which the Ambassador found the King was hardly surprising, for of all the 'invasion alerts' sounded between September 3rd 1939 and May 10th 1940, perhaps the most sinister – and certainly the most considerable in its consequences – occurred during the second week of January. Hitler had again definitely decided to attack through Belgium and Holland and was only waiting for favourable weather conditions. By now, von Hassell observes, 'all

---

* John Cudahy wrote a series of articles which appeared in the *Sunday Express* in November and December 1940. See also Cudahy's statement in *The Belgian Campaign and the Surrender of the Belgian Army*.

opposition of the military leaders to the drive-through-Belgian plan had collapsed. This in spite of the fact that Brauchitsch and Halder, as well as all the others, are convinced the result will be disastrous. But they feel they must obey. Göring also was still against it, but could not make up his mind to resist; instead, he confined himself to a certain sabotage of the plan on the pretext of bad weather.'[83] On January 10th the meteorologists promised 'ten days to a fortnight of clear winter weather beginning on the 15th' and Hitler ordered the assault for January 17th.

The Belgians were again forewarned. Colonel Oster gave his usual accurate information through Major Sas, while warnings were also received from a number of other sources including the King's sister Princess Marie-José (the wife of Crown Prince Umberto of Italy); from the Pope via the Papal Nuncio; and from Ciano (the Italian Foreign Minister and Mussolini's son-in-law), who was in the habit of sending secret notifications to Brussels. But, says Spaak, '*il était cette fois plus précis et plus pessimiste. Il était convaincu que l'attaque allait se déclencher.*'[84] On January 2nd Ciano advised the Belgian Ambassador in Rome that his country was in danger and should keep on the *qui vive*.

Blind chance confirmed these warnings. A certain Major Helmut Reinberger, commander of the paratroop school at Stendal, near Berlin, had been attached to General Student's staff to help in the preparations for an airborne operation against Holland and Belgium. Summoned to a conference in Cologne, he was delayed by jams on the railway in the Ruhr and was obliged to spend the night of January 9th–10th in Münster. Here in the Officers' Club he met Major Hoenmanns, a 1914 War pilot and commandant of the local airfield at Loddenheide. The latter, eager to combine some flying time with a visit to his wife in Cologne, offered to fly Reinberger there the following morning. He knew nothing of the top secret papers his passenger was carrying.

There was, in fact, a strict German security regulation in force forbidding an officer to fly while carrying secret documents. Yet Reinberger's papers contained the main details of *Fall Gelb* – for a massive armoured attack on Belgium in the Maastricht area, with powerful airborne assaults and landings to secure bridges and strong points, including those on the Meuse further to the south. Unfortunately for him Hoenmanns, navigating too far to the west in poor visibility, crash-landed their Messerschmitt Taifun light plane at Mechelen-sur-Meuse, on Belgium's north-east frontier with Holland, under the impression that he was on the Rhine.

After the two officers emerged from their aircraft, Reinberger was spotted by an alert Belgian soldier trying to burn some papers in a ditch, but the Belgian was able to stamp out the flames and retrieve them before escorting the Germans to a military post. There Reinberger again tried to destroy the documents, snatching them from the table where they lay and thrusting them into a lighted stove. But the officer in command, Captain

Rodrique, rushed forward and, badly burning himself in the process, recovered the damaged but still partly readable documents. Realizing his failure was final, Reinberger burst into tears and made an abortive grab for Rodrique's revolver, crying 'I am finished. Let me end things now. I am guilty of an unpardonable crime in the eyes of my country.'*

The German Air Attaché to the Low Countries, General Wenninger, who was stationed at The Hague, demanded to see the captured airmen as soon as he heard of their arrest. He was not allowed to do so until the Belgians had installed a hidden microphone in the room where the interview took place the following day. As soon as they were alone, Wenninger asked whether the documents had been destroyed and was assured that they had been. He then informed Berlin that 'the despatch case was burned for certain'. But acute anxiety was felt in Berlin and Hitler, Göring and Keitel spent hours poring over the files, trying to ascertain what might have been disclosed.

In the meantime Belgian Intelligence had translated and assessed what remained of the papers and at noon on the 11th Van Overstraeten took the results to the King, who immediately informed General Denis, the Minister of Defence, at the same time stipulating that Gamelin and the British and Dutch should be informed forthwith. Accordingly, Van Overstraeten summoned Colonel Blake and Colonel Hautcoeur and gave them copies of a document which contained a summary of all the information which could be extracted from the charred fragments. Hautcoeur was then asked to take this document to Gamelin, with an enquiry as to how soon the Belgians could expect assistance in the event of the German attack being launched.

Hautcoeur reached Paris late that night. At a conference at 10.30 next morning Gamelin and his staff weighed the issues. The French were suspicious of Van Overstraeten's motives for sending them a summary rather than photocopies of the original documents. But what they failed to appreciate was that the papers were of limited value by themselves, being so burned that it took the Belgian Intelligence Service hours of painstaking work to extract all the information which the summary contained (see page 474). Although the French General Staff suspected that the whole episode was a 'plant', the document together with the warnings they had already received clearly demanded action. A top priority alert was therefore issued to the Army, and General Champon was ordered to stand by as head of a French Military Mission to Belgium. The BEF also stood to. On the 13th Leopold's sense of urgency was increased by a message from his Military Attaché in Berlin stating that he

---

* After May 10th Reinberger and Hoenmanns were sent to England and then to Canada. In their absence they were condemned to death. Deprived of these sacrificial victims, Hitler 'sent into the wilderness' General Felmy, commander of *Luftflotte 2*, and his Chief of Staff, Kammhuber.

had discovered from a sure source (Colonel Oster) that the Germans assumed the documents had been captured. To forestall counter-measures they would therefore attack the next day, the 14th. But nothing happened, for as we now know, Hitler, impressed by the strength of the Belgian defences, by then fully alerted – having lost the advantage of surprise through the discovery of his plans – and being denied the *casus belli* that an Allied entry into Belgium would have provided, called off the assault after a stormy conference with his generals. The deterioration in the weather was another factor.

The Belgians had no doubts as to the authenticity of the documents. However, Churchill and many others were suspicious at the time and Reynaud, despite all the evidence available by 1951, wrote in his memoirs of Hitler 'manipulating the faked accident which was at the root of the affair'.[85] The vivid truth was expressed by General Keitel at the Nuremburg Trials in 1944, when he described Hitler's fury on hearing the news. 'It was the worst storm I ever saw in my life,' Keitel testified. 'The Führer foamed at the mouth and struck the walls with his fists. The shadow of executions passed over us.' And after seeing Hitler on the 12th, General Jodl wrote in his diary 'The situation is catastrophic.' The choice now lay between immediately implementing the captured plan or abandoning it for good. Göring* has also added to the story with an account of the decision taken at a General Staff Meeting at Hitler's headquarters, in which he describes how the High Command decided 'to accept the least favourable hypothesis, and to assume that our plans had become known'.

But the crucial significance of this episode lies in the fact that it caused Hitler to adopt, at the end of February, the project put forward by Manstein and von Rundstedt, which transferred the *Schwerpunkt* of the main Panzer thrust from central Belgium to the Ardennes as the final, victorious version of *Fall Gelb*. Until then virtually all the *Wehrmacht*'s armour had been allocated to von Bock's Army Group B in the North, for the *Blitzkrieg* straight through the heart of Belgium, while the subsidiary function of von Rundstedt's infantry divisions was to protect von Bock's southern flank. Under the new plan, about which Leopold and others vainly tried to warn Gamelin, the two generals' roles were reversed and seven of von Bock's Panzer divisions were transferred to von Rundstedt to enable his Army Group A to take over responsibility for the main thrust. The object was for von Rundstedt's Panzer armada to penetrate the thickly wooded area of the Ardennes, where the French refused to believe there could be a major attack, and break through their front on the Meuse in the Sedan area – the weak hinge of the Franco-British armies' right-wheel advance into Belgium. Thus, instead of pulverizing the mainly infantry forces of the Belgians, French and British in the

---

* Von Hassell noted in his diary 'From Ilse Göring I heard that Hermann was beside himself for a number of days.'

North, as planned in the earlier versions of *Fall Gelb*, the great phalanx of armoured vehicles would race westwards to the sea and scythe round the Allies' southern flank and rear with the intention of cutting them off from the bulk of the French armies and the Channel coast. The task of von Bock's three Panzer divisions, backed by his powerful infantry and airborne forces, was now to conquer Holland and break through the Belgian defences. The object there was to confirm the Allies' misconception that Belgium was the focus of the main German attack and to entice the French and British forces in the North as far into that country as possible, in order to facilitate their encirclement by the massed Panzers of von Rundstedt's Army Group A in the South.

For Leopold the paramount question now was: where did Belgium stand as regards the Allies? At this moment of extreme emergency he felt it imperative to seek undertakings from Britain and France which would safeguard her future should she be forced into war. He therefore summoned Sir Roger Keyes once again to Laeken to transmit the proposals he had in mind to the British Cabinet. Such a preliminary approach was no exceptional practice for Belgian monarchs, King Albert and his predecessors having more than once engaged in informal discussions with foreign statesmen before bringing in the appropriate Belgian Minister. Unfortunately, not all the members of Leopold's government shared his pro-British sentiments, indeed several Ministers and in particular one Gustave Sap were known to be sympathizers with Nazi Germany. As a precaution against leakages of sensitive information by these pro-Germans, it had therefore been necessary for the King to withhold from his Cabinet such facts as the secret liaison missions of Admiral Keyes and the resulting flow of Belgian military intelligence to the British. Information about the similar arrangements with the French, through Gamelin, was also kept from the Belgian Ministers, with the exception of General Denis, the Minister of Defence, who was let into the secret.

In this case, however, the King's primary reason for bypassing his Ministers in the first instance was that there was no time for the approach to be made through long-winded official channels, in view of the imminence of hostilities. He hoped, moreover, to persuade the British to make an apparently spontaneous offer direct to the Belgian Government and thus avoid giving the Germans a pretext for aggressive action against Belgium.

Thus it was that in the evening of the crisis-ridden January 13th King Leopold received Sir Roger Keyes for the third time at Laeken. In an ante-room the Admiral found General Van Overstraeten and Colonel Blake discussing the warning which had just been received from Colonel Oster in Berlin that the invasion was to be launched next day. Blake broke off to put through a brief telephone call to London, telling the War Office simply 'Balloon expected to go up tomorrow!' The King then invited the Admiral into his study and asked him whether, despite Belgium's wish for peace, were she to be involved in war beside Britain, Sir Roger thought that Britain would be prepared to offer her the same guarantees as in 1914–1918. To help with the wording of the guarantees he had in mind he called in Van Overstraeten and, taking a sheet of paper, he jotted down with corrections as he wrote:

1 *Pas d'ouverture de négociations de paix sans participation de la Belgique* (No opening of peace negotiations without Belgium's participation)
2 *Garanties de la restauration intégrale du statut politique et territorial de la Belgique ainsi que de sa Colonie* (Guarantees for the total restoration of the political and territorial status of Belgium and of the Congo)
3 *Assistance pour la restauration économique et financière de la Belgique* (Help in the economic restoration of Belgium)*

Keyes studied the terms and said that they seemed reasonable. He felt that an official request on these lines from the Belgium Government might be favourably received, but stressed that he could give no assurance of this and would have to consult the British Cabinet. With that, he left Laeken to return to British GHQ at Arras with the intention of taking a plane straight to London. But the Belgian countryside was enveloped in dense fog and when Keyes reached Arras in the small hours, visibility was still so poor that flying was out of the question and he had to spend the night at GHQ.

From GHQ early next morning, the 14th, the Admiral telephoned a report of the conversation to Churchill at the Admiralty. He read out the King's tentative guarantee proposals and explained that in view of the urgency of the crisis the King had not asked for these guarantees on behalf of the Belgian Government through official channels, because he felt that this would take too long and be difficult to arrange. The Admiral added his own strictly personal view that, if the proposals were accepted by the British, King Leopold *might* be able to persuade his Ministers to invite French and British troops into Belgium at once. Churchill thought the King's request 'reasonable' and immediately passed it to the Prime Minister at Downing Street. Chamberlain, however, refused to look at it,† contenting himself with sending Keyes the following testy reply for transmission to the King:

The British Government have repeatedly offered to come to the help of Belgium, but it is not thought that a last moment like this is the time for giving guarantees other than is implicit in the fact of an alliance in war.

* The original pencilled draft in the King's handwriting is in the Admiral's archives.
† This is an extraordinary sidelight on Chamberlain, but on his original draft of his message Keyes pencilled: 'Telephoned to Winston Churchill who thought the request reasonable and passed it over to the Prime Minister who declined to see it.'

The Prime Minister feels deeply for the King in this hour of danger, and the most useful step that could be taken would be to establish immediate Staff contacts between Belgian and French military authorities . . .

The matter came up formally, however, at that morning's War Cabinet meeting, when Churchill submitted a brief memorandum on the Admiral's telephoned report. Its last paragraph ran:

If these conditions were promised, Sir Roger thought that the King would be able to persuade his Ministers to invite French and British troops into Belgium at once.

Chamberlain – as Ironside records – 'reacted violently and said that the Belgians had no right to put such conditions under the stress of attack'. But he was persuaded to have second thoughts and at lunch-time a message was hastily sent to Sir Lancelot Oliphant, the British Ambassador in Brussels, asking him to instruct Keyes not to deliver the earlier Note but to substitute this:

It is not possible to give a definite answer: the matter is still being earnestly considered and he [the King] will hear from us again shortly.

Not until late that night did the War Cabinet reach a final decision. The Ministers assumed from Churchill's misapprehended version of Sir Roger's message that, under hourly threat of invasion, Belgium was at last prepared to waive the neutrality issue and permit the immediate entry of Allied troops *before* any attack, provided she was given the guarantees for which the King had asked. They therefore gave their approval and towards midnight on the 14th their reply went to Keyes via the British Embassy in Brussels:

We are ready to accept the invitation to British troops to enter Belgium and understand the French attitude is the same. We are asked to give guarantees to Belgium which go further than anything we have promised the French and which we might not be in a position to carry out at the end of the war. Subject to the above we are ready to promise as follows if such an invitation were given at once.

The Note then outlined the three conditions virtually as the King had proposed them, and went on:

The King will realize that the value of the invitation will be seriously discounted from the point of view of Belgium as well as ours unless the invitation is given in sufficient time to allow the British and French troops to secure a strategic advantage of position before any German attack begins.

The King did not receive this Note until the following morning, the 15th. He was appalled. The War Cabinet's reply was based on a calamitous misconception. What Keyes had mentioned in his telephoned report to Churchill as a purely personal expression of opinion – the *possibility* of the Belgians admitting troops at once, before a German attack – had been taken by the Cabinet as a firm statement of the King's intentions. According to the Note, it had even been construed as an 'invitation'. The King had in fact given neither an undertaking nor an invitation, such initiative being quite outside his constitutional powers.

How had the mistake arisen? Somewhere along the line there was wishful thinking. On the evidence, it would appear that Churchill was responsible for converting a speculation on the part of Keyes into a formal request from King Leopold. Whatever the truth, from this misapprehension flowed in the next hours an extraordinary chain of events which, but for the King's calm consistency, would almost certainly have precipitated Hitler's *Blitzkrieg* at a time when the Allied forces were even more perilously unready and weak than they were four months later.

On the morning of the 14th Winston Churchill's distorted version of Keyes' report had been quickly circulated to the Foreign Office and from there was conveyed to the French Ambassador in London, who immediately passed it on to Daladier in Paris. Daladier, recklessly eager to see the Allied armies move into Belgium at once, was delighted at the news. At 3.30 pm he telephoned General Gamelin at French Supreme Headquarters, Vincennes, to say that, according to information from Neville Chamberlain, King Leopold had declared himself ready to call in the Allies. He asked whether the Allied forces could move immediately and Gamelin answered 'Yes'. General Georges, commanding the armies of the North-East, was warned to advance his troops to the frontier preparatory to entering Belgium next morning, immediately the authorization was received. Meanwhile the French anxiously awaited the British Cabinet's approval for the BEF to move into Belgium with the French armies. But as the hours passed without word from Downing Street they became increasingly impatient. A series of agitated telephone calls from Paris to London, complaining that the Cabinet's delay in answering was jeopardizing the whole Allied plan, failed to elicit any positive answer.

Meanwhile an unaccountable action by the Belgian Chief of Staff, General Van Den Bergen, confused matters still more. At midnight on the 13th, on his own authority, he ordered the opening of the massive frontier barriers between France and Belgium for the first time since the start of the war – an act which cost the General his appointment. He was shortly replaced by General Michiels. Admiral Keyes, crossing the border *en route* for Arras early on the 14th, noted the fact with astonishment, the more so when a Belgian officer told him that he had orders to allow British and French troops to enter Belgium.

Yet even at this crucial stage – a late report from Oster in Berlin now named the 17th as the date of the German attack – the Belgian Government still adamantly refused official Staff talks. At a further meeting with Leopold on the 14th Keyes reiterated the Allies' need to have full military conversations before they were called into Belgium. A similar approach from Sir Lancelot Oliphant was equally unsuccessful. At an evening conference on the 14th the King, Spaak and General Denis decided that liaison should be confined to the respective Military Attachés.

At 9.30 next morning Sir Roger brought the British Cabinet's Note to the King's study at Laeken. Handing it to Leopold he said, with some embarrassment, 'If Belgium makes an immediate appeal for British aid, the guarantees Your Majesty proposed will be given.' The King listened to Keyes in shocked surprise. 'Is this fair play?' he asked. If he understood the Admiral right, the British would refuse the guarantees unless they were granted instant entry into Belgium – a step which, they apparently appreciated, would automatically plunge Belgium into war. This was entirely at variance with what King Leopold had proposed and showed total misunderstanding of his intentions, which had been to secure the guarantees unconditionally and then present them to his government.

The King slowly read the two blue-tinted sheets bearing the British Embassy heading and found his fears confirmed. Then he summoned General Van Overstraeten and showed him the document. Van Overstraeten declared at once that it was 'unacceptable'. Leopold turned to Keyes and pointed out that the British answer would have a very bad effect if he communicated it to his government. An invitation to the British and French forces to enter Belgium would, he said, immediately provoke a devastating German invasion and make her once again the battlefield of Europe. Though the Belgian people were overwhelmingly in favour of the Allies, they were desperately anxious to be kept out of the war and this would be a matter of terrible concern to them.

The advantage the Allies would gain by taking up strategic positions at once, the King added, would be out of all proportion to the sufferings that would be inflicted on the Belgian people if they became involved in a war fought on Belgian soil, or even on her frontiers. He pointed out that he was not a dictator and his government, consisting as it did of various parties, could not be induced to go to the length of entering the war while there was any hope of averting it. And it would not be fair to the Belgian people if they did so.

Keyes asked if the captured documents did not provide a justification. No, the King answered, not before the Germans had actually attacked. Moreover, they could quite easily adopt some other plan and repudiate the documents, making tremendous capital in Germany of the violation of Belgian neutrality by Great Britain and France. It was in the paramount interest of the Allies to leave the onus for the breaking of Belgian neutrality on Germany. Keyes then asked: was the Belgian Government ready to call in the Allies if Holland were invaded? He pointed out that the violation of Dutch territory was a direct threat to Antwerp and Belgian interests on the Scheldt, and must inevitably lead to an attack on Belgium. Leopold answered that there would be considerable delay before his government could be induced to make a decision.

The King was particularly annoyed that the British had not granted freely the guarantees he asked for – quite apart from making these dependent on a condition that was totally unacceptable. This grievance he aired to Keyes as the uneasy meeting ended. The guarantees, he declared, were no more than the undertakings given to Belgium during the last war, and it seemed to him not too much to ask when one considered that Belgium had spent vast sums of money and made an enormous military effort to deny her territory to a German occupation which would so greatly menace British security.

Sir Roger took leave of the King, disappointed at his inability to shake his determination. He had done everything in his power to persuade him to accede to the British request to allow the BEF and French armies into Belgium. But what he did not appreciate was that the King's firm stand was of inestimable benefit to Britain and France, for the Admiral had no idea of the enormous preponderance of the German ground and air forces over those of the Allies and of what would have happened if the latter had been allowed to enter Belgium, thus calling down on their heads Hitler's overwhelming mechanized might and air power. That night he cabled a summary of the King's arguments to Neville Chamberlain in a cypher telegram despatched from the British Embassy in Brussels.

Meanwhile the French, still misled by the previous day's report from London, had been acting on the assumption that the Allies would be invited into Belgium at any moment. Throughout the day the Allied formations were poised at the open barriers along the border, awaiting the order to move. At Vincennes Gamelin had been concerned since early morning at the lengthening delay that was holding up the advance. 'It is essential that the Belgian Government be made to face its responsibilities,' he urged in a note to Daladier.

In Paris Daladier himself was impatiently awaiting the formal Belgian request. His frustration mounted as the appeal failed to arrive. Early that afternoon he summoned the Belgian Ambassador in Paris, Le Tellier, and told him that the French Army was ready to move into Belgium within six hours of receiving the invitation, which he understood would be given on the strength of the guarantee which had been asked for and would be granted. The astonished Le Tellier replied that he knew nothing of any guarantee being requested by his government.

The Ambassador at once sent a coded cable to Spaak, who received it while in conference at the Foreign Office. He was as dumbfounded and puzzled as Le Tellier had been. After reading the message to his colleagues, Spaak hurried with Pierlot and General Denis to Laeken to consult the King. At 6 pm Spaak telephoned Le Tellier, who told him that Daladier insisted upon a reply by 8 pm. Spaak thereupon answered in the hearing of his colleagues: 'You surely wouldn't want us to decide to abandon our neutrality in a matter of minutes, to cock a snook at Parliament without taking its advice, and embark voluntarily on a war that the whole nation wants to see kept away from Belgian territory? You must tell M. Daladier that it's impossible for us to reply by eight o'clock!' At the conference with Leopold, which lasted over ninety minutes, the Ministers backed the King in refusing Daladier's demand that the Allies be permitted to enter Belgium. After telephoning Le Tellier with the news, Spaak sped back to Brussels to obtain full Cabinet approval of the decision.

In Paris at 8.50 pm Daladier informed Gamelin of the Belgian refusal by telephone. His words revealed his grievous misconception of what Leopold had said to Keyes in their talk on the 13th. 'The Belgian Government,' said the indignant Premier, 'has rejected the King's proposal. It does not feel able to assume the responsibility of letting the Allied troops enter Belgium!' Gamelin angrily replied that in his opinion Belgium had once more 'failed in her destiny'. But the Allied troops could not have entered Belgium as a co-ordinated force, even had the Belgians invited them. For it was not until the following day, the 16th, that the British Cabinet finally agreed to the BEF advancing with the French into Belgium.

The British Ministers had, as usual, dispersed to their country retreats for the weekend despite the gravity of the crisis, and when Ironside telephoned Chequers urgently on Sunday the 14th Chamberlain was 'too tired' to speak to him. It was not until 6 pm that a Cabinet meeting was held, at which a telephone call was received from Gamelin 'almost speechless with rage that the great opportunity would be missed through the British Government's delay in letting the BEF move in with the French Army'.[86] Nevertheless, the meeting ended without the British Ministers making a decision. It would therefore appear that they were racked with doubts about taking this potentially disastrous step.

The alarm subsided as suddenly as it had arisen. The Allied armies reverted to their defensive posture on the 16th. The bulk of the German formations, however, remained closed up near their frontier ready to strike – without the advance warning their massive forward movements in November and January had given the defenders. Amid an intensified flow of representations and explanations between Brussels, Paris and London tension relaxed and the situation reverted to the former uneasy calm. But among the French at least the five-day crisis was to leave an aftermath of resentment against King Leopold for his supposed 'change of face' in refusing immediate Allied entry into Belgium after first allegedly agreeing to or even inviting it.

In London and Paris there was puzzled speculation over the episode. Various theories were bandied about, including the suggestion that the Belgian King and his government had invited the Allies in when invasion was immiment and then withdrawn the invitation when the threat seemed past. Daladier himself made no secret of his anger. On the 18th he protested to Le Tellier that the Belgians had not only alerted the French Army with virtually no warning, but in preventing it from entering Belgium they had upset the French General Staff's plan. In support of his complaint he cited the telephone message of the 14th from Admiral Keyes to Winston Churchill, the misinterpretation of which had sparked off the crisis.

Leopold's secret approach to the British Cabinet had gone badly awry. But nothing had occurred to weaken the determination of the King and his government not to depart from their policy of strict neutrality. They therefore felt bound to continue to refuse to hold open Staff talks with Britain and France and above all to reject any question of the Allies being invited into Belgium before a German attack. As a result they unanimously turned down a second British guarantee proposal, slightly modified but basically the same as the first, which was submitted to the King at Laeken by Keyes on January 17th. On that occasion Leopold cautioned the Admiral: 'The main point is not to start on the wrong foot. Remember.'

Daladier's *démarche* of the 15th to the Belgian Ambassador in Paris implying that the King had invited the Allies into Belgium had come as a bombshell to the Belgian Cabinet and, even after they had been disabused on this score, the fact remained that Leopold had been negotiating with the British Government without their knowledge. This 'put the King in an awkward position with his government', as Sir Roger noted. The King was naturally disturbed by the turn of events and forthwith called Spaak to Laeken. After giving him a full account of what had happened, Leopold sought Spaak's advice as to how best to deal with this awkward situation. Spaak loyally assured the King that he could leave it to him to enlighten and mollify his colleagues, and he was as good as his word. To strengthen his hand in establishing the truth of the matter with the Belgian Government, Spaak suggested that the King should obtain an explicit written report from Admiral Keyes. The Admiral complied, with a detailed record of what had been done and said on the 14th and 15th 'in case', as he put it, 'the matter is reopened by any future [Belgian] Government, not so well disposed to the King as the existing one'.

Leopold was particularly disturbed because the dangerous crisis had blown up as a direct result of leakage to the French concerning his London contacts. He was baffled as to how this had occurred. The

Admiral did his apologetic best to explain in a personal letter accompanying his report: 'It would seem that after Mr Chamberlain received my telephone message [of January 14th], the French Ambassador here was consulted . . . I must confess I was very angry when I heard of it . . .' Clearly Ironside's pledge of secrecy had been forgotten or ignored by the British Ministers in the sudden excitement, following Churchill's misinterpreted report to them of his telephone conversation with Keyes. The King's anger was not allayed by the knowledge of this breach of confidence on the part of the British, a breach which failed only by a hair's breadth to bring down upon Belgium a crushing military and aerial onslaught.

Later on, Lord Halifax requested Sir Roger to report to him at the Foreign Office. At meetings on February 21st and 22nd the Foreign Secretary questioned Keyes closely. In particular he wanted to know whether the King in asking the British Government to give the three undertakings which Sir Roger had communicated through Winston Churchill had it in mind to invite French and British troops into Belgium *before* the actual invasion of Belgium by Germany. He then showed Keyes the text of the message in question, as passed by Churchill to the War Cabinet on January 14th, of which the last paragraph ran: 'If these conditions were promised, Sir Roger thought that the King would be able to persuade his Ministers to invite French and British troops into Belgium at once.'

Keyes cast his thoughts back to the tense evening of January 13th when Belgium had seemed on the verge of invasion and the King, anxious and preoccupied, had drafted in his own hand the three suggested guarantee conditions. He believed that Leopold's motives had been the same as his father's. He was asking in advance for the same guarantees that had been given in the Great War by the Allies for the restoration of Belgium, which seemed once again about to suffer the devastation which would result from the fulfilment of her reciprocal promise to resist the German onslaught with all her strength. He was certain, he said, that it had not been King Leopold's intention to try to persuade his government to agree to invite Allied troops into Belgium *in advance* of a German invasion, in return for a favourable answer from the British. The King may have felt that if he obtained the offer of the guarantees, it would help his government Ministers to make up their minds to appeal immediately to the Allies for aid if Belgium was invaded.

Sir Roger had to admit to Lord Halifax, however, that as communicated to the War Cabinet the message had been open to misunderstanding. However, Keyes reminded the Foreign Minister of the critical situation prevailing at the time: the captured plans in possession of the Belgians, the large German forces massed on the Belgian border, the reliable information the King had received from Berlin that Belgium would be attacked next morning. It was these facts, the Admiral stressed,

Prince Albert (later King George VI), King Albert, Queen Elisabeth and Prince Leopold, before their triumphal re-entry into Brussels, 1918

King Leopold, Queen Elizabeth, Princess Lilian and the Duke of Edinburgh at Argenteuil, May 1966

Leopold on the beach at La Panne

Leopold, Charles and Comte de Grunne, 1915

Leopold at Eton, 1917

King Leopold's reunion with his Eton Housemaster, S. G. Lubbock, at the author's house, 1956

Albert I, George V, Admiral Keyes, Leopold
and British generals, 1918

The King and Queen aboard a submarine with
Sir Roger Keyes, C-in-C Portsmouth, 1930

Albert and Leopold, 1917

Captain Prince Leopold marching with the First Grenadiers, 1926

The wedding group, November 10th 1926

King Albert, Prince Leopold, Princess Astrid and her father, Prince Charles of Sweden

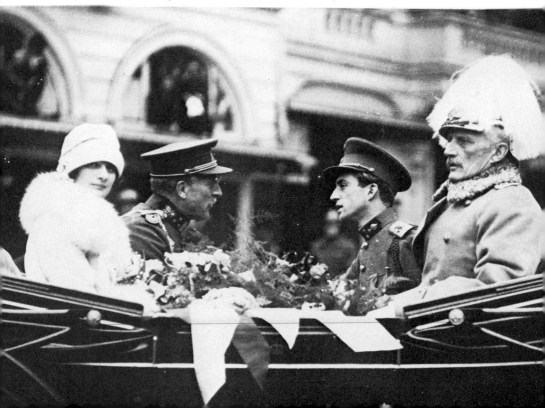

St Moritz, 1934
Prince Leopold playing in an
international golf championship

Climbing in the Dolomites, 1934

Prince Leopold, aviator, 1934

King Albert's funeral, February 1934

King Leopold swearing his Accession Oath, February 1934

Joyeuse entrée, Antwerp, 1935

Queen Astrid's funeral, September 1935

Queen Astrid with Josephine Charlotte
and Baudouin

Admiring the view, Folkestone, 1935

which led him to express the purely personal opinion that Belgium *might*, if the three undertakings were given, make an immediate appeal for assistance.

Lord Halifax now had the truth of the matter: there had never been any question of the King inviting the Allies into Belgium immediately. But the Foreign Secretary did not see fit to explain to the Admiral how and why a garbled form of Keyes' conversation with Churchill had come to be conveyed to the French, in breach of Ironside's pledge of secrecy.

In view of the confusion which had arisen, the Admiral suggested to Halifax that it would be best to await an invitation from the King before visiting Belgium again. Halifax concurred and for the duration of the *drôle de guerre* Leopold did not see Sir Roger again, Anglo-Belgian military liaison being maintained through Colonel Blake.

CHAPTER TWELVE

Neutrality Violations

'Failure at Trondheim! Stalemate at Narvik! Such in the first week in May were the only results we could show to the British nation, to our Allies, and to the neutral world . . .'

Winston Churchill,
The Second World War, Vol. 1

On November 30th 1939, the Russians, in further exploitation of the 'spheres of influence' allotted to them in the Baltic by the Nazi-Soviet Pact, bombed Helsinki and launched a heavy attack across the Finnish frontier, but this time the victims fought back so tenaciously that the Red Army was stopped in its tracks.

Russia's aggression against yet a fourth neutral country aroused the indignation and sympathy of the world and was thunderously denounced by Churchill. His praise of the Finns' brave resistance was well merited, but behind Churchill's eloquence there was a strain of enlightened self-interest. 'I welcomed this new and favourable breeze,' he wrote, 'as a means of achieving the major strategic advantage of cutting off the vital iron-ore supplies of Germany.'[87] Indeed, the British and French leadership both saw the Russo-Finnish war as an opportunity to gain control of the ice-free port of Narvik (from which Germany's vital ore supplies were shipped through the sanctuary of Norwegian territorial waters) and the Swedish iron mines at Gällivare, together with the rail link between them, on the pretext of sending 'volunteer' military aid to Finland.

Both the Allies and the Germans had already begun to develop plans to violate Norway's neutrality and occupy her territory, the first step on either side being taken by Churchill on September 19th 1939, when he persuaded the Cabinet to agree to his plan to stop the ore traffic by mining 'Norwegian territorial waters'. Then on February 5th 1940 at the Allied Supreme War Council meeting in Paris attended by Chamberlain and Churchill it was decided to land an Anglo-British force 'camouflaged as volunteers' at Narvik – ostensibly to aid Finland, but in fact to 'get control of the Gällivare ore-field'. A few days later Daladier urged that the *Altmark* incident should be used as a pretext for the 'immediate seizure of the Norwegian ports, by a sudden stroke'. In the previous month Gamelin had submitted plans to Daladier for the landing of an Allied force at Petsamo in northern Finland and the 'seizure of ports and airfields on the west coast of Norway'. Later he stated that one of his aims was 'to draw the enemy into a trap by provoking him to land in Norway'.

At meetings of the British War Cabinet in early March it was decided to launch the operation to push a force through Narvik and up the railway line to occupy the Swedish iron-fields on the 20th of that month – with only a small contingent actually proceeding on to Finland. On March 13th, however, the Finnish Government, weary of unfulfilled promises of Allied military assistance, concluded an armistice with the Russians – thus saving the Allies from the disastrous folly of going to war with Russia, but depriving them of their excuse for invading Norway and Sweden.

Commenting on the proposal made earlier by Churchill for 'a major offensive operation' designed to provoke the Germans into invading Scandinavia, Liddell Hart writes: 'He omitted any consideration of what the Scandinavian peoples would suffer from having their countries thus turned into a battleground'[88] – an observation which would apply equally well to the moves made by Churchill and the other Allied war leaders to invade, or to incite the Germans to invade Belgium and Holland. This was precisely what Gamelin was now proposing, for the French Commander-in-Chief had been swung from his policy of extreme caution to one of reckless bravado by the goading of Daladier, himself under political pressure to 'open up the war'. Accordingly, in March Gamelin sent Daladier a memorandum stating that the problem consisted of 'obliging the *Wehrmacht* to fight', one of his suggestions to achieve this aim being to 'incite the Germans to hurry things up and invade Belgium and Holland' by tightening the blockade and other means. Gamelin's long memorandum was in response to a directive from Daladier ordering him to prepare plans to hit at Russia, as well as Germany, but to keep all military operations as far away from French territory as possible.

Astonishingly, in view of France's great inferiority in military and air power, Gamelin's General Staff now proposed, in addition to the moves to provoke German reactions in Scandinavia and the Low Countries, a series of widespread and reckless operations designed to 'suffocate' or otherwise damage Germany. These included the bombardment of the Russian and Rumanian oil fields and refineries; penetration into the Caucasus; the blockading of the Danube and the Black Sea; landings at Salonica to occupy Greece; and even intervention in Persia and Afghanistan. But, ironically, on March 21st – while Daladier was studying Gamelin's plans – his government was overthrown, largely because the parliamentarians blamed him not only for his inaction against Germany, but for failing to take aggressive action of the kind proposed by the General Staff against Russia and other non-belligerents.

Daladier was succeeded as Premier by the pugnacious Paul Reynaud, who was thirsting for action to justify his promises that he would 'arouse, reassemble and direct all the sources of French energy to fight and conquer'. But Reynaud had got in by a majority of only one vote – and that, according to General de Gaulle's memoirs, the President of the Chamber regarded as suspect. Reynaud's government was received, as he himself records, 'without warmth, if not with hostility, by a part of the Centre, the Right and the Left', while friends and enemies alike urged him to resign rather than try to rule France with such a questionable mandate. But as Reynaud's friend Paul Baudouin put it, his 'love of a fight and the desire to remain in power had carried the day'.[89]

Reynaud's first action was to fly to London to urge the British leaders to wage war more energetically and in particular to act swiftly and ruthlessly in regard to Norway and Belgium. But the Allies' Scandinavian operation was fatally delayed until April 8th, too late to precede the German invasion of Norway and Denmark on the following day.

Thus, on the 8th, while the absurdly inadequate British landing force of five battalions and one brigade assigned to seize the four major Norwegian ports was being embarked in transports and cruisers (no air support was provided) and a British naval squadron was on its way to mine Norwegian waters, the German invasion fleet was steaming up the Norwegian coast. As soon as its presence was detected, the British troops were hurriedly disembarked and the cruisers sailed away from Rosyth with all their equipment. But this was only the first of a whole series of blunders, whereby every chance of defeating and driving out the Germans was thrown away, despite the immense superiority of Britain's sea power. It was Nelson who declared that 'the boldest measures are the safest', but in their Scandinavian campaign it was the Germans who put these principles into highly successful effect, while the British Admiralty remained bogged down in indecision and defensive-mindedness – for unfortunately the 'Safety First' school of Admirals was in charge.*

By nightfall on April 9th the whole of Denmark and all Norway's major ports and airfields were in German hands. On the 10th, Churchill wrote to Sir Dudley Pound, the First Sea Lord, 'we have been completely outwitted', although on the following day he told the House of Commons:

> In my view, which is shared by my skilled advisers, Herr Hitler has committed a grave strategic error . . . I cannot see any counter-advantage which he has gained . . . I feel that we are greatly advantaged by . . . the strategic blunder into which our mortal enemy has been provoked.

Although it is not within the scope of this work to follow the disastrous course of the Scandinavian campaign, the consequences of Hitler's

* For Churchill's description of how his 'great friend' Sir Roger Keyes passionately urged the Admiralty to take rapid, bold and decisive action against Trondheim, which could have routed the weak German forces there and changed the whole course of the campaign, see *The Gathering Storm*.

invasion of Norway and Denmark have a considerable relevance as far as the Belgian King and his people are concerned. It is clear, for example, from the analysis of the situation which von Hassell made in his diary, that if only the British had used their overwhelming sea power to rout the German Armada, as he and his fellow members of the opposition hoped they would, the humiliation for Hitler would have prevented him from launching his attack in the West and might well have triggered his downfall. Von Hassell also endorses the view that Mussolini's belligerence would have been much deflated if things had gone badly for Hitler in Norway – as they certainly would have done if the British Admiralty had acted in the Nelson tradition, or if Colonel Oster's timely warning giving the details, time and date of Operation *Weseruebung* to Major Sas and thus to the Chief of Dutch Intelligence had been passed on by him to Britain, France, Norway and Denmark, as requested by Oster.

Oster had made the painful decision to alert Hitler's intended victims and the Allies through Sas and thus endanger the lives of many German servicemen, because he and his fellow members of the opposition believed that the complete failure of Hitler's Scandinavian gamble would at least deter him from committing any further acts of aggression – and also increase their chances of overthrowing him. But when, due to the Allied leadership's belated, inept and feeble response to *Weseruebung*, Hitler's boldness was triumphantly vindicated and his venture was crowned with success, his reluctant generals and the anti-Nazi opposition lost all hope of stopping him and the attack on Belgium, Holland and France became inevitable.

Another aspect of Hitler's Scandinavian venture which had an important bearing on the future of King Leopold and his people was the conduct and fate of the two Royal victims of his aggression – King Haakon of Norway and King Christian of Denmark. In both cases Hitler planned to capture the Monarchs and their governments and allow them to continue in power under a mild form of supervision – and in the case of Christian he succeeded. In his memoirs von Weizsäcker explains how Hitler imposed different systems of rule on the countries he conquered, according to the situation he found when he took them over. The method depended upon whether or not the rulers and their administrations had fled, and ranged from the bestial regimes under SS Gauleiters that he imposed on the leaderless Poles, Norwegians and Dutch to the lighter rein which was used in Belgium, Denmark, France and the British Channel Isles, where some or all of their respected leaders remained on their native soil.

In the case of Denmark, the German Foreign Office and the *Wehrmacht* were allowed to arrange matters to the exclusion of Himmler's SS and so the Danes, according to von Weizsäcker 'managed to preserve the sovereignty of their country almost intact . . . and enjoy more liberty than any other country occupied by Hitler'. At 4 am on April 9th, the German

Minister, von Renthe-Fink, called on the Danish Foreign Minister, Dr Munch, and informed him that Germany was 'coming as a friend to prevent an imminent British attack on Norway and Denmark' and that unless German demands were accepted at once 'the consequences for Denmark would be disastrous'.

At 5.30 am the almost bloodless occupation of Denmark began and shortly after 7 am King Christian and his government capitulated. The King then received Renthe-Fink and General Kurt Himer, who thus described the scene:

> The seventy-year-old King appeared inwardly shattered, although he pre-
> served outward appearances perfectly and maintained absolute dignity during
> the audience. His whole body trembled. He declared that he and his govern-
> ment would do everything possible to keep peace and order in the country and
> to eliminate any friction between the German troops and the population. He
> wished to spare his country further misfortune and misery. General Himer
> replied that personally he very much regretted coming to the King on such a
> mission, but that he was only doing his duty as a soldier. It was Denmark's
> misfortune to be placed between the two great warring powers . . . Germany
> wished to prevent England plunging the country into war and devastation. We
> came as friends . . .

The Danish position was well defined by Christmas Mølle, the Danish elder statesman:

> No document of capitulation exists, nor is there any written agreement with
> Germany. Denmark chose to lay down her arms in the face of German threats
> to devastate her cities. The German Minister, speaking for the Reich Govern-
> ment, and the Commander-in-Chief, on behalf of the *Wehrmacht*, made the
> most solemn promises to respect our internal liberty. They also promised that
> our country would not be used as a base for attacking Britain, that we should
> regain our political independence, and that our territorial integrity would be
> respected . . .
>   In deciding not to defend herself, Denmark acquired a peculiar position
> amongst the countries invaded and enslaved by Germany. I want you to
> understand that the way we acted on April 9th 1940 made it possible for
> Denmark to keep her King, her Government and her Parliament, thus permit-
> ting internal administration to remain exclusively in Danish hands . . .

Since the Germans were able to secure the co-operation of the King and his Socialist government, their occupation of Denmark was not at all onerous until later in the war, when a change of policy was brought about as a result of a 'laconic' letter King Christian wrote to Hitler, to which the latter took offence.

The position in Denmark was analogous to that in the equally vulner-able British Channel Islands, after the latter had surrendered to the

Germans on June 30th 1940, on the orders of the Government. Here also the Germans imposed a moderate regime under a decent military Governor, Count von Schemettow, who remained in control until 1945, when he was removed after Nazi complaints that he was 'too magnanimous to the islanders'. (He survived, despite the Gestapo's displeasure, thanks to the protection of his uncle, General von Rundstedt.) Guernsey's (Attorney-General, Major Ambrose Sherwill, gave this advice to the islanders:

> We are, let us remember, under enemy occupation, and are treated with consideration. So long as we refrain from provocative behaviour and go quietly about our task, there is no reason to fear harm to anyone. May this occupation be a model to the world. On the one hand tolerance, courtesy and correctness on the part of the occupying forces, and, on the other, dignity, courtesy and exemplary behaviour on the part of the civilian population. Conformity – the strictest conformity – with orders and regulations issued by the German Commandant and civil authorities.

In consequence the islanders enjoyed a relatively easy existence with British 'Bobbies' doing the Germans' bidding and postmen collecting the mail from the traditional red pillar-boxes. Indeed, von Schemettow, according to English press reports, received a 'friendly welcome' from the islanders when he revisited Jersey as a tourist in 1963, being 'greeted warmly by the Jersey people, for they remember him as a kindly and humane man'.

Meanwhile in Oslo, shortly before 5 am on April 19th, the German Minister, Dr Curt Braeuer, presented the German ultimatum to the Norwegian Foreign Minister, Dr Koht. After a brief consultation with the Cabinet, Koht refused to surrender and declared that 'the war is already going on'. Indeed, at that same moment the sound of heavy gunfire and explosions could be heard as the guns and torpedoes of the forts guarding the Oslofiord, fifteen miles from the capital, halted the German invasion squadron.

The battlecruiser *Blücher*, which was now burning and sinking, was not only the fleet flagship, but carried the military commander, General Engelbrech, his Staff and a large body of troops, with their vehicles and equipment. The capital was thus given a few hours' reprieve and at about 7.30 am the Royal family and the Government, who otherwise would certainly have been captured, escaped by train to Hamar, seventy miles to the North. Braeuer now made an appeal to the Norwegian Government to open peace negotiations on the basis that Norway's political and territorial integrity would be respected, to which the Storting agreed. At the same time two companies of German paratroops under the command of the Air Attaché, Hauptmann Spiller, set off in commandeered buses, hoping to round up the King and his government. But they were repelled at a barricade set up by the Norwegians on the road and their leader was killed.

Despite this episode, King Haakon and Dr Koht received Dr Braeuer at Elverum on April 10th and there is little doubt that agreement would have been reached for the King and Government to remain in power, as in Denmark, had Hitler not insisted against Braeuer's advice that the traitor Major Quisling, who had already broadcast from Oslo claiming to be the Head of the Government and cancelling Norwegian mobilization, should be accepted as such. This was, of course, totally unacceptable, and negotiations collapsed. The King therefore placed himself at the head of his troops and made a fighting withdrawal to the North.

On June 20th, shortly after arriving in London with King Haakon, Dr Koht broadcast to the Norwegian people, now under Nazi rule, to explain why their King and Government had abandoned them to their fate. He told them how, after many dangerous adventures, towards the end of May they had made an approach to the German Government, through that of Sweden. Their proposal was that the King and the Government should be allowed to rule an unoccupied zone in Norway with 'a demarcation-line being drawn between the part of Norway then in German hands and the northern part of Norway still held by the Norwegians'.[91] (The proposed arrangement was similar to that subsequently accorded to France under the terms of her Armistice with Germany.) The King and Government naturally did not want to desert their homeland and their people, but after the Allies had evacuated Norway and having received no reply from the Germans to their *démarche*, they were persuaded* to allow themselves to be evacuated from the port of Tromsö, along with a number of Norwegian troops, by the cruiser *Devonshire* and came reluctantly to England, where they established their government-in-exile. For the Norwegians the consequences of their King's absence were that instead of a mild surveillance by the *Wehrmacht* and the Foreign Office, as in Denmark, or a moderate military governorship, as in Belgium and the Channel Islands, they suffered under the heel of the ruthless SS Gauleiter, Josef Terboven. But even worse would soon befall Holland, where the repellent Gauleiter Seyss-Inquart turned the screw – after Hitler had found the Dutch people leaderless, their government having fled and their Queen having been evacuated to England against her will. Although both these monarchs – like Leopold – regarded it as their duty to remain with their people to share their hardships and use their influence over Hitler to protect them against his occupation forces, Allied propaganda suppressed the fact that they had been unwilling to abandon their countries and people to their fate. Instead, flight to

---

* Sir Alexander Cadogan's diary entry for June 5th 1940 reads as follows: 'King of Norway sent tiresome message. Prepared to do a "Leopold". Drafted reply urging him not to be an ass or a traitor. Got it approved by W.S.C. and Neville.'

England was presented as the only honourable course of conduct for rulers whose countries Hitler had overrun. Paradoxically, however, neither King Christian and his Socialist government nor the Channel Islands' leaders were ever criticized for remaining in office during the German occupation of their national soil.

Here then were two distinct types of behaviour on the part of leaders of invaded territories. The first, passive acceptance of the *fait accompli* – with the result that the administration was left almost undisturbed and the people called upon to endure very little beyond the moral disadvantages of a foreign occupation. The second, flight, involuntary or otherwise – with great material and propaganda advantages for the British, for which the deserted peoples, leaderless and unprotected, were made to suffer grievously under the brutal SS regimes which Hitler always imposed under these circumstances.

The King of the Belgians was to provide a third and quite distinct type – for he never considered bowing to the Germans, fought at the head of his army until it could resist no longer, then elected to remain as a prisoner with his people in the hope – justified as it turned out – that his conduct would earn the respect of the conquerer and that his presence might help mitigate their hardships and provide a rallying point for national pride and resistance. Moreover, another favourable consequence of Leopold's decision to remain in captivity in Belgium was a decent and honourable military governor, instead of a Gauleiter. In contrast to the fate of the Poles, the Norwegians and the Dutch, this was of enormous advantage to the Belgian people.

CHAPTER THIRTEEN

An Ultimatum for Belgium

'Had discussion with Halifax, Strang and Makins about Chiefs of
Staff paper regarding going into Belgium without Belgian consent
and without waiting for German attack. Attended Cabinet 11.30
. . . Decided to tell Belgians that if Holland attacked and they
(Belgians) do nothing, we will nevertheless go in.
                                        Sir Alexander Cadogan's Diary,
                                                        April 12th 1940

'General agreement has been reached, that, as soon as the Germans enter Holland, a sort of ultimatum should be presented to
Belgium . . .'
                                        General Gamelin, April 15th 1940

On March 27th 1940, shortly after becoming Prime Minister of France,
Paul Reynaud flew to London to urge the Allied Supreme Council to
'open up the war' and to take ruthless action in regard to Norway and
Belgium. But he found that the British political leaders needed no urging,
for they had already abandoned all pretence of protecting the inviolability
of those and other neutral nations. Within a few weeks, on May 4th, Sir
Alexander Cadogan would be writing in his diary: 'Planning conquest of
Iceland for next week.'[92] (Concidentally the conquest of that small
neutral country by the Royal Navy and Royal Marines took place on May
10th, the same date as the German invasion of the Low Countries and
France.) Now that Churchill's friend, the equally bellicose Reynaud, was
ruling France, the decisions taken at that meeting will evoke no surprise.
Even the hitherto pacific and morally scrupulous Chamberlain was,
according to Churchill, by now 'much inclined to aggressive action'.[93]
Indeed, Chamberlain opened the meeting by strongly supporting Churchill and Reynaud's plans to violate Norway's neutrality and to break the
Allies' 1937 treaty guaranteeing Belgium's independence and integrity.

As Churchill records in his memoirs, it was decided at this Council to
launch the Norwegian operation on April 5th and that:

. . . if Germany invaded Belgium, the Allies would immediately move into that
country without waiting for a formal invitation; and that if Germany invaded
Holland and Belgium did not go to her assistance, the Allies should consider
themselves free to enter Belgium, for the purpose of helping Holland.[94]

Quite apart from the gross impropriety of this decision, it is ironical that just as the Germans had completely redesigned their *Fall Gelb*, following the Belgians' capture of the earlier version, to draw the French and British armies as far as possible into Belgium and thus facilitate their encirclement by von Rundstedt's massed Panzers, the Allies were doing their utmost to effect an advance into the trap which the Germans had prepared for them.

On the morning of April 9th, a few hours after the German invasion of Norway and Denmark forestalled the Allies' plans to land their own forces, Reynaud presided over a meeting of the French War Committee in Paris. It was unanimously decided to seize what they considered to be a favourable moment to move into Belgium. Gamelin announced that he was *partisan de l'action en Belgique*: he believed that the diversion of the *Luftwaffe* to Norway was of critical importance and declared himself, with General Georges' agreement, ready to undertake the operation. '*Les malheureux*,' writes Benoist-Méchin, 'they did not realize that this was exactly what the enemy wanted . . . In short, the French Army, which was designed for positional warfare, wanted to undertake of its own volition a war of movement . . .'[95] When the French Air Chiefs protested against the decision to enter Belgium because of the Germans' overwhelming air superiority, Gamelin told them that it was not too late to take that into consideration since formal requests to allow the entry of the French and British Armies were already on their way to the Belgian Government. The Committee finally decided that if the Belgian reply was negative, the Allies 'would avoid provoking German reactions before our Air Force is ready'

In 1942 at the Riom trials and in his voluminous memoirs, Reynaud claimed that in Norway he had only applied his predecessor's plans and that he had been opposed both to this operation and to the entry of Allied troops to Belgium, although Gamelin and France's other military and political leaders later affirmed that they had never heard him say so at the time. 'It would have been much better,' Benoist-Méchin continues, 'if instead of saying afterwards that he had disapproved of these operations, he had opposed them at the time.' 'Why,' asks Méchin, 'when he knew better than anyone the extent of our unpreparedness . . . did he hurl himself headlong into these hazardous adventures . . . ?'

It sprang from his impatient temperament . . . He had presented himself as a man of energy and decision . . . He had scourged Daladier's waiting policy too violently not to take the opposite of his temporizing action. It was necessary for him to accelerate the rhythm of events and pass rapidly from a cold war to a hot one if he wanted to maintain his reputation . . . No more '*drôle de guerre*' . . . He would lead France to combat whatever the consequences . . . To keep himself in the saddle and maintain the power that a precarious majority had put in his hands, he would not hesitate to risk the whole life of the country on one single throw of the dice . . .[96]

One of the many who advised Reynaud that it would be disastrous to try to rule France and wage energetic war with such a divided, weak and unrepresentative ministry was Paul Baudouin, who became – after advising Reynaud to resign – his *confidant* as Secretary of his War Cabinet and an Under Secretary of State. Baudouin remained in this key position until Reynaud handed over the premiership to Marshal Pétain on June 16th 1940. He then served as Foreign Minister until January, 1941. The chronicle of events and the character sketch of Reynaud in Baudouin's *Private Diaries* are therefore of particular interest. After describing the 'almost insolent incisiveness' of Reynaud's remarks, his 'preference for fighting alone', his 'contempt for Parliamentary traditions' and his 'consuming ambition, with frequent surrenders to his faults', Baudouin puts his fingers on a 'powerful and permanent' factor behind Reynaud's drive to the top of the political ladder and his resolve to cling to that position of power. This was the determination of his wealthy mistress, the Countess Hélène de Portes, 'to see him head of the Government'. Baudouin describes this 'impatient, impulsive and insatiable' woman, without exaggeration, as 'the controller of the Cabinet'.[97] An example of the manner in which France was governed during the last weeks of the Third Republic has been given by Pierre Lazareff, the editor of *Paris Soir*. At the end of April Lazareff wanted to see Reynaud about an urgent matter and telephoned for an appointment, to find the Countess on the line. She told him that Reynaud was in bed with *la grippe*. '*We* are horribly busy, my dear,' she said. 'But come over anyway.' When Lazareff arrived, he recounts:

> I found Hélène de Portes sitting behind Paul Reynaud's desk, surrounded by generals, high officials, parliamentarians and functionaries, she was presiding over a Council. She did most of the talking, speaking rapidly in a peremptory tone, advising and giving orders . . .

When Lazareff asked if he could see the Premier alone the Countess replied: 'No, he is ill. I'm doing my best to replace him.' A moment later she left the room to confer with Reynaud. As soon as the door was shut, Lazareff recalls, everyone started to curse her for trying to run the government. They blamed her and the Marquise de Crussol – Daladier's equally domineering and interfering mistress, with whom she was at daggers drawn – for the fact that the two principal Ministers of France (Daladier had become Defence Minister in Reynaud's cabinet) were by now barely on speaking terms. While the Countess was out of the council chamber, one of the officials described how these two rich and titled rivals had recently 'nearly come to blows'.[98]

Thus, in the last few weeks before the *Blitzkrieg* struck and the collapse of France, her fate was in the hands of Reynaud and his *bête noire*, Daladier, who – as Georges Mandel, the Minister of the Interior, later told General Spears – was being 'egged on' in his opposition to the Premier 'by that infernal woman who is pursuing her harridan quarrel with Madame de Portes over the corpse of France'. Spears further comments:

> The rift between Reynaud and Daladier was known to be widening, the latter not even keeping the former informed on current military events. Reynaud, we were told, was reduced to getting his war news from the communiqués. The Marquise backing the one and the Comtesse backing the other were having a grand time, all claws out and no holds barred. On his side, Reynaud was obviously determined to get rid of Gamelin, and preparing to face the ministerial crisis which would inevitably follow.[99]

On the afternoon of April 9th, following their decision to invade Belgium by force of arms if not invited in, Reynaud and Daladier, accompanied by Admiral Darlan, the head of the French Navy, flew to London for a meeting of the Supreme War Council. The Council ratified the morning's decisions, sending instructions immediately to the British and French Ambassadors in Brussels and to Hautcoeur to insist that the Allied armies should forthwith be allowed to march into Belgium.

In his memoirs, Gamelin describes another decision taken at this Council 'by both our Governments . . . that an ultimatum to Belgium should be prepared and given to both our Ambassadors in Brussels, to be used if circumstances arose'. On April 14th General Georges wrote to Gamelin: 'May we conclude that, as soon as we are aware that Holland has been invaded, the Commander-in-Chief North-East Front will be enabled *ipso facto* to give the order to the Franco-British forces to advance into Belgium?' To this Gamelin replied: '. . . General agreement has been reached that, as soon as the Germans enter Holland, a sort of ultimatum will be presented to Belgium. But she would only be given a short time to reply.'[100] Although Gamelin had shown no scruples about 'inciting' the Germans to invade Norway and Belgium, he seems to have been perturbed by the prospect of having to order the Allied armies to invade the latter country, for he immediately sent a private warning to the Belgian Defence Minister, General Denis. This was an honourable gesture, but served only to confirm the suspicions the Belgians already harboured about France's covetous attitude towards their territory. Denis replied that if Holland were invaded, Belgium would certainly invite the Allies in.

The upshot was that until the Allies decided, a few days later, to dispense with their ultimatum and march into Belgium without warning or discussion, the British and French Ambassadors were carrying round with them a kind of time-bomb with a short-delay fuse. Meanwhile, in accordance with the Allied Council's directive, the French and British diplomatic representatives in Brussels roused Spaak just after midnight on April 10th and – after informing him that an attack on Belgium was imminent, perhaps within the next few days, and that maps of Belgium and Holland had been distributed to the troops on the German frontier – demanded that the Franco-British forces should be allowed to enter Belgium immediately.

At 10.30 am Spaak summoned a ministerial meeting. Its unanimous rejection of the Allies' demands was endorsed by a full Cabinet at 11 am and ratified by the King. It is to be noted that it was the Cabinet, not the King, who first agreed on rejection. As there had been a press leak, the Belgian radio broadcast a statement at 1 pm: '*Le gouvernement a été une fois de plus unanime dans sa volonté de persévérer fermement dans la politique d'indépendance et de neutralité qu'il a suivie depuis le début du conflit européen.*'* In those words there is not the least hint of a Royal *politique personnelle*.

The Belgian Government's refusal to allow the Allied armies entry infuriated Churchill and Reynaud and further prejudiced them against that country and her King. As Paul Baudouin points out in his book, Reynaud would particularly have welcomed such a spectacular coup in order to consolidate his shaky ministry. The result was the Allied leaders' decision taken at their Supreme Council Meeting in Paris on April 22nd (as Churchill records in his memoirs with some satisfaction) 'that the Allied armies should at once advance into Belgium, without further approaches to the Belgian Government' – and thus without even delivering the ultimatum which they had prepared, 'in the event that Germany invaded Holland'.[101] Brian Bond comments as follows:

> Thus the frustrations of the Phoney War, humiliating failure in Norway, and the reluctance of small nations to offer themselves as a battlefield caused the Allies to adopt a highly questionable policy towards Belgium. Although the eventual result was bad enough, it was a small mercy that Hitler attacked Holland and Belgium simultaneously, otherwise there might have ensued the unedifying spectacle of the Allies fighting their way through the territory of one small neutral country in an effort to bring assistance to another.[102]

Winston Churchill had revealed his attitude to the small neutral nations who were resisting the Allies' attempts to embroil them in hostilities, in a radio broadcast three weeks before. On March 30th he referred to the

---

* As Pierlot very reasonably pointed out in the Senate on April 16th, after eight months of war Britain, France and Germany still kept their forces and their territories intact, but from the very first day of hostilities Belgium would be completely ravaged.

neutral countries as 'frightened' and 'sitting on the fence'. 'They bow humbly in fear to German threats of violence, comforting themselves meanwhile with the thought that the Allies will win . . . each one of them hopes that if he feeds the crocodile enough, the crocodile will eat him last . . .' This broadcast caused grave offence to the neutral countries, particularly the Belgians, whose rearmament effort had been relatively so much greater than that of France and Britain. The true attitude of the Belgian people was demonstrated a few days after their rejection of the Allies' demands when Spaak, to prolonged applause from all parts of the Chamber except the Communist benches, declared:[i]

The Belgian people may be sure that the Government will accept no suggestion tending to make it abandon the course which it has chosen, a choice approved by the vast majority of the country . . .

We too, in the Government, have our preferences and our friendships, but long before our friendships stands our duty . . . The country wants peace, the country wants neutrality. If the necessity arises, the country will do its duty all the better for the complete conviction that its leaders have done all in their power to preserve both.

His sentiments were echoed by *Le Peuple*, the official organ of the Socialist Party:

The Belgians are all resolved, with no exceptions, Flemings and Walloons alike, to reply to an attack when it comes, to appeal to their guarantors when the time comes – but not before . . . except for an infinitesimal minority, to whom the Allied newspapers lend far too attentive an ear, no one in Belgium wants preventative intervention. The population does not want it, because it knows that the whole country would then become a battlefield.

The *Soir*, a 'middle of the road' newspaper, but which adopted an anti-Leopold stance after the war, had this to say:

It is certainly in our interests to desire that the war may end one way rather than another, but we bear not the least responsibility for its origins and any policy tending to place us against our will in the front line would be profoundly unjust. If the Allies were to bring us to this pass, they would at one blow lose millions of ardent supporters.

On April 17th Belgium's national solidarity was expressed dramatically during a debate in the Senate, when a vote on the policy of independence was almost unanimous – 131 in favour, with three Communists against and two abstentions. The mood of the House and the people was summed up in a particularly moving way by a Walloon Socialist Senator, François André: 'I am the more qualified to say what I think of this policy, in that I was opposed to it at the beginning. Confusing independence with neutrality, I told myself that neutrality was something shady and cowardly . . . I have realized that I was mistaken, and for the past eight months I have felt sure that our young King was right and, old Republican as I am, I thank him.' The Government would not have been able to carry the Nation with it on any other policy, even if it had wanted to.

Time was now running out. As Spaak puts it in his memoirs, '*d'incident en incident, de péripétie, d'alerte en alerte, nous allions vers la guerre*'. On May 4th the Papal Nuncio urgently requested an audience with Leopold and told him that the Vatican believed an invasion of Belgium to be imminent. Next day the Pope himself warned Prince Umberto and Princess Marie-José, and the latter passed the word on to Leopold. The Pope had been given full details of Germany's war plans and intentions by Josef Müller, an agent of the German opposition sent by Admiral Canaris. The Pope also warned the Allies of the impending offensive.[103] Ciano was silent, because this time he had been kept in ignorance by the Germans. On the 7th Baron van Harixma, the Dutch Minister in Brussels, told the Government that 'according to the German informer of their Berlin Legation' (Colonel Oster) the invasion might take place any day. On the 9th Oster told his friend Major Sas: 'This time there's no doubt. That pig [Hitler] has just left for the Western Front. It means a general offensive.' By 9 pm the message had reached Brussels, where the staff of the German Embassy had already burned their papers.

As a constitutional monarch, Leopold could only employ the human material made available by Belgium's political party system. Yet it is not too much to claim that when the supreme test came, it was thanks to the policy which he had championed since 1936 that Belgium was more united and better armed than she had ever been in her history. The King's resolution, courage and foresight had gained precious time for the Allies to remedy their appalling military unpreparedness, but it was not his fault that they had failed to take much advantage of it. Moreover his robust stand had deterred Hitler and postponed his onslaught on the West – although it did not prevent it. Only a similarly dynamic policy and build-up of armed strength on the part of the Allies could have done that.

The Spirit of Irony, looking down on the cockpit of Europe, must have observed during these days one episode very much to its liking. Pierlot, it will be recalled, tried to resign on April 25th on the trivial issue of linguistic reform and only remained in office because Leopold appealed to him not to abandon his responsibilities. The King's action was widely praised, a special tribute being paid in the *Vingtième Siècle* by William Ugueux – another who would later turn and vilify his Sovereign:

One might have thought that the tragedy of 1914 . . . had exhausted the reasons for the gratitude which we owe to our Sovereigns. Yet the new reign of Leopold

III has already plunged the Nation so deeply into a debt of gratitude that the Belgians will never be able to pay it off.

This time as before, in foreign affairs or in internal disputes alike, it is from our Sovereign that has come the truly wise and truly Belgian solution, expressed with as much discretion as decision . . . For a long time to come we shall turn back to the words of yesterday's letter . . . They thrust back into the darkness the pettiness and bickering of those always incomprehensible politicians . . .

Not to be outdone, Pierlot made a speech at Charleroi on May 5th in which he stated: 'In these circumstances, as at other decisive periods in our history, the monarchy's judgment has been both accurate and timely. That judgment is a sure guide, with its sense of the permanent interests of the Nation, and the experience which, handed down from father to son, has enabled our Kings to draw upon so strong a tradition . . .' Within a few weeks the Prime Minister would be playing a very different tune.

CHAPTER FOURTEEN

*Blitzkrieg**

> 'This considerable success has been achieved thanks to the exemplary action of the *Luftwaffe*. For all the bravery and offensive power of our ground forces could only have been fully exerted in the space protected by our air power.'
>
> Communiqué issued by the
> German High Command, June 1940

War burst on Belgium in the tranquil early dawn of Friday May 10th, when Hitler's ground and air forces invaded Holland, Belgium and Luxembourg in a concerted assault stretching from the North Sea to the Moselle. Although Germany made no declaration of war, the Belgians, thanks to all the warnings they had received and their excellent Intelligence Service, were (unlike the British and French, who had discounted all such reports) in a state of full alert when the blow was struck. Nevertheless, the Germans were able to achieve three spectacular successes that day: the destruction of the best part of the Belgian Air Force on the ground, the capture by glider-borne shock troops of three of the Albert Canal bridges and their audacious airborne assault on the linchpin of the Belgian defence system, the vast stronghold of Eben-Emael.

The tribute quoted above, which was paid by the German Army to the *Luftwaffe* after they had, acting in unison, conquered the Netherlands and Belgium, routed the French Armies at Sedan and driven the British Expeditionary Force into the sea, was well merited. Without the *Luftwaffe*'s legions of fighters and flak batteries which protected the ground forces from airborne attack, without the swarms of Stuka dive-bombers to blast a path for the Panzers and without the landing of thousands of parachute and glider-borne troops to seize vital bridges and strong-points these German victories could not have been achieved so rapidly and decisively.

Supporting the ground forces in their assault on Belgium were the two Air Fleets of Kesselring and Sperrle, comprising about 3,700 planes. An overwhelming force of fighters, bombers and reconnaissance aircraft was thus at the disposal of the military commanders on the ground and the Stukas, protected by fighters, could be used by them as super-heavy and rapidly deployed artillery. So efficient and direct were their communica-

* See map page 470

162

tions that within minutes of a radio call from the military, groups of Stukas would come screaming down upon their objectives with deadly accuracy, thus clearing the way for an immediate penetration by tanks and infantry.

The situation was very different on the Allied side, for neither the French Air Force nor the RAF had established any form of close collaboration between their air and ground forces like that employed with such deadly effect by the Germans. Indeed, as Major Ellis records, the RAF was 'neither organized nor equipped, nor indeed was it trained, except in some small "army co-operation elements" for close collaboration in a moving battle'. Thus, while the German field commanders down to the lowest level were in constant and direct communication with their supporting air formations, there were no similar links on the British and French side and requests for air support from the military had to go through the most complicated channels – even through London at a later stage of the batle – entailing long delays which frustrated their whole purpose.*

The British Army and the Royal Navy would continue to suffer throughout World War II from the Air Ministry's policy of minimal involvement in the activities of the other Services and its doctrinal obsession that wars could be won by strategic bombing alone. Thus, in May 1940 it rejected all the desperate appeals which were made for the RAF's heavy-bomber force to attack the highly vulnerable but fleeting targets presented by the German Army's close-packed columns as they poured into Holland, Belgium and France. The anguish felt in Allied military circles as the reports came in of the RAF's nightly bombing of such targets as Hamm and Essen, hundreds of miles inside Germany, instead of the endless and rapidly encroaching columns of tanks, guns and troops, is the recurrent theme in many chronicles of the campaign.†

Another dire result of the Air Ministry's policies was that the RAF aircrews, whose fighting spirit was of the highest, were at a grave disadvantage not only from the lack of co-ordination with the military, but because their aircraft were greatly outnumbered by and inferior to those of the Germans. Indeed, the Hurricane was no match for the Messerschmitt 109, the Blenheim light-bomber was slow and vulnerable, and the Battle single-engined bomber was an obsolete death trap. As for the *Armée de l'Air* it was, as we have seen, so ill-equipped and low in morale that its Chief, General Vuillemin, had predicted that it would be wiped out within a fortnight of the outbreak of hostilities.

The morale of the Belgian Air Force was high – but, for the reasons given earlier, it possessed few modern aircraft and was not a strong arm. Moreover, the fact that the Germans attacked Belgium without a declaration of war enabled the *Luftwaffe* to bomb her airfields with impunity. An overwhelming force of German bombers had fallen upon every airfield in

* See Appendix IV.
† See, for example, *The Diary of a Staff Officer*.

Belgium at first light, and during the day the *Luftwaffe* launched seventy-five further strikes on them. By nightfall on May 10th the Belgians had lost over half their total fighting strength. All nine of their Hurricanes and the majority of their Gloster Gladiators were destroyed during the day. Nevertheless, as Robert Jackson records, 'the Belgians fought on tenaciously with their surviving obsolescent equipment' against the modern aircraft of the *Luftwaffe*, which enjoyed complete mastery of the air. 'By May 14th, the Belgian Air Force had to all intents and purposes ceased to exist, its bases were graveyards of wrecked aircraft, caught on the ground between sorties. By May 16th, it was all over – only nine elderly biplanes remained and these were ordered to withdraw to France.'[104]

The Belgians had been least inclined, perhaps, of all the Western nations to underestimate the potential power and rapidity of an offensive by the German Army – as the King had demonstrated – but what neither he nor his advisers had expected was the impotence of the French and British Air Forces against the *Luftwaffe* and their failure to protect the Belgian Army and its key positions from the overwhelming assaults which were launched upon them by swarms of tanks, dive-bombers and airborne shock troops. Moreover, they could have no preconception of the novel and audacious methods for seizing vital bridges and overcoming the most powerful fortifications from the air which the Germans were able to execute with such devastating success thanks to their unchallenged air superiority.

At the start of the battle the Belgian Army had twenty-two divisions. Of these, ten were in the defensive positions along the Albert Canal and the Meuse and at the fortified bases of Antwerp, Liège and Namur. Two manned the frontier canals in the North and two were east of the Meuse in Belgian Luxembourg. In the rear, one division stood on the main defence position, the K-W Line, between Antwerp and Louvain, while the remainder were in reserve. The divisions in the Albert Canal-Meuse-Liège-Namur positions – Belgium's first line of defence – had a vital initial function to perform. Within the framework of Gamelin's Plan D the Belgians were expected to withstand the full shock of the German onslaught and hold the line until advancing Allied troops had occupied their pre-arranged sectors on the K-W Line in their rear. Only then would the Belgians retire to their own allotted sector of that line, between Antwerp and Louvain, filling the gap between the French Seventh Army in the North and the BEF on their right. In the South, at the outlets of the Ardennes forests, the Chasseurs Ardennais had a delaying role, which they performed with courage and effect.

As the map on page 470 shows, Belgium's first line of defence, or delaying position, ran north-eastwards along the Meuse from Givet, where it flows out of France, through the fortified towns of Namur and Liège to the point where it joins the Albert Canal. Since the Meuse runs through the Dutch town of Maastricht and its surrounding territory in this sector, the Albert Canal, which was completed two years previously, was built to bypass this stretch of the river. The Belgian defence line therefore followed the Albert Canal north and north-westwards to its outlet, the great fortified port of Antwerp. Although the broad and deep Albert Canal constituted a formidable obstacle to a German invasion, in the areas of Liège and Maastricht it hugged the Belgian frontier with Holland so closely that no outposts were possible.

The considerable strengthening of Belgium's defences and fortifications in the Liège and Namur area* had obviously turned the Germans' thoughts to making their main thrust further north near Maastricht, which involved crossing the narrow 'appendix' of Dutch territory in violation of Holland's neutrality and forcing a crossing of the Albert Canal at a point fifty-five miles due east of Brussels. The crucial importance to the Belgians of the Dutch bridges spanning the Meuse (known by them as the Maas) at Maastricht and giving access to the roads leading to the three great Belgian bridges over the Albert Canal needs no emphasis. Since the outbreak of war all these bridges had been mined and Belgian and Dutch Sappers had been constantly manning the concrete casemates, ready to explode the charges upon the approach of the German invaders.

In order to command these vital crossing-points over the Albert Canal, the Belgians had built at a cost of over one million pounds the fortress of Eben-Emael – the largest and what was regarded as one of the most impregnable strong points in the world. It embodied all the lessons learned from the great sieges of the 1914 war, particularly that of Verdun, and included a superstructure proof against the heaviest bombs then in service. Eben-Emael measured 1,000 yards long and 700 yards wide and on its north flank it ended in a sheer 130 foot drop into the canal. Its other flanks were protected by anti-tank ditches and obstacles and a maze of barbed wire, covered by blockhouses mounting searchlights, heavy machine-guns and anti-tank weapons. Inside the perimeter the heavily-reinforced concrete structure bristled with guns – sixteen of 75 mm calibre and two of 120 mm in armour-plated turrets, which covered every inch of ground with their field of fire.

Eben-Emael was indeed invulnerable to every form of attack except the unprecedented method used by the Germans. Its designers had no more allowed for a landing on the roof of the fortress by troop-carrying gliders, than had the constructors of battleships anticipated boarding

---

* When the Germans invaded Belgium in 1914 (without violating Dutch territory) they had been able to cross the Meuse north of Visé without too long a delay, because the ring of Liège forts had not been completed. Accordingly, under the stimulus of King Albert and King Leopold, the Belgians had at great cost modernized all the existing fortresses ringing Liège and Namur, and built the three great modern forts of Neufchâteau, Battice and Pépinster, to complete a system designed to guard against a similar move and bar the eastern approaches to Liège.

parties from rowing boats. In order to overcome this formidable obstacle to their advance and capture the three Belgian bridges over the Albert Canal, the Germans had formed an élite task force known as 'Assault Detachment Koch'.* These 424 'specialists' (including pilots) were carried in forty-two heavy assault gliders, towed by Junkers 52 transport planes. The men – all young volunteers – had been training for six months with full-scale models of their objectives until each man had learned how to do his individual task blindfold.† Moreover, they knew that the whole success of the German invasion of Belgium depended on their achieving their objectives.

The four Storm Groups – 'Granite', 'Concrete', 'Steel' and 'Iron' – took off at 03.25 am from an airfield near Cologne. Shortly after four o'clock the Ju 52s released their forty gliders at a height of 7000 feet twenty miles from their objectives and began to drop dummy parachutists festooned with fire-crackers to confuse the defenders. Groups of ten gliders landed near the western end of each of the three Albert Canal bridges carrying the main roads from Maastricht into Belgium – Vroenhoven, Veldwezelt and Briegden. The fourth group landed on top of Eben-Emael itself. As the gliders landed with Teutonic efficiency exactly on schedule, ten minutes before the zero hour of 5.35 am, each disgorged nine men, heavily armed with sub-machine guns, flame-throwers, grenades and explosives. The three groups assigned to the Albert Canal bridges at once attacked the rear of the casemates in which the Belgian sappers stood ready for an assault from the East. At Canne, a mile north of Eben-Emael, the German attack failed and the bridge was destroyed by a switch inside the fort. Tragically, however, at Vroenhoven and Veldwezelt the Germans were able to surprise and wipe out the sappers before they could throw the demolition switches.

At Briegden the charges failed to explode and the bridge remained intact – for a time – the officer responsible for its demolition being found shot at his post. As dawn broke, the Germans launched the greatest bombing attack ever delivered upon the Belgian defenders of the Albert Canal bridgehead. All 400 Junkers 87 Stukas of VIII *Fliegerkorps* were used to pound this restricted area. Not only was it soon reduced to rubble by the rain of 1000-pound bombs, but the survivors of this devastating onslaught, even those protected by dug-outs and blockhouses, were stunned and concussed. In addition, the military telephone exchange and many underground cables were destroyed, disrupting communications, so that outlying posts remained without orders.

* Hitler took a personal interest and helped in the planning of the surprise capture of the Belgian and Dutch bridges and strong points, in the teeth of his High Command's scepticism and doubts about the feasibility of these *coups*.
† A Belgian lieutenant and cartographer, Joseph Dombret, had treacherously sold the plans of Eben-Emael and other fortresses to the Germans before being arrested and sentenced in 1939. See German plan on page 474.

When, through the fog and tumult of battle, the appalling news that the three vital Belgian bridges were still intact reached the general commanding the Belgian 7th Division, which was drawn up facing the Albert Canal, he ordered their immediate destruction. A first attempt, made by a strong detachment, was beaten back. But another succeeded in destroying the Briegden bridge, through the heroism and self-sacrifice of Major Tillot, who filled a haversack with explosives and set off alone under enemy fire with a Bickford fuse and a box of matches. The bridge was destroyed, but Tillot was never seen again. Yet the bridges at Vroenhoven and Veldwezelt remained in German hands despite further desperate Belgian counter-attacks.

Meanwhile, the seventy-eight assault pioneers of Storm Group 'Granite' were swarming all over the upperworks of Fort Eben-Emael. They had brought with them 2½ tons of a new and powerful type of 'hollow-charge' explosive which blew large holes in the fort's armoured gun turrets and spread flame and choking gas within. Smoke-bombs were also thrown down the ventilators and flame-throwers inserted at the gun ports and other openings, driving out or incinerating the guns' crews. Soon the Germans were in possession of the fort's upper galleries and the whole installation was operationally blind. As a desperate measure the commander of Eben-Emael telephoned neighbouring forts and artillery batteries requesting them to lay a barrage on the upper-works of the fortress in order to dislodge his tormentors. This forced the attackers to take cover in the shattered bunkers. For hour after hour the battle raged, with the Germans receiving excellent support both from paratroops dropped from transport planes and from Stuka dive bombers there being no Allied fighters on the scene to oppose these highly vulnerable aircraft.

While the German airborne troops were desperately holding out at the two Albert Canal bridges and on the superstructure of Eben-Emael, a strong force of specially trained infantry and combat engineers was racing to their relief across the Maastricht Appendix. The Germans had used a variety of tactics in their attempts to seize the Dutch bridges before they could be blown up. Strong sabotage units of German shock troops had infiltrated across the frontier near Roermond and Maastricht some hours before zero hour with this object. The Maeseyck bridge was nearly taken at daybreak by a German detachment which, according to the German XI Corps diary, drove captured Dutch soldiers along in front of them 'to provide cover against enemy fire'. Happily this ignoble stratagem failed. But another unit succeeded in preventing the destruction of the main Maastricht bridge, thus opening the way for ground forces to reach the Belgian bridges over the Albert Canal.

The Germans also forced a crossing of the Maas in rubber boats, and by mid-afternoon on May 10th the vanguard reached the two Albert Canal bridges and relieved the hard-pressed German airborne defenders. But it was not until the morning of May 11th that the German relieving force succeeded in crossing the Albert Canal – after finding the bridge at Canne destroyed – and reinforced the exhausted assault pioneers on the superstructure of Eben-Emael.

After the capitulation of the Belgian Army fanciful stories were published by the Allied press seeking to explain the fall of Eben-Emael[j] and the 'surrender' of the Albert Canal bridges, many of them alleging that these losses were due to 'Belgian treachery' and had actually caused the French military catastrophe at Sedan and the subsequent encirclement of the Northern Armies. Professor Cammaerts gives an example, in *The Prisoner at Laeken*, describing how one well known author proclaimed that the 'non-destruction' of the 'Maastricht bridge' through 'Belgian folly or treachery' was to blame for the defeat of the French armies on the Meuse and all the military disasters which followed.[105] But he remained to the last doubtful about the exact location of the offending bridge. Once it appeared as 'in front of Maastricht', on another occasion as 'above that town' and on yet a third as 'probably near Visé', the only consistency in his accounts being the alleged Belgian responsibility for its non-destruction. Had he checked his facts he would have found that the Maastricht bridge is in Holland, that its defence was never the responsibility of the Belgian forces and that the capture of the Dutch and Belgian bridges had no bearing on the *débâcle* on French territory far to the south.

The truth is that none of these bridges was 'surrendered'. Their destruction was certainly prevented through treachery, but the treachery was that of the Germans who, without a declaration of war and in some cases disguised as Dutch soldiers or civilians, surprised and liquidated the bridgehead guards at their posts. Only some of the desperate ruses employed by the Germans succeeded, to be exploited to the full, but the unconventional methods used by the long-rehearsed 'specialists', coupled with the successes they achieved behind the lines, provoked fantastic accounts of the omnipresence of a mythical Belgian fifth column, which in turn gave rise to spy mania, parachutist-phobia and distrust, suspicion and misunderstandings between the Allies. Contemporary stories published in all seriousness about German soldiers disguised as nuns and priests make strange reading today, but they were believed at the time, often with fatal consequences for innocent civilians. These stories appeared in 'responsible' newspapers and the 'nun' story was given credibility in Lord Gort's *Despatches*.

At 11.30 on the morning of the 10th, the Belgian Air Force attempted to destroy the three intact bridges over the Albert Canal with the only bombers that had survived the dawn attacks – nine Fairey Battles, obsolete single-engined planes carrying 100-pound bombs, operating from Aeltre. The Belgian pilots pressed home their suicidal attacks with the greatest heroism in the face of murderous fire, on the bridges at Veldwezelt, Vroenhoven and Briegden, but six were shot down by the intense flak which surrounded the bridges and the small bombs of the remaining three failed to do any vital damage. However, as the War Diary of the German XVI Corps for the 11th records 'considerable delays' resulted from these attacks.

As soon as Belgian GQG learned that the bridges over the Maas and the Albert Canal had been captured by the Germans, they began to make a series of desperate appeals to the French and British Military Missions for the *Armeé de l'Air* and the Royal Air Force to destroy them. But there was no response until the third day of conflict, for the reasons given above and because the RAF was reluctant to commit its slow and vulnerable light-bombers to battle in the face of the Germans' overwhelming air superiority. And when it came, the RAF's reaction, although supremely gallant, was too little and too late to be effective. Indeed, as Van Overstraeten noted on the afternoon of May 11th:

> The British Mission announce that in response to our requests the RAF is to undertake powerful action to clear the Maastricht region. Too late! The absence of Allied bomber aircraft deprived us of the most powerful element on which we relied to delay, disperse and demoralize the enemy's advancing columns. Instead of being able to constrain the enemy by a costly delaying action, our troops are obliged to carry out a hurried retreat under unfavourable conditions of complete domination by the enemy's mechanized forces and mastery of the air.[106]

With only a handful of aircraft left to the Belgian Air Force and no air protection or support forthcoming from either the British or French Air Forces, it is hardly surprising that the Germans were able to consolidate so rapidly the breach they had blasted in the Albert Canal defences. When next day Air Marshal Barratt finally gave orders for 114 Blenheim Squadron to stand by for an attack on the bridges, the entire squadron was wiped out on the ground in less than a minute by a squadron of Dornier 17s, before the startled defences had had time to fire a shot.

Because of the paralysis of the French High Command, it was not until about 6 pm on May 11th, more than thirty-six hours after the *Blitzkrieg* had struck, that the French day bombers flew their first mission of the war – an attack on the Dutch bridges at Maastricht. Indeed, General Gamelin only agreed late on the 11th to remove the restrictions he had placed on the Allied Air Forces and ordered them to 'put everything to work to slow up the German columns in the direction of Maastricht, Tongres and Gembloux, and not to hesitate to bomb towns and villages in order to obtain the required result'. As a result of this order, ten French medium bombers, escorted by eighteen fighters, tried to bomb the Maastricht bridges. One bomber was shot down and all the others badly damaged, without any hits being scored. A similarly abortive air attack was made on these bridges before nightfall on the 11th, by two Blenheim squadrons based in Britain – four aircraft being shot down and all the rest damaged, again without any hits being achieved.

At 7.00 on the morning of May 12th, the Advanced Air Striking Force's sole surviving Blenheim Squadron attempted to attack a Panzer column advancing towards Tongres, but they were caught by fifty enemy fighters and cut to pieces. The annihilation of the AASF's two Blenheim squadrons meant that the slow and vulnerable single-engined light bombers of the Battle squadrons had to be sent into action by day, although this was known to be a one-way trip to disaster, as the Belgians had already discovered. Thus it was that no Allied bombing attacks were made on the intact Belgian bridges until the morning of the third day of the invasion – and by then it was too late.

An overwhelming armoured and mechanized force had already flowed across the two Belgian bridges, and the Germans had had time to establish a superabundance of flak batteries round them. Recognizing the suicidal nature of the mission, Barratt stressed that the attack on the bridges by the Battles was to be a task for volunteers. Although the whole of 12 Squadron volunteered, the Squadron Leader chose only six volunteer crews, three Battles being detailed to attack the bridges at Veldwezelt and Vroenhoven. Fighter cover was provided by three squadrons of Hurricanes which, outmatched and greatly outnumbered by the swarms of Messerschmitt 109s covering the bridges, got the worst of the dog-fight that ensued and were unable to protect the gallant Battles. This courageous attack was, like that of the Belgian Battles, a massacre; all six planes were shot down. Some hits were, however, scored by 250-pound bombs and Flying Officer Garland's plane crashed into the western end of the bridge at Veldwezelt with a tremendous explosion – both he and his observer Sergeant Gray being posthumously awarded the Victoria Cross. The bridge was damaged – but not destroyed, as claimed at the time – and the flow of German traffic was only interrupted for thirty minutes. (The *Official History* of the campaign comments that the bombs used were far too small to damage seriously a modern steel or concrete bridge.) This heroic but foredoomed operation can be summed up in the words of the German officer who interrogated one of the shot-down crew:

> You British are mad! We capture the bridge early on Friday morning. You give us all Friday and Saturday to get our flak guns up in circles all round the bridge, and then on Sunday, when all is ready, you come along with three aircraft and try to blow the thing up.

Later that Whit Sunday the last attempt by the RAF to attack the Dutch bridges in the Maastricht area was made by twenty-four home-based Blenheims of Bomber Command, but ten were shot down and no hits were scored. Of the 135 Blenheims and Battles of the British Advanced Air Striking Force there remained only seventy-two that evening.

Although Belgian infantry units continued to counter-attack gallantly, the reinforced German airborne troops and brilliantly co-ordinated dive-bombing attacks repelled them. During the morning of the 11th Eben-Emael was completely neutralized and surrounded. But the fortress did not succumb until that afternoon, when the 1200 survivors of the garrison surrendered. The way was now open for the spearheads of von Reichenau's Sixth Army to cross the two captured bridges over the Albert Canal. The 500 tanks and the motorized division of Höpner's XVIth Panzer Corps, followed by an endless stream of vehicles, guns, troops and material, had crossed the Dutch frontier at zero hour. Fighting their way across the Maastricht Appendix, with their attendant swarm of Stukas and fighters overhead, they were, by noon on the 11th, thundering across the bridges of Vroenhoven and Veldwezelt into Belgium. After smashing through the Belgian forward positions, which had just been devastated by the tremendous dive-bombing attacks already described, the powerful shock force fanned out and took them in the flank and rear. With von Richthofen's* 'Stuka Circus' acting in close concert and blasting a path of destruction ahead of them, Höpner's Panzers reached Tongres within the hour.

The fighter element of VIII *Fliegerkorps* flew 340 sorties to protect the intact bridges over the Maas and the Albert Canal on May 11th. But when the Allies broke off their attempts to destroy them, the full fighter strength reverted to its task of escorting the swarms of Stukas, which were acting as heavy mobile artillery for Höpner's Panzer armada. The whole of the dive-bomber strength of the *Luftwaffe* had been concentrated on the Belgian defences, not only to pulverize them but to convince the Allies that this was the focal point of the main German invasion of the West.

'The Belgians were painfully surprised at Eben-Emael and the nearby Albert Canal bridges,' writes Telford Taylor, 'but the shock gave way not to a desperate confusion, but to a most determined and well-directed defence.'[107] The Belgians certainly fought on stubbornly against these hopeless odds and the Germans were made to pay dearly for their success. No order to retreat was given. Many Belgian units standing in the way of the German onrush fought to a finish where they stood. The heroic actions fought by the Belgians were legion. To mention only two, a Grenadier regiment held on when attacked from all sides in the smouldering ruins of the village of Eben-Emael. And an infantry battalion held the approach to Laeselt for thirty-six hours, commanded by a major who,

* Von Richthofen was a cousin of the First World War air ace.

with a handful of survivors, only yielded after exhausting all his ammunition under the combined assault of infantry, tanks and dive-bombers.

The Panzer spearheads launched by the enemy in the direction of Hasselt and St Trond threatened two Belgian infantry divisions with encirclement, but a light cavalry regiment succeeded in frustrating this move in the nick of time, causing the Germans to veer to the south-west, where they were again halted by a cavalry division between Tongres and Waremme. The two days' fighting caused the virtual elimination of the Belgian 7th Division, which had borne the main brunt of the onslaught. At 8 pm on the 11th it was recorded at the King's GQG that small groups of survivors from this division were making their way back in retreat – 1,000 or 1,500 men in all. Eventually, the survivors proved to be some 3,500.

Leopold had spent the night of May 9th–10th at the Queen Mother's little house in the grounds of Laeken. After dinner the telephone rang continually, with news that grew steadily more threatening. The need for instant decisions became pressing, so a bed was improvised for the King on a couch beside the telephone. Following the final warning which had come from Colonel Oster via the Belgian Military Attaché in Berlin at 9 pm, a stream of reports from the frontier of troop movements, the noise of engines, marching feet and words of command were telephoned to Belgian GQG and just after midnight the code word 'René', signifying that an attack was imminent, was signalled to the Army.

Between five and six am came the first news of invasions: the bombing of Belgian and Dutch airfields, German units crossing the two countries' frontiers, airborne landings on Fort Eben-Emael and near the Albert Canal bridges. As dawn broke and the sleeping capital was aroused by the wailing of sirens, followed by anti-aircraft fire and the crash of bombs, Leopold bicycled across the park to Laeken Palace under a sky streaked by tracer shells. From there he motored to the Palais de Bruxelles, where at 7.30 am he received his Ministers, Pierlot, Spaak, and General Denis. A year later in London, Spaak described the scene in an article published in *La Belgique Indépendante* on May 8th 1941:

> *Le Roi est ferme, calme, décidé. Aucune discussion n'est nécessaire. Nos coeurs battent à l'unisson . . . J'ai le coeur serré et, pourquoi le cacher, les yeux pleins de larmes au moment où il me serre la main. Quand nous reverrons-nous?*

In his memoirs published in 1969, which are stuffed with special pleading, distortions and inaccuracies, Spaak repeats his 1941 article almost word for word and, although describing the King as 'calm, master of himself and resolute', introduces a passage stating that the King 'rejected' his Ministers' demands that he should address Parliament when it assembled that afternoon. But what Spaak's memoirs fail to reveal is that he and his colleagues were in full agreement with the King that the pace of the *Blitzkrieg* obliged him as Commander-in-Chief of the Army to go at once to his Headquarters to take command of the battle – and thus prevented him from attending and addressing Parliament as his father had done in 1914. As the Ministers well knew, the circumstances were quite different in those statelier days, for King Albert had had time to address Parliament before Belgium was invaded – to inform its members of the terms of the German ultimatum, which had not yet expired, and obtain their support for his rejection of it. Thus Albert was already at the head of his troops when the Germans launched their invasion of his country.

The allegation that Leopold had refused to address Parliament because of his undemocratic and anti-Allies leanings, was one of the many slanders trumped-up after the war, when the campaign to discredit and overthrow the King was launched by politically motivated men – including those who, having deeply wronged him, sought to rehabilitate themselves at his expense. Another line of attack which they subsequently adopted was to accuse the King of having imposed himself on the Army, asking: 'Why couldn't he have left it to the soldiers?' But under Article 68 of the Constitution, the King was, like his predecessors, Belgium's chief soldier and bound by his oath to command the Belgian Army in the field.

Foremost among those who would act on the principle of 'let us our sins . . . lay on the King' were, of course, Pierlot and Spaak. Yet, when addressing the Assembly that same afternoon, they paid homage to the King and gave his line of conduct the Government's full support. Indeed, when Pierlot spoke on behalf of his Sovereign in the Chamber, his declaration that the King was 'at the head of his troops, where the Commander-in-Chief must be, once the battle has started', was greeted with tumultuous applause. 'The King would have liked to have addressed Parliament,' the Prime Minister continued, 'but the rapid development of events has prevented him from doing so.' Nevertheless, in the course of his interminable attempts to justify himself after the war, Pierlot did not scruple to attribute quite different motives to the King. 'I have always thought,' he wrote, 'that he did not want to make a statement or even by his presence seem to associate himself with statements that would have committed him more deeply to the Allied cause than he cared to be.' This was a line to which Spaak subsequently lent some support, despite his statement that the Ministers' 'hearts beat in unison' with the King and his eulogistic references to him in the Chamber that afternoon. After describing his own part in the morning's events in glowing terms and reiterating Pierlot's statement 'that there could be no question of peace until Belgium's independence had been reconquered', Spaak declared that the Belgian Army was safe in the hands of the son of the King who had led his forces to victory in the previous conflict. The acclaim which greeted this peroration was equally fervent when the Speaker summed up the unanimous sentiments of the Assembly:

> Obeying his duty with the same firmness and self-denial as his illustrious father, the King has immediately put himself at the head of his troops. We have the most complete confidence in his spirit of decision . . . He can count on our indestructible fidelity.

By their response to all these loyal and patriotic affirmations the Belgian Parliament made it abundantly clear that they and the people supported their Sovereign's leadership of the Nation and its armed forces as wholeheartedly as they had done in King Albert's time.

Meanwhile from his headquarters the King addressed a Proclamation to his people:

> Belgians, for the second time in a quarter of a century, Belgium – a loyal and neutral country – has been attacked by the German Empire in spite of the most solemn undertakings contracted before the whole world. The Belgian people, who are fundamentally peaceful, have done everything in their power to prevent this, but between sacrifice and dishonour the Belgian of 1940 will hesitate no more than the Belgian of 1914 . . .
>
> France and Great Britain have promised to help us. Their advance troops are already pushing forward to join up with ours. The fight will be hard. Great sacrifices and deprivation will be asked of you. But there can be no doubt about the final victory. I intend to remain faithful to my constitutional oath to maintain the independence and integrity of the territory. Like my father in 1914, I have put myself at the head of the Army with the same faith, the same clear conscience. The cause of Belgium is pure. With the help of God it will triumph.

Within an hour of the attack being launched Spaak, as Foreign Minister, had called personally on the British and French ambassadors to request, under their countries' 1937 Guarantees, the entry of their troops into Belgium which they had so long and pertinaciously sought to achieve. (At the British Embassy Spaak caught a glimpse on the staircase of Lady Oliphant in her night attire. '*C'est la seule fois durant toute ma carrière*,' he noted in his memoirs, '*que j'eus cette vision d'une ambassadrice d'Angleterre.*')

In the early hours of that morning Ribbentrop had summoned the Belgian Ambassador in Berlin, Vicomte Davignon, who – according to von Hassell's diary – gave the German Foreign Minister 'a piece of his mind'. When told that Belgian resistance was useless, Davignon replied that his King was a man of courage and honour and that Belgium would keep her word to defend her frontiers. 'Davignon's dignified words,' wrote von Weizsäcker in his memoirs, 'made a profound impression on me. But at the same time, I knew that any Belgian blood that would be shed would be shed in vain.'[108]

The King's *Grand Quartier Général*, which he described to the author as 'my fort', was the grim pile of Breendonck, twenty miles north of Brussels – a place which later achieved infamy as an SS prison. When Leopold and Van Overstraeten arrived there at 8.30 am, they found a bustle of unloading lorries and shouting men, as supplementary staff moved in. Here in his quarters in the dark casemates with their windows overlooking the moat, the King received from his Chief of Staff, General Michiels, the latest news of the battle which had been raging since before dawn.

The picture Michiels drew was far from reassuring. As already described, much of the small Belgian Air Force had already been destroyed on the ground and many other significant targets were being continuously bombed, while the 4th and 7th Divisions on the Albert Canal were under tremendous pressure from swarms of dive-bombers and airborne storm troops. Critical bridges were being lost over the waterways and the fortress of Eben-Emael was being heavily assaulted.

The German attack had, of course, been made without any declaration of war. It was not until 8.30, after Spaak's meeting with the King at the Palace, that he was visited by the German Ambassador, von Bülow-Schwante. Spaak thus describes the scene:

> The strongest emotion of my life. My heart beats terribly in my breast. Von Bülow enters. Consolation: he is even more upset than me. Without giving him time to say a word, I read in a choking voice the few lines of protest which I have just written. He listens in silence to my indignant phrases. In his turn he starts to read his government's Note . . . In the middle of his discourse I take the paper from his hands and glance through it. I have nothing further to say to him; my reply, that of Belgium, has already been given.[109]

The German Note read as follows:

> In order to forestall the invasion of Belgium, Holland and Luxembourg, for which Great Britain and France have been making preparations clearly aimed at Germany, the Government of the Reich is compelled to ensure the neutrality of these three countries by means of arms. For this purpose, the Government of the Reich will bring up an armed force of the greatest size, so that resistance of any kind will be useless. The Government of the Reich guarantees Belgium's European and colonial territory, as well as her dynasty, on condition that no resistance is offered. Should there be any resistance, Belgium will risk the destruction of her country and the loss of her independence. It is therefore in the interests of Belgium that the population be called upon to cease all resistance and that the authorities be given the necessary instructions to make contact with the German Military Command.

The Note then went on to enumerate at great length Germany's complaints against those nations. These included accusations that the Belgian and Dutch press 'have even surpassed the British and French in their anti-German attitude'; that 'leading personalities in public life . . . have increasingly asserted that Belgium's place was at the side of France and England'; that 'the military measures taken by the Royal Government of Belgium speak an even clearer language', the Belgians having 'fortified only their frontier with Germany' and not that with France; that the two countries had 'mobilized exclusively against Germany'; that they had 'secretly sided with France and Britain' and that the latter had 'assembled a powerful offensive motorized army on the Franco-Belgian border'. Finally the Note declared:

The German troops are not coming as enemies of the Belgian and Dutch peoples, for the Reich Government has neither wished for nor brought about this development. The responsibility falls upon England and France, who have prepared the offensive against Germany on Belgian and Dutch territory, and upon the Belgian and Netherlands governments who have tolerated and favoured it . . .

Furthermore the Reich Government declares that Germany has no intention, now or in future, of touching through these measures the sovereignty of Belgium and the Netherlands, either with regard to their European or their extra-European possessions. Even today the Belgian and Netherlands governments have it in their hands to safeguard the well-being of their peoples by seeing to it that the German troops will meet with no resistance whatsoever . . . Should the German troops be offered resistance in Belgium or Holland this resistance will be broken with all means. The governments of Holland and Belgium would be held solely responsible for the consequences and for the then unavoidable shedding of blood.

Meanwhile, in Berlin Ribbentrop was telling the German and foreign press representatives that it was an 'act of criminal arbitrary power by Great Britain and France which forced this war on Germany', and referring to 'an act of despair by which the present leaders of Great Britain and France wished to save their Cabinets, which had been endangered by their past failures'. From now on, he said, the German Army would speak to them 'in the only language which their rulers seem to understand'.

For once the Nazi leader spoke the truth, at least in part, since the Prime Ministers of Britain and France were indeed struggling to save their Cabinets and their political lives. Neville Chamberlain was on the point of being ousted and Reynaud had, on the 9th, informed the President that his government was dissolved. A leading part in bringing about the downfall of Chamberlain and his replacement by Winston Churchill was played by Sir Roger Keyes, in his role as an MP. In the House of

Commons on May 7th, Keyes, wearing his Admiral of the Fleet's uniform with its six rows of medals, delivered a passionate denunciation of the Government's inept conduct of the war and a plea for a change in leadership, thus spearheading the attack which so swiftly led to Chamberlain's resignation and his succession by Churchill.* This 'absolutely devastating attack,' as Harold Nicolson described it in his diary, 'is by far the most dramatic speech I have ever heard and when Keyes sits down there is thunderous applause.'[110] 'The intervention of Sir Roger Keyes in full uniform,' writes Chamberlain's biographer, 'which was the turning point, seemed to denounce the loss of that offensive spirit which had achieved our ancient glory.'[111] And General Sir Edward Spears, who was also an MP, recalls:

> Roger Keyes provided one of the sensations of the afternoon . . . In fact, Churchill, winding up the debate, said it was the best speech Keyes had ever made in the House . . . He was cheered and cheered again . . . This warmth was in strong contrast with the icy gloom prevailing on the Government Front Bench. Keyes obtained his greatest success from his peroration in favour of Churchill. The whole country, he declared, looked to him, Churchill, to help win the war. This was a great relief. His enemies, particularly on the Government Benches, would now find it harder to try to fasten the blame of our failure on him.[112]

On the following day Churchill loyally defended the Government's performance and declared 'I take complete responsibility for everything that has been done by the Admiralty', at which Lloyd George interjected 'The Right Honourable Gentleman must not allow himself to be converted into an air-raid shelter to keep the splinters from hitting his colleagues.' The debate continued throughout the 9th and it was not until after the *Blitzkrieg* struck next morning that King George sent for Churchill and called upon him to take the helm.

Meanwhile, on the morning of the German attack, France was without a government. Reynaud's quarrel with Daladier had come to a head the previous day and he had submitted his government's resignation in the expectation that the President would ask him to form a new Ministry, from which Daladier could at last be excluded. Reynaud had also been persistently trying to get rid of Gamelin – that 'nerveless philosopher', as he called him – but Daladier had fiercely protected the Commander-in-Chief and Reynaud had shrunk from forcing the issue of his dismissal. The Secretary of the Cabinet, Paul Baudouin, wrote that he was 'thunderstruck by the pitiful spectacle of the Prime Minister's impotence to break the political chains which bound him; thunderstruck also by his obvious

* The Admiral's speech evoked over 400 letters, all expressing appreciation, admiration and gratitude – several of which echoed the view of one of his constituents that 'Mr Churchill has you to thank, very largely, for his present position.'

preference for keeping silent rather than risking his place as Head of the Government'.[113] The French politicians were therefore still jostling and wrangling for seats in the new Ministry when the German offensive was launched on the 10th, but the President insisted that the Government should continue in office. Thus, in France's bleakest hour Reynaud clung on as Prime Minister, but with his two *bêtes noires* Daladier and Gamelin still in power as War Minister and Commander-in-Chief.

CHAPTER FIFTEEN

A Trap for the Allies

'When news came that the enemy was advancing along the whole
front I could have wept for joy: they had fallen into the trap . . . We
had made them believe that we were remaining faithful to the old
Schlieffen Plan.'

Adolf Hitler

Before leaving for his Headquarters, the King had made a private
sacrifice. He had arranged for his children to leave Belgium at once for a
safer refuge in France. After moving farewells Josephine-Charlotte and
her two young brothers set off, in the care of the trusted Vicomte du Parc
and a tutor. But they soon met signs of war. Near Mons they passed the
British and French vanguards moving east, and 25 miles to the south they
ran into an air raid. As the German planes flew overhead they were
hurriedly led to a shelter while the bombs fell. After various vicissitudes
they were at last compelled by the German advance to retire to a remote
château in the Department of Lot, where they remained until the French
collapse at the end of June. Queen Elisabeth had also departed from
Brussels on May 10th for La Panne, where she occupied the villa in which
she had lived with King Albert from 1914 to 1918. Leopold was thus left
entirely alone to bear the immense burdens of Head of State and
Commander-in-Chief.

Alone, except that he was almost immediately joined by Sir Roger
Keyes, whom he subsequently described to the author as 'the best friend
any man ever had'. On the morning of the 10th Keyes was summoned to
the Admiralty by Winston Churchill, who was still First Lord, but would
within a few hours attain the leadership of the Nation. The Admiral of the
Fleet was asked to get into his uniform and stand by to fly to Belgium at
once as 'Special Liaison Officer to the King of the Belgians'. At the
Admiralty Churchill briefed him for a few minutes after a Cabinet
meeting at which he was given the nominal appointment of 'Additional
Naval Attaché to the British Embassy in Brussels', although he was
assured that this was to give him diplomatic status and that he would be
independent of the Ambassador. At 3.30 pm Keyes left Hendon in an
RAF communications plane for Amiens, which he was told was as near to
Brussels as it was practicable to go. Three Hurricanes escorted the

Admiral's plane as it approached the French coast and it landed safely at Amiens at four-thirty. His diary takes up the story from there:

> May 10th: . . . I then drove to Arras in a military staff car, and thence to the new GHQ at Wahagnies, where I saw Lord Gort, who took me to his château in which he lived and gave me dinner. At 9.30 pm I started again for Brussels. My car was overtaking lorries, guns, tanks, buses full of troops of the BEF throughout the night. The road was marked by little lights on the ground about 200 yards apart, along the whole route to be taken by the BEF, and the controls and arrangements generally were excellent.* Our only difficulty arose when I left this route, when it diverged from the main road to Brussels and was no longer marked. Parachutists had already been active, and I was treated with great suspicion on two or three occasions. Brussels – which was a blaze of light when I was there in January – was absolutely blacked out, and it was difficult to find one's way. Eventually I came across a gendarme and I asked him to direct me to the British Embassy. He said he would do so from the running board, but he took me instead to the *hôtel de ville*, where I was surrounded by gendarmes and suspicious officials, who would not even accept my passport until they had telephoned to the Embassy – where I eventually arrived at 2 am. The Ambassador told me that German planes had been flying over Brussels and the neighbourhood all day, and had dropped bombs about three hours before the German Ambassador had informed the Foreign Minister that Germany had taken Belgium under her protection, but that the casualties only amounted to about 300 killed and 60 injured.

Next day the Admiral received a warm welcome from the King at Breendonck. Leopold was 'delighted', as Van Overstraeten noted, 'to have at his side this distinguished sailor, the hero of Zeebrugge and old friend of King Albert'. From then on Keyes would maintain the closest contact with the King, living under the same roof, following his direction of military operations, sharing his confidences, burdens and anxieties. His testimony is therefore of unique authority and historical importance, for no other British individual nor indeed any Belgian except General Van Overstraeten was so close to Leopold during the eighteen days of tragedy which were to follow. The Admiral not only kept a meticulous record of events for the purposes of the official report which he rendered to the Government, but described his day-to-day experiences in guarded terms in letters which were sent by 'safe hand' to his wife. His records throw a revealing light on the story of the Belgian campaign and squarely refute the charges which were levelled against Leopold and his army after its capitulation.

Every day, while the King and the Admiral were at Breendonck, they would have a five-minute walk to the mess for lunch through a magnifi-

* This was the happy result of the Belgians' secret collaboration with the British, which most British accounts ignore or deny, although 'Monty', a stickler for perfection, told Alan Brooke that his advance 'had gone like clockwork'.

cent field of corn of exceptional height. The King described to the author the radiance of those May days: 'The sky was a deep blue as it is in Italy. There was an intensity about everything, with the birds singing and only the distant rumble of artillery, the occasional scream of dive-bombers and the wailing of sirens to bring one back to reality. The nights were warm and beautiful and the full moon was so bright that one could read a newspaper by it.' The sense of unreality was heightened when Leopold returned during a lull in the fighting to the almost deserted Palace of Laeken for a bath and some clean linen. There was no escape from the whining of sirens, which went on almost continuously, despite the acceptance of Brussels as an open city – on condition that no military traffic passed through it – as announced by the German High Command on May 11th. The King felt, like many others, that the effect of this ghastly noise was far more demoralizing for the population than actual bombing would have been.

Admiral Keyes' diary graphically presents the atmosphere on May 11th. He records that the King told him that enemy airborne formations had put the fortress of Eben-Emael out of action and prevented the demolition of two of the three Albert Canal bridges, while only seven fighters had survived the *Luftwaffe*'s dawn attacks on the Belgian airfields. Keyes then describes how: 'Tanks, armoured cars, and mechanized troops poured across the bridges, accompanied by low-flying bombers. This formidable force had broken through the Belgian troops in that sector and for the last thirty hours, the King told me, German bombers had been bombing and machine-gunning them and the fugitive civilians who crowded the roads. This breakthrough and the gap in the Albert Canal defence line had jeopardized the Belgian troops holding it, and it was absolutely essential to withdraw to the line of the Dyle without delay.' Leopold, as the Admiral recalls, was becoming worried by the complete absence of Allied planes overhead.

> The King told me that repeated appeals had been made through the British and French missions for air support, but none had been sent, and he feared an absolute *débâcle* if nothing could be done to check the low bombing attacks, which had a most demoralizing effect. The Germans were indeed pursuing exactly the same tactics as they did in Poland, and the Belgian Army had neither tanks nor aircraft to compete against the German onslaught, and very few anti-aircraft guns.
>
> I knew that the BEF's co-operation squadrons would be quite insufficient to deal with the formidable attack which was being launched by the Germans* and which threatened to overwhelm the Allied Armies before they had time to

---

* 'I felt', Gort wrote in his *Despatches*, 'that the resources of the Air Component would prove insufficient for the requirements of the Force during operations'; and later, 'Tactical reconnaissance became virtually impossible without fighter support.' By May 12th the fighter Group of the BEF's Air Component was reduced to only 50 aircraft.

consolidate the positions they were taking up, and it seemed to me vitally important to get adequate air support for both the British and Belgian Armies at the earliest possible moment.

I told the King that I would go into Brussels and get into communication with Mr Churchill. I was provided with a car and the King gave instructions that after I had done what I wanted in Brussels, it was to bring me to Château Melis, near Lippeloo, about four miles from the Belgian GQG, where he was living and where, he said, a room would be found for me.

All that day German planes were flying low over Brussels and the approaches, without any opposition to speak off, as nearly all the Belgian anti-aircraft guns were defending military positions. It is true that the enemy did not deliberately attack the civilian population of Brussels as they had the previous day, but they were observing everything from a very low altitude and thoroughly dominated the air. Air-raid warnings and all-clear signals followed one another in such quick succession that no one paid any attention to them before long.

On arriving at the British Embassy, the Air Attaché got me through to the Air Ministry in London, which passed me on to the Admiralty, and I told Mr Churchill how critical the situation was, and that the Belgians' appeal for air support had remained unanswered for two days.* He passed me on to the Chief of the Air Staff, who told me he could not accept my statement that no British aircraft were helping the Belgians. I was not able to speak to Mr Churchill again, as he had gone to a meeting, but I told his Secretary (Mr Seal) to tell him that the Norwegian catastrophe would pale into insignificance in comparison with that which awaited the BEF, unless the RAF could provide an effective answer to the German air menace. I then sent the following message to Mr Churchill, who I learnt had become Prime Minister:

Chief of the Air Staff does not accept my statement that the RAF has done nothing whatever to assist the Belgians to stem the German advance over the Albert Canal west of Maastricht, but it is a fact.

The Royal Air Force were provided with all the necessary photographs to ensure effective co-operation on the 17th January. In fact I handed them over at GHQ, BEF, on that date. Arrangements have been made to refuel fighters here.

At 10 am yesterday the Belgian Headquarters asked both British and French for air support, in view of the serious losses they had incurred. I understand that they have only about seven fighters left. Prompt and sufficient help would probably have enabled them to prevent the Germans

---

* On May 5th 1943, in a House of Lords debate in which Lord Beaverbrook was vainly trying to overcome the Air Ministry's opposition to dive-bombers, Keyes described the scene: 'I foresaw disaster . . . and called the Prime Minister . . . At first I got no sympathy and no help, and being a bit annoyed I held my telephone out of the window and said, Can't you hear the nasty things? It's a constant roar all day long.'

In *Unexpected* General Brownrigg writes that he found the British Military Attaché 'scarcely recovered from the effects of a conversation he had overheard in his office between Sir Roger Keyes and the Prime Minister in London. The Admiral had apparently spoken in no uncertain terms on what he considered the inadequate air support we had given the Belgian Army.'

making good their hold over the two bridges, the destruction of which was prevented by parachutists. No help however has been given either by the French or the British, in spite of repeated appeals, with the result that German bombers have been flying round at will. They have practically wiped out a Belgian Division and all its communications . . .

Unless a tremendous effort is made by the RAF and the French Air Forces to break up and destroy the two German columns which are advancing into Belgium with unchallenged air support, the Allied Armies in Belgium are faced with a major disaster. The BEF will certainly be fighting for its very existence in positions they have not had time to consolidate and with their communications continually threatened by air attack.

It is absolutely necessary to gain command of the air in this battle . . . I do beg you to be guided by this advice, to act immediately and spring a tremendous surprise on the Germans at dawn tomorrow.

I then motored back to Château Melis and told the King what I had done. It was then about 9.30 pm and finding that I had had no dinner, the King sat with me while I had a meal . . .

Keyes' personal approach did in fact produce an immediate, if temporary effect. Next day he noted in his diary that 'the Prime Minister acted with characteristic vigour' and that at dawn the RAF had 'arrived in force and cleared the sky'. But unfortunately this was only a flash in the pan, for throughout the rest of the eighteen-day campaign British planes were conspicuous by their absence over the battlefield. The British airmen had performed prodigies of valour against the overwhelming odds they had to face, but by nightfall on May 15th the RAF in France had lost a total of 205 out of 416 aircraft. The operation of fighters from Continental airfields was abandoned three days later because they were in the path of the advancing enemy. Of the 261 Hurricanes in France only 66 were repatriated; 74 were lost on operations, the remainder either destroyed on the ground or abandoned for lack of pilots to fly them home. From May 20th onwards the surviving Hurricanes, being based in Kent, were unable to operate effectively over the battlefields, due to their limited range and because their briefing reached them belatedly via the War Office, the Air Ministry and their home base. It is not surprising, therefore, that the author of the Belgian Government's 'blue book' should have written: 'For eighteen days the Belgian Army had the depressing feeling that it was manoeuvring and fighting under a sky that belonged exclusively to the enemy.'[114]

Thus the King had constantly to face situations in which his troops, deprived of their own Air Force and under heavy pressure from the German Sixth and Eighteenth Armies, were exposed to the full rigours of dive-bombing and strafing from the *Luftwaffe*. The BEF, on the other hand, came under no comparable pressure on the ground or from the air during their advance to the K-W Line and their retreat towards Dunkirk, as the casualty figures dramatically show. (Ironside later informed Churchill that the BEF had, by May 21st, suffered only about 500 battle casualties.)

At Lord Gort's widely scattered GHQ in and around Arras,[k] all had been peace on the night of May 9th–10th, since the spate of alarming reports about the impending invasion of Belgium and Holland which had alerted those two countries had been ignored by the Allied High Commands. The BEF, now comprising ten divisions,* had spent an undisturbed winter improving the defences on their thirty-mile sector on the Franco-Belgian frontier between Halluin and Maulde and large numbers of troops had recently been sent home on spring leave. But as dawn broke on the 10th, Gort and his multitudinous staff were rudely awakened by the roar of planes overhead and the thunder of bombs falling on the town and nearby airfields. 'GHQ seem to have been caught off their guard,' wrote a senior staff officer at the headquarters of BAAF in his diary on the 10th: 'Quite a lot of people away on leave . . . There is no news of our troops or aircraft. No messages, no intelligence summaries, no telephone.'[115] In his diary Pownall admits that 'interest . . . was concentrated on the political crisis at home' and that 'being in no state of previous *alerte*', the BEF would not be able to move till 1 pm.[116]

In response to the Belgian appeal for aid the French High Command ordered the immediate execution of Plan D at 6 am. Although some French units entered Belgium shortly afterwards, seven hours elapsed before the 12th Lancers (the only armoured-car regiment used in the campaign) got under way and crossed the Belgian frontier, followed by five other mechanized cavalry regiments. Still later came the infantry divisions, much surprised at the absence of the *Luftwaffe*, in a move which was sheduled to take eight days to complete. The advanced formations made good time, since Gort – ignoring the terrible danger of German air attack – had ordered his army to advance in closely packed columns by day, unlike the French, who had prudently decided to restrict the movements of their main bodies to the hours of darkness. Gort's decision could have resulted in a massacre, had the *Luftwaffe* bombed and strafed the BEF as heavily as they had the Belgians on the Meuse and Albert Canal. But the Germans had no intention of impeding the Allied advance, since the object of their revised *Fall Gelb* was (as Van Overstraeten and General Georges had suspected) to draw (*aspirer*) the maximum number of Allied troops as far as possible into Belgium, the better to cut them off with von Kleist's scythe-like Panzer sweep round their right flank and rear. Hitler's reaction has been recorded: 'When

---

* One 'green' division was stationed behind the Maginot Line, to gain battle experience and 'convince the French soldiers that there really was a British army in France', as Gort's biographer, J. R. Colville, puts it in *Man of Valour*.

news came that the enemy was advancing along the whole front, I could have wept for joy; they had fallen into the trap!'

The point was taken by, amongst others, Kim Philby, the Soviet spy, who was covering the advance of the BEF for *The Times*[1]. 'It went too damn well,' he remarked to a colleague. 'With all that air power why didn't he bother us? What is he up to?' At the Advanced HQ of BAAF the anonymous diarist wrote on May 13th: 'A strange and I feel very suspicious feature has been the extraordinary lack of any German bombing of the BEF and the French Armies in their advance . . . It looks almost as if the Germans want us where we are going.' Colonel de Villelume, Reynaud's link with the High Command, was also worried by the absence of air attack on the advancing columns, and voiced his fears to the Prime Minister: 'Are they letting us fall into a trap?' But Gort and Pownall remained blind to such a possibility, for as Gort's biographer records 'It occurred to nobody that the Germans might not wish to deter the Allied armies from their eastern progress.'[117]

In the North the French Seventh Army's futile thrust was equally unimpeded. By the end of the day, Giraud's patrols were across the Antwerp Canal and pushing towards Breda in Holland, while the British mechanized cavalry screen was established on the seventeen-mile-long front to be occupied by the BEF along the River Dyle between Louvain and Wavre, only ten miles to the east of Brussels. Here they awaited the arrival of the three infantry divisions which were to hold it – the remaining six being deployed in great depth, with two stationed forty-five miles in their rear, behind the River Escaut (or Scheldt).

Meanwhile, on the right of this narrow British front General Prioux's Cavalry Corps was covering the French First Army's twenty-five mile front known as the 'Gembloux Gap' – the plain between Wavre on the Dyle and Namur on the Meuse. Here, unlike those of the Belgians and the British, Blanchard's ten divisions would enjoy no waterline protection – only the system of steel 'Cointet' anti-tank obstacles, the concrete gun emplacements and the minefields which had been established by the Belgians. Namur, on which his right wing rested, however, was surrounded by a powerful system of Belgian-manned fortresses, which would hold out long after the French had withdrawn.

From Namur the front to be held by Corap's ill-fated Ninth Army, which was now moving up to it, continued southwards across the Meuse to Sedan – to complete the link-up with the Maginot Line and its extension. Thus, while the three French armies, with the BEF in their midst, wheeled forward to the main Belgian defence line, with their pivot at Sedan, they were sheltered from the massive assault of von Reichenau's Sixth Army by the Belgian Army, whose resistance to overwhelming attacks by dive-bombers, tanks, artillery, infantry and airborne shock-troops has already been described.

On the second day of the battle the reports reaching Leopold at his Breendonck Headquarters were even more disquieting than on the first. At midday the Chief of Staff, General Michiels, reported to the King, who was in conference with his Minister of Defence, General Denis. Michiels' report was followed by a long silence. All agreed that in view of the breach made by the Panzers and Stukas, which was outflanking Belgian positions, the delaying action on the Albert Canal could not be protracted. The King therefore gave orders that the Belgian divisions should begin, that night, their pre-arranged fighting withdrawal to their allotted positions on the K-W Line to the left of the BEF. This involved the complicated and difficult manoeuvre of retiring under constant enemy pressure from their delaying positions along Belgium's 250-mile-long eastern frontier to a forty mile front on the left of the Allied line.

The Albert Canal had never been considered more than a delaying position, on which the enemy might be held for a few days at most. Nevertheless, the decision to abandon it, on the second day of the conflict, was a hard one. But since it was an essential element in the German master plan that the Allied armies in Belgium should remain as far forward as possible, the orderly retirement of the Belgian Army to take its allotted place on the main defence position was a vital contribution to the Allied cause. Moreover, the stalwart defence of the Belgians against a massive and technically brilliant attack, carried out with full control of the skies, gave the BEF and the French First Army sufficient time to occupy painlessly their prescribed sectors of the K-W Line.

Lieutenant-Colonel George Davy, who had been GSO 1 to the Mission headed by General Sir Richard Howard-Vyse with the French High Command at Vincennes before taking charge of the British Liaison Mission at Belgian GQG on May 17th, comments as follows:

> In March Gamelin explained to Howard-Vyse his plan for the advance into Belgium, including what he wished the Belgians to do. This was *to retire intact from the Albert Canal* to the left of the British on the Dyle line. He did not look for a prolonged resistance on the Albert Canal. He wanted a strong Belgian Army on his left.

The Belgian move was in any case inevitable, since the British and French armies would advance no further than the K-W Line and the forty mile gap on the British left had to be filled. But Gort and his Chief-of-Staff had not only failed to apprehend from the absence of the *Luftwaffe* overhead that they were being drawn into a trap, but totally ignored the fact that the absence of the *Wehrmacht* in front of them was thanks to the resistance of the Belgian Army, which was bearing the full brunt of a massive aerial and Panzer *Blitzkrieg* more than a hundred miles to the east. Indeed, far from giving their Belgian companions-in-arms any credit for their brave stand, which was protecting the three British front line divisions from the enemy onslaught, as they occupied their diminutive sector of the K-W Line, the British generals were fostering the legend of cowardly Belgians in disorderly retreat, and blaming them for all their troubles.

Pownall in particular, as his diary reveals, remained from first to last blinded with prejudice against the Belgians, regarding them as 'lesser breeds without the law'. This anti-Belgian line is followed by Sir John Colville, whose biography of Lord Gort draws heavily and unquestioningly on Pownall's distorted version of events – which is surprising in a book written over thirty years later, when the slanders about King Leopold and his army had long since been disproved. In contrast, Dr Brian Bond, the editor of Pownall's diaries, which were published in the same year as Sir John's work, is careful to point out that 'the diarist's references to King Leopold III and his army are consistently prejudiced and unjust . . .' The editorial note continues:

> The diary fails to make it clear that the Belgian Army, virtually without air cover, bore the brunt of the German 6th Army's attack while the BEF had a comparatively easy withdrawal to the French frontier. Indeed, but for the prolonged resistance of the gallant Belgian Army, the evacuation of the BEF from Dunkirk would have been impossible.[118]

Already on the second day of the campaign Pownall was writing: 'What troubles are arising are due to the Belgians', a gibe which Gort's biographer echoes and elaborates: 'Such problems as arose during the next four days were caused neither by the Germans nor by the French, but by the Belgians . . .' On May 13th Pownall wrote 'A lot of flap during the day from Belgian GQG . . . They were wild with fear – by "they" I mean the King . . .' Next day he was referring to 'the King of the Belgians, who like the rest of the Army is in a complete state of wind-up, their morale is just terrible . . .' Colville caps these strictures with the equally baseless accusation (apparently referring to May 10th) that: 'The Belgian Army, which in October, 1939, Gamelin had deemed capable of holding the Albert Canal for at least two days and Georges for seven, immediately recoiled in headlong retreat. King Leopold and the Belgian High Command gave way to panic . . .' But Colville really gives his imagination free rein with his allegation that on May 14th 'there was streaming westwards an apparently endless line of Belgian soldiers, some in boots and some in carpet slippers, a few, but very few, still clutching their rifles, practically none wounded and not an officer to be seen'. 'It was the penalty,' Colville asserts, 'for trusting in neutrality and for the refusal of even clandestine Staff conversations.' The biographer had previously observed: 'It was distressing that the Belgians, for fear of offending the Germans, would still allow practically no reconnaissance of their territory which their friends and deliverers* would be invited to occupy.'

Nevertheless, although much maligned, the Belgian Army was not entirely without protagonists. Indeed Colonel Davy, from the moment he took charge of the British Liaison Mission at Belgian GQG on May 17th, made strenuous efforts to counteract the false impressions of the Belgian Army's morale and performance which were being so widely disseminated by Gort, Pownall and other senior officers of the BEF. On the following day, for example, his Mission sent a message to the War Office which was published in the press and broadcast by the BBC:

> Morale of Belgian troops still extremely high in spite of continued withdrawal and realization that it is for reasons beyond their control.
>
> Magnitude of Belgian achievement in withstanding full onslaught of German attack by new methods of warfare and then withdrawing their troops intact across Belgium is not generally appreciated at home.
>
> Belgian Staff work is excellent and their movements well executed.

Moreover, on September 4th 1949 Colonel Davy wrote as follows in reply to a letter from General Nuyssens, the head of the Belgian Military Mission at Gort's headquarters:

> The Belgian Army, after its resistance on the frontier, conformed very well with General Gamelin's intentions and rather more effectively than he himself had envisaged. In fact it never ceased to have contact with the enemy and immediately on its withdrawal from the Albert Canal, took its place beside the British on their left. Unfortunately however, a number of stragglers without weapons passed through the British troops, mingled with the stream of refugees. It is an unfortunate fact that an army is judged by the individuals whom one sees. There was for some time an impression in the British Army . . . that the Belgian Army was defeated. This idea persisted and led to a considerable nervousness about their left flank, which was without foundation. If there had been closer liaison between our armies right from the beginning this false impression would have been quickly dispelled. Unfortunately liaison was sadly lacking . . .

It was indeed unfortunate that the British High Command showed no desire to liaise with the Belgians, and that the reports and sightings of non-combatant stragglers from the Belgian Army's rear-areas in disorderly retreat, should have created such a false impression of the morale of the army as a whole – especially since similar conduct was reported in

---

* Winston Churchill also convinced himself that the Allies' entry into Belgium, which they had decided to make forcibly, if not invited in, was in the role of 'deliverers', as his memoirs clearly demonstrate: 'The First Army Group, with the British in the centre, instead of standing behind their fortifications, leaped forward into Belgium on a vain, because belated, mission of rescue.' *The Second World War*, Volume II.

all the armies engaged in the 1940 campaign. In fact, there are numerous accounts of French, British and even German troops in panic-stricken retreat. For example, the official and personal reports which have only gradually come to light over the years, reveal that in the chaos of the BEF's flight to the sea and evacuation, there was disorder and indiscipline among its troops, particularly from the rear-areas, including desertion, drunkenness and looting – and that a number of them, including some officers, were shot on the spot or while trying to rush the evacuation craft.

Although Vice-Admiral Sir Bertram Ramsay, the overall commander of the evacuation of the BEF, was more restrained in his criticisms of such behaviour by the military than some other observers, his official *Despatches*, which he submitted on June 18th 1940, were suppressed for eight years until July 15th 1948. In his report he wrote:

> As regards the bearing and behaviour of the troops . . . it must be recorded that the earlier parties were embarked off the beaches in a condition of complete disorganization. There appeared to be no military officers in charge of the troops . . . It was soon realized that it was vitally necessary to despatch Naval officers . . . with armed Naval beach parties to take charge of the soldiers on shore . . . Great credit is due to the Naval officers and Naval ratings for the restoration of some semblance of order. Later on when troops of fighting formations reached the beaches these difficulties disappeared.

In his account of the earlier evacuation from Boulogne of a large number of troops from the rear-areas of the BEF by British destroyers Admiral Ramsay wrote: 'On the quay a panic-stricken rabble . . . tried to rush the ship, but were driven back by the demolition party at the point of the bayonet. Many of them were drunk.' On a less serious note, Peter Hadley gives an eyewitness account of how a 'disorderly mob' of British soldiers fled, on hearing a false report that enemy tanks were close behind them: 'They hurried on, looking (if the truth be told) very much like the popular conception of the Italian Army.'[119]

Unfortunately, when the soldiers of one of the embattled armies observed those of another behaving badly, they tended to form an unfavourable opinion of that army as a whole. This was particularly marked in the case of the British, many of whom adopted a contemptuous attitude towards their Belgian and French comrades-in-arms, although the French were just as critical of the British, after they had embarked for home without warning their allies. Only the Belgians, although even more cavalierly treated by both the British and the French, would refrain from recrimination.

Although generally prejudiced in his writings about the Belgians and their King after the capitulation, William L. Shirer's contemporary diary entries, made when the Germans took him on a conducted tour of conquered Belgian territory in 1940, were sympathetic and laudatory: 'May 20th: – You were immediately struck by the difference between Holland and Belgium. As soon as we crossed into Belgium we started running into blocks of pulverized houses along the road. Obviously the Belgians were of a different metal from the Dutch . . . they fought like lions. From house to house.' After passing through a number of utterly devastated towns, including St Trond, Tongres and Louvain, Shirer was granted an interview by General von Reichenau, who told him: 'The hardest fighting the first days was along the Albert Canal.' Summing up on his return to Berlin, Shirer noted: 'May 28th: – I saw at the front last week the terrible punishment the Belgian Army was taking; saw all of Belgium, outside of Brussels, laid waste[m] by the German artillery and Stukas.'[120]

CHAPTER SIXTEEN

Allied Command and Communications

'We British sometimes have a reputation among our smaller Allies
of riding roughshod over their susceptibilities . . . above all we
must remember and never forget that we are an Ally ourselves.
Perhaps the British may sometimes fail fully to realize this.'

General Sir Richard Gale,
in a lecture on 'Co-operation with Allies'

Admiral Keyes' appeal for air support had been the first demonstration of
what would prove to be the value of his presence at King Leopold's side.
It was through him alone – because of his special relationship with
Churchill – that the King's point of view was effectively presented to
London. It was unfortunate that this point of view was habitually ignored
– although not for want of statement – and that the truth about Leopold's
conduct and character was perverted or suppressed after he was forced to
surrender his army. But thanks to the careful notes which Keyes made on
the spot, the King's record can be established authoritatively and incon-
trovertibly.

In fact, during the most crucial days of the campaign the King had
virtually no channel of communication with the British other than Keyes.
The British Ambassador in Brussels, Sir Lancelot Oliphant, accompanied by Colonel Blake, left the country in haste a few days later and
disappeared, in circumstances described below. Although Major-
General Needham, a former Military Attaché, had arrived in Brussels on
May 10th to head the British Military Mission to the Belgian GQG, he
was soon repatriated, following a motor accident.* It was not until the
17th that the admirable Lieutenant-Colonel George Davy replaced
General Needham and thereafter performed his vital task in the teeth of a
hostile and suspicious British GHQ, with sensitivity, dedication and
enterprise.

Much bitterness and many misunderstandings would have been
avoided if the British generals in Belgium had followed the precepts
which the intrepid and unchauvinistic General Gale, who led the parachute assault before the 1944 Normandy landings, expounded after the

---

* After General Needham returned to England he wrote to Sir Roger that in his opinion
King Leopold 'sized up the situation a good deal better than those responsible for the Allied
endeavours in Belgium did'.

war. In addition to the advice quoted above, he declared that good relations with allies depended on a knowledge of their language, an understanding of their problems, tact and patience: 'At all times, not only military considerations have to be taken into account. National pride, national outlook and national habits have to be borne in mind.'[121] Unfortunately, these qualities were notably lacking in the higher echelons of the BEF, with Pownall taking the lead in 'riding roughshod' over his Belgian allies' susceptibilities.

Despite all the efforts made by Keyes, Davy and his excellent liaison team to foster good relations with the Belgians, Pownall and certain like-minded senior officers persisted to the last in their suspicious, scornful and overbearing attitude towards them. It was tragic that the men occupying the key positions at the heart of the BEF should have been so disposed, for this hostile attitude towards the Belgians radiated throughout the British forces and as far as London – where, of course, it already existed. This meant that in what was now *de facto* an alliance proper liaison was impossible to achieve. In some cases the British treated the Belgians more like the inhabitants of an enemy country which they were occupying than those of a friendly nation to whose 'rescue' they were supposed to be rushing, since many of their plans had been drawn up on the assumption that their entry would be made by force of arms.* In his biography, *Alexander as a Military Commander*, General Sir William Jackson frankly admits: 'British commanders reflect their country's view and will always place the safety of their troops above considerations of an alliance. Mistrust of foreigners runs deep and inevitably comes to the surface in times of crisis.'

The British General Staff kept themselves in almost studied ignorance of what the Belgian Army was actually doing, and invariably assumed that their motives and conduct were of the worst. And by their deliberate avoidance of frank exchanges with the Belgians they exacerbated the chaos caused by the lack of communications within the BEF itself and also externally with their allies. In his *Memoirs* Montgomery records that 'wireless communication within the BEF was never efficient; outside the BEF it hardly existed. Because of this, inter-communication within the Allied forces was almost entirely by civil telephone and this was always "insecure".'[122] Moreover, the operators tended to desert their posts during air raid alerts. Within a few days most of the main land lines were cut by enemy action. Thus all telephonic communication ceased between

---

* After the war a Belgian historical researcher, J. Verhaeghe, was informed by the former Press Attaché at the British Embassy in Brussels that on May 11th 1940 he received a visit from two British officers from Gort's GHQ, who brought with them posters bearing instructions for the Belgian population. The Press Attaché considered the wording to be offensive and more suitable for an enemy than a friendly country. With the Ambassador's approval, therefore, he made substantial alterations to their texts.

the headquarters of Gamelin, Georges, Billotte, Gort and King Leopold. In consequence, as Montgomery recalls, 'there was no co-ordination between the operations of the Belgians, the BEF and the First French Army; the commanders of these armies had no means of direct communication except by personal visits'.

When Gort, who was 'thirsting for battle', decided to abandon his vast and cumbrous Headquarters at Arras and establish his Command Post as close as possible to the front line, 'signal communication was so inadequate,' writes Montgomery, 'the Command Post could be set up only at places – few and far between – where the international buried cable system came to the surface . . . The traffic consequently thrown on the wireless was too great for the few available sets to handle. And the size of the Command Post grew and grew.'[123]

In *Man of Valour* Sir John Colville describes as 'an administrative disaster' Gort's action in taking with him to his Command Post his Chief of Staff, Pownall, and the majority of his senior staff officers, for, as he points out: 'An already imperfect system of communications deteriorated to such an extent that the link between Gort and the nucleus of his Staff [the hundreds of officers and administrative personnel at GHQ] was all but severed.'[124] In his *Memoirs*, Montgomery ascribes the 'breakdown in the intelligence organization' to what he calls 'an amazing decision' whereby Gort sent, on May 16th, Major-General Mason-MacFarlane, the head of the Intelligence Staff and the latter's senior staff officer, Lieutenant-Colonel Templer, who were with him at his Command Post (and thus separated from their organization at Arras), to take charge of a scratch force to protect the right rear of the BEF. Next day the entire GHQ organization at Arras was hurriedly transported to Boulogne in two special trains, to be evacuated by sea in the nick of time to avoid capture by Kleist's Panzers.

In a scathing summing-up Montgomery describes 'the command and control' of the French and British Armies in May 1940 as 'a complete dog's breakfast', for which he blames Gort and Pownall as much as Gamelin:

> They should never have allowed the British Army to go into battle with such a faulty command set-up; knowing the hopeless organization of the High Command, they should have organized GHQ in a more professional way.

'The distribution of Staff duties between GHQ and the Command Post,' Montgomery continues, 'was badly organized from the very beginning; the Staff plan was amateur and lacked the professional's touch.' 'Moreover,' he concludes, 'GHQ of the BEF had never conducted any exercises, either with or without troops, from the time we landed in France in 1939 up to the day active operations began in May 1940 . . . The result was a total lack of any common policy or tactical doctrine through-out the BEF . . . and there was no firm grip from the top.'

Montgomery was not the only senior officer in the BEF to be appalled by the deficiencies and shortcomings throughout the force and its High Command, and to lack confidence in the C-in-C and Chief of Staff, whom he later described as 'completely useless'. Indeed, his fellow-generals and in particular Alan Brooke (later Field Marshal Lord Alanbrooke) shared his views. Both these outstanding generals were frank in their criticisms of their leaders, as well as castigating the command structure. And both let it be known that, although they and their colleagues liked and admired Gort as a brave fighting soldier, they found him incompetent as an army commander.

Of Gort, Montgomery wrote in *The Path to Leadership*: 'He was unfitted for the job – and we senior officers all knew it.' And in his *Memoirs* he commented that 'Gort's appointment was a mistake; the job was above his ceiling'. (Gort's highest previous command had been an infantry brigade.) 'He was not clever,' Montgomery continues, 'and he did not bother about administration . . .'[126] To this Alanbrooke adds: 'Unfortu-nately his brain was geared to detail all the time. The important points . . . he left entirely to his Staff, whilst he dealt with details such as platoon log-books, carrying of sandbags, booby traps . . . Repeatedly Dill and I called for conferences to discuss specific important points . . . but when we met, all these points were handed over to Pownall or Neame to deal with. He took practically no part in the discussion . . . As the time passed, these failings became more and more disconcerting . . .'[125]

It was not until 1981, when extracts from Montgomery's pencil-written diary of the campaign were published in Nigel Hamilton's massive biography, *Monty, The Making of a General*, that the full story of the inept command and control of the BEF by Gort and Pownall was disclosed. After describing their command structure as 'chaotic' and Gort as 'arguably the bravest but most incompetent British army commander of the twentieth century', Hamilton reveals that Montgomery was so incensed by the two generals' mismanagement of the BEF that he went straight to the War Office on his return from Dunkirk and demanded an interview with the CIGS, General Dill. Montgomery's diary note records that he informed Dill 'as to the condition of Gort . . . on the evening of May 30th' and said that 'the events of the past few weeks had proved that certain officers were unfit to be employed again and should be retired'. In a description of Gort's 'condition' on the 30th, Montgomery wrote that he was a 'pathetic sight' and was, 'in my opinion, finished. He was incapable of grasping the military situation firmly, and issuing clear orders. He was incapable of instilling confidence or morale. He had "had it" . . .'*

---

* Letter written by Montgomery on August 25th 1952 to Gort's biographer, J. R. Colville, but not quoted in *Man of Valour*.

Montgomery also gave Dill his opinion 'that the BEF had never been "commanded" since it was formed, and that for the next encounter we must have a new GHQ and a new C-in-C'.

A few days later Montgomery received a private letter from Pownall cautioning him about wagging tongues bringing discredit to the BEF. This, Nigel Hamilton suggests, was a vain attempt to 'silence' Montgomery by a 'veiled threat that Gort might not recommend him for an honour or future command', if he did not desist from criticizing the C-in-C and the Chief of Staff of the BEF. Across the bottom of Pownall's letter Montgomery pencilled: 'He was completely useless' – an assessment which Field Marshal Templer endorsed during an interview with Hamilton in 1979, as the latter recalls.[127]

And what of the French Supreme Commander, under whom Gort and Pownall served? Gamelin was the very antithesis of the schoolboyish British Commander-in-Chief, being 'like a savant testing the chemical reactions of his strategy in a laboratory', as General de Gaulle describes him, 'in a setting which suggested a convent, attended by a few officers, working and meditating without mixing in day-to-day duties'.[128]

Gamelin was the senior service officer on the Supreme Allied Council, of which Gort was not even a member, because the BEF was so small that it constituted only one of the four armies in the French No. 1 Army Group stationed on the Belgian frontier. Thus Gort was subordinate not only to Gamelin, but also to Georges, the Commander-in-Chief of the North-East Front, and to Billotte, the commander of No. 1 Army Group. Gort did in fact have access to Gamelin, although their meetings were few and far between. An amusing account is given by Brigadier L. A. Hawes of their encounter at the first Anglo-French Staff talks which were held in France in 1939. 'There were no interpreters present and General Gamelin spoke so quickly that I am quite sure half of what he said was not understood by the British . . . General Gamelin would talk at great length very rapidly for some minutes . . . and General Gort would reply at once: "*D'accord.*" '[129]

Although Pownall was hardly in a position to criticize in view of the deplorable state of his own Staff organization and command structure, he described in his diary that of the French as 'a really clownish arrangement'. In *Assignment to Catastrophe* General Spears describes how 'for lack of a definition of powers, there were in fact two Commanders-in-Chief of the land forces, Gamelin and Georges' – between whom, he observes 'the struggle was extremely bitter'. As we have seen, Gamelin and his protector, Daladier, had on the eve of the German attack narrowly escaped being eliminated by Reynaud, who strongly championed Georges. Gamelin was the Supreme Commander of the land forces, but – disliking direct responsibility – had delegated to Georges

command of all the field armies (including the BEF) on the North-East
Front. As Spears recalls:

> So ridiculous had the quarrel become that the absurd solution was adopted of
> creating yet another Staff half-way between Gamelin's Headquarters at Vin-
> cennes, near Paris, and Georges' at La Ferté-sous-Jouarre. It would have been
> comical had the issue been less grave than the conduct of a war in which the life
> of a nation was involved.[131]

The French system of High Command from three isolated headquarters was made infinitely worse by the archaic methods of communication that were used between them. Despite the advances in telecom-
munications in the nineteen-thirties, there was no teletype service between the three headquarters and the armies in the field, and the
inadequate telephone system was soon put out of action. At Vincennes
Gamelin did not even had a radio.* Nor even, as one of his staff officers
complained, any carrier pigeons. The main method of communication
was by motorcycle despatch-riders who, General Beaufre recalls, frequently failed to get to their destinations due to accidents, in which a
number of them were killed, on the congested roads.

The Supreme Commander thus found himself isolated in a headquarters which de Gaulle described as 'his ivory tower' and one of
Gamelin's staff officers likened to 'a submarine without a periscope'.
Having no radio himself, and due to the paucity of wireless equipment in
the French Army and Air Force (there were no radios in their tanks and
very few in their aircraft), Gamelin was unable to receive direct reports
from other headquarters or to intercept radio messages to keep in touch
with the situation. For the same reason there were long delays in the
transmission of orders. For example, it would take at least six hours for
instructions to get through to the Air Force Command to attack a specific
target – and when they arrived, operations were greatly hampered owing
to lack of radio communication and other shortcomings. When Gamelin
was asked by the Parliamentary Investigating Committee: 'Since, as you
said in several of your orders, "It is a question of hours", how long did it
take before they were executed?' he replied: 'From the echelon of a
Commander-in-Chief, even of a theatre of operations, to the executory
echelon on the actual front, it generally took forty-eight hours.' It is
hardly surprising in these circumstances that Montgomery should have
written in his *Memoirs*: 'From the point of view of command and control
of the forces available in France in May 1940, the battle was really almost
lost before it began.'

But it was Montgomery as Commander of 3rd Division and Brooke as

---

* 'At the echelon where I was,' wrote Gamelin in a letter to *L'Aurore* in November 1949,
'of what use would a radio have been?'

his Corps Commander, who played the leading parts in an episode which provides a lamentable example of how Anglo-Belgian relations were poisoned by poor communications and by the imperious attitude displayed by the British towards their smaller ally. Readers of Montgomery's *Memoirs* and Alanbrooke's diaries in *The Turn of the Tide* will be familiar with the somewhat facetious British versions of the Louvain incident. But from the Belgian point of view it was certainly no joke. In January 1940 Van Overstraeten had learned from Blake and Hautcoeur that it was Gamelin's intention that the BEF should occupy a narrow front to the east of Brussels and including Louvain, if his 'Plan D' were to be implemented. The King discussed the matter with Pierlot and his other Ministers and military chiefs and all were agreed that the defence of Brussels and the ancient town of Louvain, which had suffered so terribly at the hands of the Germans in 1914, should be undertaken by Belgian rather than Allied troops.

On February 15th Van Overstraeten conveyed a note to Hautcoeur which dealt with a number of matters concerning Belgian co-operation with the Allies in the event that they were invited into Belgium, following a German attack. These included measures for preventing civilians from leaving their homes, keeping the roads clear of refugees for the benefit of Allied military traffic and the exclusive allocation of the Belgian railway system, rolling stock and locomotives to them for the same purpose. As far as the Brussels area was concerned, the note stated that 'The Belgian Government maintains formally that the Brussels agglomeration should remain exclusively in the Belgian zone.' The note then proposed that the northern limit of the British front should be Louvain, but *not* include that town, which would remain a Belgian responsibility. On February 22nd Hautcoeur acknowledged this Belgian proposal on behalf of Gamelin and told Van Overstraeten that the Generalissimo considered it to be 'only natural'.

On March 15th Van Overstraeten made similar representations to Blake and finally delivered a formal Note dated March 18th to him and the French Military Attaché, General Laurent, which declared that the King and the Government 'expressly desire that the agglomeration of Brussels should be included in the zone of operations of the Belgian Army and that in principle no foreign troops should penetrate or sojourn in this agglomeration'.

General Laurent readily agreed that Louvain was 'the key to Brussels' and must obviously be defended by Belgian troops. Colonel Blake, after consulting Gort at British GHQ, accepted on his behalf that the Brussels area, including Louvain, should be outside the British zone. But the King never received any formal acceptance of his *démarches* from either Gamelin or Gort. Thus when Montgomery's 3rd Division reached Louvain on May 11th, it found already in occupation the Belgian 10th

Division, whose Commander told Montgomery that he had been entrusted with its defence by his King and would not leave unless ordered to
do so by him.

'I decided that the best way to get the Belgians *out*,' writes Montgomery in his *Memoirs*, 'and my Division *in* was to use a little flattery . . . I
would therefore place myself under his orders. He was delighted! The
news got to GHQ and there was terrific consternation; my Corps Commander came to see me. But I told him not to worry as I was about to get
the Belgians *out*, and I would then be in front and be the responsible
Commander.'[132] When, as he records in his diary, Brooke asked Montgomery 'what he proposed to do if the Germans started attacking', he
replied: 'Oh! I'd then place the Belgian Divisional Commander under
strict arrest and I'd take command.'[133] Although presumably intended as
a pawky jest, Montgomery's boast was revealing of the supercilious and
high-handed attitude he and some of his fellow-generals displayed towards the Belgians. This frame of mind is further revealed in Montgomery's version of the incident's outcome: 'When the Germans came within
artillery range and shelling began I had no difficulty in taking over the
front from the Belgian Division' – the implication being that the Belgian
troops would immediately retreat in panic on coming under enemy fire. In
fact, when the Belgian division handed over this sector to the British it
was on the orders of the King and not as a result of enemy action or
Montgomery's heavy-handed gambit.

Indeed, Brooke had gone to Belgian GQG some hours before his
meeting with Montgomery at Louvain to sort the matter out. On his
arrival there he met Sir Roger Keyes, who immediately took him in to see
King Leopold. Brooke gives this account of what followed in his diary:

> As I came in I saw no one else in the room, and Roger Keyes withdrew and left
> me alone with the King. I explained to him my difficulty . . . in English. I found
> him charming to talk to, and felt that I was making progress . . . when I
> suddenly heard a voice speaking French from behind my right. On turning
> round I found an officer there who did not introduce himself to me, but went on
> speaking in French to the King. His contention was that the Belgian Division
> could not be moved, that the whole of the BEF should be stepped further south
> and be entirely clear of Brussels.[133]

It was, of course, Van Overstraeten, and although his discourtesy was
inexcusable, he did have cause for exasperation on finding that the British
had ridden roughshod over the King's proposal that the sector of the K-W
Line covering Brussels and Louvain should be defended by Belgian
troops. Although Gamelin and Gort had agreed totally to this proposal,
Pownall's attitude towards the Belgians' wishes concerning the defence of
their capital and their cherished medieval town of Louvain was clearly
expressed in his diary entry for May 11th. On hearing that a Belgian

division was occupying the Louvain sector he wrote: 'They were told three weeks ago, when they raised this through Gamelin, that *we* proposed to hold it. Nevertheless, we find them there on arrival.'

According to Brooke's diary, he 'turned on' Van Overstraeten and informed him, in French, 'that the 10th Belgian Division was on the wrong side of the Gamelin Line'.* Van Overstraeten was surprised to find that Brooke was a fluent French speaker and had understood every word he had spoken to the King. The forceful English general was not the most diplomatic of men and the argument which now developed with the equally obstinate and outspoken Van Overstraeten convinced Brooke that the Belgians were 'no better than the French', of whom he had a very low opinion. The two generals were mutually antagonistic and neither was able to see the other's point of view. In fact, the King later agreed, for the sake of Allied unity, that his 10th Division should yield the Louvain sector to Montgomery's 3rd Division, when asked to do so by Billotte on behalf of Gamelin, but the whole episode created bad feeling on both sides. Although Brooke never saw the Belgian Army or Air Force in action and neither he nor the BEF experienced massed Stuka and Panzer attacks like those suffered by the Belgians, his diaries are suffused with derogatory comments about them. The distinguished American historian, Telford Taylor, comments as follows:

> Brooke, who seems to have had unfavourable preconceptions about the Belgians, was constantly nervous about his left flank, which adjoined the Belgian front. These worries were reflected in Brooke's diary by a stream of critical references, from which one would conclude that the Belgian staffs were totally incompetent and the troops wholly lacking in 'fighting spirit'. But Brooke did not support his harsh comments with any specific instances of poor Belgian performance in combat . . . In fact, the Belgians never broke, and Brooke's left flank remained firmly anchored until the very end . . .
>
> Whatever Brooke may have thought of the Belgian soldiers, the Germans became most respectful . . .[134]

As to Van Overstraeten's attitude towards the British, it is hardly surprising that General Needham should have found the atmosphere at Belgian GQG on that day 'by no means cordial', as he wrote to Admiral Keyes later.

The chief event of May 12th was the momentous meeting which King Leopold and Van Overstraeten attended at the Château Casteau, near Mons. One of its main purposes was to try to bring some order into the Allies' ambiguous and ill-defined command structure. Others present

---

* Brooke's diary comment shows that he was under the erroneous impression that the Belgians had been agreeable, since the inception of 'Plan D', to 'the boundary between the Belgian and British forces . . . known as the Gamelin Line', running 'east and west on the north side of Brussels and Louvain'.

included Daladier, the French Minister of National Defence, General Georges, the C-in-C of the North-East Theatre of Operations, his subordinate General Billotte, commanding No. 1 Army Group, and General Pownall, representing the C-in-C, BEF. The Belgian Army was, of course, under the independent command of King Leopold.

After Daladier, in gaiters and breeches, had paid an eloquent tribute to the courage of the Belgians and their King, Georges asked whether Leopold and Gort would accept the authority of Billotte as the 'Co-ordinator' representing himself – Gamelin having just delegated to Georges the command of all the armies in the field, including the BEF. Pownall could not consult his chief, having been forced to come to the meeting half an hour late without him, since Gort – not for the first or last time – had left his Command Post and could not be found or contacted, because (as his biographer observes) 'the BEF was so singularly ill-equipped in signals'.[135] The British Chief of Staff nevertheless accepted Georges' proposal on Gort's behalf and the King also agreed without demur. This is unquestionable, though it was a favourite line of Leopold's detractors that he 'refused' or was 'reluctant' to accept French command. In fact the King observed at Casteau that it was 'an obvious necessity'. But inevitably, this cumbrous chain of delegated responsibility, with its almost non-existent communications, resulted in muddle and confusion, followed by complete paralysis. Meanwhile, Pownall's diary reference to King Leopold was typically insensitive and derogatory:

> The King of the Belgians seemed pretty dazed and hardly spoke. He had some conversation afterwards with Georges and Billotte but didn't seem to have a gracious word for anyone else, although educated at Eton! I don't wonder he's feeling pretty queer. His country overrun again and his policy broken down.[136]

But Leopold was normally reserved on official occasions and he was now carrying the immense double burden of a Commander-in-Chief in the field and a Head of State whose country was being overrun and devastated. Also, of course, it was his Staff Officer, Van Overstraeten, who naturally spoke on matters of detail as they arose at the conference. But to such considerations Pownall was blind.

Pownall himself reported to the conference that the forward movement of the BEF had gone smoothly, except for the difficulty which had arisen at Louvain. During the course of the conference it was reported that when the French moved up to fill in 'the Gembloux gap', they had found that the anti-tank defences were not as they had expected them to be. Pownall had commented in his diary when he originally heard this: 'Trust the Belgians to bog it', but after hearing the explanation given by General Van Overstraeten at the conference, he wrote in his official account that the 'Cointet' anti-tank obstacle:

had originally run northwards from Namur via Gembloux towards Wavre. This was the shortest possible line and had been selected at a time when they were short of materials. Later, when more material was available it had been decided to move forward this obstacle on the line Namur-Pernez, east of the Forest of Meerdael to Louvain. The southern portion of this had been completed, there were about a dozen uncompleted gaps amounting to a total of 5 Km. In a week's time this work would have been finished.

Commanders preparing for or engaged in battle naturally find it difficult to look far beyond the interests of their own units or to remember that confusion and misunderstanding are a permanent aspect of the relations between allies. They tend to expect a standard of perfection in others even when it is missing in their own command. And the Belgians, of course, were not perfect. Despite their intensive 'round-the-clock' efforts, they had just failed to complete the anti-tank defences across the Gembloux gap. They had been surprised and shaken by the Germans' new and devastating methods of attack. But in a larger perspective it can be seen that by resisting so staunchly they had by May 12th fulfilled their essential task of shielding the Allies' advance from the assault of von Reichenau's Sixth Army. It was not for the French or the British to throw stones. Compared with the deplorable state of the Allies' command and communications systems and the abysmal poltroonery which was shortly to be displayed by the French Ninth and Second Armies on the Meuse, the Belgians' deficiencies seem trivial. And the British who by May 10th had been able to produce on the Continent only ten ill-equipped divisions, not one of which was armoured, were not best placed to criticize the war efforts of others. It was indeed inappropriate that the leaders of an army which the British Official Historian of the campaign admits 'was too small a force to affect the final issue', should have acted so high-handedly towards the soldiers and people of a small nation whose contribution to the battle in progress, in terms of men under arms, suffering and casualties, was proportionately so much greater than theirs.

Nevertheless, thanks to the acceptance by the King and Pownall of Billotte as the 'Co-ordinator', the Casteau conference ended without overt animosity. But Billotte already showed signs of misgivings. Speaking on behalf of his superiors, he drew attention to the immense preponderance of German aircraft and ended with these words:

> The approaching battle may be decisive, and will certainly be difficult. We must expect Belgium to be the focus of the main German attack. Common sense tells us to prepare for the worst. We shall have to envisage retreat to some position further to the rear, without announcing the fact, while yet being resolved to fight to a standstill.

This was not a very inspiring message from the Allied Supreme
Command. It is not surprising that in the car on the way back to
Breendonck the King observed to Van Overstraeten: 'Confidence in
success would appear to be limited.'

All through the fourth day of battle, despite heavy loss of life and the
relentless pressure of the German ground and air forces, the Belgian
Army maintained its orderly fighting withdrawal towards its allotted front
on the left of the BEF on the K-W Line. The retiring Belgians, who for
two days had held the extended delaying positions along the Albert Canal
and the Meuse, had to side-step right across Belgium to fit themselves into
their forty-mile section of the main defence line between Louvain and
Antwerp. This was a remarkable feat of planning as well as execution, as
can be seen from the map, and great credit is due to the Belgians for
having successfully completed it by the following day.

As the Belgian troops withdrew, they fought many fierce actions and
made the enemy pay dearly for his gains. The infantry on the enemy's
right wing, after forcing a crossing of the Albert Canal north-west of
Antwerp, was halted by the sturdy resistance of the Belgian forces
deployed along the River Gette. The Belgian infantry, cavalry, artillery,
Lancers and *Cyclistes* particularly distinguished themselves, while the
Chasseurs Ardennais inflicted bloody losses on the Germans during their
long fighting withdrawal. Many Belgian units, including the Air Force,
added fresh laurels to the battle honours they had won in the 1914 War.

, Notwithstanding Pownall's gibes about the King and his army 'being in
a complete state of wind-up', the morale of the Belgian troops and their
leaders in fact remained 'extremely high', as Colonel Davy reported to
the War Office a few days later. Moreover, the appearance of their
popular young Sovereign in the most threatened parts of the battle-front
acted as an additional stimulus to the troops' spirits. The King made a
practice of visiting the front line as often as he could and on the 13th,
having heard that Antwerp was under attack, he spent the afternoon with
the Vth Corps which was defending that sector. As for Breendonck, there
was no dejection there, as the diary entries made by Keyes and Van
Overstraeten, who was certainly no optimist, make clear. Indeed, the
Admiral signalled to London on the 13th that the King and Van Overstraeten 'expressed their confidence in the Allied armies being able to
hold the line covering Antwerp and Brussels, if adequate air support was
provided', and on the 14th he noted in his diary 'I found the King and Van
Overstraeten even more confident in the morning.' Nor, indeed, was
there anything faint-hearted in the Order of the Day which Leopold
issued to the Army on the afternoon of the 13th, before setting out to visit
the defenders of Antwerp:

Soldiers,

Brutally assaulted by a stunning surprise attack, at grips with forces better equipped and supported by a formidable air force, the Belgian Army has for three days been carrying out a difficult manoeuvre, whose success is of the utmost importance for the general conduct of operations and the outcome of the war.

This manoeuvre demands from everyone, both officers and men, exceptional efforts sustained day and night, in the midst of a moral stress heightened by the sight of the devastation caused by a ruthless invader.

However severe the trial you will surmount it valiantly . . . we are closing our ranks; in the decisive days to come you will stiffen your resolution, accept every sacrifice, to halt the invasion.

As on the Yser in 1914, the French and British troops rely on this; your country's safety and honour demand it.

LEOPOLD.

Moreover, the 'Personal and Secret Instructions' which the King addressed to his generals on the following day were in the same spirit, for he enjoined them to defend their positions to the bitter end. The front held by the Army, he declared 'protects the heart of the Country and must be *defended at all costs*'. (These words were underlined in the original document by the King.) The Belgian divisions had by now completed their fighting withdrawal and were drawn up in battle array on the K-W Line – and they were in good heart, as the King confirmed on his visits to the front. The Belgian troops knew that every 350 metres a strong concrete bastion containing a 47 mm anti-tank gun provided protection against the enemy's advance, as did the River Dyle and the Cointet anti-tank barrier which stood in front of them.

Although the Belgian Army Corps defending Liège was forced to evacuate the area to avoid encirclement, all the fortresses in that heavily fortified zone – now forty miles behind the German lines – held out like islands in the German tidal wave. The enemy was thus forced to tie up considerable forces to contain them and suffered from the continuous barrage of shellfire from the forts and the consequent disruption of his communications. After retiring from Liège, the troops of the Belgian III Corps integrated themselves with the French forces commanded by General de Fornel de la Laurencie, who paid them this tribute in his official report:

With a high conception of their duty, they fought at the side of their French comrades with an heroism which commands admiration. Although the fortunes of war were against her, as they were against us, Belgium can be proud of her sons, I was there to testify to it.

The resistance put up by the Liège and Namur forts, isolated and with no hope of relief, also came up to the highest expectations of the King and the Army. Of the former, Chaudfontaine did not fall until the 17th, Pontisse and Barchen until the 18th, Evegnée until the 19th and Neufchâteau until the 21st. Pépinster did not cease fire until May 29th, the day after the Belgian capitulation. This so impressed the Germans that they allowed the garrison to march out with the honours of war. At Namur, the fort of Marchovelette held out until the 18th, Suarlée until the 19th, St Heribert and Malonne until the 21st; Dave, Maizaret and Andoy until the 23rd. On May 15th, after an NCO had escaped from one of the beleaguered Liège forts and reported that they were all holding out and that 'the morale of the garrison was high', the King ordered that a personal message should be broadcast to them on the National Radio:

> Colonel Modart, Commander of the Fortress Regiment of Liège, officers, non-commissioned officers, and soldiers of the fortified position of Liège: resist to the end for your Country. I am proud of you!
>
>   LEOPOLD.

In order to maintain the closest possible contact with Winston Churchill, Sir Roger Keyes motored into Brussels three times on the 13th. This he was able to do without the transport difficulties he had previously experienced, since he had acquired a Packard motor car, a civilian driver and a police officer, who had been attached to him as a bodyguard on the orders of the King. (In a letter to his wife the Admiral described him as 'a most charming, good-looking and magnificent young man, armed to the teeth'.)[11] As the Admiral saw for himself, the Belgian population was greeting the French and British columns with cheers as they headed up the roads to fight alongside their own soldiers, but the passage of British troops through the centre of Brussels caused great annoyance to the Belgian High Command, which had specifically requested that they should not do so. The Germans, who were maintaining constant aerial observation over the Capital, had announced on May 11th that they would recognize it as an open city and abstain from bombing it *on condition that no military traffic passed through the city*. Five days later the German radio proclaimed 'should Brussels continue to be crossed by British troops, the city will be bombed'. By this date they were of course proceeding in the reverse direction. This situation even caused some friction between the King and the Admiral, as the latter noted in his diary:

> May 13th: That evening after dinner I had rather an argument with the King and Van Overstraeten. They had complained a good deal about British troops going through the middle of Brussels . . .
>
> I had heard many complaints since I arrived, but I thought they should appreciate our point of view . . . Colonel Blake had told me that . . . he had been assured that additional bridges would be made to enable the BEF to avoid going through Brussels to take up their positions.

Van Overstraeten said that there certainly had been difficulty in providing these, but in any case it was possible for our troops to reach their destination without going through the main boulevards . . . As far as Colonel Blake's complaints were concerned, he . . . reminded me that they had agreed, in compliance with my request, to any British officer, from the C-in-C downwards, being taken anywhere in plain clothes by Colonel Blake, to see for himself the whole terrain . . .

The King told me that General Gamelin had said that he personally was quite satisfied with the information given to his Military Attaché in Brussels. I do not think that our Military Attaché had much to complain of, and I am quite sure that there would have been no grounds for complaint if my liaison with King Leopold had not unfortunately been broken, after my visit to Brussels in January, owing to the Belgian Government getting to know of it . . . and fearing that it would compromise their neutrality.

Before going to bed I said that the BEF had kept its schedule and apparently the French Seventh Army had done likewise, and I hoped all differences would be wiped out, and we could look forward to a good alliance in the future. They cordially agreed, and expressed their confidence in the Allied armies being able to hold the line covering Antwerp and Brussels, if adequate air support were provided.

But though the morale of GQG and most of the Belgian troops was steady, that of the Government and the civilian population, which looked in vain to the Administration for a lead, was less so. According to the official report which was drawn up from the notes of the King, the chaos in Brussels on May 14th was 'indescribable'. The Government had made no effort to stop the ever-increasing stream of refugees who encumbered the roads and impeded military operations. As they crossed the city they spread the most alarming rumours, with the result that in the absence of any guidance from the authorities the city began to empty. Whole streets were soon deserted by their inhabitants.

The previous night shooting had started in the park and rumours had quickly spread that parachutists had landed in the city. It was said that some had been seen on the roof of the Electrobel building and that they had attacked the Palace guards. But although the Prime Minister, Pierlot, in a broadcast speech declared 'no parachutists, I repeat, no parachutists, dropped on Brussels yesterday or last night', he refused to take steps to keep the refugees off the roads. *'Ce serait livrer nos populations aux fureurs de la barbarie teutonne.'* ('This would be to abandon our populace to the furies of Teutonic barbarism.') The Admiral's diary describes the events of this day:

May 14th: . . . I learnt that the Belgian Government already wished to leave the capital and had made arrangements to do so; however, they had been requested by the King to remain, and he asked me to beg our Ambassador not to leave. I went into Brussels and found that the British Ambassador had already made arrangements to leave that afternoon, and that the archives were being burnt in the courtyard. I gave him the King's message. Sir Lancelot Oliphant then got into communication with his French colleague and saw the Prime Minister and Minister for Foreign Affairs, and I was glad to learn from him that the flight of the Government and the Allied Diplomatic Corps had been arrested for the moment.

Finding Lord Gort and his Corps Commanders in the Military Attaché's office, I telephoned to the King to let him know of Gort's presence. He replied that he would be delighted to see him, and Gort accompanied me to GQG that afternoon.

The buoyant Gort, revelling in the thought that battle was about to be joined, made a good impression on the King. '*Jeune, aimable*,' noted Van Overstraeten, '*il assure sa Majesté de son concours absolu*.' Then Billotte, whom Leopold had first met with Queen Astrid many years before in Indochina, turned up, but in contrast to Gort he was the personification of despair. The Army Group Commander told the King that he was worried by the enemy's advance in the direction of Sedan. 'The Germans have forged an instrument to win this war,' lamented Billotte, 'this instrument we have not got.' The King had already heard about the crossings of the Meuse south of Namur and, as we have seen, his secret intelligence sources had convinced him that the Germans' main thrust would be made in this region. But it was not until next day that he became aware, from the reports of his liaison officers, of the extent of the French military disaster on that river. Billotte went on to say that German air attacks on the roads leading from Philippeville to the Meuse had reached such a pitch of violence that all troop movements had been brought to a standstill. These were sombre truths and Keyes signalled forthwith to Churchill another plea for air support:

> The battle will be settled by the ability or otherwise of the Allied Forces to command the air, and in order to do this effectively fighters are absolutely essential . . .

The Belgian Command was still confident that the main Belgian defence position could be held against all attacks, but the intervention of the RAF over the battlefield following the Admiral's appeal to Churchill had raised false hopes that the necessary air support would be forthcoming from the Allies. They were soon to be disillusioned.

Another fact of life that Leopold would now have to face was that the Allies' ability to hold the K-W Line was becoming irrelevant. It was no longer the fighting in central Belgium that was of paramount importance, but what was happening on the front held by the French Ninth and Second Armies south of Namur.

That evening the King learned that German tanks, having crossed the

Meuse, had put the French to flight in the region between that river and the Sambre and caused them to abandon their artillery. Later the King received another disturbing report from General Galet, a distinguished Belgian soldier and old friend of King Albert, whom Leopold had appointed as liaison officer at George's GQG. The General's report confirmed the King's view that the main German thrust was aimed at the junction point of the two groups of armies at Sedan, with the object of cutting off all the Allied forces north of this point. His supposition that the object of the attacks on the Belgian and Dutch fronts was to lure the Franco-British armies deep into those countries was also correct. Only Galet's conclusion – that the French disposed of sufficient reserves to halt the enemy advance – was ill-founded. The French had in fact misled him on this score, for in answer to Winston Churchill's question two days later: *'Où est la masse de manoeuvre?'*, Gamelin would have to admit that he had none, since he had frittered away his only mobile reserve – the seven divisions of Girand's Seventh Army – by sending them on a wild goose chase into Holland. Gamelin's only other 'reserve' formations were thirteen static divisions in the Metz region, but these did not constitute a mass of manoeuvre, being intended only as reliefs for tired divisions in the front line. Since like the bulk of the French Army they had hardly any transport of their own, even of the horse-drawn variety, and depended for their movements on the railways, they became completely immobile when the *Luftwaffe* paralysed the system by relentless bombing.

There was another uncomfortable fact for the King to digest that evening (the 14th). After nearly five days of resistance by the Dutch Army, its Commander-in-Chief, General Winkelman, broadcast a proclamation of military surrender. This meant that Keuchler's Eighteenth Army, which included one Panzer, one motorized SS division and eight infantry divisions, would now be released to add their weight to the German assault on the Belgian Army's front. As in all the *Wehrmacht*'s operations, speed was the watchword and even before Holland was fully occupied the bulk of the invasion forces, headed by the 9th Panzer Division and most of the SS motorized units, were following hot on the heels of the French Seventh Army as it retreated into Belgium. This had been the only Allied military aid to reach Holland, but it had received little or no air support, despite Giraud's desperate appeals to the RAF. After taking a beating from Panzers and Stukas, the French forces retreated southwards in some disorder through Belgium right across the rear of the Allied armies on the K-W Line to France. The German Eighteenth Army, after its redeployment, thus became the right wing of von Bock's Army Group B, pressing hard on the Belgian-held sector of the front, less than one division being left to hold Holland.

The use of a small number of airborne troops in Norway had alerted the Dutch to the danger, but a month was insufficient to prepare for this new form of attack – let alone for the vastly greater force which now blanketed the whole country. Almost two divisions of airborne infantry were landed by transport planes and 4,500 trained paratroops were dropped at key points in the rear of the Dutch defence positions to open the way for the Panzers and infantry of the Eighteenth Army. As in Norway, Denmark and on the Albert Canal, the key to the Germans' success was surprise, speed and daring – and, above all, mastery of the air. And as in those assaults, the Germans' spectacular successes spawned highly-coloured stories that their victims' countries were riddled with fifth columnists, traitors and saboteurs, although as Telford Taylor writes in *The March of Conquest* 'Careful investigations since the war have abundantly proved that . . . the reports of subversion and sabotage were uniformly exaggerated and often utterly groundless.'[137]

CHAPTER SEVENTEEN

Queen in Exile

'I will be responsible for everything except that no harm is to be done to Queen Wilhelmina, who is so popular with her people and with the whole world!'

Adolf Hitler, in his orders to General Student, before the German invasion of Holland

Within a few hours of the invasion of Holland the principal Ministers of the Dutch Cabinet arrived in London by air, and were soon joined by the rest of the administration. But it was not until the fourth day of battle that Queen Wilhelmina joined her government, thereby creating another legend which adversely affected Leopold's reputation. If she could escape to England and in London embody the spirit of free Holland, why could not Leopold do the same for Belgium? So the argument runs, but it is based on a number of false assumptions. In fact the Queen was determined to remain with her people to share their fate and to face the invader, and she never had any intention of going to England, as she records in her memoirs.[138]

At 5 am on the 13th the Queen telephoned King George VI with a desperate appeal for military and air support, and in particular for fighter planes to help in the defence of her country. But apart from a few sorties by the RAF and the landing at the Hook of a handful of Royal Marines and a Guards battalion, which were withdrawn on the 14th without even seeing the enemy ground forces, none was sent. There was, however, a group of elderly British destroyers operating in Dutch waters (the author was serving in one of them as a sub-lieutenant) and HMS *Hereward* was alongside at the Hook when Wilhelmina arrived there later on the 13th. Since German troops were hemming her in, and the port was being bombed, the Queen calmly boarded the destroyer and asked to be taken to Flushing or Breskens in Zeeland Flanders, where her forces were holding off the enemy.

As the *News Chronicle* reported on May 18th: 'Perfectly calm, despite the din and the fires ashore, the Queen walked up the gangway. Her first words to the commander were: "I want to go to Flushing, please" . . . "I have never seen a lady so calm and unruffled", was the comment of a naval officer.' When the *Hereward* was at sea, however, difficulties arose about the minefields protecting Flushing and the Captain received orders from the Admiralty to proceed to Harwich. On arrival there the Queen refused to budge and telephoned King George to insist that she be returned to Holland and also reiterated her appeal for military aid. Both requests were turned down, and she was eventually prevailed upon to accept the *fait accompli* and to go to London in the train provided for her.

Queen Wilhelmina arrived in London at 5 pm, with a single suitcase, clutching the steel helmet she had been given aboard the destroyer. She was greeted with warmth and sympathy and taken to Buckingham Palace by King George, who recorded in his diary:

> I met her at Liverpool Street Station and brought her here . . . She told me that when she left The Hague she had no intention of leaving Holland . . . She was naturally very upset, and had brought no clothes with her.[139]

President Roosevelt's special representative, Harry Hopkins, was given a first-hand account of Queen Wilhelmina's involuntary arrival in England by the King and Queen in their air raid shelter at Buckingham Palace after lunching with them on January 30th 1941. After describing the circumstances related above, Hopkins noted in his diary:

> The Queen said she was a fine courageous woman, and it was perfectly clear from this conversation that she arrived in England entirely by accident and not by intent on her own part.[140]

'I imagined,' wrote Queen Wilhelmina in her memoirs, 'that I should be able to remain at my post in The Hague for some time at least and that if the worst came to the worst I should accompany the army southward, as King Albert had done in his day . . . If the . . . parachute troops had not cut off all connections with the army fighting on the Grebbe, I could have joined it to share the fate of the soldier . . . Of course I was fully aware of the shattering impression my departure would make at home.'[141]

Now that the Queen of the Netherlands was in London, there was nothing she could do except put the best face on it and make use of the facilities of the BBC to explain her departure as best she could to her embattled countrymen. But before she was able to do so, the Dutch people were shattered to hear the bald announcement on their radios as an 'item of Court news' that their Queen was staying with the King and Queen of England at Buckingham Palace. No one was aware that the Queen's arrival in England had been involuntary and the fact was kept carefully concealed by Allied propaganda, which built up her presence in England into a legend. But what that legend, which persists to this day, fails to comprehend is the effect of the Queen's departure on her fighting troops and the consequences for her country during the long years of occupation.°

The Dutch people, who were convinced that their Sovereign would share their fate whatever it might be, and sturdily confront the invader, were stunned by the news that she had left them. A wave of anger and grief swept through the country. One typical Dutchman remarked to a British newspaper correspondent: 'How *could* she? When this becomes generally known, it will lead to a complete collapse of morale – it certainly means the end for us.' He was right, for on the afternoon of May 14th, the day after the involuntary departure of Queen Wilhelmina, with not a single Government Minister remaining in Holland, General Winkelman decided on his own initiative to surrender the main body of his army. The Dutch troops still holding out in Zeeland, where their Queen had tried to join them, were not included in the surrender. The Dutch Royal Navy had escaped to friendly ports by the 14th.

King Leopold would soon find himself in much the same predicament as General Winkelman, for neither C-in-C was able to consult any member of his government, all having fled the country. Moreover, in neither case were any political terms involved – the capitulation referring only to the armed forces. The Dutch C-in-C announced the cease-fire in the following terms:

Germany has this afternoon bombed Rotterdam. Utrecht was also threatened with destruction. To save the civil population and to prevent further sacrifice of life, I feel justified in ordering the troops concerned to lay down their arms . . . The fight in Zeeland is continuing.

I appeal to the population to maintain a dignified and peaceful attitude during the forthcoming occupation and so compel the respect of the enemy.

By a vast superiority of the most modern arms, the enemy has been able to break our resistance. We have nothing with which to reproach ourselves.

Ultimately the Netherlands will rise again as a free nation. Long live our Queen!

Later that evening General Winkelman broadcast again:

Practically unsupported . . . we could not see our way to go on fighting . . . The war was completely one-sided. To have gone on would only have meant that still more innocent victims would have fallen . . .

Our new lot must be endured with courage and determination. We must have confidence in the future. We must show this in our behaviour. We must set ourselves to reconstruct our damaged country. Long live Her Majesty the Queen! Long live the Fatherland!

The bombing of Rotterdam caused a wave of horror and indignation throughout the world. The Dutch defenders, finding themselves abandoned by their Queen, their government and their allies, lost heart and were actually discussing surrender with the Germans when the blow fell.

The red flares sent up by the Germans to call off the attack were largely obscured by the smoke of battle and only a proportion of the bomber formation turned back, the remainder pressing on to wreak appalling damage on the city. This was but a pale shadow of what would have befallen Brussels, had the Germans fulfilled their threat to bomb that defenceless city on account of the passage through it of British troops.

So ended the five days' campaign in Holland. The resistance of the Dutch forces had only resulted in considerable loss of life and the devastation of their country. But this was as nothing compared to what the Dutch people were to suffer for the next five years, under the reign of terror which Hitler imposed on them, on finding no Head of State or government left on Dutch soil with whom to negotiate or run the country. In Holland, as in Poland and Norway, Hitler appointed a *Reichskommissar* responsible only to himself, the infamous Dr Artur von Seyss-Inquart, to head a tyrannical administration of SS men. On the day her country was invaded Queen Wilhelmina had made a stirring proclamation which, *The Times* correspondent reported on May 14th 'made a great impression', he then described how a man remarked to him 'that even if the Germans did penetrate The Hague it would only have begun their troubles, for they would still have to face "Wilhelmintje".'

There is no doubt that Hitler had an almost reverential attitude towards certain Royal personages and for Wilhelmina in particular he had considerable respect. General Student, who commanded the German airborne forces in Holland, described to Liddell Hart after the war how at a briefing by Hitler before the invasion the Führer gave him special instructions 'to ensure that no harm was done to the Queen of Holland and members of the Royal Household. In conclusion, Hitler said: "I will be responsible for everything except that no harm is to be done to Queen Wilhelmina, who is so popular with her people and with the whole world!" To emphasize the importance of the order it was handed to us in writing.'[142]

The German officer chosen for the mission of capturing Queen Wilhelmina and 'ensuring her safety' was Captain Otto Begus. Begus subsequently described how Hitler planned to capture 'those Heads of State who were much loved by their people'. His special *Kommando* unit landed as planned by parachute and in transport planes near Ruygenhoek Palace, but Queen Wilhelmina had left half an hour earlier. A few weeks later Begus was instructed to prepare an airborne operation to capture the British Royal family. The task force of 500 paratroops was to be dropped in the grounds of Buckingham Palace. Its members were briefed as follows: 'On entering the presence of Their Majesties you are to salute in the manner of the German armed forces, NOT the Nazi salute . . . Members of the Royal family are not to be subjected to physical search without the most pressing reason. At all times they are to be treated with respect and with courtesy.'[143] This plan was not as wild as it sounds, for Buckingham Palace was virtually unprotected against this type of coup in those early days. In fact a number of equally bold strokes, including the rescue of Mussolini by Colonel Skorzeny's airborne task force from his 'unapproachable' mountain-top prison in Italy, were entirely successful.

Had Queen Wilhelmina remained in Holland, as she intended to do, to share the fate of her subjects and shield them from the occupying power, it is almost certain that Hitler would have established a moderate military regime, like those in occupied France, Denmark, Belgium and the British Channel Islands, and the Dutch people would probably have been spared much of the suffering which was to be their lot for the next five years under the heel of the SS.*

The most immediate effect of the retreat of the French Seventh Army and the Dutch surrender was to expose the Belgian left flank and greatly increase the threat to Antwerp. Admiral Keyes' diary for the 15th reads:

> The King told me that a strong attack on the Antwerp sector from the North was developing, and a number of tanks had been located approaching from the East in the direction of Malines. He thought that the ground situation was good and well defended: everything depended on getting command of the air over the battle, which is now developing. I went into Brussels that morning and telegraphed to the Prime Minister to the foregoing effect, adding: 'These two attacks must be broken up, if the position is to be held.'
>
> I received the following reply from him:– 'Many thanks for your excellent reports: we are doing our best to help in the air, in accordance with General Gamelin's request. He is commanding the whole battle and alone has a complete view. Pray give my warm regards to our friend [King Leopold].'

But Churchill's confidence in the omniscience of the Allied Supreme Commander was sadly misplaced, for Gamelin, virtually blind in his Vincennes retreat, was making no attempt to 'command the battle', having delegated that function to Georges, who had in turn passed it on to Billotte. In fact, the whole cumbrous and illogical French command structure had by now become completely crippled. Indeed Major Archdale, the British Liaison Officer attached to Billotte's headquarters, commented that 'no command in fact existed' and recalled:

> There were no wireless communications whatsoever in the First Group of Armies. The French relied entirely on physical liaison and on telephones, but within four days of the battle opening, telephone communication had virtually ceased. Co-ordination of operations, planned movements of troops or of

---

* In *Une Tragédie Royale* Fabre-Luce states that figures compiled in Britain show that 300,000 people died at the hands of the Nazis in Holland during the occupation, while the figure for Belgium, where their King's presence as a prisoner helped to protect the people, was 23,000.

supplies, had simply become impossible, for lack of the means of communicating orders or information.[144]

Although the German strategy was for von Bock's Army Group B to break through the Belgian defences and then hold the Allied armies in the North as far forward as possible, while von Rundstedt's Army Group A struck the mortal blow at the pivot point of the Anglo-French wheel forward, von Bock did not take kindly to the secondary role allotted to his force, and was eager to pursue the offensive. Accordingly, he allowed his troops to maintain their pressure on the fronts held by the French First Army and the Belgians.

Meanwhile the whole of the Belgian Army's front was holding well, with the troops fighting back tenaciously against attacks at many points. The troops covering Antwerp, who had been withstanding heavy pressure from the East by the German IX Corps, for example, were now successfully resisting attacks from the North by the spearheads of Kuechler's Eighteenth Army, fresh from their victory in Holland. As the Germans continually probed the Belgian defences, a series of violent artillery duels, in which the Belgian artillery consistently outclassed that of the Germans, were fought all along the front.

At the same time, in the East the troops manning the Belgian fortresses which ringed Liège and Namur maintained the tradition they had established in 1914 by continuing their fierce resistance far behind the enemy's lines. Pownall's diary entry for the 15th was therefore yet another perversion of the truth: 'Belgian morale, already thoroughly bad from top to bottom. They are simply not fighting . . .' On the contrary, it was thanks to the fact that the Belgians *were* fighting so well that, until the fifth day of battle, there had been no fighting for the BEF to do. Indeed, all had been quiet on their narrow front, sandwiched between the embattled Belgian and French armies, until the night of the 14th. It was not until then that the Germans made their first probing attack on the positions held by Montgomery's 3rd Division.

The attack penetrated as far as Louvain railway station, but Montgomery thought so little of it that, having given instructions that he 'was never to be disturbed except in a crisis', he was 'angry' with the staff officer who woke him up and peremptorily ordered him: 'Go away and don't bother me. Tell the Brigadier in Louvain to turn them out.' After which, in his own words, Montgomery 'went back to sleep again'.[145] On the 15th the attack was renewed, while lighter exploratory probes were made on the other two British divisions in the front line – all being vigorously repelled with the help of heavy fire from the well-placed artillery emplacements which had been reconnoitred by General Davidson. On their less densely held and waterless front on the right of the British, however, the French First Army was taking heavier punishment and, after fierce fighting in which the Germans breached the front held by the crack 1st Moroccan Division, the First Army began to withdraw.

Meanwhile, the British Admiralty, fearing that Antwerp might soon fall to the enemy, had sent over the destroyer HMS *Brilliant* with a demolition party on board. On the morning of the 15th Commander Sandford, who was in charge of the operation to evacuate everything that floated and if necessary destroy the port's facilities, the oil, petrol, etc., reported to Sir Roger, who noted in his diary: 'He told me that everyone there was confident of being able to hold it.' The Belgian authorities therefore regarded Sandford's intentions as somewhat premature and had been making difficulties. So, Keyes continues, 'I took him to see the King, who was much impressed, as I was, by his personality, and gave orders to the Belgian General in command at Antwerp to help him in every possible way, and Sandford had no more difficulties.'

Amongst the charges levelled against Leopold for political reasons after the war was the allegation that the King deliberately prevented the ports of Antwerp and Zeebrugge from being put out of action. In fact, the Admiral involved himself personally in the blocking and destruction of the two ports (in the case of Zeebrugge for the second time in history) with the full approval of the King – and nearly lost his life in the process. *

At Belgian GQG, amid almost continuous conferences and a non-stop flow of signals, reports and calls for fresh orders and decisions, the King and his Staff were under ever-increasing pressure. As Head of State, Leopold also had to maintain constant contact with his Ministers and almost every day one or more of them visited him at his Headquarters to discuss matters beyond the purely military sphere. On the 15th, for example, the King asked the Prime Minister what were the intentions of the Government. Pierlot replied that its members were looking to the King for guidance on the line to follow. But, he told the King, the maintenance of the seat of government in Brussels was becoming increasingly difficult. Van Overstraeten's diary for that day summarized Pierlot's remarks in this conversation with the King:

> Brussels is in a nervous state. The sirens sound ceaselessly, frightening the public unnecessarily, and often without justification. Refugees are pouring in, some voluntarily, some forcibly ejected by the French and British. Government officials fear that their retreat by car will be impeded by the damage done to the roads by the German bombs. The hysterical phobia about parachutists leads to the most pitiful mistakes . . . The Government and its officials feel incapable of working under the ominous disturbance of the sirens, the fear of parachutists, the dread of bombs and the prospect of departure.[146]

The Prime Minister was anxious that the Government and the Administration should quit the capital without delay and establish itself at

* See Appendix VI.

Ostend, but the King emphasized the moral influence which the continued presence of the Government and foreign diplomatic missions should exercise in the capital. He was insistent that the Government ought to remain in the capital as an example and pointed out that, having been accepted as an open city, it was undoubtedly the 'safest shelter in all Belgium'. The Prime Minister promised that the Government would not leave Brussels immediately, but asked the King to assume responsibility for telling its members when the time came for them to depart. Meanwhile, unknown to the King, Spaak was strongly urging the British and French Ambassadors and their staffs to quit Brussels as soon as possible – 'in order', Leopold was to comment later, 'to justify their own flight'.

On motoring into Brussels that day the Admiral was dismayed to find how deeply the alarm had bitten. At the British Embassy he found a situation which, he wrote to his wife, 'embarrasses me very much'. In his diary he noted:

> May 15th: On my arrival at the Embassy I was shocked to see a notice pasted on the door, to the effect that it was the property of HM Government, and was now under the protection of the United States Ambassador . . . I was told that the whole Embassy staff was leaving at once . . . I told the Ambassador on his return that the King attached great importance to keeping up the morale of the capital, and doing nothing to shake belief in the ability of the Allies to defend it. I told him that the King had asked the Government to remain and I begged him to reconsider his decision to go. The Ambassador said he felt he ought to go, in view of the [Belgian] Government's wish . . .

The Admiral had privately asked Colonel Blake, whose contacts and experience were invaluable, to remain behind even if the Ambassador were to depart, but the latter insisted upon Blake accompanying him. Sir Roger later wrote to his wife that 'only the Third Secretary showed any spirit and desire to hang on'. At GQG next morning, Keyes' account continues: 'I learnt from the British Mission that the Embassy and all its staff had left at 8 am for an unknown destination! At that time the King and GQG and the Allies were confident of being able to withstand any attack which the enemy could deliver. I telegraphed to the Prime Minister: "Owing to the flight of the British Embassy, only means of communication now through Needham Mission."' The Admiral then drove into Brussels to see 'how matters stood' at the British Embassy:

> . . . I found it shut up, but the Military and Air Attachés' office, which had been established in a large house opposite, was occupied by a Corporal's guard of eight men, who turned out very smartly to receive me. There were also two young English civilians, who were dressed in private's battle dress, and one (F. C. Russell) had taken charge and had collected large numbers of papers (many of which he thought were confidential) ready for destruction. He and his

companion had been answering telephone messages from various Consular Authorities and others, who were asking for instructions and information from the Ambassador, but they could only reply that the Embassy had left for an unknown destination before they came on duty that morning, and then listen to the scathing comments in reply.

Admiral Keyes was much impressed by the conduct of the young soldiers and the two junior clerks put into uniform by the Military Attaché who were the only representatives of His Britannic Majesty's Diplomatic Mission now to be found in Brussels. He particularly admired young Russell for his initiative in taking charge of the situation which followed the sudden disappearance of his superiors. Russell spent the best part of the day at the Embassy dealing firmly with endless problems and enquiries concerning the Ambassador's whereabouts. When the Admiral returned to England, he received from Russell a vivid account of the situation in the rapidly emptying capital, from which it is clear that the young clerk was much concerned about the effect on British prestige of the precipitate departure of the Embassy staff:

At about 3 pm *The Times*' War Correspondent* came in and took refuge in our cellar. I told him that if a word was printed in *The Times* about his last day in Brussels I would have him shot . . .

He had no means of leaving Brussels, so I requisitioned a bicycle for him and sent him off. Shortly afterwards a Gendarme appeared and informed me that the Military Command had left Brussels, and requested us to look after the 400 German prisoners in the Petite Isle, as he was afraid they were escaping. Messages came through asking for arrangements to be made for the blowing up of the Wireless Transmitting Station near Louvain.

The news of the departure of the Government and the Military Command spread quickly, and there was a tendency for groups to form in front of the Embassy. I therefore caused our front door to be opened, and the guard to be visible from the outside. This gave the people confidence, as they saw we had not left and we were able to keep them calm.

After prodigious efforts in burning documents, smashing up teleprinter equipment etc., and handling Embassy problems, and after having been repeatedly arrested on account of his lack of military credentials, this resourceful young Englishman eventually reached England.

Meanwhile, the Ambassador and the Embassy staff had reached Ostend, which was being bombed – causing the Belgian Government to move, on the 18th, to La Panne, where they paused until the following morning, before resuming their flight to Le Havre in France, over 200 miles to the south-west. However, instead of staying in contact with the

---

* Possibly Kim Philby, the Soviet spy, who was then *The Times* War Correspondent with the BEF.

four principal Ministers whom the King insisted should remain with him
on Belgian soil, Oliphant raced off by car to France with the object of
joining the remainder of the fugitive Government. Despite Colonel
Blake's protests Oliphant insisted that he went with him. In his memoirs
the Ambassador justifies his flight by declaring that he promised to
'return, if necessary, by aeroplane . . . whenever M. Spaak wished'. The
pair were allowed across the frontier, but after various ineffective per-
egrinations in northern France found themselves blocked by the German
advance on the coast north of the mouth of the Somme. After some days
of lying low, which included hiding under juniper bushes on the dunes and
during which their car was stolen, the Ambassador 'reluctantly agreed' to
Colonel Blake leaving him to continue his journey alone. Blake duly
reached England, but by then the campaign in the North was over.
Although Sir Lancelot knew that the British diplomats in Norway and
Denmark had been correctly treated and repatriated by the Germans, he
remained in hiding in the village of Fort Mahon, and did not give himself
up to the Germans until June 2nd.

The overtones of the story are both comic and ignominious, and the
undignified circumstances in which the Ambassador was found were
exploited to the full by the Germans to ridicule him – with consequent
damage to British prestige.[P] But from the practical point of view, the
Ambassador's removal of himself and the Military Attaché from the
scene meant that King Leopold was deprived of their diplomatic and
military liaison services with the British at a time when these lines of
communication were of crucial importance. Ironically, Oliphant would
have been much better off, and perfectly safe, had he stayed in Belgium,
for the Belgian Premier and the Foreign, War and Interior Ministers all
remained until May 25th, while Sir Roger Keyes and the senior officers of
the British Military Mission did not leave for England by sea until the
early morning of the 28th, the day on which the Belgian Army was forced
to capitulate.

CHAPTER EIGHTEEN

Sedan

'With ruin upon ruin, rout on rout,
Confusion worse confounded.'
Milton, *Paradise Lost*

When Julius Caesar fought the Germans among the hills and narrow
valleys of the Ardennes, he described the area as 'a place full of terrors'.
Now, while the much publicized attack on Belgium and Holland diverted
attention from the real danger point in the Ardennes, the Germans were
about to emerge from those forests and spread terror among their
opponents.

Sedan bears an ill-omened name in French military history. It was here
that McMahon's forces were routed by the Prussian armies of Moltke in
1870 and Napoleon III surrendered, spelling the end of Imperial France.
During the 1914–18 War the stronghold was again overrun by the
Germans and remained occupied by them throughout the conflict. Here
once again, in May 1940, was struck the blow which was to cripple
French resistance and lead to one of the greatest military defeats in
history, but this time the defences of Sedan crumbled under a rain of
bombs from Stukas, while Kleist's Panzers tore a mortal breach in the
French front along the Meuse. This assault would rout the French armies
on that river and lead to the evacuation of the BEF, the capitulation of
Leopold's Army and the surrender of the whole French Nation.* Within
something over twenty-four hours the Germans had won the whole
campaign.

There were four main factors in this new catastrophe: the drastic
change made by the Germans in *Fall Gelb* after the Belgians had captured
the earlier version; their bold exploitation of the new form of warfare they
had developed; their unchallenged mastery of the air; and the incapacity
and low morale of the French. The Germans had been able to keep the
Allies in complete ignorance of the fact that they had changed the
Schwerpunkt of their main attack from central Belgium to the Ardennes,

---

* The French Ninth and Second Armies were routed on May 14th–15th; 'Operation
Dynamo' commenced on May 26th; the Belgian Army capitulated on May 28th and the
French Armistice was signed on June 21st 1940.

by remaining silent about their advance in the latter area and writing up
their offensive in Belgium and Holland in their communiqués.

'We were badly informed,' observes Gamelin mildly in his autobiography, *Servir*, 'on the advance of the enemy in the direction of Dinant and
Sedan.' In fact, French reconnaissance aircraft reported as early as the
night of May 11th that the approach roads to the Meuse in the Ardennes
were crammed with vehicles moving rapidly westwards with headlights
ablaze and confirmed next morning that a vast armoured force was
approaching that river. But Gamelin and his staff persisted for six days in
their blindness to all such evidence, for they had 'made a picture' before
the battle started, ruling out the possibility of a serious penetration
through the Ardennes, despite the warnings they received from King
Leopold and others that this was the focus of the main attack.* British
GHQ was equally blind, in spite of the anxieties expressed about the
defences in this sector and the warnings sent to the War Office by the
Howard-Vyse Mission at Gamelin's Vincennes Headquarters.†

'The Germans have two Armoured Divisions down there,' Pownall
wrote in his diary on May 12th. In fact, there were no less than seven in
Kleist's *Panzergruppe* of three Corps – comprising 2,270 armoured
vehicles, including 1,800 tanks, the remainder being self-propelled field
and AA guns, troop carriers and armoured cars – the whole closely
supported by thirty-seven divisions of motorized and conventional infantry. This vast array of military power was advancing westwards towards
the Meuse arranged in three great phalanxes, the whole column being a
hundred miles long, with its tail fifty miles east of the Rhine. These enemy
columns winding nose-to-tail along the narrow roads through the Ardennes presented unbelievable targets for the Allied Air Forces to bomb.
'Yet, because of the French terror of *Luftwaffe* reprisals,' writes Robert
Jackson, 'the opportunity to hit the invaders hard was being thrown
away.'[147] While the French High Command floundered in blindness,
timidity and indecision, the Allied bombers were kept on the ground.

On the night of the 12th Georges told Gamelin that 'the defence seems
well assured on the whole front along the River'. The French generals *had*
to believe this. In their 'picture' the Meuse was only of secondary
importance and they were committed to the idea stated by Billotte and
Daladier at the Casteau Conference that the Allies 'were within sight of
the decisive battle of the war in which Hitler was staking his all' and that

* On April 30th the French Military Attaché in Berne learned from German opposition
sources and the Swiss Intelligence Service that the *Wehrmacht* would attack in the West
between May 8th and 10th, with Sedan as the 'principal axis of the movement'. This
information was immediately conveyed to Gamelin and Georges, with a personal visit to the
Generals by the Attaché's deputy on May 3rd, to ensure that they had received it. The same
intelligence was passed to French GQG from several other authoritative sources, but
ignored.
† See Colonel Davy's report in Appendix V.

this was about to occur in the North between Namur and Antwerp, as predicated in Gamelin's Plan D.

At zero hour on May 10th the three Panzer divisions of Guderian's XIX Corps had crossed the Luxembourg frontier, while further to the north four others, including Rommel's 7th, rolled forward closely followed by a solid mass of guns, vehicles and troops. Guderian's corps traversed Luxembourg without incident (according to General Blumentritt the local police even helped to direct the traffic). But when the Panzers reached the Belgian frontier they were held up by the extensive road blocks, felled trees, demolitions and minefields there.[q] According to Guderian 'the destruction of the roads in Belgium did much to delay our advance' and he recalls that his spearheads 'had not been able to advance deep into Belgium owing to extensive road-demolitions which could not be bypassed in that mountainous terrain'.[148] Rommel also commented on the effectiveness of the Belgian Army's delaying tactics in his *Papers*: 'much of the Belgian demolition work had been done with consummate skill: bridges so well dynamited that their remains provided little of use for emergency bridges; roads blown with charges so deep into their foundations as to make them completely impassable.'[149] After describing the stiff resistance on the Belgian frontier, General Blumentritt writes:

> First and foremost, the brave Belgian Ardennes Rifle Division, together with a suddenly advancing French cavalry division, in country very favourable to delaying actions, offered serious opposition. But all the bravery in the world was of no avail against the Panzer and infantry masses, which were advancing along every road and track, as well as across country.[150]

Indeed the progress of the closely packed columns of German tanks and vehicles along the winding roads through the mountainous and thickly wooded Ardennes was constantly impeded and harassed by the 1st Division of the Belgian Chasseurs Ardennais, which, with the help of French cavalry units, fought a series of fierce delaying actions throughout the whole depth of the Ardennes and did extensive demolition work as they withdrew. Nevertheless, after the defeat of France, certain Frenchmen, including Daladier and Reynaud, persisted in alleging that the Belgian units in the Ardennes had withdrawn to the North 'without fighting' or carrying out the destructions of bridges etc., which they had undertaken to do. The repetition of these slanders finally stung the Belgian Minister of National Defence to issue this communiqué in July 1947:

> In the field of destructions no country has made a greater effort, nor agreed to more onerous sacrifices than Belgium . . . In May 1940, all prepared destructions were carried out with the exception of a few which were made impossible

by tactical surprise (the bridges of Vroenhoven and of Veldwezelt) . . . If, in his reported declaration, M. Daladier has in mind the Ardennes, his error is even more glaring, as all the demolitions were carried out in this region and all the bridges on the Meuse were blown up in time. These destructions were at times carried out in extremely difficult conditions . . . and greatly slowed down the advance of the German armies. All construction works of strategical importance were destroyed; and the destructions of a tactical nature handicapped the enemy no less. The Germans have admitted this many a time . . .

The seventy miles that separated the German start line from the Meuse were covered by most of the armour and motorized infantry in three days. The infantry were not far behind, having covered the distance remarkably quickly by forced marches. By the evening of May 12th enemy advance units had reached the Meuse all the way from Dinant to Sedan and the great build-up of tanks, guns and troops began on this forty mile front. The following morning hundreds of German tanks were commanding the wooded heights to the east of the Meuse. All was quiet that sunny morning, for the Germans had reached the river obstacle before the bulk of the French defenders.

The crossing points on the river between Namur and Dinant had remained under the guard of small detachments of the Belgian Chasseurs Ardennais, anxiously awaiting the arrival of the French Ninth Army, which was wheeling forward to join up with the right wing of the French First Army at Namur. Meanwhile, according to German testimony, a small Belgian unit which had established itself in a flanking position at Houx had held the advancing Panzers in check for several hours. It was the Belgians who destroyed the bridges when the van of Rommel's 7th Panzer Division reached them on the afternoon of May 12th, for the bulk of the French defenders had still not yet reached their positions. At Yvoir two German tanks were actually on the bridge when a Belgian lieutenant blew it up, causing bridge and tanks to plunge into the river.

Instead of waiting for the slower-moving artillery to catch up, to cover the crossing of the river, as the French expected, the Germans decided to use swarms of Stukas to soften up the French defences on the west bank. Hitler had promised the maximum support of the *Luftwaffe* and according to Guderian's operation order 'almost the whole of the German Air Force' was to be employed to cover the crossing of the Meuse by the Panzers. Three Air Fleets (*Luftflotten*) were in direct support; and Richthofen's VIIIth *Fliegerkorps*, consisting of twelve squadrons of dive-bombers, which had just pulverized the Belgian defences on the Albert Canal, was switched to launch equally devastating attacks on the French positions west of the Meuse. This vast concentration of bombers were ordered to pound the French positions for eight hours. (Kleist referred to 'about 1,000 aircraft' appearing on the scene on the afternoon of May 13th.) The morale of the French soldiers was completely shattered by the intense bombardment. 'During this time,' the French Colonel de Bardies wrote, 'there were no French planes in the sky. The soldiers felt abandoned.'[151] As in the case of the BEF, the French Army's air support was utterly inadequate. General Huntziger had only twenty-four fighters available to him.

The French 55th and 61st Divisions which received the full shock of the *Blitzkrieg* were low-grade units composed of largely untrained over-age reservists, who were badly under-equipped and hardly knew how to handle their weapons. Each division had to cover a ten-mile front and the defenders were therefore much too thin on the ground. The first crossing in strength was made on May 13th by Kleist's group to the east of Sedan by one of the 1st Panzer Divisions' Rifle Regiments accompanied by Guderian in person. That same afternoon the fortified town of Sedan was captured by a powerful force of Panzers. By dawn on May 14th a pontoon bridge was completed and Guderian's tanks poured across it to establish a considerable bridgehead.

The Royal Air Force, at last released from the restrictions put on it by Gamelin, and a few French planes now put in an appearance and delivered courageous but ineffective attacks on Guderian's pontoon bridge, the aircraft being mostly obsolete and pitifully few in number. The *Luftwaffe*'s highly mobile flak batteries and the swarms of Messerschmitt 109 fighters which protected the ground forces shot down over 50 per cent of the attacking Allied aircraft. Of 71 Battles and Blenheims that attacked during the afternoon, 40 were destroyed – the highest loss-ratio of the war.

Guderian's bridgehead was also attacked by a French tank force, but this was repulsed with a loss of seventy French tanks. The German bridge remained intact and the Panzers continued to pour across, whilst swarms of Stukas pounded the French positions. At Sapogne, where the fronts of the French Ninth and Second Armies met, the French artillery was suddenly overrun by hundreds of German tanks. 'It must be emphasized,' writes Colonel de Bardies, 'that many of our gunners in the rear echelons had absolutely no weapons at all . . . It was found that out of a total of six divisions, 15,000 men had no means of defence whatsoever: not a rifle, nor a revolver, not even a knife.'[152] Yet at the Riom trials it emerged that vast quantities of arms of all types remained unissued in French depots, 'because no one asked for them'.

Meanwhile, the whole operation was proceeding in the warm May sunshine as though the Germans were on manoeuvres. As soon as the 1st and 2nd Panzer Divisions were safely across the Meuse on May 13th, Guderian ordered them to turn right and strike westwards. This blow shattered the extreme left wing of Huntziger's Second French Army at its point of juncture with Corap's Ninth Army, driving a great breach between the two French armies. By the evening of May 14th the German bridgehead was thirty miles wide and fifteen miles deep. Further to the north Rommel's 7th Panzer Division, with the 5th on his right and the 6th and the 8th belonging to Kleist's group on his left, were achieving equally spectacular results against Corap's Ninth Army. As Rommel's personal record recalls:

> Soon we began to meet refugee columns and detachments of French troops, a chaos of guns, tanks and military vehicles of all kinds, inextricably entangled with horse-drawn refugee carts, covered the roads and verges . . . The French troops were completely overcome by surprise at our sudden appearance, laid down their arms and marched off to the east beside our column. Nowhere was any resistance attempted. Any enemy tanks we met on the road were put out of action as we drove past. The advance went on without a halt to the west. Hundreds upon hundreds of French troops, with their officers, surrendered at our arrival. At some points they had to be fetched out of vehicles driving along beside us . . .

The official history of Rommel's division records that the losses suffered during the Meuse breakthrough amounted to only 35 killed and 59 wounded. At the same time the division captured 10,000 prisoners, 100 tanks, 30 armoured cars and 27 guns. The record concludes laconically: 'The division had no time to collect large numbers of prisoners and equipment.' It was not until some days later that 50,000 of Corap's men were rounded up as far back as Compiègne. One of Gamelin's staff officers who was sent to reorganize them reported:

> Total rout. Out of 70,000 men and numerous officers, no unit, however small, is under command; they are a numbed and haggard herd . . . Ten per cent, at most, of the men have kept their rifles and there are no automatic weapons . . . Nevertheless the losses sustained appear to have been slight. No wounded amongst these runaways (*fuyards*) . . . These people are routed . . . The sight of a plane fills them with terror . . .[153]

The same officer quotes a lieutenant who had fled by car as far as St Quentin as saying: 'The sudden appearance of German tanks causes the most indescribable panic everywhere. In 1814 the cry was "*Voilà les Cosaques*"; in 1870 "*Voilà les Uhlans*"; in 1940 the cry is "*Voilà les blindés*" [tanks] – and everyone runs away.' In *Servir* Gamelin recounts a terrible episode where the French fired on their own comrades-in-arms. Georges described to him later how on May 14th 'Huntziger informed me that from the heights one could see, in the Meuse valley below, French soldiers coming out of their casemates, their hands raised in surrender. He had ordered his own artillery to fire upon them.'

The French High Command system was so powerless and their forces so disorganized that they were never able to mount any serious counter-attacks. It will be remembered that the French had no mass of manoeuvre – only thirteen badly placed and static divisions resting in the rear – compared with the Germans' well sited and mobile reserve of forty-five divisions. Most of the French Army's armour, motor transport and best equipment had been allocated to the Seventh Army (which had lost a large proportion in its abortive sortie into Holland) and to the First Army in the North, where the French expected the main attack. The remainder of the Army, therefore, had to rely on horse-drawn transport and the railway system for mobility. The vast German bomber force, having secured the crossings of the Meuse and bombed the French airfields, now shifted the weight of its attack to the lines of communication behind the front, with devastating results. By now, as Billotte had informed Leopold, the roads and railways were under such merciless air attack that all French troop movements were stopped.

'After crossing the Meuse and turning westward,' writes Liddell Hart, 'Kleist's drive met with little resistance. His tanks rolled along what was virtually an open corridor, behind the back of the Allied wing, in Belgium. There was no "Battle of the Bulge", such as the official commentators described so graphically at the time. It was a smooth run . . . Soon there were 100,000 prisoners and countless material captured . . . There were only two men killed per 1,000 and moreover these were hit in the general stampede. Fifteen French divisions had ceased to exist. Manstein's strategy had succeeded beyond his wildest dreams. Unless the Anglo-Franco-Belgian Armies of the North could break out their fate was sealed.'

Meanwhile, on May 14th Gamelin, isolated from the battle at Vincennes, remained blissfully unaware of the seriousness of the situation which was developing on the Meuse. At noon on that day he assured General Touchon that the battle in the Sedan area was only 'a local incident' and that in a few days the reinforcements levied from the Sixth Army would be 'available again for other missions'. The following morning the Generalissimo reassured Daladier about the progress of the battle. But the scene was quite different at General Georges' Headquarters in the early hours of the 14th, as André Beaufre, a staff officer who accompanied General Doumenc there, recalls:

> The atmosphere was that of a family in which there had just been a death. Georges got up quickly and came to Doumenc. He was terribly pale. 'Our front has been broken at Sedan! . . . There has been a collapse.' He flung himself into a chair and burst into tears . . . It made a terrible impression on me . . . Georges, still pale, explained; following terrible bombardment from the air the two inferior divisions had taken to their heels . . . Here there was another flood of tears. 'Well, General,' said Doumenc, 'all wars have their routs. Let us look at the map and see what can be done.'[155]

In *Servir* Gamelin writes that Georges 'seemed completely overworked at the time. I hoped, I admit, that the depression I found in him . . . would be passing and that it was due to his visible fatigue.'[156] The anonymous author of *The Diary of a Staff Officer* describes another conference which took place that day, at which he and high-ups of the two Air Forces, including General Vuillemin (the head of the *Armée de l'Air*) and Air Marshal Barratt, were present:

> The conference was a tragic affair. Most of the French officers were in tears, some quite openly sobbing at having to admit the shame they felt in acknowledging the appalling fact that the French had walked out of their fortified positions without any attempt at general resistance.[157]

Similar scenes of French officers breaking down and weeping as the news of the *débâcle* on the Meuse came through were observed by Major Archdale at Billotte's GQG. Even making every allowance for the appalling deficiencies in French communications and the lack of aerial reconnaissance, it is almost unbelievable, but nevertheless a fact, that not until the evening of May 15th did it dawn on Gamelin that the Ardennes had been the route of the Germans' main attack – and that by sending his best troops into Belgium he had delivered them into an enormous trap. Upon returning to Vincennes from a War Committee meeting in Paris late in the day, he was horrified to see the disastrous reports which had been coming in throughout the afternoon. 'Until then,' writes Pertinax, 'he seems to have nurtured the illusion that everything could be sealed up [*colmaté*] – an expression borrowed from the vocabulary of the 1914–18 War . . . Suddenly his eyes were opened to reality.'

Gamelin recalls in *Servir* how the awful truth burst upon him: 'On the evening of May 15th the Ninth Army was in full retreat. A breach had been opened between the First and Second Armies on a front of nearly 100 kilometres. One could say that the battle of the Meuse was definitely lost.' At 8.30 pm Gamelin telephoned Daladier to inform him of the desperate situation. William Bullitt, the American Ambassador, was present when Daladier received the call at the War Ministry. Later he recorded what transpired. Their conversation was interrupted by the telephone call from Gamelin, speaking from Vincennes. Suddenly Daladier (who had been present at the War Committee at which both Gamelin and Reynaud had expressed every confidence in the outcome of the battle) exclaimed 'No! What you are saying is not possible! You have made a mistake!' Gamelin had informed him that a German armoured column had broken through all the French defences and was between Rethel and Laon, sixty miles from Paris. Daladier was stunned, but when he recovered himself he cried: 'We must attack at once!' 'Attack? What with?' retorted Gamelin, 'I have not enough reserves.' Long explanations followed ending with Gamelin stating baldly: 'I have not a single corps of troops at my disposal between Laon and Paris.' The telephone conversation ended with Daladier saying 'But that means the destruction of the French Army?' To which Gamelin agreed without qualification – and admitted that he had not prepared or manned a line to fall back upon.

The American Ambassador immediately cabled Cordell Hull, the Secretary of State: 'It appears that failing a miracle like that of the Marne, the French Army will be completely crushed.' He added 'the British are beginning to distrust the French and are not throwing all their resources into the battle.' 'The situation of the Allied armies was fatally compromised – they were never able to recover . . . It is no exaggeration to say that we lost the war on that day,' concludes Albert Kammerer, a former French ambassador, in his book *The Truth about the Armistice*, and recalls:

At the same time members of the Generalissimo's entourage were spending the night warning the leading figures of the State: Herriot was woken up at 4 am by a colonel from GQG. Baldly telling him the news, he advised him to make immediate preparations for the evacuation of the Chamber of Deputies. When Herriot asked: 'Is the situation desperate, then?' the Colonel . . . replied: 'Yes, the army, riddled with Communism, is not holding anywhere.'[158]

The torpor and pusillanimity of the French High Command, from which the British suffered as much as the Belgians, was no more than a faint reflection of the panic which swept through the Administration in Paris on May 15th. If the previous two days were the military turning point of the campaign, the 15th was the psychological turning point, for it was then that the French Prime Minister and his Cabinet definitively lost hope. At 7.30 in the morning Reynaud telephoned Winston Churchill in London and said baldly: 'We have been defeated; we are beaten; we have lost the battle.' In spite of Churchill's encouraging reminder of Foch's principle that offensives come to an end after a while and are then ripe for counter-attack, Reynaud could only reiterate 'We are defeated; we have lost the battle.'

At the Cabinet meeting in Paris later in the day it was seriously proposed that France should turn for help to Italy, offering as a bribe international status for Gibraltar. 'The situation has never appeared so grave,' wrote Major Minart, 'the centre of the country is threatened and it is tragic to think that, even if the Government is no longer in ignorance of the danger, the whole nation knows nothing of the immensity of the peril.'[159] This is a reference to the rigid censorship which had been clamped down by the French Government on all bad news.

The optimistic and evasive communiqués issued day by day by the 'Military Spokesman' as the extent of the *débâcle* increased make astonishing reading. At the daily press meetings correspondents could obtain only such soothing handouts as 'The situation is favourable on the whole', with the result that the world remained in ignorance of the fatal march of events. This policy was to prove disastrous, for when the terrible truth burst upon the French they were quite unprepared for it and began to howl for scapegoats, which Reynaud was only too ready to provide. His first sacrificial victims were fifteen generals, headed by the luckless Corap,* who were thereupon blamed for the *débâcle* on the Meuse and summarily sacked – and soon the French Commander-in-Chief himself would suffer the same fate. Indeed, from this moment until the end of his days Reynaud would indulge in an endless outpouring of exculpatory writings in which he heaped the blame for all the disasters which befell his country on everyone but himself.

The press were not the only ones to be kept in ignorance of developments. Not only were the British and Belgian liaison officers who had been appointed to the various French headquarters kept in the dark by the French High Command, but according to Baudouin, the Secretary of the War Cabinet, the Prime Minister of France and his government received the same treatment. When Reynaud rang Daladier – he did not like to call Gamelin direct, for fear of offending the War Minister – and asked the latter what were the Generalissimo's counter-measures, he was told 'He has none.' 'Each day,' writes Baudouin, 'with increasing anxiety, the Premier has had to put up with the impossibility of obtaining information and of exercising any influence over the High Command, in which he has no confidence.' After Colonel de Villelume had tried for the fourth time to obtain some news from Colonel Petitbon (Gamelin's Chef de Cabinet) the latter, Baudouin recalls, 'made an emphatic protest against the curiosity of the Prime Minister's representative. "If this goes on," he said, "I will not give any information at all." The Prime Minister exploded on being told of this, and declared, "It is time to put an end to this comedy. I must be Minister of National Defence; Daladier will have to go to the Ministry of Foreign Affairs or resign." '

Early on the 16th Reynaud heard Gamelin confirm on the telephone to Daladier 'that the Germans could be in Paris this very evening'. In his memoirs Reynaud refers to the *grande peur* that prevailed on this day. 'It was certain that pessimism was general,' he writes, 'I learnt that there was talk of an armistice at GQG.'[160] At 8 am Reynaud gave Baudouin an account of the happenings of the night. 'Daladier had broken down,' he said, 'and General Hering, the aged Military Governor of Paris – in a state of collapse – had advised the Government to leave Paris without delay.

* In a radio broadcast Reynaud publicly castigated the generals and accused Corap, quite falsely, of having failed to destroy the Meuse bridges. The General, who had vainly complained about the inadequacy of his resources in men and *matériel* before the Germans attacked, was subsequently exonerated and reinstated by a Military Tribunal.

General Gamelin had declared without ambiguity, "As for Paris, I disclaim all responsibility from now, Thursday evening." ' 'Which,' the French Premier observed to Baudouin, 'is a polite way of washing his hands.'[161]

Next, Reynaud sent the following SOS to Churchill: 'Yesterday evening we lost the battle. The road to Paris is open. Send all the troops and aircraft you can.' Shortly afterwards the American Ambassador, Bullitt, cabled to Cordell Hull: 'Prime Minister Reynaud has telephoned Churchill and told him that, given the rupture of the French lines, the war could be lost in a few days.' In response to Reynaud's appeal, Churchill, accompanied by a large staff, arrived in Paris that afternoon to see for himself a situation which, he signalled that evening to the Cabinet in London, was 'grave in the last degree'. In London Neville Chamberlain noted in his diary: 'Terrible message from Winston, who is in Paris. Effect is next three or four days decisive. Unless German advances can be stayed, French Army will collapse, and BEF will be cut off.'[162] Churchill had been greeted at the Quai d'Orsay by the spectacle of bonfires of the State archives on the lawn and by the leaders of France with 'utter dejection written on every face'.[r]

At a conference later that day Generalissimo Gamelin answered Churchill's question: '*Où est la masse de manoeuvre?*' with a shrug and the word: '*Aucune.*' This was the atmosphere in which the so-called 'Gamelin Plan' (later known as the 'Weygand Plan') had its genesis. As a strategic conception it involved the assumption that the German armoured incursion could be 'pinched off' and the northern and southern groups of armies could be reunited. With the French Army in the state just described it was doomed to failure. No Frenchman believed it could succeed, but Churchill pressed Gamelin to agree that the Germans would not be able to nourish their armoured incursion and at the same time keep the flanks of their corridor adequately guarded. Gamelin even discussed the question of withdrawing some divisions from quiet sections of the front for the counter-attack, but when Churchill asked him where he proposed to attack the flanks of 'the bulge', his reply was 'Inferiority of numbers, inferiority of equipment, inferiority of method' – and then 'a hopeless shrug of the shoulders'.[163]

Whatever the misunderstandings, and they were many, which arose from the Gamelin and Weygand Plans, it is at least certain that from May 16th onwards Churchill was envisaging the evacuation of the BEF, for his message to the Cabinet in London included this significant phrase: 'I imagine that if all fails here, we could shift what is left of our own striking force to assist the BEF should it be forced to withdraw.' It is, of course, the duty of a leader to plan for every contingency and, while hoping for the best, always to be prepared for the worst. Churchill, like Leopold, was doing just that. In fact, from this point forward Churchill and his advisers showed a similarly realistic appreciation of events and thought along much the same lines as the King.

Hence, on May 17th, immediately upon his return to London from his visit to Paris, Churchill requested Chamberlain to examine with other Ministers 'the question about our ability to go on alone'. The remarkably prescient document in which the Prime Minister put the same question formally to the Chiefs of Staff, includes the following:

> In the event of France being unable to continue in the war and becoming neutral, with the Germans holding their present position and the Belgian Army being forced to capitulate, after assisting the British Expeditionary Force to reach the coast; in the event of terms being offered to Britain which would place her entirely at the mercy of Germany . . . what are the prospects of our continuing the war alone against Germany and probably Italy?

The detailed answer prepared for Churchill a few days later stated that while the RAF and the Royal Navy were in being Britain should be able to prevent Germany carrying out a sea-borne invasion, but if Germany were to gain complete air superiority, the Royal Navy alone would not be able to prevent invasion for long. It was further considered that the British land forces would be unable to deal with such an invasion. After noting that the Germans had an advantage in the air of four to one, the Chiefs of Staff concluded that '*prima facie* Germany has most of the cards; but the real test is whether the morale of our fighting personnel and civilian population will counter-balance the numerical and material advantages which Germany enjoys. We believe it will.' On May 18th and 20th Churchill telegraphed President Roosevelt to inform him of the extreme gravity of the situation and to stress how seriously the interests of the United States would be affected by the conquest and subjugation not only of France but also of Great Britain. His messages assured Roosevelt that:

> Our intention is, whatever happens, to fight on to the end in this island . . . If members of the present Administration were finished and others came in to parley amid the ruins . . . no one would have the right to blame those then responsible if they made the best terms they could for the surviving inhabitants . . . Evidently I could not answer for my successors who in utter despair and helplessness might well have to accommodate themselves to the German will.

It is clear from this that Churchill, like Reynaud, was determined not to be identified with any policy of surrender. If the worse came to the worst, he could only envisage doing what the French Premier was to do a few weeks later, namely to hand over the seals of office to someone who was prepared to accept them under such circumstances and come to terms with the enemy. Although Churchill's prognosis appears to condone the conduct of those like Pétain, Pierlot and Spaak who were prepared to treat with the enemy to obtain a political armistice and so 'accommodate themselves to the German will', it goes far beyond the purely military capitulation without terms which King Leopold was subsequently forced to accept.

In order to encourage the French Ministers and boost their shattered morale, Churchill adopted a 'never-say-die' attitude and gave them no hint of his own forebodings. But, in spite of all his brave words, he was, in Paris, preparing 'for the fact that the French may be offered very advantageous terms of peace,* and the whole weight be thrown on us' – as he wrote next day to the Chiefs of Staff, when urging that 'only half of the so-called Armoured Division' be sent to France. Furthermore, he rejected all the entreaties from the French to throw into the battle the whole weight of the Royal Air Force – although he agreed to send as many planes as could be spared 'to give the last chance to the French Army to rally its bravery and strength' – as he put it in a message to the British Cabinet, adding, 'It would not be good historically if their requests were denied and their ruin resulted.'

---

* In fact Hermann Göring had already, on May 15th, asked a Swedish diplomat to go to Paris and offer Reynaud lenient peace terms, if he made an immediate request for an armistice. (See Chapter 20, page 254.)

CHAPTER NINETEEN

Days of Retreat

'Je suis crevé de fatigue, et contre ces Panzers je ne peux rien faire . . .'

General Billotte, on May 18th 1940

On the morning of May 15th, shortly after Paul Reynaud told Winston Churchill 'We are defeated; we have lost the battle', the flow of news reaching Breendonck made the King realize, with the awful clarity of a nightmare, that the whole group of armies in the North was going to be cut off from the main French forces and encircled. On the previous day Billotte had shown his apprehension about the situation on the Meuse and now the King learned that between the breach at Sedan and the English Channel the French had no fortified line, nor reserves, nor indeed any means of stopping the onrush of German armour towards the sea.

The King was one of the first to appreciate just how calamitous the consequences of the *débâcle* on the Meuse would be both for Belgium and the Allies. For this he has been termed a pessimist, but it would be more accurate to say that he was a realist. Having measured the dimensions of the catastrophe and foreseen its effects, Leopold thereafter based his personal conduct and his direction of military operations on that diagnosis, without however diverging from the path of loyalty and duty towards the Allies and their Supreme Commander, under whom he had agreed to serve.

Characteristically, the King's first thought was to confer with his Ministers. At 1.30 pm, therefore, Pierlot and General Denis arrived at Breendonck in response to his request (Spaak had not yet returned from a trip to Paris). The King conveyed to them his forebodings and showed them a map on which were marked breaches in the French line north and south of Namur and a considerable incursion of enemy armour at Sedan. Pointing to the English Channel between Dieppe and Abbeville, the King said: 'They will be there in less than eight days.' In fact, the Panzers reached the coast in five.

Two weeks later at Limoges Spaak declared that Pierlot was 'appalled' (*effrayé*) by the King's hypothesis, but he acknowledged that Leopold had 'foretold the military developments which were to take place. He was certain the German columns would not march on Paris; he foresaw their movement to the sea and believed that not only his army, but also the Anglo-French armies, were going to be encircled.' Writing later, he added that by May 16th the King had also predicted 'the defeat of the French Army, France's demand for an Armistice and the continuation of the war by England'.

The distraught Pierlot immediately made a proposal which he was to repeat persistently in the dramatic days which were to follow. He declared that if the three national armies in the North were in danger of being cut off, as the King forecast, he must immediately manoeuvre the Belgian Army westwards and then southwards towards France to join the main body of the French forces and thus avoid encirclement. The King explained patiently that the movements of the Belgian Army depended upon the evolution of events and were also determined by the need to keep its place in the Allied line of battle – and above all by the French Supreme Command under whose orders he had agreed to serve.

In spite of Denis' agreement with the King's views, Pierlot – as he subsequently admitted – began to harbour suspicions that the King wanted to manoeuvre the Belgian Army in such a way as to dissociate its fate from that of the Allied armies. Perversely, he could not or would not understand that, having given his word, the King was in honour bound to follow the directions of the Allied Supreme Commander and this included remaining in line with his army's British neighbours.

This was the beginning of the divergence of views between the King and the Prime Minister, with Leopold realizing that in view of the military situation there was only one course of action open to him, and Pierlot, with his rigid outlook and ignorance of military matters, believing that what the King outlined was what he *wanted* to happen. This divergence would develop into an irreparable split, when Pierlot and the three other Ministers who remained in Belgium on the insistence of the King deserted and disowned him three days before the end of the battle. Denis, being a soldier, understood, but he was not a very forceful personality and was no more successful than the King in making any impression on Pierlot's closed mind.

It was not until the evening of this day (the 15th) that Gamelin at last realized that by executing his Plan D he had sent the Anglo-French armies in the North into a trap. Clearly it was imperative to order all three northern armies to withdraw without delay, yet Gamelin took no action – leaving it to Georges and Billotte to make the decisions. But Billotte, who was supposed to be co-ordinating the operations of the armies north of the breach, was a broken reed, sunk in depression and apathy.

Major Archdale, whose comments on the tearful staff officers at Billotte's headquarters have already been noted, 'had for some time noticed a staleness, a nerve strain and an absence of personal liaison with the armies of the group, all of which boded ill for efficiency in time of crisis'. The situation was no better at the Headquarters of Blanchard's First Army, which prolonged to the south the Dyle line manned by the Belgians and the British. 'There was no planned division of duties among the staff officers, who fell asleep at their desks from unnecessary over-work; no proper maps were available . . .'[164] Nor was their Commander in better shape. One of his staff officers recalls spending a whole hour in Blanchard's presence in which his chief sat in tragic immobility 'saying nothing, doing nothing, just gazing at the map between us'.[165]

By the evening of the 14th Blanchard's hard-pressed army had started to fall back, thus endangering the British right flank – an added reason for ordering a general withdrawal. But the powerless Billotte gave no instruc-tions to the British or the Belgians – only to the French First Army, which at 10.30 am on May 15th he ordered to *prepare* to retire. Leopold only heard about this order thanks to the initiative of Colonel Ronge, his liaison officer at Blanchard's Command Post, and this caused him to make immediate enquiries about Billotte's intentions at the latter's headquar-ters. Similarly, Gort sent General Eastwood there to point out that both the British and the Belgians were gravely threatened by the falling back of the French armies on their right and that he, Billotte, the Co-ordinator, must issue some orders and 'co-ordinate'.

Thus it was not until the morning of the 16th that the Belgian and British High Commands obtained orders to retire from the trap in which Gamelin's Plan D and the French *débâcle* on the Meuse had placed them. But the orders for a general withdrawal in the North were not only belated, they were only half measures, which resulted in the retreat being carried out too slowly to meet the situation. Finally, at 10 am on the 16th, an 'Instruction from the Commander of Army Group No. 1' arrived at Breendonck, from which the King learned that the whole line was to fall back, first to the River Senne that night, then on the following night to the Dendre and finally, on the 18th, to the Escaut (or Scheldt) – the front to which the Allied armies would have advanced under Plan E. The document, Van Overstraeten observed, was neither signed nor dated, which suggested '*quelque précipitation*' in the originating headquarters.

Within an hour of Gort receiving the retreat orders a conference was held at his Command Post to co-ordinate the movements of the British and Belgian armies. This was attended by General Needham, but on the way back to Leopold's headquarters he was seriously injured in a car accident. Thus it was some time before the Belgian Command knew of the steps the BEF intended to take that night in compliance with Billotte's order.

In *Servir* Gamelin makes an odd allegation concerning the retreat order: 'The King of the Belgians at first refused to order a retirement which would leave Brussels completely exposed . . . in order not to abandon the Belgian Army, General Billotte had, during the night of the

15th–16th, to maintain the British Army in position and only retire the right wing of our First Army. We thus lost twenty-four hours.' This story, which was repeated in various forms by the French leaders, is entirely without foundation – as Gamelin was forced to admit by a member of the historical service of the Belgian Army after the war.

Winston Churchill's attitude to the withdrawal of the armies in the North is also rather curious, since in his memoirs he refers only to the BEF and the French First Army being ordered to retire, and omits all mention of the Belgian Army, which was in fact larger than the other two put together, and was defending a longer front than they held. It was also the most drastically affected of these three armies, for the Belgian troops were being forced, on foreign orders, to abandon their homeland – and in most cases their families – to a ruthless invader, without making a stand in its defence.

In fact the King accepted this heartbreaking order stoically and in the spirit of a loyal ally, although it meant the abandonment by his troops of the main defence line which had been prepared at such cost and which protected the heart of their country, their exposure to heavy attack in ever more dangerous positions, the loss of most of Belgium's principal cities and towns, including Brussels and Antwerp, along with the bulk of her territory, and greatly increased hardships for millions more of his civilian subjects.

For the Belgian Army the retreat, which began that same night, involved falling back step by step towards Ghent and Terneuzen, fighting on the rivers Nethe, Rupel and Dendre and on the Willebroeck canal, and marching each day further west, due to the need to maintain their appointed place in the Allied line. Daily the enemy pressure was to increase, despite the destruction of bridges and roads, with the Belgian Army being forced to abandon province after province, able and willing to make a stand, but obliged by military events outside their borders and the Allies' requirements to conform with their withdrawal. Though the King had foreseen this development, Billotte's order was 'the moment of truth'. Its implications were extremely serious, for it might lead to a withdrawal right out of Belgium or, more probably, to a falling back on to the coast with other Allied forces cut off by a German armoured thrust into the Pas de Calais. The alternatives were so momentous that the King felt it his duty to discuss them fully with his Ministers. He therefore summoned them to Breendonck for a conference.

The King had previously asked his Ministers to make urgent representations to the British and French Governments with a view to obtaining the same kind of written guarantees covering Belgium's post-war restoration as had been secured by his father in the Great War – and for which Leopold had applied secretly to the British through Sir Roger Keyes back in January. The King had also reminded his Ministers of the importance of preserving the same independence *vis-à-vis* the Allies as King Albert's government had done, by refusing to enmesh Belgium in a political alliance with them and maintaining not only that her obligations were limited to defending herself, but that she was not bound by their war aims.*

The Ministers were unanimous in their agreement that Belgium should maintain the same posture in the present conflict. Indeed, Spaak had made it clear from the first that the guarantees of military assistance given by France and Britain in 1937 could only be invoked at Belgium's request, and that if she did so, this would not create an alliance with her guarantors – her only reciprocal obligation to them being that she would defend her territory to the limit of her resources.

As in 1914, there were no compensating advantages for Belgium in invoking the Allies' guarantees – very much the reverse in fact – for it had simply allowed them to enter her territory and use it as a battlefield, thus contributing to its ruin and devastation. Moreover, by placing his army under the orders of the French High Command, Leopold had weighted the scales even more heavily against his country's interests and in favour of the Allies. The King and his Ministers therefore felt that Belgium was entitled to receive some consideration in return for the sacrifices she had made on their behalf – at the very least, the same guarantees they had given her in the Great War.

Spaak had accordingly renewed his approaches to Britain and France and travelled to Paris to press Belgium's case in person. But he had been brusquely rebuffed. At a most unpleasant interview, Reynaud had fiercely upbraided him for his government's policy of independence and its refusal to allow the Allied armies to enter Belgium before she was attacked. Spaak was therefore back in Brussels in time to accompany Pierlot and Denis when they presented themselves at Breendonck at 2 pm on the 16th, in answer to the King's summons.

The Foreign Minister was seething with indignation when he told Leopold of the Allies' rejection of Belgium's *démarche* and of his treatment at the hands of Reynaud, whose manner, he said, had been *'plus que grossier'*. In the light of the Allies' refusal to make even this meagre concession towards counterbalancing the one-sided relationship between themselves and Belgium, the King declared – and his Ministers fully agreed – that Belgium's position must remain the same as it had been in the Great War, namely 'that of keeping out of any political alliance; Belgium would defend her independence, but she would not be bound by the war-aims of her guarantors'. It was only when Pierlot began to worry about 'the Allies hurrying to lay all the blame for the defeat on Belgium',[166] as he wrote prophetically in a memorandum to the King on

---

* In 1917 the Belgian Government, with King Albert's full approval, refused to join the Pact of London, in which France, Britain and Russia agreed not to conclude a separate peace with the Germans.

May 20th, that he and Spaak started to backtrack on their stance that Belgium's obligations to the Allies were limited to the defence of her territory.

Later, after the two Ministers had fled to France and denounced their Sovereign under pressure from Reynaud, both would pretend that this was the King's personal policy and would give slanted accounts of their conversations with him, denying that they had fully supported it. As will be seen, Spaak would be quite shameless in distorting and even falsifying the record, particularly in the course of his emotional and later-to-be-regretted outburst at Limoges two weeks later. Nor can Pierlot, although less blatant in his subsequent twisting of the facts, be absolved from rewriting history in the light of hindsight. Fortunately the King, unlike his Ministers, kept a full and detailed record of everything that was said at their meetings and this was committed to paper at the time.[167]

Meanwhile, at the afternoon's conference with his three principal Ministers, the King amplified for Spaak's benefit the dilemma of his army. Because of the direction, power and rapidity of the Germans' armoured thrust, they were likely to cut off the armies in the North and force them northwards against the sea, with the ultimate likelihood of capitulation. If the three armies were encircled, as Leopold envisaged, the only hope for the Belgian Army would be to take up a position backing on the coast, if possible in concert with the British and French forces. On the map he indicated a rough semi-circle around Zeebrugge which he termed a 'national redoubt' – a concept which was similar to that of the C-in-C of the BEF and his generals and identical to that of General Brooke – as will be seen. But Pierlot and Spaak, alarmed by the King's realistic hypothesis, passionately demanded that at all costs the Belgian Army should withdraw south-westwards into France.

They must have made a strange contrast – the pliable Spaak, the rigid Pierlot, the grave, unshakeable King.* Unfortunately the Ministers' thesis was totally unrealistic and impracticable. Indeed, the Allied military leaders never considered it possible even for the nineteen divisions of the French First Army and the BEF, which were closely engaged with the enemy, to retreat into France across an area into which von Rundstedt's forty-four divisions, under an umbrella of unchallenged air power and spearheaded by more than 3,000 armoured vehicles, were pouring. The possibility that the Belgian Army's twenty-two divisions, at the extreme

---

* On May 18th, *The Times* of London published this report from Belgium, which originated from Pierlot's office: 'The Prime Minister was received by the King. He found him calm. He is sharing the sufferings of his people, but without showing it, fully absorbed by the stern duty which confronts him. He directs the operations, looks after every one, and is filled with deep concern for the fate of his troops, whose physical and moral condition he knows full well. Each one of us should, regardless of his own tribulations, be inspired by such a heroic example. All are determined, under the command of our Sovereign, to remain firm until victory is won.'

northern end of the Allied line, could have accompanied them on such a suicidal adventure was therefore never entertained.

In June 1940, when Pownall was speculating on the possibility that the Anglo-French forces in the North could have withdrawn into France across the front of von Rundstedt's massive and rapid thrust, he commented in his diary: 'To withdraw south-west meant uncovering the Belgian Army, or if the Belgian Army conformed, leaving to the Germans the whole of north-western Belgium, the Belgian ports and maybe some of the French.' Indeed the three armies in the North had no alternative, if they were to remain shoulder-to-shoulder, but to retire *westwards* in concert – and this is what Billotte had belatedly ordered them to do. Commenting on a later proposal that the Anglo-French forces in the North should 'march' south-westwards, Pownall wrote:

> In my view had we attempted it we should have lost not only the equipment of the BEF but every man in it as well. All cohesion would have been lost and there would have been a massacre. Incidentally, what did HMG intend to happen to the Belgian Army whilst the BEF and the French First Army 'cut its way through' down south?[168]

The trouble was that the King's Ministers lacked a grasp of military truths, whereas the King had the military commander's gift of the *coup d'oeil*. Because he saw that to be cut off was inevitable and that France must certainly be defeated, he now thought and spoke in these realistic terms. He was just as accurate about what would happen if by some miracle he and some of his forces were able to withdraw to France, when he told them 'once I am in foreign territory I will have to submit to the laws of that country, as will the Army. Consequently the Belgian Command will be no longer free . . . and have no control over the interests of Belgium.'[169] This is precisely what happened to Pierlot and Spaak when they found themselves in France after the Belgian capitulation: they were subjected to extreme pressure by the French Government and forced to submit to its will. But for the moment the debate was left unresolved.

Next day, the 17th, Leopold's GQG was transferred from Breendonck to Ghent. Meanwhile in France, as Albert Kammerer wrote: 'From that day on General Gamelin considered the situation as lost.* He declared to Paul Reynaud that he could only guarantee the security of Paris for the next day and for the following night, adding that it was advisable henceforward to consider an armistice.'[170] On this day, also, after some hesitation on the part of the German High Command, the momentum of the Panzer thrust towards the Channel coast was renewed. Von Rundstedt had put a brake on the advance (causing Guderian to tender his

---

* On the morning of May 16th, according to *The Ironside Diaries*, in a telephone conversation with the British CIGS Gamelin used the expression '*tout est perdu*'.

resignation) because of fears of a French counter-offensive,
failed to materialize and reports on the low morale of the
reached the C-in-C, he authorized von Kleist to press
River Oise. The diary entry of the anonymous British sta
day is illuminating:

> May 17th, 1200 hours: The fog of war grows thicker, but nonetheless, there
> emerges the gloomy bulk of the fact that many units of the French armies are
> not really fighting. The German armoured divisions are too much for them . . .
> Talk of the BEF withdrawing to England. This seems deplorable . . .[171]

Whether deplorable or merely realistic, that eventuality was already
being envisaged and prepared for by, amongst others, the British political, naval and military leaders. It was as early as the 16th that Churchill
predicted the forthcoming collapse of France and the evacuation of the
British forces, while on the following day the CIGS proposed to the
Admiralty (as the editors of *The Ironside Diaries* reveal) that all available
small vessels should be assembled for this purpose. Ironside's diary
entries for the 17th make clear why he took this timely step on that same
day:

> If Billotte cannot stop this broadening to the north we shall find ourselves cut
> from our lines of communication in Amiens. That means that we shall be trying
> to evacuate the BEF from Dunkirk, Calais and Boulogne. An impossible
> proposition . . . I cannot see any of the BEF equipment coming out of Calais,
> Dunkirk and Boulogne. We simply must get the line back to something
> reasonable to cover our communications. Otherwise there is no hope of any
> evacuation, not to speak of collecting any of the Belgian Army . . .
>   At the moment things are very black indeed and we stand faced by a
> completely Nazified Europe . . . What chance have we in reality of continuing
> the struggle by ourselves with the French knocked out? . . . Could we get
> enough of the BEF men and equipment back to England to ensure security
> against air invasion?
>   Very grave days indeed. It seems hard to think that we are up against the
> crashing of the Empire.* And yet we are most surely. Nothing could be more
> certain. We have lived in a fool's paradise. Largely depending upon the
> strength of the French Army. And this Army has crashed or very nearly
> crashed. The turning point in history. Our own faults . . . At the moment it
> looks like the greatest military disaster in history . . .[172]

Gort's vast main GHQ in and around Arras lay directly ahead of the
advancing Panzers – necessitating its immediate evacuation. The whole
cumbrous organization was therefore hurriedly moved to Boulogne on
the 17th in two special trains and evacuated by sea. 'If I had chosen some

---

* Ironside did not just confide this to his diary. On May 19th he said to Anthony Eden: 'This
is the end of the British Empire,' as the latter records in his memoirs, *The Reckoning*.

intermediate spot,' writes Gort's Adjutant-General, General Brownrigg, 'as I very nearly did, I doubt if many of the personnel of GHQ would have got away at all.'[173] Meanwhile, Gort's advanced headquarters staff had moved back to their original billet at Wahagnies.

Like Ironside, Gort and Pownall were by now acutely aware of the mortal peril in which the German armoured thrust placed the BEF, with its undefended communications lifeline stretching across the enemy's line of advance and its exposed right flank and rear. And, just as Churchill and the CIGS were doing in Whitehall, they had to think in terms of the BEF being evacuated, which meant abandoning all its equipment. But in the meantime their minds were concentrated upon taking emergency defensive measures. To this end they hastily deployed in the path of the rapidly advancing swarm of Panzers the three half-strength and only partially armed Territorial 'divisions' which had been sent to France for training, digging and labour duties. One division scraped up thirteen field-guns – some of which could only fire over open sights, others with no sights at all. These weak and scattered British units fought well, but were soon brushed aside or overwhelmed by the highly mobile German formations equipped with tanks, armoured vehicles, self-propelled guns and troop transporters on a scale undreamed of for a British division, and closely supported by the *Luftwaffe*.

At the same time, GHQ set about organizing further improvised forces to defend key points in their rear. Guns and vehicles were withdrawn from training or repair depots and troops from base areas, searchlight and headquarters units. Even a Mobile Bath Unit is mentioned in Gort's *Despatches* as having been sent into action. To command these scratch forces, Gort and Pownall sent off a number of their remaining senior staff officers including their Director of Intelligence – thus incurring the strictures of General Montgomery, Major Ellis and Sir John Colville (Gort's biographer) for depriving their already 'badly organized' advanced headquarters organization of so many of its key members. The resulting breakdown in the British staff and intelligence organizations, coupled with the loss of Gort's main headquarters staff organization when it was evacuated through Boulogne, was disastrous. Indeed the deplorable state of 'command and control' of the BEF, coupled with GHQ's obstructive attitude towards Anglo-Belgian liaison, would have fatal repercussions for the Belgian Army.

On this critical day, however, there arrived to head the British liaison mission at Belgian GQG, Lieutenant-Colonel George Davy of the 3rd Hussars. Henceforward this refreshingly unconventional, enterprising and outspoken officer would do his utmost to improve the almost non-existent liaison between the two armies – in the teeth of British GHQ's hostile and suspicious attitude towards the Belgians. Davy's eye-witness testimony from behind the scenes on the state of affairs within the British as well as the Belgian High Commands and the relationship between them, in which he played a vital role, is therefore of first-class historical importance. Indeed without it many of the facts here revealed would never have emerged. Fortunately Davy, unlike most of the members of his Mission, survived to record his experiences not only in two official reports, but also in an informal personal account and in correspondence.

On May 16th Davy, a fluent French speaker, having served as GSOI of the British liaison mission to Gamelin's GQG at Vincennes,* was in London on the point of departing for Norway, when he was ordered to Belgium to 'strengthen' the Needham Mission. 'The impression I got in the War Office,' Davy recalls in his memoirs, 'was that they had been surprised in two respects: first the rapid collapse of Dutch resistance; secondly the unexpectedly firm resistance of the Belgians, who had in fact withdrawn fighting to the left of the British, which was just as Gamelin had hoped. That the Belgian Army had remained intact for over a week also surprised GHQ in France, as a week had been allotted as their life span.'[174]

On arrival in Brussels next morning Davy found that the badly injured General Needham had been repatriated and immediately took command of the Mission. But Davy made an error. 'In order not to confuse people,' he wrote, 'I decided to put the name Needham in all my signals to GHQ and the War Office. I found later that this had been a mistake. GHQ had thought Needham to be ineffective and had taken little notice of his signals, and as few of them realized that he had gone, I think many of mine still bearing the name Needham were not taken seriously enough.' The Admiral's diary takes up the story:

> May 17th: GQG had taken possession of a convent (Saint-Denis-Westrem) at Ghent, and the British Military and Air Missions were provided with offices in it. Colonel Davy, who had arrived in Brussels from England to join the Military Mission just before we left, was now the Senior Officer and took charge of it.

Davy's first call was at the GHQ of the BEF, where he had what was hardly an encouraging initiation in a session with Gort and Pownall. Pownall, Davy noted, 'did most of the talking. I gathered that the Belgian Army was useless and Pownall said I must get the Belgians to change their dispositions at once so that their regular divisions (1 to 6) were next to the British and no other; he also said that the Belgian Chief of Staff was pro-German and so was the Queen Mother.' The value of Davy's witness is that he came to his task with no pre-conceptions, and yet the closer and longer he stayed by King Leopold's side, during the tensest period of the

---

* See Appendix V.

campaign, the more his admiration for him grew and the greater the distaste he felt for the way his superior officers in the BEF treated the Belgians and their King.

After his return to England Davy was shocked to find that these same senior officers were compounding their iniquitous treatment of the King and his army by laying on them the blame for their own force's misfortunes and defeat. In addition to his official report, therefore, Davy wrote a frank and revealing account of his experiences, headed 'Supplementary Report by Head of No. 6 Military Mission. Attitude of GHQ BEF to the Belgians'. In the introduction Davy stated that he had refrained from criticizing GHQ in this connection in his official report, but went on: 'Now that the C-in-C [Gort] has followed the lead of M. Reynaud in attacking the King of the Belgians and in making scathing comments on the Belgian Army . . . I feel justified in writing more candidly on the attitude of GHQ towards the Belgians.' To ensure that the truth would emerge, even in the event of his death, Davy placed copies of this document in the hands of individuals he could trust to reveal them at the appropriate time, including Sir Roger Keyes.

In September 1943, however, Davy decided to deposit his *Supplementary Report* at the War Office for the use of the Official Historian. In his covering letter Davy reiterated that he had intended to avoid criticizing such senior officers as Gort and Pownall, but 'the savage and lying attacks' made on King Leopold by the French Premier, the British press and 'prominent military persons who found in him a profitable and unresponsive scapegoat', had made him feel 'that the truth should not be suppressed for ever'. He concluded '. . . in the interests of accurate historical fact I think I should leave the document as I wrote it and trust you to use it as you think fit, bearing in mind that the British Commanders and Staff were all tired and short of sleep.' There are however no signs of its use in the *Official History* of the campaign, which is characteristically uncritical of the British.[175]

Davy describes in his memoirs how he met Sir Roger Keyes for the first time soon after his arrival at Belgian GQG in Ghent. The two men quickly established a friendly relationship based upon mutual trust and respect 'in which nothing was held back on either side', as Davy put it. From then on they worked closely together in the cause of improving Anglo-Belgian relations, with Davy enjoying the Admiral's strong support in his uphill efforts to establish and maintain a good liaison between the two armies, despite the hostile and uncommunicative attitude of the officers of the GHQ, BEF towards the Belgians.

Davy was presented to Leopold by the Admiral, to whom, the Colonel recalls, 'I owed my immediate acceptance by the King'. From then on Davy was almost as intimately associated with Leopold as was Keyes, since the King accorded him open access at all times. Davy's account goes on to describe his meeting and subsequent relationship with the King:

> In the next ten days I had several interviews with him, sometimes in his office, sometimes the two of us walking round the garden of his headquarters. He sent for me if there was anything he wanted me to know and I could always go to him if I had an urgent message . . .
>
> The King's taciturn manner since the death of his wife had been common knowledge since before the war. The years of anxiety under the Hitler threat, the struggle to keep up a neutral appearance during the phoney war, the invasion of Belgium and now the visible imminence of French collapse had done nothing to brighten his outlook. The only time I saw him smile was when I assured him, at our first meeting on May 18th, that there was no intention to move the BEF back to England . . .
>
> The King was [later] much maligned by irresponsible correspondents. The 'childish tantrums' of which one 'historian' accused him were a malicious fabrication. He always behaved with the dignity which becomes a monarch, and he never failed to tell me in advance what he wanted to do.

Unfortunately the same co-operative spirit and willingness to provide information was not a characteristic of the British General Staff, as Davy's account reveals:

> It was at once apparent that liaison between GHQ and Belgian GQG had broken down . . . There was no point, in this fast-moving campaign, in starting a series of telegraphic exchanges with the War Office demanding an improvement in liaison arrangements and there was nothing for it but to get on with it myself. The King was trying to do his best to help Gort; British GHQ suspected everything Belgian . . .

Colonel Davy's *Supplementary Report* continues the sorry tale:

> I always had difficulty in getting information for the Belgians regarding the situation and intentions of the BEF. When I went to GHQ myself I badgered someone or other until I was given the situation . . . An ally cannot co-operate unless he knows what you are trying to do, any more than a flank formation of your own army can. And GHQ distrusted their Belgian ally . . . probably I found out too much, and I was a nuisance in the process. I certainly discovered all I could . . .

As a result, a Staff Colonel told Davy that Lord Gort wanted him to remain at Belgian GQG and that all liaison therewith was in future to be carried out by British GHQ's liaison officers. These were known as the 'Twelve Apostles' but, as Davy records in his memoirs, 'they were not provided with any means of communication and on their long journeys to and from GHQ they were out of contact with all information coming from any direction'. He therefore ignored 'that rebuff', which 'did not keep me away from GHQ when I wanted to be there'. Davy's account continues:

> Flank liaison was certainly unsatisfactory, and to the lack of it much of the underrating of the Belgians was probably due. It was not always the same corps which were on the left of the BEF and the right of the Belgians . . . The official comments on the operations state that flank liaison with allies was 'universally unsatisfactory'. I agree that it was poor, and that either more or better liaison officers should have been provided by GHQ. The Belgians themselves were a little slow to provide liaison officers, but they were quicker than our own formations, and were often handicapped through being unable to find out the location of British headquarters.

In his memoirs Davy wrote: '. . . as regards the junction between the two armies . . . there were occasions when I was able to establish contact between the left British division and the right Belgian one; this was largely due to the Belgian GQG always knowing the exact location of every division and brigade; for me to get the British divisions' locations was much more difficult, and I usually had to go and search for them.' Davy's *Supplementary Report* gives some disturbing details of the hostile and uncooperative attitude shown by the BEF towards his and the Belgians' attempts to establish effective liaison between their respective flanking formations and how more than one Belgian was shot by the British, while attempting to do so.[5]

As to the organization of the staff at British GHQ, the workings of which Davy found 'by no means easy to follow', he wrote: 'In contrast to the Belgian GQG it always seemed harassed, hurried and untidy . . . method seemed to be lacking and information did not circulate . . .' He further records: 'The Operations Section at Belgian GQG was tidy and methodical . . . The order and calm at GQG is all the more commendable when one remembers that only one officer in the 2nd Section knew where his wife and family were. All that the others knew was that their families were among the refugees.'

When he first called at Gort's headquarters, Davy was ordered to inform the BEF 'if at any time the Belgians were going to withdraw' and was told that 'on the withdrawal from the Dyle the Belgians had gone first, leaving the flank of the left British division exposed'. Davy's memoirs describe what followed:

> In my first conversations with the Belgian Staff, I checked the movement of the right-hand division on the date in question and found that it had withdrawn a day later than the British division on its right; the apparent lack of troops on its left was due to the simple fact that the Belgians were fifteen miles nearer the enemy! The void on the British left was not a 'no-man's-land' but the void of the Belgian rear area.

This was the first of three occasions when exactly the same thing happened, and I still have the map, marked at the time and showing this. I showed it to King George at Buckingham Palace when he sent for me after the Belgian surrender, when all too many people were trying to make a scapegoat of King Leopold who, being then a prisoner of war, could say nothing to refute the malicious attacks of Reynaud and others.

The incidents cited by Davy were by no means the only cases where the British fastened undeserved blame on the Belgian Army for their own blunders and poor staff work – incomparably the worst being the tragic happening on the River Dendre on May 18th. No mention of any of these miscarriages was made in Gort's *Despatches* and it was not until 1953 that it was belatedly admitted by the Official Historian that one such 'costly mistake' made 'at some point or other' in the British Command – for which the Belgians had been much abused and blamed at the time – was no fault of theirs, but was entirely due to a British blunder.

By 9 am on the 18th the retiring Belgian Army had effected a junction with the British on the Dendre-Escaut line, but a British force remained out in the open under orders to protect the Belgian flank. They were soon surrounded and cut to pieces by the advancing Germans, after fighting gallantly. The few British survivors who managed to extricate themselves, having been led to expect that the Belgians would be on their left front, were convinced that they had retreated without warning their British neighbours, thus leaving them exposed.

This was not so. The Belgians had retired early on the 18th, entirely in accordance with the plan agreed between the two General Staffs. But troops of British II Corps had been ordered to remain forward as a covering force for them throughout the day – in the mistaken belief that the Belgians would not be withdrawing until that night. Someone on the British staff had neglected to inform the British units concerned of the correct time of the Belgian withdrawal. Yet Major Ellis comments: 'No record exists to prove whether the Command Post or II Corps was initially responsible for this mis-statement of Belgian intentions, and the question is unimportant now.' It might, however, be considered as important to the Belgians that the British military leaders allowed them to bear the blame for this particular disaster for twelve years, thus fuelling the far greater antagonism which was so unjustly aroused against them later.[t]

It was at this point that Davy became aware of the fact that Gort's headquarters' staff were pursuing the policy of deviousness towards the Belgians and deliberate concealment of their intentions, which would persist throughout the campaign. On May 18th, Davy recalls, 'the King asked me whether there was any possibility of our withdrawing further than the Escaut line. This with the Ghent bridgehead was his last prepared line of defence and here he hoped to be allowed to stand and fight. If, tempted by the excellent defences, we were to withdraw from the Escaut to the frontier line which we had worked at from October to April, the Belgians would be forced to conform by withdrawing to the Lys, on which nothing was prepared at all.'

Davy immediately sent a message to Pownall giving the gist of Leopold's question. He received a reply from Pownall's Deputy, General Eastwood, which informed him in writing that *there was no intention either at that time or in the future of withdrawing from the Escaut.* This he passed on to Van Overstraeten, who was much relieved, as was the King.

On the following day, the 19th, Davy motored to the GHQ of the BEF at Wahagnies with Admiral Keyes, who had been asked by the King to ascertain Gort's intentions in the event that the three armies in the North became cut off from the main French armies in the South and whether he was experiencing the same lack of direction from Billotte as were the Belgians. When Davy called on Pownall and Eastwood, he told them how relieved the Belgians were to know that the British were not going to withdraw from the Escaut. 'As a matter of fact we *are* going to,' said Eastwood. 'Yes, we are,' said Pownall. 'But don't tell the Belgians.' Davy naturally protested about the Belgians not being told and pointed out that they intended to fight on the Escaut under the impression that the British would do the same. 'Let them go on thinking that,' said Pownall, 'otherwise they will go and leave our flank exposed.'

Davy was torn between loyalties. But 'I never had any doubt in my own mind. This fear of the Belgians bolting was an obsession in the minds of the whole staff at GHQ and had permeated to other parts of the BEF . . . Personally, I had more confidence in the Belgians. So on my return [on the 20th] I told the King that we were going to leave the Escaut and retire to the frontier positions the following night. He was disappointed, and said so. But he expressed no disgust, and showed none of the "characteristic and childish pettiness" or other unroyal moods attributed to him [later] by the more disreputable elements of the British press.' Davy's account continues:

> He was forced to conform with our withdrawal, although it entailed leaving his last prepared line without a struggle, and although he recognized that the movements of his army and the BEF on diverging lines of withdrawal would weaken the junction and mean lengthening his line.
>
> In spite of all this – of course he never knew that the decision to withdraw had been taken 24 to 48 hours before he was told of it – he and Van Overstraeten co-operated fully with the BEF.

The King would have been even more disappointed if he had known of the current developments in British military thinking – which were, of course, deliberately withheld both from him and the French. On May 16th Winston Churchill had envisaged the re-embarkation of the BEF, with the Belgian Army covering their retreat, and next day Ironside, as CIGS, had asked the Admiralty to assemble the necessary vessels. But it was not until the 18th that Gort and Pownall faced up to the harsh realities of the situation and took the practical steps, including the issue of orders which resulted in nearly 28,000 troops being evacuated *before* 'Operation Dynamo' began on May 26th.

The event which concentrated the minds of Gort and Pownall was the visit of Billotte, the so-called Co-ordinator, to their headquarters at Wahagnies late on the night of May 18th. Gort's biographer describes how, on the 19th, the C-in-C added to a letter he had written on the previous day to his friend Lady Marjorie Dalrymple-Hamilton (in which he referred scathingly to the Belgians as having 'evacuated the forward positions on the Albert Canal all too hurriedly' and to 'the speed with which allies suddenly evaporate without warning') the following post-script: 'I am afraid I am not feeling at all optimistic today . . .' The normally boisterous and confident Gort had every reason for feeling despondent, for Billotte had told him that 'he had no plan, no reserves and little hope'.[176]

Major Archdale, appalled by the supine futility of Billotte and his Chief of Staff and the contempt which their subordinates expressed towards them, had decided that the only way to awaken Gort and Pownall to the danger was to arrange for Billotte to visit them at GHQ, BEF. In his diary Archdale noted that during the car journey the French General kept on repeating '*Je suis crevé de fatigue, et contre ces Panzers je ne peux rien faire.*'[177]

On arrival at Gort's Command Post Billotte made no attempt to conceal his deep depression. He produced a situation map on which the spearheads of ten Panzer divisions were shown to be little more than fifty miles from the Channel coast, with no French troops between them and their objective. Although 'not a very clever man', Gort was essentially a realist – and it was obvious from Billotte's despairing remarks that the Panzer thrust could not be halted and thus the possibility that the BEF could now retire 'to the line of the Somme as far as its mouth', with this overwhelming armoured force across its path, had to be ruled out. (It will be remembered that in 1939 Gort, on learning that the Germans had ten Panzer divisions on the Western Front, had remarked to his ADC, Lord Munster, 'in that case we haven't an earthly chance'.) Moreover, it was recognized at GHQ, as Gort's *Despatches* record, that even if this manoeuvre had been possible 'It would obviously be unwelcome to the Belgians who would be faced with the alternatives of withdrawing with us and abandoning Belgian soil; fighting on a perimeter on their own, or seeking an armistice.' As to the possibility 'of the gap being closed by successful counter-attacks made simultaneously from the north and south', this too had to be discounted, as the *Despatches* make clear.

The British Commander-in-Chief was therefore squarely faced by the fact that there remained only one plan of action which offered any hope of salvation for his army. This was the eventuality which Leopold had so shocked his Ministers by envisaging on May 15th and 16th. And it was of course the plan which was eventually implemented – but only after being almost fatally delayed by the embargo which was placed on it by Churchill in London and the French political and military leaders in Paris. In the words of Gort's *Despatches* the plan was for

> withdrawal north-westwards or northwards towards the Channel ports, making use of the successive river and canal lines, and of holding a defensive perimeter there, at any rate sufficiently long to enable the force to be withdrawn, preferably in concert with the French and Belgians . . . It involved the virtual certainty that even if the excellent port facilities at Dunkirk continued to be available, it would be necessary to abandon all the heavier guns and much of the vehicles and equipment.[178]

As a result, Pownall telephoned the War Office in London at about 11.30 am on the following day, May 19th, Trinity Sunday. Speaking 'in camouflaged language' to the Director of Military Operations, he told him that the BEF might soon be forced to evacuate via Dunkirk. (At 1.30 pm he rang again to say that a withdrawal via Bruges and Ostend was an alternative.) Following Pownall's first call, a joint Service meeting was immediately convened in the War Office, at which Vice Admiral Dover (Bertram Ramsay) was present – and, in the words of his *Despatches*, 'the genesis of the "Operation Dynamo": the Dunkirk evacuation took place'. That same morning Gort's Corps Commanders were summoned to a conference – 'a momentous one', as General Brooke described it. The GHQ plan was for a situation in which the Germans had reached the Somme and involved the retirement of the BEF to Dunkirk, round which a defended area would be established for the evacuation of personnel, without stores and equipment. Brooke proposed the alternative of building up a defensive hedgehog round the harbours of Ostend and Zeebrugge, which gave a better chance of keeping contact with the Belgians. (This was one of the eventualities which Leopold forecast to his Ministers on and after May 15th, and which aroused their suspicions that he wanted to separate his army from those of the French and British.)

That morning Gort informed General Brownrigg, his Adjutant-General, 'that the evacuation of the personnel of the BEF with the sacrifice of its material was the best that could be hoped for, unless the French . . . could hold up or cut off the German armoured formations'. He then ordered Brownrigg to evacuate what he described as 'every useless mouth' forthwith through the ports of Boulogne, Calais and Dunkirk.[179] These 'useless mouths' included the personnel of Gort's vast main headquarters, whom the Adjutant-General had whisked out of the path of the onrushing Panzers on the 17th, and the disorganized and often unarmed groups of British soldiers dispersed throughout the back areas, who had been caught between their own retreating army and the tide of enemy forces sweeping round its flank and rear.

The Adjutant-General immediately called a conference and 'explained to the representatives of nearly every branch at GHQ that they must prepare for the evacuation of the BEF, although the final decision had not yet been taken'. His two assistants were immediately sent to take charge of the evacuation, one to Calais, the other to Dunkirk. From May 19th onwards, thanks to this initiative and Admiral Ramsay's brilliant organization, the flow of British troops evacuated by the vessels of the Royal and Merchant Navies grew to a flood – but not without heavy casualties in ships and men, mostly from air attack.

It is thus evident that the idea of evacuating the BEF had become so definite by May 17th that the CIGS had asked the Admiralty to assemble the necessary shipping, while two days later the C-in-C, BEF had ordered the immediate evacuation of thousands of troops through the northern ports – and had felt impelled to ask London to prepare for the evacuation of all his personnel by the same route, thus initiating a joint Service meeting on the 19th at which plans to this end were made and immediately put into effect. Yet *at no point*, even after the full-scale British evacuation began on May 26th (two days before the Belgian capitulation), was King Leopold informed by the British Government or its military leaders that the BEF was seeking safety in flight and abandoning their Belgian comrades-in-arms on the field of battle.

By May 18th, when Antwerp fell, the Germans had overrun the major part of Belgium – and the homes and families of the majority of Leopold's soldiers were in enemy hands. Most of the Belgian Army's supply depots had been left behind and there remained only two weeks' war supplies and provisions. On the 18th too Richthofen's 'Stuka Circus', which had pulverized the Belgian defences on the Albert Canal, now fresh from the 'kill' on the Meuse, was switched back to the Belgian Army's front – just as the last of the RAF fighter planes based on the Continent were withdrawn to Britain.

Due to the refusal of the Belgian Government to insist that the civilian population should stay put, hordes of refugees were encumbering the roads. That day Admiral Keyes described their pitiable ordeal in a letter to his wife:

The roads are terribly congested with troops, transport and hundreds of thousands of refugees, old men, women and children, on bicycles, on foot and in farm carts: it is simply heart-breaking. Every now and then the road is bombed and low-flying aeroplanes dive down and machine-gun the roads. I must say the people are brave and plod along doggedly. For instance one sees a young woman being dragged in a small handcart and 100 other tragic combinations . . . They nearly all carry a little bedding, or a blanket, but that is all. This trek has been going on ever since I arrived. I have never watched anything more hateful. I wish our smug-faced 'Peace at any price' people could see all this and realize how fortunate they are that they have – up to the present – been spared war, because of the armed forces they have done their best to get rid of as 'incentives to war'.*

The Admiral then added: 'I think the calm courage of the King and Van Overstraeten and the behaviour and morale of the Belgian troops is quite splendid . . . Luncning with the King today we listened to the 1 o'clock news and heard a great deal about the British and French – nothing about the Belgians . . .' On this day too Keyes recorded in his diary:

May 18th: I motored back to Ghent in the morning with the King, and we passed a long column of Chasseurs Ardennais on bicycles, with horse transport, in very good order. He told me that they had been fighting in the Ardennes since the morning of the 10th, then for two days at Namur, and since had been retreating. Their physique and bearing were excellent.

If the King could be proud of the behaviour of his front-line troops, he was less gratified by the conduct of his government. On the 18th Leopold gave orders that his GQG should be moved immediately from Ghent to Bruges to ensure that his Ministers, now in Ostend, could keep in close touch with him. But at 12.30, as this was being organized, a message came to say that the Government had left Ostend in haste and, heading westwards down the coast, was now in La Panne, close to the French frontier. The following day the King learned that the entire administration, including thirteen of the seventeen Ministers (only Pierlot, Spaak, Denis and Vanderpoorten remained on Belgian soil, on the King's insistence) had crossed the French frontier (as their predecessors had done in 1914) *en route* for the sanctuary of Le Havre, far to the south-west in France.

Meanwhile, on the morning of the 18th, the King received a letter which Pierlot had written after the Council of Ministers in Ostend the previous day. 'If the Army cannot avoid encirclement,' wrote the Prime Minister, 'the unanimous view is that the King must, at all costs, escape in time from the danger of being made a prisoner.' Pierlot argued that the question was not simply military. 'We here find ourselves involved in the sphere of the constitutional responsibilities incumbent on the King's Ministers.' Then came a statement which has a rich irony in view of the

* A reference to the various left-wing 'Peace' (or pacifist) organizations which, like their modern equivalents, had been demanding that their country should disarm itself unilaterally.

persistent attempts the Ministers would themselves subsequently make to treat with the victorious Hitler. 'A peace treaty could only be fatal for us. It would be the end of our national existence.'

It so happened that when the King received his Prime Minister's letter he was deeply involved in the military questions which Pierlot failed to comprehend, but which were of crucial importance so far as the future of his army, his people and his Kingdom were concerned. Leopold and Van Overstraeten had accordingly sat down at a table and were weighing all the available information. 'The exalted imaginations and anxious minds' of the Ministers – as Van Overstraeten put it – could not grasp realities, but for the King and his military staff the realities were self-evident. The Belgian Army was under the orders of the French High Command and it was unquestionably its duty to maintain its position in the Allied line of battle, which meant keeping in alignment with the British on their right. Even if it had been permissible for them to act independently as the Ministers demanded and fall back towards France, such a move was quite out of the question. Their transport was in any case fully committed and their rear was being crossed by Giraud's French Seventh Army, which was streaming back towards France in considerable disorder.

The King and his Staff also had to consider the fact that during the withdrawal from the Antwerp-Louvain line a number of units had been badly shaken and these needed time in a stable position to recover themselves. In what was so much a non-regular army all this was not surprising, nor was it characteristic of the whole. More importantly, as if to underline the realism of the morning's assessment of the military situation, a message arrived reporting that several Panzer divisions were advancing at unheard-of speed towards Abbeville and Boulogne. When, therefore, Pierlot, Spaak and Denis – at the King's request – arrived at Ghent that afternoon and proposed that the Belgian Army should retire urgently to the west of the Somme, while Gamelin should be forced to promise that it should not at any cost be allowed to become cut off from the main French forces, the King was well equipped to reply. But when he reiterated the points which had emerged during the morning and re-minded them that his army's movements were determined by the orders of the French High Command, the Prime Minister retorted: 'That attitude does not suffice. If you have the impression that the orders given you are inadequate, you should evoke others, if necessary take the initiatives essential to save as much as possible of the Army.'

However, the King firmly refused to follow this course, which was inconsistent with the statement in Pierlot's letter of the 17th that the dominating preoccupation of the Government was to see that the Belgian Army shared the fate of the Allied armies. Then the King must avoid being taken prisoner, the Ministers insisted. Leopold's position as Head of State, they argued, had priority over his function as Commander-in-

Chief. But the King took his stand on his belief that in case of capitulation honour required a Commander-in-Chief to remain with his troops. There could be no immediate compromise between these attitudes, and the meeting ended inconclusively. The tone of the discussion nevertheless reflected an unworthy suspicion in the Prime Minister's mind that the King was voluntarily allowing himself to be pushed back to the sea, so as to be compelled to surrender and thus not have to leave his national territory. At least the four Ministers would be able to watch at close hand, for the King insisted that they should not flee the country, as the rest of the Government had done, but remain at Bruges near his new headquarters, which opened up that evening.

CHAPTER TWENTY

The March to the South

'Situation desperate . . . Personally I think we cannot extricate the BEF.'
General Ironside's diary entry on May 21st 1940

'To remove a general in the middle of a campaign – that is a mortal stroke,' wrote the great Duke of Marlborough. But that is precisely what Reynaud planned to do as the *grande peur* in Paris reached its zenith. Indeed he would now proceed to sack Gamelin, the Allied Supreme Commander, as well as cashiering no less than fifteen generals as scapegoats for the Meuse disaster. On May 17th the Premier secretly recalled the seventy-three-year-old General Maxime Weygand from his command in the Eastern Mediterranean, to which he had been appointed on the outbreak of the war after five years in retirement. At the same time he summoned to Paris the eighty-four-year-old Marshal Pétain from his post as Ambassador in Madrid and on the 18th appointed him Deputy Premier. At that evening's Cabinet reshuffle Reynaud managed at last to dislodge Daladier from the War Ministry, which he thereupon took over himself, relegating his *bête noire* to the Foreign Ministry. Next day he dismissed Gamelin and appointed Weygand Generalissimo in his place.

Reynaud's appointment of these two aged martial figureheads met with a chorus of praise from the press and the public. 'Pétain's nomination has given the country an immense sense of security,' said one newspaper, while another spoke of the incomparable prestige of his name and referred to the extraordinary lucidity of his mind. Weygand's appointment was also popular; he was greeted as 'the soul of Foch'. The famous columnist Madame Tabouis went so far as to announce that his appointment was the thing Hitler feared most. But Alexis Léger, the former Secretary-General at the Quai d'Orsay, 'was convinced that on May 18th Reynaud had lost all hope, and wanted to bring Pétain into the Cabinet because he thought that a surrender would be more easily accepted if men like the Marshal would serve as a front', as he told William L. Langer. Certainly, as General Spears records, Reynaud told him (in almost the same words as Churchill had used in the telegram he sent to President Roosevelt on that same day) that 'whatever happened he would go on to the end, but that the time might come when others, who held different

253

views, might replace him and treat with the Germans'. 'According to General Laure,' Langer continues, 'the Marshal, as he was leaving Madrid, felt that his mission would be not so much to carry on the war as to try to obtain an honourable peace. In the same way Weygand had said, on leaving his command in Syria, that "the military situation in France was already so irremediably compromised that it would be necessary to accept a reasonable armistice . . ."'[180]

The same idea had occurred to the Germans as early as May 15th, the day on which Reynaud had told Churchill 'we are defeated', but it was not until the 20th that the Premier agreed to receive their emissary. This was Raoul Nordling, the Swedish Consul-General in Paris, who records that he was briefed in Berlin by Hermann Göring on the 15th in the following terms: 'Let M. Reynaud make us armistice proposals right away. He must hurry up if he wants to avoid the total occupation and destruction of his country. In a few weeks it will be too late. The offer I am authorized to make today will not be renewed. The longer France delays in acknowledging what is inevitable, the more severe our conditions will be.' Reynaud, who Nordling describes as being in a nervous and emotional state, was much displeased and, after threatening to have him arrested, put him on his honour not to mention Göring's peace offer to anyone.

When Weygand arrived in Paris on May 19th after being given a report of the military situation and seeing a map showing the German advance, he exclaimed, according to Spears: 'If I had known the situation was so bad I would not have come.' When Weygand was asked by Reynaud to take over as Supreme Commander, Paul Baudouin, the Secretary to the French Cabinet, heard him reply: 'Very well, I accept the heavy responsibility you have given me. You will not be surprised if I cannot answer for victory, or even give you the hope of victory.'[181]

Weygand had been put in an impossible position, for the military situation was already irreparable, with a large part of the French Army routed and the Allied armies in the North cut off by Guderian's thrusting armour, which was approaching Arras on the 19th and would sweep on to capture Abbeville and reach the Channel coast the following day. Though remarkably brisk and energetic for his seventy-three years – in contrast to the enervated Gamelin – Weygand had never held a field command. His main military experience had been that of a staff officer far from the front line – his fame having been won as Marshal Foch's right-hand man in the Great War.* In his memoirs Weygand admits that he had lost touch with

---

* Ironically, Maxime Weygand could have been a blood relation of the Belgian Kings, since it is widely believed that his mother was the Empress Charlotte, widow of the ill-fated Maximilian of Mexico and sister of Leopold II. He was obviously proud of his supposed Royal birth, which he would never confirm or deny. His birth was registered in Brussels in 1867 as 'sans origines' and he was brought up in France as a wealthy young man, passing out of St Cyr into the 4th Dragoons in 1888.

military affairs during his retirement and that he had only a 'superficial knowledge' of the situation when he took over as Supreme Commander.

Weygand's first action was to visit Georges at his GHQ. From this interview he drew the following conclusions: 'The conditions prevailing in the higher ranks of the Army were chaotic, while in the lower ranks that staunchness of spirit that had in 1914 enabled them to stand up against the disaster of the first few weeks, seems no longer to be there.'[182] Weygand later told Reynaud that Georges had 'disappointed and even disquietened him. He was like a man who had received a violent blow in the stomach and found if difficult to pull himself together again. He took a narrow and timid view of things . . .'[183]

When, on the 20th, Gamelin handed over his heavy responsibilities, with obvious relief, he did not 'turn over' his command in the normal fashion, but merely stalked out of the office after the exchange of a few words. In view of the illogical and inefficient command structure Weygand inherited and the almost non-existent communications, it is hardly surprising that he was never able to get a proper grip of the military situation, in spite of beginning his day at 5 am and travelling almost continuously. Moreover, the daily visits he was ordered to make to Reynaud and Pétain in Paris further hindered his efforts to gain control of the rapidly deteriorating situation.

In a discussion with Reynaud, Weygand declared that he had been struck by the panic the Germans had created with their aircraft and tanks. 'It was not only part of the army which had taken to flight, but also the civilian population, and in many districts troop movements had been rendered almost impossible by the exodus of the civilians.' Furthermore, Weygand told him, 'Communications with the North are broken, and I am only in contact with General Billotte through London; beyond London the communications are worked by the English.' 'Our whole system of communications,' Weygand wrote in his memoirs, 'had already reached a stage not far removed from complete breakdown. My orders, and also, incidentally, reports to me from 1st Army Group, had to be transmitted by the most unlikely and devious ways.'[184] When Reynaud asked Weygand what orders he intended to give the Allied armies, he replied that he would not issue any until he had seen the position for himself.[185]

Winston Churchill has claimed, although Weygand has denied, that his first action was to cancel his predecessor's 'Personal and Secret Instructions Number 12'. This outlined the so-called 'Gamelin Plan' and was the only operational order Gamelin had produced since the start of the battle. It had been issued in circumstances which can only be described as ludicrous. On the morning of the 19th, knowing that he was on the point of being relieved by Weygand, Gamelin motored to Georges' headquarters and, on leaving, handed him a single sheet of paper on which he had pencilled some vaguely worded 'suggestions of a nature to put matters right'.

In *Servir* Gamelin writes that he found Georges 'in a state of depression which rendered him incapable of taking the helm'. Yet Gamelin's 'Instructions' which he addressed to Georges and Vuillemin, with copies to Reynaud, Pétain and Daladier, placed all the responsibility for directing the operations of the three Allied armies on Georges. It began: 'Without wishing to interfere in the conduct of the battle in progress, which depends on the authority of the C-in-C of the North-East Front, and approving all the orders he has given . . .' and continued in imprecise and general terms to outline measures which Gamelin considered appropriate. These included the 'need' for the French armies in the East to maintain contact with those in the West, while at the same time covering Paris, and for both groups to attack the flanks of the German armoured incursion. One paragraph declared that 'all French and British aviation should aim to participate in the battle . . . in order to keep the mastery of the air . . .' Gamelin appeared to be unaware of the incapacity of the *Armée de l'Air*, or that the remnants of the Advanced Air Striking Force of the RAF had been withdrawn from the Continent the previous day, while what was left of the Air Component of the BEF was in process of doing so. Gamelin's timidly expressed document ended with the observation: 'The whole thing is a matter of hours.'

In his account of this episode Georges describes Gamelin's document as 'an umbrella' and 'a Parthian shot', rather than an order, and declares that the object was to lay the responsibility on him – without giving him the necessary powers of a C-in-C, thus 'leaving the way open to disown me if the occasion arose'. He also points out that some of the suggested measures were already in course of preparation, while others had been considered, but were quite incapable of being implemented, due to the 'inadequacy or absence' of the necessary material means. It is not surprising that the Allied army commanders remained without orders and in the dark as to the Supreme Command's intentions, since Gamelin would not give specific instructions to his delegate Georges, whose authority had in turn been delegated to Billotte, and since the latter was overwhelmed by his responsibilities and unwilling to make decisions on his own initiative.

That evening, in the gloomy moated Château of Kervyn, near Bruges, with its great hall and fourteenth-century armour guarding the telephone switchboard, Leopold received a message from Weygand to say that he had replaced Gamelin as Generalissimo and would come north to confer with the King and the other C-in-Cs on the 21st. The attitude of the King at this stage is well illustrated by the tenor of his daily orders. At 8.30 that morning, for example, he issued a directive to his Chief of Staff, Michiels, that no territory must be abandoned except to superior enemy forces and that the movements of the Belgian Army must be scrupulously tied to those of the British. At exactly the same time on the 20th he reiterated the order that no ground must be willingly yielded.

The King's positive thinking is reflected in the notes Van Overstraeten made that morning. As they had received no communication from Billotte, 'the Co-ordinator', or the French Supreme Command, they could only speculate on its policy. But they agreed that it was more than ever imperative that all three armies in the North should immediately manoeuvre in the way the King had postulated to his Ministers on May 15th and 16th and create something akin to the Lines of Torres Vedras – Van Overstraeten's analogy – in the Peninsular War. That is, to take up defensive positions on as wide a perimeter as possible, behind the succession of curving waterlines which covered the Channel coast and ports. There the Belgians must fight to the last; if they succumbed, the important thing was to do so with honour, after every effort had been exhausted. The King and his military staff were not to know that on the previous day the British C-in-C and his generals had opted for a similar move – albeit as a prelude to the BEF escaping from the trap by sea, rather than 'fighting to the last' – or that the British High Command did not regard themselves as 'scrupulously tied' to the Belgians, as Pownall had just revealed to Davy. But, as became evident in the early hours of the 20th at GHQ, BEF, the Prime Minister in London had decided that the BEF should forthwith embark on a manoeuvre of quite a different kind.

When Churchill had learned on the 19th, as a result of Pownall's two telephone calls to the War Office, that Gort was considering a retreat to the coast and evacuation, he reacted strongly against these realistic representations. (A few days later he wrote to Eden and the CIGS: 'Are you sure there is no streak of defeatist opinion in the General Staff?')[186] The Prime Minister was burning to go over to France himself, but was persuaded to send the CIGS over to Gort instead. The Chiefs of Staff regarded Ironside's mission as one of enquiry, since very little was known in Whitehall about the situation at the front due to the abysmal communications and the general confusion. But Churchill had no such doubts and, while hurriedly briefing the CIGS at the Admiralty that evening just before Ironside's train left for Dover, he dictated the following instructions, which he described as 'Cabinet Order A', to two staff officers, who took them down in longhand:

1 The Cabinet decided that the CIGS was to direct the C-in-C BEF to move southwards upon Amiens attacking all enemy forces encountered and to take station on the left of the French Army.

2 The CIGS will inform General Billotte and the Belgian Command making it clear to the Belgians that their best chance is to move tonight between the BEF and the coast.

The reaction of those present is graphically described in the memoirs of Marshal of the Royal Air Force Sir John Slessor, who accompanied Ironside to France that night:

> There was a short silence. Someone suggested that, as the BEF was under the orders of General Georges, he should be consulted. A paragraph was added to the effect that the War Office would inform him. The same thought was probably passing through other minds than mine – was the War Cabinet in a position to direct operations of the BEF from London, not really knowing the latest situation? What would be the reactions of the French Command, of whose forces it formed only a relatively small part? If the situation was as black as it looked, was there in fact any prospect of this order being carried into effect?[187]

This appears to be the first – but by no means the last – occasion on which Churchill intervened directly in the conduct of military, naval and air operations. On becoming Prime Minister he appointed himself without parliamentary approval 'Minister of Defence', being careful, as he put it in his memoirs, 'not to define my rights and duties', quoting Napolean's dictum that 'a Constitution should be short and obscure'.[188] General Ismay, whom Churchill appointed his Chief of Staff in this new 'Ministry' which, it has been said, 'had no constitutional existence', records: 'the practical effects were revolutionary. Henceforward the Prime Minister . . . exercised a personal, direct, ubiquitous and continuous supervision, not only over the formulation of military policy at every stage, but also over the general conduct of military operations.' As for the Cabinet to whom 'Order A' was attributed, Churchill was equally careful to consolidate the almost limitless powers which he had taken, by excluding his three Service Ministers from his War Cabinet* and restricting it to himself and four compliant civilian political figures: Neville Chamberlain, Lord Halifax, and the Labour Party leaders Clement Attlee and Arthur Greenwood.

It is hardly surprising, therefore, that Churchill's first attempt to direct a distant military campaign from London should have been so potentially disastrous. When he assumed his one-man overlordship, the system for the control and co-ordination of military, naval and air operations by committees 'faithfully repeated', according to Ismay, 'the worst shortcomings of the First World War'.[189] Such meagre information as was placed before Churchill was out of date or incorrect and, as he himself admits in his memoirs, he did not yet 'comprehend' the new form of high-speed warfare that was being waged by the Germans. The assumptions and the decisions he made would therefore be based on wishful

---

* Under Churchill's new system of virtual single-handed direction of the war, the three Service Ministers were neither members of his War Cabinet, nor did they attend the Chiefs of Staff Committee meetings, nor have any responsibility for plans or operations.

thinking – and a persistent blindness as to what was actually happening on the battlefronts in France and Belgium. Pownall's reaction to Churchill's Order A was recorded in his diary:

> May 20th: CIGS came as the bearer of a message from the War Cabinet that we should retire south-west towards Amiens. A scandalous . . . thing to do and in fact quite impossible to carry out . . . Luckily even the CIGS was rapidly convinced of the folly of it, though how he could have allowed the Cabinet at a meeting at which he was present . . . to issue such an order not only puzzles me but also proves his futility.[190]

When Admiral Keyes, who was at GHQ on the 19th, learned that the CIGS was expected next day, he accepted Gort's invitation to spend the night. He was therefore present when Ironside arrived early next morning and observed the shocked reactions of Gort and his Staff to Churchill's order for the BEF to attack southward and 'take station on the left of the French Army'. Keyes was immediately struck by the disastrous consequences for the Belgian and British armies if the order brought by the CIGS was obeyed, as his diary reveals:

> It was only too evident that the orders he brought from the Government had caused consternation at GHQ. I found it difficult to understand why Lord Gort did not insist on being left free to take such action as he considered necessary to extricate the BEF from the dangerous position into which it had drifted, through no fault of his . . . It was clear to me that those responsible for these instructions were quite out of touch with the local conditions, and that if such an attack was carried out in conjunction with the French in their present mood it was unlikely to succeed, and in any case it would almost certainly lead to breaking contact with the right flank of the Belgian Army – a contingency which the CIGS admitted to me was likely and probably inevitable.

That 'contingency' was referred to even more bluntly in Ironside's diary that day. 'It meant' he wrote 'abandoning the Belgians'.[191] And in a telephone call to Anthony Eden, the Secretary of State for War, the CIGS declared that one of the consequences of the southward move would be 'that the enemy now approaching in considerable strength will certainly slip through any gap round the BEF's left'.[192] Gort also telephoned and signalled to Eden giving his reasons why 'withdrawal south-west' was, unless the French could restore the military situation in the South, 'entirely impossible'. But Churchill seems to have taken little notice of Gort's, Ironside's or Eden's representations and persisted in demanding that his orders should be obeyed.

Reflecting on what he had learned from Gort and Pownall about the prospects for the counter-attack which had been ordered, Admiral Keyes made a significant and prophetic comment in his diary:

The impression I formed was that if this failed, which was almost certain, the BEF would have no choice but to withdraw towards the coast and embark at Dunkirk, Nieuport and Ostend, with little prospect of saving much material, and that every day's delay added to the danger.

The state of affairs at the British and French general headquarters on this critical day is graphically described by Sir John Slessor. He records that when Ironside produced Churchill's handwritten Order A 'it caused a mild sensation' and that Gort and Pownall, after pointing out the impracticability of 'the march to the South', had said that 'there was no possibility of the Belgian Army being able to conform with any such movement'. In a 'gloomy conversation' with Slessor that morning Gort made it clear that 'the British Army was in a desperately precarious position'. They then discussed evacuation and Gort told him that 'he was thinking of using Ostend, Nieuport and Dunkirk'. Slessor writes that after hearing further details of the BEF's desperate plight 'it really dawned on one that there was every chance of the BEF being rounded up and captured *en masse*, without a round of ammunition to enable them to continue fighting'.

The atmosphere was even gloomier at Billotte's headquarters at Béthune, which – Slessor recalls – 'made my blood run cold. It was like a morgue.' He found some 'utterly dejected-looking officers wandering listlessly about or sitting staring at the wall' and heard such words as '*rien à faire*', '*fini*' and '*armistice*', which caused him to ask himself 'What hope for the BEF if this is the staff of the Army Group [which is] supposed to be controlling their destinies?'[193]

In *Their Finest Hour* Churchill writes that Ironside was instructed that the Belgians should be urged to conform to Gort's march to the South or 'that we would evacuate as many of their troops as possible from the Channel ports'.[194] But there is no record that Ironside or anyone else mentioned this possibility to Keyes or the Belgians, either then or later. Churchill's Order A had merely instructed the CIGS to inform the Belgian Command 'that their best chance is to move tonight between the BEF and the coast' – whatever that meant. The Admiral was intensely loyal to his own country, but equally loyal to Leopold and vividly aware of the sacrifices the Belgians were making in the Allied cause. His diary entry continues:

The danger of further procrastination was frightfully apparent to me, and after hearing Lord Gort's views I had the following telegram to the Prime Minister cyphered at GHQ and transmitted through the War Office:

20.5.40. To the Prime Minister from Admiral of the Fleet Sir Roger Keyes.

I understand that the orders to BEF brought by the CIGS amount to abandonment of junction with Belgian Army and to fight southwards. In this

case the Germans will quickly drive wedge through to north of BEF and there
is the present threat to south flank by tank attack now proceeding. BEF very
tired congestion on roads with refugees makes movement very difficult and I
gather that any reorganization of British divisions to south-westward of Lille
area can only develop very slowly. Am returning to Bruges and I do not
propose to tell the Belgians that the BEF intends to desert them yet.

The historical significance of this appreciation is that the wording was
Gort's, except for the last sentence, but he refused to let the Admiral
reveal that it represented his own views. Had Gort done so, of course, it
would have enormously strengthened Sir Roger's hand – since he would
not have appeared to be simply an advocate for the Belgians, but would
have been expressing a criticism of an unsound military idea which the
Commander-in-Chief himself held. In the vigorous letter Keyes sent to
Gort after they had both returned to England (the author, then a
sub-lieutenant RN on leave, delivered it by hand) he wrote:

The orders given to you on the 20th May by the CIGS for an offensive to the
southward in co-operation with a thoroughly demoralized French Army, at a
moment when your communications were cut and you were running short of
food, munitions, and everything needed for further offensive action, was
deplorably misjudged. For this the War Cabinet must bear all the responsibility
. . . The CIGS having apparently been unable to dissuade the Cabinet from
putting forward such a hopeless plan, you were put in the difficult position of
having to carry out an operation which you knew was doomed to failure, or of
declining and refusing to jeopardize your army any further by delaying its
withdrawal to the northward.
   You may remember what I said at the time: Why don't you tell the
Government to go to the devil, and insist on being given a free hand to extricate
your army from the appalling situation into which it had been placed, through
no fault of yours? After all, you bore all the responsibility for success or failure,
and you alone were in a position to judge . . . whether it was possible to carry
out the Government's orders or not. I offered to do anything I could to help,
and you helped me to write a military appreciation but you would not let me say
that you had seen it and approved of it, which would have strengthened my
hand when I tackled the Prime Minister about it . . .

Before Ironside arrived at GHQ, Gort and Pownall had issued orders
for all the forces they could scrape up to carry out an operation which, the
Official Historian writes, 'was not planned as a "counter-attack" but as a
large-scale mopping-up operation . . . The general aim was to ease the
enemy's pressure on Arras and to delay his encircling movement round
the rear of the British Expeditionary Force . . .' Moreover, in the orders
which GHQ gave General Franklyn, the commander of the force,
'nothing was said about a counter-attack or any larger objective, nor was
there any suggestion that the French would be associated in the opera-

tion'. Nevertheless, at their morning meeting Gort and Pownall told the CIGS that they had 'had plans in hand to counter-attack with the 5th and 50th divisions to the south of Arras' and that this force 'would be ready to attack on the following morning'. But in fact 'Frankforce', as it was called, consisted not of two divisions (for both were under-strength) but of only two battalions and 74 tanks with worn-out tracks – all that was left of the BEF's only tank brigade – of which 58 were armed with machine-guns only. Having thus committed almost all their available reserves for this limited operation, the British generals decided to ask the King if he could relieve the British 44th Division at Audenarde – the junction between the two armies on the line of the Escaut – in order to provide them with one division in reserve. Accordingly, Keyes and Davy returned at once to Belgian GQG to make this request. '*Le Roi*,' Van Overstraeten records, '*marque son agrément immédiat.*'

After their conference at GHQ, Ironside and Pownall went to see Billotte at his headquarters at Lens to urge him to support the 'counter-attack' which, they told him, was going to be launched at Arras 'with two divisions' next day. Ironside noted in his diary: 'I found Billotte and Blanchard . . . in a state of complete depression. No plan, no thought of a plan . . . *Très fatigués* and nothing doing. I lost my temper and shook Billotte by the button of his tunic. The man is completely beaten . . . Gort told me when I got back to his headquarters that they would never attack.'[195] Nevertheless, Billotte and Blanchard did agree to support the British operation with two of their divisions in an attack towards Cambrai to be concerted with General Franklyn. 'Imperceptibly,' writes Major Ellis, 'General Franklyn's operation now began to be thought of at Lord Gort's Command Post as a preliminary move in the projected attempt to close the gap, but no fresh orders were issued to General Franklyn, who was not told that his operation was now regarded as related to a bigger counter-attack in which the French were involved.'[196]

At a subsequent meeting Franklyn, in ignorance of this enlarged concept, puzzled the French generals by refusing to vary or co-ordinate with them the operation which he had been ordered to carry out next day. The French generals undertook, nevertheless, to launch their own attack towards Cambrai as soon as possible and the combative Prioux offered to operate on Frankforce's right flank with the remnants of his mecha-nized cavalry division. Thus two brave but uncoordinated attacks were launched, without air support: that by Frankforce backed with gallantry and effect by Prioux's cavalry on the 21st, and that by some elements only of the two French divisions on the 22nd. These were the only offensive moves that were made by the BEF and the French First Army during the entire campaign.

Meanwhile at Château Kervyn, after obtaining the King's approval for the Belgians to relieve the British 44th Division, Keyes simply told him that the BEF and the French force in the North were going to operate in a southerly direction and that the British Government hoped that the Belgian Army could retain touch with the left wing of the BEF. After a discussion with his Chief of Staff and Van Overstraeten, the King asked Keyes to let the British Government know his views on the broader issues – including, as the Admiral wrote in his diary, 'his anxiety to help our magnificent army to extricate itself from the impossible position into which it had been placed by the French reverse to the southward'. Keyes therefore signalled Churchill:

20.5.40. On my return to Belgian GQG I told the King of the proposal to extend the BEF southwards so that part of it could operate in a southerly direction. The King pointed out that the Belgian Army existed solely for defence, it had neither tanks nor aircraft and was not trained or equipped for offensive warfare. He also told me that in the small part of Belgium left there was only sufficient food for fourteen days, possibly less, owing to the influx of refugees. He did not feel that he had any right to expect the British Government to consider jeopardizing perhaps the very existence of our ten divisions in order to keep contact with the Belgian Army. He wished to make it clear that he does not want to do anything to interfere with any action which may be considered desirable for the BEF to undertake towards the south, if the circumstances made it necessary. He realizes, of course, that such action would finally lead to the capitulation of the Belgian Army. The King asked me to try to ascertain the intentions of the British Government, if the German thrust towards the sea succeeds in separating us from the main French forces in the South. It must not be thought that he has lost heart or faith, but he feels he owes it to us to make his position perfectly clear. I have sent a copy of this to Lord Gort.

Van Overstraeten writes that Sir Roger remarked, when he showed him this signal, 'This message bears the stamp of a *man*.' Certainly it is in incontrovertible documents like these that the true image of Leopold is to be found, rather than in the splenetic comments of Pownall, painting a picture of cowardly Belgians always whining for help, or of Alan Brooke, harping on the notion of an untrustworthy ally. But the real significance of the King's warning message – and it would not be his last – was that it put before both the British Prime Minister and his Commander-in-Chief, unambiguously and without complaint, the plain truth that if the BEF separated itself from the Belgian Army, the latter would be faced with inevitable capitulation.

The CIGS had been rapidly convinced (according to Pownall) of the 'folly' of ordering the BEF to march off to the south and readily agreed that the limited sortie by Frankforce, which he had been led to believe was 'a counter-attack by two divisions', should take its place. On his return to London next day Ironside reported to Churchill, according to the latter's account, 'that confusion reigned in the French High Command in the North, that General Billotte had failed to carry out his duties and appeared to have no plans, that the BEF were in good heart and had so far had only about 500 battle casualties'.[197] It is not clear how forcefully the CIGS tried to convince the Prime Minister that the situation on the spot made the march to the South impossible. But, whatever his representations were, Ironside's lack of enthusiasm for it may well have cost him his job, for Churchill rejected them and thereupon replaced him with his deputy, General Sir John Dill, who, as the Official Historian points out, 'had not seen Lord Gort and . . . had therefore an imperfect knowledge of the situation in the North'. In practice Dill took over as CIGS on the 22nd, although his appointment was not announced until May 27th. However, on the 20th Dill was on the other side of the breach, conferring with Weygand and Georges at the Generalissimo's headquarters at Vincennes. Thus, while Ironside was agreeing with Gort at the latter's GHQ that the southward move was impossible, Dill was assuring Churchill by signal that he shared his belief that 'a move southwards by the armies acting under General Billotte was the only means of restoring the situation', although he had been told that Billotte's intentions were limited to 'blocking holes'. But, in a more realistic vein, Dill's message continued that he had told the French generals that if the BEF's communications were cut – no one at Weygand's GQG seemed to know that this had already occurred – 'we should then have to take what steps we could independently for the security of our forces and this might involve withdrawing to cover the Channel ports'.

The reports which flowed in to Leopold's GQG that day had only served to highlight the appalling dangers which now faced the French, Belgian and British armies. The arrival of Guderian's Panzers on the Channel coast to the west of Abbeville during the evening meant that the northern armies were now completely cut off from the main French forces. The following day at lunchtime the German radio announced, without exaggeration:

> In the West the greatest offensive operation of all time has attained its first stage . . . We have entirely defeated and broken the French Ninth Army – its chief is our prisoner. The spearheads of our armoured detachments and of our motorized units have captured Arras, Amiens and Abbeville. North of the Somme and in the direction of the Channel ports we have cut off the rear of the French, English and Belgian troops . . . In Belgium . . . the enemy has again deployed to the east of Ghent and further south on the Escaut to give battle.

The Belgians had indeed 'given battle' and their new line on the Escaut remained unbroken. The Belgian Army's brave stand on that river brought forth tributes from 'political and military circles in Berlin' who, according to the Swiss newspapers (as quoted in *Figaro*), 'recognized the heroic resistance and staunchness of the Belgian soldiers'. Early on the 20th von Bock's Army Group B had launched heavy assaults on the Belgian Army's front and left wing of the British line in the region of Audenarde. Although the Belgians successfully repelled these attacks at Syngem and Quatrecht and even maintained fighting patrols on the eastern bank of the river, in the sector held by the British 44th Division the enemy managed to cross it unnoticed in the morning mist and drove deeply into its positions. The appeal which Gort and Pownall made to Leopold later that day to relieve this British division was urgently repeated next morning (by which time the enemy incursion had increased) by a message via Davy insisting that its relief should take place that night. Van Overstracten replied that every effort would be made to comply and that the Belgians were expecting that the British 4th Division, *'qui sera alors à notre droite, défendra l'Escaut à fond'.*

It was not surprising that von Bock now concentrated his attention on the point on the British front where his forces had achieved this penetration – for, as his War Diary shows, it was here that he considered his best chance lay of breaking through between the two armies and effecting a pincer movement with von Kleist's Panzers in the West to cut off the BEF* and the French First Army from the sea. Next day his forces enlarged the bridgehead they had formed on the west bank of the Escaut and pressed forward with great determination, overrunning other British positions. In the course of its enforced retreat the 44th Division suffered heavy losses in men and, as a result of 'the confusion and misunderstanding of orders' (*Official History*), lost, among much other equipment, thirty-four field guns – an ominous development for the BEF.

Amid the traffic of urgent military reports at Belgian GQG on the 20th – all transforming the situation for the worse – the King had to deal with a morning visit from Pierlot, Spaak, Denis and the fourth Minister whom he had asked to remain at Bruges, Vanderpoorten. As their spokesman, Pierlot returned tenaciously to the point that the King must not be taken prisoner, buttressing this argument with their faith in the certain survival of France as a combatant. The King remained non-committal, simply asking the Ministers whether they had reflected on the possibility that the Allied armies on the Continent might be defeated. How could he not, since an hour or so earlier his liaison officer with the French Ninth Army, General Nuyten, had telephoned to say that it was cut to pieces and that its commander, Giraud, who had succeeded Corap, was believed to be dead? (Giraud had actually been captured on the 18th, while trying to take control of the remnants of the army he had been sent to command.) And a little later, in the afternoon, General Delvoie returned to Château Kervyn from his liaison duties with the French First Army to report that it was 'no more than an accumulation of debris'.

* See maps on page 471.

Since the Ministers were criticizing the King for the attitude he had adopted in the light of these dire facts, having misinterpreted his calm realism as defeatism, it should be recalled that others with heavy military responsibilities were even more sombre in their assessment of the situation. Take, for example, Ironside's diary comments on May 17th, that the evacuation of the BEF was 'an impossible proposition' and that 'nothing could be more certain' than that 'we are up against the crashing of the Empire'. Or his entry on the 21st: 'situation desperate . . . personally I think we cannot extricate the BEF'.[198] And Alan Brooke's forebodings on May 23rd: 'Nothing but a miracle can save the BEF now, and the end cannot be far off.'[199] The task of a Commander-in-Chief is to view military situations objectively, perceiving not what he wants to see but what is there.

In the evening of this disastrous day the King and the Admiral were able to have a confidential talk. Leopold described to Keyes his grave misgivings arising from the success of the thrust and the collapse of French morale. He then said, as the Admiral recorded in his diary: 'he could not understand why we [the British] did not realize that the only chance now of extricating the BEF was to swing to the north-westward at once, strengthen its contact with the Belgian Army, and cover Dunkirk and the Belgian ports by occupying the Lys-Gravelines line.' This was of course exactly that the British General Staff wanted to do, but were prevented by the political leaders in London and Paris from doing until it was too late. Leopold had seen from the beginning that this was the only hope for the three northern armies and, as was to be proved in practice, that the plan for 'the march to the South' was an impossibility. Though Gort shared this view, he would be driven by pressure from Churchill and Weygand to continue in pursuit of the unattainable until, after five days of wasted time and empty gestures in which the situation of all three armies in the North became increasingly imperilled, he finally rebelled against his orders and acted on his own initiative 'to save the BEF'.

The conversation that evening between the King and Admiral Keyes deserves careful attention. It explains why during the days to come Leopold loyally accepted demands on his army which were designed to facilitate a southward move by the British, although he knew he was being asked to weaken his army's position and endanger its existence for the sake of a strategy he believed to be not only impractical, but potentially disastrous for all concerned. Nor was there anything to encourage the King or Keyes in Churchill's reply to the Admiral's first signal of the day, which now arrived:

> Cannot understand what sort of solution you have in mind. BEF will make every effort to sustain and shield the Belgian Army during movements which are indispensable to its life and further action. Please acknowledge.

As Leopold well knew, the BEF was getting so perilously short of supplies that it could hardly sustain itself – while the southward march stipulated in Churchill's Order A, far from shielding the Belgian Army, would inevitably lead to its isolation and defeat. The drift of events during the day offered the King not the remotest prospect of either shield or sustenance. Nor did Winston Churchill's outlook. The Prime Minister was certainly struggling with every weapon he could clutch to keep France in the fight – even at the risk of losing the entire British Expeditionary Force – but Belgium ranked low in Churchill's scale of priorities. It was unfortunate that at their pre-war meeting he and Leopold had not achieved a mutual understanding. On the 18th Keyes had sent a personal signal to Churchill: 'British wireless extols British and French morale no mention of Belgian war effort. Calmness and bearing of King and General Van Overstraeten is admirable. Plight of refugees on bombed and machine-gunned roads is tragic.' But on the following evening, Trinity Sunday, Churchill again demonstrated his attitude to the Belgians when he declared in a broadcast that everything depended on the British and French armies. His only mention of Belgium was as the last on the list of nations whose liberty had already been extinguished, ignoring the fact that hers was the only army which was still fighting at the side of the British and French – and now more for her allies' sake than for her own, since the Belgians had been compelled to yield the bulk of their territory to the Germans on French orders.

Although occasional references to the Belgian Army were now made in the Allies' news bulletins,* there was certainly no build-up of King Leopold and his troops. And they were unable to keep the world *au courant* with their story because there were no Allied war correspondents attached to them and once they had left the main centres such as Brussels and Antwerp they no longer had direct contact with any radio stations from which to broadcast communiqués. The Belgian Radio was allowed some facilities in Paris, but all the bulletins were issued by the out of touch and disorganized refugee Belgian Government and subjected to censorship by the Allies. Since the populations of France and Britain heard little about the Belgians and were kept completely in the dark about what was actually happening to their own armies, while being constantly told that 'the situation was favourable on the whole' or that counter-attacks (which never materialized) would restore the situation, they would react violently when the Belgian Army was forced to capitulate. 'The Belgians have done damn all, and now they have deserted us' – and '*Nous sommes trahis!*' became the popular cries in Britain and France.

By now, at Belgian GQG, Admiral Keyes was deeply worried by

* On May 23rd the British communiqué announced: 'The Belgian Army contributed largely to the success of the battle now taking place' and on the following days British and even some French newspapers praised the courage of the Belgian troops.

Churchill's dangerous misunderstanding of the real situation in Belgium and determined to correct this. He noted in his diary:

> May 21st: Telephonic communication was now established between London and the British Mission to the Belgian GQG at St André near Bruges, but it was of course unsafe for confidential communications. I found, however, that it was possible from La Panne, about 40 miles from Bruges, where the cable entered the sea, safely as far as Belgium was concerned, and I spoke guardedly from there,* and did everything in my power – apparently without much success – to make the Prime Minister realize that the situation of the BEF was very dangerous. It seemed that I was held responsible for suggesting that the order sent to Lord Gort would inevitably result in a break with the Belgian Army. Actually it was not I who suggested this, but the CIGS [Ironside], and of course he was right. I asked the Prime Minister to let King Leopold have a reply to his question in my second telegram of the 20th [i.e. the intentions of HM Government in the event of the German thrust towards the sea separating us from the main French force in the South] . . . as soon as possible. I received the following reply in time to give the Prime Minister's message to the King, just before a conference with General Weygand at Ypres that afternoon:

> 21.5.40.
>
> Weygand is coming up your way tomorrow to concert action of all forces. Essential to secure our communications southwards and strike at small bodies intruding upon them. Use all your influence to persuade your friends to conform to our movements. Belgian Army should keep hold of our left flank. No question of capitulation for anyone. We greatly admire King's attitude. German thrust towards Lille must not succeed separate us from main French forces. Have complete confidence in Gort and Weygand, who embody offensive spirit vital to success.†

Naturally Churchill admired the King's attitude, since the signal to which he was replying made plain Leopold's unselfish reaction – that he did not expect the BEF's movements to be inhibited out of consideration for the safety of the Belgian Army and the need to maintain contact with it. But the rest of Churchill's message demonstrated just how blind he was to the actual situation in Belgium and France. For there were of course no longer any 'communications southwards' nor could that vast array of military might (including ten Panzer divisions under an umbrella of unchallenged air power), which had already separated the northern armies from the 'main French forces', accurately be described as 'small bodies'. The reference to 'German thrust towards Lille' which lies sixty miles to the north-east and therefore that distance *behind* the point on

---

* This 'safe' telephone was in the Royal villa in which Queen Elisabeth was residing, having been installed for King Albert's use in World War I.
† This signal was apparently dictated by Churchill on May 20th, but dated and despatched next day. Weygand made his trip northward on the 21st.

the coast already reached by that thrust, suggested either incompetent map-reading or an absolute ignorance of what was happening on the battlefields. Moreover the Belgians, by being required to 'keep hold' of the BEF as it moved southwards, were being asked to do the impossible.

Keyes viewed Churchill's attitude with dismay. In his judgment – and in this he was supported by Gort – the southward move was entirely impracticable and if attempted would be disastrous for the Belgians as well as the British and French. Three weeks later, in the letter he wrote to Gort after their return to England, he described the strenuous but unsuccessful efforts he made from this day onwards to enlighten Churchill about the realities of conditions in Flanders:

> On 21st May and during the next few days, I motored hundreds of miles in order to speak to Churchill from La Panne, and I did my utmost to make him understand the gravity of your position. He would not listen, and even abused me for the statements in the military appreciation you gave me. If I had only been free to say it was really yours, I might have been more successful. He would not accept my contention that, if this counter-attack to the southward was insisted on, it was bound to separate the Belgian and British armies, as it did; for it cannot be denied that although your attack was never delivered, the preparations for it dangerously weakened the line held by the Belgian Army, laid it open to an overwhelming attack, and delayed the withdrawal of the BEF for six precious days.

CHAPTER TWENTY-ONE

Weygand's Plan

'At this point the C-in-C was somewhat disturbed at the prospect of leaving the Belgians in the lurch, but he looked on it as inevitable.'
Colonel Davy's diary note of a
conversation with Lord Gort,
May 21st 1940

'Do the Belgians think us awful dirty dogs?'
Lord Gort to Sir Roger Keyes,
later the same day.

After his discussions with Georges, Gamelin and Reynaud, Weygand had decided to issue no orders until he had seen the situation for himself. Since direct communication with the commanders of the three armies in the North was impossible, Weygand decided to visit them to establish personal contact. Accordingly, on the 19th, despite opposition from Reynaud, who asserted that the Generalissimo should remain at the Government's side, he despatched signals to Leopold, Billotte and Gort asking them to attend a conference to be held in Ypres on the 21st. Initially it was arranged that Weygand should go as far as Abbeville by rail and from there by car – the French staff being unaware that the Germans were on the point of entering the town. As a result Weygand's cars, which had been sent on ahead, narrowly escaped capture and he was forced to undertake the perilous journey by air.

'The deplorable conditions,' Weygand noted, 'in which my journey took place gave me an idea of the negligence prevalent in the armies.'[200] His troubles began at Le Bourget aerodrome in the early hours of the morning of May 21st, where he found to his fury that nothing was known about his journey and no preparations for it had been made. He was sent 'from one end of the airfield to the other' and wasted an hour before an aircraft and fighter escort were produced.

Once in flight, the General's aircraft was fired on from La Canche – unwelcome proof that the enemy were already established on the Channel coast and had completed the severance of the northern and southern fronts. On landing at Norrent Fontès near Béthune, Weygand's exasperation was increased when he found that there was no one to receive him and saw evidence that its abandonment two days before by the British and French had been 'precipitate'. (There were, for example, a number of

270

apparently undamaged Hurricane fighters on the airfield.) The only living soul to be found was one small and 'very dirty' French soldier who had been left in charge of 20,000 litres of petrol and whose great concern was what he should do with it. Nor were there any telephones in working order on the deserted airfield. 'So,' Weygand continues, 'the general who had just been invested with the command of all the theatres of operations and with the highest responsibilities found himself, through the incredible negligence with which his journey had been organized, alone in the countryside with his ADC, without the means of getting into touch with any of those whom he had come to meet in Flanders, and to whom his visit had been announced.'

The deeply humiliated and indignant old general set off in a decrepit lorry driven by the French soldier in search of a telephone. After forcing a passage against a tide of refugees and suffering many frustrations, he found a serviceable telephone in a half-deserted village where 'after long efforts' he gained 'abominably bad' contact with the French 1st Army Group staff. He learned that General Billotte, who was supposed to have met him, was searching the countryside for him, 'though nobody could say in what direction he had gone'.

On his return to the airfield and while his ADC was making arrangements for the aircraft to fly him to Calais airfield, Weygand, 'tortured by hunger', visited an inn nearby. His forebodings were not lessened when he noticed a lithograph on the wall showing himself in the famous scene at the signing of the Armistice in the wagon-lit dining-car at Compiègne on November 11th 1918. Taking off once again from Béthune, it was midday before the Generalissimo's aircraft touched down at the heavily bombed airfield at Calais. Here after more telephoning it was arranged that Leopold would meet him at 3 pm in the Mayor's office at Ypres Town Hall and that a car would be sent for him.

When Weygand reached the Town Hall, shortly before the King, he was surprised to be waylaid by the Belgian Ministers Pierlot and Spaak, since he had not invited them to the conference. They had learned of it 'by chance' and had resolved to attend unasked at some sacrifice to their dignity. In the next hours, as the talks proceeded, they were obliged to occupy what Spaak later described as 'a humiliating position' in an ante-room to the Mayor's office, from which they would suddenly emerge when anyone likely to possess information passed the door. In later years Pierlot and Spaak complained bitterly that the King had excluded them from the conference room, but it was Weygand, not Leopold, who had invited the commanders of the three armies to meet him to discuss strictly military matters. The Generalissimo had not asked any political or civilian representatives of the three countries involved and there was no reason why he should have allowed the Belgian Ministers to attend the conference.

Before the King arrived there was a short discussion between Weygand
and the three Ministers. 'When I told them,' wrote Weygand, 'that in my
opinion the Belgian Army was remaining too long in the East, their faces
cleared with satisfaction and they exchanged a few words with one
another that showed me that on this point they could not be in agreement
with the King or his advisers.' This was a most improper intervention by
Weygand, who as yet had not even met Leopold and could have no idea of
the factors in his mind. It was equally improper for the Ministers to
disclose to Weygand – as they did – their King's confidential prediction
about the imminent downfall of France – an indiscretion both disloyal and
harmful to Franco-Belgian relations.

When the King arrived at the Town Hall there was no sign of the French
or British Commander-in-Chief, so he and Weygand went upstairs to a
large *salon* for a preliminary talk, pending the arrival of Billotte and Gort.
They were not strangers. They had met briefly several times before during
the First World War and in 1938 in Brussels, where they had had a long
conversation. Meanwhile, the Belgian Ministers outside buttonholed
Van Overstraeten. 'Why is the retreat so slow?' Pierlot demanded
sharply. 'We follow the instructions of the Allied C-in-C.' 'Get new ones.'
'Why?' 'To avoid being cut off from France.' 'But, Prime Minister, we *are*
cut off.' (This exchange is sometimes used to indicate Van Overstraeten's
defeatism, but his statement was literally true – at 8.30 that morning,
GQG had intercepted a German wireless message that Abbeville had
been captured the previous evening.)

Time was passing and neither Billotte or Gort could be contacted, since
Billotte was somewhere out in the countryside, vainly searching for
Weygand, and Gort was once again out of touch with his headquarters,
which was now at Hazebrouck. The Official Historian, Major Ellis,
declares that there is no record that Weygand's message to Gort, that he
was coming to Ypres to confer with the Allied commanders on May 21st,
was received, but Pownall's diary entry for May 20th – 'Weygand comes
here tomorrow' – proves that the Generalissimo's advance notification
was received by the British High Command. However, Gort evidently
considered the emergency situation which was developing that
day on his left wing, where the enemy was driving the 44th Division
back from the Escaut in some disorder, to be of more immediate
concern than a conference with the new Allied Supreme Commander,
and had hurried off to confer with his Corps commanders near the
front.

Although the presence of Gort and Billotte was essential if the conference was to have any value, Weygand decided to start with the Belgians
alone. Generals Van Overstraeten, Michiels, and Champon (the head of
the French liaison mission at Belgian GQG), were accordingly summoned to the conference room.

In his own words, Weygand opened the proceedings by describing 'the plan of action on which I have decided'. Since Weygand admits in his memoirs that he had only 'a superficial knowledge of the situation' and had announced in Paris that he would take no action until he had ascertained the position from the Allied commanders in the North, to have 'decided' on a plan before giving a hearing to those who would have to execute it was a fine example of putting the cart before the horse. Nevertheless the Generalissimo launched into a description of what became known as the 'Weygand Plan'.

Weygand stipulated, according to Van Overstraeten's account,[201] that massive attacks should forthwith be launched from the North and South on the enemy's flanks in order to 'destroy the spearhead of the enemy offensive' – and for this purpose it was necessary to muster as many divisions as possible, 'even the whole British Army'. This was, of course, absurd. A moment's thought reveals the impossibility of disengaging an entire army, all of which was in the line, and mounting an attack with it in the opposite direction to which it was facing. But unfortunately Gort and Pownall were not there to point out Weygand's misconceptions and the unfeasibility of his plan, which were well illustrated when he signalled to Gort two days later that the counter-attacks he had ordered to be made from north and south 'should close the breach and bar the return journey of the Panzer adventurers in the North'.

Weygand now declared that time was pressing and it was necessary to act before the German infantry caught up with their tanks. He went on to claim, with quite unfounded optimism, that a counter-attack by three French divisions would be launched northwards from the southern side of the breach on the following day (in fact, no serious counter-attack was ever delivered from that quarter), to link up with the thrust which was already being made from the north by the BEF. This, Weygand told the King, was a 'counter-attack by two British divisions' which was in progress at that moment in the Arras area. Here again he was under a delusion, for the only action taking place was the spirited but short-lived sortie by the 74 dilapidated tanks and two infantry battalions of Frankforce, which by that evening had been repulsed with heavy losses and was never to be renewed. (This courageous operation, commanded by Major-General Martel, which was launched without air support and uncoordinated with the French, in the face of heavy dive-bombing and fierce resistance by greatly superior enemy forces, including Rommel's 7th Panzer Division, nevertheless inflicted severe casualties on the Germans and had a jolting effect on the nerves of their High Command quite out of proportion to the small size of the British force.)

Having described his 'plan' to Leopold, before being able to ascertain from Billotte and Gort whether or not it was acceptable or feasible,

Weygand asked for the co-operation of the Belgian Army. His official account states his intentions as follows:

> The situation requires that, under the cover of the Belgian Army, which will assure their protection on the east, and, if required, on the north, the available French and British forces should take offensive action southwards in the region of Cambrai and Arras and in the general direction of Saint-Quentin, so as to fall on the flank of the German armoured divisions at present engaged in the pocket of Saint-Quentin–Amiens.[202]

Weygand declared that that Belgian Army's front was too long and too far to the east to be in a position to cover this Anglo-French offensive towards the South and called upon the King to bring his army back, by a series of steps, behind the Yser. In fact the French and British armies in the North consisted mainly of infantry and had insufficient reserves, supplies or air support even to hold their threatened fronts, flanks and rear successfully – let alone embark upon an attack into an area swarming with armoured, mechanized and infantry forces under an umbrella of unchallenged air power. But neither the British nor French C-in-C was there to bring these facts to Weygand's notice. Thus, on the false assumption that offensives could be launched from the north and south, Weygand called upon the Belgian Army further to weaken and endanger its own position in order to cover an operation which none of the potential participants believed possible and which was destined never to take place.

According to Weygand's memoirs Van Overstraeten, 'a man of great distinction of manner expressing himself with eloquence and clarity . . . apologized with a few kind words for not agreeing at all with my opinion'.[203] In replying, the King's Military Adviser was in some difficulty – for, unlike the Generalissimo, he was fully *au fait* with the situation in the North and realized that the whole basis of Weygand's demand that the Belgians should abandon their relatively strong positions on the Escaut, where they were well placed to form part of a wide Allied defensive perimeter covering the coast, would disappear if he could be persuaded that the southward move was an impossibility. He could only hope, therefore, that Billotte and Gort would soon arrive and convince him. In the meantime he would do his best to awaken Weygand to the realities of the situation in the North.

Van Overstraeten first explained to Weygand the reasons why it was undesirable for the Belgian Army to withdraw any further. Already it had been compelled – on French orders – to abandon the greater part of Belgium without being allowed to make a decisive stand. Recent successful actions had heartened the troops, but the fighting spirit of the soldiers was weakened in proportion to the amount of their homeland left to defend. The Belgian troops were worn out after the succession of night marches. The roads were hopelessly encumbered by the ever-growing multitude of refugees, whose distress and suffering increased daily. And with the bright moonlight and brief hours of real darkness, it was an illusion to suppose that there was any advantage in movement by night. Such a withdrawal as Weygand suggested, across open country to unprepared positions, under continuous air attack, would inevitably incur both severe losses and increasing dislocation.

A retirement to the Lys would be bad enough – but a withdrawal to the Yser would be disastrous, both materially and from the point of view of morale, since it could involve the abandonment of virtually the whole of Belgium and the supply and ammunition depots upon which the Army depended for its existence, all of which lay to the east of that river. But above all it would mean ceding to the enemy without a fight the vital ports of Ostend and Zeebrugge, as well as the Channel coastline right up to Nieuport, where the Yser enters the sea, only seventeen miles to the east of Dunkirk – a particularly serious matter for the British as well as the Belgians, who depended on these ports for their supplies. (In fact the British generals had already earmarked those ports for evacuation.)

Van Overstraeten concluded by guaranteeing that in its present position the Belgian Army would fight well; but if it was asked to undertake a further withdrawal in depth to unprepared positions, he could not answer for the consequences. At this point General Champon was seen to nod his head in agreement. According to the carefully tailored accounts Weygand gave of the conference after the war, Van Overstraeten suggested as an alternative that the Belgian Army's left wing should stand fast, while its right could curve back 'so as to place it in a vast arc with the sea behind it'. The Belgian general's proposal, he implies, was that the Belgian Army *alone* should form a bridgehead round Ostend, which would entail its separation from the British and French forces, and that he turned it down for that reason. But the King and his military staff had, of course, only envisaged having to form such a defensive perimeter on their own, in the event that the BEF and the French First Army separated themselves from the Belgian Army by their southward offensive, which Weygand had just stipulated must immediately be launched.

What Van Overstraeten actually proposed on behalf of the King was the 'Torres Vedras' concept, which they had considered to be the only viable course of action ever since the Meuse breakthrough – the formation by all three armies in the North of the widest possible perimeter waterline with their backs to the Channel. Indeed, on the previous day the King had expressed his surprise to Admiral Keyes that the BEF was not manoeuvring in this way – both men having been kept in the dark by Gort and Pownall about the decision they had made to that effect two days before (on the 19th), after concluding that a retreat to the Channel ports and 'holding a defensive perimeter there . . . sufficiently long to

enable the Force to be withdrawn' represented the only hope of salvation
for the BEF. In his memoirs Van Overstraeten describes the conversation
he had with the King after the conference, when they expressed their
regret that Gort's failure to turn up for this crucial discussion meant that
their realistic concept of a *vaste tête de pont* could not be discussed in the
joint presence of the British C-in-C and the new Allied Supreme Commander. The King and Van Overstraeten felt that such a bridgehead
could hold out with the help of British sea and air power (although at
terrible cost to the Belgians in view of the dominance of the *Luftwaffe*),
thus frustrating, for a time, the enemy's 'obvious intention of seizing the
whole Channel coast and its ports – so vital to the English and their army'
– and at the same time posing a serious threat to his flank and rear.[204]

Van Overstraeten's representations appeared to have had some effect,
for Weygand now declared that an immediate choice would have to be
made between two courses of action: 'either to maintain at all costs the
continuity of the Allied Front, which is what I desire; or to cover the
Channel ports, which involves accepting the severance of the fronts – a
serious step.'[205] At this remark Van Overstraeten asked Weygand in
some astonishment whether he was unaware that the Germans' arrival on
the Channel coast the previous evening had already severed the Allied
fronts. According to Van Overstraeten, Weygand professed his ignorance of this development, of which he had of course already been made
aware.

At this point the King intervened to say that Weygand's question as to
whether the Belgian ports were to be covered or abandoned was of such
cardinal importance to the British that it was essential that Gort should
participate in the conference. He felt that it was vital that before
committing himself further Weygand should give a hearing to the British
case. Accordingly Van Overstraeten was requested to make contact with
Gort and get him to come to the conference. The meeting then broke up
so that he could do so.

When Weygand emerged from the conference room he had a talk with
Keyes, who was the only Englishman present. In his memoirs, Weygand
expresses great admiration for the Admiral, referring to him as 'an old
friend of almost legendary fame' and 'of having given evidence of
extraordinary intrepidity and decision'. But Weygand could not prevail
on Keyes to help him persuade the King that his 'plan' was feasible and to
support it. It was hardly surprising that Weygand 'gave up hope of help
from him', since the Admiral shared the views held by the Allied
commanders in the North – which Weygand had not yet heard – that the
southward offensive was impractical and that their only hope lay in an
immediate move to cover the Channel coast and ports in as wide a
perimeter as possible. Although an Admiral of the Fleet and the most
senior officer in the whole theatre of war, Keyes had no command and it

was not part of his liaison duties to anticipate the representations of the British case, which he felt sure Gort and Pownall would soon make in person.

It was fully half an hour before Van Overstraeten was able to report back, for he had found the only telephone-box occupied by two talkative French officers. He had been unable to gain contact with Gort, but had learned from the Needham Mission that he was away from his new headquarters at Hazebrouck and was not expected back until 6 pm. Weygand was already fuming because there was still no sign of Billotte and his time was running out. It was not until 5 pm that the distraught Billotte, accompanied by General Fagalde, put in an appearance. He had been vainly searching for his chief since early that morning. Weygand thought that 'the fatigues and anxieties of the past two weeks had left a deep mark on him'.[206]

Talks were at once resumed and Billotte was asked to describe the situation in the North. He began by giving a harrowing account of the plight of the French First Army, which he declared was in a state of disintegration and exhaustion. He insisted that the onrush of the Panzer divisions, with their closely concerted air support, was 'irresistible'. Ordinary conventionally equipped divisions stood no chance against this new combination and were rapidly overwhelmed. Billotte went on to say that nine or ten Panzer divisions, which he estimated to consist of between 3,000 and 3,500 tanks, had been identified between Amiens and Cambrai. This vast armoured force was advancing at undreamed-of speed, backed by a mass of motorized and conventional infantry divisions, whilst the sky was dominated by the *Luftwaffe*.

When Billotte learned that Weygand was calling for counter-offensive action from the North, he declared that the French First Army was barely capable of defending itself, let alone undertaking offensive action. He claimed that only the British Army, which was intact and which had not yet been engaged in any serious fighting, was capable of launching an attack. It is true that the BEF was virtually unscathed,* but Billotte well knew that GHQ had no uncommitted reserves at its disposal; that the BEF was cut off from all its supply depots and desperately short of food and ammunition, while its left wing on the Escaut was falling back under enemy attack.

Seizing upon Billotte's exaggerated assessment of the BEF's offensive capacity, which Gort was not there to discount, Weygand – who appreciated that little could be expected from his own country's forces – readily determined that the British Army should undertake the principal offensive role in his 'plan'. Accordingly, in the absence of any representative of

---

* This was the day on which Ironside reported to Churchill, according to him, that the BEF 'had so far had only about five hundred battle casualties'. *Their Finest Hour*.

the British Army or Government, he brushed aside Billotte's representations about the plight of the French First Army and imposed his 'solution' on that helpless and unhappy officer. 'I had no difficulty,' Weygand later declared, 'in persuading him of the essential nature of the following three points:

1 That at all costs contact between the Belgian Army and the main Allied body must be preserved.
2 Covered by this army to the east, an attack, comprising all available units – say about seven infantry and three mechanized divisions – to be made from the neighbourhood of Arras in the general direction of Bapaume-Péronne.
3 That this attack should be started as soon as possible, in order to profit from the comparative vulnerability of the Panzers before their infantry supports could catch up with them.'[207]

Billotte was well aware of the impossibility of carrying out these unrealistic instructions. Weygand was demanding the deployment of ten Allied divisions, despite Billotte's statement that only two of his divisions retained any cohesion and the fact that Gort had only nine, all in the line. But Gort and Pownall were not there to disillusion Weygand, and Billotte lacked the character and inclination to argue with his forceful chief. 'General Billotte did not inform me of anything that could turn me from my project,' Weygand later declared. As to the Belgian Army's role in his plan, Weygand admitted that he had thought at first that it could with advantage be withdrawn behind the Yser, but he now conceded the validity of the objections raised by the Belgian Command and agreed that such a move was undesirable and impractical. But all interests could be reconciled, he claimed, if the Belgians would agree instead to retire only to the Lys and relieve some British divisions, so as to enable them to take part in 'the counter-attack in the Arras area'.

The King agreed to these suggestions and offered for good measure to release the French General Fagalde's XVI Corps, which was stationed behind his left-wing divisions, to let it join in this offensive action. But Billotte declined the offer and instead asked the King to take it under his command. The King then repeated his observation that nothing could be settled without the British. He therefore proposed that someone should be sent to try to locate Gort and bring him to the conference. The meeting broke up with Van Overstraeten, accompanied by Keyes, setting off by car to search for the elusive British C-in-C.

As time passed, Weygand expressed increasing annoyance at Gort's non-appearance. 'I could not go back without meeting him,' he wrote in his memoirs, 'as that meeting was one of the principal reasons for my journey . . . To leave the North without renewing contact with him in my new capacity and without having exchanged views with him and personally informed him of my programme, in the execution of which the forces he commanded had a very important part, seemed to me to be out of the question.'[208] Reynaud had insisted that Weygand should be back in Paris by the following morning to take part in the meeting of the Supreme Council which Winston Churchill was to attend. 'I therefore decided,' Weygand told his son, 'to wait a bit longer . . . and to fly back at night or at the latest first thing on the morning of the 22nd.'[209] But the French Admiral Abrial now appeared and informed Weygand that the Calais airfield had been bombed again and his aircraft and its fighter escort had been sent back to Le Bourget. Abrial suggested that the only way for Weygand to get back to Paris was by sea and placed a small French torpedo boat at his disposal. Although a message had been received that Gort was on his way, Weygand decided to leave at once and, after bidding the King farewell, departed.

As Weygand told his son, he and the other French leaders were angry with Gort, for they concluded that he had 'purposely abstained from coming to the Ypres conference'.[209] In this connection General Spears quotes Georges Mandel (the French Minister of the Interior) as asking: 'Why did your Commander-in-Chief not meet Weygand, when he had made such an effort to go north to see him? The military and others are persuaded this was a deliberate slight, a sign that the British will not accept French orders.'[210] From this time forward, as Spears and others record, the French political leaders and generals, with Reynaud and Weygand well to the fore, would revert continually to the theme of British 'duplicity' and 'defection', in order to lay on them – and on Gort in particular – the blame for their own failures, until both nations found a convenient scapegoat in the Belgians. But while the French leaders made an issue of Gort staying away from the Ypres conference, the King and his entourage gained the impression (as he told the author) that Weygand had deliberately departed before Gort's arrival, because he did not relish the prospect of a confrontation with the British C-in-C or the task of persuading him to undertake a major offensive with his small and heavily committed force in the reverse direction to that in which its only chance of survival lay.

Leopold's impression could well have been correct, since Weygand admits in his memoirs that when Winston Churchill telephoned Reynaud two days later in an unsuccessful attempt to persuade him to abandon the Weygand Plan and agree to a withdrawal to the northern ports, 'Mr Churchill expressed the intention of communicating direct with me, but I forestalled him by informing him [by telegram] that I was fully aware of the situation but maintained my decision.'[211] Yet elsewhere in this same book Weygand blames the British Prime Minister and C-in-C, BEF for not 'communicating direct' to him the factors which made the realization of the Weygand Plan impossible and complains bitterly that, although Gort 'differed' from his plan, he never 'attempted to make contact' after

failing to meet him at Ypres. And in *The Role of General Weygand* the
Generalissimo was even more specific in blaming his British allies for his
own fatal mistake in brushing aside the advice he was given at Ypres and
persisting in the wrong course of action for the next five crucial days:

> The Commander of the BEF would certainly have informed me of the
> difficulties which he thought stood in the way of the realization of my pro-
> gramme . . . Failing the interview that day . . . should not Lord Gort, in view
> of the gravity of the questions involved, have come to me . . . ?
>
> Since this initiative had not been taken by Lord Gort, it was for the [British]
> Prime Minister who had known since the 19th that the Commander of the BEF
> considered a serious southward offensive to be impossible . . . to bring about
> this meeting, so that Lord Gort could explain his reasons for not agreeing to my
> plan of action. One of two things – either I would not have deferred to those
> reasons and would have held to my orders . . . or I would have recognized the
> force of the arguments brought forward by Lord Gort and would have
> examined with him the decision to be adopted.
>
> In that case it might have consisted of withdrawing the Allied forces on May
> 22nd to the north of the Lys, and installing them in a huge and solid bridgehead
> in front of the three northern ports. I would, in fact, have adopted some days
> earlier, in conditions which the position of the Belgian Army at that date
> rendered very different, the decision to which I was driven on the 26th. It might
> have enabled the whole of the troops and their most valuable equipment to be
> saved.

Meanwhile, Keyes and Van Overstraeten had made good progress in
tracing Gort's whereabouts. On hearing that his GHQ had moved from
Wahagnies to Hazebrouck, they drove there and found Major McKenzie,
a member of the Needham Mission, who suggested that the C-in-C might
be found at Premesques, south of Armentières. Luckily the Admiral not
only succeeded in getting through on the telephone, but learned that Gort
had just returned and was able to speak to him. He strongly urged the
C-in-C to come at once to the Ypres conference and the latter agreed to
do so. At about 7 pm all arrived back at Ypres Town Hall simultaneously.
The Admiral and Van Overstraeten were pleased with the success of their
mission, but were dismayed to find that Weygand had just left.

The apparent indifference shown by Gort and Pownall to this crucial
conference, upon which the fate of all three national armies in the North
depended, is partly explained by their contemptuous attitude towards the
French and their leaders, under whom they were supposed to be serving,
and is shown by the omission from Gort's *Despatches* of the fact that the
new Generalissimo had convened the meeting and flown north specifically to confer with Gort and the other Commanders-in-Chief.

So, as darkness fell, the third and final conference began at Ypres,
without the presence of the Allied Supreme Commander who had
convened it. Sitting round the table in the Mayor's office were King

Leopold, with Generals Van Overstraeten and Michiels; Generals Billotte, Fagalde and Champon; and the latecomers, Gort and Pownall.
Billotte started by telling the British generals what had been discussed
and decided in their absence and relayed the orders the Generalissimo
had given for the execution of the Weygand Plan. It was immediately
apparent to Gort and Pownall that Weygand was completely out of touch
with the realities of the situation in the North. But they had just missed
the opportunity to disabuse him of his grandiose misconceptions and to
persuade him to adopt the realistic alternative which he had considered
and they desired – the formation of a vast *tête de pont* covering the coast.
They had come to Ypres reluctantly and with many anxieties and
preoccupations on their minds. Not the least were the lack of any reserve
formations and the dangerous situations that were developing on their
eastern front and in their rear. That afternoon, while conferring with their
three Corps commanders, Gort and Pownall had learned that von Bock's
thrust across the Escaut had driven the 44th Division back to Petegem
and, as Gort's *Despatches* put it:

> All felt that they could not now hold on for more than 24 hours. We discussed a
> withdrawal to our old frontier defences, where advantage could be taken of the
> existing blockhouses and trenches and of the anti-tank ditch. This move would
> have little effect on the French on our right . . . but would seriously affect the
> Belgians, who now held the line of the Escaut from Audenarde to Ghent and of
> the canal from Ghent to the sea at Terneuzen.

In fact, it will be recalled, Pownall had told Davy that the decision for
the BEF to retreat from the Escaut to the security of its old fortified
frontier line in France had been taken three days before. In some notes
Admiral Keyes made on Gort's *Despatches* he commented on the above
passage as follows:

> From this it is clear that Lord Gort fully appreciated the sacrifice the Belgians
> would have to make in order to allow the British Army to retreat to the security
> of its old frontier defences.
> It meant, in fact, that King Leopold would have to withdraw from his
> well-prepared position on the Escaut, abandon his bridgehead, stores and
> ammunition at Ghent and extend his army in the open behind the Lys on a front
> of about 90 kilometres, in order to allow the BEF to retire behind their old
> frontier positions.

During the winter and spring the BEF had constructed over four
hundred concrete pill-boxes and had done an immense amount of work
creating a comprehensive system of earthwork defences, anti-tank ditches
and telephonic communications along the twenty-five mile line on the
French frontier between Halluin and Maulde. It is hardly surprising,

therefore, that Gort and Pownall had long since decided to move the BEF
back behind this heavily fortified and shorter front – the decision which
they had, on May 19th, ordered Colonel Davy not to communicate to the
Belgians, since (as subsequently admitted in Gort's *Despatches*) it would
'seriously affect' them. This was putting it mildly, for (as can be seen from
the map on page 471) their old line along the French frontier stuck out like
a sore thumb at an angle of 90 degrees from the Lys – the unprepared line
to which, in order to maintain contact, the Belgians would be compelled
to retire from their well-prepared defences on the Escaut. Thus the BEF
would be wheeling back away from the path of the attack launched by von
Bock on their left wing, until they were parallel to it and safe behind their
powerful fortifications. The strong British and the weak Belgian fronts
formed an inverted right angle; as a result, the enemy's thrust would be
diverted from the British 44th Division (which Leopold had agreed to
relieve) and funnelled on to the southern end of the Belgians' line, which
they would have to leave dangerously thin and extend, in order to connect
with the British left at Halluin, where the latter's fortifications ended.
Consequently, the full weight of von Bock's offensive would fall upon the
Belgian right wing and prise it away from the point at which it joined the
end of the BEF's static front, driving the Belgians north-westwards away
from the British. An appropriate analogy would be that the BEF's
manoeuvre was like a man in a room taking cover behind a heavy open
door and calling upon his companion to bar the path of an intruder by
stretching across the doorway and holding onto the handle, so that the
wrist and forearm of the defender would become the logical target for the
assailant to strike.

   The British generals, and Pownall in particular, had shown scant
consideration for Belgian interests and the decision they had made to fall
back into France would force the Belgian Army to give up another
expanse of Belgian territory and retire to weak, over-extended and
unprepared positions. But they should have appreciated that it also had
considerable perils for themselves. Although their forces would be safe
from attack behind the shorter frontier line, because of its strong fortifications and parallel alignment with the enemy's line of advance (and they
could consequently reduce the number of divisions behind it), there was
the great danger that von Bock's breakthrough attempt – now transferred
from the British left to the Belgians' right wing – would separate the two
armies, turn the British left flank and join up with the Panzers advancing
from the West, thereby cutting off the BEF and the French First Army
from the coast.

   But Gort and Pownall were intent on a further problem for the BEF
which could be solved by another Belgian sacrifice. The positions to
which the British 44th and 4th Divisions were to retire (the 44th was
already being driven back by the enemy) were on the Lys, north-east of

Halluin and still right in the path of von Bock's *Schwerpunkt*. But if the King could be induced to relieve the 4th, in addition to the 44th, both divisions could be rushed to secure positions behind their old fortified frontier line – leaving it to the Belgians to face the full fury of the enemy's onslaught in the exposed and unprepared positions on the Lys which the two British divisions had vacated. The decision made by Gort and Pownall to retire to their old frontier line, in spite of all these dangers to their own army and the Belgians, was thus a measure of their concern to reduce the number of their divisions facing the enemy on their eastern front, in order to create a reserve from which reinforcements could be rushed to protect the BEF's increasingly threatened southern flank and rear – and in particular to the Canal Line, which guarded the western side of their escape corridor to the Channel coast and Dunkirk.

The British C-in-C was still under orders from 'the Cabinet' to march off to the South and when Billotte ordered him, in Weygand's name, to launch a major offensive in that direction, Pownall replied that there were no uncommitted British reserves available for such an operation. The British generals, upon whom the onus was being thrust to play the major role in Weygand's plan, considered (as they later told Leopold) that its chances of success were virtually nil in the present situation, which they described as 'desperate'. They could not simply decline to obey these utterly unrealistic orders, so they decided to pay lip-service to the Weygand Plan – but in such a way as to gain their objectives, including an escape route to the sea.

Accordingly, Pownall proposed to Billotte that if the BEF abandoned its positions on the Escaut, which he said it was now compelled to do, 'due to the shallowness of the water'*, and retreated behind the fortified frontier line – and if the Belgians and French each relieved two British divisions – the four divisions so released would be used for the southward offensive demanded by Weygand. The British generals must have given this undertaking with tongue in cheek, for not one of the four British divisions relieved by Belgian and French divisions for this specific purpose were so deployed or used for other than purely self-defensive purposes. The British 2nd and 48th Divisions, after their relief by the French, were sent straight to the Canal Line to reinforce the British scratch units which were all that defended the BEF's rear against the Panzer armada advancing rapidly from the South-west. Here they were joined by the badly shaken 44th Division after it had rested in the rear, following its relief by the 3rd Belgian Division. The British 4th, after its relief by the 1st Belgian Division and having similarly side-stepped von Bock's attack, took shelter behind the fortifications on the left of the

---

* The 'shallowness' of the Escaut was considered by Billotte, Van Overstraeten and the Official Historian, Major Ellis, amongst others, as an invalid pretext for the BEF to retreat from that river line.

British frontier line up to Halluin. (In an aside to Van Overstraeten Gort had grumbled that the 44th and 4th Divisions, which the Belgians had agreed to relieve on the nights of the 22nd and 23rd respectively, were not his best – '*ne sont pas fameux*').

The French, who had on the 19th refused to relieve any British divisions, because Billotte's staff believed that the intention was to further Gort's evacuation plans, agreed to do so on being assured at Ypres that this would release two British divisions for 'participation in the counter-offensive' and also enable two 'tired' French divisions to withdraw behind the British fortifications along the frontier line. To this compromise solution, after some discussion, all agreed – although the King expressed his grave concern about the feasibility of Weygand's plan and the vulnerable position in which the British withdrawal would place his army.

The final request the British generals made to Leopold revealed that they were prepared to forfeit to the Germans the ports of Ostend and Nieuport – which Gort had just told Slessor he intended to use for evacuation – and accept the narrowing of their beach-head on the coast to only twenty-eight miles, for the sake of furthering their immediate plans, for they asked him to consider withdrawing his army to the Yser. Since the whole issue of this retirement has been much misunderstood and misrepresented, it deserves careful examination. The most one-sided view – that the BEF was 'the only one in step' – was taken by Major Ellis, who argues in his *Official History* that the right angle between the malorientated British front and that of the Belgians at Halluin should have been straightened out not by the BEF and the French falling back to the Lys-Gravelines waterline, which covered the maximum length of coastline and all the Channel ports in a great arc, but by the Belgian Army wheeling all the way back to the Yser (a journey of fifty miles for its left wing), which if achieved would have handed over to the Germans without a fight the whole coastline to within seventeen miles of Dunkirk and all the ports except the latter.

But the crowning absurdity is Major Ellis' contention: 'In maintaining that the Belgian Army could not withdraw to the Yser, the King and Van Overstraeten were in effect accepting defeat.' In the event, it was extremely fortunate that Leopold declined to attempt this potentially disastrous manoeuvre, for it would have prematurely narrowed the BEF's escape corridor to and the perimeter round Dunkirk, thus adding an extra 500,000 Belgian soldiers to the 'unbearable congestion' which (according to Admiral Ramsay's *Despatches*) resulted when a million-and-a-half people, consisting of Belgian refugees and British and French troops, compressed themselves into the contracting area round the port – now the only outlet for the BEF's escape by sea.

It has often been claimed that the King did agree to fall all the way back to the Yser at the Ypres conference, but even Gort's *Despatches* make it clear that when Billotte asked Leopold whether he would retire behind the Yser, if he was forced to withdraw from the Lys, the King did not agree to do so, but simply replied that 'no alternative line existed'. Exactly what the King had agreed to do was confirmed by the Belgian High Command in a memorandum later handed to the heads of the British and French Missions at GQG:

> At the Ypres conference it was established by the King that the Belgian Army would defend itself to the last . . . on the line of the Lys, and its canal from Deynze to the sea, and that it would relieve two British divisions on its right and also extend its front as far as Halluin, the point of juncture with the frontier position occupied by the British.

The third Ypres conference came to an end after dark at about 9.30 in an atmosphere of profound gloom and despondency, with the French generals trying to encourage the hope, which neither Gort nor Pownall supported, that British offensive action could still save the day. 'You must do it, Sir,' pleaded Fagalde of Gort, but as the latter left the room he remarked to the King 'It's a bad job, Sir.' Undoubtedly Gort's conscience was troubling him on account of the adverse effect of the BEF's move on the Belgians and the sacrifices the latter were making to its advantage – for Keyes noted in his diary that on coming out of the meeting Gort asked him 'Do the Belgians think us awful dirty dogs?' 'I answered that the King's main concern was to help the British Army to withdraw and escape the disaster which faced it, if it became encircled. I told Lord Gort that this was made clear in my second telegram of 20th May, a copy of which I had sent him, but which he had not apparently seen.' The thought at the back of Gort's mind had come into the open during the afternoon in a significant conversation with Colonel Davy which the latter recorded in his memoirs:

> I had a quarter of an hour in the garden at Premesques with the C-in-C. He was in two minds whether to go south . . . or to retreat to Calais and across the Channel . . . We discussed the effect on the Belgian Army and I told him they would help him as long as possible but that they must inevitably capitulate if he left them. Sir Roger Keyes had already told him this . . . At this point the C-in-C was somewhat disturbed at the prospect of leaving the Belgians in the lurch, but he looked on it as inevitable . . .

The Belgian Ministers – particularly Pierlot – were, however, in a more truculent mood. During the *entr'acte* before Gort arrived at the Ypres conference they engaged in a somewhat acrimonious discussion with the King. In his *procès verbal* of this meeting the King describes them as 'aggressive and disagreeable'. The Ministers were annoyed at not being present at the military discussions and were anxious to find out what had passed. Leopold himself became angry when they let slip that they had given Weygand their version of his confidential prediction about the imminent downfall of France, which they interpreted as defeatism.

The King then told the Ministers exactly what had transpired at the military meetings and tried to get them to understand the realities of the situation, but was met with outright disbelief by the overwrought and suspicious Pierlot. Van Overstraeten had explained to them before the main meetings began why it was undesirable that the Army should retreat from the Escaut, including the fact that the troops needed time to rest and re-form after their arduous fighting withdrawal. But Pierlot, invoking his experience as a *fantassin* (an infantryman) in the 1914 War, declared that this standstill was 'inadmissible'. The longer the troops remained on the line of the Escaut, he declared, the greater the difficulties of retreating into France would become. He had visited various parts of the front and found that the morale of the soldiers was good and that they were perfectly capable of making this move, which he and his colleagues had been urging the King to undertake from the first.

The King tried once again to convince Pierlot that the 'retreat into France', which would involve the Belgian Army disengaging itself from the British and French armies and crossing their rear, had never been a practical proposition – and now that the Panzers had cut off the whole group of armies in the North it was even less so. It would in any case be 'inconceivable', the King declared, 'to decide on a retreat which left the British flank exposed'. He then reiterated that the movements of his army were not only tied to those of the BEF but subject to the overall control of the French Supreme Command, which had so far sent him only one directive – to retire behind the Escaut. He expected the new General-issimo to issue some orders, but not before Gort's arrival. Yet Pierlot continued to rail at the King for 'passively awaiting orders' and for not 'invoking' them, or acting independently, if none were forthcoming, 'in order to avoid the capture of the Belgian Army'.

The King could make no headway in the face of Pierlot's rigid outlook, even with the help of General Denis, and found to his dismay that Pierlot was actually accusing him of wanting to disengage his army from those of the Allies with the object of holding on to the maximum amount of Belgian territory and then making a separate peace with Germany. After the war, when Pierlot was trying to justify his conjectures and actions,* he wrote of this day: 'The King considered the position of the armies in

---

* The accuracy of Pierlot's articles, written so long afterwards, is suspect, because he states that the Ministers 'immediately met Generals Weygand and Billotte' upon their arrival at Ypres at 3 pm and describes their conversation, although Billotte did not in fact arrive until 5 pm.

Flanders almost if not quite hopeless' – a view expressed by Gort and his Corps Commanders that same afternoon.

After his final meeting with Gort and Pownall the King informed the Ministers, according to Pierlot's account, of Gort's agreement to attack towards the south in accordance with Weygand's plan and of the decision that the Belgian Army should retire to the line of the Lys. 'This position,' Pierlot quotes the King as saying, 'is less advantageous from several points of view . . . but it is impossible to do anything else, because the Escaut position is, according to Lord Gort, already too deeply penetrated. The British general considers that the chances of the manoeuvre in which he is going to take part are practically nil. The situation is desperate.'[213]

This should have left the Ministers in no doubt as to the true position, but Pierlot gave Leopold the impression that he was unconvinced. The King was so disturbed by the Prime Minister's obstinate misunderstanding of the position that he summoned General Denis to GQG next morning and explained the military situation with the help of maps. Denis thereupon expressed his entire concurrence with the King's military policy, which he agreed was '*la seule possible*'. Having thus gained the Defence Minister's understanding and approval for his strategy, the King wrote a letter to Pierlot, the dignified language of which hardly concealed his anger. Their meeting the previous day 'in the presence of M. Spaak and General Denis' had, he wrote, left 'a most painful impression'. He did not believe 'that he deserved the reproach of following a policy whose object was to lead the country to the conclusion of a separate peace with Germany'.

The King then patiently described the true situation of the Belgian Army. 'In accomplishing my constitutional duty as Commander-in-Chief of the Army,' he continued, 'I have above all the task of defending the national territory, endeavouring at the same time to co-operate, as far as possible, in the struggle of the Allied armies, and to prevent the fate of our army from being compromised . . . I cannot admit, moreover, that the Ministers, whose competence does not extend to the conduct of military operations, should pass judgments on the capabilities of the Army.' He then refuted the Ministers' reproaches that he had kept them in ignorance of military developments, by reminding Pierlot that he had, from the first, drawn their attention to the fact that the way events were unfolding on the battlefield could lead to an outcome quite different to that which they thought probable.

The King went on to underline the essential difference between himself and the Cabinet which had existed ever since Breendonck. 'You deem that there can be no question of my binding my fate to that of the Army under any circumstances. I replied that it was impossible for me to exclude a hypothesis which would justify such an attitude.' Leopold's next point was that since he was keeping the Ministers fully informed about the course of military operations, he expected them to keep him *au courant* with developments in foreign affairs and the political sphere. But he well understood, the King continued scornfully, that the Ministers were in some difficulty here, because of the 'ridiculous haste' with which all the government departments and some provincial and communal services had betaken themselves to France. This exodus of almost the entire civil authority had deprived the country of any form of government.

The King's pointed letter evidently brought home to Pierlot that he had tried his Sovereign's patience too far, for he replied at great length in the most deferential and apologetic terms. His reply began: 'In the midst of the heavy preoccupations of which the King bears the load, the keen desire of my colleagues and myself is to do everything that depends on us to alleviate his burdens. We are deeply distressed if something in our attitude has caused an increase in the King's anxieties.' The Prime Minister then attempted to explain how the Ministers' own anxieties had been aroused. He had 'gathered' from his visits to Breendonck that the King's intention was that the Belgian Army should 'retreat into a redoubt backed by the sea and separated from the Allied armies, without any other future than capitulation . . . an eventuality . . . which was preferable to the disadvantages of leaving Belgian territory . . .' But, wrote Pierlot, 'it appeared at the audience which the King granted us at Saint-André, that we had not quite understood what was in his mind. I offer my apologies for this misunderstanding which has been painful to Your Majesty, and I sincerely regret that it should have incurred his displeasure.'

Pierlot then hastened to assure Leopold that 'M. Spaak and I must have expressed ourselves badly if the King interpreted our words as a reproach that we have been kept in ignorance of the military situation' and went on to 'regret that we have not been able, during these last days, to keep Your Majesty in better touch with the state of our foreign policy'. But Pierlot could only reply haltingly to the King's point about the flight of the civil administration, for he knew that the Government had been shockingly neglectful of their duty towards the population since May 10th. He did, however, accept full responsibility for the Government's precipitate departure from Belgium. After apologizing for the length of his letter, Pierlot expressed the hope that 'it would convince the King that his Ministers had no other thought but his service, nor any other inspiration than their attachment to his person and their devotion to their Country' and signed himself 'Your Majesty's very respectful, very faithful, very obedient servant'.

Tragedy followed close on the conference. The late arrival of Gort and Pownall compelled all the participants to drive home in darkness. Writing to his wife two days later, Keyes described the perils of driving by night on the congested roads and the fatal consequences for General Billotte:

> By the time we left it was dark and we had a hideous drive home. Billotte said he was nervous because it seemed possible that the Germans had got through and might be unpleasantly close to the route he had to take . . . Half an hour later he was mortally injured in a motor smash. My friend's [King Leopold's] chauffeur drove too fast . . . It was moonlight, but we could not use lights – we were passing farm carts of refugees and every sort of vehicle going our way and the opposite way – guns, lorries, etc. etc. . . .
>
> Over and over again we were saved by seeing one of the motor cyclist gendarmes . . . swerve over to the right and use his brake, which fortunately showed a fairly bright red light – then we swerved and missed something going the other way by inches . . . So after watching two or three narrow escapes I lay back, closed my eyes and soon went to sleep and woke up 1½ hours later at our Château.
>
> But we heard before we finished dinner that Billotte was fatally (probably) injured . . . It was cruel luck. The Almighty is chastening us properly – *everything* goes wrong. My friends are playing up splendidly and my friend could not be finer – but the others [the French], not so good . . .

There was now nobody – and even Billotte had been better than nobody – to attempt to concert the operations of the three national armies in the North. It was assumed that Blanchard, the commander of the First Army, would replace Billotte. But Weygand did not appoint him until four critical days had passed and Blanchard was 'a military professor type' (according to Spears), rather than a man of action, and no less inert and ineffective than Billotte. After meeting Blanchard on May 24th, General Brooke wrote in his diary: 'He gave me the impression of a man whose brain has ceased to function . . . and hardly aware of what was going on around him . . . I was badly shaken and felt that if he was to take over the tiller in the present storm, it would not be long before we were on the rocks.'[214]

'What had been largely true from the beginning of the offensive now became patently true,' writes Major Ellis, in his *Official History*. 'The conduct of Allied operations was not determined by the Supreme Command but by commanders on the spot.'[215] This is not to say that one commander on the spot did not make his voice heard in distant higher places. Keyes' diary for May 21st records:

> King Leopold pointed out that the well-prepared frontier line to be held by the British troops on his flank was unlikely to be seriously attacked, but that to be held by the Belgian troops was weak and would be comparatively lightly held and thus invite attack. He feared that if it were seriously assaulted with strong air support, the Germans would break through, sever the connection between the two armies and overwhelm the Belgian Army. He asked me to send the

following reply to the Prime Minister's message, which I had given him at Ypres that afternoon:

21.5.40.

Reference to your telegram, the King feels that you do not appreciate the difficulty of keeping in touch with the left flank of the BEF if it operates to the south as you suggest. He would like above all things to co-operate with the BEF if this were possible; but it is a physical impossibility under the existing geographical conditions. Moreover the Belgian Army has now provisions for 13 days only.

His government are urging him to fly with them to Havre before the Army finds it necessary to capitulate. Of course he has no intention of deserting his army and he considers that he can serve his Country better by staying here, ˙rather than as a fugitive with a government which represents no one while outside the Country.

The King asked me to thank you for your message and to say that if the British Government understands his motives, he does not care what others may think.

The King had further commented to Sir Roger in private that in regard to the southward attack by British and French divisions which Weygand had ordered 'he was very loath to throw doubts on the ability of the British and French armies to close this gap "since the offensive spirit was in the air", although he was tempted to point out that the offensive had been delayed too long'. By agreeing to take over the Lys front as far as Halluin (in the belief that the two British divisions he was to relieve were to be used to counter-attack in the South) the King would be forced to fall back to unprepared positions on the Lys, which Colonel Davy had seen and describes 'as hardly an obstacle at all . . . in some places it was packed so tight with boats and barges that it could be crossed dry shod'. Moreover, he would have to extend his front to a length of sixty miles and put virtually the whole Belgian Army in the line. And it should be remembered he had not only agreed to do this, but had offered to release the French 60th and 68th Divisions on his left wing.

The 'offensive spirit in the air', with all its dangerous implications for Leopold and his army, was very soon to be intensified. The commanders of the armies in the North were not to be let off the hook. During the next day, the 22nd, Churchill arrived in Paris for discussions with Reynaud and together they drove down to Vincennes at noon. Here in the map room Weygand, 'brisk, buoyant and incisive', captivated the two Prime Ministers with a grandiose exposition of his 'plan'. Not only were the northern armies to drive south-eastwards into the German flank – 'their rear would be protected by the Belgian Army, which would cover them toward the East, and if necessary towards the North' – but also a new French army under General Frère would concentrate along the Somme, 18 to 20 divisions from Alsace, the Maginot Line, Africa, 'and from every other

quarter'. This would push via Amiens to Arras and link up with the
northern group. Here was heady matter, which Churchill and Dill, now
for all practical purposes the new CIGS, agreed they 'had no choice, and
indeed no inclination' other than to accept – as they did, uncritically and
immediately. The French minutes of the meeting describe Churchill and
Dill as giving 'frequent indications of their approval' and showing 'that
their conception of the situation corresponded in all respects with that of
the Generalissimo . . . Mr Churchill stated more than once his conviction
that the reopening of communications between the armies in the North
and those in the South . . . was urgently necessary, . . . that all the depots
upon which the BEF was dependent for its supplies . . . were between
Calais and St Nazaire, and that what had been throughout uppermost in
Lord Gort's mind was to keep his connection with this vital base open.'

'It is hard to avoid the conclusion,' writes Brian Bond, 'that Weygand
misled the Prime Minister, though Churchill's determination to see a
silver lining in the darkest cloud may also have contributed to the
confusion.'[216] In fact, General Frère's force, which was spread out over a
front of sixty-five miles, comprised only six divisions, three of them
incomplete – and, according to the minutes and the vaguely-worded
orders Weygand issued that day, it was not expected to do more than
recapture the Somme crossings and 'increase the pressure on the enemy
armour in the region of Amiens, Abbeville and Arras'. Moreover, as
Weygand admitted later to his son, 'I was too well aware of the weakness
of the numbers at my disposal . . . to allow myself to indulge in any
illusions regarding the strength of the thrust from the South . . . But I
calculated that however feeble it might be, it would at least create an
additional threat to the German flank, and thus increase the chances of
success for the northern offensive.' He added that Frère's force took so
long to assemble that 'when the VIIth Army did eventually launch its
attack it hardly progressed beyond its prepared positions'.[217]

After the conference Churchill signalled to Gort:

The conclusions which were reached between Reynaud, Weygand and
ourselves are summarized below. They accord exactly with general directions
you have received from the War Office . . . It was agreed:

1 That the Belgian Army should withdraw to the line of the Yser and stand
there, the sluices being open.
2 That the British Army and the French First Army should attack south-west
towards Bapaume and Cambrai at the earliest possible moment, certainly
tomorrow, with about eight divisions, and with the Belgian Cavalry Corps on
the right of the British.
3 That as this battle is vital to both armies and the British communications
depend upon freeing Amiens, the British Air Force should give the utmost
possible help, both by day and by night, while it is going on.
4 That the new French Army Group which is advancing upon Amiens and

forming a line upon the Somme should strike northward and join hands with the British divisions who are attacking southwards in the general direction of Bapaume.

Pownall's reaction to this 'extraordinary telegram from Winston' was explosive, as his diary entry shows:

We have had *no* directions from the W.O. if one excepts the scribbled paper [brought] by Tiny [Ironside] telling us to do an impossible *sauve qui peut* to Amiens . . . Here are Winston's plans again. Can nobody prevent him trying to conduct operations himself . . . How does he think we are to collect eight divisions and attack as he suggests . . . He can have no conception of our situation and condition. Where are the Belgian Cavalry Corps? How is an attack like this to be staged involving three nationalities at an hour's notice? The man's mad. I suppose these figments of the imagination are telegraphed without consulting his military advisers, indeed it says little enough for them if they had any hand in it.

The Vincennes conference and Churchill's signal to Gort require careful consideration, for if at this stage both Prime Ministers and the Allied Supreme Commander could be so abysmally ignorant about the true situation not only of Leopold's troops, but also of their own armies, it is no wonder that they could later condemn the Belgians for failing to live up to expectations which only their own blind optimism had aroused. However was an attack on an army scale to be planned, prepared and launched 'certainly tomorrow'? Who had agreed that the Belgian Cavalry Corps should participate in the counter-offensive? Which were these other eight divisions to be so employed – there being not a single uncommitted division in the northern armies? Was not Gort scraping the very bottom of the barrel to find men for the defence of his southern flank and rear, as the Panzers began to swing up into the Pas de Calais? If the Belgians were to retreat to the Yser, how could they conceivably cover their Allies 'towards the East, and if necessary towards the North'? And had it not been agreed at Ypres that the Belgian Army should retire only to the Lys? After all that had happened since May 10th, how could it be imagined that a new French army from Alsace, Africa, the Maginot Line and elsewhere could ever be assembled, still less make any impact on ten battle-tested German armoured divisions, backed by a great mass of mechanized and infantry forces, operating under a canopy of overwhelming air power?

It was unfortunate for the BEF and also for the French and Belgian armies in the northern theatre, all of whom were adversely affected by this misconceived directive, that Churchill did not have at his side to restrain him a wise and robust adviser such as General Sir Alan Brooke would later prove to be – a man who, without hesitation, would have torn Weygand's wishful fantasy to shreds.

CHAPTER TWENTY-TWO

Anglo-French Disunity

'The situation is very serious, for the English are falling back on the ports instead of attacking in the South . . . It is impossible to command an army which remains dependent on London in the matter of military operations.'

General Weygand, May 24th 1940

'General Weygand seemed to me overcome by the defection of the English.'

Paul Baudouin's diary, May 24th 1940

Early on the morning of the 22nd at GQG the King approved the plans for retirement to the Lys which had been drawn up overnight by Van Overstraeten and Michiels. 'But,' he declared, 'we must defend ourselves there without thought of further retreat.' With scant satisfaction he and his military staff had been deliberating on the previous day's talks. They were under no illusions about the attitude of the French and British leaders. 'We must expect the Belgian Army,' the King observed, 'to be abandoned, isolated, left to its fate.' But these mordant reflections did not prevent him from carrying out to the full the undertakings he had given at Ypres – and even going beyond them in his efforts to help the British. Indeed, as Admiral Keyes noted in a memorandum:

> The Belgian Army held on to its position on the Escaut for twenty-four hours after the BEF withdrew; moreover they moved two divisions to cover the withdrawal of the British 44th Division, which had taken a considerable knock at Audenarde and had allowed the Germans to cross the Escaut there.

It will be recalled that Leopold had agreed to relieve the British 4th and 44th Divisions on the understanding that they would be used for the 'counter-offensive' to the South. On learning from his Deputy Chief of Staff, General Dérousseaux, that the 44th Division was being driven back in some disorder towards the Lys, the King ordered that the two Belgian divisions which were to have relieved the British divisions after they reached their allotted positions on the river, should instead be rushed there immediately. As a result, the Belgians not only allowed the two British divisions to withdraw from the battlefield through their ranks to the safety of the BEF's heavily fortified frontier line, but by replacing them in the unprepared positions on the Lys in which they would otherwise have had to stand and fight the pursuing enemy, the Belgian Army took over from the BEF the full weight of von Bock's thrust between the two armies. (See the map on page 471.)

Here again was true co-operation according to King Leopold's principles, but the extension of his line to replace the two British divisions inevitably weakened his whole front, and proved a sacrificial gesture when von Bock developed the full power of his assault. But the nature of the Belgians' sacrifice was not appreciated by the BEF. Pownall refers in his diary to the retreat of the 44th: 'the division is of course a long way from being a properly trained one', but he fails to acknowledge Leopold's unselfish assistance. And he again demonstrated his cavalier attitude towards the Belgians in a conversation he and Gort had with Colonel Davy while walking in the garden of GHQ at Premesques on the 23rd, as the latter recalls:

> By this time they had almost decided to evacuate by Calais or Dunkirk; the projected offensive in the South had gone out in the betting owing to the ineffectiveness of the French. I again raised the question of what was wanted of the Belgians and whether they could be evacuated, or some of them, with the BEF. 'We don't care a bugger what happens to the Belgians,' said Pownall; and Gort made no comment; so I suppose he did not disagree with the sentiment.

Although Davy had already been made aware of Pownall's hostility towards the Belgians, this remark shocked him – for his own view, based on his first-hand experience, was that 'the King did his best to co-operate in every way and complied with every request from the BEF, whether to take over more frontage or to re-adjust a boundary. Only once did he insist on having the use of a particular road up to a certain hour, and by that hour the road was free.' Pownall's remark coarsely summarized the truth – that by now the British had ceased even to pay lip-service to Belgium's interests and were considering only their own.

As the situation worsened, Belgium was consistently being cast as the victim. The Belgian Army had already been denied the use of the bases of Gravelines, Dunkirk and Bourbourg in favour of the French and British. Now it was threatened with the loss of its two remaining ports. Next day Major Cockburn of the Needham Mission was sent to GHQ, BEF in response to Belgian complaints that the British were 'commandeering civilian hospitals and food, which were required by the Belgians'. On his return he noted the General Staff's reaction to his representations: 'The Belgians do not yet know [about the forthcoming evacuation]; we must have free disposal of the ports of Nieuport and Ostend, our only outlet now. As for the hospitals, food, etc., the British are just going to commandeer what they require, though very sorry for the Belgians . . .'

On the morning of May 22nd, when von Bock's assault on the left wing of the BEF south of Audenarde was renewed, no attempt was made to dislodge the enemy bridgehead, for the whole British front was now wheeling rapidly back to the security of their fortified line behind the French frontier – thus exposing the Belgian right flank. By that night the BEF's seven front-line divisions were all back in the positions in France from which they had dashed forward into Belgium on May 10th. But now the enemy was behind as well as in front of them.

In order to assist the British the King had thinned and extended his line right across Belgium from the Escaut estuary to the French frontier. To defend this sixty-mile-long front, on which nothing had been prepared for defence, was beyond the strength of the Belgian Army. Nor was there any hope of Allied ground or air support. It might have been expected that the Belgian troops would lose heart at this point; that they did not do so was largely due to the leadership of their Sovereign, who constantly urged them to maintain their resistance for the sake of their Allies.

The King's generous gesture in rushing two of his divisions to replace the British 44th and 4th on the Lys had unfortunate results, for it denuded his front in the Ghent sector, where the German XXIVth Corps launched a powerful attack next day – before the Belgian replacements arrived. Under the cover of a tremendous bombardment by dive-bombers and artillery, the enemy established a number of bridgeheads across the Terneuzen Canal north of Ghent and the Belgian positions soon became untenable. That evening Leopold was forced to order a general withdrawal from the Ghent-Terneuzen line to the Derivation Canal, which covers Bruges and Zeebrugge to the east.

From his vantage point at Belgian GQG, Admiral Keyes was as keenly aware of the BEF's predicament as he was of the Belgian Army's. In his eyes their fates were linked, for if disaster was to be avoided it was vital that they should maintain contact with each other and remain shoulder-to-shoulder in order to cover the Channel coast and ports – on which the northern armies now depended for their continued existence. Above all, he saw the suicidal futility of the southward sortie attempt and the perils inherent in the lack of communications and a unified command, from which all three armies were suffering. His diary for that day records:

May 22nd: After a very short night, accompanied by Colonel Davy, I went to the GHQ Command Post at Premesques, in order to find out if I could help Lord Gort in any way, by getting direct contact with the Prime Minister through La Panne. I found the BEF were on half-rations and short of munitions, not very favourable conditions for the Army to launch an offensive into the blue, with all its communications cut.

Lord Gort then arranged to send his ADC, Lord Munster, with me to La Panne to speak to the Prime Minister . . . Unfortunately the Prime Minister was away [in France]; however we both spoke to the Secretary of State for War

[Anthony Eden] and did our best to make him realize the gravity of the BEF's situation – and I think succeeded . . . I told Mr Eden that it seemed essential to appoint a Chief to co-ordinate the action of the three armies, since General Blanchard was evidently quite incapable of doing so . . . that it was vitally important that some military authority should be sent out to see for himself the existing conditions, and said that I understood that a visit from General Dill would be much appreciated by GHQ.

As Keyes later wrote to his wife, Gort, frustrated by Whitehall's refusal to recognize the realities of the BEF's situation, had asked him to get Dill sent out to see it for himself – 'they didn't want anyone else' the letter concluded. The pessimism at British GHQ at this moment is well illustrated by a letter dated May 23rd which Keyes received from Lord Munster, who had been Under-Secretary of State at the War Office and a peace-time Whip in the Chamberlain government, before becoming Gort's ADC. Referring to the 'counter-attack', Munster wrote 'If that fails we might as well pack up shop!' Incredibly, this revealing statement was sent openly on GHQ headed notepaper.

Meanwhile, Keyes was having some exasperating and dangerous experiences in the course of the daily journeys he made back and forth on the bombed and congested roads between Bruges and La Panne, in his efforts to keep Churchill fully informed by means of the safe telephone line. When he arrived there on the morning of the 23rd he waited in vain for Munster – GHQ having moved yet again, owing to a scare about approaching German tanks. But, he recorded in his diary, 'I told the Prime Minister, on behalf of Lord Gort, what I had said to Mr Eden.' Churchill then asked him to return to La Panne that afternoon, but after keeping him waiting until 10 pm, the Prime Minister merely asked him to return next morning. Being thus forced to motor back to Bruges late that night without lights, Keyes had some hair-raising near-misses when he encountered a demoralized French formation going in both directions. This was the 68th Division, which the King had, in agreement with the French, sent in Belgian vehicles to defend the Gravelines line in his rear – now threatened by the Panzers advancing from the West. 'On crossing the Yser,' the Admiral recalls, 'they heard a rumour that German tanks were already in Dunkirk, so they had turned and fled back, meeting the remainder of the column and causing great confusion on the road.'*

On his visits to La Panne, the Admiral was warmly received by the Queen Mother, who (as Keyes recorded in his diary) 'seemed to spend all her time in the hospital, and helping to look after the thousands of refugees who . . . had been refused entry into France.' For nearly a

---

* In a letter to his wife Keyes wrote: 'My journey home was quite frightful and I do not mean to be caught on the road again at night. I told Winston next morning that if I was more use alive than dead, he had better not let me in for it like that again!'

fortnight, this intrepid lady, wearing a red-cross armband, but scorning a steel helmet, had been a much admired figure in this heavily-bombed area, as she went about her relief work in her small Fiat car. But as the German tanks raced up the Channel coast she was forced to leave La Panne and join Leopold at the Château of Wynendaele, near Thourout, to which the King and his suite moved next day. GQG was established nearby at St André.

The military situation of the Allies was now desperate and chaotic. Because of the dangerous misconceptions of Churchill and Weygand and the orders they had given, the three northern armies were compelled to remain in an elongated and highly vulnerable pocket seventy miles deep, with its narrow mouth on the sea and the enemy pressing in from both sides. The eastern side was held by the Belgians on their over-extended front – hard pressed by von Bock's forces. (The four British and two French divisions behind the fortifications of the frontier line were undisturbed by the two German divisions which were all that faced them.) The bottom, or southern section was manned by the French First Army, now in a state of disintegration. The western side was defended only by a few scratch and improvised units of the BEF, hastily deployed on the Canal Line in an attempt to stem the remorseless intrusion of the Germans into the Pas de Calais. Now that the French airfields in the North were all captured or abandoned and the RAF was operating from British airfields, there was virtually no air support for the three armies in the North, as the German ring swiftly tightened round them. With von Rundstedt's forces – nine Panzer, six motorized and numerous infantry divisions – operating virtually unopposed under an umbrella of unchallenged air power in their rear and on the flanks, the BEF was now completely cut off from its supply bases – all being to the west of the Somme. It was running desperately short of food and ammunition, and attempts to create new bases in the northern ports were being frustrated by heavy bombing.

On the afternoon of the 22nd von Kleist's Panzers entered Boulogne, sweeping on to invest Calais and reach Gravelines, at the sea end of the Canal Line only ten miles west of Dunkirk, next day. The Panzers were now much nearer the BEF's main evacuation port than was the bulk of that force. But Dunkirk was temporarily reprieved – thanks to the famous 'Halt Order' given by Rundstedt on the 23rd and endorsed by Hitler on the 24th, whereby the Panzer divisions were held back for three crucial days on the Canal Line and their advanced units, which actually entered the outskirts of Dunkirk on May 23rd, were ordered back across the Canal du Nord.

By now No. 1 Army Group was little more than a name. Around 4 pm on the 22nd General Delvoie, Leopold's liaison officer with Billotte, returned from the latter's headquarters at Béthune and reported that his condition was desperate (he died later that day) and that the staff had been left without orders. Moreover, the staff of Blanchard's First Army were 'worn out and depressed' and the army itself was *'ruiné'*. Its eleven divisions were now equivalent to three. Panic reigned everywhere. Béthune had been severely bombed and was in an indescribable state, with corpses lying in its streets. As for the area west of Arras (ten miles south-east of Béthune), Delvoie reported this to be undefended. For miles there were no troops and no demolitions had been carried out.

The possibility that any counter-attack from north or south would succeed in closing or even narrowing the gap had now become even more remote. This was underlined by the failure of the French advance from south of the Somme to materialize, and the short-lived nature of the French counter-attack in the Cambrai area on May 22nd, which Blanchard had been unable to launch on the previous day in conjunction with the Frankforce sortie at Arras. Instead of his Cavalry Corps and two infantry divisions, he was able to deploy only one infantry regiment and two small armoured units. They attacked gallantly and reached Cambrai that evening, but fell back after suffering heavy dive-bombing. So ended the only offensive effort by Blanchard's broken First Army.

Next day (the 23rd) Ironside noted in his diary: 'We have sent complete discretion to Gort to move his army as he likes, to try to save it . . . Gort is very nearly surrounded and there is just the possibility that he may be able to withdraw through Ypres to Dunkirk . . . I cannot see that we have much hope of getting any of the BEF out.' But Winston Churchill, now back in London after his sortie to Paris, remained as determined as ever that Gort should launch the southward attack. When he learned that no offensives from the south or north had yet begun, he fired off to Reynaud (with a copy to Gort) a brusque 'demand' that the 'most stringent orders' for the immediate execution of the Weygand Plan should be issued. By that afternoon, his eyes having been partly opened to the desperate situation in France and Flanders by Keyes, who had managed to get through to him from La Panne and reinforce the message he had given Eden, Churchill was beginning to have his doubts. At 4.50 pm he telephoned Reynaud and (according to the latter's memoirs) asked if, in view of Gort's lack of orders from Blanchard – now assumed to be Billotte's successor – and of the encroaching Panzer forces, it might not be better for the British and French armies in the North to retreat to the northern ports. Both Reynaud and Weygand vigorously rejected the suggestion. This was the occasion when Weygand 'forestalled' Churchill's attempt to speak to him direct and signalled that the Weygand Plan must proceed.

It was Weygand who fired the next shots in the war of words between the French and the British leaders, which would become increasingly acrimonious as the situation deteriorated on the battle-fronts. Having found, as he later admitted to his son, that the Seventh Army had 'hardly progressed at all beyond its prepared positions',[218] Weygand signalled to Gort that 'the attack in progress from the South towards Albert is going very well. This movement combined with that of the BEF and General Blanchard's army should close the breach and bar the return journey of the Panzer adventurers in the North.' Weygand concluded by urging Gort 'to continue the manoeuvre with the energy of a tiger'. He then reported to London that the great re-formed army he had envisioned on the Somme 'was advancing successfully' and had already 'captured Péronne, Albert and Amiens'. This was wholly untrue. In fact, the French forces in the South did not even reach the Somme, on which Amiens stands – the other two towns being to the north of that river. General Spears, who was present when Churchill received this false report, recalls: 'The Prime Minister's cigar was waving cheerfully now . . . Wonderful. This really looked like business. Every optimism was justified.'[219]

By 10.30 pm, however, when King George, deeply worried, summoned him to Buckingham Palace, Churchill had shed his rosy illusions. As George VI recorded in his diary: 'He told me that if the French plan made out by Weygand did not come off, he would have to order the BEF back to England. This operation would mean the loss of all guns, tanks, ammunition, and all stores in France . . . The very thought of having to order this movement is appalling, as the loss of life will probably be immense.'[220] In the course of the evening, therefore, Churchill signalled Reynaud:

> General Gort wires that co-ordination of northern front is essential with armies of three different nations. He says he cannot undertake this co-ordination, as he is already fighting north and south and is threatened on his lines of communications. At the same time Sir Roger Keyes tells me that up to 3 pm today (23rd) Belgian Headquarters and King had received no directive. How does this agree with your statement that Blanchard and Gort are *main dans la main*?
>
> Gort further says that any advance by him must be in the nature of a sortie, and that relief must come from the South as he has not (repeat not) ammunition for serious attack. Nevertheless we are instructing him to persevere in carrying out your plan . . .

As Weygand admits, he had no expectation that a counter-attack of any strength could be launched from the South but he hoped 'that however feeble it might be, it would at least create an additional threat to the German flank and thus increase the chances of success for the northern offensive'.[221] Thus, while Weygand sought by dissimulation to encourage the British to launch the main attack from the North, Churchill and Gort were insisting that it would have to come from the South. But worse was to come. Next day the French leadership began to insure themselves against France's defeat by scoring debating points which could be used in future propaganda to prove that the British were responsible. During the night of the 23rd, Gort cancelled his instructions to the British force at Arras, whose briefly successful sortie had been repelled, that they should hold the town 'to the last man and the last round' – and ordered its immediate retirement to positions behind the Haute-Deule Canal in the North. Unfortunately he omitted to inform Blanchard until next day and the French First Army was left in a dangerously exposed salient. Weygand and Reynaud seized their opportunity in a flash. In an angry riposte to Churchill, Reynaud signalled that Weygand had informed him that

> contrary to his formal orders, confirmed this morning, the British Army has decided upon and carried out a withdrawal of forty kilometres in the direction of the ports, at a moment when our forces from the South were gaining ground towards the North to join up with the Allied armies of the North.
>
> This withdrawal has naturally compelled General Weygand to modify his whole plan. He is now compelled to give up his attempt to close the breach and establish a continuous front. It is unnecessary to stress the gravity of the consequences which may result.

This was the old French line of 'perfidious Albion'. In fact it was not the 'British Army', but the two under-strength divisions, the 5th and 50th (now further depleted after the costly Frankforce sortie), which had withdrawn – to Carvin, behind the Canal Line, a distance of twenty-six kilometres as the crow flies. Moreover, the claim that the French forces in the South were 'gaining ground' was fictitious, for they had made no appreciable progress towards the Somme, which was strongly held by the enemy with several bridgeheads across the river. But Reynaud and Weygand had established their debating point '*pour l'histoire*'.

The two incidents on the previous day – Churchill's proposal for a withdrawal to cover the ports, and the two British divisions' hurried retreat from Arras without warning the French formations on their flanks – provided the French leaders with a useful stick with which to beat the British. 'General Weygand seemed to me overcome by the defection of the English,' noted Paul Baudouin in his diary for the 24th, and describes how the Generalissimo told him that morning 'The situation is very serious, for the English are falling back on the ports instead of attacking to the South' and complained 'It is impossible to command an army which remains dependent on London in the matter of military operations.' Later that day Weygand telephoned Baudouin and said that because 'the English Army had . . . retreated forty kilometres', he was 'compelled to abandon Wednesday's plans' – concluding that he was 'by no means sure' that it would be possible 'to avoid an early capitulation of the armies in the North'.[222]

Meanwhile, the British Ambassador in Paris was summoned by Reynaud, who read him a lecture on the theme that 'British generals always made for the harbours in an emergency', as General Spears learned next day, when he arrived in France as Churchill's liaison officer with Reynaud. From now on, as Spears recalls in his memoirs, British 'defection' and their 'making for the harbours' was to be the recurrent theme amongst the French leadership.[223]

Much exasperated by Reynaud's recriminatory message and the lack of information about the BEF, Churchill had at once replied: 'We have every reason to believe that Gort is still persevering in the southward move . . . Nothing in the movements of the BEF of which we are aware can be any excuse for the abandonment of the strong pressure of your northward move across the Somme . . .'

While the withdrawal of the two British divisions northwards, blowing the bridges behind them, had hardly improved the northern armies' prospects for the 'southward move', it certainly provided a pretext for General Besson, commanding the Sixth and Seventh Armies, south of the Somme, to abandon his 'offensive' from the South and for Weygand to authorize Blanchard to call off his sortie attempt from the North. On the 24th Besson telephoned Frère to say that the withdrawal by the northern armies had compelled him to call off the attack, while the Generalissimo signalled Blanchard that day saying that if the British withdrawal had made the counter-attack impossible, he should form as wide a bridgehead as possible, covering the three northern ports.

Unfortunately, the confusion caused by almost non-existent communications, false information, orders and counter-orders was now so great that Blanchard failed to take advantage of this permissive cover to execute the already fatally delayed 'vast perimeter' plan. Instead he was inveigled into planning with the British another southward sortie, to be launched on May 26th. Despite Weygand's claim that the British retreat from Arras had forced him to give up his 'plan', heavy pressure was applied from Paris and London (by Dill in particular) whereby Blanchard and Gort were induced to waste more precious time going through the motions of preparing another attack to the South. Gort even agreed to contribute 'two divisions', although these were the same battered and depleted 5th and 50th whose hurried retreat northwards behind blown bridges had caused all the fuss, and which were therefore hardly well placed or in fit condition to take any offensive action. Blanchard likewise agreed that the French First Army would contribute one division of infantry and its Cavalry Corps, although both were similarly depleted and incapable of taking the offensive after several fierce actions. Fortunately, this new 'southward move' never got beyond the theoretical stage, for the British and French units had forthwith to be withdrawn or deployed for urgent defensive purposes.

There is a peculiar irony in the events of May 24th, since it was on this day that Reynaud, in conversation with Baudouin, 'wondered if, even in the event of an offer of a moderate peace by Germany, the state of public opinion would permit of it being rejected' – to which he added 'In that case, since I have always advocated war to the end, I would resign.'[224] Of May 24th, despite what he said to Baudouin, Reynaud wrote in his memoirs: 'From that moment the idea was born in the mind of Weygand, and *a fortiori* in that of Pétain, that the hour was approaching when France ought to lay down her arms.'[225] As a quid pro quo to Reynaud's accusations of defeatism, Weygand charges him in his own memoirs with doctoring the official minutes of the War Committee meeting next day, by deleting certain passages referring to the prospects of the enemy granting France an armistice.[u]

Although Reynaud was chary about such words as 'armistice' and 'capitulation' being attributed to him, they are recorded as being bandied about between Pétain, Weygand and himself, in his room that evening (the 24th) – words which would soon be used like swords against Leopold. They were used again at the War Committee meeting chaired by President Lebrun later that evening and at that of the War Cabinet next morning, at which the Generalissimo introduced an emissary from Blanchard, Commandant Fauvelle. In reply to Reynaud's opening question on the state of Blanchard's army, the Commandant declared: 'I believe in a very early capitulation.' Questioned by Weygand, Fauvelle reported that the First Army was 'stupefied by the air bombardment' and described how neither armoured vehicles nor horse-drawn transport nor heavy artillery remained, while food and ammunition supplies were running dangerously low. Only three divisions retained any cohesion, but their movements were paralysed by refugees. Fauvelle then repeated: 'I think that a capitulation must soon take place.'[226]

Weygand's reaction was to announce that he would immediately order Blanchard to retire to cover the ports – 'the only course open to him'. But Reynaud stopped him, on the score that Blanchard was 'attacking southwards at this moment' and must therefore believe that he could break through. When asked about his chief, Fauvelle described him as '*très fatigué*', which meant (as General Spears explains) that he was 'no longer capable of exercising his command'.[227]

At the War Committee meeting that evening, in a bleak survey of the situation, Weygand declared that France had made the cardinal error of entering the war without the necessary military material or technique. 'She would probably have to pay dearly for that culpable imprudence.' The Committee then proceeded to a general discussion in which it envisaged the early loss of all three armies in the North, the abandonment of Paris, the surrender of the French forces and the conclusion of a separate peace with Germany. The Committee, though admitting the necessity of informing Great Britain of any steps which they might later decide to take, criticized her severely for contributing only ten divisions, as compared with the eighty French, and for not affording more effective air support. The disastrous situation of the Belgian Army and people was never once mentioned by any of those present.

When the President of the Republic asked Weygand if it would not be better for the Government to examine offers of peace from the Germans before the French armies 'were dispersed and destroyed' as Weygand envisaged, the latter expressed his complete agreement. 'Certainly,' the President continued, 'we have signed engagements which forbid us to make a separate peace. If, however, Germany should offer us relatively advantageous conditions, we ought to examine them very closely, and deliberate coolly on them.' Campinchi, the Minister of Marine, then remarked 'that if the present Government had given its word to England, another Government would find it less awkward to sign a treaty of peace without prior agreement with her. The present Government need only resign.' Reynaud, who still made no mention of Göring's peace proposals, was finally asked by the Committee to go to London forthwith to give the British Government a full and frank statement of France's 'painful situation' and sound them out on the possibility of her making a separate peace with Germany.

Although the French Premier was later reproached by his colleagues for failing to be sufficiently frank at his meeting with the British Cabinet next day, Chamberlain noted in his diary for the 26th: 'the blackest day of all . . . plain from his [Reynaud's] attitude that he has given up all idea of serious fighting, and if we are to go on, we shall be alone.'[228] After the meeting Churchill told Sir Alexander Cadogan that Reynaud had not actually said that France would capitulate 'but all his conversation goes to show that he sees no alternative'. 'W.S.C. seemed to think,' Cadogan's diary continues, 'we might almost be better off if France did pull out and we could concentrate on defence here.'[229]

But in reply to a letter from General Spears (who, to his annoyance, had been left behind in Paris by Reynaud) reporting that the French Government was 'talking about capitulating', Churchill wrote that day instructing Spears to 'resist all suggestions by Reynaud of cutting out [of the war]'. The Prime Minister then related how Reynaud had told him that 'French means of resistance were exhausted and that they considered the struggle was hopeless'.[230] In a postscript Churchill added that no doubt France would be offered favourable peace terms by the Germans. But Reynaud never revealed either in conversation or in writing that he had received such an offer from Göring.

Cadogan's *Diaries* further record that although Halifax, the Foreign Secretary, had called on the Italian Ambassador in London the previous day with an offer to make concessions to Italy in the Mediterranean in an attempt to 'stave off war' with that country, Churchill was opposed to Reynaud's more far-reaching plan to make a 'final appeal' to Mussolini and to use him as an intermediary to obtain peace terms from Hitler.

To the King it now seemed certain that his own hour was approaching. On the 24th, as he had predicted, the enemy launched an all-out assault on the southern end of the Belgian line on the Lys, with an abundance of air support. This was the follow-up to the attack von Bock had launched to drive a wedge between the Belgian Army and the BEF and which had breached the British front on the Escaut near Audenarde on the 20th. But it now fell not on the British troops, but on the Belgian divisions through which they had withdrawn from the battle. Throughout the morning a heavy concentration of artillery and swarms of Stuka dive-bombers continuously pounded the Belgian positions. In the afternoon two German corps, the IVth and XIth, launched a determined assault on the Belgian line with four divisions of regular infantry. Even Sir John Colville, who generally echoes the unfair denigration of the Belgians by Pownall and Gort in his biography of the latter, concedes that 'the best elements in the Belgian Army fought well against superior arms and odds'. But under immense pressure the line was breached both north and south of Courtrai – incursions which the Belgians were only able to check by throwing in their last remaining reserves.

On his return to La Panne that same day, Keyes managed to speak to Churchill, and after reporting that the Belgian front was under heavy attack, tried once again to persuade him that the southward offensive spelt disaster for the BEF as well as the Belgian Army, and to get him to agree to a withdrawal to cover the Channel coast and ports. But the Prime Minister told him 'that the counter-attack would be carried out by the BEF as planned by General Weygand'. Keyes then renewed the request Gort had asked him to make, and 'begged' Churchill to send out General Dill, suggesting that he should come by Motor Torpedo Boat to Ostend. Dill was brought to the telephone and agreed to come. He arrived at nightfall and after sleeping at Colonel Davy's Mission went to GHQ at dawn.

But Dill's visit to GHQ disconcerted Gort and Pownall, for he hinted that there was criticism at home of the performance of the BEF, and insisted that it must carry out the southward offensive in accordance with the Weygand Plan. All at Belgian GQG were similarly 'dismayed by his apparent optimism', as Keyes noted, when he presented Dill to the King there later that day and the CIGS announced that the British Government had ordained that Gort's southward offensive 'was on no account to be modified'. The King warned Dill of the critical situation which was developing between the two armies' fronts and of the impossibility of the Belgians holding their line and at the same time maintaining contact with the BEF, unless the latter rendered strong assistance. He had thrown in

King George VI and his Ministers greet King
Leopold on his State Visit in 1937

The two Sovereigns' carriage drive to
Buckingham Palace

King Leopold's State Visit to Paris, 1937

The King and Paul-Henri Spaak, 1937

Greeting foreign Air Attachés, 1938

The King and Princess Josephine
Charlotte, 1938

Decorating a cadet for bravery

Liège, 1939

The King inspecting a parade of the 5th Royal Inniskilling Dragoon Guards, marking his appointment as their Colonel-in-Chief in 1937

The Belgian Army on parade, 1939

Eben Emael fortress on the Albert Canal

May 10th 1940, German paratroops dropping i
the Albert Canal area

Eben Emael firing on a German assault
craft

Eben Emael after the battle

German tanks crossing a Belgian river

Right: A Stuka dive-bombing

The ruins of Ostend

A bridge demolished by the Belgians

elgian refugees

The King and the Admiral in the garden
of GQG

Conferring at Wynendaele

Admiral of the Fleet Sir Roger Keyes, Director
of Combined Operations, and Winston
Churchill, Prime Minister, watching an
amphibious exercise in June 1941

The King, Van Overstraeten and Sir Roge
Keyes at Wynendaele, May 25th 194

Paul-Henri Spaak in 1939

Right: Weygand, Baudouin,
Reynaud and Pétain

Left: General Pownall

Right: Lord Gort, VC.

Bottom right: General von
Reichenau escorting General
Dérousseaux to his car

Bottom left: Von Reichenau
telephoning Hitler with the news
of the Belgian capitulation, May
28th 1940

The memorial at Zeebrugge

Sir Roger Keyes, portrait by de Laszlo, 1923

The *Vindictive* Memorial at
Ostend

Block-ships in the Zeebrugge
Canal, 1918 (right) and
(below) 1940

all his reserves and feared that it would be impossible to stem the enemy's breakthrough towards Ypres, which was likely to be exploited by a tank formation now reported to be approaching. When the Admiral begged Dill to get the BEF to relieve the pressure on the Belgians' right wing, the latter promised to arrange for the British II Corps to do so. After complimenting the King on the 'magnificent bearing and spirit' of the Belgian 2nd Cavalry Division, which he had encountered on the road, Dill departed.

That morning (the 25th) the enemy stepped up pressure all along the Belgian front on the Lys. In the North Kuechler's Eighteenth Army pressed forward, while the IXth Corps established a bridgehead across the Derivation Canal north of Deynze. But the main effort was still concentrated on the Belgian right wing, where von Bock, in order to strengthen his breakthrough attempt, threw in the Xth Corps and a fresh infantry division between the two Corps already engaged. 'The Belgian Army made a valiant effort to seal the breach,' writes Brian Bond, 'but was driven inexorably northwards by an enemy superior in numbers and in total command of the air.'[231]

At GHQ that afternoon Gort, who had been reared in the tradition of 'theirs not to reason why', at last decided (as Keyes had urged him to do five days before) to rebel against 'the Cabinet's' orders, which Dill had renewed that morning, and act on his own initiative to extricate his army from what Keyes generously described in his subsequent letter as 'the appalling situation in which it had been placed through no fault of yours'. At 5.30 pm Major Archdale found Gort, 'looking rather bewildered and bitter', complaining that he had 'had a raw deal from the Allies' and 'no direction or information from the High Command'. Shortly afterwards, Gort received from General Brooke ominous news of the heavy assaults by enemy ground and air forces on the Belgians' right wing. This was followed by information obtained from a captured order of the German Sixth Army that two more enemy corps were to be thrown in against the Belgians next day – one north-westwards towards Ypres, the other westwards towards Wytschaele – a development which caused Churchill to ask in his memoirs 'How could the Belgians withstand this double thrust?'

The danger that the Germans, having driven a wedge between the Belgian and British armies, would then swing south-westwards behind the latter to join up with the Panzer forces which were advancing north-eastwards, thus encircling the BEF, had at last become clear to Gort. He therefore decided at 6.30 pm on the 25th, as his biographer recalls, 'without wasting the hours which finding and consulting Blanchard would entail' to cancel the BEF's counter-attack, to rush the 5th and 50th divisions to protect his left flank and to withdraw his entire force with all speed to the coast, with the object of evacuating it by sea. Having

refrained from consulting or informing his allies about this withdrawal of
his army from their midst, it is indeed strange that this same brave soldier
would shortly join the chorus of those who falsely accused King Leopold
of capitulating without warning his French and British fellow-
combatants.

Gort's biographer excuses the C-in-C's failure to mention to his allies
the 'delicate matter' of the decision to evacuate the BEF, on the grounds
that 'he was expressly ordered not to do so' by Anthony Eden, the
Secretary of State for War. Eden had signalled Gort, endorsing his
decision to march to the coast, where 'all beaches and ports east of
Gravelines will be used for embarkation', and stating that Churchill would
inform Reynaud, but 'in the meantime it is obvious you should not discuss
the possibility of the move with the French or Belgians'. Yet Churchill did
not tell Reynaud of the decision to evacuate the BEF, only that the
counter-attack had been called off. 'Gort may perhaps be excused for not
informing the Belgians,' writes Brian Bond, 'but there is no defence for
the [British] Government's silence.'[232]

Next morning there was a conference at Blanchard's GQG – to which
no Belgian representatives were invited – attended by Gort and Pownall.
But, as the latter recorded in his diary, 'we did *not* discuss any question of
going to the sea . . . we spent the whole day, one way and another, laying
on the arrangements not only for the withdrawal by bounds but also for
the other end . . . It's going to be the hell of a business, the most difficult
embarkation problem that any army has been called on to perform.'[233] At
11.30 am, accepting the *fait accompli* of Gort's decision to call off the
British counter-attack, but kept in ignorance of his plans to re-embark his
force, Blanchard issued an order in which he was careful to blame British
non-participation, and the critical situation on the Belgian front, for his
cancellation of the northern half of the Weygand Plan. The order then
stipulated that 'The French, British and Belgian armies will regroup
behind the waterline demarcated by the Aa Canal, the Lys and the
Derivation Canal, so as to form a bridgehead covering Dunkirk in
breadth' and concluded: 'This bridgehead will be held without thought of
retreat.'

Here at last was the Torres Vedras concept, but it had come a week too
late and by now the British were thinking only of retreat – and of 'cutting
their way home to Blighty', as Churchill put it in a signal to Gort next day.
That evening (the 26th), at 6.57, the British C-in-C received the historic
signal 'Operation Dynamo is to commence' – although the operation had,
in fact, begun at 3 pm. (Nearly 28,000 British troops had already been
evacuated in the last week by the Royal and Merchant Navies, in
accordance with Gort's instructions on the 19th to evacuate all 'useless
mouths'.) But at no point was the King informed by the British that the
BEF had been ordered to race to the coast and embark for home, or that a

full-scale attempt to evacuate the whole force had begun that day. And the Belgian High Command was not only kept deliberately in the dark about the BEF's flight from the battlefield, but they were led to believe that Gort was at last going to collaborate in forming the vast perimeter backing on the coast which Van Overstraeten had advocated at the Ypres conference. Indeed, they had gained that impression from the news Davy had brought from GHQ on the previous day. '*C'est la solution de la tête de pont; tardive certes, mais non désesperée,*' Van Overstraeten commented when he received it, to which Davy replied 'Yes, it is rather in accordance with your own ideas.' But next day (the 26th), on finding that GHQ, BEF was rejecting his appeals for a counter-attack on the enemy's exposed flank, the General wrote in his diary:

> Although intact, the BEF has not executed the offensive from Arras. It has not been attacked on the 'frontier position'. Though it has the same interests as the Belgian Army, in not letting itself be thrown back into the sea, and is concerned to cover Great Britain directly, it refuses to participate in our battle – a battle that will decide its fate as much as ours! By dint of procrastination the English will lose their army, after wearing out its magnificent troops in marches and counter-marches without actually having been engaged to the benefit either of Belgium or the Allied cause. All this because, apparently, General Weygand and the governments presumed to regulate operations from a distance and persist in an unworkable plan. The saying of an English general – Sir Ian Hamilton – keeps coming into my mind: 'When politics interfere in strategy, the armies are heading for disaster.'[234]

Although bitter in tone, Van Overstraeten's observations accurately reflect the concern felt at GQG about the prolongation of efforts to make the unworkable Weygand Plan work and the refusal by the British to support them in the desperate battle they were fighting for the benefit of the Allies, now that their own cause was so palpably lost. But they would have been even more disturbed had they known that the British were concealing the fact that they were in process of abandoning the Belgian Army to its fate. Even without this knowledge the future looked black enough, for in the face of von Bock's full-scale offensive resistance was weakening and there were no more reserves. As Brian Bond sums up: 'by persisting in attempts to implement the Weygand Plan, Britain and France were instrumental in precipitating Belgium's collapse through over-extension to assist the BEF'.[235]

CHAPTER TWENTY-THREE

The Parting of the Ways

'In spite of all the advice I have received to the contrary, I feel that
my duty impels me to share the fate of my army and to remain with
my people.'

King Leopold III, in a letter to King George VI,
written on May 24th 1940

During the last few days, while the King tirelessly conducted his army's
last-ditch stand, his mind had been running on the gravest matters
affecting his own and Belgium's future. With the Weygand Plan obviously
stillborn, his front beginning to crack and defeat looming ahead, he had
become increasingly preoccupied with the choice he knew he must make:
whether to leave Belgium with his Ministers or stay with his army and his
people. The issue was not complicated by personal considerations, such
as the fact that his children were in France. The sole question was: what
was his duty to his country? In this he had a clear precedent. During the
1914–18 War King Albert had always declared that he would never leave
his country, even if the Germans overran it completely; for he considered, as one of his Ministers recalls, that to do so 'would be tantamount
to treason'. And he was in fact fortunate in that his army had been able to
hold on to a small patch of Belgian territory, which he never left
throughout the war.

The King's discussions with his Ministers had helped him to focus on
the essentials. With his Military Adviser, too, he had conferred on his
agonizing problem. 'The King abhors the role of an idle refugee
monarch,' wrote Van Overstraeten, 'cut off from the Belgian people as
they bow under the invader's yoke . . . Even as a prisoner of war in
Germany, his prestige could impress itself on the Germans and deflect
them from fatal decisions.'[236] On the evening of the 24th, therefore, after
weighing all the factors in a final anxious appraisal, the King made his
irrevocable decision: he would remain in Belgium. That night he wrote a
letter to King George VI.

Regarding this fateful letter Leopold had, as so often on crucial
matters, sought Admiral Keyes' advice. But it was only a break-down of
Sir Roger's car as he left La Panne, after telephoning Churchill, that
enabled the King to get in touch with him. In a guarded letter to his wife,
dated May 24th, the Admiral wrote:

. . . if I had not been stopped by the roadside I would have gone on to Ostend and back to Bruges, and have missed my friend [King Leopold] who wanted me very much – at quite another place [the Château de Wynendaele], in which my friend, his Mother and Van O. are living. The K., Q. and I dined in her bedroom – the others in quite a big mess. Before dinner I helped him to write something – after dinner we listened to the 9 o'clock wireless and were immensely impressed with King George's inspiring speech. I must go to bed, I am dead dog weary . . .

On a sheet of plain quarto paper, carrying the typed heading '*Commandement de l'Armée Belge, Grand Quartier Général*', Leopold had pencilled the following draft opening for his formal letter to George VI:

Your Majesty,
Belgium has held to the Engagement she undertook in 1937 by maintaining her neutrality and by resisting with all the forces at her disposal, the moment her independence was threatened. Her means of resistance are now nearing their end.
After the first reverse of the morning on the 10th of May, when my country was treacherously attacked without warning, the Belgian Army succeeded in withdrawing and establishing a good line of defence in co-operation with her Allies. But retreat from day to day was imposed upon the Allied armies in Belgium by military events which took place outside the country. The Belgian Army withdrew in good order until it reached the position it is now holding. It is impossible to retreat further. The development of the battle now in progress is wearing out my army. The whole cadre of officers and staff being in action, there is no possibility of creating a new military force. Therefore the assistance we can give to the Allies will come to an end if our armies become encircled.

Keyes then took over from the King, pencilling from his dictation as follows on a second sheet:

In spite of all the advice I have received to the contrary, I feel that my duty impels me to share the fate of my army and to remain with my people. To act otherwise would amount to desertion. Whatever trials Belgium may have to face in the future, I am convinced that I can help my people better by remaining with them rather than by attempting to act from outside, especially with regard to the hardships of foreign occupation, the menace of forced labour and the difficulties of food supply.
By remaining in my country, I fully realize that my position will be very difficult, but my utmost concern will be to prevent my countrymen from being compelled to associate themselves with any action against the countries which have attempted to help Belgium in her fight. If I should fail in that endeavour, and only then, would I give up the task I have set myself.

Typed and bearing King Leopold's signature, this dignified declaration was entrusted to General Dill when he arrived at GQG next day to be delivered, on his return to London, to King George VI. In an affectionate covering note to his cousin, Leopold expressed his personal feelings and his faith in the future:

Mon cher Bertie,
Je suis persuadé que j'agis au mieux des intérêts de mon pays. Nous avons tous été très émus par ton impressionnant discours d'hier soir. Moi aussi j'ai une foi entière dans l'avenir.
Que Dieu te bénisse.
Affectueusement à toi et à la chère Elizabeth.
                                                          LEOPOLD.

The original pencilled text of the King's formal letter, in his and the Admiral's handwriting, is in the late Lord Keyes' archives. This document, a photograph of which appears on page 473, is valuable as evidence, for after the war Leopold's traducers alleged that he had written it under the 'sinister' influence of Henri De Man, who was to collaborate with his country's conquerors after the capitulation. It is therefore important to note that De Man, who spoke excellent English, states in his autobiography, *Cavalier Seul*[237] (in which he claims that he was awarded the British Military Cross in the 1914–18 War), that the King had already prepared a rough draft of this letter and asked him to help with the wording before Admiral Keyes arrived at Wynendaele. The typewritten letter, which was despatched on and dated May 25th, is identical to the handwritten text quoted above which the King and the Admiral finalized the night before.

The part played by De Man in the last three days of the Belgian campaign was greatly misrepresented and exaggerated by the Socialists and their Communist allies in their post-war campaign to dethrone the King. This was ironic, for in May 1940 De Man was not only an Army officer, an ex-Minister, a Senator and a Minister of State,* but was also. the popular and respected President of the Socialist Party.

It was even more ironic that after the capitulation many of the Socialists who later slandered Leopold by propagating the fiction that De Man was his 'close friend' and that the King had followed his 'collaborationist' and 'defeatist' advice, transferred themselves from the Socialist Party, when De Man dissolved it, to the pro-German 'New Order' movement which he formed in its place – and were only re-converted to a fervent pro-Allied stance when Hitler destroyed the Nazi-Soviet Alliance by invading Russia, in June 1941.

In May 1940 there was, of course, no reason for the King or anyone else to doubt De Man's loyalty or patriotism. As an Army Captain engaged in relief and welfare work in the La Panne area, De Man had attached

---

* The equivalent of a British Privy Councillor.

himself to the Queen Mother 'to look after and protect her'. Or, as he said to the King when he arrived at Wynendaele on May 24th, having driven her there from La Panne in his car: *'Je m'occupe de votre mère.'* Although Leopold was undoubtedly grateful to him for acting as a combined *aide*, bodyguard and even chauffeur to his peripatetic mother, he had no great liking or esteem for De Man, whom he found 'pushing and full of self-importance'. But as a conscientious constitutional Monarch, it was entirely natural and proper that he should discuss with De Man the political aspects of the crisis, after the last of his Cabinet Ministers had deserted him, since De Man was then the only respected and experienced political figure within reach.

But contrary to the subsequent statements of certain left-wing politicians and writers, De Man's role at Wynendaele during the last three days of hostilities was relatively insignificant. Indeed De Man himself makes no claim in his memoirs to have influenced either the King or the course of events. The unsupported assertions of such writers to that effect are therefore baseless, as are the allegations that the King received De Man at Laeken several times after the capitulation – and even gave his approval, in June 1940, to De Man's collaborationist presidential address to the Socialist Party. In fact, De Man makes no mention in his memoirs of having even seen Leopold after May 31st, for the truth is that the King refused to receive or have anything to do with him when he revealed himself as a collaborator.

'Like a Greek tragedy the end seems inevitably to come closer and closer with each succeeding day and event,' wrote Pownall in his diary on Saturday May 25th – the day on which Gort decided to evacuate his army. But the most tragic event, in the true Greek sense, had occurred in the early hours of that morning. By the previous day the Germans had advanced to within six miles of Bruges, where the four remaining Belgian Ministers were installed. From there, in mounting anxiety, they telephoned several times to the King, who was urgently occupied issuing orders to counter the new German assault around Courtrai – imploring him to join them in their flight from Belgium, for which they had now made the arrangements with the British. To all their importunities Leopold replied that he had decided to share the fate of his troops. Not having managed to meet the King all day, the Ministers resolved to see him before they began their journey into exile and make one last attempt to persuade him to accompany them. Around 11 pm Van Overstraeten was roused in his quarters at Wynendaele by an orderly reporting that Pierlot was on the telephone asking to be received by the King. Soon after, General Denis made another call – to the Deputy Chief of Staff, General Dérousseaux – to discover the latest battle situation. Dérousseaux reported that the front was penetrated at a number of points and that reserves and ammunition were dangerously short. 'It is the end then,' exclaimed Denis. He passed the news to his colleagues, but they decided to call at GQG on the way to Wynendaele to confirm the military position for themselves.

The record of what occurred at GQG in the early hours of the 25th has been preserved in the form of a declaration signed later by the two staff officers who received the Ministers:

Declaration

   On the 25th May 1940, at 3.30 in the morning, Prime Minister Pierlot, the Ministers Denis, Spaak and Vanderpoorten, presented themselves at *Grand Quartier Général* at St André (Bruges). They were received by Major B. E. M. Defraiteur* and Captain Ducq, of the 1st Section of GQG. As soon as they arrived, they enquired about the situation of the Belgian Army, and about the operations of the previous day. Having examined the operational map, and having been given the information required, they expressed their appreciation of the fact that our army would be unable to offer more than a brief resistance to the enemy – either one or two days. Major Defraiteur offered to acquaint the Chief of the General Staff of their presence, but they stated that they did not wish to see him. On the other hand, they enquired about the state of the roads leading to France, and the condition of the various bridges. It is therefore certain that, on the morning of the 25th, the Ministers readily accepted that the Belgian Army would be unable to offer more than a brief resistance to the enemy – either one or two days. Nevertheless, on May 28th M. Pierlot no longer admitted the necessity for the suspension of hostilities.†

From GQG the Ministers hurried to the Château de Wynendaele, where they arrived at five o'clock and were shown into a large ground-floor drawing-room. The King appeared shortly, dressed in uniform, and received his Ministers. In addition to King Leopold's own record there are a number of accounts of this 'tragic and painful meeting', as he described it, written by the Ministers at different times, when they were in different circumstances and states of mind. The concise account given by the King has the advantage that it was written at the time and reflects the exact meaning of his words. The account given by Spaak to the American *United Press* in France on May 31st 1940, and that of Pierlot in *Paris Soir* on June 1st 1940, are self-justificatory and prejudiced against the King – to suit French public opinion, which had been inflamed against him by Paul Reynaud's charges of desertion and treachery, a few days earlier. The formal account which Pierlot wrote of this seventy-minute meeting some years later is so long and detailed that the 1946 *Commission d'Information* suggested that it might have been embellished with hindsight.[238] On July 13th 1947 Pierlot published another self-

_____

* Major Defraiteur became Minister of Defence in a post-war government.
† A reference to Pierlot's subsequent broadcast from Paris condemning the King for capitulating without due cause or warning.

justificatory account in the Belgian newspaper *Soir*, in reply to the findings of that *Commission*. Then there is the *procès verbal* of the histrionic and factually inaccurate diatribe which Spaak delivered, with much emotion and without notes, during the stormy meeting of the refugee parliamentarians at Limoges six days later. This 'account'* is largely discounted by those of the Prime Minister and the King. In contrast, the version given in Spaak's memoirs, published in 1969,[239] is brief, uncontentious and low-key, as is that in his famous television interview that same year.[240]

All these accounts agree that the discussions began with Pierlot declaring that, as the situation was desperate and the Army was on the point of capitulation, he and his colleagues had decided to leave Belgium rather than be captured. They had therefore come to make a last appeal to the King to leave with them and avoid being taken prisoner. By staying in Belgium, Pierlot declared, he would divide the country and in any case be powerless to do any good during the occupation. After a silence, Pierlot recalls, the King replied 'with a visible effort' that he had never in his life gone through such hours of anguish. In deciding to stay in his country with his army and the vast majority of his countrymen, he judged that he was fulfilling his duties as Head of State and Commander-in-Chief. His conscience dictated that he should act in this way. To leave would be desertion. He believed that he could serve his people better in the country than outside it. He felt that if he left he would never return.

The King then told his Ministers that in order to reveal to them more clearly the attitude of mind which had led him to decide upon this course of conduct, he would read them the letter he had written to King George the night before. This letter, of which he gave them a French translation, is of great significance, for in it he had set out unequivocally his thoughts, motives and intentions – nine hours before this last meeting with his Ministers and eighty hours before his army was forced to lay down its arms.

The Ministers were thus put in possession of the fact that the King had written to his fellow Monarch warning him and his Allies that defeat was imminent and that he had decided to remain with his army and people, with the firm intention of using all his influence to protect them from the rigours of enemy occupation and prevent them from collaborating with the enemy or acting against the interests of Britain and France.

It was a great misfortune, as Spaak's biographer, J. H. Huizinga, points out, that the Ministers paid so little attention to this clear statement of the King's attitude and intentions and that the meeting did not end at this point, as Leopold clearly desired, for the suspicions and misapprehensions which entered their minds during the long and confused

---

* See Chapter 28, page 391.

debate which ensued might never have arisen. Although the Ministers realized that the King was immovable in his decision to stay in Belgium and wanted to terminate the discussion, they continued to argue and plead with him. Of those present, the most affected by the stress of the occasion was Spaak. When the King had finished speaking Spaak asked permission to be seated. They then all sat down. It was clear that Spaak's nerves were strained to their limit. He was, as the King noted, 'completely prostrate'. He lay full length in his armchair, head thrown back, legs dangling, uttering disconnected phrases and constantly repeating 'Do you realize that Belgium is lost?' He wondered if it would be better if all four Ministers resigned. 'I don't want to desert the King but I don't want to be a Minister under the occupation . . . let us all resign . . . Our colleagues won't resign . . . Never mind . . . I don't know what to do.' In his memoirs Spaak claims that he was so devoted to Leopold that he very nearly decided to stay with him, but was deterred by the reproving look he received from Pierlot. 'What would have happened to me,' he writes, 'if I had stayed at the King's side? I prefer not to think.'[241]

The fateful talks dragged on, as a brilliant dawn lightened the sky, bringing with it another of those perfect May days in which the battle of Flanders was fought. Little new was being said by the five tired and overstrained men gathered in the gloomy *salon* at Wynendaele. Leopold had made his position abundantly clear and the arguments put forward by the Ministers had all been stated and restated at previous meetings.

As we have seen, the fundamental difference between the Ministers and the King lay in their unshakeable belief that France would continue in the war and provide the Belgian Government-in-exile with a safe haven, as she had done in 1914, whereas the King knew and had warned them that France was rotten both politically and militarily and would very soon succumb. For the Ministers, if France fell, then Germany would have won the war; for, as events would prove, it never occurred to them that Great Britain would fight on alone – indeed she had hardly entered their thoughts. But the King, with his first-hand knowledge of the British and their stubbornness in adversity, was convinced that the Commonwealth and Empire would continue to wage war and would base his personal conduct on that conviction – as his letter to George VI had shown.

The Ministers' attitude towards England is explained by Spaak's biographer, who records that one of the Ministers of the Dutch Government which had established itself in London nearly a fortnight before tried in vain to persuade the Belgian Ministers to remain in London when they arrived there later that day. Spaak, the Dutchman later declared, 'could make nothing of the English, he was a fish out of water in their country'. 'France the Ministers knew and in France they had fastened all their hopes,' writes Huizinga. 'They were bound to underestimate the home of the "contemptible little army" just as the Kaiser had done and, like him, they were to live to regret it. For it was due to this ignorance of the islanders' strength and tenacity that barely three weeks later they, who were so indignant about their King's defeatism, showed themselves ready to throw in the sponge.'[242]

In his account Pierlot describes how in answer to the question 'What part does the King think he will be able to play in Belgium?' the King said he could not tell what he might be able to do, but he hoped to maintain at least a minimum of economic life in Belgium, including an adequate food supply, and save his compatriots from the worst sufferings, such as deportations. The King then declared: 'In a short time, perhaps in a few days, France must in her turn give up the struggle . . . I have no doubt that England will continue the war, although not on the Continent . . . this war will be long.' He added that it could last 'for many years', during which Belgium might be allowed some kind of restricted national life, while awaiting the happier outcome which might result from as yet unforeseeable events.

When the Ministers realized that Leopold was adamant about remaining in Belgium, they asked him: 'What does the King think we ought to do?' To this question he replied that he left it to them to follow the dictates of their consciences and would not stand in their way if they wanted to leave. Pierlot's lengthy account of what followed reveals that, having decided to leave him, the Ministers became anxious about the possibility that after their departure he might form a government to replace them. It also reveals that the King had not yet clearly thought out his role – apart from the hope that he might be able to mitigate the sufferings of his people under the occupation. In fact his thoughts had not moved beyond the problems of the imminent military capitulation and of his own duty when that moment came. He was, after all, in the last stages of conducting from hour to hour a fierce modern battle, moving from telephone to conferences and from conferences to the field. There had been no time or respite for planning the future. He saw clearly the one thing he must do, but its consequences were veiled.

In an attempt to find out the King's intentions, the Ministers now plied him with a series of questions on hypothetical situations which might arise. The King's answers, according to Pierlot, 'were given with precision, but each time after a moment's reflection, which seemed to indicate that the various eventualities raised by the Ministers had not been contemplated by the King, or at least had not yet been thoroughly examined by him'. Thus it was that when Spaak asked him point-blank whether or not he would form a government after the four Ministers had left the country, in Pierlot's words, 'before answering, the Sovereign reflected, giving the impression that he had never asked himself that question'. He replied, however, 'Obviously; for I have no wish to be a dictator.' This answer would later be used to 'prove' that Leopold

intended to form 'a collaborationist government' and make a separate
peace with the Germans. But of course no government of that or any
other kind was formed in occupied Belgium – for the very reason that the
King stayed in his country and prevented this from happening. But he was
caught in a trap, for had he replied to Spaak's question in the negative, the
Ministers would probably have assumed that he intended to violate the
Constitution and assume dictatorial powers. On this subject the 1946
Commission d'Information, after weighing all the evidence, concluded:
'Judging from all the documents in our possession, it seems clear to our
Commission that . . . the King had no intention of forming a government
in Brussels, or making a separate peace with the Germans, or of under-
taking any negotiations whatsoever.'

After once again considering whether or not they should resign, the
Ministers – who were visibly perturbed by the prospect that if they did,
the King would replace them – declared simply that they felt their place
was with their colleagues in France. According to Pierlot's version, he
then warned the King that under the Constitution the Ministers were
responsible for the acts of the Crown and, since the King had not followed
the advice of his Government, 'it would be unjust to lay on us a
responsibility in which we should bear no part'. 'We do not wish,' his
account continues, 'to appear in the eyes of history to have been the cause
of the catastrophe which we foresee. We shall therefore be obliged, if the
King persists in his intentions, not only to cease to cover him, but publicly
to dissociate ourselves from him.' According to Pierlot, Leopold replied: 'I understand your position. You have a conviction. I know it is
sincere. You will act according to it.' Finally, when the Ministers
asked 'Is capitulation avoidable, and if not how long could it be postponed?' the King's answer was 'Inevitable; within forty-eight hours at
the most.'

It was after six; the time for separation had come. In response to a final
emotional appeal from Spaak, the King declared: 'The decision I am
taking is terribly painful. I should have an easier life, certainly, if I
withdrew into France, if I went to live there with my children while
awaiting the end of this torture; but I believe that when two paths lie
before us, that of duty is the harder. It is that path which I have chosen.'
There was nothing more to be said. After shaking hands with their
Sovereign the ministerial quartet departed to board the British Motor
Torpedo Boat which had been sent to take them to England, whence they
would immediately hasten to France, on whose future they pinned their
faith.

It must be recognized that in pleading that Leopold must avoid capture
Pierlot and Spaak had before them two precedents: King Christian and
his government, who remained (in power) in Denmark, and Queen
Wilhelmina and her government, who had fled their country. It was

Wilhelmina's example they urged Leopold to follow, for they did not regard the situation of defenceless Denmark as comparable and were probably not aware that the Dutch Queen had been unwilling to leave her country. Moreover, King Haakon was still fighting with his troops against the invader in northern Norway and the fact that he too was determined to remain with his people – to the point of approaching the Germans to that end – was as yet unknown. The Belgian Ministers were also desperately keen to ingratiate themselves with the Allies; to avoid their reproaches and to divest themselves of responsibility for the catastrophe which was about to befall their country. They therefore blindly clung to their conviction that the French would fight on – and that they would be allowed freedom of action in Paris, despite the King's warning that they would be caught up in the collapse of France and would no longer be free agents.

Most writers have criticized Leopold for his 'unconstitutional behaviour' in not conforming with his Ministers' demands to flee the country with them – ignoring the fact that he also refused to do so when, after the fall of France, they tried desperately to come to terms with the victorious Germans, in the hope that they would be able to persuade the enemy – and their King – to countenance a resumption of their government in occupied Belgium. As far as Leopold was concerned, his duty was clear. He had sworn to preserve his country and his country was about to be conquered. He had asked his army to die for their King, their Country and their Allies. He had no doubt that while his men were still dying he must stay with them, and that when his country was subjugated he must remain to do his best for his captive people. It would have been easy enough to escape. In fact, the Germans were already profiting from this possibility. During the last few days the *Luftwaffe* had been dropping leaflets over the battlefields containing a dramatic map of the encircled Allies and the emotive appeal in French and English:

> *Camarades!*
> *Telle est la situation!*
> *En tout cas, la guerre est finie pour vous!*
> *Vos chefs vont s'enfuir par avion.*
> *A bas les armes!**

Before they reached GQG, Leopold told Van Overstraeten that the moment had come to make a declaration assuring his troops that he had no intention of abandoning them. In the stirring proclamation he now made, the King urged his army to fight on with the utmost energy in the fierce battle now raging on the same ground where it had victoriously held the invader in 1914 – and promised 'Whatever happens, I shall share your

* See page 474.

fate.'* There is no doubt that this knowledge stiffened the resistance of his hard-pressed troops along the Lys. Most British and French accounts fail to recognize the magnitude of the Battle of the Lys or the fact that here the Belgian Army suffered 40,000 casualties (over half its total for the campaign, of 7,976 killed and 53,813 wounded). Yet it may well be asked what would have happened to the BEF and the French First Army, if these men had not been prepared to face wounds or death, and monopolize the attention of fourteen German divisions, which otherwise would have had nothing to stop them from cutting off the two Allied armies from the coast. In Holland the news of Queen Wilhelmina's 'desertion' had profoundly affected the morale of the Dutch forces, which then capitulated after only five days' fighting – and it is most unlikely that the Belgian troops, had they learned that their King had fled the country, would have fought on in a situation thus recognized to be hopeless.

That afternoon the King received a cryptic message from the Belgian Ambassador in London indicating that the four fugitive Ministers had arrived there: '*Les quatres gros paquets sont arrivés.*' Meanwhile at GQG General Michiels and the Staff were outraged when they found that General Denis, who was a serving officer as well as the Minister of Defence, had departed without handing over his duties to anyone, thus burdening them with much additional and unfamiliar work. The precipitate departure of the four Ministers had also imposed a heavy extra load of responsibility on the King, for it had deprived the country of the last vestiges of a civil administration. Thus the responsibility for taking care of the vast throng of civilians who were compressed, under terrible conditions of danger and hardship, into the restricted area of Belgian territory to the rear of the Army, devolved upon the King. It was urgent that some kind of civil administration should be set up for this purpose. After conferring with his military staff, the King summoned the Advocate-General, Hayoit de Termicourt – the highest legal authority available – to consult him about the constitutional aspects of the crisis caused by the departure of the entire civil administration and Government. At the same time the King recalled two members of his civil household, Comte Capelle, his Secretary, and Lous Frédéricq, his Chef de Cabinet, who were with the Government in France, for he found himself diplomatically and politically isolated, now that his entourage was entirely military.

When the Advocate-General arrived at Wynendaele, a conference was held under the trees in the garden of the castle. De Termicourt told Leopold that grave disquiet had been caused amongst the troops by the rumour that the King had fled the country, but as soon as Leopold's pledge to remain with his army and people became known, it had been

* As a further spur for morale, a broadcast was made to the troops telling them that though their Ministers had found it right to depart abroad, the King was still with them and that he was now 'even more than previously the incarnation of a free and independent Belgium'.

universally applauded and had greatly heartened them. If the King were to depart, he was certain that the disillusionment and collapse of the Army would result. As to the flight of the Ministers, the King was now powerless in all non-military matters for, without the signature of a Minister, he would be unable to deal with the multitude of such problems which were pressing for urgent solution. It would therefore be necessary to appoint one or more Ministers to cope with such matters; at least one Minister should be appointed to assume the portfolios of National Defence and Supply, and one to combine the functions of Minister of the Interior and Justice.

As Van Overstraeten records, the King replied that even though the four Ministers had spoken of resigning before their departure that morning, the Ministers-in-exile 'should retain their powers because they represented Belgium'.[243] De Termicourt then put forward the names of some suitable candidates for these temporary appointments, including two eminent jurists and ex-Ministers, Joseph Pholien and Albert Devèze, who were serving as Reserve officers nearby.

After some further discussion, during which it was agreed that no immediate action on this matter need be taken, they moved on to the crucial question of the King's constitutional position when the time came to surrender. His Cabinet Ministers had all abandoned him. Could he surrender without them? The King had been struck by Pierlot's contention that morning that he could not capitulate without a ministerial counter-signature. But the Advocate-General ruled that while, as C-in-C of the Army, the King could order a purely military capitulation, the signature of a serving Minister would be necessary to cover any non-military terms or conditions which might be imposed by the Germans. Hayoit de Termicourt accordingly advised the King to obtain from the Ministers in Paris or London, two blank decree forms, duly countersigned by a Minister, to cover this or any other contingency which might arise up to the moment of the Army's capitulation.

The whole affair of the *arrêtés royaux en blanc* was later blown up to enormous proportions and became the subject of fierce controversy, with the King's enemies alleging – for political motives – that his object in asking for the decrees was to enable him to form a collaborationist government in occupied Belgium. Ironically Spaak, after using this accusation as the spearhead of his attacks on the King in his post-war campaign to oust him from the Throne, would finally admit that it was baseless, twenty-nine years later. On January 15th 1969, after the television appearance in which he 'came clean' – as Sam White put it in an *Evening Standard* article* – Spaak wrote to the Editor of *Le Soir*† in order to 'clarify public opinion'. After explaining that the Ministers in France

* See Appendix IX.
† It was published on January 29th 1969.

had turned down the King's request for the *arrêtés en blanc*, because they believed 'in all good faith' that he intended to use them to form a government in Brussels, Spaak summed up the whole affair accurately and fairly:

> It is now established that in requesting this blank decree King Leopold's intention was not to form a new government in Brussels. When the Ministers left him on the morning of May 25th, the King immediately consulted M. Hayoit de Termicourt . . . The latter, as he would confirm a few days later, in a written consultation signed, in addition, by MM. Devèze and Pholien, indicated to the King that although he was entitled, in his capacity as Chief of the Army, to make all decisions connected therewith, he was not permitted to make any other kind of decision without a ministerial counter-signature . . .
>
> It was under these conditions that the King made the request in Paris for a blank decree signed by a Minister, to enable him eventually to cope with one situation or another, the precise nature of which could not at that moment be foreseen, but which might concern the Army or the refugees.
>
> Given the confusion that prevailed at this time and the difficulties in communications . . . the King's request was not explained with all the necessary clarity . . .

Henri De Man claims in his memoirs that the King sought his advice after the conference with the Advocate-General and asked him if he was prepared to become a Minister if it became necessary, 'perhaps with one or two other personalities . . . in order to resolve certain questions in connection with the capitulation'. De Man writes that he agreed, and suggested that 'the temporary and transient character of this measure' should be underlined by appointing as Ministers such non-political figures as General Tilkens, the Head of the King's Military Household, and Hayoit de Termicourt.[244]

De Man declares that Leopold replied that it was first of all imperative to obtain the co-operation of at least one Minister-in-office in regard to the blank decrees, in accordance with the Advocate-General's advice, and that the King then asked him to take the necessary steps. It was, however, Comte Willy de Grunne, the Master of the Queen Mother's Household, who telephoned the Belgian Embassy in London at 9 pm, on the 25th. De Grunne hoped to speak direct to Camille Gutt, the Finance Minister, who was on a visit to London, but found that he had just returned to France. The consequences were disastrous, because the message was then relayed to the Ministers in Paris in a form which did not make clear the precise purpose of the King's request. (Unfortunately he neither saw nor approved the message before it was transmitted.) At a Cabinet Meeting next morning the Belgian Ministers unhesitatingly turned it down, as in the panic-stricken atmosphere of the time Pierlot and Spaak, who already harboured unworthy suspicions about the King's intentions, jumped to the conclusion that he had asked for the blank decrees to enable him to dissolve their government and form a new one in Belgium. It was this misapprehension on their part which tipped the scale in what became known as the *malentendu tragique* between the King and his government, and caused Pierlot and Spaak to embark on a course of conduct which immeasurably harmed the reputations of their King, their country and themselves.

Meanwhile, Winston Churchill was showing his awareness that the capitulation of the Belgian Army was imminent, and his anxiety that Leopold should escape and join the other leaders of defeated nations whom he had gathered under his wing. It had become his overriding concern to persuade such leaders to set up 'free' governments in London, to join the Allied cause and to hand over to the British such resources as were still at their disposal. Late on the 24th, therefore, Churchill sent Sir Roger Keyes an urgent telegram, which reached him next day, after the King had told his Ministers (and the Admiral) of his unalterable decision to remain in Belgium with his army and his people. The text read:

24.5.40.

Following for Sir Roger Keyes from Prime Minister:

We are naturally much concerned to ensure safety if things go badly of King, Queen, and members of Belgian Government still in Belgium. Necessity has not yet arisen, but if and when it does, it will no doubt be necessary to act very promptly. We can of course understand what must be the King's feelings about position he holds in the middle of the Army, but from wider international point of view, and from point of view of carrying on the war, we would emphasize that it would be essential in the circumstances contemplated that King should move to place of greater safety. We earnestly hope he would take same view and would be prepared to take decision quickly should need arise.

   Please impress on him the importance we attach to this. We shall have arrangements ready for evacuation at short notice.

'But King Leopold said he had made up his mind,' the Admiral noted in his diary, 'and that his mother was determined to stay with him.' Keyes replied as follows:

25.5.40.

The King was told last night by his Ministers that Lord Halifax was telegraphing to me to persuade His Majesty to withdraw with his government. I have now received your message of 24th May.

   For the last eleven days the Ministers have been urging the King to fly with them. The four who by his orders have remained here spent some hours last night urging him to go with them at once; thus deserting his army at a moment when it is fighting a stern battle to cover the left flank of the BEF. Deprived of the King's leadership, the capitulation of the Belgian Army would inevitably be hastened and the BEF endangered. King Leopold has written to the King to explain his motives for remaining with his army and people if our armies become encircled and the capitulation of the Belgian Army inevitable. Dill takes this letter and a special Order of the Day from the King to his army.

I trust that HM Government will not be unduly impressed by the arguments of the Belgian Ministers who, apparently, have had no thought but the continuation of a political regime, whose incapacity and lack of authority have been only too apparent during the last fortnight. Their example has been followed by nearly all the local authorities and the result has been absolute confusion. Moreover they urged the British and French Ambassadors to precede them, in order to justify their own flight – a course which did not add to the prestige of the two countries.

CHAPTER TWENTY-FOUR

Exit the BEF

'Everything is complete confusion: no communications and no one knows what is going on, except that everything is as black as black. Boulogne taken, Calais heavily besieged. Dunkirk more or less open, and that's the only exit for our BEF, if they can ever be extricated. Meanwhile they have little food and practically no munitions.'

Sir Alexander Cadogan's diary entry for May 25th 1940

Events were now moving swiftly to a climax, with the BEF hell-bent on escaping from the rapidly closing trap by sea and the Belgian Army under almost insupportable pressure. Throughout the 25th the battle on the Belgian front raged with mounting violence. At GQG Colonel Davy was given a map on which a line was drawn to the west of Menin through Gheluwe and Zonnebeke, marking the extreme limit of the line the Belgian Army could hold. He was asked to convey this information to British GHQ. Since the fall of Ghent, with its vast supply depots, the Belgian Army's stocks of food and ammunition had been running dangerously low. Moreover, the sea-borne supplies they had been promised failed to materialize, owing to the Allies' requisition of the Channel ports and the heavy bombing attacks on them by the enemy.

Since May 23rd the Belgian Army had been suffering from intensive dive-bombing and strafing attacks from the air and a ferocious and ever-mounting assault on the ground from von Bock's infantry and artillery. It is not surprising therefore that they should have been forced back, and that the gap between their right wing and the end of the static British front at Halluin was gradually widening. The four BEF divisions, snug behind their fortified frontier line, had suffered no such ordeal and were in an ideal position to relieve this tremendous pressure on the Belgian front (and, incidentally, reduce the danger of being outflanked themselves), by striking at the vulnerable flank of the enemy forces streaming across their front in full view, on their way to attack the Belgians. The Belgian High Command therefore sent a series of increasingly urgent messages to Gort and the French Supreme Command by every conceivable means, including Admiral Keyes and Colonel Davy in person, to that effect and appealing to the BEF to counter-attack the

323

enemy forces which were driving a wedge between the two armies. But all they received in return were brusque denials that the BEF had any forces available for a counter-attack and a series of carping messages from Gort and Pownall, complaining that the Belgians were responsible for the gap and thus for exposing the British flank.

The British generals seemed to be blind to the fact that the breach on their left was the inevitable consequence of their inability to hold their positions on the Escaut; their side-stepping of von Bock's thrust after being relieved by the Belgians, and their occupation of their fortified front *parallel* to his line of attack and *at right angles* to the semi-circular defensive waterlines which covered the Channel coast. The rejection of all these Belgian appeals, Brian Bond suggests, was due not only to the BEF's own problems, but because 'the British commanders were confirmed in their anti-Belgian prejudices and would be unwilling to take risks to assist them'.[245] Some pertinent entries are to be found in Pownall's diary. On May 26th, for example, referring to Gort's decision of the previous evening to evacuate his army, which had been deliberately kept from the Belgians, he wrote:

> We need not fear the Germans following us up. What we have to fear is a Belgian break . . . The Belgians show every sign of running fast northwards . . . We have sent them every message we can think of to try and get them to stand where we want them. But they are rotten to the core and in the end we shall have to look after ourselves.

Next day Pownall wrote of King Leopold: 'Throughout the day he had been screaming for *us* to counter-attack to relieve pressure on *him* . . . We have indeed done enough to help both the Belgians and the French . . . it is useless for them to expect more . . .'[246] Such was GHQ's attitude; they refused to help the Belgians (and themselves) by relieving the pressure of von Bock's breakthrough thrust between the two armies, but expected the Belgians 'to stand where we want them' to facilitate the BEF's escape from the Continental battlefield.

As a result of GHQ's policy, the four British divisions, which had remained undisturbed except for some shelling since they retired behind the fortifications of the BEF's malorientated frontier line, were forced to stand impotently by and watch 'considerable bodies of enemy troops moving northwards across their front'. The British artillery was even forbidden to engage these wonderful targets in order 'to husband ammunition' and so the Belgian Army's attackers were allowed 'to pass unmolested'.[247] All these British guns were subsequently found by the Germans abandoned on the battlefield, for on the 26th Brooke (II Corps) informed Montgomery (3rd Division) that the BEF was to retreat post-haste to the coast and embark, leaving all their guns and heavy equipment behind.*

The growing separation of the two armies was increasing the danger that the Belgian Army would be completely cut off from the British; and that von Bock's thrust would now swing left round the British flank to link up with the armoured push from the West – and so encircle and capture the BEF and the whole French First Army. But instead of using the 5th and 50th divisions, which he had rushed northwards, to 'plug the gap' and support the hard-pressed Belgian right wing, Gort placed them in purely defensive positions along the Ypres-Comines Canal to protect the northern side of his path of retreat to the sea. The Belgians, who had been led to believe by Dill and others that British and French forces were being sent to their assistance, were dismayed when the BEF blew all the bridges between themselves and the Belgians – thus making their self-defensive purpose abundantly clear.

Gort meanwhile continued to reject all the urgent appeals from the French and Belgian High Commands for a counter-attack to relieve the intolerable pressure on the Belgian right wing, complaining that he had no forces available for such a move. Indeed most of his forces were now otherwise engaged, for since his *sauve qui peut* decision of the previous evening his sole aim had been to re-embark as many of his troops as possible and to protect both sides of their escape corridor to Dunkirk. As Churchill observes, thanks to their mechanical transport the four British divisions in the fortified frontier positions on the right of the Belgians 'came back with surprising rapidity almost in a night', while 'by fierce battles on either side of the corridor the rest of the British Army kept the path open to the sea.'[248] What Churchill does not mention, however, is the fact that the British never informed the Belgians that they were abandoning these positions, thereby dangerously exposing the Belgian Army's right flank.

But the BEF's French neighbours in the Lille area were not so fortunate as the British. Not only were they less mobile (their transport being mainly horse-drawn), but General Prioux, the First Army's spirited new commander, refused to join in the BEF's race to the sea, but insisted upon obeying Blanchard's orders – now endorsed by Weygand – to stand on the Lys 'without thought of retreat'. When Blanchard asked Gort and Pownall if they intended to retreat from the Lys, knowing that they would be going without the French First Army, Pownall replied that they must do so, since they were now acting under the orders of the British Government. Consequently, when the enemy's pincers subsequently

* On August 20th 1940 Montgomery wrote to Keyes, then Director of Combined Operations, that he had received these orders – 'the first news' that the BEF was being evacuated – at 4.00 pm on the 26th. His letter concluded: 'If you want a good fighting Corps to hit someone a crack overseas, I hope you will not forget me!'

closed at Armentières, five French divisions – nearly half the First Army – were encircled and, after putting up a fierce resistance, were forced to capitulate. (As a mark of their respect, the Germans accorded them the honours of war.) Even so, by holding out for four days Prioux diverted the attention of seven German divisions from the BEF and thus, like the Belgians, made an invaluable contribution to its escape, as well as saving the rapidly-contracting Dunkirk perimeter from the even more 'unbearable congestion' which their presence would have caused.

As the enemy pressure towards Ypres increased, the Belgians tried every expedient. During the night of the 25th, for example, they brought up and placed end-to-end 2,000 railway wagons to form an anti-tank barrier on the railway line from Roulers to Ypres. Next day a fresh German division was thrown in towards Ypres, threatening the total separation of the Belgian and British armies. A cavalry and an infantry division moved from the Belgian left flank blocked this attempt, and together with another infantry division held the attackers in front of the Ypres-Roulers line. Meanwhile, the front was breached at Iseghem and other points. The 1st Division of the Chasseurs Ardennais largely re-established the position by fierce fighting, but the battle suddenly spread northwards beyond Eecloo, fifteen miles east of Bruges. This was followed by the Germans forcing their way across the canal at Balgerhoek. All the Belgian reserves had now been thrown in, including scratch units armed with 75 mm guns taken from training depots, which were rushed to threatened points. 'The King had given the order to his army to hold the line of the Lys to the end,' Keyes recorded; 'their artillery had been told to stand to their guns, until either their ammunition was expended or their guns had been overrun.' His diary continues:

> The Belgians had no reserves; a Mechanized Cavalry Division, which was hurried down from the left flank, was practically wiped out in its efforts to support the right flank; and they had brought up the ill-equipped 15th Division (infantry without artillery or machine-guns) from the Yser, and thrown them into the battle. These elderly second-line troops were much shaken by low bombing attacks, and were probably the Belgians of whom one has heard our troops speak contemptuously. That night (the 26th) King Leopold gave orders for the French 60th Division, which was still under his direction, to be moved across the Yser to Nieuport in Belgian lorries and buses. At the time it was open to question whether the Yser would be reached first by the Panzer divisions driving east along the coast, or by the German divisions attacking Belgium from the eastward.

That evening the Admiral motored once again to La Panne to report the critical situation to Churchill by telephone:

> I told the Prime Minister that the Belgian Army was sorely pressed again, and had been subjected all day to the most frightful aerial bombardment from

low-flying German bombers, unmolested by the Royal Air Force. I told him that it was trying for me to listen with my Belgian friends to the BBC telling of the amazing achievements of our splendid airmen, while the issue of the battle which was raging on land was being settled by the German military machine, with its aeroplanes, tanks, mechanized vehicles and troops working together as one unit.

The Prime Minister put me on to the Secretary of State for Air – Sir Archibald Sinclair – and I told him that unless the RAF could do something to counter the German low bombing attacks and lighten the Belgian Army's burden, it was bound to crack, and was unlikely to stand another day, having endured three without respite. I also telephoned to the VCNS (Vice Admiral Phillips) and suggested that two or three MTBs should stand by to come to Nieuport, to bring off the last flight, in case the Belgians had to capitulate.

Little of what was happening on the Belgian Army's front was visible to the British, as they concentrated all their efforts on their retreat and on protecting both sides of their avenue of escape to Dunkirk. Inevitably, due to the 'sore thumb' alignment of the British front, the Belgians' right wing was being driven northwards, away from it, thus creating what Brooke called 'an eerie void'. It was this blindness to the tremendous battle which the Belgians were fighting for their Allies' benefit to the north of them which led Brooke and others to pass the unjust strictures on the Belgian Army's fighting performance which have since gained so much credence. But the critical situation on the Belgian front on the 26th was all too evident to the King and his Staff, as they studied the incoming messages from the battlefield. The position was now so grave that they despatched further urgent signals to Weygand and Gort, reiterating their appeals for a counter-stroke on their attackers' exposed flank and warning them that the Belgian Army's resistance could not be sustained much longer. At midday General Champon successfully passed, at the King's request, the following message to Weygand, to which he received no reply:

For the last three days the Belgian Army, holding a total front of more than ninety kilometres, has been engaged in a full-scale battle on the Lys from Menin to the north of Deynze, without co-operation of any kind except for certain interventions by British aircraft.

We are defending the ground step by step, and inflicting considerable losses on the enemy. Our reserves are exhausted and the attack . . . thrusts irresistibly at the junction of the British and Belgian armies in the direction of Ypres, thus placing the Belgian Army, the British Army, and the ports of the Pas-de-Calais in the greatest possible danger.

The Belgian Command made known at the Ypres conference its intention to defend to the last extremity the line of the Lys and the Deynze Canal to the sea. It agreed to . . . relieve two British divisions, and also announced its determination not to fall back on the Yser, by reason of the irremediable dislocation which would result for the Army.

The Belgian Command is convinced that it has rendered to the Allied armies all the services which the Belgian Army is in a condition to render, in inflicting upon the attacking German troops considerable losses and precious delay to the profit of operations of all the Allied armies. For the rest, the Belgian Command has found itself without instruction of any kind from the inter-Allied Command, except for the approval which General Billotte expressed during the Ypres conference.

The Belgian Command requests you make known to the Allied Supreme Commander that the situation of the Belgian Army is extremely grave, and that while its Commander-in-Chief intends to sustain the fight until the total exhaustion of his resources . . . the limits of resistance have very nearly been reached.

Neither the French nor the British High Commands could now have had any illusions about the Belgian Army's desperate plight, for similar warning messages were also sent by Belgian GQG to Blanchard and to Gort via Sir Roger Keyes, Colonel Davy and General Nyssens, the head of the Belgian Mission at GHQ. An example was the message handed to Davy that day reporting that in resisting the several violent attacks on their front the Belgian Army had exhausted all its reserves and therefore 'no longer had any forces available to bar the approaches to Ypres'. The idea of withdrawing to the Yser also had to be ruled out, the signal continued, since it would destroy the Belgian forces more rapidly than fighting where they stood – and without loss to the enemy. It concluded by informing Gort that all preparations for flooding had been completed and that this had been ordered on the east bank of the Yser, with a prolongation on the Yperlee, at nine that morning.

As he makes very plain in his *Despatches*, Gort had simply written off the Belgians. 'By this time,' he wrote, 'the position of the Belgian Army was so obscure that the possibility of its being included in the bridgehead was not taken into account, though the perimeter could of course have been extended eastwards to include them if necessary.' Gort had even withheld from Keyes the news that he had cancelled the counter-attack to the South and intended to re-embark his army as quickly as possible at Dunkirk, despite the fact that the Admiral of the Fleet was the British Government's special representative with the Belgian King. When Keyes arrived at Premesques on the morning of May 26th, after being bombed and machine-gunned on the road, he saw Gort for a few minutes and 'asked if there was anything I could do to help'. But Gort did not tell him that the BEF was being evacuated – only that he was 'too busy' at a conference with his Corps commanders to inform the Admiral 'what he proposed to do'. But Gort again made the impractical suggestion that the Belgian Army should retire behind the Yser.

The Admiral accordingly sped to GQG in Bruges (he had to take a circuitous route to avoid Ypres, which was being heavily bombed and threatened by the German advance) in order to give Gort's message to the King and Van Overstraeten. They said they would do their best about withdrawing to the Yser, but reiterated that this was a practical impossibility, since the only railway line was out of action and the few roads were not only under constant dive-bombing and machine-gunning attacks but were blocked by tens of thousands of refugees. They again stressed the point that Gort had apparently overlooked – that to retreat to the Yser meant giving up all the Channel ports except Dunkirk and attempting the impossible task of compressing the three armies and about a million refugees into the 28-mile-wide strip between that river and the Canal Line, in which Dunkirk is sandwiched.

Since Gort and Pownall had deliberately kept Leopold, Keyes and even Davy in ignorance of the decision to evacuate the BEF, no one at Belgian GQG was aware of the fact that the Weygand Plan had been called off and that the BEF was hurriedly abandoning the frontier line and in full retreat to the sea. Much time and effort was thus wasted in making plans and appeals based on the belief that the BEF was standing firm or was even engaged in offensive action. The King and Van Overstraeten therefore again urged that the British should strike at the enemy's communications and bridgeheads on the Lys, declaring that the British troops on their right, who had not been attacked on the ground or from the air, were ideally placed to launch a counter-attack – with, as Keyes wrote in his diary, 'every prospect of inflicting a considerable defeat on the enemy, and relieving the pressure on the Belgian Army, which had suffered tremendous and ceaseless low bombing attack without respite'. 'Nevertheless,' his diary continues, 'they had made several counter-attacks, slain some thousands of Germans and taken several hundred prisoners.'

Believing that the southward offensive was still on, Van Overstraeten conceded that Gort's commitment to it meant that less resources would be available for the counter-attack in the North, but he felt that any stroke, however weak, would be beneficial. 'He stressed,' Keyes records, 'that it was the one possible chance of saving the Belgian Army from annihilation, and for the British Army to inflict a defeat on the German infantry; also that a success here would ensure the retention of Ostend and Nieuport for some time . . .' The Belgians had already sent Gort 'at least five' appeals to that effect, both by messenger and signal, without result. Keyes and Davy therefore drafted further messages, explaining why withdrawal to the Yser was impossible and the counter-attack so imperative. These were then rushed to British GHQ by Captain Durham, a member of the Needham Mission, who was instructed to stress their importance. Davy's 'military appreciation', which supported the Admiral's signal, included the following:

26.5.40.

Van Overstraeten is desperately keen for strong British counter-attack. Either north or south of Lys could help to restore situation . . . There can be no question of Belgian withdrawal to Yser. One battalion on march NE of Ypres was practically wiped out today in attack by 60 aircraft. Withdrawal over open roads without adequate fighter support very costly. Whole of supplies are east of Yser. They strongly represent attempt should be made to restore situation on Lys by British counter-attack for which opportunity may last another few hours only.

The Admiral then hurried to La Panne by car to speak to Churchill on the telephone. He was 'much relieved' to learn, for the first time, from the Prime Minister that 'the attack to the southward was off'. Churchill purported to be astonished that Gort had not told Keyes or Belgian GQG 'of the instructions he had received'. But he cannot have been unaware of the fact that his War Minister had specifically ordered Gort *not* to apprise the Belgians or the French of his instructions to re-embark his force. He conceded however 'that it was only fair that King Leopold should know these instructions as soon as possible' and promised 'to send a cypher message at once to the British Mission at Bruges'.

Churchill did not, however, tell Keyes that Gort's 'instructions' in-cluded orders for the evacuation of the BEF – or that this operation had already begun at Dunkirk. Nor did he despatch the promised message until the following day, by which time the evacuation was in full spate. In consequence his signal never reached Leopold; and Keyes himself only received his copy after his return to England on the morning of the 28th, some hours after the Belgian capitulation. Churchill admits all this in *The Second World War*, but adds 'the fact is not, however, important'. It might nevertheless seem important that at no time did King Leopold receive any warning from the British military or political leadership that the BEF was abandoning the Belgian Army to its fate – and seeking safety in flight from the battlefield by sea.

Considering that Anthony Eden was the Secretary of State for War at the time, his memoirs are remarkably evasive about these matters of fact, principle and honour. Like so many other British writers, he does not make it clear that the order for and the execution of the BEF's full-scale re-embarkation preceded the Belgian capitulation (the former being on the 26th and the latter on the 28th May). He does, however, state that he *wrote* to Churchill on the night of the 26th to remind him 'that we had ourselves told the Belgians nothing about the change of plan . . .' Eden's letter suggested that Churchill should 'advise the King [George VI] personally to send the news, or that he should do so himself'.[249] This was some hours *after* the BEF had begun its full-scale evacuation. The following day Churchill drafted two messages – one for Gort, the other for Keyes – and sent them off with a copy of the latter attached to that for the C-in-C. The text of the telegram to the Admiral, which he only received after his return to England on May 28th, was as follows:

27.5.40.

Impart following to your friend [King Leopold]. Presume he knows that British and French are fighting their way to coast between Gravelines and Ostend inclusive, and that we propose to give fullest support from Navy and Air Force during hazardous embarkation. What can we do for him? Certainly we cannot serve Belgium's cause by being hemmed in and starved out. Our only hope is victory, and England will never quit the war whatever happens till Hitler is beat or we cease to be a State. Trust you will make sure he leaves with you by aeroplane before too late. Should our operation prosper and we establish effective bridgehead, we would try, if desired, to carry some Belgian divisions to France by sea. Vitally important Belgium should continue war, and safety of King's person essential.

In his message to Gort, also dated the 27th, Churchill asked: 'Presume troops know they are cutting their way home to Blighty?' After suggesting that 'cannon ought to kill tanks, and they might as well be lost doing that as any other way' and making the unrealistic proposal that Gort should occupy Ostend and relieve the hard-pressed British and French troops defending Calais – which had, unknown to Whitehall, surrendered on the previous day – Churchill instructed Gort:

It is now necessary to tell the Belgians. I am sending following telegram to Keyes, but your personal contact with the King is desirable. Keyes will help. We are asking them to sacrifice themselves for us.

Although Gort received both these messages, he did not 'tell the Belgians', nor did he inform Keyes or invoke his help in breaking the news of the BEF's abandonment of the Belgians to Leopold. Indeed, his last communication to the King was in quite a different spirit, as the Admiral's diary records. During the night of 26–27th May he received the following message from Gort to Leopold:

2155 hours, 26.5.40.

His Majesty the King of the Belgians has on two occasions been good enough to assure Lord Gort that the safety of the BEF was a primary consideration in his mind. Lord Gort is bound to observe that the proposed movement of the Belgian Army, which dangerously exposes the left flank of the BEF, is a breach of His Majesty's expressed intention.

'I need hardly say,' Keyes' diary continues, 'that I did not show this to the King, as the only movement of the Belgian Army had been forced on

it by enemy pressure, which the BEF had been unable to relieve . . .'
Considering that the BEF had for the last seven hours been making an
all-out effort to save its own skin via Dunkirk, without a word of warning
to its allies, Gort's signal showed the most remarkable degree of blink-
ered self-interest and hypocrisy. Although Keyes had been kept in
ignorance about the BEF's retreat and evacuation and did not therefore
appreciate the full enormity of this message, he was deeply shocked by its
tone. He admired Gort as a brave soldier and thought at first that
Pownall, of whose baleful attitude towards the Belgians he was aware,
must be its author. But he did not then know that Gort's attitude towards
his Belgian allies was hardly less prejudiced than Pownall's.

Next morning, however, when Captain Durham returned from delivering the messages from Keyes and Davy to Gort at his GHQ, the Admiral
learned more about the C-in-C's state of mind, for Durham reported that
he had found Gort's attitude carping and abusive. The two officers'
reports on the Belgian Army's inability to retreat to the Yser and the
further request for a British counter-stroke were not well received. Gort
declared that he had nothing with which to attack. In the classic tradition
of chastising the bringer of bad tidings, the C-in-C described the
Needham Mission as 'useless' and roundly abused the Belgians. He
claimed that they 'had absolutely failed to keep their promise to protect
the British flank' and also repeated his demand that the Belgian Army
should withdraw behind the Yser and 'on no account in a northerly
direction'.

In a memorandum on the subject of relations between British GHQ
and Belgian GQG, Keyes wrote: 'On two or three occasions I heard both
Gort and Pownall complain that they got no help from the British
[Needham] Mission. I can only say that they and I did everything in our
power to strengthen the liaison between the GHQ and GQG, and
endeavoured to make the former appreciate the Belgian Army's difficulties. I even offered to get the Belgian Liaison Officers attached to GHQ
changed, since Gort and Pownall complained that they too were useless,
but they did not wish me to do this. I feel very strongly that GHQ made no
effort to "play the game" and in fact let the Belgian Army down badly.'

There was, however, now no more the Belgian Army could do to affect
'the safety of the BEF', except continue to fight and to die where it stood,
thus distracting von Bock's Army Group B and the *Luftwaffe* from the
British forces and preventing the enemy from breaking through and
cutting them off from the coast. Nor could this continue for long. That
evening at 6.30, when General Blanchard, steel-helmeted and accompanied by General Champon, arrived at Belgian GQG, he received a
personal warning from the King of 'the extreme gravity' of his army's
situation and 'the imminent danger of its annihilation'. Blanchard's news
was also bad, for he announced that Gort had absolutely refused to

'counter-attack the Germans who were crossing, in full view, in front of his troops manning the frontier line on the Belgians' right. Blanchard further reported that the British were now abandoning those positions and retreating rapidly, but he offered to throw in a light mechanized division to help the Belgians plug the gap which this withdrawal was creating. (But this French unit, described by Weygand and Churchill as 'an armoured division', had been reduced from 100 to 15 light tanks and was never able to help the Belgians, for it was immediately commandeered by General Brooke to help him defend the northern side of the BEF's escape corridor to Dunkirk.)

'On the evening of the 26th,' wrote Colonel Davy, 'both Keyes and I, from our separate sources, deduced that the end was in sight . . . I knew what was coming from the faces of the staff in the usually cheerful operations room . . .' After being told by the King that his army was nearing the end of its resistance, the Admiral asked Davy to drive at once to Gort's headquarters at Cassel, near Dunkirk, and warn him about the Belgian Army's imminent defeat. After an unpleasant drive without lights, Davy arrived at Cassel early next day and sought out Pownall. At about 9 am he told the British Chief of Staff that the Belgian Army's situation was desperate and warned him that in his opinion 'they would have packed up within 24 hours'. Pownall did not, however, tell Davy then or later that the British had abandoned their positions on the Belgians' right flank and were in full flight to Dunkirk – with the object of 'evacuating the maximum possible numbers' – and that they had been doing so since the previous afternoon.*

---

* It is a curious fact that Pownall never once mentions Colonel Davy, nor any of his officers, nor indeed the Needham Mission, in his diary account of the campaign. The fact that 'Operation Dynamo' began on May 26th is also omitted – the impression being given that the retreat and re-embarkation of the BEF only started two days later.

CHAPTER TWENTY-FIVE

The Belgians' Last Stand

'Our last reserves have been engaged and we have only three weak regiments left. Liaison with the British is maintained at our expense. By noon large breaches were made, in the North towards Maldegem, in the centre towards Ursel, on our right between Thielt and Roulers. The enemy is infiltrating hour by hour and reaching our Command Posts. In the Thielt region, six or seven kilometres of front are undefended. The enemy has only to thrust into the gap to reach Bruges, where our GQG is situated. Our losses are heavy, there are many wounded, the hospitals are overflowing and numerous artillery pieces are without ammunition . . . The circle of fire is contracting, thousands of refugees and the civilian population are milling about in the narrowing space, completely exposed to the enemy's artillery and aviation . . .'

General Michiels' Report, May 1940

'The great battle joined on the Lys in the Courtrai region of Belgium on Sunday, was still raging with extreme violence yesterday afternoon.' Thus ran a report in *The Times* on the 28th based on 'French military sources'. It continued: 'After attacking throughout the night, the Germans yesterday morning continued to hurl masses of infantry, supported by strong artillery fire, against the Belgian lines. The attacks were carried out on a front of 25 miles, with complete disregard for losses on the German side.' In other reports quoting the French 'military spokesman' *The Times* described the Belgian Army as 'having counter-attacked with great dash and vigour' and 'borne the brunt' of 'tremendous attacks', which the Germans had launched with 'a heavy concentration of tanks and aircraft, supported by infantry *"marchant à tombeau ouvert"* '.

As these reports describe, the Germans were continuing their all-out assault on the Belgian positions with increasing ferocity. They were thus able to widen the Menin-Courtrai breach and smash through the Belgian line between Roulers and Thielt, while further north they made serious breaks in the line at Ursel and Maldegem. The Belgians made desperate efforts to keep contact with the British forces, but the latter were now pouring back towards Dunkirk – leaving only flank and rearguards, and all their heavy equipment, behind them. As the relentless pressure of von Bock's forces and the closely-concerted attacks of the *Luftwaffe* forced the Belgians back north-westwards, the gap to the east of Ypres gradually widened. The Belgian artillery constantly outclassed the German, which throughout the war was indifferent. Guns were fought to the last, even when unsupported by infantry. But ammunition was low, and such desperate measures could only postpone temporarily the inevitable defeat.*

Meanwhile, the *Luftwaffe* maintained undisputed mastery of the air, with 'groups of 50 to 60 dive-bombers' escorted by fighters wheeling constantly overhead, completely unmolested. Any movement attempted by the Belgians was immediately pounced upon by a swarm of Stukas. Early that morning Keyes had asked Van Overstraeten if there was anything he could do to help. In reply the General made the oft-repeated request (the King would make it again later that day) that the RAF should provide fighter aid to purge the skies of the omnipresent *Luftwaffe*, and also bomb the attacking enemy. The Admiral promised to do his best, but his telephoned appeals to London were almost in vain – for, as the *Official History* records, 'the Royal Air Force could do but little for the Belgians in view of their other commitments'.[250] These were, of course, to give the BEF all possible air support during its hazardous evacuation – in accordance with Churchill's promise – and every available fighter (all of which were now based in Britain and therefore at the limit of their range) had been sent to form a protective umbrella over the Dunkirk beachhead, from which the BEF was being embarked in ever-increasing numbers. Nevertheless, one air strike was made that morning, in response to the Admiral's appeals, by eighteen British bombers under fighter escort on enemy targets in the Courtrai area.

For the much-tried Belgian Army events were moving swiftly towards the last act of the drama. For eighteen days it had been fighting desperately against a determined and better equipped enemy supported by overwhelming and unopposed air power. Its defeat had been made certain not through any fault of its own (it had faithfully carried out such orders as it received), but through the massive collapse of the French armies guarding the Meuse, which had placed the whole group of armies in the North in an untenable position. Since this reverse their predicament had been aggravated by absence of proper command, belated, indecisive and ill-judged orders from the French High Command, unrealistic political intervention from London and Paris, and almost non-existent communications. Now, as Leopold had predicted on the 22nd, his army was indeed 'abandoned, isolated and left to its fate'. And to compound this bitter result for the Belgians, there was the cynical lack of candour and confidence shown by the British military and political leaders towards the King and his General Staff – and their callous disregard for the fate of his army and people.

The final grim logic of the situation was that, while it was open to the BEF and part of the French First Army to escape by means of Operation Dynamo (now, unknown to the Belgians, in full swing), the sole option

* See Appendix VII.

left to the Belgian Army was to stand its ground, alone, and fight to a finish. To add to Leopold's sense of isolation there arrived early that morning a stiff and formal reply to his letter of the 25th to King George VI. In accordance with a practice established in the reign of George V for letters from the Monarch to other Heads of State, it was drafted at the Foreign Office, probably by Sir Alexander Cadogan.

26.5.40.

Following from His Majesty for King Leopold.

I am very grateful for your letter. I note that Your Majesty considers it to be your duty to your people and to your Allies to remain with your army in Belgium. In taking this decision Your Majesty will not have overlooked the extreme importance of establishing a united Belgian Government with full authority outside territory occupied by the enemy, and while playing tribute to Your Majesty's devotion, I and my Government must express our grave concern at your decision.

While it would be presumptuous of me to advise you in respect of your duty to your people, I can say that as regards the Allies and the fulfilment of their joint purpose in war, I do not feel that Your Majesty is called upon to make the sacrifice which you contemplate.

Moreover I am bound to put to Your Majesty another point. If it were possible for you to remain in Belgium at liberty to mix with your people, and to act and speak for them, there might be great value in the establishment of such a rallying point necessary to the Belgian Nation. But I can hardly hope such would be the outcome of Your Majesty's decision to stay with the Army. It seems to me that Your Majesty must consider the possibility, even probability, of your being taken prisoner, perhaps carried off to Germany, and almost certainly deprived of all communication with the outside world. Such a position would leave your people bereft of their natural leader, without so far as I can see any compensating advantage.

(Signed) George R.I.

'I gave this message to King Leopold,' Keyes' diary records, 'and he took it into Queen Elisabeth's bedroom. Later he told me that they had decided to remain in Belgium, at any rate as long as they were allowed to. He remarked that of course the message did not represent King George's views, but those of his Government, and only repeated the arguments which his own Government had been using for several days. I went to La Panne and telephoned to the Prime Minister to give him King Leopold's reply. I also told him that I did not think that the Belgian Army's resistance could be maintained much longer . . . I then returned to Bruges.'*

* In spite of Keyes' unwelcome communications about Leopold, Churchill took the trouble to write to his wife on the 27th: 'My dear Eva, this is only a line to let you know I talk to Roger every day. He is doing wonderful work. I thought you would like to know. P.S. Presently he will be ordered home.'

George VI's chilly official reply (in private he was much more sympathetic) only served to increase Leopold's feeling that his predicament
and the desperate situation of his army was not appreciated by his Allies.
And in a mid-morning message brought from GHQ by an officer of
Davy's mission the old demand was reiterated for him to order a
retirement to the Yser. Gort and Pownall seemed not to comprehend that
behind the Belgian front was an area normally occupied by nearly a
million people into which a million more were pouring in search of refuge;
that the road system was limited; that without reserves the King could not
withdraw an army fully engaged all along the line; and finally that all
movements were inhibited by the *Luftwaffe*'s almost continuous and
unopposed dive-bombing and strafing attacks. The Belgians must fall
back to suit the BEF but it would do nothing to help them – that in effect
was the one-sided proposition.

All that morning the Belgian Command received reports of ever-
increasing gravity from the front. Enemy infantry was infiltrating the
Belgian line at several points – and losses in men and material, chiefly
from the massive bombing attacks, were mounting dangerously. At about
10.30 am GQG issued orders for the Army to retire methodically, step by
step, to a specified line.

Behind the exhausted and desperately battling troops struggled that
other army, the million-strong host of refugees. The plight of these
people – almost entirely women, children and the aged – was pitiful.
Owing to the closing of the French frontier against them, they were
herded into an overcrowded and contracting area in conditions of acute
hardship and danger. Casualties among them were said to be higher than
among the fighting men. Starving refugees could be seen tearing up roots
in the fields and eating them raw, while children were following the Army
field-kitchens, begging for food.

By midday the reports from the Belgian front had become even more
disturbing. The I Corps commander announced that the enemy had
penetrated the barrier of railway wagons on the line Ypres-Roulers,
which were burning at several points. His right at Frezenburg was under
heavy attack, and his corps was in danger of being surrounded. GQG had
now lost touch with a number of corps headquarters and from those still in
contact the news was extremely grave. The Belgian Army was rapidly
disintegrating. Besides being the helpless victims of continuous air attack,
the troops were running short of food and ammunition.

For Leopold and his General Staff it had been a morning of mounting
tension and anxiety. At one o'clock there was more bad news: the V and
VII Corps fronts had been broken and the VI Corps front was under
violent attack. The situation, Michiels reported, was becoming critical.
The King accepted this fresh blow calmly, though its significance was
obvious. Keyes told the King that he wanted to drive to Zeebrugge to

check that the demolitions he had organized there had been properly carried out. 'Too late,' replied the King. 'The front is broken.'

At 10.05 am General Champon had succeeded in getting through to Weygand and informed him that the Belgian Army was on the point of disintegrating. 'Late that morning' (according to the *Official History*), Gort received via Keyes a warning message from the King, the generous and uncomplaining tone of which was in sharp contrast to the recriminatory communications which had been sent to him from the GHQ of the BEF:

27.5.40.

From King Leopold to Lord Gort.

He wishes you to know that his Army is greatly disheartened. It has been incessantly engaged for four days and subjected to intense air bombardment, which the RAF have been unable to prevent. The knowledge that the Allied armies in this sector have been encircled, and that the Germans have great superiority in the air, has led his troops to believe that the position is almost hopeless. He fears a moment is rapidly approaching when he can no longer rely upon his troops to fight or be of any further use to the BEF. He wishes you to realize that he will be obliged to surrender before a *débâcle*.

The King fully appreciates that the BEF has done everything in its power to help Belgium, and he asks you to believe that he has done everything in his power to avert this catastrophe.

The Admiral noted that at the time of sending this chivalrous message the King 'hoped to be able to hold on for another day, but the enemy broke through in several places that afternoon'. At 2.30 pm Van Overstraeten told the French Generals Champon and Koeltz (Weygand's representative, who was visiting Belgian GQG): 'We have reached the extreme limit of our resistance. Our front is giving way like a worn-out old rope.' Half an hour later Colonel Davy's Mission succeeded in getting another warning message through to Gort's headquarters, describing the desperate straits of the Belgian Army and concluding: 'Situation still very confused, but indications are that the Belgian front may be crumbling.'

The official communiqué issued soon afterwards by the Belgian High Command summed up the situation:

The Belgian Army has totally exhausted its capacity for resistance. Its units are incapable of renewing the struggle tomorrow. A retreat towards the Yser cannot be considered. It would aggravate the pile-up of the Allies, already appallingly congested between the Yser, Calais and Cassel.

The appalling moment of decision came shortly after three o'clock, when Van Overstraeten and Michiels reported to the King in his office.

The Chief of Staff first gave his formal estimate. 'I believe,' said Michiels, 'that the Army is finished. The time has come to send an envoy to stop the fighting, if we are to avoid total disaster.' The King turned to his Military Adviser and asked: 'What is the opinion of General Van Overstraeten?' According to both his books of memoirs,[251] the General replied:

> From the national angle, all our units have been fully engaged, no more reserves remain, and the front has been broken in several places. Having thrown in everything, I believe that the Army has done its duty to the full; honour is safe.
>
> But from the international point of view we are under an obligation to gain as much time as possible for the Allies' sake. By sending an envoy now, we will give them a breathing-space overnight and tomorrow morning.
>
> We propose to release the French 60th Division and get it away in Belgian lorries to Dunkirk. The flooding of the Yser is in progress and the bridges are prepared for demolition and guarded. In these circumstances we have also done our utmost from the international point of view.

The King answered, simply, 'We must send the envoy at once.' He then ordered that the British and French liaison officers should be informed. Most accounts incorrectly state that he did not inform them of this decision until after the departure of the envoy at 5 pm, but the records of Admiral Keyes and Colonel Davy clearly establish that they and General Champon were informed at least an hour and a half before the envoy left GQG.

The choice for this repugnant mission fell upon General Dérousseaux, the Deputy Chief of Staff. His authorization required careful drafting, and the Advocate-General was summoned. The final form of words was designed to delay the proceedings for as long as possible. Signed by General Michiels, 'in the name of the King, Commander-in-Chief', it empowered General Dérousseaux 'to discover the conditions for a cessation of hostilities between the German Army and the Belgian Army . . .' Finally, at 5 pm, the General's white-pennanted car set off for the German Lines. At the same time arrangements were made for the flags of the Belgian Army to be delivered for safe keeping to the nearby Abbey of St André.

In his unpublished memoirs Colonel Davy describes how he heard of the King's decision from Admiral Keyes after he arrived back at GQG from Cassel, where he had personally warned Pownall about the imminent collapse of the Belgian Army. The Admiral had been told the news by the King at about 3.15 pm, after he emerged from the conference with his General Staff. Davy writes that he went immediately to the Operations Room, where he found a number of officers – 'all very upset' – including Michiels and Dérousseaux, who was preparing himself 'to carry the white flag'. The French General Champon, Davy declares, 'was just leaving in a cloud of froth, which was all he ever produced'. After sending off 'the necessary signals to GHQ and London', Davy continues, 'Keyes and I decided that we must go to the direct telephone at La Panne and talk to our respective bosses.'

Amid the shock felt by all at GQG and the British Mission, there was a grim realization of the inevitability of Leopold's decision. The Admiral had seen with his own eyes that no other course of action was possible. There was a bond of warm friendship and mutual respect between the two men and when the King told Keyes of the decision he had just made, the Admiral expressed his sympathy and understanding as best he could. Then he said that he must go at once to La Panne to inform Winston Churchill direct by telephone, but promised to return to GQG as soon as possible. In his diary for May 27th, Keyes wrote:

> The situation had now arisen which the King and Lord Gort foresaw on May 20th. Being unable to be of any further use to the BEF, having flooded the Yser [five days earlier], mined its bridges and removed all the French troops across the Yser, he asked for a cessation of hostilities to avoid the further slaughter of his sorely tried people, who crowded every town, village or road and were being ruthlessly bombed.

After being informed of the Belgian Command's decision to send an envoy to the Germans, Champon was unable to get a message through to Supreme Headquarters at Vincennes until 6.05 pm, when Weygand received it. But he failed to find or contact Blanchard, whose Command Post, like that of Gort, had moved to an unknown destination. Before leaving Belgian GQG, Champon expressed his sympathy to Van Overstraeten, but said that he felt negotiations should not be opened except by common agreement between the three armies of the North. Van Overstraeten replied that no steps had been taken to open negotiations: the envoy's mission was limited to an enquiry as to the conditions for a suspension of hostilities. No other decision had been made. Moreover, General Nyssens had confirmed General Champon's own findings in a note brought by General Delvoie which reported complete 'disarray' in the British and French commands and that neither of the C-in-Cs nor their headquarters could be found. How then could Gort and Blanchard be consulted?

Having duly warned his British and French allies, the King now despatched a trusted agent with instructions to try to get through to Brussels with a letter for the American Ambassador, John Cudahy, requesting that he should come at once to St André. Leopold wished to explain to the Ambassador the reasons for his action and also give him a letter for President Roosevelt. But, not surprisingly, Cudahy never received the King's letter. On the way to Brussels (almost entirely through German-held territory) the messenger was captured three times, and though each time he managed to escape in the confusion, finally he was caught and imprisoned under a strong guard.

The Admiral's diary next recounts how he motored to La Panne with Davy and gave Churchill the news on the telephone at 5 pm:

> The Prime Minister was not at all surprised, in view of the repeated warnings, but he told me that I must make every endeavour to persuade the King and Queen to come to England with me, and he dictated a message which he said I ought to have received that afternoon:
>
> 27.5.40.
>
> Belgian Embassy here assumes from King's decision to remain, that he regards the war as lost and contemplates separate peace. It is in order to dissociate itself with this, that the Constitutional Belgian Government has reassembled on foreign soil. Even if present Belgian Army has to lay down its arms, there are 200,000 Belgians of military age in France, and greater resources than Belgium had in 1914, with which to fight back. By present decision the King is dividing the Nation and delivering it into Hitler's protection.ᵛ Please deliver these considerations to the King, and impress upon him the disastrous consequences to the Allies and to Belgium of his present choice.
>
> I asked that the Admiralty should be told to send the MTBs to Nieuport during the night, and was told that this would be done.

As Davy records in his memoirs, he telephoned the news of the forthcoming Belgian surrender to London twenty minutes before the Admiral gave it to Churchill at 5 pm, for when they arrived in La Panne at 4.30 pm (after a car journey which must have taken at least an hour), Keyes told him to ring first, explaining 'that under no circumstances could he telephone to the Prime Minister between 3 and 5 pm, as this was his siesta'. At 4.40, therefore, Davy rang the War Office and was put through to General Percival, the Vice-CIGS, since Dill, the CIGS, was out. As Davy recalled for the author, the conversation which followed was somewhat one-sided. When Davy made the dramatic announcement that the Belgians were sending an officer with a white flag to the enemy lines to ask for a cease-fire, Percival replied aloofly 'Yes'. And this was the only response Davy could get to his six successive statements and questions concerning the forthcoming capitulation. In each case the General's reply was a flat 'Yes' – when Davy told him twice that the Belgians were going to surrender and that he had sent a signal to that effect to GHQ; when he asked the VCIGS if he 'really understood' that the Belgians intended to capitulate; and when he requested that the War Office should inform Gort's GHQ, in case his signal from Belgian GQG had gone astray. It was only when Davy asked what he and his Mission should do, that Percival varied his response and ended the conversation with 'Come home'.*

These first-hand accounts amply demonstrate the falsity of the attacks which would soon be made on King Leopold for surrendering without warning his allies – some by those who deliberately kept the Belgians in the dark about the BEF's withdrawal from the battle and re-embarkation, which had begun on the previous day.

A progressive series of warnings had been given to the British political and military leaders since May 20th that separation from the British meant surrender and that the Belgian Army was nearing the end of its capacity to resist. As Gort's *Despatches* clearly show, he and Pownall had recognized as early as the 19th that the BEF's abandonment of the Belgian Army would lead to its capitulation. On May 20th Keyes had signalled to Churchill and Gort the King's message that he would accept with good grace any movement of the BEF which was deemed to be essential for its survival, but that 'such action would finally lead to the capitulation of the Belgian Army'. On the 21st at Premesques Davy had told Gort, who was 'disturbed at the prospect of leaving the Belgians in the lurch', that they 'would help him as long as possible, but they must inevitably capitulate if he left them'.

During this whole period Keyes and Davy were warning Churchill, Gort and Pownall almost daily that the Belgian Army would be bound to crack if no help was forthcoming from the BEF and the RAF. On the 25th Leopold had informed George VI in the clearest terms that his army's defeat was imminent and early on the 27th Davy had personally told Pownall that this was likely to happen within twenty-four hours. Less than four hours later Gort received via Keyes the King's message, transmitted on Davy's radio set, that he would be obliged 'to surrender before a *débâcle*'. To lend credence to the subsequent allegations that the King surrendered without warning his allies, it was put about that Gort never received this or any other warnings from the King prior to the capitulation – and since Gort's *Despatches* omitted all mention of them, this slander is even now still widely believed. It was not admitted until thirteen years later, in the British *Official History*, that Leopold's specific warning that 'he will be obliged to surrender before a *débâcle*' reached Gort 'late in the morning' of the 27th.

Colonel Davy's cyphered warning message to the War Office was received there at 5.54 pm, over an hour after he had given it to Percival on the telephone. But the signal he sent direct to Cassel, according to the

---

* Ironically, on February 15th 1942, the monosyllabic General Percival would, as C-in-C, surrender Singapore and his 85,000 troops unconditionally to the 30,000-strong Japanese invasion force, under far less critical circumstances. This was described by Winston Churchill as 'The greatest disaster and the worst capitulation in the history of the British Empire.'

British Official Historian, 'seems to have gone astray'. But what neither the *Official History*, Gort's *Despatches* nor Pownall's diaries explain is that on the afternoon of May 27th Gort and his headquarters became impossible to locate or contact (as the British, French and Belgian liaison officers who tried to do so, discovered), since on the reported approach of enemy tanks they had hurriedly abandoned Cassel for unknown destinations. In fact the Staff lodged overnight at Houtkerque and established a makeshift GHQ next day at Queen Elisabeth's villa at La Panne, ten miles from Dunkirk. But Gort and Pownall had set off in a different direction on a wild-goose chase after Blanchard, whose officers were, in turn, trying to locate them and British headquarters. Communications with GHQ had been bad enough, despite the fact that the main telephone cables ran underneath Cassel, but after its departure from that town they became almost non-existent, due to the lack of radio equipment and the fact that a British officer blew up the main telephone exchange at Lille, against the protests of the French officer in charge, wrecking the entire northern telephone system. Thus, it was solely due to their own poor communications and the fact that they were on the move and out of touch that Gort and Pownall failed to hear of the Belgian Command's decision to send an emissary to the Germans until 11 pm, when they arrived at Dunkirk – although neither the *Official History* nor Gort's *Despatches* nor Pownall's Diaries admit this.

Indeed, the *Official History*'s account of the circumstances leading to the Belgian surrender is highly tendentious, while those in Gort's *Despatches* and Pownall's diary are even more so. For example, Major Ellis, while admitting for the first time in 1953, that Gort received the King's warning message on the morning of the 27th, claims that 'it came as a shock' to Gort when at 11 pm in Dunkirk he heard from the French the news that a cease-fire was being sought. Ellis, like Gort and Pownall, fails to mention the tremendous ground and air attacks the Belgians were suffering, or the many previous warnings received by the two generals and Churchill, or the fact that Keyes and Davy personally informed London of Leopold's decision that afternoon and had had their messages repeated to GHQ. He further distorts the picture by stating: 'By midnight on May 27th the King of the Belgians had accepted defeat and the Belgian Army had been ordered to cease fire,' whereas the cease-fire did not in fact take place until 4 am on May 28th. But Gort's biographer, in his equally unfair and inaccurate account (he asserts, for example, that the King's action had been 'taken against the advice of his Government, which was now established on English soil'* and also omits to mention that Gort received the King's penultimate warning message on the

---

* The Belgian Government was, of course, in France and was not 'established on English soil' until five months later, in October 1940.

morning of the 27th), at least contradicts Major Ellis' assertion that Gort was shocked by the news, by disclosing that he told ins ADC that 'he had been expecting it'.[253]

But even more reprehensible, in the light of the progressive warnings Gort had personally received, was the statement in his *Despatches* that the news which reached him in Dunkirk at 11 pm on the 27th 'was the first intimation I had received of this intention . . . I now found myself suddenly faced with an open gap between Ypres and the sea, through which enemy armoured forces [sic] might reach the beaches.'[254] As will be seen, the formulation of Gort's *Despatches* became a political propaganda 'cover-up' exercise, after Gort had been packed off to Gibraltar as Governor. Indeed Sir John Colville, in *Man of Valour*, describes how the Establishment 'employed a public relations officer to write a bowdlerized edition of the despatches without referring the matter to Gort'. Nevertheless, there can be no excuse for Gort allowing his name to appear as the author of an official report, parts of which are a travesty of the truth.

Ironically, Pownall, who was initially responsible for writing up the *Despatches* and endorsed the allegations made by Gort and others, after his return to England, that Leopold had suddenly exposed the BEF's flank and endangered its retreat by capitulating without warning, refutes this particular slander in his private diary. In June, he wrote under the heading 'In retrospect':

> The attacks on Leopold and the Belgian Army are mostly political. Although Gort himself had only one hour's notice that Leopold had asked for an armistice, it did not make any *immediate* danger.
>
> The most imminent danger lay to the South . . . where pressure was continuous . . . The northern flank, when the Belgian Army surrendered, was pretty well cared for, *for the time being*. We held the Ypres-Comines Canal (where there was a lot of fighting), Ypres and north of it.
>
> We had made these dispositions in self-protection when it was clear that the Belgians were being pushed north . . .[255]

Yet Pownall continued to make slighting entries in his diary. He refers, for example, to the 'defection' of the Belgians; to their King as 'the man who packed up on us without saying he was going to do so'; and wrote that, since he and Gort only heard of Leopold's move at 11 pm, this was 'not exactly what you would call fair warning from an Allied King who had appealed for and obtained our assistance'.*

The truth of the matter was that the Belgian request for a cease-fire surprised neither Gort nor Churchill. When the decision was taken by the King to send an envoy to the enemy, Weygand, Churchill and the War

---

* Pownall's diary entry for May 31st, made after his return to England, but not included in *Chief of Staff*.

Office were all successfully notified; that neither Gort nor Blanchard heard the news until later was due to their own deficient communications and unknown whereabouts, not to any sloth or malign purpose on Leopold's part. He had kept his army fighting to the last possible moment, and the terms of his approach to the Germans were carefully designed to help his allies by holding up von Bock's fourteen divisions for as long as possible. He could have done no more.

CHAPTER TWENTY-SIX

Unconditional Surrender

If you can keep your head when all about you
    Are losing theirs and blaming it on you,
If you can trust yourself when all men doubt you,
    But make allowance for their doubting too;
If you can wait and not be tired by waiting,
    Or being lied about, don't deal in lies,
Or being hated don't give way to hating,
    And yet don't look too good, nor talk too wise:

If you can dream – and not make dreams your master;
    If you can think – and not make thoughts your aim;
If you can meet with Triumph and Disaster
    And treat those two impostors just the same;
If you can bear to hear the truth you've spoken
    Twisted by knaves to make a trap for fools,
Or watch the things you gave your life to, broken,
    And stoop and build 'em up with worn-out tools . . .*

If, by Rudyard Kipling

The missions of both Sir Roger Keyes and Colonel Davy were now nearing their end. The two officers made their way back from La Panne to take their leave of the King, but as the Admiral noted:

> The King was not at GQG and I was told that I should find him in the Provincial Governor's Palace at Bruges. He was not there, but the Queen had just arrived . . . I told the Queen of the anxiety of our Government that Her Majesty and King Leopold should come away with me. She had just seen bombs falling among men, women, children and horses in the crowded streets, and told me that people had appealed to her, to ask if nothing could be done to stop the slaughter. She said that she was sure the King would not change his mind and that she intended to stay with him: of course they could not possibly leave their people, who needed them.
> At about 9.30 pm I heard that the King had returned to the old GQG at St André and would wait for me there. I went there at once, having changed into a

* When Admiral Keyes was taking leave of King Leopold at 10 pm on May 27th, six hours before the capitulation, he remarked that Rudyard Kipling's poem 'If' seemed to be particularly appropriate for the King in the present tragic circumstances. The King then asked the Admiral if he could write the poem out for him, which he was able to do from memory. In 1952, after King Baudouin had acceded to the throne, His Majesty showed the author a framed copy of 'If' on the wall of his room.

suit of plain clothes lent to me by the Queen's Secretary, to give me a chance of escaping as a refugee, if the Germans overtook me.

I gave King Leopold the Prime Minister's message, but he said he had made up his mind that he must stay with his army and people, for the reason he had given in his letter to our King, a copy of which he then gave me. [This was the pencilled draft mentioned above.]

I asked King Leopold whether the guarantee handed to him recently by Sir Lancelot Oliphant did not bind him not to make a separate peace. The King said there was no question of his making a separate peace: his Country was overrun by the enemy, who had the power to impose on the people any terms they wished. But in any case, his government had rejected the offer and would have nothing to do with the British guarantee, as they said there were too many ifs and buts in it. All he hoped to do was to use his influence in the direction he had clearly stated in his letter to King George. King Leopold said that of course he would be attacked and condemned, and accused of having all sorts of ulterior motives, but he knew he was doing what was best for his people. He could not possibly be of any use to them as a fugitive. The refugees, including those of military age who had gone to France, would be involved in that country's collapse, which he felt convinced was imminent.

At 10 pm Sir Roger took leave of King Leopold, who saw him to his car. The King had thoughtfully provided a senior *Sûreté* officer, who was invaluable in getting the Admiral's car through the appalling traffic conditions on the road to Nieuport, which – as Keyes noted – 'was crowded with vehicles and refugees and frequently blocked. German planes roared overhead all the time and occasionally dropped bombs.' When Keyes and Davy arrived at the harbour at 1 am, they found there Major Hayley, who had come from Ostend, where he had embarked the rest of the mission in the 'bread boat', SS *Aboukir*, on Davy's orders. (The two liaison officers' concern for the Admiral's safety saved their own lives, for tragically the *Aboukir* was torpedoed, and all the members of their mission, except the Sergeant-Major, were killed.)

In case the MTBs failed to arrive, Keyes, Davy and Hayley boarded a number of fishing boats, and were about to commandeer one when two MTBs appeared. The Admiral signalled with his torch and the craft came alongside. As dawn was breaking, the MTBs roared out to sea, bound for Harwich. Before leaving, the Admiral handed Comte Capelle, the King's Secretary, who had crossed from England to rejoin his Sovereign, a farewell message to Leopold which he had scribbled in the dark.

Sir,
   We all arrived safely at Nieuport and hope to find our boats before morning. I hope Your Majesty will have the bridges on the Yser blown as some protection to our army. I pray for a happy issue.

When the King received this note he immediately gave orders for the destruction of the bridges, although they had in the meantime been placed under French control.

That Leopold himself believed in an ultimate happy issue is evident from his recorded comments, both then and later. In his discussions with his Ministers and during his last talk with Keyes he had reiterated his certainty that France would soon succumb, but that the British would continue the struggle. 'You will gain the upper hand,' he declared, 'but not before going through hell.' The King also told the Admiral he was sure that the Ministers who had deserted him 'would lose their heads' when France collapsed. In his official report to Lord Halifax, Keyes later wrote:

> On the last three nights which we spent at Wynendaele, I dined alone with the King and Queen Elisabeth and they talked freely about the future. The King said that he was absolutely convinced that the French Army would collapse before the German onslaught within two or three weeks, that there would be internal trouble in France, and that the French Government would desert us. He said that it was a tragedy that our government had failed to appreciate that every day of delay would only add to the difficulties and dangers of the withdrawal of the splendid troops of the BEF . . . The King and Queen both expressed their confidence that British Sea Power and the spirit of the people of the British Empire would prevail and ensure victory in the end.

Meanwhile, at Belgian GQG the staff had anxiously awaited the return of General Dérousseaux. The envoy finally arrived back at 11 pm after a hazardous journey, during which his car had been met by a hail of machine-gun fire while passing through the German lines, its windows shattered and the flag-bearing member of the party wounded. Dérousseaux handed General Michiels a brief document in German: '*Der Führer fordert bedingungslose Waffenstreckung.*' ('The Führer demands unconditional surrender.') The Chief of Staff, accompanied by Van Overstraeten and the Attorney-General, immediately took the German document to the King, who was at the Provincial Governor's Palace in Bruges.

The following account of what happened next is taken from the hour by hour account of the campaign which Van Overstraeten wrote at the time and published in *Albert I–Léopold*, in 1946. The variations, afterthoughts and surmises which Van Overstraeten incorporated in his second book, *Dans l'Etau*, and published in 1960, are examined below, although they do not alter the factual record he compiled twenty years before.

In his account Van Overstraeten records that all those present at this crucial meeting agreed with his own contention that 'the cessation of hostilities pure and simple has the advantage of not involving the Sovereign in the discussion of terms or conditions and not binding

Belgium to any future political course of action' and that 'the capitulation would be an exclusively military act simplified by the phrase "unconditional"'. Van Overstraeten records that the King agreed and decided that he must accept, but claims that he himself was 'filled with the desire to maintain our place in the line of battle until the following midday' in order 'to gain as much time as possible for the benefit of the Allies'. However, the Chief of Staff feared that a resumption of fighting would result in an 'immediate and complete *débâcle*', in view of the condition of the troops, and proposed that the cease-fire should take place at four or five o'clock that morning. Van Overstraeten then makes it clear that he made no objection when the King gave his decision: four o'clock.

Van Overstraeten further affirms that he was in complete agreement with the text of the reply to be sent by radio to the Germans, which the Chief of Staff drafted:

Laying down arms. Cease fire at 4 am (Belgian time) 28th May. Envoy will cross German lines at 5 am.

Indeed, his account continues: '*La formule est bonne, c'est une simple reddition. Le Roi l'approuve.*' Next he describes how he reminded the King of General Champon's protest at the lack of consultation with the French and British and quotes Leopold as replying that the Allies had received many warnings over a long period, that he had warned Lord Gort yet again at noon on the previous day through Admiral Keyes that the Belgian Army would have to surrender to avoid complete disaster. Moreover, the King pointed out, the total breakdown of communications was preventing all liaison with the French and British.[256]

Van Overstraeten's contemporary record thus confirms that the King's decisions to send the envoy to the Germans and to accept their demand for unconditional surrender were made on the advice, and with the full backing of the Chief of Staff and himself and that although he hoped the cease-fire could be delayed until midday, he did not dissent when the King accepted Michiels' recommendation that it should be at 4 am.

But in *Dans l'Etau*, which Van Overstraeten wrote in his embittered old age, he re-interprets many of the facts he had previously recorded, and introduces a series of self-justificatory afterthoughts and derogatory insinuations concerning the motives and actions of virtually all the other participants in the drama, including the King. This change of ground can only be explained by Van Overstraeten's accumulated resentment at the persistent abuse and lack of appreciation he had received from both sides of the political fence, from the military and from loyal supporters as well as the enemies of the Crown. He was also clearly motivated by the smouldering jealousy he felt for Henri De Man, who he grew to believe had supplanted him as the King's closest adviser during the three days before the capitulation. Although in his original work Van Overstraeten attributes no significance whatsoever to De Man's presence at Wynendaele, mentioning his name only twice, without comment, in his second book he subtly changes the wording and inserts a number of sentences alleging that the King was 'seduced by De Man's germanophile tendencies' and that his decisions, from May 25th onwards, were made under the Socialist leader's 'evil influence'.[257] This is ironical, since De Man did not earn that epithet (or that of a collaborator) until after the Belgian capitulation, whereas Van Overstraeten had long been described as 'pro-German' by the French and British, albeit unfairly, and would himself be accused by many who were then De Man's Socialist colleagues and supporters of having 'exercised an evil influence' over the King.

The Protocol of Surrender was duly signed by General Dérousseaux for Belgium and General von Reichenau for Germany, on the morning of May 28th. It was a purely military act of laying down arms – of which there were to be quite a number, often under far less critical circumstances, among the Allies before the tide turned in their favour.* Unlike the surrender of the whole French nation, which was soon to follow, the Protocol contained no political terms, nor was it in any sense an armistice or a peace treaty. For the King this fact was fundamental, since he was to base on it the whole character of his conduct in captivity. Its provisions were as follows:

> The Belgian Army will unconditionally lay down its arms at once and will from that time onwards regard itself as prisoners of war. A cease-fire was implemented this morning at 4 am at the request of the Belgian Command. The German operations against the British and French troops will not be suspended.
>
> Belgian territory will at once be occupied, including all ports. No further damage shall be done to the locks or coastal fortifications.

ADDITIONAL PROTOCOL

1 As a mark of honourable surrender, the Officers of the Belgian Army shall retain their weapons.

2 The Château of Laeken shall be placed at the disposal of His Majesty the King in order that he may reside there with his family, his military attendants and his servants.

---

* For example, only two weeks later, 8,000 men of the 51st Highland Division surrendered without resistance to General Rommel at St Valéry, where it was cornered with its back to the sea. A year later the German airborne invaders of Crete captured 12,000 British troops. In 1942 the British suffered even more humiliating defeats. In February came the shameful surrender of Singapore and its garrison of 85,000 troops, to a 30,000-strong Japanese invasion force. And in June Rommel captured, in one day, the fortress and harbour of Tobruk, its 33,000 defenders, and a vast stock of stores, fuel, ammunition, weapons, armour and transport. (The much reduced strength of Rommel's Afrika Korps was thereby restored, enabling him to advance into Egypt – 80% of his transport being captured British vehicles.)

Before the Protocol was signed, as the authors of *The Surrender of King Leopold* put it: 'His task was done as nearly as it could be done. In his way he had helped make possible what neither Gamelin nor Weygand had come even close to achieving – a chance to extricate the better portion of two armies from a hopeless situation. It was up to Gort and the British Navy and the British Air Force to realize upon that chance. That they did is, of course, history.'[258]

At the time of the Belgian cease-fire the Dunkirk evacuation had been in progress for thirty-six hours 'entirely without the knowledge of the Belgian Command', despite the fact that Gort had received Winston Churchill's message the previous morning telling him that it was 'now necessary to tell the Belgians' and declaring that 'We are asking them to sacrifice themselves for us.'

By the time the Belgians laid down their arms, many thousands of British troops had embarked safely. However, it was still highly uncertain whether the rest of the force would be able to reach the coast. Significantly, the chief threat to their escape was the advance of the German Panzers from the South-West, where one enemy group had come within four miles of Dunkirk and was now shelling the port. But the eastern prong of the encroaching German pincer-movement was held back by the prolonged last-ditch stand of the Belgian Army, while Gort's deployment of flank and rear-guards protected his troops as they streamed back to the coast.

On the morning of May 28th, a few hours after the Belgian cease-fire, Blanchard visited GHQ, BEF and was 'horrified', according to Pownall,* when he and Gort told him that Whitehall had ordered the BEF to withdraw to the coast. He would have been even more horrified had they been frank with him and admitted that these orders, which were for evacuation as well as withdrawal, had been received two days before, on the 26th, and that since then, their army had not only been in full flight to the sea, but had been embarking for England in ever-increasing numbers.

Because of this deceit on the part of the British political and military leaders, Blanchard remained as ignorant of 'Operation Dynamo' as were the Belgians – until the 29th, three days after it began, when Admiral Abrial first heard about it and told him, by which time over a third of the BEF's personnel had been evacuated. Meanwhile, at their morning meeting with Blanchard on the 28th, Gort and Pownall 'begged' the French C-in-C to order the First Army to retreat to the coast in concert with the BEF, but both Blanchard and its forceful new commander, Prioux, adamantly refused to do so. When Blanchard asked formally if Gort intended to withdraw the BEF, knowing that he 'would be going

---

* Pownall's account is given in Winston Churchill's *The Second World War*, Vol. II. See also *Chief of Staff*.

without the French First Army', the British generals replied, according to
Pownall's account, that 'it was necessary for the BEF to withdraw, even if
the French First Army did not do so', in compliance with the orders they
had received from London.

Gort and Pownall also told Blanchard that while the German threat to
the BEF from the North-East would probably not develop for at least
twenty-four hours, the *immediate* menace was from the massive Panzer
and infantry forces advancing from the South-West. The British generals
cannot therefore have failed to appreciate that the Belgians, by holding
up the advance of von Bock's fourteen divisions, had saved the BEF from
being cut off from the sea – although Gort and Pownall would never show
any gratitude to them, or give them any credit for thus making possible
the escape of their army from the rapidly-closing trap. Indeed the
German High Command had ordered that the two arms of the pincer-
movement by Army Group 'A' in the South-West and Army Group 'B' in
the North-East, which was designed to complete the encirclement of the
Franco-British forces, should link up at Kemmel, a town situated between them and the coast. Had this plan succeeded, the Germans would
have captured the French First Army and the BEF – the entire nucleus of
the future British Army – with consequences which can well be imagined.
That the Germans were unable to do so was primarily due to the fact
that Leopold's troops – although exhausted, abandoned, and suffering the most terrible punishment from the bulk of the *Luftwaffe* – held
up and wore down von Bock's fiercely-attacking army for four crucial
days.

And yet most British accounts, and in particular that in the *Official
History*, when describing the Germans' failure to round up and capture
the BEF as well as the whole French First Army, make no mention
whatsoever of the fact that it was the Belgian Army which prevented von
Bock's arm of the pincers closing between them and the coast. Indeed,
these accounts attribute the failure of the German pincer-movement
exclusively to the slow-down of the Panzers' advance from the South-West
caused by Hitler's four-day Halt Order and the resistance of the small
British improvised units which were flung in their path, and deployed
along the 'Canal Line' to the West of Dunkirk. While it is true that these
two factors undoubtedly prevented the Panzers from arriving in Dunkirk
before the BEF and a part of the French First Army, it is equally
irrefutable that these Allied forces could never have even reached that
coastal area, let alone embarked from it, had not Leopold's army
prevented von Bock's powerful thrust from cutting them off from the sea.

At 11 am on May 28th 1940 Colonel General Walter von Reichenau,
the commander of the German Sixth Army, presented himself at the
Provincial Governor's Palace, where King Leopold and his Staff were
now installed. The bemonocled General was accompanied by an impress-

ive entourage, headed by his Chief of Staff, General Friedrich Paulus, who would later take over command of the Sixth Army and, on January 30th 1943, surrender himself and its remnants to the Russians, in the ruins of Stalingrad.

The German C-in-C and his Staff were astounded to learn from the Belgian emissary, General Dérousseaux, that the King had not fled the country and had no intention of deserting his army. The reaction at von Reichenau's headquarters has been graphically described by one of his staff officers, Colonel Werner Kiewitz, who two days later was appointed the King's custodian and commander of his prison guard at Laeken. When Dérousseaux asked the Germans what fate they had in store for Leopold, Kiewitz recalls, 'We were absolutely thunderstruck to learn that the King was still on Belgian soil. We thought that he had fled to England, like the Queen of Holland. We soldiers found this decision of the Commander-in-Chief of the Belgian Army worthy of our admiration, and I must say that the German officers spoke of the King with great respect.'

Von Reichenau and his officers were also taken aback, Kiewitz continues, because 'the King's presence raised a problem which we had not previously considered, and which we could not resolve without reference to the Führer'. When von Reichenau thereupon telephoned Hitler, the exultant dictator was in 'a charming mood' and decreed that the 'prisoner King' was to be well treated and incarcerated in the Palace of Laeken.[259] That the Führer was at first favourably disposed towards the King and his army was confirmed by the German radio bulletin on the 28th, which announced that the Belgian Army had capitulated, and declared:

> The Führer has ordered that the King of the Belgians and his army be given treatment worthy of the brave fighting soldiers they have proved themselves to be.

When von Reichenau and his retinue arrived at the Governor's Palace, he clearly intended that the meeting between the commanders of the victorious and the vanquished armies should be a dramatic and well-publicized spectacle, for he brought with him a large number of newsreel cameramen, press photographers, journalists and radio reporters. But they were all disappointed, for the King sent word by Major Van den Heuvel, the Commandant of the Royal Palaces, that he would receive only the German C-in-C and would not meet anyone else or make any public appearance.

Commandant Hubert Rombauts, the Secretary of the King's Military Household, who was later to play an active role in helping to form a number of Resistance groups inside the Royal Palaces, helped Van den Heuvel to persuade von Reichenau that he would have to forgo a *manifestation spectaculaire* in his hour of triumph, and has described what followed.*

The German C-in-C was accordingly shown, alone, into the *grand salon* on the first floor of the Governor's Palace, where Leopold awaited him. After saluting the King, who was standing stiffly behind a writing table at the far end of the room, the General advanced towards him with his hand outstretched, but the King's cold and unresponsive demeanour brought him to a halt, at a distance of about twenty paces, from where he made this formal statement:

> I have the honour to command the army which fought against that of your Majesty. I desire to testify to the courage of the Belgian troops who have fought most valiantly – to the resistance of its fortifications and the efficiency of its demolitions. I deplore the fate of your army, which was not due to any inferiority.
>
> I must also tell you that the Führer has expressed his admiration and esteem for the Belgian Army, which has fought very bravely.

When von Reichenau had finished speaking, the King asked him 'What will happen to my army?' The General replied that he had not yet received any instructions in this regard, but for the time being they must be considered as prisoners of war. 'In that case,' the King retorted emphatically, 'I must ask you to consider me as your first prisoner.' When the General reminded the King of the Führer's edict that he must live at Laeken, he replied: 'Tell Hitler that King Leopold wants no special favours, and that he will share the lot of his army – a palace is not the right place for a King whose soldiers are in prisoner-of-war camps.' But von Reichenau insisted that the King must conform with Hitler's orders and all his subsequent efforts to get the Germans to place him in a more modest place of detention were in vain.

Von Reichenau also assured the King – and thus misled him – that his officers and soldiers would be sent back to their homes and allowed to return to civilian life 'as soon as possible'. Since Leopold was aware that the Dutch armed forces had been allowed to do so after their surrender, he had no reason to doubt that his own troops would be treated in the same way, particularly in view of the Führer's order that their treatment must be worthy of their brave fighting performance. For many Belgian soldiers, however, especially the Walloons, 'as soon as possible' would prove to be a long time.† In his diary account of the confrontation von Reichenau wrote:

---

* In his book *Le 18e Jour*[270] the French author and Resistance hero Colonel Rémy quotes from a description Commandant Rombauts gave of this episode in 1966 at a reunion of one of the Resistance groups of which they had both been members.
† See Appendix VII.

Today my army scored a great triumph: a gallant adversary has laid down his arms. He was forced to do so by our superiority . . . Arrived to see the King this morning at 11 am. He kept me waiting 40 minutes – not an easy morsel to swallow! A frank interview. Hats off to this man! He did not hesitate to say what he thought. Nor did I. He deserves correct treatment . . .

Then, entirely misreading the situation, von Reichenau added 'If we are clever, and don't act the Prussian, we can gain Belgium's friendship . . .' This was an early indication of the policy of appeasement which at first characterized the German occupation of Belgium.

Before quitting Bruges von Reichenau told Colonel Schuler, the officer detailed to take charge of the King, 'See that all goes well at Brussels; I am very keen that it should . . . Remember the King is Belgium and Belgium is the King . . . we can have nothing but the greatest respect for that man.'* Schuler arrived at the Governor's Palace about four o'clock and immediately installed himself in a room with a radio set tuned in to the Führer's headquarters. A column of German infantrymen marched singing across the nearby Place du Bourg. In the Palace courtyard a guard post was set up and, watched by incredulous Belgians, two German sentries ordered the gendarmes of the Royal escort to move out and took possession of the ceremonial entrance-gate. Intermittent rain added to the gloom of defeat hanging over the old city. Meanwhile, King Leopold made a final proclamation to his army:

GQG, May 28th 1940

Officers, Non-Commissioned Officers and Men,
    Plunged unexpectedly into a war of unparalleled violence, you have fought courageously to defend your homeland step by step.
    Exhausted by an uninterrupted struggle against an enemy very much superior in numbers and material, we have been forced to surrender.
    History will relate that the Army did its duty to the full. Our Honour is safe.
    This violent fighting, these sleepless nights, cannot have been in vain. I enjoin you not to be disheartened, but to bear yourselves with dignity. Let your attitude and your discipline continue to win the esteem of the foreigner.
    I shall not leave you in our misfortune, and I shall watch over your future and that of your families.
    Tomorrow we shall set to work with the firm intention of raising our country from its ruins.

LEOPOLD.

On the same day, before his voice was silenced in German captivity, the King wrote moving personal letters to the Pope and President Roosevelt in which he was at pains to explain the facts of the Belgian tragedy and his reasons 'for sharing the lot of my army and my people'. Belgium, he

* In 1949 the German magazine *Der Stern* published an article by Heinz Schroter, one of the attendant war correspondents, describing this historic meeting.

declared, had fulfilled her duty and upheld her international engagements
by 'scrupulously maintaining her neutrality and then by defending, foot
by foot, the entire extent of her territory'. The King then described how
his army, after withdrawing in concert with the armies of her guarantors
and after fighting a four-day battle 'without counting the cost', with its
back to the sea, had been 'broken under the weight of a crushing
superiority of troops and aviation'.

> We found ourselves finally encircled in a very restricted area which already had
> a dense population and had been invaded by several hundreds of thousands of
> civilian refugees, who were without shelter, without food, without water and
> were being driven from one place to another by aerial bombing . . .
>   .Requested for several days past to quit my soldiers, I refused, since I felt that
> this would be desertion on the part of a Commander-in-Chief of an Army.
> Moreover, by remaining on my native soil, I intend to stand by my people in the
> trial which they will have to go through.

The two letters, which were in the same terms, were given wide
circulation in Belgium, but their publication was suppressed by the
censorship in Britain and France and was also withheld in the USA.

At 10 am on May 29th Albert Devèze, the leading jurist and ex-
Minister who was serving as an Army officer nearby, arrived at the
Governor's Palace. The King had summoned him for a consultation and,
after outlining the circumstances leading to the capitulation, said to him:
'I consider myself a prisoner, and as long as I remain a prisoner I shall
abstain from all political activity.' But he felt an urgent need to establish
authoritatively the legal and constitutional propriety of the capitulation.
In particular, he sought assurance that the absence of a Minister's
signature was not irregular. Devèze thereupon advised the King to
commission himself and two other distinguished legal experts who were
serving in the Army, Hayoit de Termicourt (the Advocate-General) and
Joseph Pholien (a former Minister and eminent jurist), to draw up a legal
assessment of the capitulation. The King readily agreed, and by May 30th
the three jurists produced a detailed report which confirmed the legal and
constitutional correctness of the King's actions.

These juridical findings were of crucial importance, owing to the
unimpeachable authority of the authors and the moment at which they
were drawn up. They have never been disputed and, when known, would
have a far-reaching effect in establishing the truth. A particular point
made in their lengthy note was that the capitulation had been a purely
military surrender. The King had neither treated with the enemy nor
signed any convention of a political character. His only act had been to
give the order to lay down arms, and 'when the Ministers have all left the
national territory, and when any communication with them has become
impossible, the Chief of the General Staff becomes invested with the

power of deciding, with the approval of the King, all matters of a military nature'. In such a situation a ministerial counter-signature was not required.

The jurists further examined the King's new situation and concluded that, having chosen as Commander-in-Chief to become a prisoner of war, along with his soldiers, he was now 'temporarily in the impossibility of ruling' under Article 82 of the Constitution. Nevertheless, they declared, 'preferring the accomplishment of his military duty to all the advantages which would have resulted from his departure from the national territory, we consider the Sovereign to have given a splendid example of courage and personal disinterestedness'.

Meanwhile, on May 29th, Colonel Schuler had reported to the King at the Governor's Palace and stated that for high-level political reasons he was to proceed to Laeken at 11 pm. The Germans had decided to make the move at night to avoid loyal demonstrations and also, though this was not revealed to the King, because Hitler was to pass through Brussels next day and intended to inspect his Royal victim. Luckily for Leopold there was a change in Hitler's plan and the meeting, which as a prisoner he could not have avoided, did not take place.

That night the King, with Van Overstraeten, was removed in a German car with a German driver and escort. The seventy mile journey from Bruges to Laeken took five hours, owing to the appalling destruction along the route. When the exhausted party finally reached Laeken, there were German sentries guarding the gates and the German flag was flying above the Palace. All was in darkness, due to a breakdown of the mains. In the cavernous hall a single candle was burning and the King saw in the gloom the silhouette of a man whom he described as 'more than two metres tall' standing inside the door. This was General von Bock, the commander of Army Group B which had opposed the Belgian Army, in full dress uniform, complete with sword. He wished to be presented to the King and to pay his tribute to a gallant adversary. Von Bock had been waiting for some hours. When Leopold entered the Palace he crashed to attention, paid homage to the King and his army for their brave resistance in words similar to those used by von Reichenau, then clanked out into the night, never to reappear. For Leopold all this had an air of utter unreality. He found no signs of disturbance in the Palace: everything was just as he had left it an age ago. But now he was a prisoner in his own home.

When Leopold rose later that morning, he was anxious to get some exercise after the cramped conditions under which he had been living, but Schuler insisted on accompanying him on his walk in the park. With the corpulent figure of the German on his right and the sprightly Van Overstraeten on his left, the King set off briskly. Platoons of infantry were encamped in the park all round the Palace, many of the soldiers being stripped to the waist in the hot sun. The King maintained a smart pace and soon the German was perspiring freely and panting for breath. As Leopold and Van Overstraeten proceeded at undiminished speed up the steep slope leading to the Palace, Schuler lagged further and further behind. 'I hope he understands,' murmured the King to his companion. This was the last he saw of Schuler, for that afternoon Colonel Kiewitz presented himself and reported that he had been sent specifically to attach himself to the King's person.

Kiewitz's first interview was brief, with the King stating simply that he wished to share the fate of his soldiers if they were to be made prisoners of war. The German apologized for the crude behaviour of Schuler and his minions. He had just evicted them from the Palace; they would trouble the King no more. Leopold was lucky in his overseer. Kiewitz, an elegant former diplomat and a fluent French-speaker, was tactful enough to keep out of the King's way except when duty demanded. But on occasion he, like others, had reason to feel the King's cold disapproval. He later described his first meeting:

> King Leopold received me extremely stiffly, with a most forbidding expression. He looked as I was to see him look so often thereafter, at which times I said to myself: 'The King has slammed down the curtain again today.' It was an impenetrable gaze that could stop you short at six paces. It did that to me. I stopped six paces from the King, saluted, and introduced myself.[261]

At ten that morning a Belgian general succeeded in getting past the German guards, who had been ordered to allow no one in without a pass, by wearing a Red Cross brassard. The general brought the King a loyal address from the Procurator-General and a description of a demonstration of fidelity by the entire magistrature which had taken place at the Palace of Justice. Typical of such manifestations was the loyal address rendered by the Burgomaster of Brussels, Van de Meulebroeck. It was signed by 2,441 burgomasters of other cities and towns throughout Belgium.

> Sire,
> Belgium, for the second time a victim of the tragic and undeserved fate against which its army, under Your Majesty's orders, has valiantly defended it to the extreme limits of its strength, wishes to affirm in the face of the world, through the voice of its communal Mandatories who have remained in the country, its moral unity with, and its indefectible fidelity to, the person of its Sovereign, and to the Dynasty which has made the greatness of the country.
> In presenting to Your Majesty, in these painful hours, the deferential homage of our ardent and indefectible loyalty, we are certain that we express the profound sentiments of the whole population, which retains its confidence in its destiny as a free and independent people.

Many thousands of similar messages from all parts of the country now began to pour in – from civilian and military organizations of every conceivable kind, as well as individual citizens and soldiers. A photostatic collection of these letters and messages was published in 1949. Some were just a scrawl, others well presented and elaborately phrased, but all affirmed their senders' loyalty and absolute faith in their Sovereign's courage, integrity and honour. Meanwhile, in a traditional Belgian tribute, a vast mass of flowers was laid at the gates of the Palaces – until all such demonstrations were stopped by the Germans. Undaunted, the people took to wearing lapel badges or brooches bearing an 'L' as a sign of their patriotism and fidelity to the Crown. Laeken now assumed the appearance of a prison. Orders were issued that no Belgian was allowed to enter or leave it. The guards were doubled on all the gates.

Next day, May 31st, the King received a visit from the importunate Dr Gebhart, this time accompanied by Minister of State Meissner, the Chief of Hitler's Secretariat, who bore a number of messages from the Führer. The German Ambassador to Belgium, von Bulow Schwante, described this meeting when interrogated by the Allies at the end of the war: 'I remember very clearly that one of these messages was a proposal for a meeting between Hitler and the King, a proposal which the latter resolutely refused. This refusal greatly prejudiced Hitler against the King.'

Later in the war, after Leopold's second marriage, Gebhart reappeared at Laeken claiming to be an emissary of Hitler. As the King recalled to the author, his wife, Princess Lilian, was present when the Doctor was shown in. They were 'frozen with horror' by Gebhart's boastful account of the experiments he had carried out in the name of science on human guinea-pigs (he was later hanged for these crimes). He added a cold-blooded description of some of the viler things being done by his Nazi colleagues. Gebhart even produced some phials of cyanide, explaining that all the Nazi leaders carried them. He then offered them to the Royal couple, saying: 'But of course you won't need them to take your own lives, will you?' The King and his wife had the uncomfortable feeling that he did not expect them to live to tell the tale. Having sent Gebhart packing, the King summoned Kiewitz and expressed the horror and disgust the Doctor had aroused, to which the Colonel replied that in fact Gebhart was not sent by Hitler, although he was a close personal friend of Himmler. Kiewitz then said that there was no need for the King to receive Gebhart in future and that he would keep him away. On the next occasion that Gebhart tried to see Leopold, Kiewitz fulfilled his promise and refused to admit him. This decision was to cost the Colonel dear, for it earned him the implacable enmity of Himmler's friend.

On the following day, June 1st, the King drew up a memorandum establishing the principles to which he committed himself for the duration of the enemy occupation of his country:

> Situation of Belgium vis-à-vis England and France:
> To this day, we have fulfilled all our engagements of neutrality and of war.
>
> Now, for as long as our territory is used for hostilities, it is our duty not to allow our Country to be associated with any action against those who were at our side in the battle.
>
> Situation of Belgium vis-à-vis Germany:
> Constrained by force, we can only submit to our territory being used for military operations.
>
> Therefore no negotiations are possible for as long as Belgian territory is used for hostilities.
>
> Situation of the Head of State:
> Difficult, on account of the attitude of many Belgians, as a result of the position taken up by the Government in Poitiers.
>
> Thus, for as long as Belgian territory serves as a base for military operations, the Head of State cannot take any political action.[262]

Two days later the King laid down a code of conduct for his compatriots as well as himself, when Paul Tschoffen, a Catholic ex-Minister from Liège, sought his guidance on behalf of its leading citizens on the attitude that patriotic Belgians should adopt during the occupation, particularly in regard to working in industry and commerce. After his audience, Tschoffen wrote down exactly what Leopold had said and, after receiving Comte Capelle's confirmation that his text 'correctly interpreted' the King's declarations, included it in a letter to W. Hallam Tuck at the American Embassy in Brussels:*

> 1 The King, a prisoner with his army, finds himself in the impossibility of freely exercising his functions of Head of State. For as long as this situation lasts, he will not in any circumstances exercise his powers. Temporarily the King does not reign.
> 2 Belgium has conscientiously fulfilled her obligations towards her guarantors. One duty remains: for the duration of the occupation, Belgium must not do anything in the military, political, or economic sphere, which could harm the Allied cause.
> 3 If the last phrase of the Royal message to the Army declares that Belgium – which is still at war – will return to work, that does not mean that the King

---

* W. Hallam Tuck, a leading member of the American community and businessman who had lived in Belgium for twenty years, was attached to the US Embassy. Tuck's valuable account of events in Belgium during this period appears in *The Belgian Campaign*,[264] published by the Belgian-American Educational Foundation, of which he was the Brussels Representative.

advises or agrees that Belgians should work for the enemy. This sentence must be interpreted as meaning that only work essential to the life of the Belgian people should be resumed. In the event that work undertaken to this end also serves the interests of the occupying power, it will be necessary to examine, in each particular case, in what degree the prospective work is essential to provide for the needs of the Belgian population and in what degree the occupying power will benefit. In deciding whether or not to resume or continue such work one should consider the best interests of Belgium as a whole and her position in the conflict.[263]

Thus at the very start of his captivity, when the future was obscure, the King laid down the principles for the irreproachable attitude he adopted for the duration of the occupation, in regard to his constitutional position, his people, the Allies and the Germans – principles from which he would never deviate.

CHAPTER TWENTY-SEVEN

The Great Lie

'Then went the jury out, whose names were Mr Blind-man, Mr No-good, Mr Malice, Mr Love-lust, Mr Live-loose, Mr High-mind, Mr Enmity, Mr Liar, Mr Cruelty, Mr Hate-light and Mr Implacable; who every one gave in his private verdict against him among themselves, and afterwards unanimously concluded to bring him in guilty.'

John Bunyan, *The Pilgrim's Progress*

It was Adolf Hitler who laid down the precept that 'the masses will always fall victim to a great lie, for while most people indulge in little lies, they are ashamed to tell really big ones, and therefore cannot conceive that anyone could have the effrontery to pervert the truth in such an outrageous manner.' It was, however, the Prime Minister of France, Paul Reynaud, who used this tactic with the most devastating and far-reaching effect.

At 8.30 in the morning of May 28th 1940 Reynaud, his high nasal voice filled with venom, broadcast to the world a diatribe in which he alleged, *inter alia*, that the Belgian Army had

surrendered suddenly and unconditionally, in the midst of battle,* on the orders of its King, without warning its French and English fellow combatants, thus opening the road to Dunkirk to the German divisions . . .

Eighteen days ago, this King, who until then professed to attribute the same value to the word of Germany as to that of the Allies, made an appeal to us for help. We answered that appeal according to a plan which had been drawn up last December by the Allied staffs.

Now we are faced with the fact that, while the battle was raging, King Leopold III of Belgium, without warning General Blanchard, without a thought or word for the French and English soldiers who had answered his

---

* The phrase '*en rase campagne*' denotes utter shame and dishonour to the French. Indeed, when General Georges was questioned by the Parliamentary Investigating Committee about Premier Reynaud's subsequent attempt to persuade Generalissimo Weygand to surrender the whole French Army to the Germans *en rase campagne*, he declared that such a capitulation 'is infamous for the chief of an army . . . Article 234 of the Code of Military Justice punishes it with death and with military degradation.' He went on to recall the surrender by Marshal Bazaine of his army at Metz in 1870, for which he was sentenced to death. Yet Weygand and Georges incurred no blame or penalty for authorizing General Condé to surrender the 400,000 men of the 2nd, 3rd and 5th Armies, when they were encircled on June 22nd.

anguished appeal by coming to the help of his country – King Leopold has laid down his arms. This is an event unprecedented in history . . .

Reynaud then declared that 'the Belgian Government has informed me that the King's decision was taken against the unanimous feelings of the responsible Ministers, and that it has decided to place all the resources of its country at the disposal of the common cause . . .'

Shortly afterwards Paris Radio announced that Leopold had been deprived of his *Légion d'Honneur* by Government decree.*

At 6.00 that evening, in circumstances which will be described later, Pierlot, the Belgian Prime Minister, followed Reynaud's broadcast with one which was no less slanderous and untruthful:

> Setting aside the formal advice of the Government, the King has just opened negotiations and has begun treating with the enemy. Belgium will be stunned, but the fault of one man cannot be imputed to a whole nation. Our army has not deserved the fate to which it has been subjected . . .
>
> The King, breaking the ties which bind him to his people, has placed himself under the power of the invader. Hence he is no longer in a position to rule . . .

That Reynaud alone was responsible for spawning the black legend of Leopold's defection and treachery which spread throughout the world following the Belgian capitulation is beyond dispute. Had his broadcast not falsely accused Leopold of surrendering the Belgian Army 'suddenly, *en rase campagne*, without warning its French and English fellow-combatants' and 'without a thought or word' for them, the reputations of the King and his army would have remained of the highest. Indeed, if Reynaud had told the truth, which he knew, the acclaim and sympathy the free world had been heaping on them would undoubtedly have continued – if not increased. For, on the same morning that Reynaud publicly vilified them, the British and world press was full of praise for Leopold and his troops. In addition to the military communiqués quoted in Chapter 25, praising the Belgian Army for its gallant and prolonged resistance on the Lys in the face of overwhelming ground and air attacks, most British newspapers on May 28th carried a Reuter report of a radio broadcast from Paris at 7 pm the night before (repeated on the BBC) in which Leopold was eulogized by the Belgian Prime Minister.† After announcing that his government had just met on French soil and was

---

* After the fall of France the French Government formally reinstated King Leopold's *Légion d'Honneur* on General Weygand's insistence.
† Diligent research by a Belgian investigator, J. Verhaeghe of Belgian Radio and Television, has only recently established that this broadcast was made, at 7 pm on May 27th in French and Flemish, on the 1293 metre band of the Paris transmitter which had been allocated to Belgian Radio, and that it was monitored and rebroadcast by the BBC that evening.

'unanimous in affirming its will to continue the struggle whatever happens, at the side of the Allies', Pierlot's speech paid this handsome tribute to the King for his leadership of the Belgian nation and armed forces:

> For the Belgian people, amid the terrible trials which are afflicting them, one figure, towards whom all our thoughts turn, dominates: that of the King.
> More than ever he is the incarnation of the Nation. We are deeply grateful to him because he has made every possible effort to spare his country the horrors of war.
> Now we see him in a new role, that of a soldier. Worthy successor of the Soldier King, he has taken the place which that personage assumed twenty-five years ago. For many years he has been preparing himself for that role. The hard school of war was his initiation. At the age of sixteen he fought in the mud of the Yser as a private soldier, second class.
> The arduous life he has lived since then, the physical exertions of his mountain-climbing, have tempered his heart and spirit.
> Even when peace seemed assured, he never ceased to devote himself to strengthening the Army and representing it as the sole safeguard of the Nation's independence. When the hour struck, he placed himself at the head of his troops. For the last three weeks he has not left them. All those who have returned from the front have testified that Leopold III is a man and a leader. Notable among these are the veterans who knew his father.

There was no mention of Pierlot's broadcast tribute to his King in the French newspapers next day, because they had been forbidden to print it by the censor. But there was no British ban on its publication and it was given wide press coverage in Britain on May 28th. The *Daily Mirror*, for example, reported as follows:

KING LEOPOLD'S THREE WEEKS WITH HIS ARMY

King Leopold of the Belgians has not left his troops for three weeks.
M. Pierlot, Belgian Premier, in a broadcast last night, said: 'Leopold III is a man and a leader. In his grave trial one figure dominates all our thoughts – that of the King.
'We are grateful to him for having done everything to spare our country the horrors of war. Now he is among his soldiers as a worthy successor of his noble father, who twenty-five years ago was fulfilling the same duty.
'When danger loomed he put all his energies into strengthening the Army.' – Reuter.

However, the references to Leopold in the next issue of the *Daily Mirror* and in other British newspapers which appeared the day after Reynaud denounced the King and his army on the radio were of a very different nature. A few hours after Reynaud's broadcast Winston Churchill told Parliament that the Belgian Army had 'fought very bravely and both suffered and inflicted heavy losses' and advised against passing a hasty judgment on the action of the King of the Belgians. That evening, Duff Cooper, the Minister of Information, in a broadcast to the Nation, declared:

> Not ours to apportion the blame, but only to acclaim the heroes of the battles, who are not less heroic because their efforts were unsuccessful. The Belgian Army are unable any longer to continue. They have fought bravely, they have suffered heavily, they have yielded only before overwhelming odds. This is no time for criticism or recrimination . . . In this connection, beware . . . of one of the most insidious forms of German propaganda, which is to persuade us to put the blame on the French and to persuade the French to put the blame on us.

Yet next morning (the 29th) the *Daily Mirror* took the lead in rejecting the two Ministers' advice and in the virulence with which it pursued the campaign of hysterical abuse initiated in France by Reynaud the previous day. Indeed, the comments of this sensational left-wing tabloid far exceeded in scurrility those of any other British publication – and even outdid some French newspapers.

Alongside a caricature depicting Leopold as a snake wearing a crown surmounted by a swastika, the *Daily Mirror* ran a vitriolic leader headlined 'KING OF THE FIFTH COLUMN'.* After referring scornfully to Pierlot's broadcast description of the King as 'the incarnation of the Nation' and 'a man and a leader', it denounced him as 'a skunk' for ordering the surrender of the Belgian Army, and as 'the most distinguished and accomplished of all the Generals of the Fifth Column in any European country up to date'. It then declared that the broadcast which Pierlot had made, following Reynaud's, 'confirmed the treachery and denied that his government had any share in the former King's capitulation . . .' On another page of the *Daily Mirror*, under the headline 'I SHALL BETRAY', *Cassandra* wrote:

> Until yesterday, a Norwegian traitor by the name of Major Quisling held all the dirty records. This unsavoury reputation was apparently looked upon with covetous eyes by royalty, and finally proved to be irresistible to Leopold the Third, King of the Belgians. Quisling was hurled from the Throne of Traitors and a greater regal Judas took his place . . .
>
> Leopold, by his faithless and terrible act, has besmirched the reputation of his house and disgraced his father's splendid name. What would King Albert think of his son today, were he alive to witness this abominable desertion! . . .
>
> In the King's hour of peril when he was invaded, the Allies rushed to his aid. Those very soldiers who came to his rescue, he has cynically and brutally left to their fate. Stubbornly and indignantly this wretched monarch refused to discuss a military alliance with the Allies . . . a ghastly explanation unfolds as the significance of King Quisling's treachery becomes more and more apparent. It

* See page 475.

looks as if the pass was sold before the battle began . . . The indignant refusal of the King's Ministers to be party to his capitulation, adds weight to Leopold's direct responsibility for this cowardly decision. The Belgian Prime Minister himself has rejected the decree whereby the Belgian Army has laid down its arms . . . The stealth of the act whereby his emissaries were on their way to the German High Command, without one word being said to the Allied generals, who were, after all, his comrades, adds horror and disgust to this melancholy operation.

The shock of this collapse becomes more intense in view of the reputation which had been built up around this young King. He was physically handsome and conducted himself with a fine show of brave dignity. His courage was unquestioned and his integrity remote from the breath of suspicion. In a night all this vanished. And the hero stood revealed as the architect of one of the greatest pieces of desertion in history.

Cassandra then took the opportunity to fire some further shots in the venomous campaign waged throughout the war by the *Daily Mirror* against the civilian and military leadership of the Nation which caused the Government to threaten to suppress it.[W] After declaring that all the countries attacked by Hitler had been 'corroded and corrupted from within by a Fifth Column', he alleged:

> Such men are at work in England today. Wealth, Honour, Fame and Reputation must no longer be allowed to protect them . . . They may be in the House of Lords. They have been proved to be in the House of Commons. It is certain that they are in Finance. Unless we cleanse ourselves of this disease then Hitler has us where he wants us. Now is the time to act. Let there be no mercy or discrimination when so much is at stake.*

On that same day every newspaper in France and Great Britain, and many throughout the world, having accepted Reynaud's great lie and Pierlot's subsequent endorsement as the truth, condemned Leopold with varying degrees of vehemence and embellishment, for deserting the French and British soldiers who had rushed to his country's succour, without a word of warning to them. For example, under the headline 'LEOPOLD . . . ROYAL QUISLING?' the Conservative *Daily Graphic*'s *Candidus* roundly declared 'Leopold has laid down his arms and has covered his name in infamy to the last syllable of recorded time.'

Vernon Bartlett in the Liberal *News Chronicle* asked if Leopold should be 'added to the list' of traitors headed by Quisling, and 'become known as the unworthy son of a great father?' 'The Prime Minister urged that we should not at once pass judgment,' wrote Bartlett, but went on to allege that 'once more Hitler has won a victory by Fifth Column methods'; that

---

* On June 2nd the *Mirror's* sister paper, the *Sunday Pictorial*, declared: 'Then came the stab in the back. King Leopold, a traitor who had been virtually confined to his palace because of his Nazi sympathies when I stayed in Brussels a week before, surrendered his country, his army and his honour to the enemy. He thought he'd also surrendered the BEF.'

Leopold had shown 'scant sympathy for democratic methods', and that the Belgian Government had planned to demand his abdication 'if he hesitated to resist'. The same newspaper's leader declared: 'The British are a tolerant people, always anxious to make allowances, seldom harsh in their judgments. But King Leopold's surrender . . . is bound to seem to them an act of unparalleled betrayal.'

That morning in the right-wing *Daily Express* a William Hickey article entitled 'FROM KING TO PAWN' was concerned to contrast Leopold, who was described as 'pro-German', with his father:

> Albert was pro-French. He died in a peculiar mountaineering accident. Nazi agents were blamed: no evidence was published. Nazis were also blamed for the car-smash in which Leopold's wife, Astrid, was killed. It was said that they had tampered with the steering-wheel – a technique they had used in other notable bumpings-off.
> Leopold, discrediting these rumours, remained pro-German; after his wife's death spent all his holidays with his mother's relatives in Bavaria; showed great reluctance to visit Paris . . . Early in the war Leopold chose to stage his army manoeuvres near his French not his German frontier . . .

Among the very few newspapers which paid some heed to the advice given by Churchill, Keyes and Duff Cooper and were relatively restrained in their censure were the *Daily Telegraph* and *The Times*. The latter, after quoting verbatim Churchill's moderate statement to the House, and the 'bitter comment' made by 'M. Reynaud on the wireless . . . in biting phrases of cold contempt', commented in its leader:

> The strictures passed upon King Leopold by M. Reynaud and others yesterday were necessary, if only in justice to those who, despite the defection of their leader, are resolute to continue the fight.* There is, however, no reason to reject the plea for a suspension of final judgment until the full facts are known. This is certainly no time for useless recrimination . . .

The Times was almost alone in referring to the great fight put up by the Belgian Army, although its Military Correspondent's final conclusion was somewhat ambiguous:

> Recriminations help no one. All that is necessary is to note dispassionately that the Belgian Army fought admirably for a considerable period of time and that the Germans hurled themselves upon it with particular violence. If during the last few days its resistance weakened somewhat, the Army none the less gave a good account of itself; if shame there be it does not fall on the troops.

The *Daily Telegraph*'s strictures too, were relatively moderate, although its attempts to explain Leopold's decision to surrender (it

---

* A reference to the refugee Belgian Ministers in France.

accepted without question Reynaud's statement that he had given his allies no warning) had a certain unconscious irony:

> Though surrender was totally unexpected, diplomatic quarters knew that the King of the Belgians took up an uncooperative attitude shortly after the war began . . . Apparently, resentment had been rankling in his mind, coupled perhaps with an unworthy suspicion that he was about to be abandoned, and had better bargain his way out.

Such was the British press coverage of the Belgian surrender generated by Reynaud's and Pierlot's broadcasts. On this day too, the Earl of Derby was moved to declare at a meeting of the Liverpool Chamber of Commerce:

> King Leopold's cowardice – the son of a brave father – his utter disregard for the welfare of his country and for the safety of the Allies whom he called in to help him, shows him to be a mastermind of perfidy and treachery . . . This is very strong language, but I feel that through the treachery of one man, the lives of many who are dear to us are in danger.

Meanwhile, in the House of Lords the Government's statement on the Belgian capitulation was interrupted by Lord Marchwood (the former Deputy Chief Whip, Sir George Penny) exclaiming: 'Although we are asked to suspend judgment, I feel that history will say that the action of the King of the Belgians is that of a base, cowardly traitor.'

As Spurgeon observed, 'a lie has gone half-way round the world before truth has got its boots on'. Hence the *Capital* journal in Calcutta, as yet so remote from the war, announced next day:

> When the history of our times comes to be written, King Leopold's capitulation to Adolf Hitler will stand out as the supreme act of treachery in a long chapter of deceits, lies and corruption . . . He has been bought off, just as the Nazis in their long record of bribery and blackmail have purchased other men who named their price . . . No other explanation fits in with what has been definitely established; and this includes the hard, irrefutable fact that the Belgian Cabinet unanimously opposed the decision to lay down arms.

But many months would pass before even a breath of the truth could emerge, for the honourable men who knew it, and wanted to refute Reynaud's lies, were muzzled by the French and British governments, while the knowledge that Leopold, as a prisoner, was powerless to defend himself only emboldened his traducers to indulge in even greater excesses of scurrility. But before giving some examples of the calumnies which now proliferated *urbi et orbi*, the question of how one man was able to instigate such a torrent of poisonous abuse and turn, in the eyes of the world, a brave and much-admired soldier-King into a cowardly and treacherous Fifth Columnist must be examined.

Conditioned by highly-coloured, but largely false stories about the Fifth Column in Norway, Denmark, Holland and Belgium – and with the name Quisling constantly before their eyes – the public found Reynaud's denunciation of Leopold only too plausible. His evil words were swallowed hook, line and sinker, and fevered imagination embroidered upon the framework of calumny which he had created. The King could do no right. Everything he had ever done, and a great number of things he had never done, were twisted round and produced as 'evidence' against him. No one questioned for one moment the word of an Allied leader carrying all the weight and authority of the Prime Minister of France, particularly where it concerned the King of a small neutral state which had only joined the Allies under pressure of dire necessity. Public opinion had been kept carefully in the dark about the corruption and defeatism behind the façade of France's power: the morals of her politicians, the ineptitude of her military leaders and above all the magnitude of the military defeats she had sustained. Due to the soothing and reassuring tone of the Allies' communiqués, the public had no conception that France was nearing total collapse, that the three Allied armies in the north were encircled and trapped, with little hope of avoiding surrender, and that the BEF was in full flight, with the desperate attempt to rescue its personnel via Dunkirk already in progress.

When a crime is committed – and Reynaud had stooped to the particularly despicable crime of character assassination – it is usual to investigate the culprit's motives, opportunity and accomplices. It is only necessary to go back a few days to find ample evidence that Reynaud had all three. It will be recalled that on May 15th he had informed Churchill without equivocation that France was defeated. From then on, while publicly expressing his determination to fight on, he had been admitting privately, to General Spears and others, that he would shift the onus for negotiating France's surrender on to other shoulders, when that inescapable moment was reached. He had, moreover, set up Marshal Pétain as his Deputy for that very purpose.

On May 25th, after the War Committee had heard the Generalissimo's report on France's hopeless military situation and the President's proposal that the Government should examine Germany's peace terms before the total disintegration of the French armies, its members enjoined Reynaud to fly to London and ask if the British Government would release France from her undertaking not to make a separate peace with Germany. Next day the British Cabinet Ministers gathered from the French Premier that he regarded France's situation as 'hopeless' and that he saw 'no alternative' to her giving up the struggle.

Reynaud was now War Minister as well as Premier and therefore, like

Weygand, received the incoming stream of warnings that the Belgian Army's situation was critical and also the laudatory French reports on its desperate resistance to the 'overwhelming' attacks of the German Army and Air Force.* Weygand and Reynaud also received, on the 26th, via General Champon, Leopold's specific warning that 'the situation of the Belgian Army is extremly grave' and that 'the limits of resistance have very nearly been reached'. On that day too, Reynaud received an even more direct and specific warning that the capitulation of the Belgian Army was imminent – from Paul-Henri Spaak, who had begged a lift in the plane in which the French Premier flew back to Paris, after his fateful meeting with the British Cabinet in London. During the flight Spaak told Reynaud that the four Belgian Ministers had separated themselves from the King at Wynendaele on the previous day because the hard-pressed Belgian Army was about to be overwhelmed and forced to capitulate and that Leopold had decided to stay with his army and people.

Next morning (the 27th) at 10.05 am Weygand received Champon's message that the Belgian Army was on the point of disintegrating, and at 6.05 pm – ten hours before it capitulated – there arrived at Vincennes a telegram from 'Colonel Morel, North-East Front' reporting that Champon had telephoned to say: 'The King of the Belgians has sent an envoy to the German High Command to enquire under what conditions hostilities between the Belgian and German Armies might be concluded.' The message then said that Champon had informed the Belgian Chief of Staff that the discussion of these conditions ought to take place in the presence of qualified representatives of the three national armies, since they formed one *bloc*. Champon's message concluded by requesting that General Blanchard should be informed (he was unable to locate or contact him) and asking for orders.

Unlike Colonel Davy, who got one of his warning messages through to the War Office by telephone from La Panne, twenty minutes before the Belgian mission had left, Champon did not succeed in getting his signal through to Paris until after its departure. Weygand himself has described the 'unlikely and devious' means which had to be used to pass messages back and forth, due to the appalling deficiency of communications. Indeed, the only links he now had with the army commanders in the North were via the French Admiralty's wireless connection with Admiral

* After the War Colonel Thierry, who was in charge of the communications department of the French Prime Minister's secretariat, made the following statement to Professor Jacques Pirenne in Geneva:

'My service intercepted all the telephonic communications of King Leopold with General Blanchard . . . in which he informed him of the desperate situation of the Belgian Army and the imminence of its capitulation. These messages – transcripts or on gramophone records – were immediately transmitted to the Prime Minister and to the War Ministry. M. Paul Reynaud therefore knew, before he had made his announcement on May 28th, that it was not true that the King had capitulated without warning his allies.'

Abrial in Dunkirk, with whom Champon maintained a precarious and indirect contact by telephone, and 'sometimes even through the French Ambassador in London'.[265]

'The news came like a thunderclap, as nothing had enabled me to foresee such a decision, no warning, not a hint of it,'[266] wrote Weygand untruthfully in his memoirs, ten years later, with a pretence of surprise which is almost ludicrous in view of the many warnings he had received from the battlefront. Indeed, these had led him to inform the French Government two days earlier that *all three* of the encircled armies in the North were faced with imminent defeat and capitulation. Moreover, a few hours earlier, at his morning conference with Reynaud and Pétain, Weygand had declared, according to Baudouin, who was present: 'Not only do the English not attack, but they retreat, and the Belgians are giving way. How are we to avoid disaster?'[267]

Shortly after receiving Champon's message, Weygand hurried to Reynaud's office at the War Ministry. With the Premier he found the aged Marshal Pétain and General Spears. In his memoirs the latter throws a revealing light not only on the rottenness of the Third Republic, but also on the behaviour of its political and military leaders in its last calamitous days. In the chapter covering this particular day, Spears records his annoyance with Weygand for attributing 'the disaster in the North' to Gort's 'refusal to fight' and for speaking of 'English defection', and notes 'my suspicion that come what might, Weygand meant to place the blame for the present disaster on Britain had become a conviction'. In this the Generalissimo was fully supported by Reynaud and his ministerial colleagues, who – as Spears recalls – also kept harping on the theme that France's crumbling military situation was attributable to Gort's retreat from Arras towards the ports and the inadequacy of Great Britain's contribution in ground and air forces.

A few hours earlier Spears had found Reynaud 'pale, lacking in buoyancy, weary, dejected', as he described his discussions with the British Cabinet in London on the previous day. The Premier agreed that he had told the British Ministers that Paris could be taken any day by a Panzer column, and that France's military situation was 'desperately serious'. He had been further depressed, Spears learned, by the prospect of Italy entering the war and of the Belgian Army's capitulation, which Spaak had warned him was imminent. When Reynaud declared for the second time that although he would 'go on to the end, others, who held different views, might replace him and treat with the Germans', Spears was 'thoroughly alarmed' and reacted strongly. He told the Premier ·bluntly that the British were throwing all their resources into the struggle (he only learned two days later that the Dunkirk evacuation had been in full swing since the previous afternoon) – but that they would be unlikely to continue doing so, if they thought that Reynaud was going to hand over responsibility to those who intended to throw in the sponge. Indeed, he warned the Premier, that would be regarded as 'a roundabout way of betraying us as well as France'.[268]

Reynaud was clearly nearing the end of his tether and his morale can hardly have been improved by Spears' homily, for he knew that France's defeat was imminent and, since he had sworn not to give up, he would soon have to hand over the office of Prime Minister to Pétain – an act which the English general had told him would be regarded as a betrayal. So it was that, with this word ringing in his ears and despair about the future in his heart, Reynaud received from Weygand the news that Leopold had sent an envoy to the Germans.

The Premier's reaction to the Generalissimo's pronouncement was instantaneous. Here was a heaven-sent opportunity to shift the blame from himself and others who would be held responsible for France's defeat on to the Belgians, who were in any case of no further use to him except as scapegoats. Hitherto that role had been filled by the sixteen French generals (including the Commander-in-Chief) whom Reynaud had sacked and defamed, and then by *perfide Albion* for her 'desertion' and 'retreat towards the harbours'. Now, if the British could be persuaded to support his anti-Belgian line, this hatchet could be buried – for the time being at least – and the two Allies, instead of putting the blame on each other for their failures, could join together in heaping it all on to their smaller ally's army and King, who as prisoners of war, would be unable to defend themselves.

Accordingly, without a moment's hesitation and with a great show of astonishment and indignation, the man who had so recently sponsored France and Britain's plan to invade Belgium by armed force – and thus dishonour their guarantees to protect her inviolability – launched into a histrionic diatribe in which he castigated her King 'in a voice of fury' for his 'betrayal' and for capitulating 'without a word of warning'. 'There has never been such a betrayal in history,' Reynaud cried; 'to think that this is the man to whose succour we flew is unbelievable. It is monstrous, absolutely monstrous.'[269] Reynaud had been presented with the perfect scapegoat. From now on he would proceed mercilessly and unscrupulously to stigmatize the King as a traitor and deserter, thus inaugurating the legend that was to blacken Leopold's name for years to come.

In the course of the discussion which followed Weygand said that the King's 'act of desertion', as he described it in his reply to Champon, was 'a good thing, since we shall be able to lay the blame for defeat on the Belgians'. In his memoirs Reynaud refers to 'the insulting opinion' which the Generalissimo 'passed on the Belgian Army' on this occasion. (It was not until four years after the war that Weygand would make a partial *amende honorable* to a group of Belgian officers.)[x] The meeting then decided upon the wording of a signal to the Allied Commanders-in-Chief, and sent it off via the French Admiralty at 8 pm: 'The French and British Governments agree to instruct their Commander-in-Chief, General Blanchard and Lord Gort, to defend the honour of their flags by dissociating themselves entirely from the Belgian armistice.'

Later that evening Weygand reported to the emergency Council of Ministers which was assembled at the Elysée Palace. With complete disregard for the truth, the Generalissimo reiterated that he had received no warning of the Belgian cease-fire (which had not yet occurred) and claimed that it 'had destroyed all possibility of implementing his plan'. He added that it had greatly increased the likelihood of disaster for the French armies which he had foreshadowed at the War Committee on the 25th. He had, of course, long since called off the Weygand Plan, on the grounds that the British 'retreat to the harbours' had compelled him to do · so, although neither he nor Reynaud had yet been told that Operation Dynamo, the full-scale attempt to re-embark the BEF, had been under way since the previous afternoon.

It is thanks to the subsequent publication by the Germans of the French State papers, which they found in some abandoned railway wagons, that we know exactly what transpired at that evening's meeting of the French Cabinet. The official *procès verbal* thus describes the proceedings:

M. Frossard [the Minister of Information] suggested that the Belgian Government which had escaped to France should depose King Leopold.

M. Georges Mandel proposed even stronger action: 'The most effective reply to the King's capitulation is to mobilize the 400,000 Belgians who are capable of being mobilized. The Belgian Government must put them at our disposal.'

M. Paul Reynaud: 'But what power has the Belgian Government without the King's signature? It cannot even issue a decree! But there is the Belgian Congo, and I reserve the right to make that convertible currency!'

At one point Frossard declared: 'I am considering the repercussions of the Belgian capitulation on French public opinion . . . What can we do to avoid a collapse of French morale? We must provoke a psychological reaction.' To this Reynaud replied meaningfully 'I will broadcast at 8.30 tomorrow morning.' Here was his motive and his opportunity. It only remained for him to co-opt his accomplices.

Before launching his attack on the King and his army, Reynaud took care to obtain the endorsement of the refugee Belgian Ministers. Pierlot, Spaak and Denis (accompanied by Le Tellier, the Belgian Ambassador) were accordingly summoned before Reynaud, Pétain and Weygand, who greeted them stonily *comme des statues*. Here, 'as if in front of a tribunal',* the uneasy quartet were harangued by Reynaud in rancorous

* These phrases were used in a letter subsequently written on Spaak's behalf to Sir Roger Keyes. See page 463.

terms about the delinquency of Belgium's King and army. In the face of
this tirade Pierlot humbly promised that the Belgian Government would
fight on beside France and Britain. In fact the Belgian Council of
Ministers, knowing that their army's defeat was imminent, had so resolved earlier that day – and Pierlot's broadcast announcing the fact,
followed by his eulogistic references to the King's inspiring leadership,
had been made from Paris Radio less than an hour before. Although
General Denis protested tearfully at Reynaud's denigration of the Belgian Army and its Commander-in-Chief, in a remarkable volte-face
Pierlot declared (according to Paul Baudouin, who was an eyewitness)
that he was 'in complete disagreement with the King, who had betrayed
Belgium'.[270]

Later the softening-up process continued. In the early hours of the
morning Pierlot and Spaak were roused from their beds and carpeted at
Reynaud's private residence. Here, according to Spaak's account, the
French Premier told the Belgian Ministers that in a few hours he was
going to broadcast the news of the Belgian capitulation to the French
people 'in such terms that the security of the two million Belgian refugees
in France would be endangered'; that his speech would inevitably
'unleash popular fury' against them; that he could not answer for their
safety and the Belgian Government had better declare without delay
where it stood. 'What were we to do?' wrote Spaak, 'On foreign soil,
treated as guilty parties by its chief Minister, we were hardly in an
enviable situation.' Hardly enviable, but precisely what Leopold had
predicted for them if they sought refuge in France.

The Belgian Ministers had two courses open to them: either to stand up
to Reynaud and refuse to endorse his slanderous attack on their head of
state and army, or to submit abjectly in the face of this blend of bullying
and blackmail. Unfortunately, they instantly chose the latter course –
although Spaak claimed later that Pierlot did at least reject the French
Premier's demand that the Belgian Government should announce the
dethronement of the King and the adoption of the French Constitution.
After obtaining Reynaud's permission for Pierlot to speak on the radio
immediately after him, the two Ministers hurried back to the Belgian
Embassy. Here they prepared a speech in which they went even further
than Reynaud in destroying their Sovereign's honour and good name, for
they now pretended that they had been opposed to the actual capitulation
and that the King had acted in defiance of their advice.

Spaak has described how he dictated the statement to a boy scout at the
Belgian Embassy and said to him 'My dear boy, what I am going to dictate
to you is neither pretty nor cheering.' 'It was indeed not pretty,' writes
Spaak's biographer, 'for he could no more afford to be truthful than
Reynaud. There was too much at stake and the truth was too complex to
be serviceable for the purpose of regaining the esteem of public opinion.

And so he allowed it to be understood that he and his colleagues shared the general condemnation of the King's military capitulation, instead of defending the latter against the slurs cast upon his military honour, by explaining that capitulation had become inevitable and that the Ministers had only opposed his decision to stay with his troops.'[271] The first, and mildest, draft of the speech which Spaak and Pierlot prepared announced:

> The King has just opened negotiations with the enemy with a view to a cessation of hostilities. This decision has been taken contrary to the formal and unanimous advice of the Government. It does not bind the country, since the King cannot exercise any power without his Ministers. Belgium will learn of this disastrous news with stunned grief.

Reynaud had promised the Belgian Ministers that their broadcast would follow his. But just before eight o'clock he telephoned to say that Pierlot could not speak till midday. When Reynaud spoke on the wireless half an hour later, every phrase and every inflexion of his voice was designed to make his threat to arouse 'popular fury' against his Belgian ally come true. Without a word of praise for the Belgian Army's stubborn and sacrificial resistance, or sympathy for her subjugated people, Reynaud poured forth the vitriol of his invective against the Belgians. At one stroke he destroyed the immense prestige they had earned in the 1914–18 War and turned them into 'the polecats of the world', as Pierlot put it.

Reynaud not only reviled Leopold, but implied that the whole Belgian Army was dishonoured: 'We think of our soldiers – *they* can say that their honour remains unsullied . . . they have given thousands of examples of their heroism . . . our generals and our soldiers form a *bloc* in which the Nation has complete confidence and which will gain the admiration of the world.'

It was with this amalgam of lies, half-truths and distortions that Reynaud misrepresented the Belgian disaster to the world. The great lie was well on its way. In his memoirs Spaak declares that he listened to Reynaud's speech with more copious tears than he had shed since childhood, and that he felt an extraordinary sense of collective shame. But after Reynaud's broadcast he and Pierlot set about altering the text of the speech they had prepared so that it would not merely echo the vicious note which had just been struck but even outstrip Reynaud in the false charges they made against their King.

'The white lie,' writes Spaak's biographer, 'had to be made blacker still . . . Where the Frenchman had only denounced him – by implication and tone of voice – for having put down his arms, they now added the far graver charge that he was "treating with the enemy".'[272] Thus 'The King has just opened negotiations with the enemy, with a view to a cessation of hostilities' in the original draft became in the speech which Pierlot finally delivered 'Setting aside the formal advice of the Government, the King has just opened negotiations and has begun treating with the enemy.' That, in addition to ordering the cease-fire in opposition to his government, was now 'the deed which we deplore'. 'Belgium will learn of this disastrous news with stunned grief' became, 'Belgium will be stunned, but the fault of one man cannot be imputed to the whole nation. Our army has not deserved the fate to which it has been subjected.'

It was not until 6 pm that the French Premier finally allowed Pierlot to broadcast his speech, after several postponements during which Reynaud insisted upon amendments to make it even more unfavourable to the King. As delivered, it can have given Reynaud nothing but satisfaction – for it not only lent credence to his falsehoods and appeared to justify his own indictment of the King, but actually augmented it. In addition to accusing Leopold of having capitulated against his government's advice and treating with the enemy, Pierlot branded the King's alleged actions as illegal and unconstitutional. He then declared that since Leopold had 'placed himself under the power of the invader' he was 'no longer in a position to rule' and the Government therefore freed all Army officers, diplomats, government officials and civil servants from their oath of allegiance to the King. By denouncing his Sovereign and issuing this edict Pierlot aroused against himself and the other Ministers-in-exile the furious detestation not only of the Belgian population, but in particular of all loyal servants of the Crown, both civilian and military. A staff officer thus describes the scene at Belgian GQG when the news of Pierlot's edict came through:

> The Royal decision did not arouse the slightest criticism, indeed our loyalty to our Chief was only equalled by our admiration for him . . .
>
> An incredible and monstrous story was spreading from mouth to mouth: the French Radio had informed Belgian officers that the Pierlot government had released us from our oath of allegiance to the King.
>
> This latest outrage surpassed all the previous ones in heinousness; many officers expressed their anger and disgust openly . . . General Michiels, the Chief of the General Staff, assembled all the officers, and in a few words denounced the vile accusations of felony levelled against the Commander-in-Chief of the Army. In a hollow and choking voice he asked us to close our ranks round our Chief, the King, and to renew our oath of loyalty and obedience to him.
>
> All the officers present shouted with intense emotion and conviction: 'We swear it! Long live the King! Long live the King!' Many of us had difficulty in restraining our tears. The room vibrated with an indescribable exaltation.

Similar manifestations of allegiance to the King – and castigation of his traducers – took place throughout the Army. In Belgium, France and the Congo officers of all ranks refuted the accusations which had been made against the King and the Army; paid tribute to both for their brave and honourable conduct, and called upon their men to remain loyal to their Sovereign.

Because of the extreme prejudices which were aroused against the King of the Belgians and his army throughout the world, particularly in France and Britain, by Reynaud's slanders, one must look to their German opponents and to certain unbiased American, French and British observers for a just and impartial appraisal of the part they played during the eighteen days' campaign of May 1940. Most British accounts are infected by the splenetic fulminations against the Belgians and their King to which Pownall persistently gave vent. His diaries were not published until 1972, but Gort's *Despatches*, Winston Churchill's war memoirs and above all the *Official History*, were all written under his editorial influence. As a result, the unfair and inaccurate statements which pervade these publications have been perpetuated by the chain of unwary authors who have since repeated them – and each other – in their writings on the subject.

In contrast, the testimony of eyewitnesses such as Admiral Keyes and Colonel Davy has gone largely unheeded. In addition to Davy's reports, memoranda and recollections, from which extracts have been given, he wrote as follows to the Belgian General Nyssens in September 1949: 'Informed military opinion was very much impressed by the performance of the Belgian Army in 1940. Some had expected it to be engulfed in a week in the first German rush . . . There were few who expected of it as much as it gave. There were none at all who expected that all the nineteen divisions, of which six had only been raised a few months previously, would be used as though they were veteran formations.' Davy concluded by expressing his confidence, which would unfortunately prove misplaced, that when the *Official History* of the campaign came to be written, 'the Belgian Army will be given full credit for its very gallant performance'.

Amongst the handful of British historians who have taken the trouble to study such first-hand evidence and have done justice to the Belgians and their King – pointing out that without their prolonged resistance there could have been no deliverance for the BEF – are Sir Basil Liddell Hart and Dr Brian Bond, whose writings on the subject are models of accuracy and fairness.

Another important eye-witness – this time an American – was Lieutenant-Colonel Duncan Brown, the United States Military Attaché to Belgium, who made this statement after the battle was over:

The Belgian Army fought doggedly on successive retreat positions and at last found themselves completely cut off with their backs to the sea. Their artillery had fought with extreme brilliancy, their large units were well led. However, they were cut off and they had virtually no air power or anti-aircraft artillery protection against German air might. The Belgian King's capitulation on May 28th was the only thing that he could do. Those who say otherwise didn't see the fighting and they didn't see the German Air Force. I saw both.

Surprisingly some of the King's most fervent champions were Frenchmen, prominent among them a certain Captain Maupeou, commanding the French naval units operating at Ostend. On May 30th 1940 he wrote to his wife from London: 'Everywhere I am defending King Leopold, whose name is being foully dishonoured. His Ministers have no right to claim to represent Belgium better than him. I saw them at Ostend, terrified by the bombing, like deserters, while the King remained bravely in the battle-zone among his troops. It is untrue to say that he is a traitor. The situation was in any case desperate and through no fault of his. I implore everyone to wait before judging, and I believe people are paying some attention to what I've been saying. I've seen Admiral Keyes in London. He believes likewise, as also do all honest eyewitnesses who were on the spot . . .'

Another French officer who felt impelled to vindicate the courage and honour of Leopold and his soldiers was the gallant wartime Resistance leader and author, Colonel Rémy.* Indeed Rémy actually wrote *Le 18e Jour* in order to 'make public amends' to the King and the Belgian Army because of his sense of outrage, as a Frenchman, that the 'tissue of deliberate lies' and 'vile calumnies' which dishonoured them originated in France – from the lips of the head of her government. Rémy's book therefore provides not only a well-documented chronicle of events and a complete vindication of the King and his army, but a scathing indictment of Reynaud and his French and Belgian 'accomplices' who, by vilifying Leopold, 'turned French anger against a King whose loyalty to our country and Great Britain was never in doubt for a single instant.'[273]

Among the few writers in the English language who give a fair and accurate account of the Belgians' performance is the distinguished American historian Telford Taylor, whose comments on their 'most determined and well directed defence' and 'retreats skilfully carried out . . . despite a murderous rain of bombs', have already been quoted. In his final summing up he writes: 'The verdict on the Belgian Army must

---

* Other French authors whose books vindicate King Leopold and show up the falsity of Reynaud's accusations include Alfred Fabre-Luce: *Une Tragédie Royale*, Benoist-Méchin: *Soixante Jours qui énbranlèrent l'Occident* and Robert Aron: *Léopold III, ou le Choix Impossible*. (The author assisted M. Aron by providing him with information and documents, but tragically Aron died before completing his manuscript and checking with the author the material he had incorporated in it. As a result, the book unfortunately contains a number of inaccuracies and misapprehensions concerning the missions of Admiral Keyes and Dr Stein as well as other matters.)

certainly be "well done" . . . For eighteen days Leopold's army held out against the German tide, fighting gallantly long after the course of the larger battle had spelled Belgium's doom. If the quality of the Belgian performance had been duplicated in other lands, the German march of conquest might have been shorter.' Telford Taylor chides Lord Alanbrooke for the stream of derogatory references to the Belgian Army which he makes – without offering any supporting evidence – in *The Turn of the Tide* 'from which one would conclude that the Belgian staffs were totally incompetent and the troops wholly lacking in "fighting spirit".'[274]

In his excellent biography General Sir David Fraser describes Alanbrooke, for all his great qualities, as pessimistic and hypercritical. These characteristics were predominant during the pre-Dunkirk stage of the BEF's inauspicious sojourn on the Continent, when General Brooke was tired out and deeply depressed by the deficiencies of the BEF and its High Command, compounded by his lack of faith in the French and Belgians and by anxiety about his son, who was critically ill.

General Fraser is, however, more charitable than Alanbrooke and most other British soldiers in his references to the Belgian King and his army. Although he does not go as far as acknowledging that there could have been no escape for the BEF but for their courageous and prolonged resistance, he concedes that 'The Belgian Army was having a hard time, subject to bombing attacks without respite.' Fraser also points out that although the British Government ordered Gort to evacuate the BEF on May 26th, they did not inform the Belgians, and it is therefore 'churlish' and 'irrational' to criticize the King for capitulating on the 28th. He then comments:

> It is particularly churlish when we consider that as early as 20th May King Leopold, judging the strategic situation accurately and foreseeing the British dilemma of how to maintain contact with Allies on both flanks, explicitly stated that he did not feel that he could ask for any actions by the BEF to maintain contact with him which would prejudice their safety . . .[275]

In contrast to this partial and belated recognition of the Belgians' self-sacrificing contribution to the BEF's escape – the first by a British General after forty-two years* – the Germans were, as Telford Taylor recalls, 'most respectful' and lost no time in expressing their admiration

---

* In an interview with Barry O'Brien (the *Daily Telegraph*, September 30th 1983), shortly after the death of King Leopold, Lady Allenby revealed that her friend General Sir Otto Lund had always maintained that the King had helped to save the BEF by his personal warnings to Alanbrooke (in Lund's presence) and by prolonging the resistance of his army for as long as possible. Lund had therefore been 'furious' at the unjust accusations that Leopold had surrendered without warning and exposed the BEF's flank. Lady Allenby continued that she had been 'haunted for years' by this testimony, and the injustice which had been done to Leopold, but that General Lund had felt that 'it would not be correct' to make these facts public in defence of the King.

for the gallantry and fortitude of the Belgian troops. Indeed, Hitler himself was moved to declare: 'On the Western Front, due allowance being made, it was the Belgians who offered the fiercest resistance to the Germans and inflicted on them the heaviest losses.' He showed his admiration for the Belgian Army and Commander-in-Chief by ordering 'that they be given treatment worthy of the brave fighting soldiers they have proved to be'; and in a letter to Mussolini he wrote 'The Belgian soldier in general fought very bravely. At the outset his tenacity was astounding . . .' In a similar vein, General Westphal commented in *The German Army in the West*: 'It was astonishing to see that the Belgians fought with increasing tenacity the nearer the end approached.'

As far as the invading Sixth Army was concerned, von Reichenau affirmed that 'the hardest fighting in the first days was along the Albert Canal', while von Bock wrote in his war diary that 'the twenty-two Belgian divisions defended their country with great courage and tenacity, making good use of their numerous fortresses and fortifications . . .' Another enemy opinion (albeit unfair to the British) was expressed in the history of the German 18th Division, *Our Route to the Sea*: 'The Belgians, who covered the cowardly retreat of the English with extraordinary bravery . . . put up an obstinate resistance to our pursuit.' Finally, the distinguished German dissident, Ulrich von Hassell, quotes a friend as saying 'Amongst our adversaries the Belgians fought the best,' in a diary note.

The Germans were no less recognizant of the fighting qualities of the front-line British soldier, when he came under pressure; indeed Hitler declared in his letter to Mussolini that they had maintained the standards of the First World War, being 'very brave and tenacious in defence' (although he added that they were 'unskilful in attack and miserably commanded'). But as even Pownall had to admit in his *Diary*[276] 'We have not had to bear the same weight of attack that was brought to bear on others.'* That these British troops would have another chance to demonstrate their fighting qualities to the Germans, was, however, in large measure due to the cover afforded to their escape by the Belgian Army, under what Admiral Keyes described as 'King Leopold's inspiring leadership'.

Although the British military establishment has never publicly acknowledged that King Leopold and his army, by their prolonged resistance, saved the BEF, a Commonwealth general who attended a course for senior army officers in England after the war has revealed that the official doctrine was that the Belgians' brave stand against overwhelming odds had prevented the whole nucleus of the British Army from being cut off

---

* The Diary's Editor notes: 'This was very true and should have caused the diarist to be more charitable in his comments on the Belgians and the French First Army.'

from the coast, thereby enabling it to escape and 'live to fight another day'. But the world-famous military expert Liddell Hart saw no reason for such reticence as far as the public was concerned and, as *The Times* reported on November 10th 1960, delivered a lecture at King's College, London in which he bluntly declared that 'The British Army at Dunkirk was saved from destruction by King Leopold of the Belgians'. The report continued: 'Captain Liddell Hart said that Sir Arthur Bryant's claim that the saving of the British Army was mainly due to Lord Alanbrooke did not stand up to examination. One saving factor was that von Rundstedt temporarily halted the German Panzer forces on the canal line just short of Dunkirk, and that Hitler converted this halt into a three-day stop. Another was that "the unfortunate Belgian Army" absorbed the weight of the German frontal attack from the North. By the time the Belgian front was turned the British had slipped out of reach and were nearing shelter at Dunkirk. The pressure and danger on Alanbrooke's front was "never so great as he imagined". But if King Leopold had left Belgium on May 25th 1940, as his Ministers and Mr Churchill urged, the Belgian Army would probably have surrendered immediately, instead of fighting on until late on May 27th. If so, the British would have had very little chance of escaping encirclement, so that it could very reasonably be claimed that they were saved by King Leopold, who was then violently abused in Britain and France.'

CHAPTER TWENTY-EIGHT

The Scapegoat

'Let us . . . our sins lay on the King!'
William Shakespeare, *Henry V*

Meanwhile in Paris, in order to round off his character assassination of the Sovereign who had modelled himself so closely on his father, Pierlot led a group of Belgian Ministers and Members of Parliament to the statue of King Albert in the Place de la Concorde. Here in front of the monument, which had been draped in black for the occasion, in the presence of the world press and a large crowd, they indulged in a 'ceremony of expiation' amid cries of 'coward' and 'traitor', while Pierlot laid a wreath at its base. Next, with the object of bringing Belgium's diplomatic and consular representatives throughout the world into line with the Belgian Government's anti-King policy, Spaak sent out from his Foreign Ministry a series of telegrams presenting an *ex parte* account of the breach between the King and his government, alleging *inter alia* that he intended to play a political role in the invaded country.

Although Pierlot's broadcast caused the free world's reprobation to be deflected from his government on to the head of the King, its effect was counter-productive in Belgium itself, where Leopold was revered as a hero and where the great majority of the population remained. Indeed, when the Belgian people heard Pierlot's philippic following Reynaud's broadcast, a storm of horrified indignation burst throughout the country and in their eyes the absentee Ministers now appeared as 'cowards', 'traitors' and 'deserters'. As Pierlot and his colleagues soon learned, by his vilification of their Sovereign he had aroused amongst their fellow countrymen in Belgium even greater hatred than had Reynaud.

'The conviction was practically universal,' wrote Paul Struye in his excellent chronicle of the occupation, 'that the capitulation was both inevitable and wise . . . M. Pierlot reached the summit of unpopularity. Never in our history of violent party struggle was a statesman so detested by the great majority of his fellow countrymen.'[277] As Spaak recalls, the absentee Ministers' unpopularity in their occupied homeland was forcefully brought home to them a few days later, when the first of their compatriots to arrive from Belgium, a Red Cross official by the name of Pelgrims de Grand-Bigand, told them: 'You must have no illusions,

Belgium in its entirety is behind the King, you are detested – or, to use a rather coarse expression, you are spewed out [*vous êtes vomis*]. They consider that you have acted in an atrocious manner.'[278] In contrast, as Jean Stengers recalls: 'The popularity of Leopold III was immense. For many it amounted to idolatry. Everyone was grateful to him for having put an end to a massacre which had become purposeless, they admired him for having shared the fate of his soldiers. And since he had suffered outrages which were considered utterly vile, they were deeply in sympathy with him.'[279] And Paul Struye adds: 'Virtually the entire country rallied round the King. This was a manifestation of a spontaneity, unanimity and fervour which is quite exceptional in our history. Without doubt there has never been such an exaltation of dynastic loyalty.'

The prisoner at Laeken was greatly heartened by the evidence that his people were united as never before in their loyalty to their King, which poured into his prison Palace in an ever-increasing flood of messages of devotion and support – accompanied by an avalanche of flowers. But far from feeling bitter, Leopold was thinking in terms of dissipating misunderstandings and healing the breach with those who had deserted, disowned and denounced him.

When the American Ambassador, John Cudahy, visited the King at Laeken on May 30th, he recalls that although grief-stricken by the brutal devastation of his country, and the suffering of his people, 'there was about his demeanour no hint of weakness. His eyes held the same unwavering honesty, and unchanged was his erect military bearing, which would always distinguish him as a soldier. At length and in full detail he spoke about the *débâcle* which had brought such disaster upon his country. Without a trace of bitterness he mentioned his hostile critics and their condemnation as if, with the wages of war, calumny was to be expected.'[280] Another who noted the King's Christian attitude towards his traducers during this tragic period was the Baroness Carton de Wiart, one of the Queen Mother's Ladies-in-Waiting. After the war the Baroness told the author that when she was walking in the park at Laeken with the King soon after the commencement of his captivity she remarked that he must be furious with the Ministers who had fled to France and turned against him. Yet the King replied 'No, I am not angry with my Ministers – indeed I only wish that they were in Belgium, to defend themselves against the far worse accusations which are being made against them here.'

Shortly after the capitulation the Belgian Primate issued an important pastoral letter and ordered that it be read in all Belgian churches. It had a most beneficial effect on public opinion both in Belgium and in other countries where it received publicity, although these did not include France or Britain, where it was suppressed by the censorship, or in the USA, where it was ignored.

Our Very Dear Brothers,

The tragic trial through which we are going is being aggravated in the extreme by the very painful accusations formulated in Paris against His Majesty King Leopold III. These have greatly shocked the majority of the Belgian people.

In order to dissipate, if possible, the unfortunate misunderstanding and to give, from a direct source, the clarification necessary, we deemed it our duty to call upon the Sovereign in person. The King has given us permission to make public the following statements:

1 The decision which he had to take, on the morning of May 28th, to lay down the arms of the Belgian Army was imposed upon him by a situation that had already become absolutely untenable. Irremediably surrounded, without hope of effective aid from the Allies, our troops, if they had continued the fight, would have been exposing themselves to complete annihilation, without any military advantage, dragging to their fate hundreds of thousands of civilians crowded into a tiny stretch of territory.

2 This decision of an essential military order was taken by the King as Supreme Chief of the Army, in full accord with his Chief of Staff and following his advice. He has not performed any political act nor has he concluded any treaty or pact – even of a military nature – with the enemy. He acted because, as has been corroborated by the unanimous judgment of three eminent Belgian jurists, he was convinced that he had the right to do so by virtue of the powers that the Constitution confers on the King in this matter.

3 It is contrary to the truth to affirm that the High Commands of the Allied Forces had not been made aware of the necessity of ceasing hostilities. The odious accusation of felony is, therefore, false . . .

For our part, knowing that our sentiments are in accord with those of the almost unanimous mass of the Belgian people, we vouchsafe to our King our respect, our loyalty and our trust. We ask our priests to continue reciting the liturgical prayers prescribed for the King . . .

We wish that all Belgians, aware of the gravity of the hour, remain united and firm behind the King, the supreme personification of our Motherland in danger . . . More than ever, let us confide ourselves to the infinite mercy of the Sacred Heart of Jesus, and let us say with the Psalmist: 'For though I should walk in the midst of the shadow of death I will fear no evil, for Thou art with me.'

In sorry contrast to these manifestations of the Belgian people's fidelity were the statements and actions of Pierlot and Spaak. While the King, incarcerated at Laeken 'under the power of the invader', was acting with meticulous propriety and refusing to take any compromising steps, in Paris the pair pursued their campaign of denigration. To explain this as the result of shock and confusion would be charitable but wrong, for it was unsupported by a single shred of evidence. It followed from the realization, provoked by panic on the night of May 27th, that submission to the demands of the French Premier represented their softest option.

All the two Belgian Ministers' acts and statements were now aimed at ingratiating themselves with the French and diverting the fury roused by Reynaud from themselves on to the head of one who was unable to defend himself or reply to their charges. The honour of their King had become expendable. Some months later, Spaak would try to justify their conduct in throwing Leopold to the wolves by claiming that 'the Government's statement avoided a disaster' and that it had earned Pierlot 'the gratitude of countless Belgians who had felt the menace of [French] concentration camps, and perhaps still worse, hanging over them.' But, ironically, the Ministers' abject submission to the French Premier did little to mitigate the hysterical outbursts of vituperation and violence against '*les sales Belges*' which his broadcast had incited, for by endorsing and adding to his false charges they had increased its credibility and effect. Indeed, the persecution of the vast throng of pitiful Belgian refugees in France continued virtually unabated. These helpless people were evicted from their accommodation, stoned, bullied, jeered at, spat upon and molested, while their cars and often their other possessions were taken from them. A number of Belgian airmen were manacled and flung into jail, while the 200,000 young men of military age who had been sent to France for training were confined to barracks and treated like concentration-camp prisoners.

In spite of chaotic wartime conditions, communication by various means still existed between France and Belgium. Above all there was the radio, particularly that of the Vatican and neutral countries such as Switzerland and Sweden, which broadcast news and bulletins from both the belligerents' camps. Consequently, the captive King and his people rapidly became aware of the defamatory line which was being taken by their government-in-exile, while the latter in turn could, if they cared to do so, receive the latest news of developments in Belgium both from neutral and enemy sources. The German radio bulletins, for example, which were widely disseminated, had announced in laudatory terms that the Belgian Army had laid down its arms in honourable surrender after fighting gallantly against greatly superior forces; that the Führer had decreed that they should be treated accordingly, and that their Royal Commander-in-Chief should be incarcerated at Laeken. There was no mention of the King parleying with his country's conquerors.

But in their eagerness to appease the French and justify the black legend they had helped Reynaud to create, Pierlot and Spaak turned deaf ears to the growing evidence that the charges they had made against the King were false and set about reinforcing them in the slanted interviews they gave to the press. 'The Ministers,' writes Spaak's biographer, 'were carried irresistibly forward from insinuation to half-truth, from half-truth to untruth, from untruth to insult.'[281] Although Spaak would admit six weeks later that the Belgian Government 'had not opposed the surrender of the Army, which had become inevitable', he declared in an interview granted to the American United Press Agency two days after the capitulation, that the military situation had not justified it and 'for this reason we did not agree with the idea of capitulating, nor could the Cabinet remain any longer at Wynendaele, as it would have made it appear that the surrender had our full support'. By thus perverting one truth, however, Spaak unwittingly laid bare another – that the four Belgian Ministers' main motive for separating themselves from the King had been to avoid being held responsible 'in the eyes of history', as Pierlot had said at Wynendaele, for making the inescapable decision to capitulate.

In other statements to the press Spaak declared that 'the King had submitted to the pro-German influence of General Van Overstraeten, a veritable *éminence grise*', and much else of a disloyal and defamatory nature. This appears to have inspired a Belgian journalist living in Paris to write in *Le Journal* next day that Leopold was 'a coward' (*un lâche*), who was guilty of 'organized felony' and 'treason', and to indict Henri De Man as 'the King's accomplice' together with General Van Overstraeten, 'another traitor'.

This eagerness on the part of the Belgian Ministers to gain the widest possible publicity for their version of events, in which they appeared as the heroes and the King as the villain, resulted in the official French news agency *Havas* obligingly publishing just such an account. Since it was attributed to 'Belgian political sources' and described proceedings at which only the King and his four remaining Ministers were present, it clearly emanated from the latter and was accepted as a factual statement made by the Government of Belgium, backed by that of France. It therefore provided an apparently authentic source from which publicists throughout the world derived and embellished even more scurrilous stories about the King.

The *Havas* despatch began by declaring that 'the treason of the King must not be considered only from the military aspect. One is faced with a pre-meditated felony.' It then stated that for years Leopold had pursued 'a very personal policy . . . through his Ministers, whom he deceived'. It further declared that the King had 'forbidden his Ministers to go abroad and especially to France, to prevent at all costs personal contacts from being made . . .' *Havas* then asserted that 'to suppress public opinion which in Belgium was favourable to the Allies King Leopold tried to impose censorship on the press'. The King was also accused of having refused his Ministers' requests that he should 'denounce the invader' in Parliament, as King Albert had done in 1914, or 'even contact the Government' on May 10th.

There then followed a highly distorted version of Spaak's and Pierlot's accounts of their relations with the King during the eighteen days' campaign. According to this, Leopold's object in trying to keep the Government and 'all the representatives of moral and economic forces' in

Belgium was to 'lay them open to being taken by the enemy'. After declaring that the Ministers had pressed the King to 'leave with them if the necessity arose' and 'reproached him for not following General Weygand's orders', the despatch quotes the King as having said that the Army was too tired to do so and the Ministers as having replied that 'the King's information was incorrect – the Army's morale and fighting ability being excellent'. General Denis was then said to have told the King that 'capitulation *en rase campagne* was absolutely contrary to military regulations' and that by breaking them he would disgrace Belgium.

The despatch then declared: 'The Prime Minister made a last effort to try to stop the King from capitulating. The King replied that he was determined to make peace in order to retain a certain measure of independence. In a last attempt, M. Pierlot warned the King that he was going to violate the Constitution which he had sworn to observe. With great difficulty the Ministers then managed to reach England.' The Belgian Government's receipt in Paris on May 26th of the King's request for blank forms signed by a Minister is then described and 'an important Belgian political figure' is quoted as saying that 'this was another act of deceit before the final felony'. Finally, the King is said to have given his army the order to cease fire 'with the complete agreement of his accomplices, General Van Overstraeten and M. Henri De Man'.

With the sponsorship by the two governments, the calumnies proliferated. Accusations of the foulest kind were hurled at the scapegoat from every quarter of the globe. Not surprisingly, the French media took the lead. Leopold was not only denounced as a coward, a traitor, a felon, a Fascist and Fifth Columnist, but reviled as a libertine and accused of having caused the deaths of his father and his wife.

Just how successful the Belgian Ministers were at exculpating themselves at the expense of their King is shown by an article in *L'Action Française* in which Léon Daudet wrote 'Nothing could equal either in horror or splendour the firm words of M. Pierlot, announcing to the whole world by radio, an act of insane ignominy commited by the felon son of the Roi Chevalier.' In another edition this newspaper declared 'When the Belgians have judged, condemned and executed this deserter, the Monarchy will regain all its virtue.'

Not to be outdone, a group of nineteen Belgian journalists and editors who had fled to France – one of whom was appropriately named Hasty – issued an *ordre de jour*: 'King Leopold has betrayed his country . . . By capitulating he has blotted out the noble page which King Albert, his father, wrote in our history. Murdered Belgium today feels covered with shame, but she cannot accept the disgrace which has been brought upon her by a traitor. She hopes that France will not judge her in the same light as a felon King . . . The King is dead. Long live Belgium.' Another manifesto was published by three left-wing professors from Brussels universities who were in Paris, denouncing 'the abominable treason of ex-King Leopold III . . . the despicable son of Albert I'. Even Maeterlinck, one of Belgium's foremost writers, who had eulogized King Albert in verse during the Great War, published a signed statement in *Marianne*, 'the weekly for the intellectual élite'. This appeared beneath a cartoon parodying a famous Goya painting, depicting Leopold on the scaffold, emblazoned with a swastika and with a garrotte round his neck. Having echoed Reynaud's allegation that 'the treason was unprecedented in history', Maeterlinck attributed this act to Leopold's German blood and, after denouncing its 'stupidity and baseness', declared that 'the name of Judas is too good for its perpetrator'. He ended by paying a tribute to 'the Belgian Government which by its attitude has saved the honour of our Belgium'.

In Britain too the anti-Leopold witch-hunt, which had started in the press on May 29th, was now in full cry. 'The foul desertion' of 'Leopold the Renegade' had been due to his 'Hohenzollern blood'; he was under the sinister influence of his Wittelsbach mother or his 'fascist sister', the Italian Crown Princess, herself promoted by Mussolini. He had had 'a German mistress planted on him by the Gestapo'. The 'thirty pieces of silver' with which the Führer intended to reward this 'Royal Judas Iscariot' was 'the crown of a combined Holland, Belgium and Luxembourg'. Léon Degrelle, the Rexist leader, was described as Leopold's best friend and accomplice. No parents, one journalist wrote, 'would christen their son Leopold for the next two hundred years'. Cartoons showed Leopold stabbing John Bull in the back or leading Hitler to the Channel: 'Sorry Sir, this is as far as I can guide you, Sir.' The vision of an agonized Astrid appeared to no less than four London spiritualists. But was the guilty man real? One ingenious illustrated paper stated, with photographic support, that when Astrid died in 1935 her husband had perished with her and been replaced by a likeness called Gustav Oldendorff. 'This plan was worked by Hitler himself, and has been applied to other Kings, Generals and statesmen.' The old men joined in. Lloyd George wrote that 'you can rummage in vain through the black annals of the most reprobate Kings of the earth to find a blacker and more squalid sample of perfidy and poltroonery'. And H. G. Wells announced 'If he is guilty he should die. What is one life to the sweetening of the world by such an execution!'

At the forefront of the muck-rakers was, surprisingly, the well-known British journalist Alexander Werth, who would pursue his vendetta against Leopold in the columns of the highbrow leftist media well into the nineteen-fifties. On May 28th 1940 Werth wrote: 'God, I always thought Leopold a bad egg, pro-Nazi, pro-Degrelle, pro-Mussolini, and he did a lot of dirty work during the Abyssinian business . . . The BEF people say he has a German mistress provided by the Gestapo – I heard them say so long ago . . . Well I suppose he'll be back in his Royal palace complete with German girl-friend, etc. . . .'[282]

But of all the manifestations to which Reynaud's broadcast gave rise, one of the most obnoxious was Dennis Wheatley's novel *The Black Baroness*. Into this fictional tale of the adventures of his Secret Service hero, Gregory Sallust, he put a number of real-life characters, including Leopold, and stirred in all the ingredients he had culled from the most slanderous outpourings concerning him. Putting copious 'appropriate' dialogue into the King's mouth, he portrayed him as a craven-hearted, hysterical, Hitler-loving weakling, ensnared by the voluptuous Black Baroness, who has been planted on him by the Gestapo, while his mother, Queen Elisabeth, is described by one of the characters as 'a rabid pro-Nazi'.[y]

As we have seen, within a few hours of Pierlot's public accusation that the King had treated with the enemy, Leopold had disproved that charge. Following his consultation with Albert Devèze, the three eminent jurists had declared that 'the dramatic error of accusing the King of having treated with the enemy and thus having violated his oath, should be corrected by all possible means and without delay. We feel in all conscience that in the interests of the Nation . . . the truth should be established and the prestige of the King fully restored.'

As his visitors had observed, Leopold, although deeply grieved and distressed, felt no bitterness or animosity towards his errant Ministers. He thought in terms of misunderstandings to be cleared up, and a breach to be healed, rather than a dividing rift. Thus, in order to apprise the refugee Government of the true facts and of the support which he had received, not only from the people of Belgium, but also from the highest authorities of the Law, the Army and the Church, the King sent his Chef de Cabinet, Louis Frédéricq, accompanied by his Aide de Camp, Colonel Van Caubergh, to Switzerland. They were provided with a comprehensive dossier of documentary evidence designed to establish that the King had not capitulated prematurely or without warning his allies; nor had he treated with the enemy, as had been falsely alleged, and that as a prisoner of war he could not reign, but bequeathed his powers to the Government as the sole representatives of Belgium. The documents included, *inter alia*, the Chief of Staff's Report on the campaign, all the King's Orders of the Day, and the full text of the findings of the jurists.

The King naturally felt that when his Ministers learned the truth, the breach between them could be healed. Moreover, if they published these facts to the world, as would be proper, some of the damage which had been done to the reputations of himself, his army and the Nation might be repaired.

Frédéricq was unable to enter France to deliver the dossier to the Ministers in person, as he had no visa. He was, however, able to arrange for Vicomte Berryer, the Counsellor at the Belgian Embassy in Paris, who had a visa for Switzerland, to come to Berne and meet him at the Belgian Legation. Here on June 2nd in the presence of the Belgian Minister, Comte Louis d'Ursel, the Royal emissaries had a meeting with Berryer at which they gave him a detailed briefing and the file of documents to be handed to the *émigré* Ministers in France.

Considering the terrible injury which Pierlot, Spaak and other members of the Government and Parliament had done to the King, his forbearance was quite remarkable. Indeed Frédéricq began by telling Berryer: 'The King has no intention of entering into conflict with the Government. His attitude is more dignified, he will not reply to an injury with an injury. The King appreciates the difficult situation which was created for the Belgians in France by Paul Reynaud's accusations.'[283] The Chef de Cabinet then affirmed, according to Berryer's account of this meeting, that 'the King recognizes the legality of the Government and is morally at its side against the invader'. Frédéricq further declared that the King accepted and would strictly adhere to the ruling of the three jurists: that while he remained a prisoner of war he was '*dans l'impossibilité de régner*', under Article 82 of the Constitution, and that he would not engage in any regal or political activity whatsoever while he was in captivity and the country remained under enemy occupation.[284]

Under Berryer's questioning, Frédéricq laid particular stress on the falsity of the accusation that the King 'was treating with the enemy', which Pierlot had made in his broadcast from Paris on May 28th. The Chef de Cabinet also explained that the King had only asked for a ministerial counter-signature on a blank form in case he was subsequently required to perform some unforeseen act 'for the benefit of Belgium' in the absence of all his Ministers, and not with the object of forming a new government under the occupation.

Having satisfied himself as to the true position and intentions of the King, Vicomte Berryer immediately despatched a coded message to the Ministers in France giving them full details of the information and documents which he had received from the Chef de Cabinet and informing them of the King's desire to end the *malentendu tragique* which was dividing the Belgians at home from those abroad. The Vicomte then returned post-haste to France to report to the Belgian Government. Before he could arrive, however, a lamentable sequence of events had carried Pierlot and Spaak into even deeper waters. Grave damage had already been done by the seditious acts and pronouncements which they had perpetrated, since taking leave of the King at Wynendaele. 'It was not until a full week had passed, however,' writes Spaak's biographer, 'that the final damage was done and direct public insult was added to the heavy injury already caused to the King's honour by the half-truths and untruths his Ministers had allowed to fall from their lips.'[285]

On Saturday May 31st a session of both Chambers of the Belgian Parliament was convened in the Town Hall at Limoges, 120 miles north-east of Bordeaux. Such was the indignation and hostility aroused by Pierlot and Spaak amongst the Belgian parliamentarians in France against the King that many of them – particularly those on the Left, with their innate Republicanism – were crying out for his deposition or even his execution and for the complete abolition of the Monarchy in favour of a Republic. The whole idea of such a session was most unwelcome to Pierlot and his Ministers – but, because they were afraid it might get out of hand without them, 'The Government felt,' as Spaak mellifluously observed, 'that it would be imprudent not to be present.'

No better method could have been chosen for demonstrating to the French that Belgium's politicians collectively endorsed Reynaud's condemnation of their King. It was not a full assembly, since only 72 Senators attended out of a possible 167 and 114 Deputies out of 202, but their numbers were large enough to create the effect of an impressive solidarity. When the Belgian Ministers arrived in Limoges from Poitiers, to which they had recently moved their government-in-exile, they were greeted by a large crowd and shouts of 'Long live the Belgian Republic' and 'Long live Pierlot'. 'At the cost of traducing their King,' observes J. H. Huizinga in *Mr Europe*, 'they had become popular heroes.'[286]

The tone was established at the outset by the left-wing Mayor of Limoges, who headed a reception committee of local dignitaries and made a speech of welcome. This was a mixture of abuse for the King and praise for the exiled Belgian Government. The Mayor passionately denounced Leopold as 'a traitor not only to his allies but to his people,' and spoke of 'the French conscience, disgusted by the King's felonies'. There were no protests from the Belgian politicians present nor, more significantly, from their Prime Minister. Indeed, they applauded the Frenchman and Pierlot made a speech in reply thanking the municipality for their welcome. The President of the Belgian Chamber, who three weeks earlier had assured Leopold of his Parliament's 'indefectible fidelity', did likewise; and echoing the Mayor's denunciation of the King, said that 'he had violated the concepts of military honour'.

The proceedings began with Spaak being called upon to tell the assembly what had happened since Parliament had last met in Brussels on May 10th. As his biographer observes, it might have been expected that Spaak would use this opportunity to tone down the accusations he and Pierlot had made in public 'for reasons of state', since a week had passed without any reports coming in that the King had actually done any of the things of which they had accused him. 'In fact,' Huizinga recalls, 'Spaak did the contrary. He added insult to injury . . . this was no carefully prepared speech, no calm recollection and judgment of recent events . . . but an improvised account spoken without notes, in the telling of which the speaker relived all the emotions of the dramatic period . . . to the point of being carried away by them.'[287] Spaak's prolonged and rambling discourse did him little good at the time and less afterwards. Highly wrought, emotional, confused, inconsequential, he tried to provide his audience with a blow-by-blow account of the relations between Leopold and his government during the events leading up to capitulation, which by throwing all blame on the King would win for the Ministers the assembly's endorsement of their actions. 'We have lived through ten such terrible and sad days,' Spaak began, 'harrowed by such anxieties, with the horror of seeing the gradual dawning of political ideas and resolves so insensate that we have, I believe, exhausted every possible emotion and feeling of indignation.' As Spaak worked himself up to what was neither his first nor his last exercise in mob oratory, he was frequently interrupted from the floor of the Chamber.

Spaak's subsequent statements show that he came to regret his ill-considered utterances, although he would never retract or apologize for them. Instead, both he and Pierlot would later behave as though they had never denounced their Sovereign or cast a single aspersion against his conduct and moral character. Indeed, they would even claim that they had from the first defended the King and protested at 'these odious accusations', as Pierlot later described them. 'The members of the Government,' wrote Spaak only six weeks later, 'never thought and never said that the King had been guilty of betrayal; on the contrary, they vigorously combated this absurd and insulting thesis.' And in February 1941 Spaak wrote to a correspondent in Lisbon: 'We collaborated in every possible way in the Sovereign's defence . . . Most certainly a grave injustice was committed in France and even in England . . . They sought and found someone to blame.'

The *procès-verbal*[288] of the assembly, however, reveals that at Limoges Spaak twice accused the King of having committed treason – 'a word', he said, 'that burns my lips and sticks in my throat' – although he charitably conceded that 'those who held that this treason had been long meditated were wrong.' Spaak also spoke of 'the collapse of all moral sense' in the King; of 'the insults' they had flung in his face; of the 'horrible words dishonour, desertion and betrayal they had used in the very presence of he who was about to accomplish this act'. Spaak then declared that the four Ministers had considered the King's arguments 'mad, stupid, criminal', had told him that he would be 'dishonoured and a traitor' if he abandoned the Allied cause, and that they had found themselves faced with a case of 'physical and moral deficiency'. He even said derisively that the King was 'no general'. As to their last meeting at Wynendaele (where he himself was in a state of emotional collapse), Spaak described the King as 'dishevelled, haggard, his eyes full of tears, his jaw set.' Soon Spaak was denouncing the King for predicting 'with a perspicacity which now seems horrible' the actual course of the battle and for obeying too precisely the French Supreme Commander, under whose orders the Belgians, like the British, had promised to operate.

By their interjections the other Ministers present supported Spaak's account. Since members of the Government were the only ones with first-hand knowledge, it is not surprising that the Senators and Deputies believed they were hearing the truth and readily endorsed the Government's acts. Nor is it surprising that when the real truth became evident they sought, in large numbers, in shame and embarrassment, to convey to their Sovereign their apologies and affirmations of loyalty and devotion.

The temperature of the debate rose rapidly. After an uncontested acceptance of the view that the King was unable (and, many, including Spaak, claimed, morally unfit) to reign, there was much heated discussion, amid cat-calls and jeering interruptions, about the appropriate procedural steps to take. 'Forfeiture of the crown' was a suggestion fervidly supported. The Marxist extremists, including Max Buset* and Arthur Gailly, were more explicit. 'Let him be executed!' (The record shows 'Hear, hear!' from parts of the audience.) A number of responsible speeches, including one by the oldest parliamentarian present, Comte Carton de Wiart, scarcely affected the general mood of hysteria, though Pierlot, who avoided being carried away, did persuade the meeting that it lacked the legal right to remove the King's crown; indeed he warned his colleagues against a motion remitting such a decision to some future full assembly – for, as he pointed out, the full Houses of Parliament meeting at some future date in a properly constituted place might well make it a reproach that the decision had been pre-judged.

Curiously – and this, as his biographer observes, 'was typical of his emotionally confused state of mind' – Spaak then urged his audience to suspend judgment on the very charges he had just made against the King and also refrained from repeating the accusation of capitulating without due cause, which had been made in Pierlot's broadcast and more specifically in the two Ministers' press statements. Indeed, when Spaak came to this point in his story, he told the assembly 'I have nothing to say about these events.' And yet he and Pierlot voted in favour of the resolution which the President of the Chamber put to the assembly: 'The Senators and Deputies resident in France, unanimously: stigmatize [*flétrissent*] the capitulation for which Leopold III has taken the initiative and for which he bears the responsibility before history . . . declare their solidarity with the Government, which has established the legal and moral impossibility of Leopold III reigning.' On leaving the Town Hall the Senators and Deputies of Belgium, fresh from denouncing their King, were cheered by the citizens of Limoges. The damning resolution they had passed was

* Later President of the Socialist Party, and one of those mainly responsible for the King's overthrow after the war.

forthwith communicated to the media and circulated by Spaak's Foreign
Ministry to all the Belgian diplomatic posts abroad.

By their participation in the hysterical assembly at Limoges Pierlot and
Spaak had hung round their necks a chain which quickly became an
embarrassment and even after the war proved difficult to remove. By
their own admission they still had no evidence that the King had acted
unconstitutionally or improperly. But in a panic that went far deeper than
concern for the Belgian refugees in France, they had yielded to
Reynaud's pressure (as, it is fair to say, Churchill was soon to do) and
from expediency had publicly dishonoured their King. Almost immediately, the consequences of their action were brought home to them.

The Limoges assembly had been convened too soon. It was hardly over
when Vicomte Berryer returned to France from Berne and delivered to
the Ministers the communications with which he had been entrusted by
the King's Chef de Cabinet. Berryer's account of this meeting[289] is rich in
human comedy, since it is clear that the evidence vindicating the King
which he presented, together with Leopold's self-effacing acceptance of
themselves as Belgium's legal Government, stunned Pierlot and the
members of his Cabinet. What had they done? One observes a ghastly
realization dawning that they had gone too far too quickly down the
wrong road.

At first Pierlot tried to justify himself by arguing that the King had
changed his attitude since his Ministers left him at the battle-front. That
cut no ice with Berryer – and the Prime Minister, with his precise legal
mind, soon admitted that he was satisfied with the position the King had
adopted and with the jurists' findings. Camille Gutt argued that the King
had altered his views to fit a belief that the Allies would be victorious.
Spaak, characteristically, declared himself 'enchanted'. For the moment
his warm feelings for his Sovereign, never entirely buried by his accumulated disloyalties, welled up again and he dashed off to call on Paul
Baudouin, the new Secretary of State at the Quai d'Orsay, to request
'that France should stop impugning the King and the operations of the
Belgian Army'. Auguste De Schrijver, strongly supported by Comte
d'Aspremont Lynden, insisted that the quarrel with the King must be
ended forthwith; that the Belgian refugees should immediately be informed and the documents brought by Vicomte Berryer be made public
throughout the world. Another Minister, Franz Van Cauwelaert, told
Berryer privately that he now accepted the King's case but felt gravely
embarrassed by his own participation at Limoges. This, he said, had been
because he had been misled by the Government (i.e. by Pierlot and
Spaak) – and they should take the blame. Such varied and revealing
reactions evoke a fascinating group portrait of Ministers united in
Cabinet responsibility for a misguided policy, but behaving according to
their individual temperaments when confronted with the truth.

Yet Pierlot and Spaak, after their brief vision of reality, however much they may have been temporarily affected, refused to alter course. The acid test of their integrity was their attitude towards publication of the new documentary evidence, the validity of which they had accepted. This was what Leopold had intended. This was what Berryer, De Schrijver and the other Ministers urged. But Pierlot and Spaak quickly realized that they were caught in a trap of their own making. After the broadcasts of May 28th, their defamatory statements to the world press and the outrageous assembly at Limoges, how could they publish the truth without self-destruction? The jurists' findings alone would have demolished the tissue of falsehoods which they and Reynaud had woven. Pierlot and Spaak therefore not only withheld publication of the evidence vindicating the King, but stubbornly resisted the pressure which their fellow-Ministers and certain parliamentarians put on them, publicly to restore his honour and good name.

With hindsight it can be seen that their failure immediately to rehabilitate Leopold was gravely damaging to the King as well as to the reputation of Belgium and her army. Time was of the essence. On June 2nd and 3rd, British and American opinion about the King, though wavering and disenchanted, had by no means settled.* Churchill's first announcement of the capitulation had left the issue open. Had the Belgian Prime Minister, with the full support of his government, immediately released the conclusive evidence produced by Vicomte Berryer, the favourable consequences throughout the world would have been immense, for their country as well as their King. If Pierlot had had the courage and integrity to proclaim the truth as he now knew it, Churchill could not possibly have denounced Leopold in Parliament on June 4th – no matter how intense the pressure from Reynaud to induce him to do so. It is doubtful whether the black legend would have been immediately and completely erased, but had Pierlot published the true facts and had Churchill continued with his line of sympathetic understanding towards Belgium and her King, Reynaud's lies would have recoiled upon him.

But Pierlot and Spaak, as the latter's biographer observes, 'were in too deep by now to make a public recantation of their "dramatic error" . . . they had publicly accused their King of treating with the enemy and capitulating without due cause. Now that they knew both charges to be

---

* On May 30th the Belgian Ambassador in London, Baron de Cartier de Marchienne, telegraphed Spaak: 'Admiral Keyes has defended the attitude of the King before a Cabinet meeting. As a result the Prime Minister has suspended his judgment. The Admiral and the British liaison officers at Belgian GQG are full of praise for the King and are vindicating him. Our situation, according to them, was desperate, due to the over-extension of the front and despite the heroic resistance of our army. The rumour of treason is false. The King is remaining to share the fate of his troops.

'I consider that one should safeguard the future by avoiding all injurious action against the King . . . Beware of the violence of French reactions, because British opinion is much more reserved.'

unfounded it was too late to re-establish the truth and thus do justice to
their martyred sovereign.'[290] Moreover, being now totally committed to
dependence on France, the publication of material justifying the man
whom Reynaud had chosen as a scapegoat would have been 'inexpe-
dient'. Instead, on June 8th, Pierlot made a broadcast in which he merely
reiterated that, as the King was debarred from ruling, all executive
functions rested with the Government. 'How grateful we are,' he said of
the French, 'for the generous and fraternal hospitality which they have
lavished on our refugees!' But this was simply another effort to curry
favour with the French – for the Belgian refugees were still being treated
as outcasts, although the two Ministers' toadying to Reynaud may have
helped to alleviate their lot to some small extent.

CHAPTER TWENTY-NINE

The Black Legend

'The first casualty when war comes is truth.'
Senator Hiram Johnson, in a speech to the US Senate in 1917

At about 8.30 am on May 28th, just as Reynaud was making his infamous broadcast from Paris, Sir Roger Keyes and Colonel Davy stepped ashore from their Motor Torpedo Boat in Harwich. They returned from the Belgian holocaust to a country as yet unawakened to the grimmer realities of war – a nation completely unaware of the gigantic reverses suffered by the Allies in France and Flanders, or that a desperate attempt to rescue the BEF via Dunkirk had been in progress for the last two days. The safe arrival of these two officers in England is of crucial importance in King Leopold's story, for they were the only men whose eyewitness evidence could have destroyed the black legend at its source – had they been allowed to give it. Reynaud's whole indictment of the King was based on the falsehood that he had surrendered without warning his allies. Had Keyes and Davy not been muzzled by the authorities, they could have cleared Leopold of this basic charge, together with all those of desertion, treachery, cowardice, pro-Nazism et cetera, which sprang from it.

From Harwich the two officers went straight to London by train to make their reports. Davy's experience was dramatic.

I arrived in the War Office looking fairly scruffy. I was walking . . . towards the CIGS's room when I ran into the Public Relations Officer. He was carrying the official communiqué for the morning issue to the press. 'You'd better see this,' he said . . . I looked at the communiqué, which was maddening. It talked of the treachery of the King of the Belgians, the surrender without notice, and other aspects of the Belgian surrender . . . 'You cannot publish that,' I told him. He told me that it had been approved by the CIGS. I told him I was just on my way to see the CIGS and I kept it firmly in my hand. The CIGS was not in his office, so I was steered to Sir James Grigg, the Under-Secretary of State. I told him that the communiqué was nonsense and he said it had been approved by the Secretary of State, and he took me to see Eden. He was not there: he was at No. 10. So Grigg took me there too. Grigg went into a room through a green baize door and presently came out with Eden and Dill.

I said again that if such nonsense were published the British would never live it down. They went behind the door again and after another few minutes Dill came and told me to come in. I was very sleepy and it had not occurred to me that

this was a Cabinet meeting until I saw Winston in the middle of the table. I was
put between Eden and Dill and the PM opened up with: 'What's this, Colonel
Davy? I hear you don't like my communiqué.' I explained my objections and the
difficulty of living down such atrocious distortions of the truth. He asked me a
number of statistical questions such as the number of Belgian casualties . . .
He started to write and then read out a completely fresh communique which
included the words 'It is early yet to judge . . .' and cut out all reference to
treachery and the absence of warning.

   He looked at me and said, 'How about that, Colonel Davy?' 'That's better, Sir,'
I replied and the whole room laughed. WSC smiled at me and I went out, went to
our flat in Dolphin Square, shaved and had a kipper for breakfast.[291]

Meanwhile, as Admiral Keyes describes in his diary, he was met at
Liverpool Street Station and driven straight to 10 Downing Street, where
he saw the Prime Minister alone for a few minutes. He was then
interviewed by the Cabinet for five minutes only 'without having had any
time to prepare a report'. 'There was no question,' wrote Keyes, 'of
blaming King Leopold for having capitulated.' Indeed, he found that the
Prime Minister did not know that the telegram he had so belatedly
despatched at 3 pm on the previous day, indicating that the British and
French were in process of abandoning the King and his army to their fate,
had not reached Leopold or Keyes. (The latter had only received a copy
after landing in England earlier that morning.) Churchill could hardly
have expected that Belgian resistance would be sustained for long after
the receipt of his message, which, as the Admiral commented in his diary,
'gave the King every right to take any action he thought necessary to spare
his army further sacrifice and punishment' and 'should, in all fairness,
have been communicated to the King on the morning of the 26th, when
Lord Gort received his orders to withdraw to the coast'.

   How could the British Ministers criticize or blame Leopold and his
troops, in the presence of the man who had kept them so well informed
about the great battle the Belgians were fighting to enable their allies to
escape to the coast, and the fact that they were being overwhelmed and
must soon capitulate? Had not Churchill signalled 'we greatly admire the
attitude of the King' and 'we are asking the Belgians to sacrifice themselves for us'? Indeed, the Ministers – and particularly Anthony Eden –
far from having grounds for complaint against Leopold must have felt
guilty about their deceitful treatment of him and the Admiral. They had,
after all, deliberately kept them in the dark about the BEF's desertion of
the Belgian Army and had actually ordered Gort not to inform them of
the fact, two days before.

   When the sixty-eight-year-old Admiral of the Fleet arrived straight
from the station at 10 Downing Street to report to the Prime Minister, he
was extremely tired, after a period of 'pretty strenuous effort, without any
real sleep', as he later wrote to Churchill, 'and without any preparation or

time to collect my thoughts'. It was a worry to Keyes that he was unable, in the few minutes he was allowed, to give a proper account of what had happened in Belgium and to do justice to the King and his army for their courageous and prolonged efforts 'to shield the BEF's movements'. Indeed the Cabinet was too preoccupied to give the Admiral a proper hearing, for it was under the enormous pressure of the greatest emergency in the nation's history – with the whole future of the British Army and indeed of the Commonwealth hanging in the balance.*

Although the Prime Minister then made no criticism of Leopold for capitulating, he was, as Keyes recalls, 'very indignant that the King should have declined to come away with me'. Churchill's existing prejudice against the Belgians for refusing to allow the Franco-British forces to enter their territory before it was invaded was now compounded by his sense of pique at being unable to gather Leopold under his wing, like the other refugee Royals and statesmen. It was at this meeting that Churchill expressed what Brian Bond calls 'to say the least, a rather selective view of recent Anglo-French-Belgian history'.[292] 'No doubt,' the Prime Minister declared, 'history will criticize the King for having involved us in Belgium's ruin. But it is not for us to pass judgment on him.' At a Defence Committee meeting the previous evening (the 27th), Churchill had said that Leopold could not be reproached for asking for a cease-fire, but that his action 'completed the full circle of misfortune into which our Allies had landed us . . .' And at a Cabinet meeting later that night he declared that although the King's action was 'not heroic', if he made a separate peace with Germany this 'might well be the best that he could do for his Country'. Churchill had further commented that the Belgian capitulation 'might sting the French to anger' and arouse them from 'their present stunned and bewildered state'. As for the British, the announcement of the Belgian surrender would 'go a long way to prepare the public for bad news'.[293]

But these comments were mild compared to the views which Churchill expressed about Leopold and the Belgians in private and in his numerous minutes. Indeed some of these were so 'vitriolic, not to say libellous', according to a *Times* article on May 19th 1981, that Whitehall ordered that they be suppressed until 1996. But due to an oversight by the 'weeders', some of these communications, which reveal the magnitude of Churchill's prejudice against, and misconceptions about, the King and his

---

* On the previous day the Cabinet had considered Halifax's proposal that Mussolini should be asked to mediate with Hitler for a 'general settlement', since he believed that, provided Britain's 'independence' could be preserved, it would be better 'to accept an offer which would save the country from avoidable disaster' than to take the risk of two to three months of air attack. Halifax declared, according to the *Colville Papers*, that 'our aim can no longer be to crush Germany, but rather to preserve our own integrity and independence'. According to the minutes, Churchill 'did not raise any objection to some approach being made to Signor Mussolini'.

people, were recently discovered in the Public Records Office by historical researchers. In a minute dated April 8th 1945, for example, Churchill
described Leopold as 'rather a feeble specimen . . . and thus thoroughly
representative of the Belgian nation which vainly hoped to keep out of
this war, no matter what they owed to those who saved them in the last
war'. And on May 27th 1944 Churchill wrote to Anthony Eden, the
Foreign Secretary:

> Considering that there are millions of French and British graves in Belgium,
> and that she was saved from all the horrors of German incorporation by our
> exertions, I thought her attitude in the years preceding the war singularly
> ungrateful and detached . . . Indeed I think they were the most contemptible of
> all the neutrals at that time . . . This however did not prevent me from speaking
> in more considerate tones about the surrender of the Belgian Army by the King
> of the Belgians without the slightest regard to what happened to all the forces
> that had come as fast as they could, in view of Belgium's policy, to the rescue of
> that country. In fact I have very little sympathy for them beyond what I feel for
> all countries invaded and trampled down by the Huns.[294]

When Keyes spoke so briefly to the Cabinet, he did not as yet know that
Reynaud had denounced King Leopold for treachery and for surrendering without warning his allies, or that Churchill had approved a communiqué echoing the French Premier's slanderous falsehoods. And it was only
after this meeting that he learned from Davy of the latter's dramatic
experience at 10 Downing Street. Although both officers were worried
because they felt that they had been unable to do as much as they would
have wished at the Cabinet meeting to establish the truth about events in
Belgium and thus nail Reynaud's lies, their success, albeit temporary, was
greater than they expected – for when Churchill addressed the House of
Commons that afternoon he spoke in relatively restrained terms:

> I have no intention of suggesting to the House that we should attempt at this
> moment to pass judgment upon the action of the King of the Belgians in his
> capacity as Commander-in-Chief of the Belgian Army. This army has fought
> very bravely and has both suffered and inflicted heavy losses. The Belgian
> Government has disassociated itself from the action of the King, and, declaring
> itself to be the only legal Government in Belgium, has formally announced its
> resolve to continue the war at the side of the Allies . . .

Soon after their arrival in London it was made clear to both Keyes and
Davy that, as serving officers,* they were absolutely forbidden to make
any public statements about their mission in Belgium. The Government
even went so far as to send an officer from the MI5 division of the Secret

---

* In March 1940 Keyes and the other Admirals of the Fleet had been restored to the Active
List.

Service to call on Keyes at his house in Chelsea to remind him of this veto and to demand that he should hand over all the papers relating to his mission. Realizing that if he did so he would never be able to establish the truth, the Admiral of the Fleet told the officer to come back in a few days, when he would have had an opportunity of sorting out his files after the recent hectic weeks – and then put the bulk of his papers in places of safety. The officer on his return was fobbed off with a few token offerings. Considering Sir Roger's status, this was a sinister and disquieting episode.

Although as a loyal officer Keyes could not make public any details of his liaison mission, he was also a Member of Parliament and as such he made a statement to the lobby correspondents of the House of Commons, in which he said 'Some very hard things have been said in this country and France about King Leopold. I trust that judgment will be suspended on a very gallant soldier until all the facts are known' – advice which was widely reported in the world's press.

Such appeals for restraint did not recommend themselves to one particular newspaper, and on May 30th the *Daily Mirror* published another vitriolic leader – this time aimed at both King Leopold and the Admiral. Sneering at Keyes's appeal (but not those of Churchill or Duff Cooper) for a suspension of judgment, it assailed him for defending the King. Keyes could not be said 'to belong to the Silent Service', it declared, 'since he has often betrayed a regrettable tendency to chatter and to express "views" which no one has invited'. (As an MP he had frequently spoken out in favour of strengthening the Nation's defences and against Labour's call for 'total unilateral disarmament', as well as the Chamberlainites' policy of abject appeasement.) As to the Admiral's appeal to wait 'until all the facts are known', the leader asked 'What facts? Are the facts not known? These facts? That this "very gallant soldier" did not, before the war, seek preventive help from the Allies: that he refused to confer with them: and that he protected certain Fascist influences in Belgium.' Next it alleged that after putting further strain upon the Allied forces by calling them into Belgium, Leopold had laid down his arms without a word of warning to them, thus 'betraying his Commander-in-Chief' and 'exposing himself to be shot as a deserter and traitor'.

The leader then addressed itself to Sir Roger ('if he can stop chattering in order to listen for a moment'): 'What the deuce were you up to in Brussels? Did you not sniff the Rat King? Smell any stench of treachery? Lost your nose and guts, man? Don't know a damned deserter when you see one? Surely *you* were not boot-scraping and bowing on Brussels carpets in a Rat King's Palace?' It then told the Admiral not to 'come gabbling here about gallant soldiers and suspended judgment' and said that he should deny the report. 'Until you do, we must revise our own views of gallantry. Until you take back your words we must suspend judgment about you.'

The Admiral took the view that though this diatribe was mainly directed against a man unable to reply, he himself was free to challenge its libellous assertions in the courts and, by revealing what had really happened in Belgium, vindicate not only himself but also, far more important, the King. He therefore issued a writ against the *Daily Mirror*. But in the meantime he must use other channels. One might be a public declaration by the Prime Minister. As it happened, Churchill was due to make a parliamentary statement on the war situation on June 4th – an excellent opportunity, the Admiral felt, for him to proceed from his temporizing remarks of May 28th to a complete rebuttal of the charges against Leopold. On the morning of the 4th therefore, Keyes sent round a letter: 'My dear Winston, I know what a heavy burden you are bearing . . .' in which he reminded Churchill that he had been unable, in the few minutes that were made available to him, adequately to report on the course of events in Belgium. He therefore gave a concise review of the salient points of the campaign, with particular reference to Leopold's 'continuous efforts to facilitate the operations of the BEF' and to the fierce and costly battles the Belgians had fought, to cover its retreat to the coast. 'This Army,' he wrote, 'was held together thanks to the inspiring leadership of King Leopold and fought bravely for eighteen days, under dispiriting conditions of retirement forced upon them.' He then reminded Churchill of what might have happened to the BEF 'had the King left, as his Ministers ceaselessly urged him to do . . .' and of all the warnings the King had given that his army would be forced to surrender, once it was abandoned by its allies. In conclusion Keyes hoped that the Prime Minister would no longer allow 'the vilification of a brave King to go on unrestrained, "in order to raise the morale of the French", for whose failure on the Meuse, both the Belgian and British armies have had to pay so dearly.' In a postscript he told Churchill that he had issued a writ against the *Daily Mirror*.*

The House of Commons that afternoon was crowded and tense, for it was at 2.23 pm that the Admiralty formally announced the completion of 'Operation Dynamo' and the end of the evacuation from Dunkirk. But as Keyes sat expectantly in his place, he found himself listening with astonishment and horror to a denunciation of King Leopold which went even further than Reynaud's. It was punctuated by cries of 'shame' and 'treachery' from Members.

> Suddenly, without prior consultation, with the least possible notice, without the advice of his Ministers and upon his own personal act, he sent a plenipotentiary to the German Command, surrendered his army and exposed our whole flank and means of retreat.

---

* In 1951 Winston Churchill himself sued the *Daily Mirror* for libel, after it had implied that he was a war-monger. The newspaper apologized and paid damages and costs.

I asked the House a week ago to suspend its judgment because the facts were not clear, but I do not feel that any reason now exists why we should not form our own opinions upon this pitiful episode. The surrender of the Belgian Army compelled the British at the shortest notice to cover a flank to the sea of more than thirty miles in length, otherwise all would have been cut off and all would have shared the fate to which King Leopold had condemned the finest army his country had ever formed. So, in doing this, and exposing this flank . . . contact was lost inevitably between the British and two of the three corps forming the First French Army who were still farther from the coast than we were, and it seemed impossible that any large number of Allied troops could reach the coast.

To complete his destruction of the honour and good name of a brave ally, whose loyal and unselfish conduct he had so recently 'greatly admired' and of whom he had asked that the Belgians should 'sacrifice themselves for us', Churchill told the House: 'Had not this ruler and his government severed themselves from the Allies who rescued their country from extinction in the late war, had they not sought refuge in what has proved to be a fatal neutrality, the French and British armies might well at the very outset have saved not only Belgium but perhaps even Poland.'*

Since Winston Churchill chose scornfully to heap all the blame on King Leopold and his army by alleging that their capitulation had 'exposed our whole flank and means of retreat' – before describing for the first time 'the miracle of deliverance' at Dunkirk, having omitted to mention that the Belgians' resistance had protected the BEF's flank and escape-route to the coast until nearly two days after that 'deliverance' had begun – he created the completely false impression that the Belgian cease-fire had preceded, imperilled or even caused the evacuation of the BEF. And yet Churchill knew perfectly well that the escape of the BEF would not have been possible but for the Belgians' prolonged resistance. Then, for good measure, Churchill added the equally false charge that the Belgian capitulation had caused about half the French First Army to be encircled and forced to surrender. Churchill, moreover, condemned the King for following the same course of action that he had authorized for the BEF in similar circumstances, when he gave Gort, and later Brooke and Alexander, discretion to surrender 'to avoid useless slaughter'.

Thus the black legend of King Leopold was even more solidly established. Churchill's endorsement of Reynaud's fabrications and the addi-

* In Churchill's minute of May 27th 1944, mentioned earlier, he further reveals his prejudices and misconceptions in regard to Belgium: 'Had she acted vigorously with France, French action might have been stimulated. Anyhow at the outbreak of war her armies could have been placed in a far better strategic position than was subsequently possible, and the hideous gap at Sedan might have presented a very different aspect to the enemy. Without going so far as to say that Belgian action might have changed the sombre course of events, I have no doubt whatsoever that up to the time when they were fallen upon and invaded, our account with them was expressed by "Thank you for nothing".'

tional charges he brought against the King went swiftly round the world
and have remained in circulation ever since. For all in 1940 and for a great
many people subsequently, his words were authoritative and unquestioningly accepted. Even today the true facts are appreciated by few. If
Churchill had told the truth, of which he was fully aware, Reynaud's
broadcast would have been obliterated – for Reynaud was soon totally
discredited[z] – and Leopold's name would have been cleared. This was
demonstrated a year later, when a simple statement of the facts made in
the High Court of Justice at the conclusion of Admiral Keyes' libel case
against the *Daily Mirror* would achieve a worldwide vindication of King
Leopold's loyalty, honour, courage, and good name.

Since the fatal words defaming and dishonouring the King of the
Belgians had been uttered in all solemnity by the Prime Minister in
Parliament and duly recorded in *Hansard*, they could only be wiped out
by a full and formal retraction – which, of course, Churchill was never
prepared to make. This bedevilled the whole situation thereafter and
remained an embarrassing impediment to any official *amende honorable*
being made. The Government's policy of silence was the result.

After the fall of France, the discrediting of Reynaud and the vindication of Leopold in the High Court of Justice, however, private individuals, writers and occasionally even members of the British Government were careful to remind the public that Winston Churchill had
advocated a suspension of judgment on the King until the facts were
known. They had either forgotten, or tactfully omitted to mention, that
the Prime Minister had almost immediately gone back on his own advice.

Why then did Churchill deliver this verdict, which he knew to be false
and monstrously unjust? He did so deliberately, as an act of political
expediency. And his prejudice against Leopold was such that he was no
longer averse to joining Reynaud's campaign to make the Belgians and
their King the scapegoats for France and Britain's misfortunes, failures
and military defeats. Furthermore, the heaping of abuse upon this small
nation and its Sovereign by the two Allies effectively reduced or diverted
the flow of acrimony between them and provided a defenceless whipping-
boy for both great powers.

That Churchill's denunciation of Leopold did not enjoy the support of
his Cabinet colleagues and advisers is shown by the attitudes adopted at
the time by Duff Cooper, Anthony Eden, Lord Halifax and even Sir
Alexander Cadogan. All these men – and they were not the only ones –
urged that there should be no recrimination over the Belgian capitulation. When, for example, the Belgian Minister, Camille Gutt, called on
the Foreign Secretary on May 30th and promised 'the Belgian Government will fight on to the end whatever happens,' Halifax thanked him and
declared 'I have no intention of pronouncing harsh words against your
King. I am certain that his decision was dictated by honourable motives.'

Cadogan too had 'urged no recrimination' as Foreign Office policy, when he heard of the Belgian capitulation, as he records in his diary.[296] He and his chief had, after all, read Leopold's letter to George VI of May 25th and had drafted the latter's reply.

Whether or not Churchill had read Keyes' letter of June 4th before he made his damning statement is irrelevant, for he was already in full possession of the facts, even if allowance is made for the statements which Gort and Pownall had made, after their return to England, laying the blame on the Belgians for the defeat of their army.* In his memoirs Churchill glosses over this discreditable episode and omits all but one short passage from his second statement to the House. The explanation he gives for his volte-face from moderation to denunciation is that the French Government 'expressed its concern' that his earlier statement had been 'in sharp contrast to that of M. Reynaud'. He writes that he therefore felt impelled 'in justice not only to our French ally, but also to the Belgian Government now in London [it was, of course, in Paris, and its rump did not establish itself in London until five months later] to state the truth in plain terms.'[297]

In fact the references to Leopold III and his army which appear in Churchill's *The Second World War* are so unfair and misleading – due as much to his omission as to his misstatement of the facts – that his son Randolph angrily told him, according to Archduke Otto Hapsburg: 'What you have written on the subject is nothing but a pack of lies, as you well know.' The Archduke, who was present, describes this heated exchange in his book *Naissance d'un Continent*, recalling that Churchill defiantly admitted: 'Of course they were lies but you must not forget that the history of a period is what its best author writes about it. I am and will remain that author and consequently what I have written will be accepted as the truth.'[298] On the same subject Churchill told Stalin at the Teheran Conference in November 1943: 'In wartime the truth must always be surrounded by a bodyguard of lies.'†

That Churchill's statement to the House on June 4th came into that category needs no emphasis. In fact the pressure which was put upon him by the French to pervert and suppress the truth had begun a week before

---

* The chief orchestrator of the campaign to blame the 'bloody foreigners' for the BEF's defeat was General Mason MacFarlane, Gort's Director of Military Intelligence and head of Press Relations (and later a Labour MP). As early as May 27th the General, fresh from Dunkirk, told Sir Harold Nicolson of the Ministry of Information, as the latter recorded in his diary, that he wanted to save the reputation of the British Army by blaming the Belgians and the French. But since the Ministry's policy was to 'resuscitate the reputation of the French,' as Ian McLaine recalls in *Ministry of Morale*, Mason MacFarlane concentrated on blaming the Belgians at a series of 'off the record' press briefings.

† After the war when the King and Princess Lilian met Randolph Churchill in the USA, he said: 'I am surprised that you are prepared to shake hands with a member of my family,' and when they asked him why, he replied 'because my father behaved abominably towards Your Majesty'.

he made it. On May 29th the Cabinet received a signal from Sir Ronald Campbell, the British Ambassador in Paris. This ran as follows:

1 Press Councillor reports that French Minister of Information has urgently appealed to him to do everything possible to prevent prominence being given in the British press and radio and to omit any reference whatever in BBC news transmissions in French to Admiral Keyes' statements in the lobbies of the House of Commons urging the suspension of judgment on King Leopold.
2 Monsieur Frossard fears that line, as stated by Admiral Keyes, will be taken as condonation of, and therefore conducive to, defeatism here at the moment French opinion has been roused to anger (with consequent improvement of morale) by disgust at the apparent treachery.*
3 French official circles are more and more convinced of the King's treachery but quite apart from the merits of the case I trust you will do all you can to meet Monsieur Frossard's requests.

'The apparent treachery' and 'quite apart from the merits of the case' reveal that the originators of this request were by no means convinced that the French Premier's statements were true. In a sentence which is almost a gloss on Sir Ronald's third paragraph, General Spears wrote in *Assignment to Catastrophe*: 'Quite apart from the merits of the case it was obvious that the French Government hoped to gain something from this disaster, at least a scapegoat, and the chance to distract the minds of their people from the shortcomings of their own military leaders.' Spears then relates that Reynaud was angered and upset by the considerate references to King Leopold and his army made by Churchill, Duff Cooper and Keyes on May 28th, and how for the next week he constantly badgered Spears to put pressure on the British Prime Minister to conform with his propaganda line, and join him in heaping the blame on Leopold, which Spears obligingly did. On May 30th after Reynaud had threatened that French opinion would be *déchaînée* against England, if the French were not evacuated in equal numbers with the British, he again expressed his annoyance and resentment at Churchill's attitude towards Leopold. Spears explained that since Britain was a monarchy the approach of the British Prime Minister must necessarily be different to that of the Premier of the French Republic.

Meanwhile in London, Sir Alexander Cadogan was writing in his diary for the 30th 'P.M. off to Paris tomorrow morning. French look like running out and putting blame on us. And he must hearten them and keep them in the fight or we must cut out and fight alone.' Cadogan had already noted, *before* news of the Belgian capitulation came through, that Churchill had expressed the view that Great Britain might be better off

---

* All statements showing any consideration or sympathy for King Leopold and his army, including those of Churchill, Duff Cooper and Keyes, were ruthlessly suppressed by the French censorship.

without the French, and that the diarist and others in high places felt the same way.

On the following day in Paris, at the Supreme War Council which had been called to discuss the desperate military situation, particularly in the Dunkirk perimeter, Reynaud seized the opportunity to urge the British Prime Minister yet again to join him in blaming Leopold for the Allies' military disasters. 'It must not be forgotten,' he said, 'that the fearful danger the troops were running at Dunkirk, and the loss of many French divisions which had jeopardized the safety of France, were directly attributable to the defection of the Belgian King . . . These were facts which in fairness to the armies and to the French and British people should not be passed over.' And so, in his desperate anxiety to appease Reynaud, to keep France in the fight for as long as possible, and in the hope that he would be able to obtain control of the French fleet when she succumbed, Churchill yielded to his demands. Indeed, on June 4th he castigated Leopold in even harsher terms than had Reynaud – for what seemed to him the right priorities – and thereafter found it impossible to recant or make any kind of *amende honorable*.

From Winston Churchill's many sayings it is possible to gain some understanding of his motivation for resorting to the basest means to gain his ends – and his unwillingness to admit that he had done so, or show any remorse. In 1942 he quoted an old Greek Orthodox proverb to explain away the British Government's dubious deal with the Vichy Admiral Darlan: 'My children, it is permitted you, in time of grave danger, to walk with the Devil until you have crossed the bridge.' On another occasion he declared 'If Hitler invaded Hell, I would make at least a favourable reference to the Devil in the House of Commons. I have only one purpose, the destruction of Hitler, and my life is much simplified thereby.' In this regard he criticized the Foreign Office for 'trying to enter into refinements of policy unsuited to the tragic simplicity and grandeur of the times and the issues at stake'. Finally, on the subject of recantation, he declared in Parliament on December 2nd 1954 'I hope the House will remember that I have done what I have rarely done – formally to express my regret for an observation I made . . . in a speech.'

Sir Roger Keyes was so shocked by his lifelong friend's unjust and untruthful attack on King Leopold that he wrote to King George's private secretary, Sir Alexander Hardinge, enclosing a copy of his letter to Churchill, with the request that it should be handed to the King. And as soon as Keyes completed his comprehensive dossier on his mission, he sent this round to Buckingham Palace also. His Majesty had summoned both the Admiral and Colonel Davy separately to Buckingham Palace immediately after their return to England and had obtained from them a full account of the Belgian campaign and of Leopold's conduct throughout. Upon being apprised of the true facts and after questioning the two men closely, the King expressed his sympathy for Leopold, and declared that his conduct of military operations had been above reproach. He made much the same comment to Harry Hopkins on the occasion, mentioned earlier, when they retired to the air raid shelter at Buckingham Palace and discussed Queen Wilhelmina's involuntary departure from Holland. 'He expressed a good deal of sympathy for the King of the Belgians,' wrote Hopkins to President Roosevelt, 'and had little or no criticism of him as C-in-C, but as King he thought he should have left the country and established his government elsewhere.'[299] This is ironic, for King George always maintained that he himself would never leave England, come what may. Indeed when it was suggested to Queen Elizabeth that the two Princesses should go to America, Her Majesty was quoted as replying: 'The Princesses could not go without me: I could not leave the King; and of course the King will never leave.' In this connection it is significant that Churchill, as Prime Minister, should have declared in the Humble Address which he delivered in Parliament on May 15th 1945:

. . . if it had come to a last stand in London, a matter which had to be considered at one time, I have no doubt that His Majesty would have come very near to departing from his usual constitutional rectitude by disregarding the advice of his Ministers.

Having ascertained the facts from Keyes and Davy, King George now knew that his cousin was not only innocent of the charges levelled against him by Reynaud, Churchill and others, but had been responsible for prolonging the Belgian Army's brave resistance, which made possible the evacuation of the BEF, until nearly two days after this had begun. Consequently there never was 'a breach' between the British Royal family and King Leopold, as was so often alleged thereafter by the media. Indeed, whenever an occasion arose, King George, and later Queen Elizabeth II, demonstrated that their feelings of affection and regard for him remained undiminished. As George VI's official biographer records, the King 'had a sincere liking for his young Belgian cousin' and this 'feeling of friendship was reciprocated'.[300]

Leopold was, however, distressed that George VI had been unable to prevent Churchill from supporting, with the full authority of the British Government, the campaign of denigration which Reynaud had initiated against him. Leopold had, after all, written to his fellow-monarch on May 25th, frankly warning him and the Cabinet about the imminence of his army's capitulation and of his intention to share its fate. He therefore felt that George VI might have insisted that his Prime Minister should uphold, rather than pervert, the truth concerning these circumstances. Had the existence of Leopold's warning letter to George VI, or even a paraphrase of its contents been made public, for example, Reynaud's allegations would have been demolished. But as we have seen, Churchill's prejudice was such that he had decided to reinforce the French Premier's false charges instead of refuting them. And, having virtually taken over the single-handed direction of the war, Churchill was paying scant attention to the representations of his Cabinet colleagues – or anyone else.

As far as King George was concerned, Admiral Keyes was told privately that His Majesty was 'furious' with those responsible for fostering and perpetuating the defamatory campaign against Leopold, but it is not known whether or not he remonstrated with Churchill for so doing. Although his father, George V, had frequently and forcefully intervened with his government, particularly in regard to foreign monarchs such as King Constantine of Greece,[301] his son may have felt unable to intervene in the political field – now completely dominated by Churchill.

King George did, however, put his foot down firmly over matters which came within his own Royal prerogatives. Thus, when it was suggested that the Belgian King's appointment as Colonel-in-Chief of the 5th Royal Inniskilling Dragoon Guards should be revoked, the King sternly refused and ordered that Leopold should continue to receive all the honours, privileges and respect due to him as such. The same thing happened, again with the full approval of the Regiment, when Whitehall suggested that King Baudouin should replace his father as Colonel-in-Chief, on his accession to the throne in 1951. Similarly George VI firmly rejected the proposal that Leopold should be struck off the Roll of Knights of the Garter, and that his banner in St George's Chapel, Windsor, should be hauled down.

Thus it was in fulfilment of King George's wishes that the 'Skins' provided a guard of honour at King Leopold's funeral on October 1st 1983 and proudly carried his coffin to the crypt at Laeken – and that a moving Memorial Evensong and Presentation of his Garter banner, attended by the Queen, the Duke of Edinburgh and the Prince and Princess of Liège, was held in St George's Chapel, a few weeks later.

In his next effort to clear the King's name, Keyes was again thwarted. He had learned that when Gort got back from Dunkirk he attributed the defeat of the BEF to Leopold's surrender. On the busy day of June 4th therefore, he visited Gort to try to persuade him to present an objective and undistorted picture, and left with the feeling that their talk had 'cleared the air a bit'. But when the Admiral heard that Gort and his officers were still making these accusations against the Belgians and their King, he reacted vigorously. On June 12th he wrote to the former C-in-C:

Since I spoke to you, I have heard that you have been attributing most of the blame for your misfortunes to having had your left flank exposed, without any warning from King Leopold that he was about to capitulate.

Do you really think that that is a fair statement, in view of the repeated requests made to you on the 26th–27th May, for help from the BEF to prevent the Belgian Army's right flank being turned, which you were unable to give; and in view of the warnings to you and the Government from 20th May onwards, that the King would be forced to capitulate if the British and Belgian armies became separated, which he regarded as inevitable, if the British attack to the southward was persisted in – [this being] an opinion shared by the CIGS and you at the time?

To this Keyes attached a detailed account of events in Belgium from May 19th onwards, together with copies of relevant signals between himself, the Prime Minister and Gort, and British and Belgian Headquarters. It demonstrated anew that if Leopold had not rejected his Ministers' appeals to desert his army and had failed to keep it fighting until May 28th, Gort's army could hardly have escaped from the battlefield. The answer was unconvincing: Gort could only claim that Keyes' account contained certain passages that were at variance with his own 'recollections'. Having lost most of his own records in the chaotic retreat to Dunkirk* he was unable to substantiate his own version of events or refute any of Keyes' facts. Gort concluded by agreeing with the Admiral's original appeal that judgment should be suspended until all the facts were known. 'There,' he wrote, 'I feel it will be better to leave the matter until hostilities are over.' Keyes tersely replied:

I was all for leaving the inquest until after the war. But in the meantime, so many officers of the BEF and others are saying what you said – before I sent you documentary evidence to show how unfair you were in your condemnation of King Leopold – and I think the truth will have to be made public, if these stories persist.

Less than a month after the Belgian capitulation and the Dunkirk evacuation, France fell. Britain was now preoccupied with her own survival. But for Admiral Keyes, burning with a sense of injustice, one thing mattered above all: the establishing of the historical truth and the clearing of Leopold's name without delay – especially since, after the collapse of France, there no longer remained any pretext for suppressing the facts – except to protect the reputation of the BEF and its C-in-C. On July 1st, therefore, he made another approach, laying an even more comprehensive dossier than that delivered to Gort before Lord Halifax – under whose orders he had officially been placed as Special Liaison

---

* According to the *Official History*, many were deliberately destroyed, some were left behind in Boulogne, some were lost at sea and others accidently burnt.

Officer to King Leopold – with the request that the Government should make a statement rehabilitating the King of the Belgians. But from the Foreign Secretary Keyes got no more satisfaction than from Churchill or Gort. In every case his pleas and submissions met a blank wall.

It was plain that the Government was determined not to reopen the matter. For Churchill and his compliant Cabinet colleagues – now facing the Battle of Britain – the lamentable events of May 1940 in France and Belgium were a great embarrassment, over which it was essential to draw a veil of silence. For if the case of the Belgian surrender were to be re-examined openly, not only would Churchill's second statement on the subject in Parliament be shown up as a gross misrepresentation of the facts, but the shortcomings in the Army's training and equipment, the inept control of the BEF by Gort and Pownall and the fact that they abandoned their Allies on the field of battle without warning them, would all become public knowledge. It therefore seemed that there was little hope of any official rehabilitation of Leopold and that while the war lasted he would remain the black legend's 'traitor King'.

CHAPTER THIRTY

The Odyssey of Pierlot and Spaak

'The name of the one was Obstinate and the name of the other was
Pliable.'

John Bunyan, *The Pilgrim's Progress*

As King Leopold had forecast, the total collapse of the French armies was
not long delayed. Fifteen days after the Belgian capitulation, Hitler's
divisions entered Paris. On June 16th they were approaching the Loire. In
the East, the Maginot Line was not only outflanked but broken through.
The Panzer divisions were rolling on towards Lyons and Valence.
Already on June 14th, the day the Germans entered Paris, Reynaud had
reached the point of proposing to Weygand that he should order the
whole French Army to capitulate, since this would 'bind only the Army
and leave the Government freedom of action' – the very act for which he
had castigated Leopold only a fortnight earlier! Weygand rejected this
proposal contemptuously: 'I refuse to bespatter our colours with this
shame!' And when Reynaud renewed his appeals and even offered to give
the C-in-C a written order to surrender the Army to the Germans,
Weygand resolutely refused.

Pierlot and Spaak were now in an even greater dilemma. At Wynendaele Sir Roger Keyes had noted that the King 'was absolutely convinced
that the French Army would collapse within two or three weeks, that
there would be internal trouble in France and that the French Government would desert us'. Moreover, as Leopold had told the four Ministers,
one of his principal reasons for refusing to go to France with them was that
he was quite sure that they would be caught up in that country's collapse –
in which it would be unwise for him to become involved. To Keyes the
King had also confided that in this situation he was certain that the
Ministers 'would lose their heads'. This prediction had already come true,
but worse was to follow. Indeed Pierlot and Spaak would now reverse
course yet again on a journey which would prove to be as tortuous as the
wanderings of Odysseus.

As the French *débâcle* drew to its climax, Pierlot and Spaak had one of
two courses open to them – and unhesitatingly chose the less honourable
one. For it was not to France alone, it was to the *Allies* – to Great Britain
as well as France – that the Belgian Government had rededicated itself

after the capitulation of their Army. This was the promise in Pierlot's first broadcast on May 28th. When Spaak held forth at Limoges on the 31st, he announced amid applause that he and his colleagues would support the Allies with all their strength, come what may – '*A côté des Alliés*,' he cried, '*jusqu'au bout!*' But instead of fulfilling these pledges, which would have meant announcing, when France fell, that they would carry on the war with their remaining ally and would themselves leave for London, the Ministers decided, before the French surrender had even occurred, that 'all was lost' and that like France they must try to come to terms with the Germans.

The moment can be pinpointed precisely. The young Minister of Health, Marcel-Henri Jaspar, has graphically described the crucial meeting of the Belgian Government which took place on June 18th.* The council chamber was, in his words, 'a miserable dirty hole' in a 'sordid house' in Bordeaux. 'It stank of cheap cigars . . . the ceiling was filthy, the door did not shut . . .' 'As we had moved from one town to another our meeting places had grown increasingly squalid in keeping with the decaying spirit of the Government . . . Our own disintegration seemed to be reflected in our surroundings . . . The air was heavy with lassitude and despair. The struggle was over. I could read in the faces of my colleagues that their nerves had gone to pieces and that their spirits were failing . . .'

At 12.30 pm on the previous day Marshal Pétain made the poignant broadcast in which he announced that he had taken over as Prime Minister and intended that day to approach the Germans with the object of putting an end to hostilities. Shortly afterwards Paul Baudouin confirmed privately to Spaak that France was on the point of collapse and that an armistice was being sought. Pierlot's reaction was immediate and definite. At the Cabinet meeting he read out a memorandum which he had prepared: 'I have considered the problem from all angles. We shall not go to England. France has thrown in the sponge. We abandon the struggle with her.' Spaak then declared 'Our mandate is fulfilled. We have done our duty.' 'But what about the Army?' Jaspar enquired. 'The Army,' General Denis replied, 'will receive and obey the same orders as the French Army.' 'It was all over,' Jaspar's account continues, 'the capitulation was complete and irreparable. These men were broken. In vain I invoked the decisions Parliament had taken on May 10th in Brussels and confirmed on the 31st in Limoges. I quoted what the Ministers themselves had said at Poitiers . . . The Prime Minister's proposal was accepted by an overwhelming majority. M. Spaak supported it firmly . . . I took a diametrically opposite view to that of my colleagues, with the exception of De Vleeschauwer and Gutt who supported me . . . I resolved that I would never support a policy of capitula-

* The Franco-German Armistice was not signed until June 21st.

tion . . . I wanted to carry on the war . . . I left for England.'[302] But the fact that Jaspar left hurriedly (with his wife, aboard a British vessel) without a word to anyone and then, on June 23rd, broadcast from the BBC in London a grandiloquent 'appeal to all free Belgians' to continue the struggle under his leadership infuriated Pierlot and his colleagues. The Government could not in practice dismiss Jaspar, since this was the King's prerogative, but Pierlot issued a communiqué stating that, as Jaspar had 'abandoned his post and his administration without notifying his colleagues' and had 'gone to London for personal reasons' (the implication being that he had done so because his wife was Jewish), his powers had been transferred to the Minister of the Interior and he was no longer regarded as a member of the Government. Pierlot further proclaimed that the Government 'absolutely disavowed' all Jaspar's 'declarations and initiatives' and that – contrary to his assertion – it was established in France, not England.

Bordeaux had been chosen as the seat of the Belgian Government-in-exile, because the central French administration was already installed there and the policy of Pierlot and his Cabinet was to stick like leeches to the French. Yet they were not in Bordeaux unavoidably. They were not trapped. They could have left for England with the greatest of ease, since Belgium possessed a large merchant fleet, and they had commandeered for accommodation purposes a Belgian vessel moored in the Gironde, the SS *Baudouinville*, which was perfectly capable of taking them and their families to England. Moreover, the British had made available both air and sea transport (including a cruiser) to evacuate the Belgian administration and their families, only to have their offers turned down by Pierlot and Spaak. The evidence for this refusal is provided by Albert De Vleeschauwer, the Catholic Party Minister for the Colonies, who – like Gutt and Jaspar – had 'energetically protested' against their colleagues' decision to throw in the sponge and to negotiate a peace treaty with Germany and had pronounced in favour of the Government rallying to England to continue the struggle at her side.

On the previous day De Vleeschauwer had been astonished by a question from Francis Aveling, the British Chargé d'Affaires, who had remained in contact with the refugee Belgian Government, the Ambassador having placed himself in German hands.* 'Why are your colleagues not going to London?' Aveling then explained that the British Government had put three aircraft and a cruiser at their disposal, 'but they refuse to come'. De Vleeschauwer was staggered, because Pierlot and Spaak had told him nothing about this facility, of which, clearly, they were not going to take advantage.

---

* In a Foreign Office minute dated June 10th 1940 Aveling recorded that Pierlot had admitted to him that Leopold's surrender of the Belgian Army had been fully justified and constitutionally irreproachable. His government, moreover, approved of the King's recognition of the fact that while he remained a prisoner he was unable to reign.

The Congo was now Belgium's greatest free asset and De Vleeschauwer was determined not only to protect its interests, but to ensure that its immense resources were placed behind Britain's war effort in order to support her in the continuing struggle. He therefore decided to leave France and his defeatist fellow-Ministers immediately, for that purpose. He could not, of course, reveal his real intentions to Pierlot or to the majority of five Ministers who supported the Prime Minister's decision to submit to the Germans instead of going to England – for if he had, they would never have let him go. Ironically, Pierlot not only agreed to De Vleeschauwer's immediate departure for America 'to safeguard the interests of the Congo', but appointed him 'Administrator-General of the Colonies' (the Congo and Ruanda-Urandi) with plenipotentiary powers equal to those of the King and in addition gave him two letters confirming his absolute authority over the Colonies. The Pierlot group's motives for giving De Vleeschauwer these powers were revealed by two members of the Cabinet who would later join him in London. On a visit to Washington in November 1942 De Schrijver told a colleague 'We decided to send De Vleeschauwer to the Congo with maximum powers to protect it against the English', while Comte d'Aspremont Lynden declared in October 1944 'De Vleeschauwer was sent off to "save the Congo", but in reality it was to prevent it falling into the hands of the British or French'.[303] (It is now known that the Belgian Government had heard rumours of the Chamberlain administration's plan to buy off Hitler with their offer of parts of the Belgian Congo in March 1938.)

Armed with these sweeping powers, the steadfastly loyal and patriotic De Vleeschauwer* left Bordeaux that same afternoon, crossed the Spanish frontier on June 19th and reached London, via Lisbon, on July 4th. It is no exaggeration to say that when De Vleeschauwer left France, he carried with him the honour and destiny of Belgium, for it was thanks to his initiatives and those of the equally redoubtable Belgian Ambassador in London, Baron de Cartier de Marchienne, that Pierlot and Spaak were finally induced – after five months of defeatism and vain attempts to persuade the Nazis to accept the subservience of their government – to come to London and there realign it on the side of Great Britain and her allies.

Meanwhile, in Bordeaux, Pierlot, Spaak and their forlorn Cabinet took refuge aboard the *Baudouinville*. Here, on the ship's bridge, the demoral-

---

* De Vleeschauwer had not been in Paris when Reynaud had induced Pierlot and Spaak to denounce and disown King Leopold nor had he been present at Limoges when they incited the assembly to castigate the King, for he had gone straight from Belgium on May 18th to organize the seat of the Government-in-exile at Sainte Adresse, near Le Havre, where it had been established in World War I. Indeed, De Vleeschauwer never wavered in his loyalty to his Sovereign and would, until his death in 1971, stoutly uphold the King's honour and good name. As Minister of the Interior in 1949, for example, he organized the *Consultation Populaire* on Leopold's return from his enforced exile, as well as the return of the King to Belgium in the following year, when he was responsible for law and order.

ized Ministers argued and disputed – and, as Spaak characteristically commented, 'we all missed having the King to concert our differences!'[304] On June 19th the *Baudouinville*'s main saloon was actually prepared as a conference room in which the Belgian Ministers could 'await with dignity' the German delegates who, so they hoped, would soon arrive and negotiate with them a peace treaty.

The wheel had come full circle. The self-righteous Ministers who had denounced their Sovereign for defeatism and 'treating with the enemy', were now themselves trying by every possible means to do just that. They had come to realize that without the King's co-operation they were constitutionally impotent. So, forgetting all they had said about their Sovereign's moral and juridical incapacity to reign and the Limoges assembly's resolution to that effect, they now addressed themselves to the King as though he were still in possession of his full Royal prerogatives – and called upon him to support their efforts to come to terms with the Germans, so that they might return to occupied Belgium.

It does not seem to have occurred to either Pierlot or Spaak, however, that an apology was due to the King for the searing insults they had hurled at him so publicly. Indeed, they would simply pretend that they had never uttered a word against him and would never make any expressions of regret or recantation.

First, on June 18th, the Belgian Government despatched a telegram for forwarding to the King at Laeken via the Argentine Minister in Berne; and next day two more were sent – one by the same means, the other via the Papal Nuncio. These reported the Government's decision to cease all hostilities against the Germans; that the fate of the Belgian officers and soldiers 'must be identical' to those of the French; and 'to send one of its Ministers to the King so that he could with that Minister's signature form a government competent to open peace negotiations with Germany'. After these preliminaries Spaak wrote on the 24th to Paul Baudouin at the Quai d'Orsay:

> As soon as the armistice between France and Germany has come into effect, I would be grateful if you would advise the German Goverment that the Belgian Government is anxious to get into contact with it to negotiate, within the limits of the conditions of the Franco-German armistice, questions relating to Belgian officers, soldiers, and civilians at present in France.
> The Belgian Government is also ready to negotiate the conditions of an armistice between Germany and Belgium, but before engaging itself in this respect, it considers that it is indispensable to get in touch with the King and requests, to this effect, a safe-conduct for two of its members.

Spaak followed this up with two more identical messages to Berlin; the first being sent through the Spanish Ambassador in France, the other by radio via the French High Command to that of the Germans. Fortunately for Pierlot, Spaak and the Belgian Government, the Nazis completely ignored these and all the other appeals to accept its submission and collaboration with which they were bombarded by every conceivable channel of communication in the ensuing weeks.

On June 20th Spaak, in the words of the Belgian author Jean Stengers, 'said goodbye to the British' when he sent a telegram to the Belgian Ambassador in London, Baron de Cartier de Marchienne, asking him to inform the British Government that the Belgian Government had decided to give up the struggle, but thanked Great Britain for having honoured her guarantee to Belgium.

De Cartier was the doyen of the Diplomatic Corps in London and enjoyed immense prestige. He was staunchly pro-British and utterly loyal to his King and country. He is rightly described by Jean Stengers as '*un grand seigneur diplomate – un roc.*'[305] When, therefore, the Baron received Spaak's defeatist message, he modified it to make it appear less definitive before taking it round to the Foreign Office and 'reading' it to Lord Halifax. This enabled de Cartier to reply to Spaak that same afternoon, in the following terms:

> The Secretary of State asks me to urge you to defer an immediate decision until you have been able to make direct contact with the British Government. He suggests that the Belgian Government comes here, or at least some of its Ministers, and observes that if you give up now, you lose everything, whereas if you continue the struggle, you safeguard the future, because the British Empire has a good chance of triumphing in the end. He adds that if you abandon the fight now, our overseas interests will be compromised and our Colonies irremediably lost.[306]

In Lord Halifax's account of this meeting with the Belgian Ambassador he records that de Cartier told him that he had always regretted that the Belgian Government had installed itself in France rather than in England. It was obvious, the Baron continued, that that Pierlot administration had been profoundly affected by the French *débâcle* and the pessimism in France – and, as he felt strongly that an independent Belgian authority should continue to exist, he asked for Britain's help in persuading his government to adopt a firmer attitude. Halifax accordingly instructed the British Ambassador in France, Sir Ronald Campbell, to put strong pressure on the Belgian Ministers to come to England; and warn them that if they went over to the Germans, the British would 'wash their hands' of Belgium's interests and would ensure – if necessary, by military action – that the Congo did not fall under German control.[307]

Although these adjurations had little or no effect on the defeatist Belgian Ministers in France, de Cartier's initiative at least prevented the door between the two governments from being closed. But in the meantime, far from believing that the British had any chance of survival, let alone of winning the war, Pierlot and Spaak were behaving as though they were already defeated. (In a note written in February 1941 Spaak attempted to justify his government's defeatist reactions on June 18th by declaring that Paul Baudouin had convinced them that the British too would probably sue for peace, since American intervention was unlikely.) Because of this attitude Belgian shipping which could have assisted during the evacuation was withheld. No effort was made to transfer Belgian troops across the Channel – even though ample Belgian and British shipping was available.* On the contrary, all such moves were vetoed. The 2,400 troops of the 7th Belgian Infantry Division, for example, waiting at St Nazaire and Brest to embark for England, were prevented from doing so by the Belgian Government. When Italy declared war on France there were Belgian troops in the South, yet these were not allowed to fight – on the grounds that Belgium was not at war with Italy.

Even before France fell the Belgian Ministers had rejected a proposal from the British Government that if the personnel of their Air Force crossed to England, they would be trained and equipped to fight anew. This refusal soon sharpened into a denunciation of Belgian servicemen who had escaped across the Channel – some in their aircraft – as deserters. Several of these airmen fought with gallantry and distinction, for which they were decorated, and some were killed in the Battle of Britain. By mid-July persecution of these courageous men took concrete form. On the orders of the Pierlot regime a Belgian Air Force court martial sentenced a number of pilots to be degraded and to harsh prison terms and fines for 'desertion' (i.e. escaping to England) and 'theft of equipment'. It was not until 1948 that this monstrous judgment was rectified by the Belgian Ministry of Defence, in an announcement which praised their conduct and cleared the names of seven Air Force officers and NCOs and one artillery lieutenant.

From the first day of their arrival in Bordeaux the Ministers had become increasingly desperate. It was clear that now France had succumbed the Pétain government, like the Germans and their own countrymen, had no use for them. When they sought interviews they suffered humiliating delays in outer offices and were received by junior officials. 'The chaos around us,' wrote Spaak in *Combats Inachevés*, 'threw our spirits into disorder.' Towards the end of his life Spaak was remarkably frank about the state of despair into which he and some of his colleagues sank. In an interview on Belgian Television in 1968, for example, he confessed that while in France 'We committed a number of errors . . . we thought that we were defeated . . . that we had lost the war – that it was finished . . . it was a rout.'[308] Spaak went on to admit that he was so demoralized that he showed his indifference to his fellow-Ministers' discussions in Vichy by 'lying on a sofa with my face to the wall' – or, as he

* On June 18th Churchill gave instructions 'to lay forcible hands on all Belgian shipping within our reach'.

put it to his biographer, Huizinga, 'I turned the sofa against the wall to show them my backside.'[309]

The Ministers were already moving steadily down the slippery slope towards total surrender to and collaboration with the Germans. By contrast, King Leopold was adhering firmly to the principles he had set himself: eschewing all political activity, refusing all contact with the Nazi hierarchy and advising enquirers such as Paul Tschoffen that the country was still in a state of war; that Belgians should only undertake such work as was essential for the life of the people; and must do nothing militarily, politically or economically which might harm the Allied cause. When the King's Chef de Cabinet, Baron Frédéricq, asked whether he should allow his son to join the Belgian Army in France, Leopold replied 'Of course'. When the Head of his Military Household, General Tilkens, set about recruiting young men for active service in Britain, the King gave his approval. There is bitter irony in this contrast of attitudes, for it was not the Ministers, Pierlot and Spaak, but Leopold and his Household who, after Belgium's liberation in 1944, were accused of defeatism and having collaborated with the enemy.

Next, on June 24th, Pierlot and Spaak sent two further messages to Laeken via the Papal Nuncio in Vichy and the former Spanish Ambassador in Belgium reiterating their desire to re-establish contact with the King 'with a view to regulating Belgian interests with the German Government'. Meanwhile Pierlot, having so far received no reply to his formal messages to the King, tried a more personal approach. On June 26th he summoned Vicomte Berryer and gave him a letter and an oral message to be conveyed to the King via his Chef de Cabinet at Laeken: 'We think there are two urgent things to be done,' wrote Pierlot, 'to negotiate with the Germans for the return of the Belgian soldiers and refugees in France, and to negotiate the terms of an armistice or peace treaty.' Pierlot then declared 'We do not wish to do anything without hearing the opinion of the King. If he considers it useful to form a new government, we are naturally ready to resign.'

In the document summarizing Pierlot's oral message which Berryer handed to Frédéricq, he wrote that he had been charged with 'explaining the Government's position to the King' and asking 'if His Majesty would, in due course, receive two Ministers'. He had also been instructed 'to offer the resignation of the Pierlot Cabinet, in order to facilitate the King's actions for the future welfare of the Nation'. The Ministers had, moreover, asked Berryer to obtain the King's 'advice and orders' and had 'all expressed their desire to return to Belgium to explain their conduct, in spite of their unpopularity there'.[310] This was indeed eating humble pie, yet Pierlot was too proud and obstinate to apologize or make amends for the slurs he had cast on his Sovereign's honour and moral character.

Thus all responsibility would have reverted, had he so wished, to the King. The fictions invented during and after the war, which represented him as a monarch collaborating with the Germans, could have been instantly rebutted on the basis of Pierlot's letter, or on the basis of the numerous other approaches that were made during the next few months by worthy and well-intentioned men, including serving and former Ministers, who wanted the King to form a government in Brussels. Nothing would have been easier or more constitutional than to accept the Prime Minister's offer to dissolve his government in France, and to adopt his suggestion that the King should form a new government in Brussels – not necessarily collaborationist in character, but acceptable to the occupying power – and to settle peace terms with the Germans. And yet, despite the fact that the King stuck to the principles which he had laid down for himself and rejected all such propositions, his entrenched critics are, to this day, still condemning him, illogically, for pursuing policies which were firmly opposed to those of his defeatist refugee government.*

Before the Ministers could receive the King's reply to their messages – indeed, as soon as Berryer had left for Brussels with them – they decided on direct action, without the King, to achieve their objective of coming to terms with the enemy. On June 27th Pierlot broadcast a speech 'to all Belgians' telling them that the war was over, that their Government had set about reaching an understanding with Germany and intended to repatriate them. The text of Pierlot's statement appeared in the French press next day.

Next, as part of the plan to get Belgium functioning again under the Nazis' New Order, the Belgian Government in collaboration with 'the occupying power' made every effort to get all their civilian and military manpower back to occupied Belgium. Accordingly, on June 30th a decree was issued over Pierlot's signature instructing all the Government departments and their staffs which had been evacuated to France, including Finance, Agriculture, Public Works, the Foreign Ministry and the Prime Minister's office, to return forthwith to Belgium. A more useful move, from the German point of view, was the Ministers' decision to demobilize and repatriate all the Belgian troops in France. Having refused to ship them to England, they rejected the proposal of General Van Daele, the commander of the Belgian forces in France, that they should be sent to the Congo, via Morocco. Instead, they obtained the co-operation of the German Armistice Commission in returning all of them to Belgium.

In a proclamation to the Army General Denis, the Minister of Defence, declared 'Today there is no longer any question of fighting – we must all work to rebuild the Country' and, in another, 'Everyone must

---

* See, for example, Jean Stengers' *Léopold III et le Gouvernment: Les Deux Politiques Belges de 1940*, published in 1980.

understand that we all, from the highest to the lowest, want to return home, and that nothing will be neglected to achieve this as soon as possible.' Denis even persuaded the Germans to allow a Belgian Military Delegation to return to Brussels in order to expedite the repatriation, demobilization and handing over of the troops to German control in Belgium – whence many of them were sent to *Stalags* in Germany, or, later on, to forced labour there.

So, in addition to all the Belgian military and civilian manpower, back poured all the Government services and all the evacuated material – motor transport, factory machinery, railway rolling-stock, equipment and staff, together with the technical resources and personnel of the Belgian Radio. The return of the last was personally supervised by the Minister of Communications, Antoine Delfosse (the only member of the Government to be left behind in Belgium – his flight having been blocked by the enemy's advance), whom the Germans allowed to travel to France for the purpose. Agents in this return traffic were sometimes dubious. The leading Belgian Communist Lahaut,* for example, was given a car and a special pass by the Germans to tour France for the purpose of rounding up Belgian workers and inducing them to return to Belgium, to be put to work for the New Order or to be sent to 'voluntary' or forced labour in Germany. Following the 'Unholy Alliance' between Stalin and Hitler and until the Germans invaded Russia, the Nazis and Communists worked hand-in-glove. Indeed, Stalin sent his 'warmest congratulations' to Hitler on the 'splendid success' of his armies in conquering Holland, Belgium and France, before presenting, on June 26th, an ultimatum to Rumania and annexing Bessarabia – in accordance with the secret 'spheres of influence' clauses of the Nazi-Soviet Alliance – on the following day.

Pierlot now made yet another effort to come to terms with Nazi Germany. On July 3rd he arranged a meeting with the former Belgian Ambassador in Berlin, Vicomte Davignon, and with much amiability but great insistence asked him to go to Berne, contact the German Minister and open up armistice negotiations with the Reich. He described regretfully his previous failures to do so through various diplomats and Spaak's approach to Paul Baudouin. The French Government had promised to lay their appeal for peace talks before the Franco-German Armistice Commission at Wiesbaden – but nothing, alas, had materialized.

Davignon, a loyal servant of the King, was naturally wary. Pierlot's ingratiating approach was unusual, and the air of urgency suspicious. So the Ambassador declined to undertake the mission on the grounds that it was unclear whom he would be representing – the King's views being

* It was Lahaut who shouted '*Vive la République*' at King Leopold's accession ceremony and again at that of his son and successor, King Baudouin. Shortly afterwards Lahaut was assassinated by an unknown assailant.

unknown, since Vicomte Berryer was not yet back from Brussels. Pierlot nevertheless telephoned to arrange a Swiss visa for Davignon – but his efforts were in vain, for shortly afterwards the Vicomte returned to Belgium again to report to the King.

Another sign of the deliquescence of the Pierlot government was that its members had not once since the notorious assembly in Limoges communicated with the Senators and Deputies who had established themselves there. Having been left in complete ignorance of their government's policies and actions, the parliamentarians sent Raymond Leyniers, the Vice-President of the Senate, to Vichy, where the Ministers had now moved for closer association with the Pétain administration, to demand a long-overdue statement. When he reported back to a session of the two Chambers at Limoges on July 8th, Leyniers declared that Pierlot had spoken '*avec clarté, précision et compréhension*'.

But the message Pierlot conveyed to the parliamentarians, though clear, was hardly inspiring. It must be understood, he had said, that the Belgians should accustom themselves to a new mentality – the outlook of a conquered people. At the best, it might be expected that Belgium would continue to exist with a qualified independence, absorbed inside a *Zollverein* and governed by a Gauleiter. Leyniers then repeated with emphasis that the Government begged the parliamentarians to get into their heads ('*mettre dans la tête*') that they were a defeated nation and must adapt themselves to the fact.

In the midst of these activities, on July 10th, Vicomte Berryer arrived with a reply from Laeken which cut the ground from under the Ministers' feet. Leopold's answer, transmitted through his Chef de Cabinet, was uncompromising. 'The King's position is unchanged. He undertakes no political acts and receives no political figures. The Red Cross is handling the repatriation of Belgians from France.' M. Frédéricq had 'indicated', Berryer said, that the King did not favour the return to Belgium of Pierlot and his colleagues – indeed he considered that 'if they were to be consistent with themselves, they would go to England'. Spaak himself later admitted that the King's attitude 'saved us' and that he 'prevented us from committing '*une faute très grave*'.* It was indeed fortunate for them that the King rebuffed their importunities – for had he not done so there is no knowing how far they might have followed down the slippery road taken by Pétain and Laval – although it is unlikely that Hitler would have had any truck with the Pierlot government, even if the King had given them his support. For German policy required a submissive, tranquil Belgium, a zone of productivity for the *Reich*, and it was well known in Berlin that Pierlot and his colleagues were spurned and execrated by the people of their occupied country. Why should the Germans have

---

* See also Appendix IX, for Spaak's 'confession' on television in 1969: 'We were saved by the King's refusal to listen to us.'

bothered with these men of straw? But there can be little doubt that, had the Führer accepted their collaboration, they would have gone down in history as Quislings.

Since well before the end of June Pierlot, Spaak and most of their ministerial colleagues had been issuing statements declaring that the war was over for Belgium and seeking through every possible channel to persuade the Germans to talk terms. Now, on July 10th – the day King Leopold's message was received – Spaak wrote what can only be described as a crawling letter to Señor Aunos, the Spanish Ambassador in Brussels. After describing how he had retreated to France 'to continue this war which I considered avoidable, mad and ill-conducted', Spaak told the Ambassador that though a number of attempts had been made to make contact with the Germans, all had failed. 'The Government of the *Reich* ignores us completely. In its eyes we don't exist.' And yet, Spaak continued with magnificent presumption, 'our sole desire is to help our King to rescue something from the disaster we have suffered.' Could the Ambassador, could Franco's government lend their aid?

The even deeper state of apathy and despair into which the refugee Ministers sank after the return of their administrative staffs to Belgium and after all their attempts to parley with the Nazis had failed is well described in an account of Antoine Delfosse's meeting with Comte Capelle in Brussels on July 18th. The Minister of Communications had just arrived back in Brussels after supervising the return of all Belgium's evacuated radio and communications equipment and personnel from France and was seeking an audience of the King.

In Vichy Delfosse had encountered his colleagues, Spaak, Eugène Soudan, Léon Matagne and Comte d'Aspremont Lynden, who all asked him to tender their resignations to the King on his return to Belgium. According to Capelle's *compte-rendu* of this interview, Delfosse found that his colleagues, bereft of their ministerial assistants, were 'extremely depressed, disheartened and completely inactive' and that 'they viewed the future with apprehension'.[310] Delfosse asked Capelle to inform the King that he was at his disposal, as a Minister endowed with his full powers, to countersign his decrees – in particular those covering the resignation of these four members of the Pierlot Cabinet and the appointment of new Ministers.

Here was another example of how the King stuck to his principles, for had he wished, with Delfosse's counter-signature, he could have resumed his prerogatives, dissolved Pierlot's administration and formed a new government in Brussels – all in perfect conformity with the law and the Constitution. But the King politely declined to grant Delfosse an audience – because he was 'a prisoner and had made it his rule not to receive any politicians', as Capelle wrote in his letter of refusal to the Minister, thus antagonizing him greatly.

It will have been noted that all attempts to initiate negotiations with the enemy had come from Pierlot and Spaak, and none from the German side. On July 18th Hitler issued a decisive edict:

> The Pierlot government has on several occasions applied to the German Government to start negotiations for the return of refugees and for an official armistice. The Führer's point of view is that there is no Belgian Government. All requests from the Belgian Authorities to get in contact with us must be turned down.

Two days later the German Military Governor in Brussels decreed that no member of the Belgian Government-in-exile would in any circumstances be allowed to return to Belgium. It may well have been these two crushing *Diktats* which induced the Belgian Ministers to execute the next 180° turn in their public attitude to the King. For on the next day – July 21st, Belgium's *fête nationale* – in a vain attempt to regain the favour of the Belgian people, Pierlot included this appeal in his speech to a large gathering of Belgian refugees and delegates from the Congo:

> We ardently hope that the thought that will dominate all others in the minds of all Belgians will be that of national union round the King.

This was a far cry from the spirit of the Limoges assembly, but it was this theme of loyalty to the King that Pierlot and Spaak would loudly proclaim throughout the next four years of their odyssey – until, on returning to liberated Belgium in September 1944, they once again turned against him for reasons of political and personal expediency.

In the meantime, despite Hitler's order that all approaches from the Belgian Ministers must be spurned, they made yet another attempt to make contact with the Nazi hierarchy. And it was a measure of their desperation that the Ministers should have employed for this purpose the Rexist leader, Léon Degrelle, who was destined to become one of Belgium's foremost collaborators and who was at that time languishing in a French prison, to which they themselves had consigned him!

It was therefore Pierlot, Spaak and the latter's uncle, Paul Emile Janson, the Liberal Minister of Justice – and not the Germans, as Degrelle cynically recalls in his memoirs – who interceded with Marshal Pétain to obtain his release from gaol: 'even though these modern Pontius Pilates had so villainously handed me over to the French Military Police, two months previously.'[311] It was indeed Janson who had, on May 10th, ordered the detention without trial of Degrelle and a large number of his followers, as well as Communists and other suspects, and then sent them to France – where, according to Degrelle's memoirs, they were brutally incarcerated and a number of them, including women and children, were shot by French soldiers.

As soon as the French set Degrelle free, the Belgian Ministers approached his colleague the Rexist leader and writer Pierre Daye and, with deference, thanked him for his help in liberating Degrelle; apologized for having 'wrongfully' imprisoned the latter and not only asked Daye to obtain Degrelle's 'forgiveness' and 'a reconciliation', but begged the two Rexist leaders to enter the negotiations on behalf of their government with Daye's friend Otto Abetz, the former Fifth Columnist in France, who was now German Ambassador in Paris. On July 25th, before the two Rexists left for Paris, Janson wrote formally to Daye on Ministry of Justice headed paper and, after reiterating the Ministers' gratitude and pleas for a reconciliation with the Rexists 'in an atmosphere of national concord', declared:

> I confirm that we are all prepared to submit our resignations and definitively to renounce all political activity. As M. Pierlot declared in his speech on Sunday, the Government considers that its last task is to ensure the return of the Belgians to their homeland.
> All this you can say in our name, both in Brussels and in Paris, where we strongly urge you to institute the envisaged negotiations.
> Lastly, in regard to the press in occupied Belgium . . . if you can preserve, in the journals which are published in Brussels, a character that is as Belgian as possible, you will incontestably render a signal service to your country.

This renewed attempt by Pierlot, Spaak and Janson to ingratiate themselves with the Nazi hierarchy was, however, as fruitless as all the others. On August 1st, moreover, the nadir was reached when the Bank of France refused to cash the Belgian Government's cheques and, on the same day, Pétain was ordered by his conquerors to break off diplomatic relations with countries under German rule. The Ministers were thus unwanted by the Nazis, unwanted by France, unwanted by their King and execrated by the people of their own homeland. But their compatriots in Belgium were not the only ones to turn against Pierlot and Spaak – for, as the latter's biographer puts it, the parliamentarians and the other Ministers who had sought refuge in France 'were rapidly leaving Pierlot's sinking ship'.[312] These Ministers had been much troubled by the persistent refusal of Pierlot and Spaak to make a public announcement rehabilitating the King, after they had learned that the charges against him were false. They would all later write letters of apology to Leopold claiming that they had been misled by the Premier and Foreign Minister – and in one of these letters De Schrijver described the unsuccessful efforts to persuade them to restore the King's honour and good name. But it was not until after Pierlot and Spaak left France some weeks later that their Cabinet colleagues were able to make a unanimous declaration repudiating the 'unspeakable' ('*inqualifiable*') accusation of treason which had been made against the King, and calling for national union round the Throne.

The parliamentarians who had so noisily vilified their King at Limoges had also quickly realized that they had put themselves horribly in the wrong and had backed the wrong horse. And they too blamed their discomfiture on Pierlot and Spaak for misleading them. 'We publicly pronounced judgment in a tragic moment . . . based mainly on M. Spaak's speech,' declared Frans Van Caulewelaert, the President of the Chamber, 'we must acknowledge that we were mistaken.'

Of the 150 Senators and Deputies who took part in the infamous Limoges debate, 114 subsequently recanted and apologized to the King, while the great majority of all parliamentarians similarly made honourable amends, both individually and collectively. Ironically, one such letter of apology was signed by a group of Socialists headed by Achille Delattre, who five years later would demand the King's abdication in pursuance of the Left's post-war campaign to overthrow him.

The situation in which Pierlot and Spaak found themselves was not a happy one – for after being 'spewed out' by the Belgian people and by the Nazis, rebuffed by the King in their attempts to come to terms with the enemy and treated with contempt by the French, they had now alienated themselves from their fellow-Ministers and the members of both Chambers. Whither to swing next? Hopes of returning to Belgium with the approval of the King and of the Germans had been shattered. Resignation? Perhaps they might slip back home as private citizens – but the hostile and contemptuous attitude of their compatriots made this an unwelcome prospect. There was no thought in their minds of betaking themselves to England in response to the growing number of appeals to that effect which reached them from overseas – because, as Pierlot said to one of his compatriots, Hugh Ansiaux, with his head in his hands: 'How can we possibly renew the struggle, having said that we had abandoned it?'[313] Moreover, as Pierlot admits in his memoirs, they recognized that without the King 'we no longer represent anything.'[314]

In the different capitals of the world Belgian diplomats and other representatives were complaining that they had not heard from their government since June 21st, nor received any response to their messages of enquiry. One diplomat, after several vain attempts to make contact with Spaak (he even tried a reply-paid telegram), observed 'Vichy shows no sign of life.' And the Belgian Minister in Berne, Comte d'Ursel, reported to Comte Capelle that the Government had not communicated with him since it left Poitiers, nor remunerated him and his colleagues in other capitals since May 10th.

It was ironic, but fortunate for Pierlot and Spaak, that at the very time when they were trying so desperately to persuade the Nazis to accept their collaboration, their ministerial colleague De Vleeschauwer was devoting his energies to collaborating wholeheartedly with the British. Indeed, he had begun to do so from the moment he arrived in Lisbon on June 24th. De Vleeschauwer's first action was to call on the British Ambassador, Sir Walford Selby – and, after establishing his credentials as the Administrator-General of the Colonies and the only legally-empowered Minister in the free world, asked him to convey to Whitehall that he was 'determined to afford the utmost assistance to the British cause'. At the same time he telegraphed to the Belgian Ambassador in London that he had decided 'to co-operate unreservedly with England'.

The unexpected arrival of De Vleeschauwer in a free country was a tremendous relief to Baron de Cartier, since he had been 'holding the fort' as the only legitimate representative of Belgium, in the appallingly difficult situation which had been created by Reynaud's vilification of Leopold and his army, and which had now led to the deliquescence of the Pierlot administration in France. And here was an undefeatist Belgian Minister, who was not only endowed with exceptional powers, but, like de Cartier himself and the loyal Belgian community in Britain, was dedicated to upholding the honour and dignity of their King and Country, and to ensuring that Belgium and the Congo remained at the side of Great Britain and her allies.

Only a few days had passed since de Cartier had relayed to Lord Halifax, albeit in modified form, Spaak's defeatist *message d'abandon* – and during that time there had been an increasing danger that the British Government would 'write off' the legitimate but potentially collaborationist Pierlot government and recognize an illegal regime headed by the dismissed Minister, Marcel-Henri Jaspar, comprising a number of extreme left-wing Belgian politicians who had fled to England.

There had, of course, never been a 'Belgian Government' in London, although Winston Churchill would reiterate after the war in *Their Finest Hour* the erroneous declaration he had made in Parliament on June 4th 1940 that the Belgian Government was 'now in London'.* The Prime Minister had, since before the Belgian capitulation, been anxious to make his wishful-thinking come true, by establishing a 'Free Belgian Government' in England as had been done in the cases of Czechoslovakia, Poland, Holland, Luxembourg and Norway. Indeed, it was vitally important to him that subservient *émigré* groups representing all the countries which had been conquered by the Nazis should place themselves under Great Britain's wing, not only for prestige reasons and to collaborate in her war effort, but above all to put their free assets at her disposal. This was particularly desirable in Belgium's case, because of her enormous wealth in gold and currency, her 450,000 tons of shipping and the almost

---

* This incorrect statement was expurgated from the serialized version of Winston Churchill's book, when it was published in Belgium after the war by *Le Soir*.

limitless resources in desperately-needed raw materials of the Congo.

Thus, when Churchill learned that the Belgian Government refused to rally to England and was attempting to come to terms with the enemy, he began to consider recognizing a 'Free Belgian Government' comprising such Belgians as were available in England to do his bidding, without too much regard to their political affiliations or reputations at home and abroad. The Foreign Office, however, was more reserved in its attitude to the motley collection of refugee politicians who were now jostling for recognition as free Belgian leaders in Britain.

As can be seen from the inter-departmental minutes which passed back and forth within the Foreign Office, the activities of Marcel-Henri Jaspar were causing some concern in Whitehall and 'considerable disquiet and enormous confusion' amongst the Belgian community in England.[315] Despite the fact that the Pierlot Cabinet had stripped Jaspar of his ministerial powers and disowned him, he was busy publishing 'decrees' in the name of 'the Belgian Government in London' and trying to set up various government departments with himself as Prime Minister. Jaspar had even asked de Cartier to be his Foreign Minister, as the Baron told Lord Halifax with wry humour at the Foreign Office on June 24th.[316] De Cartier had called on the Foreign Secretary not only to tell him about De Vleeschauwer's arrival in Lisbon and his pro-British sentiments, but to emphasize that as Belgian Ambassador he was the sole legal representative of the Kingdom in London and that Jaspar's claims to that effect were spurious.

In fact, the Foreign Office needed no convincing that Jaspar had no following among his compatriots at home or abroad and was 'quite unsuitable as a Belgian leader', as Francis Aveling put it in a report – adding that the ex-Minister was regarded 'in Belgian political circles as a mountebank and an adventurer'.[317] Indeed, reactions to Jaspar's attempts to emulate General de Gaulle as the self-styled '*premier résistant belge*' with a grandiose 'proclamation' urging all Belgians to continue the struggle under his leadership, larded as it was with such phrases as 'the time is not for tears, but for action' and 'death rather than slavery', had been negative, derisive or hostile. The American Ambassador in London, Joseph Kennedy, for example, wrote that Jaspar 'had no backing whatsoever among the Belgian people' and was 'the cheapest sort of small-time politician, personally ambitious and crooked'.[318]

The Foreign Office was faced with yet another headache and the loyal Belgian community with further 'disquiet and confusion' when on July 26th a rival pretender to the leadership of the 'Free Belgian Government' appeared in London. This was the avowed Republican ex-Minister Camille Huysmans, another left-wing extremist who weaves in and out of King Leopold's story. Huysmans immediately assumed the leadership of a group of far-Left Belgian politicians who had fled to England with the object of forming a Republican Belgian government in London. Within a few days Huysmans presided over this group when it proclaimed itself, without any semblance of legality, 'the Belgian Government in London'. It was also described as 'the Huysmans-Jaspar Cabinet', the Marxist and the Liberal-Left ex-Ministers having formed an uneasy alliance, although – as Huysmans told Lord Halifax – he would serve in a government with, but not under Jaspar.

The British Foreign Secretary was aware that the reputations of Huysmans and some of his comrades were even worse than that of Jaspar, as is revealed in the voluminous Foreign Office documentation on the subject. In a note to Aveling, for example, Halifax wrote that Huysmans had 'a very bad reputation in Belgium', where he had been the head of the Marxist Second International – and that, as Burgomaster of Antwerp, 'he had deserted his post'.[319] (Huysmans had been amongst the first to flee to France, in his chauffeur-driven Cadillac.) He was also described as being 'very unpopular' in Belgium and as having 'many enemies'. Other arguments put forward against Huysmans by his British and Belgian critics included the fact that the Belgian people, who were 'passionately devoted' to their King, would never tolerate a revolutionary Republican as a member of their government. The same could be said of most of the members of Huysmans' 'Cabinet', since it comprised such Republican-Marxist extremists as Max Buset and Arthur Gailly, who had cried out the loudest at the Limoges assembly for the setting up of a Soviet-style Belgian Republic and the execution of the King – and would persist in viciously attacking him, right up to and even after his abdication in 1950. There were also two formidable women of the same persuasion in the group: Mesdames Hubin and Isabelle Blume, a fiery revolutionary known as '*La Passionata*', of whom more will be heard later.

De Cartier and the responsible Belgian patriots with whom he was in contact throughout the world were naturally aghast at the prospect of Britain recognizing a 'government' formed by these 'undesirables' and were doing everything possible to frustrate this eventuality. Such a government, declared Georges Theunis in a telegram from Washington, would be 'illegal and eventually revolutionary in character . . . and would exacerbate discord among Belgians'.[320] And De Vleeschauwer would later write to Comte d'Ursel, the Belgian Minister in Berne, that the British Government had been prepared to recognize 'a revolutionary government composed of certain Belgian parliamentarians of whom some with frankly Republican tendencies are most active in London and to whom the gold of the Bank of Belgium would be handed over as enemy property'.[321]

When De Vleeschauwer first arrived in Lisbon on June 24th, Jaspar had been sufficiently sure of his own prospects of being recognized as the leader of a new Belgian government in London to cable the Minister for the Colonies: '*Viens, rejoins-moi, nous gouvernerons ensemble.*' De Vleeschauwer naturally ignored this presumptious message, but de Cartier de Marchienne was so worried by the activities of Jaspar, Huysmans and company that he sent a trusted emissary post-haste to Lisbon to warn De Vleeschauwer about them and to beg him to come immediately to London to restore the situation to legality.

Before flying to England from Lisbon in the British aircraft which was placed at his disposal, De Vleeschauwer sent off a series of telegrams designed to restore confidence in Belgium and her leadership. His theme was that the Belgian Government, loyal to their King, would continue the struggle at the side of the British and that all the resources of the Congo would be used for that purpose. In his messages to Belgium's overseas representatives establishing his governmental authority, De Vleeschauwer shrewdly promised to pay their salaries from the same source. He also ordered them not to accept any instructions which came directly or indirectly from enemy-occupied territory – and he included Vichy France in that category. Then, to the amazement and gratification of Belgium's creditors and those throughout the world who thought of her as defunct, De Vleeschauwer proclaimed that the Congo would pay all the Mother Country's debts.

When De Vleeschauwer arrived in London on July 4th, he was welcomed with open arms not only by de Cartier and the loyal Belgian community, but also by the British Government. Indeed the Belgian Minister found himself the subject of pressing and persistent attention, for as Administrator-General of the Congo, with its enormous riches, and the only legitimate member of the Belgian Government at large, he was a man to be wooed. Under the guidance of de Cartier, De Vleeschauwer had within a week met, lunched or dined with Winston Churchill, Lord Halifax, Lord Lloyd (the Colonial Secretary), Hugh Dalton, Lord Woolton, Sir Archibald Sinclair and Duff Cooper (the Minister of Information). De Vleeschauwer also had discussions with Clement Attlee (the Socialist Deputy Prime Minister), Sir Alexander Cadogan, Lord Camrose (of the *Daily Telegraph*) and other men of influence, including the American Ambassador and Dutch statesmen. At every one of these meetings, as De Vleeschauwer recalls, he was asked the embarrassing question 'Where is your government? Why is it not coming here?'[322]

De Vleeschauwer had been preceded by the favourable reports rendered to Lord Halifax by Sir Walford Selby, Francis Aveling and others describing him as 'a good man' who was 'on our side' and 'the only determined member of the Pierlot government', which was 'demoralized' and would probably 'soon come to terms with Germany'. He was therefore well received when he called on Halifax at the Foreign Office on the day after his arrival in London. De Vleeschauwer's first concern was to establish the basis of his co-operation with the British Government. As

Halifax recorded in a note to Aveling, the Belgian Minister declared that he had come as 'an ally and a friend', with the full powers of a member of his government, 'to offer everything he had to offer to the Allied cause'.[323] He added, however, that he was acting 'in strict legality and for my King and Country', and would therefore have nothing to do with any self-appointed and illegal Belgian 'government' or 'national committee' – or with those like Jaspar, who claimed to have formed one. De Vleeschauwer also stressed from the first that he and his associates were devotedly loyal to their King and deeply deplored the defamatory statements which Reynaud had broadcast about him. They fully approved of the position which Leopold had taken: that as a prisoner in German hands he was 'temporarily in the impossibility of reigning' and would not exercise his powers until Belgium regained her liberty.

When Halifax asked De Vleeschauwer why his colleagues in Vichy were not coming to England, he replied that they were demoralized and had 'neither the will nor the power to govern'. They felt that their task was ended, and only wanted to resign – the problem being that there was no one to whom they could submit their resignations! Above all they did not want to do anything to obstruct any action the King might want to take in Belgium. De Vleeschauwer declared, however, that he 'did not despair' of persuading some of his fellow Ministers to come to London to join him in continuing the struggle at the side of Great Britain and her allies. In the meantime, said De Vleeschauwer, he would use his powers not only to rule the Congo, but also to regulate all other Belgian Government matters, including finance, diplomacy and the Belgian armed forces in Britain.[324]

The high point of De Vleeschauwer's whirlwind visit to London was his first encounter with Winston Churchill, over lunch at 10 Downing Street on July 8th. According to the Belgian Minister's account of this crucial meeting, he was greeted warmly by Churchill, and, as they shook hands, he declared 'I bring you everything that we have and everything that we possibly can.' But, after reiterating that he was 'acting in strict legality and for my King and Country', he warned Churchill that if the British Government recognized the Huysmans-Jaspar regime 'I would withdraw and you would get nothing more from me, indeed you would not only provoke discord among Belgians, but would arouse the anger and hatred of the people in our occupied country against those whom you would be sustaining and thus, on the rebound, against yourselves.'[325] De Vleeschauwer drove this point home at a subsequent meeting with Hugh Dalton, the Socialist Minister for Economic Warfare: 'We have a legal government of which I am the representative. A committee in its place would be illegal . . . I will not collaborate in it. I will bring you everything in a legal manner; you will not obtain more, not a kilo more copper, from such a committee.'[326]

Although Winston Churchill had been in favour of recognizing the illegal 'government' of Huysmans and Jaspar and was under pressure from the Labour members of his Cabinet to do so, he was favourably impressed by De Vleeschauwer and his resolute attitude and soon declared: 'We are in agreement, we have confidence in you.'[327] De Vleeschauwer found Churchill in an emotional state, with tears in his eyes, since he had on the previous day given orders for the destruction of the French Flcct at Mcrs-El-Kébir and was anxious about reactions on the Continent. The Belgian Minister reassured Churchill as best he could, and an excellent *rapport* was established between the two men.

When Churchill asked the inevitable question about the intentions of the other Belgian Ministers, De Vleeschauwer declared '*L'activité de la Belgique, pour le moment, c'est moi*' – to which the Prime Minister replied 'But you are a bit thin by yourself!'[328] De Vleeschauwer then promised that he would try to persuade at least three Ministers, Pierlot, Spaak and Gutt, to join him in London. Shortly afterwards Pierlot, alarmed by reports that De Vleeschauwer was 'exceeding his brief' and committing the Belgian Government to collaborating with the British, sent him a telegram demanding that he should rejoin his colleagues in Vichy forthwith.

De Vleeschauwer immediately assured Churchill that he had no intention of obeying Pierlot's instruction and that he well knew what would happen to him if he were to return to France. De Vleeschauwer made no reply to this telegram and when he asked Pierlot for an explanation, after he had finally persuaded him to come to London four months later, the Premier replied lamely 'We had all decided to resign and put an end to our participation in the war, and we wanted you to be with us.'[329]

In the meantime, De Vleeschauwer sent Pierlot and his colleagues in Vichy a series of messages urging them to join him in London to continue the struggle. But having received no reply to any of them, he came to an agreement with Churchill and Halifax that he should return to the Continent – but not to France – and try to extract some of his fellow Ministers from their Vichy retreat. Before leaving, De Vleeschauwer obtained their assurance that they would not recognize any Belgian 'government' or 'national committee' during his absence, although they warned him that they might have to do so if some more functioning and co-operative Belgian Ministers did not come to England in the near future.

On July 16th De Vleeschauwer flew to Portugal and then travelled to San Sebastian in Spain, where Leopold's three children were staying. He had greeted them at the frontier during his previous visit, when they had first arrived in Spain on June 20th, and was now able to help with the arrangements for their return to Belgium, for which the Germans had given permission. De Vleeschauwer took this opportunity to write a long letter and report to the King on July 28th, which he gave to Princess Josephine-Charlotte for delivery to her father at Laeken.

The Minister began by expressing his loyalty and devotion to his Sovereign and described what he had done and intended to do 'for my King and Country'. He then brought Leopold fully up to date on everything that had happened since he had left his Cabinet colleagues in Vichy – without, however, mentioning their disloyal and defeatist activities in May and June, in which he had not been involved. He paid particular tribute to de Cartier for the stalwart support he had given to their cause '*Pour le Roi et la Patrie dans la légalité*'. This, De Vleeschauwer affirmed, was their theme and also that Belgium must bend all her efforts, within the limits of her means, to sustaining those whose victory would restore her liberty and that of her King. 'We will provide the British Empire,' he continued, 'with all the resources she needs . . . The prosperity of the Colony will be a certain proof of Belgium's vitality and will be of invaluable assistance to the Mother Country when she recovers her liberty.' De Vleeschauwer ended his letter: 'I pray to God to help Your Majesty and to protect our beloved Belgium, which I long to see free again under my revered Sovereign.'[330]

Meanwhile, from Lisbon and Madrid De Vleeschauwer continued to bombard the Belgian Ministers in Vichy with urgent messages, without evoking any response. ('They no longer bothered to read your cables, *mon cher*,' Camille Gutt told him later.) They did, however, try to 'draw' De Vleeschauwer back into Vichy France, as he put it, by obtaining an entry visa for him from the Pétain government, but he was far too alert to fall into that trap.

However, De Vleeschauwer eventually managed, with great difficulty, to persuade Pierlot, Spaak and Gutt to meet him at Perthus on the Franco-Spanish frontier. In this he was helped by two Belgian diplomats who had free access to Vichy France and by the British Ambassador in Madrid, Sir Samuel Hoare, who made available to him the services of the Intelligence personnel attached to his Embassy. De Vleeschauwer was compelled to wait beside the road on the Spanish side of the frontier throughout August 1st and the morning of the 2nd, before the three Ministers appeared, which naturally aroused the suspicion of both the French and Spanish border guards. But he managed to persuade the latter that he was a Belgian University professor (which was true) and wanted to confer with some 'parents and friends' who were living in France, without entering that country. Thanks to the amicable relations he established with these officials, he was allowed to hold a meeting with Pierlot, Spaak and Gutt in the French customs house in 'no man's land', when they finally arrived during the afternoon of August 2nd.

The two-and-a-half hour discussion which followed was of crucial importance in Belgium's history, for by the end of the meeting the reluctant Pierlot and Spaak were persuaded by De Vleeschauwer's passionate advocacy to agree to join him in London 'soon'. Although De Vleeschauwer could rightly claim the credit for inducing them to agree to do so, it would be the King's influence which would finally uproot them from their Vichy refuge, as will be seen. After this meeting Pierlot and Spaak returned to Vichy, ostensibly to tidy up their affairs and with a promise that they would come to London 'within two weeks . . . perhaps with some colleagues'.[331]

Camille Gutt, the Minister of Finance, had already been persuaded by the emissaries and messages sent to Vichy by De Vleeschauwer, de Cartier, Theunis and others to betake himself to England, and was able to enter Spain and accompany De Vleeschauwer on his return journey to London, with the aid of an ordinary traveller's visa. Gutt had, however, undergone several changes of front and mind before reaching this point of decision. Having joined his colleagues in castigating Leopold in May and June, Gutt wrote him a confused, despairing letter on July 13th regretting his disloyalty and defection, but 'demanding' that the King should recall him to Brussels. However, in the letters and telegrams Gutt sent to a friend in America that same month he declared not only that 'the war was lost' but that it was 'impossible' for him to return to Belgium, despite 'his fervent desire' to do so, because of his reputation as 'a Jew, a Liberal and a banker'. And yet Gutt gives the impression in his memoirs that he, not De Vleeschauwer, was the prime mover in bringing about the eventual reconstitution of the pro-Allied Belgian Government in London two months later.

CHAPTER THIRTY-ONE

The Turncoats

'These chameleon Ministers, worn out by their changes of colour.'
Alfred Fabre-Luce, *Une Tragédie Royale*

When Pierlot and Spaak arrived back in Vichy, their new-found resolve quickly evaporated and they began to regret the promises they had made to De Vleeschauwer. Indeed 'soon' was not immediately, for the future heads of 'the Belgian Government in London' were singularly lethargic about removing themselves from the peace and relative comfort of unoccupied France, and facing an embattled Britain. The two Ministers were infected with the defeatism which prevailed in Vichy and felt rejected by the whole world – by their Cabinet colleagues, by the Germans, by the French, by their own people and, above all, by their Sovereign. How could they act without the advice, approval and support of the King? For he was the only one who counted in Belgium – being 'almost sanctified in public opinion', as Vanderpoorten put it in a letter to a friend.[332]

The Ministers were desperately anxious to regain the King's favour, or at least not to make relations any worse than they already were by going against his wishes. Now that Hitler had forbidden any member of the Pierlot government to return to Belgium there remained only two courses of action open to them – to remain in France and resign, or make their way to England. After nearly three weeks of paralysis Pierlot and Spaak therefore decided that they would do nothing until they had 'ascertained the King's wishes and, if possible, obtained his instructions', by sending yet another emissary to Laeken. For this mission they chose Commandant Georges Hannecart – who, as their 'Commissioner-General for Repatriation', was permitted by the Germans to circulate freely between France and Belgium in the course of his duties.[333] Before any reply was received from Laeken, however, Pierlot and Spaak were bombarded anew with urgent demands from Britain and America that they should come to London without further delay.

On August 13th De Vleeschauwer and Gutt signalled that the British Government hesitated to recognize the validity of their powers, particularly in financial matters, before Pierlot and Spaak arrived in London, adding that the Foreign Office had warned that if they did not come soon, it would be forced to recognize a Belgian 'National Committee'.[334]

Three days later, on August 16th, Gutt cabled Pierlot and Spaak that 'vital financial matters were insoluble' without their presence in London and reiterated that the British 'would recognize the Jaspar Government and hand over to it the Belgian gold held in the Bank of England', if the two Ministers' arrival was further delayed. Next day an even stronger message was sent from London, signed by De Vleeschauwer, Gutt and de Cartier, 'insisting' that Pierlot and Spaak should immediately fulfil their promise – this being 'the sole means of avoiding irreparable damage to Belgium's interests'. Then on August 20th De Vleeschauwer and Gutt sent Pierlot and Spaak a virtual ultimatum:

> Your silence during the last sixteen days, despite all our cables and letters, makes us fear that you are unwilling to leave, in spite of your promise, and that you are being driven towards resigning.
>   Prolongation of the present situation will lead not only to the disappearance of the Government, which will be catastrophic for Belgium's immense material, moral and political interests, including the Colonies, but to the recognition of a Jaspar-Huysmans-Dens-Buset-Wauters government, and to their gaining possession of our [gold and currency] holdings.
>   Your remaining in France or resigning will in no way improve your position in Brussels, and will cause irreparable damage here, while the presence of a stable government [in London] will enable us to regulate the large number of urgent Belgian problems, and to prepare for a great future . . . Cable whether or not you are coming . . . We await you anxiously.[335]

It had now been made abundantly clear to Pierlot and Spaak that if they did not come over soon the British Government would not only recognize a Belgian 'government' composed largely of Marxists and Republicans, but would treat the two Ministers as being in a hostile camp, on the principle that 'if you are not with us, you are against us'. But even this pistol to their heads failed to bring the reluctant pair to the point of decision. Indeed the reply which they eventually made, on August 20th, to the spate of messages from London simply declared that it was 'impossible to decide at the moment', as they were awaiting the King's advice.[336]

Ironically, Commandant Hannecart, the emissary whom Pierlot and Spaak had sent to King Leopold to obtain his 'advice and instructions' was, on that same day, presenting himself at Laeken to General Tilkens, the head of the King's Military Household, and telling him that the Belgian Ministers in Vichy were '*très désemparés et complètement inertes*' – and that Pierlot and Spaak, in particular, were uneasy and undecided about joining their two colleagues in beleaguered London. Indeed, Hannecart reported that Pierlot had declared that he would only go to England if he was guaranteed a safe passage for his wife and eight children, while Spaak had expressed his anxiety about his family in

Belgium.[337] In the long discussion with Tilkens which followed, Hanne-cart was greatly impressed by the resolutely pro-British stance of this trusted right-hand man of the King and his confident prediction that Germany would eventually suffer defeat at their hands. At the end of the meeting Tilkens asked Hannecart to return next day, when he would be given the King's response to the Prime Minister's *démarche*.[338]

Commandant Hannecart had been charged by Pierlot with enquiring verbally if the King wanted the Government 'to resign *en bloc* and disperse on French territory' – or would he prefer that Pierlot and 'one or two Ministers should go to London to continue with the policy of aid to the Allies', after those who remained in France had resigned? Pierlot had also givcn Hannccart for dclivery to thc King a long lctter and various documents, including a 'draft proclamation' and copies of the letters which he and Spaak had received from de Cartier de Marchienne, Theunis and others, begging them to reinforce De Vleeschauwer and Gutt in London in order to 'safeguard Belgian interests' and thus avoid the danger that a Republican 'government' would be set up there.[339]

Pierlot's letter informed the King that the refugee Belgian Ministers felt compelled to 'dissolve the Government' because the French had cut off their funds and had ceased to recognize or cooperate with them. Pierlot therefore submitted for the King's approval a 'draft proclamation to the Belgian people' announcing the Belgian Government's dissolution, which he wanted to issue. This began by paying a handsome tribute to the King for the 'energetic stimulus' he had given to strengthening Belgium's military power and security against aggression through the policy of armed independence in the pre-war years.

The proclamation declared that the Army, after resisting the invasion for eighteen days, had been 'forced to capitulate, and the King, who commanded it, shared the fate of his soldiers, and was made prisoner'. After skipping lightly over the subsequent period of confusion and '*informations tendancieuses*', it stated that in exercising the Sovereign's powers under Article 82, because he was a prisoner, 'the Government had not acted against the King, but had been compelled to act without him'. The Government's efforts to repatriate the two million Belgian civilians and troops were then described, with the comment that 'the King, as a prisoner, could make no decision on this subject'. In view of the financial and other difficulties the Ministers were experiencing, the proclamation continued, they found it impossible to fulfil their duties and therefore would, after delegating the necessary powers to the repatriation committee to enable its task to be completed, 'cease to exercise their functions'. The proclamation ended with this appeal: '*Restez unis, autour du Roi, symbole de la Patrie indépendante. La Belgique vivra.*'[340]

When General Tilkens delivered to the King Pierlot's documents and oral request for a ruling on whether or not the Premier and some other

Ministers should go to London, he also passed on all that he had gleaned from Commandant Hannecart and summarized everything in his *note au Roi*.[341] Leopold was therefore in full possession of the facts concerning the Belgian Ministers, both in Vichy and London, and their contrasting attitudes. But notwithstanding the fact that Pierlot and Spaak had by their atrocious behaviour lost all credibility and respect and were now held in universal disrepute, the King still ruled in favour of their joining De Vleeschauwer and Gutt in London and there re-establishing a legal Belgian government on the side of Great Britain and her allies.

Since a number of Belgian writers with an anti-Leopold bias or a political axe to grind have either ignored, denied or twisted these facts, or sought to discredit the principal witnesses thereto, it must be emphasized that the testimony given by General Tilkens and Commandant Hannecart is unimpeachable and has never been seriously challenged.

In a fully authenticated statement[342] the Commandant records that when he returned to Laeken on the day after his first meeting, General Tilkens described the conversation he had had with Leopold. Tilkens told him that, after some discussion and having considered Pierlot's various documents and messages, 'the King said that he approved of Pierlot and Spaak going to London and of the other Ministers remaining in France'. Hannecart's account continues:

> General Tilkens said, however, that since the King was a prisoner and had eschewed all political activity, it was not possible to reveal this response in Vichy, which, if made public, might bring down terrible reprisals on Belgium.

Tilkens and Hannecart then agreed on a formula for conveying the King's reply to the Ministers. Thus, when the Commandant returned to Vichy and reported to the Cabinet on August 23rd, he declared:

> The King is a prisoner and cannot give any political advice. General Tilkens personally considers, however, that the Ministers ought to go to London. He added that he knew the position taken by the King sufficiently well to affirm that the King was of the same mind as himself.

Having made this agreed statement to the Ministers, the Commandant left them in no doubt about Leopold's wishes. Indeed, his account continues, he 'made it known that the King had given his approval for them to go to London'. Spaak then told Hannecart, according to the latter, that after some reflection he felt 'that it might be better to go to America first, and then on to London, in order not to compromise the French Government, and not to provoke reprisals against the Belgian Ministers who were going to stay in France. The pretext for going to America would be to organize food supplies for Belgium.'

Accordingly, after Pierlot had persuaded the eight Ministers who were to remain in France to place their resignations in his hands 'for submission to the King when circumstances allowed' (he and Spaak made no attempt to persuade any of their alienated colleagues to join their *exeunt* to freedom), the two Ministers obtained the Cabinet's approval for their journey 'to America to organize food supplies for Belgium', with the proviso that 'they would be free to go to England' from the USA in due course. Leopold was then informed via the Belgian Legation in Berne of 'the dissolution of the Pierlot government in France' and the fact that the Premier and the Foreign Minister 'had departed for the United States'.

The two Ministers' true motives and intentions will, however, always be obscure. It is impossible to tell whether or not they actually intended to go to England at this point, since they subsequently gave conflicting explanations as to why they had not gone to America as promised. While Pierlot declared enigmatically that a 'detour via America' to England had to be ruled out because of the length of time they were held up in Spain, Spaak admitted that they had never intended to honour the solemn undertaking to go to America that they had given their fellow-Ministers, in any case!

There is, however, no obscurity surrounding the circumstances of the two Ministers' departure from Vichy a few hours after they had received from Commandant Hannecart the King's advice that they should join their two colleagues in London and continue the struggle alongside the British. Indeed, it is clear that this was the crucial factor which finally impelled Spaak and Pierlot (accompanied by the latter's wife and eight children) to set off by car for the Spanish frontier on August 24th – since, as we have seen, they refused to budge from Vichy until they had received an answer to their request for the King's 'advice and instructions'.

The two Ministers' Spanish journey irresistibly conjures up the image of Quixote Pierlot and Sancho Panza Spaak, interminably tilting at windmills. Everything went wrong, though their predecessors had passed through unhindered. Spain was not inclined to welcome them, and they were ordered back to France. Pierlot dug in his heels however, and they had to hang about for some days in 'no man's land' between the frontiers. After arguments with frontier officials and more days of delay, rationing their food (Spaak had provided himself with a large hamper filled with such delicacies as *pâté de foie gras*), they were allowed to go to Gerona and then on to Barcelona. But they were placed under police surveillance and became virtual prisoners in their hotel, with little hope of being allowed to leave Spain. By this time Pierlot's wife and large family, whose passports were in order, had proceeded independently. Spaak's mental and physical reserves were by now near exhaustion. The author was told by a Belgian lady years later that she had seen the Foreign Minister sitting in his car, while it was held up at the frontier, in a state of tearful emotional collapse.

Meanwhile, in London De Vleeschauwer, Gutt and Cartier were holding the line with great difficulty in the face of the Foreign Office's growing impatience at the non-arrival of Pierlot and Spaak – and the campaign of intrigue waged against them by Huysmans, Jaspar and company. The latter ceaselessly tried to discredit the two legitimate Belgian Ministers and the Ambassador by letters and 'manifestos' alleging that they were 'defeatist', 'unrepresentative' and much else. *Inter alia* Jaspar, Huysmans and his fellow-Marxists complained to the Foreign Office and others that De Vleeschauwer was 'only a Junior Minister' and 'a Flemish Catholic', while Gutt was 'a non-party Jewish financier' and not even a Member of Parliament, thus the two Ministers 'in no way represented the Nation as a whole'. These arguments found some favour in certain Foreign Office quarters – if only, as one official minuted, 'as a means to force the hands of the Belgian Government in the right direction'. The Foreign Office accordingly combined its threats to recognize the Huysmans-Jaspar 'government' if Pierlot and Spaak did not arrive soon in London with strong pressure on De Vleeschauwer and Gutt (and on Pierlot and Spaak when they eventually arrived) to appoint Ministers from other political parties and racial groups.

Indeed, the Foreign Office had a low opinion of virtually all the members and supporters of the Pierlot Government, with the possible exception of De Vleeschauwer and de Cartier de Marchienne, and also regarded the latter's left-wing antagonists in London with suspicion and disfavour. Although Gutt was at first well received, because he was Belgium's Minister of Finance and was willing to place her wealth in gold and currency at Great Britain's disposal, he soon incurred the criticism of Makins, Aveling and others as 'intolerant' and 'dictatorial'.[343] Another of the Foreign Office's complaints was that the '*gouvernement à deux*' was 'still a bit thin', as Halifax put it at his first meeting with Gutt, and also that it was 'totally unacceptable', according to Makins, 'that the Belgian Government should consist of a non-party Jew and a Flamingot Catholic, without a single Walloon'.[344] But it was Pierlot and Spaak who were held in the greatest contempt by the British Government, as can be seen from the relevant Foreign Office documents.

When De Vleeschauwer, Gutt and de Cartier (who had never had much confidence that Pierlot and Spaak would keep their promise to come to London) asked Lord Halifax to help extricate them from Spain, the scornful attitude of the Foreign Office towards the two Ministers was shown in its inter-departmental correspondence. In a minute dated September 4th, for example, William Strang recorded how Sir Samuel Hoare had been instructed to ask the Spanish Government to allow Pierlot and Spaak to leave the country, but not to press the matter to the point of jeopardizing Britain's economic relations with Spain 'for the sake of this miserable Belgian government'. This was an epithet which recurred in another note which Makins wrote to Halifax on September 29th:

> M. Pierlot and M. Spaak are not deserving of much consideration, but it is certain that a Belgian government, legally constituted and established in London under our eyes, is the only satisfactory solution to the Belgian problem.
>
> However poor the material, one can only hope that they will improve . . . I therefore recommend that we bend all our efforts to extricate these miserable Ministers.[345]

Meanwhile, on September 2nd, De Vleeschauwer took the opportunity, in a widely publicized speech in Liverpool, of proclaiming his loyalty and devotion to his Sovereign:

> . . . Our first thought goes towards the Royal prisoner at Laeken, to the leader of all Belgians whether outside occupied Belgium or within its territory; to His Majesty, King Leopold III . . .
>
> Our King, after personally leading his army in battle from the very beginning, wished to share the lot of his soldiers and was, at the time of the surrender on May 28th, made prisoner just as were his troops. As is the case of the regular Army officers, he continues to be a prisoner and conducts himself under all circumstances as a prisoner, without taking any part in the government of our country's affairs . . .

This was followed a month later by a joint broadcast from London by De Vleeschauwer and Gutt in Flemish and French, in which they told the Belgian people that they were 'the only legal Belgian Government and the only Ministers nominated by the King'. They then declared: 'We want a free Belgium and a free King . . . to achieve that end we will fight shoulder-to-shoulder with Great Britain until the final victory.' After emphasizing that Belgium had neither concluded an armistice nor signed a peace treaty and describing the magnificent spirit of the British people, as well as the gallant contribution made by the Belgian aviators in Great Britain's fight for freedom, the two Ministers ended with these words:

> Belgium is a prisoner. Long live Belgium!
> The King is a prisoner. Long live the King![345]

And both Ministers lost no opportunity to refute the scurrilous attacks which were still being made on their Sovereign. In an indignant reply to H. G. Wells' grotesque diatribe against Leopold, quoted earlier, for example, Gutt wrote in a Sunday paper: 'When he remained with his army, the King was actuated by the most honourable desire to share the fate of those who had fought under his command . . . since then he has been idolized by the Belgian Army and the whole of the Belgian population.'

By now De Vleeschauwer and Gutt had lost hope that Pierlot and Spaak would reach England, and on that assumption they took decisive action. On October 1st they not only announced that they were taking over all the ministerial portfolios between them, but pledged the resources of Belgium and her Colonies to the British Commonwealth's war effort. But they firmly resisted the British pressure to appoint other Ministers and, while Gutt assumed the roles of Minister of Finance, Foreign Affairs and Defence, De Vleeschauwer became acting Prime Minister and took over all the other Ministries.

A few days later in Spain Pierlot and Spaak, whose morale had reached its nadir at the prospect of being unable to leave that inhospitable country, were galvanized into action by the fears for their safety which had been aroused by the news that Himmler was about to visit Franco. With the help of some enterprising young Belgians from the Belgian Consulate and the British Secret Service, the two Ministers contrived, on October 18th, to leave their hotel in Barcelona undetected, while their police guards were at a football match, and to escape across the frontier into Portugal – where they were given no alternative but to go to England.

The method of escape was not attractive. They were to cross Spain and the mountainous frontier in a minute hiding-place specially built behind the driver's cab of a lorry. For hours the corpulent Spaak and the rigid Pierlot sat face to face in their tiny cell, hardly daring to breathe, because a Spanish policeman had taken a lift and was sitting within inches of them. Pierlot slipped out his rosary and prayed. In his memoirs the unbeliever Spaak characteristically recalls that he invoked Mahomet, Confucius and Buddha, on the grounds that one might as well take out as comprehensive an insurance as possible. At last the customs posts were safely behind them and they were in Portugal. King Leopold described for the author how the ebullient Spaak told him at their first meeting after the war that at this point Pierlot put out his hand, with the evident intention of placing it on Spaak's knee, and then withdrew it sharply as if he thought better of such a gesture of human warmth.

On October 24th, 1940, the British flying boat which brought Pierlot and Spaak from Lisbon touched down at Bournemouth. The perturbation in the two Ministers' minds as their aircraft approached the shores of embattled Britain can well be imagined. How would they be received? They were painfully aware of the fact that they had utterly disgraced themselves by their denunciation of their Sovereign and their fruitless attempts to induce the Nazis to accept the submission of their government, and that their actions in France had irreparably damaged the reputations of their King, their country and its army. In consequence they had not only been 'spewed out' by the Belgian people, but had alienated their ministerial colleagues and were held in contempt by the British Government and the loyal Belgian community in London. The two Ministers' political futures must indeed have looked bleak.

Whatever the unhappy pair's reluctance about making their journey, once they reached England they were committed. They had been pre-empted by the loyal and pro-Allied stance of de Cartier, the Belgian community and the two Ministers, De Vleeschauwer and Gutt. There were therefore two propositions to which the Belgian Premier and Foreign Minister were now compelled to give their unqualified assent – allegiance to their King and dedication to Great Britain's cause and war effort.

Professor Cammaerts described to the author the scene he witnessed at the Belgian Embassy when the travel-weary Pierlot and Spaak presented themselves. It was a delicate moment for men whose allegiance had been so markedly mobile. The distinguished figure of Baron de Cartier was flanked by the leading members of the Belgian community as he greeted the two Ministers, sheepish and uncomfortable under the gaze of their consistently loyal fellow-countrymen. The Ambassador explained suavely that politicians who had left their country and denounced their King were not popular in Belgium, whereas Leopold commanded the devotion of his people. Spaak knew what he must do. With an air of absolute conviction and the sonority of an expert orator, the man of successive sincerities cried out: '*Je suis pour le Roi!*'

How, in view of the behaviour of Pierlot and Spaak following the Belgian capitulation, did it ever come about that they were taken into the fold by the British Government and presented to the public as loyal and consistent Allied leaders? Looking back at their rejection of Churchill's appeals to continue the struggle in England, their declarations that Belgium was a defeated nation and no longer at war, coupled with their persistent attempts to come to terms with the Nazis, the two Ministers must have been amazed and relieved to find that the British were prepared to overlook these aberrations and recognize them as the principal Ministers in the Belgian Government-in-exile. But, as we have seen, the pragmatic Churchill, despite his aversion to the delinquent pair, wanted them under his wing in London as legal representatives of the Belgian people and, above all, to place at Britain's disposal Belgium's vast overseas resources in gold, currency, shipping and raw materials. Recognizing the Pierlot Government was now the only way for the British to secure not only these desperately needed resources, but also the moral and psychological advantages of Belgium's collaboration in their war effort. The British Government therefore made it plain from the outset what was expected of Pierlot and Spaak in return for burying their reprehensible pasts and recognizing their government, and they were not slow in fulfilling their side of the bargain.

By a series of economic and financial agreements which were signed with alacrity by the Pierlot administration, all the Congo's rich resources were placed at Great Britain's disposal. All Belgium's gold and foreign exchange and that of the Congo went to the Bank of England, which was starving for both. And looming ahead was the vast uranium potential of the *Union Minière de Haut Katanga*.* There is a revealing and character- istic note in Sir Alexander Cadogan's diary for December 24th 1940: 'Went to see H. Wilson and R. V. Hopkins about our financial difficulties in US – and about Dutch and Belgian gold, which we must try to snaffle.'[347] In this design the British were completely successful – since, in addition to securing the gold and currency mentioned above, they were able to arrange for a $260,000,000 hoard belonging to the Banque de France held in the Federal Reserve Bank of New York to be seized on behalf of the Belgian Government, which thereupon made it over to Great Britain. (£65,000,000 worth of Belgian gold consigned to England aboard a French ship had been ceded to the Germans. An American Tribunal therefore authorized the attachment of the French gold.) But in these negotiations between the two Governments – in which few conces- sions were made to the Belgians – the British, who gained very substantial advantages from them, made it a condition of their co-operation that Belgium should abandon her 'reprehensible' pre-war policy of independ- ence. The thesis that this policy was to blame for the disastrous course of events in Europe was a convenient exculpatory propaganda line for the British and all the arguments which were put forward in its favour by the Belgian Ministers fell on deaf ears.

Conscious of the universal opprobrium in which they were held, Pierlot and Spaak reacted in different ways. While Spaak tried to restore his tarnished image and ingratiate himself with the British Government by doing everything that was required of him, the chip on Pierlot's shoulder was such that he maintained a high-handed and obdurate attitude towards all with whom he came in contact throughout the war years in London. That neither of these contrasting attitudes found favour with the British Establishment is shown by the comments of those who were involved with the two Ministers. Professor Malleson, for example, a senior wartime officer in SOE (the Special Operations Executive) described to the author how Pierlot exasperated those who had to deal with him, from Winston Churchill down, by his self-righteousness and churlish intractability.

The Establishment's assessment of Spaak and the use to which he could be put can be found in the report which Francis Aveling rendered to Lord Halifax after his first interview with the Belgian Foreign Minister on October 23rd. Spaak's dramatic escape from Spain had evidently uplifted

---

* When the Germans invaded Belgium they seized the existing stocks of 600 tons of uranium oxide. The uranium output of the Congo became of intense interest to the British and Americans in the later stages of the war, as the work on an atomic bomb bore fruit. See Margaret Gowing, *Britain and Atomic Energy, 1939–1945* (Macmillan).

his depressed spirits to a remarkable extent – for Aveling found him in a state of euphoria and 'full of energy and good intentions', which prompted the diplomat's suggestion that given HM Government's 'encouragement and guidance' Spaak might be steered 'in the right direction' and thus 'make a contribution to the common cause'. But Aveling went on to describe Spaak as 'a very ambitious man, not overburdened with scruples or political principles and with a reputation to "remake" ' – adding that he was 'looked on with great suspicion by the Belgian Socialists, who regarded him as a political opportunist and as the man principally responsible for the weakness shown by the Pierlot government'.[348]

Aveling was therefore not surprised to find at his subsequent meetings with de Cartier, Pierlot and Spaak that the latter reciprocated the feelings of antipathy which the Belgian Socialists had evinced towards him. In fact, as Aveling reported to Halifax, both Ministers firmly resisted the British pressure to make their government more representative by appointing additional Ministers from the Socialist and Liberal parties (including Huysmans and Jaspar), as well as from the Catholic Party. Although the two Ministers' pretext for this refusal was that such appointments would be unconstitutional, since it was solely the King's prerogative to make them, the real reason was their determination to exclude their bitter left-wing antagonists in the Huysmans-Jaspar group – and the fact that such eminent Catholic ex-Ministers as Van Zeeland, Theunis and Van Cauwelaert refused to serve in what Aveling described as 'a government as discredited as that of M. Pierlot'.

In their conversations with British officials and Ministers – including Churchill – both Pierlot and Spaak took every opportunity to denigrate their *bêtes noires*, Jaspar and Huysmans, by repeating the stories about their desertion of their respective posts and declaring that they were held in disrepute, had no following and were therefore unacceptable as Ministers.

At one meeting to which Aveling summoned Spaak to plead in vain that the government of four should be augmented by some additional Ministers, Spaak conceded that it had shortcomings and enjoyed no support in Belgium, but declared that it was at least legal and constitutional. Spaak added that in such circumstances in normal times Pierlot would have had to resign. When Aveling observed that Spaak was the only Socialist in the government, the Minister admitted that his position in the Party was 'not strong' and that he 'could not be considered as fully representative of the Party'. Huysmans, as the senior Socialist ex-Minister in London, Spaak declared, was the obvious candidate for ministerial office, but his appointment was ruled out because of his 'many enemies' and the fact that 'public opinion, which was strongly in favour of the King, would be shocked by the presence in the Cabinet of an avowed Republican'. Pierlot and Spaak would not, however, yield to British pressure and the quartet of Ministers was formally, but reluctantly, recognized by HM Government as the Belgian Government-in-exile.

It was, moreover, Aveling who elicited from Pierlot and Spaak at another meeting, on October 22nd, this résumé of their current attitude and policy towards Leopold. 'The King,' Pierlot declared, 'considers himself a prisoner of war and resolutely refuses to involve himself in any political activity of any kind.' There had been no public communication between them, Pierlot continued, although oral messages had been passed back and forth by emissaries. The Prime Minister then affirmed that the transference of the Government to England had been approved by the King (thus, incidentally, demolishing the case of such Belgian writers as Jean Stengers who still allege that Leopold did not give his approval for this move or have his wishes conveyed to Pierlot by Commandant Hannecart).

Pierlot then declared that the King was apparently being well treated, but was a prisoner in his Palace. He was not allowed to communicate with anyone, nor leave the park, nor receive anyone without the permission of a German officer. Spaak intervened to say that the situation of the King *vis-à-vis* the Germans was becoming increasingly difficult, because the Germans were beginning to consider him as an obstacle to their plans for Belgium. At the start, Pierlot continued, the Germans hoped that the presence of the King would help to make the occupation acceptable to the Belgian population, but he was certain that the King would not do anything whatsoever which could compromise the independence of the Nation and that he would firmly maintain his status as a prisoner. Pierlot concluded by saying that he had received word that the King attached great importance to the maintenance by the Belgian Government of a legal and constitutional authority.[349]

A few days after the arrival in London of Pierlot and Spaak the British Government, although inhibited by the inexpediency of contradicting Winston Churchill's denunciation of Leopold in Parliament, was persuaded by the Belgian Ambassador to make a muted gesture in line with the Pierlot government's new policy of loyalty to the imprisoned King. On November 3rd 1940, Leopold's patronymic day, the Vice-Marshal of the Diplomatic Corps, Sir John Monk, called on de Cartier to present a message of good wishes for the King. Spaak was delighted, and immediately notified Belgian diplomatic posts throughout the world of the British Government's favourable attitude. (The occupants of these posts must have been increasingly perplexed during 1940 by the stream of contradictory information with which they were furnished!) The Belgian Ambassador next sent a copy of Cardinal van Roey's Pastoral Letter to Winston Churchill, whose secretary replied 'Rest assured that His Majesty's Government understand the attitude of His Majesty the King of the Belgians.' But the British Prime Minister's prejudiced and unrepentant attitude towards the King, his unwillingness to retract the charges he had made against him, coupled with the need to protect the reputations of Gort and the BEF, effectively prevented any public refutation or amends from being made by the British Government.

The fact that Churchill did, paradoxically, write privately to Leopold in February 1940 expressing his admiration for the King's 'dignity and fortitude' only emerged with the discovery in the United States National Archives of a copy of this letter, which was sent to the Secretary of State, Cordell Hull, in Washington with the request that President Roosevelt should write a similar letter of encouragement to Leopold.

The explanation for Churchill's apparent inconsistency is that Anthony Eden, who had replaced Halifax as Foreign Secretary, had reported at a Cabinet meeting that Spaak had expressed his concern that his Sovereign might – as he and Pierlot had so persistently urged him to do – 'make a deal with the Germans and form some kind of government'.[350] Spaak should, of course, have known the King well enough to appreciate that he would never go back on his word. But on the rather insulting assumption that Leopold's resolve needed stiffening, at Eden's suggestion Churchill wrote the following letter to the King:

> Since the cataclysm of last summer when the German flood seemed likely to engulf us all, I have heard with admiration of the dignity and fortitude with which Your Majesty has declined to enter into collaboration with the invader, or to depart from your status as a prisoner of war.
>
> During the months that have passed with the shattering of the great air attack on this country . . . and with assistance from the United States rising to a flood, the prospect of victory grows even brighter. With this prospect will dawn the liberation of Belgium.
>
> It is the earnest hope of His Majesty's Government, as it is of Your Majesty's own faithful Ministers, that Your Majesty will inflexibly maintain, no matter what may be indubitably offered, your refusal to co-operate with a tyrant whose defeat is certain.
>
> In the name of the British people I send Your Majesty a message of hope and confidence.[351]

Although the British Government maintained a strict silence in public regarding Leopold, the Belgian Government in London, which had been committed to the theme of loyalty to their King, Country and the Allies by de Cartier, De Vleeschauwer and Gutt while Pierlot and Spaak were lingering on the Continent, was under no such restraint and none were more vocal Royalists than the newly-arrived Belgian Premier and his Foreign Minister. Whatever their true sentiments and intentions may have been, they would vie with one another in their expressions of devotion and loyalty to King Leopold throughout their four year sojourn in London. Spaak was quickly off the mark. One of his first acts on resuming office in London was to send a telegram, on October 27th, to the

Belgian Minister in Berne, Comte d'Ursel: 'Forced by circumstances to act without being able to consult the King, the Government is very far from acting against the King. The word of command is, on the contrary, national unity around the King. For a free Belgium, for a free King . . .'

Three weeks later Spaak indulged in a choice piece of sophism in the form of a 'directive' to all Belgium's representatives throughout the world, designed to gloss over the Pierlot government's complete reversal of policy in realigning itself with the Allied cause and reverting to its pre-capitulation attitude of allegiance to the King.

'I feel that it is essential,' Spaak began, 'clearly to establish the position of the King, the Government, Belgium and her Colony.' After 'paying homage' to the King for deciding to share the fate of his troops and describing the Ministers' unsuccessful attempts to persuade him to change his mind, Spaak wrote that they had left Belgium on May 25th 'to continue the struggle'. Moreover, they had had no contact with the King during the three days before they learned of the capitulation in 'a communication from M. Paul Reynaud', which was 'tendentious and full of inaccuracies'.

The Ministers, Spaak continued, had then received documents, including the findings of the three eminent jurists, which 'had left them in no doubt about the King's intentions and position', which he defined as follows: 'The King is a prisoner of war, and is temporarily in the impossibility of reigning.' In capitulating 'he accomplished a purely military act. He never wanted to be anything but a prisoner of the invader. He has not formed a government in Brussels. He is carefully avoiding all political action. He is not governing and has no wish to govern.'

Spaak then skipped over the five month period of defeatism which elapsed before he and Pierlot rallied to London, without mentioning the Prime Minister's defamatory broadcast or the Limoges Assembly or that the Ministers, although convinced, on June 3rd, by the documentary evidence that the King was innocent of the charges which they had made against him, took no steps whatsoever to withdraw them nor to rehabilitate his honour and good name. Not surprisingly, Spaak also omitted from his scenario the Pierlot bloc's repeated pronouncements that the war was lost and their persistent endeavours – in which they tried to involve the King – to come to terms with the Nazis.

After several pages of misrepresentation by the omission of all such discreditable facts, Spaak summed up his government's new pro-King and pro-British stance as follows:

1 The capitulation of the Army on May 28th was inevitable. A continuation of the struggle would have brought human sacrifices out of all proportion with any possible military results.

2 The King wanted to share the fate of his soldiers and his people, in order to maintain their morale and alleviate their suffering.

3 The King, a prisoner of war, does not govern, nor does he perform any political role.

4 The Government withdrew to free territory. At first to France and then to England, to continue the war, thus accomplishing the mission with which it had been entrusted by the entire Nation.

5 The Ministers meeting in Council, by the application of Article 82 of the Constitution, exercise executive and legal powers.

6 The Government is forced by circumstances to act without being able to consult the King, but it is not acting against the King. The attitude of the prisoner King and that of the Government in England do not contradict each other, nor are they opposed.

7 All those who have sworn an oath of allegiance to the King must respect that oath. In the present circumstances, this oath implies obedience to the Government.

8 A state of war still exists between Belgium and Germany . . .

9 Italy having carried out hostile acts against Belgium, the Belgian Government is regulating its relations with her on the basis of reciprocity.

10 Without being legally allied to Great Britain, Belgium is closely associated in the struggle which that country is carrying on. Belgium is providing her with all the assistance of which she is capable, with a view to the communal victory.

11 The Congo is following the same policy as Belgium.

12 The Government's word of command is:
'All possible aid for Great Britain, with a view to victory.'

> For an independent Belgium,
> For a free King.
> London, November 22nd 1940.
> Minister of Foreign Affairs,
> P. H. Spaak.

Even the most ardent Royalist would have difficulty in finding fault with those parts of this directive which deal with the King's past performance, present position and future intentions. But, when Spaak changed sides once again four years later, he would write with equal lucidity on the same subject – in diametrically the opposite sense.

It is a curious trait of Spaak's character that the warmth of the loyal protestations which he poured forth throughout his years in England was at least partially sincere. When he faced the reception committee of his loyal compatriots in the Belgian Embassy on his arrival in London and proclaimed '*Je suis pour le Roi!*' his sonorous tone had concealed a rich mixture of uncertainty and guilt. But his mercurial temperament helped him to switch his allegiance effortlessly. Underlying all his readjustments of front was a deep-rooted respect and affection for Leopold. At the time of the Belgian capitulation self-interest temporarily suppressed these feelings, but now, in London, it was with a sense of release that he found them to be once again respectable. Characteristically, Spaak appears to have felt no sense of contradiction in suddenly and continuously announcing to the world that he and his colleagues stood for Leopold. In his heart this was true, and for the time being there were no problems of self-interest to prevent him convincing himself. But after the liberation and his return to Brussels, political pressure from the Left caused him to reverse himself yet again and play a different theme. He would then maintain that his loyalty to the King during the London years had been merely a sham, due to wartime necessity, and that his pronouncements to that effect had been '*une vérité officielle alors qu'elle n'était pas la vérité*'. He may have overlooked the personal letter he had written to his Sovereign in November 1941 – or hoped that it would never see the light of day.

> Sire,
>   I eagerly avail myself of an opportunity now open to me to address a few words to Your Majesty. I am just back from a journey to the United States, where I represented Belgium at the International Labour Conference. Wherever I met our fellow-countrymen, I expounded the following few ideas, which form the basis of the policy pursued by the Government . . . The King, by his resolute refusal to collaborate with the enemy, is not only the symbol of passive resistance of occupied Belgium. He has also become an important factor in her active resistance. Be faithful to him, as we are ourselves.
>   We often think of Your Majesty, of your sorrows and your trials, of your isolation which must be so hard to bear, and I am convinced that my colleagues agree with me in telling you to have confidence in a better future . . .
>   Your Majesty and your Ministers separated in tragic circumstances; events which have occurred later have enabled us to correct, on either side, many mistakes and many misunderstandings.
>   My colleagues and I are doing all we can to work for the union of the Belgian people, for their close association in the love of their country and of her institutions, of which the constitutional monarchy is the most important, and our feeling for your Majesty's person are today the same as they were before May 10th: a respectful and loyal devotion.
>   May Your Majesty have confidence in us . . .

To those who read this letter some years later with a picture in their minds of Spaak in 1950 inciting mobs of rioters to overthrow the King, in defiance of the democratically expressed will of the majority, it is difficult to avoid feelings of distaste at such apparent hypocrisy. Yet, given Spaak's character and temperament, it is quite possible that when he wrote that letter he meant what he said – just as there is no reason to doubt that the warmth of his regard for the King was genuine.

It is to be doubted whether Pierlot's stolid, unimaginative character was stirred by such complicated emotions as Spaak's, although he must have shared the latter's sense of relief at being accepted in London by what looked as though it might eventually be the winning side. For his part Pierlot doggedly followed his government's new policy of solidarity with the Allies and loyalty to the King, like a Communist executing a 180-degree turn in his policies and attitudes after the German invasion of Russia. At the Royal Institute of International Affairs, for example, on February 14th 1941, Pierlot meticulously demolished the charges which Reynaud and he had levelled against Leopold. As to what he called those 'odious accusations', he denied that 'the Belgian Government had ever consented to associate itself with them'. 'We know that the King obeyed what he considered his duty,' he declared. 'His conduct was inspired by the highest ideals . . . The King is a prisoner of war . . . He has refused to exercise his functions as Sovereign under the control of the invader . . . This attitude constitutes a permanent protest against the accomplished fact. It is a symbol, an ever-increasing encouragement, it is the centre of all Belgium's resistance.'

Could this be the Pierlot who had argued so vehemently with his King before the capitulation, the Pierlot of Limoges, the Pierlot of Vichy, who was now proclaiming that Leopold's decision to capitulate was not taken until reiterated warnings had been given to the Allies and that the surrender of the isolated Army was inevitable and fully justified? Could this be Spaak broadcasting to Belgium on the first anniversary of the invasion? 'We are thinking of you, and of those of you who are prisoners, from the greatest of them to all the others . . . Gather closely round your imprisoned King. Be faithful to him. He represents the Fatherland for you as for us who labour here on your behalf.' These were the refrains which the chief vocalists constantly sang. At the same time Spaak took up the cudgels in support of King Leopold in a long and spirited letter to the *Daily Telegraph* on May 10th 1941. This was an indignant refutation of an article which the newspaper had published attacking the King, *inter alia*, for what were described as his 'tragic blunders' in maintaining Belgian neutrality; having 'abandoned the military alliance with France' and for allegedly having 'vetoed' her prolongation of the Maginot Line to the sea. In this succinct exposition of the facts, Spaak was at pains to justify and praise all Leopold's policies and actions since he came to the Throne.*

* See Appendix IX.

CHAPTER THIRTY-TWO

Vindication

'Let us not forget the Belgians grouped round King Leopold, who maintains with unbroken dignity his position as prisoner of war. They recreate the spirit of resistance which inspired the whole Belgian nation in a previous ordeal.'
Anthony Eden, as Foreign Secretary, June 24th 1941

Although Sir Roger Keyes' faith in Winston Churchill had been badly shaken by the latter's shameful treatment of the King of the Belgians and his army, the Prime Minister soon demonstrated that he held the veteran Admiral in even higher esteem as a result of his outstanding services on the Belgian battlefields. Undaunted by the British Army's defeat on the Continent and its disorganized and almost weaponless state after its miraculous escape to Britain, Churchill immediately decided to wage 'a vigorous, enterprising and ceaseless offensive against the whole German coastline' – as he minuted to General Ismay on June 6th 1940. Churchill also wanted help, as he later wrote to Anthony Eden, in 'giving vigour and positive direction to the conduct of the war, and in overcoming the inertia which has so far led to our being forestalled on every occasion by the enemy'. 'Churchill recognized in Keyes a fighting spirit after his own heart,' writes Cecil Aspinall-Oglander in his excellent biography, *Roger Keyes*, 'and he was determined to have him with him.'[352]

Accordingly, on July 17th, despite the opposition of certain convention-bound, defensively-minded Service officers, Churchill created a new Combined Operations Command with Keyes as its chief. (The Royal Marine General, Sir Allan Bourne, who had formed a small raiding force a few weeks earlier, willingly became Keyes' second-in-command.) 'Churchill decided,' Aspinall-Oglander continues, 'that if rapid progress was to be made and the "do nothing" policy of the faint-hearted obstructionists finally swept aside, the new formations must have at their head an officer of the highest possible standing, whose very name would ensure co-operation and whose reputation as a leader would inspire everyone concerned . . . Churchill had the highest admiration for Keyes' power of leadership and had wanted for months to get him an active command.'[353]

As the first Director of Combined Operations, Keyes built up the great organization which not only studied and developed the techniques and practice of aggressive amphibious warfare, but formed and trained a large force of Commandos, planned suitable operations and provided all the necessary ships, landing craft, weapons and equipment to carry them out.

Although Keyes enjoyed the Prime Minister's complete confidence and support, even Churchill was unable to overcome the inertia and resistance of the entrenched Whitehall bureaucracy, with its endless sub-committees, to the Combined Operations concept and to the two men's plans for a series of bold amphibious strokes against the enemy. These included 'Operation Workshop' – the capture of the poorly defended but strategically crucial Italian island stronghold of Pantellaria,* which Keyes was ready to launch in December 1940, before the Germans reinforced it with their Stukas and 'E' Boats. Churchill was determined that this operation, the effect of which he declared 'would be electrifying and would greatly increase our hold on the central Mediterranean', should be carried out. But it was undermined and frustrated after the Commandos had actually embarked in their assault ships by those whom Churchill described as 'masters of negation', headed by Keyes' former Chief of Staff in the Mediterranean, Admiral Sir Dudley Pound, now First Sea Lord, who epitomized the 'Safety First' school of officers and had not been present when the Chiefs of Staff had approved this operation. In consequence, this fleeting opportunity for a resounding victory, when Britain's fortunes were at their lowest, was lost.

The magnificent striking force of ten highly-trained and eager-for-battle Commandos which Keyes had created was similarly prevented from carrying out most of the operations which were mounted, except for a few successful raids, and the Commandos were kept in frustrating idleness – scattered abroad, frittered away on inappropriate tasks and in several cases actually disbanded.

After fourteen months of jealous antagonism, frustrations and disappointments, Keyes wrote to Churchill that he could not carry on as Director of Combined Operations unless he was given the necessary powers to function as such. But Pound and his ilk were determined to clip the wings of this charismatic, forceful and immensely senior officer. So, when Keyes was offered the post of 'Adviser Combined Operations' in September 1941, he declined it and his successor, Captain Lord Louis Mountbatten, RN, was given this title, with the rank of Commodore.†

But Churchill showed how greatly he valued the contribution Keyes had made to the successful prosecution of the war, despite the obstruction

---

* In British hands this small island, with its underground hangers, would have been an unsinkable aircraft carrier and a stepping-stone to Malta. But after the Germans moved in, it became a highly damaging thorn in our side.

† Although Mountbatten was subsequently made Chief of Combined Operations, he suffered from a similar lack of executive authority as had Keyes and was widely held responsible for the costly *débâcle* of the Dieppe Raid on August 19th 1942, though he was not in overall control of the operation.

of lesser men, by the tributes he paid him in *The Second World War* and by recommending him for the peerage with which he was honoured on January 1st 1943. And when, on April 27th 1950, with unconcealed emotion, Churchill unveiled the memorial to the Admiral of the Fleet, close to Nelson's tomb in the Crypt of Saint Paul's Cathedral, he said, in the course of his moving address:

> In the late war, as Chief of Combined Operations, he gave a most important impulse to amphibious warfare. There radiated from him the Commando spirit to which we owe so many glorious episodes. He animated and impelled from his earliest days all the vast design and construction of landing-craft of all kinds, without the timely preparation of which the greatest victories of the Western Allies could never have been gained.*

Meanwhile, as Admiral Keyes wrestled with his many problems in his Combined Operations Headquarters during the autumn, winter and spring of 1940–41, his libel case against the *Daily Mirror* was proceeding slowly through a number of stages. The brilliant and famous Sir Patrick Hastings, KC, was retained as Sir Roger's counsel. But would the case actually come to court? The *Daily Mirror* had second thoughts about its editorial – perhaps Leopold was not a Rat King or the Admiral a carpet-scraping lackey – and offered to settle the case with an open apology to Keyes. This missed the point, however, since his main object was the total public exculpation of the King. Keyes instructed his solicitor that any settlement reached must include an admission that he had been fully justified in his request on May 28th, when interviewed by the press at the House of Commons, that judgment should be suspended about Leopold's actions. Furthermore, he required that a substantial sum should be paid to charity and apologies published both to the King and himself. Negotiations continued until October, when the *Daily Mirror* prudently withdrew its defence of 'fair comment' – on the grounds that its remarks about Leopold could not be substantiated – and repeated its wish to make 'honourable amends' to Keyes.* But it also asked for mitigation of damages on the ground that it had acted on information from apparently unimpeachable sources (presumably Reynaud's broadcast).

The *Daily Mirror* declined to pay into court more than 1,000 guineas, which Keyes and his advisers considered wholly inadequate. In any case, Keyes welcomed the opportunity to refute the libels on Leopold and himself in open court and thus obtain the greatest possible publicity for a statement to be drafted and made by him from the witness-box. In it he gave a cogent summary of facts in rebuttal of the *Daily Mirror*'s charges,

---

* Despite the Admiral's writ, the *Daily Mirror* continued to slander King Leopold and his family – publishing as late as December 28th 1940 defamatory material under a headline 'TRAITOR KING'S SISTER A FASCIST'.

but carefully avoided anything which could cause embarrassment to the Prime Minister or Gort. Wishing to be fair to Churchill, Keyes sent him a copy, asking for his comments.

This friendly gesture was disastrous. A reply came on March 12th from the Secretary to the Cabinet, Sir Edward Bridges. It had been decided after careful consideration, he wrote, 'that the public interest would not be served' by ventilating the matter. The Prime Minister therefore asked that the case be settled out of court. This amounted to an official veto on the revelation of the truth about King Leopold and the surrender of the Belgian Army. Virtually the only voice in Britain able or willing to vindicate the King was to be gagged. Keyes hastened to see Sir Edward Bridges and request an explanation – only to receive another blow. Bridges informed him of the imminent publication of Lord Gort's official *Despatches*. Although he had had no contact with Gort since their unsatisfactory exchange of the previous June, the Admiral realized what this meant. Events would be described strictly from the self-exculpatory standpoint of Gort and Pownall, with no attempt to give the Belgian Army's side of the picture. Keyes was particularly concerned that this official record of the campaign should not contain inaccurate or prejudiced statements which he would feel bound to disprove publicly by quoting from his own very comprehensive records. Consequently, he wrote to Bridges on the 18th stressing how deplorable it would be if Gort's forthcoming *Despatches* were not fair and accurate, and he forwarded to him as evidence his comprehensive dossier on the Belgian campaign.

The Admiral was now becoming a thorn in the flesh for Churchill, whose one concern must have been that the unfounded attack he had made on the King of the Belgians in the House of Commons on June 4th should be forgotten. He therefore decided to delegate the silencing of Keyes. Accordingly, on March 24th Bridges wrote asking the Admiral to meet the Deputy Prime Minister (the Labour leader Clement Attlee) and the Secretary of State for War, Captain Margesson, to discuss the whole matter. On the afternoon of the 25th Keyes duly met Attlee in his room at Great George Street.

Sir Edward Bridges had failed to persuade Keyes to agree to the settlement of his case out of court. Could the two Ministers do so? The dossier presented to Bridges had made it painfully clear that if the case came to court it could seriously discredit Gort's *Despatches* and entirely demolish Churchill's charges in the House of Commons. The Prime Minister clearly considered it vital to prevent such an embarrassment at all costs. Virtually the only means of silencing Keyes was to plead 'the national interest' (as Bridges had done in his letter of the 12th). Attlee and Margesson therefore put to him the difficulties that would arise, both for the Prime Minister and for the Government, from a public hearing of the case in the midst of Britain's life and death struggle with Germany.

Keyes' loyalties were divided. Yet he could hardly ignore such an appeal
on behalf of the Prime Minister; and he was finally induced to settle the
action out of court – 'to avoid,' as he put it, 'the possible risk of being
cross-examined as to statements which were made by the Prime Minister
on the 4th June'.

But there was a condition. In return for agreeing to settle his case in this
way Keyes obtained an important verbal undertaking from the two
Ministers. This was, in his own words, that nothing would appear in
Gort's *Despatches* 'which attributed the blame for the misfortunes of the
British Army to any avoidable failure on the part of King Leopold and the
Belgian Army, or to his capitulation after the British and Belgian armies
had become separated'. On receiving this assurance, Keyes immediately
instructed his legal advisers to arrange for the settlement of the case out of
court. This meant that the Admiral had to accept the derisory 1,000
guineas the *Daily Mirror* had paid into court and forgo the much higher
damages which a jury would have been likely to award him in view of his
high repute and the enormity of the defamation, had the case gone to
trial. On hearing of this decision, Attlee wrote to Keyes in evident relief
'Margesson and I are very glad to hear that you are proposing to settle
your case without it coming to trial.'

But Keyes was in for a further shock. He now contrived to obtain –
unofficially – a copy of the draft of Gort's *Despatches*. When he read
them, the Admiral was dismayed to find that the two Ministers' undertaking of March 25th had not been fulfilled – indeed the *Despatches* were
stuffed with prejudice against the Belgian King and his army. The French
on the other hand were spared from all such criticism and censure. Not
only were the Belgian soldiers and their Commander-in-Chief given no
credit for the sacrifices they had made and the costly battles they had
fought to enable the BEF to escape from the battlefield, but it was alleged
or implied, *inter alia*, that they had refused to retreat to the Yser and had
omitted to warn Gort of the impending capitulation, which had created an
undefended twenty-mile gap on the BEF's left, thus exposing it to mortal
danger. There were, of course, no admissions of any failures or shortcomings on the part of the BEF or its High Command, nor that they had failed
to inform their French and Belgian allies about their re-embarkation.

With the object of putting as many influential people as possible in
possession of the true facts concerning the Belgian campaign, particularly
at the War Office, Keyes had already sent copies of his dossier to a
number of VIPs, including several senior Army officers. In appropriate
cases he asked them to use their best endeavours to ensure that the
Despatches gave a fair, accurate and unprejudiced account of the part
played in the campaign by King Leopold and the Belgian Army. The
reply he received from General Haining was deeply significant.

WAR OFFICE,
WHITEHALL,
S.W.1.
8th April, 1941

Dear Sir Roger,

I am returning the file which you lent me the other day after our interview. It is a very interesting story.

I am afraid I am not in a position to do anything and I know that the matter is a very political one, and is being dealt with as such. Thank you for letting me see it.

Yours sincerely,
(Signed) A. H. Haining

Admiral of the Fleet Sir Roger Keyes, GCB, KCVO, DSO, ADC,
Director of Combined Operations,
Offices of the War Cabinet,
Great George Street,
S.W.1.

The matter had indeed become highly political and, as his biographer reveals, after Gort had been packed off to Gibraltar the text of his *Despatches* was 'bowdlerized', without reference to him, by a government propaganda department. Publication was also held up until October 1941, on various pretexts, including 'the paper shortage' and the Government's desire to avoid giving offence to the 'Pétain-Weygand regime at Vichy'.[354] Indeed, as mentioned earlier, officialdom's policy was to 'resuscitate the reputation of the French' and their propaganda line was therefore to praise rather than blame the French in the aftermath of their military collapse, with the British Government even heaping high honours and decorations on such French leaders as General Weygand, General Blanchard and Admiral Abrial. Although the authors of such documents as Gort's *Despatches* accordingly refrained from criticizing the French, they were under no such restraint in regard to the Belgians, and were even encouraged by certain elements in the Military Establishment to blame Belgium's King and Army for the BEF's defeat.

After studying the draft of the *Despatches* he had obtained, Keyes made a strong protest to Sir Edward Grigg, Parliamentary Under-Secretary at the War Office. If they were published in their existing form, he wrote to Grigg on April 18th, it would be 'an outrage'. He stressed how easily certain passages could be refuted and that their publication, unaltered, would be 'most discreditable to the British reputation for chivalry and fair play'. Appealing to Grigg to urge Gort to make the necessary corrections, Keyes added that unless this were done he would feel obliged to go to the War Cabinet and do everything in his power to stop the publication of the *Despatches* as they stood.

In addition to his dossier on the Belgian campaign Keyes gave Grigg a closely argued refutation of the offending paragraphs in Gort's *Despatches*. On May 9th Grigg returned these with a 'Private and Personal' letter that made sorry reading. It had been resolved not to change anything in the *Despatches* and these would be published as soon as possible. Keyes immediately tried, without success, to see the War Minister, Margesson. On the 12th, he wrote to him in the frankest terms, ending with the warning:

> In view of your decision to publish the *Despatches* as they stand, in spite of my protest, I now consider myself free to take any steps I consider necessary in the interests of truth to uphold our reputation for honesty and fair play.

The War Minister was giving the full seal of his approval – and, by implication, the approval of the War Cabinet – to the unfair strictures and uncorrected distortions in Gort's *Despatches*. Keyes saw this as a flagrant breach of faith: he felt that he had been tricked into abandoning his libel action against the *Daily Mirror* by a Government undertaking which had not been kept. But despite his warning to Margesson that he would 'take any necessary steps in the interests of truth', he was powerless to pursue the matter further through official channels. He could not even countermand his agreement to settle his case out of court, for all arrangements for this had been completed and the court announcement of the settlement was fixed for mid-June – barely a month ahead.

Keyes now pinned his frustrated hopes on his libel case; and, as it turned out, it was to achieve for him what all his other efforts had failed to do. Listed as *Keyes v. Daily Mirror Newspapers Limited*, the hearing took place before Mr Justice Tucker in the King's Bench Division of the High Court on Friday, June 13th 1941. Keyes, wearing the uniform of an Admiral of the Fleet with six rows of medals, sat alongside his solicitor in front of his two counsel, Sir Patrick Hastings and Mr Valentine Holmes. Mr G. O. Slade represented the defendants. This being an uncontested case, the proceedings were purely formal, with no witnesses called. Sir Patrick's task was to announce the settlement and outline the facts and events which rebutted the charges made in the *Mirror* editorial. The defending counsel would then reply, tendering the appropriate apologies. But as Sir Patrick, armed with the statement prepared by Keyes, soberly outlined his story, listeners in the quiet London court-room were presented with a vivid picture of the drama that had played itself out on the Belgian battlefields thirteen months before around the figure of King Leopold.

Sir Patrick's calm recital presented the key points of the campaign, concluding with the details of the repeated warnings which had been received by the Allies from King Leopold that he would be forced to capitulate. Admiral Keyes had thus felt fully justified, Sir Patrick added, in suggesting a suspension of judgment on the King and he quite naturally resented the *Daily Mirror* article attacking him. The defendants now appreciated that their criticism of him was unfounded and 'were accordingly desirous of making honourable amends to Sir Roger Keyes, who had acted throughout in accordance with the highest traditions of honour and justice'.

Mr Slade, replying, admitted that Sir Roger's attitude towards King Leopold had been abundantly justified and on behalf of the defendants offered him a sincere apology. But, he continued, it was plain that a very grave injustice had been done to the King of the Belgians, who had also acted throughout 'in accordance with the highest traditions of honour and justice'. The defendants wished therefore to tender to the King their most sincere and respectful apology for the injustice they had done him. Mr Slade sat down. After assenting to the settlement and the withdrawal of the record Mr Justice Tucker pronounced his final words:

All I need to say is that this libel action, unlike some others, appears to have served a most useful purpose, and resulted in statements being made which will give very wide satisfaction.

Admiral Keyes left the High Court a quietly jubilant man. Apart from the satisfaction accorded to himself, after a year's thankless campaigning he had gained his main objective. What had been impossible to achieve through the British Government had been won through the staid, impartial processes of the Law.

On all counts, Sir Patrick Hastings' statement to the court was sensational. Not only did it demolish the lies that had been told about King Leopold, but in doing so it lifted the veil of secrecy imposed by the Government and boldly refuted the official versions that were to appear in such accounts as Gort's *Despatches*. To a press fed on stilted communiqués, routine war reports and Ministry of Information hand-outs, it was of the highest news value. Next day every British paper prominently featured the case with heavy headlines. 'K.C. Clears King Leopold's Name: London Told of Surrender Plan' ran one headline. Another proclaimed: 'King Leopold Warned Britain of Surrender.' The sense of all press comment was that the King had been resoundingly vindicated; and some papers expressed concern that the Government had remained silent and that this vindication had had to be achieved by a private individual. Many journalists admitted to having besmeared Leopold's reputation and made honourable amends. For example a syndicated feature article entitled 'Leopold Vindicated' declared: 'When the Huns have been smashed and the full story of this war can be written, the whole world will learn that among the loyalest and bravest of friends of the Allied cause was, and is, King Leopold of the Belgians. His name has been dragged in the mud. I, among others, referred to him as "King Quisling". We were all misled. The least we can do is to make amends, and explain precisely what happened on those fateful days which led up to the Belgian Cease-fire.'

Any belief held by British officialdom that the case's settlement out of court might avoid unwelcome publicity for the truth about the Belgian surrender had been rudely shattered. Sir Patrick's speech was hardly less effective in exposing it than the Admiral's personal testimony from the witness-box would have been. Although Keyes had been careful to spare Churchill and Gort embarrassment in his statement, parts of it might still prompt awkward questions regarding the accuracy and fairness of Churchill's speech in Parliament on June 4th 1940 and of the offending passages in Gort's *Despatches*. The Government could not censor the reporting of a case in the High Court by the British press, but it had one weapon for restricting the publicity that it could and did use; it proceeded to muzzle the BBC. Significantly Duff Cooper, who as Minister of Information had broadcast, on May 28th 1940, a tribute to the Belgian Army for its courageous resistance and declared 'This is no time for criticism or recrimination', has revealed that the main pressure to prevent the BBC from broadcasting the news about the vindication of the King of the Belgians and his army came from the War Office. As a result of this official policy to suppress the truth, Leopold's exoneration remained less widely known than it deserved. For example, many foreign newspapers, as well as large numbers of people in occupied Europe and British servicemen abroad whose news sheets depended upon the BBC's transmissions, remained in ignorance of this important development. Indeed the author, who was serving at sea in the Royal Navy, heard nothing about the case at the time. But the Admiral's wife subscribed to an international press cutting bureau and thus a stream of newspaper articles came pouring in to his home from all quarters of the globe, with headlines such as 'Leopold vindicated by London Court' and 'Leopold was a Hero' providing welcome proof of the success of his libel action overseas. But the cuttings revealed that in many cases the newspapers concerned had only heard of the King's rehabilitation thanks to the initiative of Belgians or others in London who had sent cables drawing attention to the findings in the High Court.

World opinion appeared to swing right round and much space was devoted to restoring the King's honour and good name. Amends as wholehearted and generous as those in the British press were made by newspapers of all political colours and in all parts of the free world. Many quoted in full the account which had been read to the court by Sir Patrick

Hastings, or gave a summary of the salient points. All agreed that a great injustice had been done to the King in 1940 and that the Admiral's libel action had removed the stigma from his name. A typical attitude was that of a correspondent in the *Johannesburg Star* who asked: 'Can anyone explain to me why it was necessary to withhold this information for over a year, and to leave King Leopold of the Belgians to be judged wrongly by the rest of the world?'

The Admiral was also rewarded with many hundreds of letters from all over the world, paying him warm tributes on the success of his action. They came in a steady stream from Belgians, Britons and foreigners alike, ranging from ordinary men and women to people in the most elevated positions. Most of them declared that they had never believed the lies about the King or lost their faith in him. All expressed their heartfelt gratitude and congratulated the Admiral on the success of his action, often with pungent comments about the *Daily Mirror*.

Of all these letters two brought the Admiral particular satisfaction. From Queen Elisabeth, in Belgium, he received in due course by clandestine means a note to say that she and the King had heard of the High Court action and its result. The other letter was written from 10 Downing Street on June 18th 1941.

My dear Roger,

I must send you a line to say how glad I am that your action on behalf of the King of the Belgians has been successful.

This must be a source of deep satisfaction to you . . . I hope King Leopold will know about what has happened. It will I feel be a gleam of comfort in a cheerless world.

I hope your sons are safe.

Yours ever,
Clementine S. Churchill

It is clear that Mrs Churchill, like her son, fully supported and sympathized with King Leopold, but the man who had assured Keyes that 'we greatly admire the attitude of the King' and signalled Gort 'we are asking the Belgians to sacrifice themselves for us' not only avoided every opportunity for a public withdrawal of his defamation, but continued to give currency to the discredited legend and to pursue his baseless vendetta until the end of his days.

This reflects a curious aspect of Churchill's protean personality. At the beginning of the second volume of his war memoirs *Their Finest Hour* he gives the moral of his work: 'In war: resolution, in defeat: defiance, in victory: magnanimity, in peace: goodwill.' Yet strangely, magnanimity was a quality which he seldom exercised. Inevitably, Churchill made other mistakes, misjudgments and misstatements while in office, but he showed a marked disinclination to admit to them in later years. But Churchill was at least consistent in his attitude towards Leopold – unlike the weathercock author of another of the letters sent to Sir Roger Keyes after the successful conclusion of his libel action.

Ministère des Affaires Etrangères et du
Commerce Extérieur de Belgique   13.6.41.

My dear Admiral,
    The Star reports the statement made by our counsel, that of his opponent, that of the judge, and the news that you have won your case.
    Allow me to congratulate you.
    Allow me also to thank you. I know how much my country is indebted to you for your courageous and disinterested efforts. By allowing the truth to become known, you are not only helping to do justice to a man, you are also serving the cause of an entire people.
    No Belgian, myself least of all, will ever forget it.
    Please accept, my dear Admiral, the expression of my respectful and devoted sentiments.*

                                                          P. H. Spaak.

Ever since his arrival in London Spaak had been making approaches to the Admiral of the Fleet in the hopes of establishing friendly relations with the man who was so close to the King and was now occupying the important post of Director of Combined Operations. Spaak wanted a chance to explain himself and perhaps persuade Keyes to put in a good word for him with the British Establishment, and eventually with Leopold. For Spaak had been much troubled by his failure to rehabilitate himself in the eyes of the world – and of his Sovereign. Indeed he and Pierlot, despite their outpourings of rhetoric in support of their King and the Allies, had been unable to regain the approbation and confidence of their compatriots in Belgium or overseas – or for that matter of the British and Allied communities and their leaders. As the months went by without Spaak making much progress in this direction, he had persevered with his efforts to ingratiate himself with Keyes – and now that the Admiral had succeeded in stimulating a strong public reaction in Leopold's favour, he was even more eager to do so.

Accordingly, on July 21st 1941, Spaak wrote in his own hand, in French, saying that he had often tried to have a talk with Keyes and much regretted his failure to do so. Could the Admiral not come to lunch or dine one day? But these 'fawning approaches', as Keyes described them, left the Admiral unmoved, as did a remarkable communication sent to him on Spaak's behalf. This letter came from Mrs Simone Dear, a Belgian woman married to an Englishman, who was Spaak's close companion in

---

* See page 473 for a copy of the original.

England during the war years and whom he married after the war. Ironically, while Spaak was developing his friendship with Mrs Dear in London, in Brussels the King was working for the release from German imprisonment of Spaak's wife, which he eventually achieved. (The King also obtained the release of Pierlot's brother, Canon Pierlot, by intervening with the German Military Governor.)

Mrs Dear's handwritten letter reveals that, having telephoned Sir Roger to arrange an interview, without success, she wrote the five pages of typescript which she enclosed. Mrs Dear was evidently concerned to put in a good word for Spaak – for the typescript was nothing less than a closely argued *plaidoirie* for her friend covering his years as a Minister of the Crown. In it she expressed her admiration not only for Spaak, but also for the King and the Admiral, concluding with these words:

> These lines have been written in a spirit of love for England and Belgium and with the firm belief that you are, Sir Roger, in this country almost the only man to have taken, since the very beginning, the defence of a Man I admire and believe in! King Leopold wanted to collaborate with England and he was right! But if his Ministers failed to understand his scheme and to follow his plans they must not be condemned for ever! Among them Spaak was the man the King had chosen and whom he preferred! Spaak himself is very fond of King Leopold and admires Him immensely. I am sure you will help them both to create a strong collaboration which may be badly needed by Belgium after the war is over.

After opening with a lengthy account of the pre-invasion episode when the King made his informal approach to the British without his Ministers' prior knowledge, Mrs Dear wrote: 'I have been trying to make Spaak realize that King Leopold, after all, had been right all along, but that it was his Foreign Secretary . . . who had obviously been lacking foresight and personality . . .' But the key words are her explanation of how she was 'hoping the moment may have come, at last, of a better understanding between both Governments and restoration of Belgium's reputation and credit. For if the King's policy was right, Spaak's honesty in his job, I am absolutely sure today, was thorough and his energy in pursuit of his plans inspiring.' Spaak was wrong again, she contended, when 'the invasion of the Low Countries took place. The "battle for the sea" was lost at Sedan! The King realized that at once: the politicians did not!' Next she pleaded that the behaviour of Pierlot and Spaak towards Leopold at the time of the surrender was due to a misunderstanding and the machinations of the French. She drew a colourful picture of the way Reynaud had intimidated the Belgian Ministers and induced them to make the deplorable broadcast of May 28th. She described how they had been hauled before Reynaud, Pétain and Weygand, who were standing *'comme des statues'* as if 'in front of a tribunal'.

Having given character sketches of the three other Belgian Ministers,

Pierlot, Gutt and De Vleeschauwer, Mrs Dear describes Spaak as 'the
best man Belgium ever had', adding 'A fortnight ago he had still the
impression that the King, in a way, had abandoned him. I believe I made
him realize that the King might have thought the same!' She then
described Spaak's position in London as 'no other than a fairly well-paid
unemployed'. But he was 'not at all happy' about the Belgian Government's position in England, which he felt was still 'very precarious'. 'He
has definitely the impression that the Foreign Office especially does not
keep him informed in the same way as the other Allied governments . . .
But, as every other human being of his standard who has paid a very high
price for having been in the wrong, he needs help, trust and friends.'

The Admiral's triumph in the High Court was not the full story of King
Leopold's vindication in 1941. Other blows were being struck on his
behalf that summer. A few days after the public had learned some of the
truth about the Belgian capitulation from the press reports of Keyes' case,
Leopold's name again featured in the headlines. These referred to the
publication of Professor Emile Cammaerts' book, *The Prisoner at
Laeken*.[355]

A distinguished Belgian patriot, scholar, author and poet, Cammaerts
had lived in England, to which he became devoted, since the First World
War.* His faith in his Sovereign's courage and integrity never wavered
and in concert with Baron de Cartier and other leading Belgians in
London, he had put his whole heart into upholding the King's honour,
from the moment it was first dragged in the mud. In addition to writing
articles and a booklet, he had set to work on what *The Times* review of his
book called a 'full-scale vindication of the conduct of his King'. Cammaerts had carefully assembled a mass of irrefutable evidence to buttress
his case, which was essentially a dispassionate explanation and justification of Leopold's performance from his accession to his captivity. In the
text and appendices Cammaerts included extracts from all Leopold's
relevant speeches, and he published for the first time in Britain what *The
Times* described as the 'noble letter' the King had written to the Pope and
President Roosevelt on May 28th 1940, as well as Cardinal Van Roey's
Pastoral Letter and other important documents. Much of this
documentary evidence, which was essential for a just assessment of the
matter, had long been available in Britain and America, but it had not
been published or even mentioned in the press of those countries,
presumably because it did not fit in with the legend of Leopold's betrayal
which had gained so much currency there.

Disregarding the regulations banning serving officers from writing for

* Professor Cammaerts' son Pieter, a Flight Sergeant in the RAF, had been killed in action
in March and another son, Francis, joined the Special Operations Executive and ended the
war, after brilliant service with the Resistance in France, as a Lieutenant-Colonel with a
DSO.

public consumption in wartime and the possible consequences, Sir Roger Keyes contributed an outspoken introduction to *The Prisoner at Laeken*. In an expanded version of his court statement he described point by point, as he had himself witnessed them, Leopold's thoughts and actions during the eighteen days between the German invasion and the Belgian capitulation.* All this, in mid-1941, was material which had been withheld from the public and Cammaerts' book, backed by Keyes' forceful eyewitness affirmation, gave renewed impetus to a tide which by now was running strongly in Leopold's favour. Newspapers which had joined in the general condemnation of the King now gave much space to exonerating and praising him.

Typical of the reactions to *The Prisoner of Laeken* in the popular press was that of the *Sunday Graphic* of June 22nd 1941. Under headlines 'Book of the Week Ends the Legend of a King's Betrayal' and 'Leopold of The Belgians Was No Traitor' the *Graphic* declared: 'Cammaerts tells the story of Leopold simply and painstakingly, smashing, by fact after fact, "the Leopoldian legend" of betrayal. Quietly, but effectively, he justifies the actions of his King, then confidently leaves the verdict of vindication to the reader and history . . . We can rely on his analysis of Leopold. We can rely equally on the evidence of Admiral Sir Roger Keyes, who writes the preface.' Other newspapers took up the same theme. *The Times* of June 25th 1941, for example, devoted several columns to its review of *The Prisoner at Laeken* and to a leading article entitled 'Vindication of King Leopold'. This paid tribute to him for his 'loyal refusal to cooperate with his German conqueror' which had 'established his motives as beyond reproach'. As *The Times* book review pointed out, 'The "poisonous abuse" of which Sir Roger Keyes (who, as liaison officer attached to Leopold III, was in the best position to know the facts) speaks, persists even to this day.' It then declared:

M. Cammaerts' eloquent and emphatic vindication is a vital service to the Allies; for the Germans have been trying to exploit every criticism of King Leopold to their own advantage . . . Neither by word nor by deed has he merited the accusation of quisling so freely levelled at him when he took the hard and inescapable decision to capitulate . . . M. Reynaud (M. Cammaerts argues) was looking for a scapegoat, and found one in the King of the Belgians, who by surrendering was supposed to have exposed and mortally endangered the left wing of the Allied line.

The evidence now available from M. Cammaerts and other sources is clear and incontrovertible. The Belgian troops fought bravely; the King, their Commander-in-Chief, carried out loyally the orders of the French Generalissimo, and far from withholding warning of his intentions, had urgently represented the terrible ordeal to which his soldiers were being subjected, and the

* It concluded that the Belgians had every reason to be 'proud of their King, for he has proved himself to be "a gallant soldier, a loyal ally and a true son of his splendid parents"'.

decision to which, failing swift succour, they would be brought . . . Most people, reading the case for vindication which the author submits with such scholarly conviction and sense of responsibility, will agree that King Leopold has proved himself to be a gallant and loyal ally.

Characteristically, it was Spaak who launched the next full-scale vindication of Leopold – thus touching off another wave of sympathetic press coverage. In July 1941 Spaak's Foreign Ministry in Eaton Square issued a hardbacked volume entitled *Belgium: The Official Account of What Happened 1939–1940*. (The author's copy still contains Spaak's compliments slip.) This well-written and carefully documented account leaves no stone unturned in putting straight the historical record of Belgium and her King – up to the surrender of her Army. Indeed, it has nothing but praise for Leopold and the last lines of the text read: 'As he had proclaimed in order to strengthen the courage of his soldiers at the height of battle, its Commander-in-Chief has since linked up his future with that of the Army. By his dignified attitude, in the captivity to which he has condemned himself, by his refusal to recognize the accomplished fact, he has shown himself to be the incarnation of a people which will not accept servitude.'[356]

The book begins with a convincing explanation of Belgium's pre-war policy of armed independence in the context of the international situation, and the King's part in it. Next the King's role in organizing Belgium's rearmament drive and leading his country's resistance to the threats and final assault of the Germans is described with pride. The detailed account of the eighteen days' campaign which follows is well supported by documents, maps, plans and photographs. The circumstances of the Belgian Army's capitulation, including the many warnings received by the British and French of its inevitability and imminence, are soberly set out without a breath of criticism or recrimination concerning the behaviour of the Allies' political and military leaders. All the King's orders of the day, proclamations and signals are quoted. The twenty-two Appendices comprise a series of documents of great political and military significance, many of them previously unpublished, and the book concludes with full details of Sir Roger Keyes' libel case and its outcome. There is, however, no hint of any disagreement between the Ministers and the King, no reference to the meeting at Wynendaele on May 25th 1940 or to the flight of Pierlot, Spaak and their colleagues on that day. Pierlot's slanderous broadcast from Paris on May 28th 1940 and the hysterical behaviour of the rump Parliament at Limoges are likewise omitted.

By leaving out all reference to their activities from May 10th onwards, Pierlot and Spaak evidently hoped that these would remain buried and forgotten – as in fact happened until, seven years later, their renewed attacks on the King provoked loyal Belgians into tearing apart the veil of secrecy with which the two Ministers' misconduct in France had been concealed. But in the meantime the people of the free world and even many in high places remained in ignorance of the fact that they had thrown in the sponge when France fell, and had only been saved from following in the footsteps of Pétain and Laval by Leopold's refusal to support their endeavours to come to terms with the enemy – and that it was not until he advised them to go to London to carry on the war at the side of the Allies that they had done so. It is one of the ironies of history that Spaak, the man who in 1950 would lead marches by riotous mobs which he had incited to overthrow the King, should have gone to such lengths in this official publication to establish his own complete lack of justification for his attacks on his Sovereign.

Meanwhile Pierlot and Spaak, by their continuous declarations of loyalty and devotion to the King, hoped to climb on to the bandwagon of Leopold's regained popularity – and so inflate their own sense of power and self-esteem. In August 1941, for example, Spaak's euphoria found expression in these sentiments: 'Last year the King was upheld against the Government, the Belgians at home against those who were fighting abroad. All these clouds, all these misunderstandings are dissipated, truth becomes known . . . Now is justice done to the Army, the King and the Country.' Again in November 1941, Spaak was declaring: 'The King, as prisoner of war, by refusing to co-operate in any way whatsoever with the occupying power, is a symbol to his people.'

Such, whatever its intention and its value, was the tenor of all the public pronouncements of the Pierlot government throughout the war years which it spent in London. As late as January 1st 1944 Pierlot announced the unconditional restoration of the King to all his prerogatives 'as soon as it shall be materially possible and without the loss of an hour' and further declared 'We shall remit into the King's hands the charge we have guarded to the end, and the responsibilities of power will be transmitted to our successors, according to the rule of the Constitution.' He spoke in a similar vein two months later, when he added that the Government's successors would be 'men who have lived in Belgium and are better acquainted with the wishes of the population'. Pierlot was evidently looking back with some apprehension at the fate of the self-exiled Belgian Government in 1918, when King Albert reached the liberated capital ahead of them – and his people rejected the politicians who had fled abroad, in favour of those who had stuck it out in occupied Belgium. Hence, as the day of Belgium's liberation approached, the plans which were being hatched behind the scenes by certain elements in Pierlot's Cabinet were quite contrary to those which they proclaimed with such fervour – and with such apparent respect for the Crown and the Constitution. Indeed after their return to liberated Belgium in 1944 Pierlot, Spaak and their supporters would renege on all these fine promises and the latter in particular would bend all his efforts to removing the King from the throne to which they had sworn to restore him.

Meanwhile in wartime Britain, though Churchill himself never abandoned his prejudiced attitude towards Leopold, the acceptance by the Allies of Pierlot, Spaak and their colleagues as Belgium's Government-in-exile and the vindication of the King which Admiral Keyes and others had achieved meant that, as the months passed, a succession of statements by leading figures in the Western Alliance spoke with admiration and respect for the King of the Belgians. Indeed, in Brazzaville in May 1941 General de Gaulle publicly praised King Leopold 'whom all the Free French salute with respect for the dignity with which he accepts captivity', ending his speech with *'Vive la Belgique! Vive le Roi Léopold!'* But it was not until after Keyes' vindication of Leopold that some British statesmen saw fit to pay similar tributes to him. On June 25th 1941 *The Times* leader declared: '. . . Allied opinion will agree that the King has deserved the tribute paid to him yesterday by Mr Lyttleton, and by Mr Eden in his recent speech at the Mansion House, when he said that the Belgians are in our thoughts, "grouped round King Leopold, who maintains with unbroken dignity his position as a prisoner of war. They recreate the spirit of resistance which inspired the whole Belgian nation in a previous ordeal."'

On another page, under the headline 'Tributes to King Leopold', *The Times* reported as follows:

> The toast of 'The King of the Belgians' was pledged with much enthusiasm at a luncheon in honour of the Belgian Government given by the British Chamber of Commerce in Belgium at the Savoy Hotel yesterday. The President of the Board of Trade, Mr Oliver Lyttleton, paid tribute to King Leopold for his steadfast refusal to work with the Germans and for the example worthy of his father, King Albert, which he had set the Belgian people.

As early as March 31st 1941 President Roosevelt had praised Leopold in a message to the Belgian people: 'The Belgians are wholeheartedly with their government in London and with their brave King Leopold, at present a prisoner of the hated Nazis. The Americans look forward to the future, towards the day when the King will soon be able to repeat: "Our cause is pure. Long live Belgium!"' But though, as *The Times* had declared, 'vindication is a vital service to the Allies; for the Germans have been trying to exploit every criticism of King Leopold to their own advantage', when the day of liberation finally arrived, these criticisms would be exploited by certain members of the Belgian Government-in-exile in their campaign to overthrow the King – and chief among their assistants were the Americans.

World opinion proved singularly ready to take its tone from the most vociferous politicians. It had turned against the King at the bidding of Reynaud, Churchill and Pierlot; admitted him once more to its approval when Pierlot and Spaak found it convenient to return to the Allies' side and resume their loyalty to him; and eventually, when Spaak led a riotous mob to the gates of Laeken Palace in 1950, would turn against Leopold once again.

al Plutarch an | Sacred Band ... con ... in ... the Allies ...
... fourth ... in ... the ... land ... Perichares ...
... Sparta ... ancient ... in ... Would ... against Sparta ...
same.

BLITZKRIEG

←	German attacks. May 10th - 13th
→	Movement of Allied Forces. May 10th - 13th
‑o‑o‑	Belgian outposts
‑‑‑‑	Belgian delaying position
▲▲▲	Belgian main defence position
▼▼▼	British Fortified line
⛽	German airborne landings. May 10th
★	Belgian fortresses
■	Belgian forts

Miles
0 10 20 30
0 10 20 30 40 50
Kilometres

NORTH SEA

WILHELMSHAVEN

GRONINGEN

LEEUWARDEN

Emden

Ter-Apel

Den Helder

EMMEN

NORDHORN

Alkmaar

ZUIDER ZEE

HOLLAND

GRONAU

HAARLEM

DEVENTER

AMSTERDAM

MUNSTER

THE HAGUE

UTRECHT

ARNHEM

R. Lek

EIGHTEENTH ARMY
(Von Kuechler)
6 inf., 1 cav., 1 mot. SS, 1 Pz.

ROTTERDAM

Emmerich

Bocholt

R. Waal

ARMY GROUP B
(Von Bock)
29 divs.

GUCH

DUTCH ARMY
(Wilkelmann)
10 divs.

R. Maas

Venlo

R. Rhine

DUSSELDORF

WALCHEREN

Breda

GERMANY

R. Scheldt

Zeebrugge

OSTEND

BELGIANS

Canal   OUTPOSTS

SIXTH ARMY
(Von Reichenau)
17 inf., 2 Pz.,
1 Mot. divs.

Albert   Canal

BRUGES

ANTWERP

COLOGNE

Nieuport

La Panne

DUNKIRK

R. Yser

BELGIUM

GHENT

R. Scheldt

Mechelen

DELAYING POSITION

Hasselt

MAASTRICHT

AACHEN

ARMY GROUP A
(Von Rundstedt)
45 divs.

FRENCH
SEVENTH
ARMY
(Giraud)

Ypres

Courtrai

R. Lys

BRUSSELS

Dyle

Louvain

Tongres

BONN

42 in OKH Reserve

Menin

Halluin

Eben Emael

LIEGE

FOURTH ARMY
(Von Kluge)
9 inf., 2 Pz. divs.

Bailleul

R. Escaut

R. Dender

Wavre

Neufchateau

Hazebrouck

BELGIAN ARMY
(King Leopold)
22 divs.

Battice

KOBLENZ

LILLE

R. Deule

Tournai

Ath

G

R. Meuse

Pepinster

Bethune

BEF
(Gort)
9 divs.

Maulde

MONS

NAMUR

TWELFTH ARMY
(Von List)
inc. 5 Pz., 3 Mot.
(Von Kleist Group)

Arras

GHQ BEF

R. Scarpe

Valenciennes

R. Sambre

Charleroi

Yvoir

I

Malmedy

25 inf.
divs.

R. Moselle

Cambrai

FRENCH
FIRST ARMY
(Blanchard)
10 divs.

R. Oise

Dinant

R. Ourthe

Bastogne

SIXTEENTH ARMY
(Busch)

Bad Kreuznach

FRENCH 93 divs.
BRITISH 10 divs.
BELGIAN 22 divs.
DUTCH 10 divs.
Total 135 divs.

GIVET

MONTHERME

ARDENNES

LUXEMBOURG

Trier

R. Rhine

R. Somme

Peronne

FRENCH NINTH ARMY
(Corap)
9 divs.

SEDAN

R. Semois

FRENCH
CAVALRY

LUXEMBOURG

ARMY GROUP C
(Von Leeb)
19 inf. divs.

AMIENS

StQuentin

Montcornet

R. Meuse

Longwy

Longuyon

FRENCH ARMY GROUP
No 1
(Billotte)

Laon

FRENCH SECOND ARMY
(Huntziger)
5 divs.

Montmedy

Thionville

SIEGFRIED

R. Oise

R. Aisne

FRENCH THIRD ARMY
(Conde)

Verdun

METZ

SAARBRUCKEN

MAGINOT   LINE

RHIEMS

F R A N C E

R. Marne

FRENCH FOURTH ARMY
(Requin)

NANCY

GQG
(Gamelin)

R. Marne

ARMY GROUP No 2
(Pretalat)
26 divs.

Canal

Seine

Montry

La Ferte-s-Jouarre

GQG NE
(Georges)

R. Moselle

PARIS

Vincennes

GQG Defense National
(Gamelin)

DJC

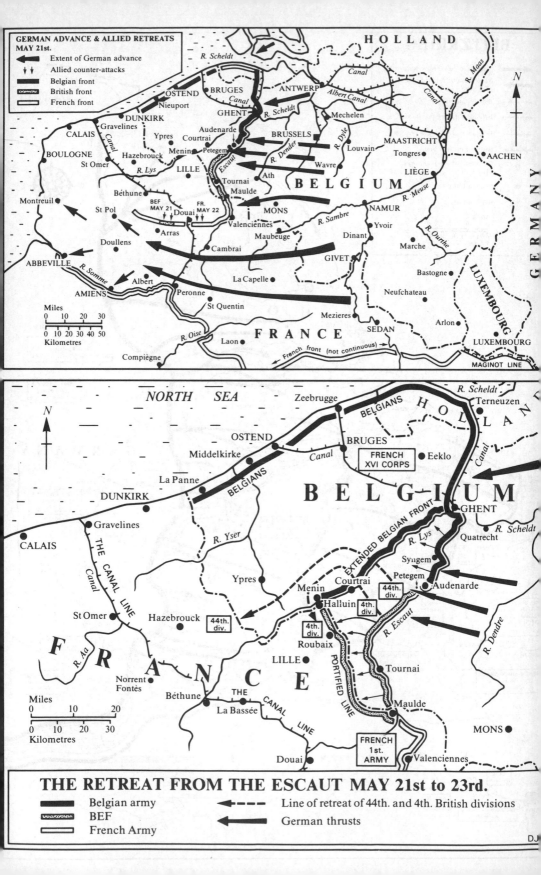

Top map legend:

GERMAN ADVANCE & ALLIED RETREATS MAY 21st.

- Extent of German advance
- Allied counter-attacks
- Belgian front
- British front
- French front

Top map labels: HOLLAND, R. Scheldt, Canal, R. Maas, Canal, ANTWERP, Albert Canal, Mechelen, OSTEND, BRUGES, GHENT, R. Scheldt, MAASTRICHT, Tongres, AACHEN, Nieuport, DUNKIRK, Audenarde, BRUSSELS, R. Dyle, Louvain, LIÈGE, GRAVELINES, Ypres, Courtrai, Petegem, R. Dender, Wavre, R. Meuse, CALAIS, Menins, LILLE, Escaut, Ath, BELGIUM, BOULOGNE, Canal, Hazebrouck, R. Lys, Tournai, Maulde, NAMUR, GERMANY, St Omer, Béthune, BEF MAY 21, Douai, FR. MAY 22, MONS, Yvoir, R. Sambre, Montreuil, St Pol, Valenciennes, R. Meuse, Marche, R. Ourthe, Arras, Doullens, Cambrai, Maubeuge, Dinant, GIVET, Bastogne, LUXEMBOURG, ABBEVILLE, R. Somme, Albert, La Capelle, Neufchateau, AMIENS, Peronne, St Quentin, Arlon, Mezieres, SEDAN, LUXEMBOURG, FRANCE, R. Oise, Laon, Compiègne, French front (not continuous), MAGINOT LINE

Miles 0 10 20 30
Kilometres 0 10 20 30 40 50

Bottom map:

NORTH SEA

Bottom map labels: R. Scheldt, Terneuzen, Zeebrugge, BELGIANS, HOLLAND, OSTEND, BRUGES, FRENCH XVI CORPS, Eeklo, Canal, Middelkirke, La Panne, BELGIANS, BELGIUM, GHENT, DUNKIRK, R. Scheldt, GRAVELINES, R. Yser, R. Lys, Quatrecht, CALAIS, THE CANAL LINE, Canal, EXTENDED BELGIAN FRONT, Syngem, Petegem, Ypres, Courtrai, 44th. div., Audenarde, St Omer, Hazebrouck, Menin, Halluin, 4th. div., R. Escaut, R. Aa, 44th. div., Roubaix, 4th. div., R. Dendre, FRANCE, Norrent Fontès, Béthune, THE CANAL LINE, LILLE, FORTIFIED LINE, Tournai, La Bassée, Maulde, MONS, Douai, FRENCH 1st. ARMY, Valenciennes

Miles 0 10 20
Kilometres 0 10 20 30

THE RETREAT FROM THE ESCAUT MAY 21st TO 23rd.

- Belgian army
- BEF
- French Army
- Line of retreat of 44th. and 4th. British divisions
- German thrusts

DJ

GREAT
BRITAIN

NORTH SEA

Ramsgate

DOVER

British garrison
surrenders
– May 26th. –

CALAIS

Gravelines

Evacuated
by British
May 23rd.

BOULOGNE

Étaples

Montreuil

ARMY GROUP A
(Von Rundstedt)

St Pol

Noyelles

ABBEVILLE

German
bridgehead

R. Somme

German
infantry
divisions

Doullens

AMIENS

German
bridgehead

OSTEND

Evacuation begins
May 26th.

Nieuport

La Panne

DUNKIRK

French
Sector

BRIDGEHEAD

Furnes

BRUGES

BELGIANS

B E L G I U M

Belgian Army
capitulates
May 28th.

Dixmude

Bourbourg

Bergues

R. Yser

F L A N D E R S

GHE

Pz.

Watten

Wormhoudt

Poperinge

2000 railway
wagons

Roulers

R. Lys

Watten

Cassel

Ypres

Courtrai

R. Escaut

St Omer

Hazebrouck

Kemmel
Comines

Menin

ARMY GROUP
(Von Bock)

Pz.

Pz.

Pz.

Aire

Pz.

Armentières

Premesques

Roubaix

LILLE

Pz.

Mot.

Béthune

La Bassée

Carvin

Fr First Army
surrenders
June 1st.

Pz.

Pz.

Mot.

Mot.

Lens

Pz.

Canal

R. Scarpe

Douai

Valenciennes

Denain

Arras

Cambrai

F R A N C E

consolidate

Canal

Peronne

St Quentin

R. Oise

German
bridgehead

La Fère

R. Serre

Canal

N

Miles
0   10   20

0   10   20   30
Kilometres

FINALE IN THE NORTH

——————— Front line, May 25th.   - - - - - - Front line, May 31st.

— — — — Front line, May 28th.

...mandement de l'Armée Belge
Grand Quartier Général

Your Majesty,

Belgium has held to the Engagements she undertook in 1937 by maintaining her neutrality and by meeting with all the forces at her disposal, the moment her independence was threatened. Her means of resistance are now nearly their end.

After the first hours of the morning of the 10th of May, when my country was treacherously attacked without warning, the Belgian Army succeeded in withdrawing and establishing a good line of resistance in cooperation with her allies.

But retreat from day to day was imposed upon the allied armies in Belgium by military events which took place outside the country. The Belgian army withdrew in good order until it reached the position it is now holding. It is an impossibility to retreat further. The development of the battle now in progress is wearing out my army. The whole cadre of officers and staff being in action, there is no possibility of creating a new military force. Therefore the assistance we can give to the allies will come an end if our armies become encircled.

In spite of all the advice I have received to the contrary, I feel that my duty impels me to share the fate of my army and to remain with my people. To act otherwise would amount to desertion.

Whatever trials Belgium may have to face in the future, I am convinced that I can help my people better by remaining with them than by attempting to act from outside, especially with regard to the hardships of foreign occupation, the menace of forced labour or deportation and the difficulties of food supply.

By remaining in my country, I fully realise that my position will be very difficult, but my utmost concern will be to prevent my countrymen from being compelled to associate themselves with any action against the countries which have attempted to help Belgium and her people.

If I should fail in that endeavour, and only would I would I give up the task I have set myself.

Leopold 25.5.40

Draft of letter to King George VI, in King Leopold's and Admiral Keyes' handwriting, May 25th 1940

M. Spaak's letter to Sir Roger Keyes, June 13th 1941

Ministère
des
Affaires Etrangères
et du
Commerce Extérieur
de
Belgique

13-6-1941.

Mon cher Amiral,

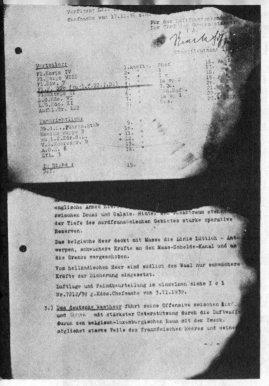

Secret German orders captured by the Belgians
in January 1940

German plan of Eben-Emael fortress

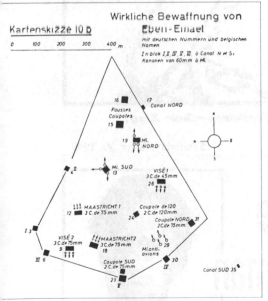

Camarades!

Telle est la situation!
En tout cas, la guerre est finie pour vous!
Vos chefs vont s'enfuir par avion.
A bas les armes!

British Soldiers!

Look at this map: it gives your true situation!
Your troops are entirely surrounded —
stop fighting!
Put down your arms!

German leaflet, May 24th 1940

Order of the Day, May 25th 1940

Soldats,

La grande bataille qui nous attendait a
commencé.

Elle sera rude. Nous la conduirons de toutes
nos forces avec une suprême énergie.

Elle se livre sur le terrain où en 1914 nous
avons tenu victorieusement tête à l'envahisseur.

Soldats,

La Belgique attend que vous fassiez honneur
à son Drapeau.

Officiers, Soldats,

Quoi qu'il arrive, mon sort sera le vôtre.

Je demande à tous de la fermeté, de la
discipline, de la confiance.

Notre cause est juste et pure.
La Providence nous aidera.

Vive la Belgique !

LEOPOLD.

En campagne, le 25 mai 1940.

TARIF DES ABONNEMENTS

Le Petit Parisien

LE PLUS LU DES JOURNAUX DU MONDE ENTIER

MERCREDI
29
MAI 1940

LES BELGES CONDAMNENT LA TRAHISON DE LEUR ROI

Un fait sans précédent dans l'Histoire...

DANS LE NORD, FRANÇAIS ET BRITANNIQUES COMBATTENT AVEC LA MÊME RÉSOLUTION

LES COMMUNIQUES

G. Q. G. français

Sur la Somme, nos troupes développent favorablement leurs opérations

LA DÉCLARATION RADIODIFFUSÉE de M. PAUL REYNAUD

LE GENERAL BLANCHARD
qui commande dans le Nord les armées franco-britanniques

Charles MORICE.

RIEN NE SAURAIT NOUS DÉTOURNER

« Le roi n'est plus

Daily Mirror

Geraldine House, Fetter-lane, E.C.4, Holborn 4321.
42-48, Hardman-street, Deansgate, Manchester, 3.
Blackfriars 2185-6-7-8-9.

KING OF THE FIFTH COLUMN

LATE on Monday night listeners heard from the B.B.C. that the King of the Belgians was "the incarnation of the Fatherland." They heard also that Leopold III was "a man and a leader."

Meanwhile, the French radio assured the Allies of Belgium's will to continue the fight —"whatever happens." The timing of these utterances was unfortunate.

For what happened, a few hours later, was that the incarnation of the Fatherland had ordered the surrender of the Belgian Army; that the man had turned out to be a skunk; and that the leader was revealed as the most distinguished and accomplished of all Generals of the Fifth Column in any European country up to date. Or perhaps the heroic broadcast may have been misunderstood! By King Leopold's Fatherland may have been meant Germany. By incarnation may have been meant camouflage.

At all events—a few hours later still—the Belgian Premier's message confirmed the treachery, denied that his Government had any share in the former King's capitulation, and said that the act of one man does not commit an entire nation.

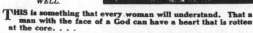

"Gentlemen—Their King!"

THE DAILY MIRROR   Thursday, May 30, 1940

The face that every woman now despises!

Today this column is written by JOHN BOSWELL.

THIS is something that every woman will understand. That a man with the face of a God can have a heart that is rotten at the core. . . .

APPENDIX I

*Winston Churchill's oration before unveiling the memorial to
Admiral of the Fleet Lord Keyes, GCB, KCVO, CMG, DSO, and
his son Lieutenant-Colonel Geoffrey Keyes, VC, MC,* close to
Nelson's tomb in the Crypt of St Paul's Cathedral, at the service of
dedication on April 27th 1950.*

We are gathered here today to unveil the tablet which preserves and proclaims the admiration of our war-torn generation for these two heroic Englishmen – the one a great naval commander, the other a young colonel awarded after his death the Victoria Cross. The tablet also expresses the enduring affection with which their memory is cherished by their many friends, and most of all by those who knew them best.

For more than thirty years I was one of the closest of the Admiral's friends. When I was at the Admiralty in 1911 he was already an officer of high distinction, and in charge of our submarine flotillas at the time when this new and terrible weapon began to break upon the naval world . . .

But we have to go back to the beginning of the century for the first occasion when the light of martial distinction shone upon the young lieutenant who, acting on his own initiative, stormed with thirty men the Chinese fort on the Pei Ho river, for which 4,000 Allied troops had been considered insufficient to attack, and thus opened the channel to the relief of the European garrisons besieged in Tientsin. From then down to the last period of his life Admiral Keyes sought glory in the face of danger and his intense impulse for action was always armed with the highest degree of naval skill and technical efficiency.

He was always in the van of naval progress, and stimulated the tactical development of the destroyer flotillas, of our submarines and most of all of the Fleet Air Arm. His exploits afloat and ashore will always excite the enthusiasm of the youth of Britain, and are full of guidance for the leaders of the Royal Navy. The splendid feat of arms conceived and executed by him thirty-two years ago, that the canal entrance to the German submarine base of Zeebrugge, from which

---

* When Sir Roger Keyes was appointed Director of Combined Operations in July 1940, one of the first to volunteer for the Commandos which were then formed, was his elder son Geoffrey, of the Royal Scots Greys. After winning the Military Cross in June 1941 for a gallant action in Syria, in which his Commanding Officer was killed, Geoffrey took command of the remnants of the 11th Scottish Commando, at the age of twenty-four, with the rank of acting Lieutenant Colonel. On November 17th, 1941, while the Commandos in the Middle East were actually being disbanded, Geoffrey was killed leading the famous 'Rommel Raid', which he had planned, not only to disrupt the Afrika Korps headquarters at Beda Littoria, 250 miles behind the enemy lines, but to capture or kill General Rommel, the enemy C-in-C, on the eve of the British 8th Army's offensive. After landing from a submarine and ascending twelve miles of mountainous terrain, the small raiding force burst into the building used by Rommel and killed and wounded several Germans. Rommel was, however, away in Italy that night, but the decoded German message to that effect arrived in Cairo too late for the raid to be called off. But it shocked and dismayed the Germans and caused them to divert a large number of troops to defend their rear areas. Geoffrey Keyes was awarded the Victoria Cross posthumously.

the U-boats sallied forth to attack our life-lines, was blocked and rendered useless, will long be famous. This outstanding example of audacity and organization is matched at every period in the sixty years of devoted service which Roger Keyes gave to the Navy and to the Nation he loved so well.

In the late war, as Chief of Combined Operations, he gave a most important impulse to amphibious warfare. There radiated from him the Commando spirit to which we owe so many glorious episodes. He animated and impelled from his earliest days all the vast design and construction of landing craft of all kinds, without the timely preparation of which the greatest victories of the Western Allies could never have been gained.

In many ways his spirit and example seem to revive in our own stern and tragic age the vivid personality and unconquerable dauntless soul of Nelson himself.

The tablet which I am to unveil adorns the walls of our famous Cathedral. The light of honour and duty which springs from it will, as the years go by, serve as an inspiration and beacon to our island race.

APPENDIX II

The Blocking of Zeebrugge, April 23rd 1918

'A small naval force, led by a leader of courage and imagination, and taught by him to disdain all thought of failure, had faced prodigious odds and achieved astounding triumph. The story of Zeebrugge, indissolubly linked with the name of Roger Keyes, will surely live for ever, not only as an instance of the value of skilful planning and faultless execution, but as an example of British heroism at its highest, and a record of one of the most daring exploits in the history of naval warfare.'

Cecil Aspinall-Oglander. *Roger Keyes*

The epic St George's Day Raid, which blocked the entrance to the Canal connecting Zeebrugge with Bruges, eight miles inland, thus bottling up the numerous warships and submarines based there, made Vice Admiral Roger Keyes, who planned and led it, world-famous overnight. But less well-known is the even greater contribution which Keyes made to eventual victory in 1918, by halting the passage through the Dover Straits of the U boats whose stranglehold on the Allies' Atlantic lifeline had brought them to the brink of defeat.

In the month of April 1917 alone, U boats had sunk more than 620,000 tons of Allied shipping. Indeed, the situation was so dire that Sir John Jellicoe, the First Sea Lord, warned the War Cabinet in June that unless the Germans were denied the use of the Belgian ports as advanced submarine bases, the Allies would be unable to continue the war in 1918, for lack of shipping.

In 1914 the Germans had secured the Belgian coastline up to Nieuport, due to the Allies' failure to appreciate its importance, and adequately to support the gallant efforts of King Albert and his army to hold on to it. The triangle of ports, Zeebrugge, Bruges and Ostend, rapidly became heavily defended hornets' nests, from which enemy light warships and submarines sallied forth to attack the Allies' patrols and shipping. By the autumn of 1917 the costly offensives by which the British attempted to recapture these bases finally floundered in the mud and the tragic bloodbath of Passchendaele.

The artificial inland port of Bruges was a priceless asset to the Germans, for it could shelter, maintain and refit up to thirty-five light craft such as destroyers and minesweepers, and thirty submarines, many being protected by concrete shelters. Since it took these U boats several days less to reach their Atlantic hunting grounds than it did for those based in Germany, as many as possible were operated from Bruges, and proceeded to their stations via Zeebrugge and the English Channel. They were able to do this with impunity until Keyes took command of the Dover Patrol, because his predecessor, Admiral Bacon, had convinced himself that no U boats were penetrating the elaborate underwater defences which spanned the Straits. In fact, enemy submarines had long been passing over the top of this barrage of nets and mines at the rate of one a night, by running stealthily on the surface.

Outrageous Fortune*

It was not until Jellicoe was replaced as First Sea Lord by Sir Rosslyn Wemyss in December 1917 that this disastrous situation was remedied. Wemyss' first action was to put his Director of Plans, Roger Keyes, in command of the Dover Patrol – promoting him to Vice Admiral at the unprecedentedly early age of forty-six. Keyes had greatly distinguished himself as a young lieutenant during the Boxer Rising in 1900, and thereafter in the important posts to which he was appointed during his meteoric promotion. In January 1915 Keyes, as a Commodore, had been posted as Chief of Staff to the C-in-C of the Anglo-French Fleet to which Winston Churchill had given the task of forcing the Dardanelles without military landings. *

The Dover Patrol was a most important force, since its tasks included supporting the seaward flank of the Allied armies – held by the Belgians – countering the intense enemy activity which emanated from their Flanders naval and air bases, protecting the shipping which carried millions of men and vast quantities of war material across the Straits and, above all, preventing the U boat fleet from using the short Channel route to the Atlantic. To fulfil these manifold responsibilities, Keyes had at his disposal a fleet of a hundred and sixty-eight warships, ranging from an old battleship and monitors carrying fifteen-inch guns to forty-knot Coastal Motor Boats. Also under his command were the ports of Dover and Dunkirk with all their facilities, including airfields and seaplane bases, and a powerful force of Royal Naval Air Service bombers, fighters, reconnaissance planes and airships.

On his arrival in Dover Keyes galvanized his new command into a state of unprecedented activity and efficiency. This resulted in the U boat traffic through the Channel being completely halted within a few months. And since the Army's desperate attempts to recapture the enemy's Flanders submarine bases had finally been abandoned, Keyes immediately started the detailed planning of operations to prevent the predators from leaving their lairs. It was typical of the air-minded Admiral that he made a personal low-level aerial reconnaissance of his objectives.

The fierce and spectacular battles which raged in and around Zeebrugge and Ostend on the night of April 23rd 1918, and the results, have been amply described in a number of authoritative books,† so only the briefest account will be given here.

The direct naval assault on these two powerful fortresses – they and indeed the whole coastline bristled with hundreds of guns – was only possible thanks to the copious use of artificial fog. The main objective was achieved at Zeebrugge when two of the three blockships (old cruisers filled with concrete) were sunk in the mouth of the canal, thus blocking it and trapping all the U boats and warships which were sheltering in Bruges. In order to divert the enemy's attention and capture the guns which dominated the blockships' hazardous line of approach through the harbour, Royal Marine and Naval storming parties were landed on the mile-and-a-half-long mole from the obsolete cruiser *Vindictive*, in the teeth of murderous fire. Meanwhile, the submarine C3, packed with explosives, rammed and blew up the steel viaduct which connected it with the shore.

The subsidiary blocking operation of Ostend that same night failed, because the Germans had moved a vital navigational buoy, as did another attempt on May 9th with the battered hulk of the *Vindictive*, when her Captain was killed at a

* See Note 'a'.
† See *The Blocking of Zeebrugge* by Captain A.F.B. Carpenter VC (Herbert Jenkins), *Zeebrugge* by Barrie Pitt (Cassell), *The Zeebrugge Raid* by Philip Warner (William Kimber) and *The Naval Memoirs of Admiral of the Fleet Sir Roger Keyes* (Thornton Butterworth).

crucial moment. But the overall issue was not adversely affected, for the Ostend canal was not navigable by the U boats, torpedo boats and destroyers which were trapped in Bruges by the Zeebrugge operation.

The effect of the blocking of Zeebrugge would have been even greater had Admiral Keyes been able to bomb the imprisoned craft with his four squadrons of twin-engined bombers. But unfortunately, three weeks before, the three thousand aircraft, one hundred and three airships and sixty-seven thousand men of the RNAS had been transferred to the RAF, which deployed them elsewhere.

Seventy-eight vessels of all sizes took part in the two Raids, with Keyes flying his flag in the destroyer *Warwick* – the only losses being one destroyer and two Motor Launches. Of the force of seventeen hundred and eighty officers and men of the Royal Navy and Royal Marines – all volunteers – two hundred and fourteen were killed and three hundred and eighty-three wounded. For their heroism, eleven officers and men were awarded the Victoria Cross, two hundred and nine received other decorations, while two hundred and eighty-three were mentioned in despatches. Roger Keyes was created a Knight Commander of the Bath, thanked by the King and the Cabinet, and showered with honours by the Allied nations. In 1919 he was created a Baronet and awarded £10,000 for his outstanding services.

The news of this sensational naval victory electrified the country, for there had been no Trafalgar in the war, and Jutland, the only major engagement, had ended in stalemate and a sense of frustration. The feeling that at last the Navy had taken positive action, and that the spirit of Drake and Nelson lived on, gave a tremendous boost to the war-weary population – as well as to the battered Army's morale. For many months the news from the front had been of ever-mounting casualties and never-ending retreat. The Germans had broken through at St Quentin on March 21st, and Ludendorff's great push was threatening Paris. On April 11th, Sir Douglas Haig warned of the terrible danger to the Nation 'at this critical moment', in his famous 'backs to the wall' Order of the Day.

Zeebrugge not only acted as a badly needed tonic for the Allies' depressed spirits, but it marked the turning point in their fortunes, and was the curtain-raiser to the five months of victory which ended with the Armistice in November 1918. Conversely, it was a shattering blow to the Germans, both psychologically and materially, for it not only halved the deadly U boat menace to the Allies' Atlantic lifeline at a stroke, compelling the Germans to operate from Heligoland Bight with a greatly reduced duration of operations, but it robbed their Army of its belief in its invincibility, and in the imminence of the Allies' collapse. Indeed, Ludendorff was so worried by the threat to his right flank that he diverted a large number of troops to protect the coastline and by June 5th his advance had ground to a halt only forty miles from Paris – soon to turn into the retreat which would end in surrender five months later.

Not surprisingly, the Germans put out false reports about the Zeebrugge Raid, claiming that it had been a complete failure, but the coded signal they sent out that morning announced that the Zeebrugge canal had been blocked, and ordered all units to use alternative ports. Although all the evidence from aerial photographs and eye-witnesses shows that the operation succeeded in bottling up a large number of U boats for a considerable period of time, and made Zeebrugge virtually unusable, there was a tendency after the war, even among some British Official Historians, to give undue credence to the German assessment of the Raid, despite its obvious unreliability. But no one denied that it was a tremendous psychological success, and the turning point in the war. Indeed, one Official Historian wrote that it 'brought about that prevision of victory which is not confined to the combatants, but comes suddenly to the whole attendant world as a revelation of the inevitable end'.

The Belgians were particularly uplifted by this stunning and humiliating blow to the German military and naval occupation force, for it raised their hopes of an early liberation. The Belgians have not forgotten, and each year they commemorate the St George's Day Raid near the carefully-tended memorials they erected in Zeebrugge and Ostend, and extend a warm welcome to the ever-diminishing band of visiting heroes. When, in 1983, only six veterans managed to attend the ceremony and the dedication of the resited Zeebrugge memorial, their leader, aged eighty-three, said: 'Unfortunately we are all getting too old for any more official visits.' The Belgian authorities and their Veteran Associations, however, declared that they would carry on commemorating the Raid 'as an act of faith by the Belgian people'.

King Leopold's Broadcast Address to the USA, October 27th 1939 (Extracts)

As I am convinced that my country is defending civilization by the attitude it has taken up towards the conflict that has broken out in Europe, I feel that I may limit myself to explaining the attitude which responds fully to the will, the courage and the honour of the Belgian people. As the Head of State, I am glad to have the opportunity of reviewing the following points:

In 1937 Belgium proclaimed her policy of independence and each of her three big neighbours acknowledged it. They went further, spontaneously gave us formal assurances that they would respect our frontiers and guarantee the independence of Belgium. The Belgian Government's declaration of neutrality, made at the beginning of the war, was the logical conclusion of our policy . . .

We have no territorial ambitions. We are concerned neither directly, nor indirectly, with the origins of the conflict which divides Europe.

If Belgium became involved, her land would be turned into a battlefield; owing to her restricted area, her total destruction would follow whatever the result of the war.

Side by side with Holland, Belgium forms an islet of peace in the interest of all. Situated at the crossroads of Western Europe, a neutral Belgium, loyal and strong as she is today, fulfils an essentially peaceful mission; she limits the extension of the battlefront . . . She constitutes . . . a citadel of peace and a means of conciliation which alone can save our civilization from the abyss towards which it would be precipitated by a general war.

We clearly see our duties and our rights; we await the future with a calm conscience; we are ready with all our strength to see that our independence is respected.

Exactly twenty-five years ago the Belgian Army, under the command of my father, King Albert, after a hard battle, checked the progress of a cruel invasion.

If we were attacked – and I pray God this may not happen – in violation of the solemn and definite undertakings that were given us in 1937, and were renewed at the outset of the present war, *we would not hesitate to fight with the same conviction*, but with forces ten times stronger, and again, the whole country would be behind the Army . . .

May I venture to hope that the American nation, to whom we are drawn by mutual aspirations and similar institutions, will help us and will support us in our attitude for the good of peace and the service of civilization.

APPENDIX IV

Memorandum by Brigadier George Davy on Army/RAF Co-operation

The RAF, as the junior of the three services which had only gained its independence in the latter part of World War I, was still suffering from growing pains. On the one hand its hierarchy had been trying to establish the existence of a separate aerial strategy, for which the time was not yet ripe. On the other hand, the same hierarchy had sought, with only limited success, to persuade the soldiers that the RAF's tactical support to the Army should be no more than tactical and artillery reconnaissance. They were consequently neither trained nor equipped for ground attack or close support bombing. These subjects, and any suggestion of combined training in their technique, were taboo in the years before the war, in such academies of free speech as Camberley Staff College; the RAF simply would not discuss them, and Army officers who felt strongly on the subject were regarded as tactless if they said too much.

So it was left to the Germans to show the way, in the early years of the war. On our side, it was a keen South African squadron in the desert, equipped with Marylands, who started close support bombing on our side, over a year later. During the Belgian campaign I well remember the disappointed and frustrated expressions of the officers of GQG as the BBC announced that the RAF had bombed the marshalling yards at Hamm and other remote places deep inside Germany.

Comments on the Same Subject by Major-General Sir John Kennedy*

As Army member of the Joint Planning Committee, I was involved, during the year before the war, in the preparation of numerous appreciations and plans . . .

A constant bone of contention in our discussions was the role to be played by the Air Force. Both the General Staff and the Naval Staff opposed the fanatical efforts of the Air Staff to press upon us their theory that the war would be decided by the action of air forces, almost unaided by the other two Services. We fought hard and unsuccessfully for the provision of adequate specialized air forces, properly trained and equipped for the support of naval and military operations. The introduction of such a policy was regarded by the Air Staff as a 'prostitution of the Air Force', so a senior officer in the Air Ministry once expressed it to me. This fight went on far into the war. The politicians were much attracted by the Air Force doctrine, and the soldiers and sailors could never persuade the Cabinet or the Defence Committee to settle the dispute in a way we thought right, either before or during the war.

* *The Business of War*. Hutchinson & Co. 1957.

APPENDIX V

No. 1 Military Mission, Vincennes

REPORT BY BRIGADIER GEORGE DAVY

This was the mission from the War Office to General Gamelin. Its head was Major-General Sir Richard Howard-Vyse. From December 1939 the Duke of Windsor was attached to the mission. I was its G.S.O.1.

Every morning the General and I went over to see General Gamelin and his 'Cabinet Partitionier'. Every day I or one of the G.S.O.2's flew to the War Office, spending one night in London and returning the following day. Twice during the winter the Duke of Windsor went on tours of the French front – the first time, accompanied by John de Salis, he went to the Maginot Line proper, south of Metz. The second time he went to the northern end of the Maginot Line and to the central part of the front, including Sedan and Mézières. On this journey I went with him.

General Gamelin and his Chef de Cabinet, Colonel Petitbon, each had a separate office. The rest of the Cabinet Partitionier, three Lieutenant-Colonels and two Majors, shared a larger room, which was also the map room. Gamelin often used to come in while I was there and expound his thoughts.

For the first few weeks the Cabinet Partitionier were a bit cagey about the French dispositions. When they got to know us however they kept their map uncovered and I gradually memorized each division of the eighty or so in eastern France until there was an almost equivalent map in the War Office.

As the pattern of the French dispositions, defences and plans emerged, and as we discussed these with Gamelin's staff and visited various parts of the front, several disquieting features became apparent. All these were reported to the War Office. The most important were:

(a) The lack of depth in the Maginot Line system itself and in its extension northwards along the Belgian–Luxembourg frontier.
(b) The poor fire-power of the major works.
(c) The absence of defences on the Meuse sector and the very sparse distribution of troops on the Ninth Army front.
(d) The absence of any prepared positions in rear of the Maginot Line.
(e) The absence of a mass of manoeuvre in reserve.

All these points were discussed very tactfully and amicably with Gamelin and his staff by Howard-Vyse and me. They were very kind and tolerant, bearing in mind of course that we were not a great military nation on dry land, such as they were. But they suffered from two incurable diseases which in combination proved fatal.

The first was Maginot-mindedness. Nothing could shake their conviction that the Maginot Line was impregnable, likewise its northward extension to the sea. 'Have you any defences in rear of the Maginot Line, for instance concerning Paris?' we asked. 'No, no,' was the answer, 'there is no need; there is the Maginot

Line!' Once, on being pressed, they pointed to a line of hills on the map and said it had been reconnoitred; no work was intended. Then we would point to a large cluster of some dozen divisions in reserve in the Metz region, and say something about a mass of manoeuvre. There was nothing of the sort. The divisions in reserve were regarded as reliefs, taking their turn in the line during the phoney war, replacing tired divisions in the line during battle. What was the need, they said, for a mass of manoeuvre? With a sweep of the hand along the frontier: 'the Maginot Line!'

As a matter of fact, some of the divisions in reserve were formed into the Seventh Army early in the new year . . . These however were not intended for use as a mass of manoeuvre in reserve, but were to play a part in the advance of the Allied line to the Dyle. The Seventh Army was to move along the Belgian coast to the help of the Dutch. This they did, although the effort was largely wasted. But there was never any mass of manoeuvre available to take counter-measures against Guderian's penetration.

The second malady was just as ineradicable and hardly less important. It amounted to a firm conviction that not more than two enemy divisions would come through the Ardennes towards the Meuse front, and that in any case the roads were unsuitable for armour. On this we did battle for some months . . .

On these grounds they discarded as impossible a German advance through the Ardennes; they agreed that, consequently, there was no need for carefully prepared defences on the Meuse sector, the river would be impassable, the destruction of the bridges was a certainty, and only a few handfuls of troops would be needed to watch this part of the front.

The War Office was kept well informed of our misgivings. On the Duke of Windsor's next tour – which included General Huntziger's front – I was sent as his staff officer. In his official report after the tour, signed by him and forwarded by Howard-Vyse to the CIGS, all our misgivings were emphasized. I doubt however if any high-level approach on the subject was ever made to the French; I also doubt whether, if such an approach had been made, it would have had any effect, so obstinate were they in their two maladies.

So the stroke which won victory for the Germans was the crossing of the Meuse. In the two or three days which followed, each French general, as he heard the news, became a beaten man, his faith gone, and without hope. Even the few who had misgivings about the Maginot system knew it was all they had and, as Reynaud himself recognized, once the line had been turned the outcome was from that moment beyond doubt.

With their leaders already defeated, it was hardly surprising that the resistance and cohesion of the troops on the Meuse front – and indeed elsewhere – should break down.

APPENDIX VI

The Blocking of Zeebrugge, May 1940

THE ADMIRAL'S DIARY

May 25th 1940

I went to the British Mission after lunch, and found two shame-faced French Naval Officers, who told me that our attempt to block Zeebrugge had failed. During the last few days, I had been in touch with the Admiralty and had visited both Zeebrugge and Ostend, to make sure that proper arrangements for blocking the canals at both places had been made. I had urged the immediate blocking of Zeebrugge, and had advised waiting to block Ostend until the last ship had left, as I had suggested that it would be quite possible to discharge ammunition and food there, and take it up to the BEF in lorries. In the meantime the French had mined the lock gates at Zeebrugge and the sluices at Ostend, under the orders of the French Admiral at Dunkirk, who had assumed command of both ports and the coast from the outset, much to the annoyance of the Belgian Military Authorities. However, the King gave me authority to do anything I thought fit.

Two blockships from England arrived during the night of 24th–25th, but the French Naval Authorities had forgotten to inform the French General commanding the troops on the Coast. On the other hand they had warned him that the Germans might attempt to land from seaward, so when the blockships and escorting destroyers arrived, they were heavily engaged by field and machine guns, and the Commanding Officer, not unnaturally thinking that the Germans were in possession and that therefore there would be no means of escape for his crews, sank his ships off the Mole, and the escorting destroyers withdrew.

I went down to Zeebrugge at once and found that, as I had directed, the outer lock gates had been blown up, and the inner one was intact; fortunately I was just in time to prevent the French blowing it up, despite the protests of the Belgian Authorities, who pointed out that at high tide the country occupied by the French and Belgian troops to the eastward would be flooded. I then arranged for a large crane to be sunk abreast the inner lock gate, which would block the canal for some time, which was the best I could do for the moment. While I was there, we were heavily bombed by low-flying German bombers, which were plastering Zeebrugge and Ostend with heavy and incendiary bombs.

I had promised to speak to the Prime Minister at La Panne that evening, and on my way through Ostend saw that the petrol tanks and waggons of the Ostend Texaco petrol installation had been set on fire by the bombers. The big Military Hospital was also ablaze.

On arrival at La Panne I talked to the Prime Minister, told him that General Dill was returning, and that nothing I could do would induce King Leopold or Queen Elisabeth to leave their Country. I also told the Admiralty that I thought the Ostend blockship should be sunk in the lock at Zeebrugge, and that if they could not produce another, we should have to rely on the French to wreck the

488 Outrageous Fortune

Ostend sluices. But by this time, I had been driven to the conclusion that it was easier to block these two ports against the opposition of the Germans, than to do it with the co-operation of the French!

In a letter to his wife Admiral Keyes described how he had escaped death by a hair's breadth when Stukas 'dropped heavy bombs *very* near to us; they circled again, but by that time we had got into one of the shelters made by the Germans against our bombing in 1918.'

After the fiasco described above, the Admiralty adopted Sir Roger's proposals, and blockships were sunk effectively in Zeebrugge and Ostend.

APPENDIX VII

THE SURRENDER AND AFTER

Extracts from an account given to *British Survey* by a Belgian Reserve Artillery Officer (a University Professor in private life), who escaped to England in July, 1940.

The Germans are not so invincible as they may look at a distance. Their infantry is good, but not as good, perhaps, as in 1918; not as good certainly as the few good Belgian regiments, such as the Chasseurs Ardennais.

The German artillery was consistently outclassed by the Belgian. Effective counter-battery was rare. Before Ghent a battery of Belgian 155 mm. howitzers, bombarded by a German battery of similar calibre, immediately opened fire, shooting much faster and better, and within fifteen minutes it had silenced the enemy's guns one by one. The Germans themselves admit the havoc played among them by Belgian shelling, which was the most effective check to their advance . . .

The surrender could not have been avoided. From May 22nd the front held by the Belgian Army was extended in order to free British troops for a counter-attack in the South, to eighty kilometres. Each weak division had 7–9 km. to hold, and there were no reserves. Intensive dive-bombing, intense enemy pressure on land, no sign of Allied aircraft . . . such were the general features of the six-day battle on the Lys.

On May 27th munitions began to fail. The artillery on my right stopped firing altogether at 3 pm. Munitions and other supplies must come from the rear; but our rear was only fifteen miles deep and only a very small fraction of the country, which explains why supplies were running low. Besides, the 800,000 people living normally in this densely populated strip of land had been more than doubled by refugees, to say nothing of the Army.

That afternoon the infantry on my right, unsupported by its guns, began to give way. By 5 pm there was an 8 km. breach in the line and HQ had not a single organized battalion to throw in. The most fantastic tactics, forced on us several times before, were again used. Artillery with no infantry to cover it took stand and held up the Germans single-handed – for a time. My own guns were in action for this last stand from 7.15 to 8.50. When ammunition gave out it was almost dark and disaster was averted for the night. We withdrew a few miles and were ready to take up the fight at 4 am. No munitions had, however, arrived. At 5 am we learned that it was all over . . . I do not think that organized resistance could have gone on for more than twelve hours. It would have cost the lives of thousands of soldiers and ten times more civilians, and that to no purpose. We waited almost a week on bad and insufficient food, most of which came from British supplies at Dunkirk. I killed three horses a day and traded a few more to the peasants for potatoes . . . There were no German guards, and our men were commanded by their own officers. Instructions eventually came for the demobilization. All Flemish soldiers were to be set free, all Walloons to remain prisoners . . . Among the Walloons were to be freed all those working in agriculture, industry, commerce and the public services, all doctors, police, etc. – in short, practically everyone except lawyers and teachers . . . In the meantime all the regulars – officers, NCOs and men – had been sent to Germany to remain prisoners until the end of the war.

There is a strong feeling of resentment against the public officials who abandoned their posts. This applies not only to local authorities, but to post office and bank officials who absconded with cash and to doctors who made off with hospital equipment and radium. It applies even more strongly to the Pierlot Government who were the first to run. This Government is hated and despised by all Belgians in Belgium. It is ignored by the Germans. It has no influence with the Belgians in Southern France who, believing themselves tricked into flight, are now fast returning home. Many stories are current about the hopeless blunders of the Government during the period of Belgian resistance and after.

Pierlot's worst mistake, however, was the attitude which he took up towards the King after the capitulation. After a moment of hesitation, born of their ignorance of the true military situation, the immense majority of the population rallied round the King . . . As Army Commander he thought it better to stick to his men and share their lot – which was, by the way, that of the majority of his people . . . Obliged to choose, he preferred the more painful course, fraught with the greater hardships, dangers and responsibilities. The King is now a prisoner. When speaking to his visitors he always insists on the purely military nature of his surrender . . .

The Germans are considered everywhere and by all as the enemies. Their present good behaviour is acknowledged, but not trusted. Everyone hopes they will eventually be defeated . . . Public feeling towards the French and British is more variable . . . . There is undoubtedly some superficial ill-feeling towards both countries, the most obvious reason being disappointment at not being effectively helped against the common enemy. Moreover, the British are accused of much wanton and useless destruction, as well as plundering . . . In a general way British troops on the Continent too often behave in a ruthless manner: this might be important to note in view of future operations, all the more so because of the restraint shown by the German occupation troops.

France and Great Britain are considered as Belgium's allies, fighting the same fight, with the same ideals. The deep-rooted traditions of the last war, enhanced by the general hatred for the Nazi Government, make this quite clear.

APPENDIX VIII

The Daily Telegraph
May 10th 1941

BELGIUM AND HER NEUTRALITY
'TRAGIC BLUNDERS' DENIED

From the Belgian Foreign Minister
To the Editor of *The Daily Telegraph*:

Sir –

In the article by Mr J. B. Firth which appeared in *The Daily Telegraph* this morning it is stated that the safety of the Belgian State had been fatally prejudiced by mistakes of policy long before war broke out.

It is further asserted that a most tragic blunder was made by King Leopold when, in 1936, he abandoned Belgium's military alliance with France and staked everything upon Belgium's strict observance of neutrality.

These allegations are in complete contradiction with the facts:

1 Belgium, who in 1920 had concluded a limited military agreement with France, has never had any alliance with that country. From 1926 she was, like Great Britain, one of the signatories of the Treaty of Locarno. Like Great Britain, she was obliged to render military assistance to Germany in the event of a French aggression as well as to France in the event of a German aggression.

2 Once more I must emphatically deny the allegation that Belgium was opposed to the prolongation of the Maginot Line.

3 Belgium was formally released from her engagements under the Treaty of Locarno by both England and France. By their joint declaration of April 24th 1937, these two Powers indicated their complete agreement with the position adopted by Belgium.

4 This position was adopted not in order to 'stake everything upon Belgium's strict observance of neutrality', but to secure the acceptance by the country of new and heavy military sacrifices: the construction of powerful fortifications on the eastern frontier and the extension to 17 months of the period of compulsory military service for all, as a result of which 46 per cent of the male population between the ages of 20 and 45 were under arms and the army in the field numbered 650,000 men. This military effort was certainly as great in proportion as that of any other Power.

The position adopted by Belgium did not prevent the Belgian Government from making it clearly understood in the autumn of 1939 that Belgium, although free from all obligations, would not remain indifferent if Holland alone were attacked. To my knowledge there is no other small neutral State which has taken a similar attitude.

5 A Franco-Belgian alliance would have prevented nothing of what happened in 1940. The fundamental cause was the crushing superiority which, especially in

the air, Germany had secured over England and France, and which prevented the assistance promised to Belgium – and which was, I can assure you, duly prepared – from being effective.

6 The Belgian Government has always, in accordance with the Constitution, assumed the whole responsibility for Belgium's foreign policy, and since 1936 the policy adopted has been increasingly endorsed by an enormous majority in Parliament. It is, therefore, a gross misrepresentation of the facts to hold King Leopold responsible for this policy.

When King Leopold was compelled, after 18 days of stubborn fighting, to surrender the Army, he did not 'throw in his hand'. He felt that he could not desert the Army he had commanded, and which had no possibility of escape or embarkation. He became a prisoner of war, and his refusal to exercise any power under the enemy is the symbol of the resistance which Belgians in occupied territory are opposing to the invader.

Your obedient servant,
P. H. SPAAK,
Belgian Minister for Foreign Affairs.
105, Eaton Square, SW1. May 9th.

APPENDIX IX

Evening Standard
Friday, January 3rd, 1969

M. SPAAK COMES CLEAN ABOUT KING LEOPOLD AND
THE MOVE TO LONDON.
Sam White's Paris

PARIS, Friday

Even though it comes a quarter of a century too late it is good of M. Paul-Henri Spaak, the Belgian elder statesman, to have finally come clean regarding the events of 1940 in which he played in the subsequent rewriting of history what might be described as a truly legendary role.

He has done this in a television appearance of almost embarrassing frankness which has received altogether too little attention in France and Britain, both of which countries shared in some of the myth-making and have since maintained a stony silence of facts.

M. Spaak, who for thirty years was either Foreign Minister or Prime Minister, directing the foreign policy of Belgium, retired from active political life in 1965. Since then he has been employed by an American business concern.

The events M. Spaak dealt with in his televised confessions are the Belgian Army surrender of 1940, the Belgian Government's subsequent flight to the French Government's temporary refuge in Bordeaux and its subsequent decision to go to London.

Some of the facts concerning these various moves have long been matters of strong suspicion.

They have never, however, been confirmed by any of the main actors in the drama – although they were rekindled as live issues during the bitter post-war disputes over whether King Leopold should be allowed to return to Belgium.

Leopold knew the facts but, to his great credit, he maintained a strict silence on them during the conflict and, indeed, until the present day. M. Spaak began by revealing that, contrary to legend, Belgium's pre-war policy of neutrality was not something imposed by a pro-German monarch on a reluctant Government but was fully supported by that Government and by M. Spaak himself . . .

M. Spaak confirms – contrary to the version invented by the French Prime Minister at the time, M. Paul Reynaud, and foisted on a reluctant Churchill – that the King, as Commander-in-Chief, gave due warning to his allies of his intention to surrender.

The most astonishing of M. Spaak's revelations, however, concerns the Belgian Government's decision to come to Britain. He makes no bones about this, saying that, after the collapse of France, the Belgian Government was convinced that the Germans had won the war. Its unanimous conclusion was that peace negotiations

493

had to be opened with the Germans. The Government then asked King Leopold's permission to return to Brussels . . .

Not being able to stay in France, not being able to return to Belgium, the Belgian Government had no choice but to flee to London. 'We were saved by the King's refusal to listen to us,' concludes M. Spaak.

Notes

a p. 22 On March 18th 1915, the Anglo-French Fleet commanded by Vice
Admiral de Robeck, with Commodore Roger Keyes as his Chief of
Staff, reduced the Dardanelles forts to impotence, but after suffering
losses from an undetected line of mines, de Robeck declined to attempt
to force the Narrows without military landings, despite Keyes' persistent urgings, and this war-winning opportunity was missed. After the
Great War the Turkish War Minister, Enver Pasha, declared that 'if
the British had shown more courage . . . they could have got through to
Constantinople' – a view endorsed by his General Staff, who admitted
that their stocks of ammunition were almost exhausted. In his book
Gallipoli Alan Moorehead sums up: 'Seen in this new light, the
campaign was no longer a blunder or a reckless gamble, it was the most
imaginative conception of the War, and its potentialities were almost
beyond reckoning.' He concluded that Keyes left behind him 'an
endless speculation as to what might have happened had he been the
Admiral in command and de Robeck his Chief of Staff'.

b p. 63 King Leopold's summing-up of the salient points in his speech to his
Ministers on October 14th 1936:
Our military policy, like our foreign policy, which necessarily deter-
mines it, must aim, not at preparing for a more or less victorious war,
following a coalition, but at keeping war away from our territory.
The reoccupation of the Rhineland, by breaking the Locarno Treaty
in both the letter and the spirit, has almost put us back to the same
international situation that we were in before the last war.
Our geographical situation compels us to maintain a military force
strong enough to dissuade any of our neighbours from making use of
our territory to attack another State. In fulfilling this mission Belgium
makes a notable contribution to the preservation of peace in Western
Europe and *ipso facto*, she creates for herself a right to the respect
and, in case of need, the assistance of all States interested in that
peace.
On these fundamental points I believe that Belgian opinion is
unanimous.
But our commitments must go no further. Any unilateral policy
would weaken our position abroad, and arouse – rightly or wrongly –
dissension at home. An alliance, even if it were purely defensive,
would not achieve the desired objective; for, however promptly an ally
might come to our aid, it would only be forthcoming after the initial
shock of an invasion, which would be devastating.
Unless she herself has a defence system capable of withstanding the

invader, Belgium would find himself, at the outset, deeply invaded and immediately laid waste . . .

That is why we must, as the Minister of Foreign Affairs said recently, pursue an 'exclusively and wholly Belgian policy'.

This policy must be firmly directed towards keeping us out of conflicts between our neighbours; it is in accordance with our national ideals.

It can be maintained by a reasonable financial effort, and it will rally the support of the Belgian people, who are inspired by an intense desire for peace . . .

Let them remember how decisively Belgium's scrupulous observance of her neutral status weighed in her favour, and in favour of our allies, throughout the War and the subsequent settlement.

Our moral position at home would have been incomparably weaker and the world would not have shown us as much sympathy, if the invader had been able to point to an alliance between ourselves and one of his opponents.

It is therefore, I repeat, solely to preserve us from war, from whatever quarter it may come, that our military system must be organized, and it is important that public opinion should receive unquestionable assurance of this.

Our military organization, which is based on the Conscription Law of 1929, although excellent in many respects, no longer corresponds to the new threat of a sudden invasion. It assures neither the permanent defence of our frontiers, nor security for the mobilization and concentration of our army. A more or less unexpected incursion might, in a few hours, seize vital keypoints and irreparably paralyse the bulk of our forces.

It is urgent that this defective organization should be remedied without delay . . . It was to decide on the means to accomplish this that I called you together.

c p. 77   In an attempt to stir up war fever, Hitler had ordered a parade of mechanized might through the capital at dusk, when the Berliners would be pouring onto the streets on their way home from work. The result was a complete fiasco, as William L. Shirer recorded in his *Berlin Diary*: 'I pictured the scenes I had read of in 1914 when the cheering throngs on this same street tossed flowers at the marching soldiers . . . But today they ducked into the subways, refused to look on, and the handful who did stood at the kerb in utter silence. It has been the most striking demonstration against war I've ever seen.' Shirer then described the scene as Hitler reviewed his troops from a balcony of the Chancellery: 'There weren't two hundred people there. Hitler looked grim, then angry, and soon went inside . . . They [the German people] are dead set against war.' Dr Schmidt, in *Hitler's Interpreter*, records a similar impression: 'The completely apathetic and melancholy behaviour of the Berlin populace which he [Hitler] observed . . . made a deep impression on him.' After Munich he noted that his master 'was profoundly disappointed that the German people, in the face of war . . . instead of showing delight at the prospect of taking up arms against the enemy . . . had demonstrated in no uncertain manner its aversion to war and its joy at the maintenance of peace.'

d p. 90   Belgium was probably the worst affected of all the European neutral
           countries by the war and the blockade. Her trade suffered grievously
           and her constant state of semi-mobilization involved enormous ex-
           penditure. Belgium has few natural resources, and her prosperity
           depends largely on her ability to import raw materials. The only way in
           which imports could be paid for was by the export of manufactured
           articles, but the Allies' restrictions on the international exchange of
           goods spelt economic disaster. The port of Antwerp was almost at a
           standstill. During September 258 ships entered the port, as compared
           with 1,025 ships in the corresponding period the previous year.

e p. 97   Erich and his brother Theo Kordt, young diplomats of strong Catholic
           faith and dedicated anti-Nazis, had long played a resistance role in the
           German Foreign Service. Indeed, in 1934 Erich had formed the core of
           the Resistance circle at the Wilhelmstrasse, the leadership of which was
           gradually taken over by von Weizsäcker when he became State Secre-
           tary in 1938. In that year Erich, in agreement with von Weizsäcker,
           formulated the appeal to the Chamberlain Government urging them to
           stand firm during the Munich crisis, which was delivered secretly to
           Lord Halifax during the night of September 7th by Theo (then *Chargé
           d'Affaires* at the German Embassy in London). Unlike most of their
           fellow anti-Hitler activists, who were massacred after the failure of
           their coup in 1944, the Kordt brothers lived to tell their tale, thanks to
           being out of reach of Himmler's executioners (Erich was in China and
           Theo in Switzerland at the time).

f p. 97   There was an almost equally sensational happening on the following
           day, November 9th, when Captain Best and Major Stevens of British
           Intelligence, who thought that they were negotiating with agents of the
           dissident German generals in the Dutch town of Venlo, on the German
           border, discovered that their contacts were SS men, who thereupon
           dragged them across the frontier into Germany by armed force. These
           two unconnected events, which were immediately bracketed together
           by Goebbels' Propaganda Ministry to 'prove' that it was the British who
           had attempted to assassinate the Führer, threw the genuine opposition
           hierarchy into confusion and disarray. (The would-be assassin was a
           lone hand, unconnected with any dissident group.) Unfortunately, the
           clamp-down on all sources of explosives, even those of the *Abwehr*,
           prevented Erich Kordt, who was relying on Colonel Oster for the supply
           of a bomb with which to assassinate the Führer, from carrying out the
           attempt they had planned to make three days later.

g p. 105 In fact, in 1940 France had at least as many tanks as the Germans in her
           army – many being heavier, but slower than those of the enemy. But
           her doctrine, like that of the British, was to scatter them in small
           numbers throughout the Army as slow-moving mobile pill-boxes for
           infantry support, as in the 1914–1918 war. Not one of the armoured
           divisions she began to form in that year was fully equipped or trained
           for battle when the *Blitzkrieg* struck France in May. Unlike the
           Germans' tanks, those of the French lacked the means to communicate
           with each other – let alone co-ordinate their operations with other
           units, including their Air Force. In contrast to a French armoured

division, which consisted of 150 tanks, a German Panzer division in addition to an average of 260 tanks comprised a brigade of motorized infantry, including a battalion of motorcycle troops, as well as armoured cars, reconnaissance vehicles, self-propelled field and anti-aircraft artillery and a battery of 88 mm anti-aircraft guns, which were also used with deadly effect against ground targets. Thus a Panzer division was completely self-supporting. Mobile workshops, squads of repair-men and fuel supplies accompanied the mechanized units and also were flown in by the *Luftwaffe* to sustain the Panzers as they penetrated far behind the enemy's lines.

h p. 127 In his diary Pownall describes Hore-Belisha as 'an obscure, shallow-brained charlatan political Jewboy'. Brian Bond, the editor of that diary, refers to the 'childish lengths' to which Gort and Pownall went in order to make life unpleasant for Hore-Belisha when he was their guest on the Western Front in 1939. At the same time Pownall was trying to influence British Press chiefs and King George's Private Secretary, Major (later Lord) Hardinge, against the Secretary of State for War, in furtherance of the 'Generals' Plot' to oust him from that office.

The jovial Lord Gort was less overtly chauvinistic than Pownall, but in describing the two generals' feud against their War Minister, which led to the latter's downfall, Sir John Colville writes in *Man of Valour*: 'Gort was much to blame', because he did not allow Hore-Belisha 'all the credit which was his due', and 'sometimes confused principle and prejudice'. Much of this prejudice against his civil chief was, according to Colville, because Gort was 'the kind of Englishman who, while accepting foreigners as a regrettable necessity, finds foreign touches and tendencies in a compatriot wholly repellent'.

i p. 159 On May Day 1940 a pamphlet drawn up by the Communist International was distributed throughout the Democracies:

> Workers of the World! In the sinister atmosphere of a new Imperialist war . . . it is becoming evident that the small neutral countries are becoming the small change of the Imperialists. In response to the brutal violation of the Scandinavian countries, Germany has sent her troops into Denmark and has occupied strategic positions in Norway. The capitalist scoundrels are dragging the nations into a new world Imperialist butchery . . . To escape the catastrophe prepared by the Bourgeoisie there is no other way but to struggle against the Imperialist war.

j p. 168 On March 4th 1941 the *News Chronicle* published an article by Pierre Jansen, described as a Dutch Army Officer resident for twenty years in Maastricht. In all seriousness, Jansen described in great detail how German workers, after helping to build the Albert Canal and having married Belgian girls, became endive farmers in the region. 'Over the years the Germans tunnelled all around and under Fort Eben-Emael . . . Tons of "fertilizer" were taken down into the caves . . . Last spring the great day came for which all these patient farmers had been working . . . At the push of a plunger the "fertilizer" was detonated and whole sections of the fort were flung skywards . . .'

k p. 184 'General Headquarters . . . was scattered amongst ten villages covering an area of about forty square miles . . . It comprised in September 1939 over 500 officers and 2,000 other ranks. By May 1940 it had grown very considerably larger . . . this scattered lay-out, combined with a most inadequate system of telephones (manned mainly by 'broad' Scots) did not make work any easier . . . I do not think that any GHQ can ever in military history have been so scattered . . .' *Unexpected*, Lieutenant-General Sir Douglas Brownrigg (then Adjutant-General of the BEF).

l p. 185 'This time at least,' wrote *The Times* on May 11th, 'there has been no strategic surprise. The armies of Holland and Belgium and those of the Allies in North-Eastern France have been preparing and maturing their plans. All of them were standing yesterday morning in a state of readiness, so that a sentence, perhaps only a code word on the telephone, would have sufficed to set the machinery in motion.' On May 29th, the day after the capitulation of the Belgian Army, however, *The Times* contradicted itself: 'The fears entertained by the Belgian Government made them refuse, before the invasion, to concert plans for their defence with the Allies, though they must have foreseen as clearly as we the probability of unprovoked attack. Nevertheless, when the assault was actually delivered, they appealed at once to Great Britain and France for help, and we could do no other than accord it instantly, and endeavour to extemporize for Belgium a defence that might have been systematically planned.'

m p. 190 DESTRUCTION IN BELGIUM DURING THE EIGHTEEN DAYS CAMPAIGN
Le Courrier de Génève of February 22nd 1941, reporting the findings of the Belgian Commission of Reconstruction, gave the following information:

> Taking the country as a whole, it is estimated that only 500 communes out of 2,500 are intact. The military action of the various armies has destroyed 9,832 houses, seriously damaged 24,156 premises, and 117,000 others less seriously. As far as industry is concerned Belgium has suffered the total loss of 352 factories. About a hundred railway stations have been hit . . . The number of bridges and tunnels blown up is double the figure given . . . for France: it reaches the high total of 1,455.
>   Finally, more than 10,000 kilometres of road have been put out of action, so that certain districts are today almost deprived of communications. (The considerable destruction of bridges, tunnels and roads was mainly carried out by the Belgian Army; however, there were some carried out by the Allied Armies.) According to the information gathered during this enquiry, the general aspect in Belgium calls to mind the destruction of the Great War, and the restoration work is immense.
>   Belgium only covers an area of 30,447 square kilometres and has a population of about 8,300,000. The extent of the damage will be better assessed if one increases proportionally these figures on the scale of a large country like France, England or Germany.

n p. 204 The author met the Admiral's Belgian driver in 1950 and learned from him that he had recently visited the Admiral's grave at Dover and placed flowers on it. He said that 6,000 kilometres were recorded on the speedometer of the Admiral's Packard by the end of the eighteen

days' campaign. His reminiscences were of a series of hectic and
dangerous journeys – frequently under air attack – at all hours of the
day and night. The two Belgians, who were indispensable to him,
formed a great attachment for the Admiral and neither was able to
conceal his emotion when he took leave of them in dramatic circumstances in the early hours of May 28th. The Admiral was deeply
touched by the devoted service of these two men, and often spoke of it
subsequently.

o p. 210 Queen Wilhelmina had to resign herself to exile, first in a cottage at
Roehampton and later in a country house called Stubbings at Maiden-
head. She spent an unhappy war, culminating in the great distress she
felt when, due to a missed opportunity, the British Army failed to
liberate the whole of her country, with the result that many of her
people starved to death. The Queen was also aggrieved when the
Allied leaders prevented the Dutch Armed Forces, which were under
their command and had made a splendid contribution to their war
effort, from liberating her overseas possessions in the East and not only
refused to lift a hand to help the Dutch regain their colonies, but
actively impeded their efforts. The Queen was much distressed by all
these cruel developments and the way that her country had been
treated by the victorious Allies, and in 1948 she decided to lay down the
burden of the Crown and abdicated in favour of her daughter, Princess
Juliana.

p p. 218 Sir Lancelot describes his book, *An Ambassador in Bonds*, as containing the 'narrative of an episode unparalleled in modern times – the
arrest, segregation, and subsequent internment of an Ambassador'.
Not surprisingly, the Germans ruled that Oliphant had forfeited his
diplomatic immunity by hiding from them, but they treated him kindly
and allowed him to lead a comfortable and comparatively unfettered
life in Germany before repatriating him sixteen months later. But,
writes Oliphant, the Germans 'aroused my indignation . . . From the
outset, therefore, I felt it my duty to adopt an intransigent attitude . . .
and to raise constant objection to my treatment.'

q p. 221 The *Daily Telegraph* War Correspondent reported on May 7th 1940
from Malmédy, near the Belgian-German frontier:
'Ingenious methods of preventing the rapid penetration of German
mechanized forces in the event of an invasion have been devised by the
Belgian Army in the wooded gorges of the Ardennes along the
Belgian-German frontier. The roads connecting Belgium with Germany have been completely blocked by the felling of trees for stretches
of 100 yards or more. The roads were nothing but a mass of pine trunks
and twisted branches and to clear away the debris in the face of fire
from the well-concealed Belgian machine-gun emplacements would be
no easy task.
'Most of this work was carried out as recently as Friday and Saturday, and roads which were still open on Thursday are now impassable,
leaving only one route free for motor traffic and another for trams. The
felling of the trees means a loss of millions of francs to the local timber
industry. At other points the roads have been obstructed by masses of

boulders and stone blocks held together with cement and placed so that a car has to slacken speed to walking pace to twist and turn between them.

'In this wild countryside of hills, pine forests, and mountain streams – very different from the flat landscape of Holland – an invading army could use only the roads and railways, and there would seem now to be little possibility of the Belgian defences being overrun by a sudden stroke.

'The spirit of the Belgian frontier forces seemed to be excellent. The Belgian Army has been trained in the tradition of their 1918 victories over the Germans at Merken, Passchendaele and Staden, and the usual neutral dread of the German war machine is conspicuously absent.'

r p. 229 'On the embankment,' wrote Alfred Fabre-Luce in the *Journal de la France*, 'the passers-by were astonished by a deluge of charred paper fragments.' Roger Peyrefitte, an eyewitness, has described the scene at the Quai d'Orsay as follows: 'On the lawn Paul Reynaud and Mandel, livid, were watching the officials sprinkle petrol over the Archives heaped up on the lawn and poking the fire with gardening instruments.'

Pertinax recalls that 'so great was the impatience of Reynaud and his circle, that when the fire did not go quickly enough they thought of having some of the papers thrown into the Seine'. 'At Warsaw and Oslo,' Fabre-Luce continues, 'the *Wehrmacht* had a rich harvest of documents. Warned by these precedents, the Quai d'Orsay wanted to avoid the publication of a new White Paper. But it was not done only to deny State secrets to the enemy. Those responsible for the declaration of war were thinking too of the High Court that would sit one day in France. It must lack proof . . .'

But all these frantic efforts by the French political leaders were in vain, for the Germans found copies of the burnt documents and other secret State papers abandoned in a railway wagon in a siding at Charité-sur-Loire, and in due course published them in the form of a White Paper, which contains some inconvenient evidence for Reynaud and others.

When criticized for having instigated and urged on the panic measures of destroying the State archives, Reynaud denied this and accused Alexis Léger, the Secretary-General, of having given the order to burn them, without notifying him. But Peyrefitte concludes 'the mistakes of the Quai d'Orsay demanded a flesh and blood victim. Paul Reynaud threw the blame for the panic on to the Secretary-General and the latter was sacrificed for having obeyed.' The unfortunate Léger was sacked the next day and had the doubtful honour of becoming the first of Reynaud's civilian scapegoats.

s p. 244 Extract from Lieutenant-Colonel George Davy's *Supplementary Report*:

'The lack of confidence of the BEF [in the Belgians] was illustrated by the rearguard on the Dendre, where Lieutenant Colonel Horrocks had disposed his rearguard facing the Germans and bent sharply back on his left towards a front where he thought there might be Belgians, but was not sure. In fact half his force was facing left. I knew there were Belgians there . . . But there was no British liaison officer with them. I went myself, despite the advice given me by a major in an anti-tank battery, who said I was going straight for the Germans. The Belgian Chasseur division promptly sent an officer to Colonel Horrocks and visits were exchanged. This resulted in some necessary re-adjustment of plans. Although it was not my job, I saw the need of intervention, and the liaison was established. Unfortunately it did not prevent one of our left-hand posts from shooting a Belgian NCO on a motor-cycle combination. The post was still facing the Belgians. If I had not taken the precaution of waving a Union Jack, which I always carried on my bit of polo stick, they would probably have shot me too, as I came back.

'Yet again, 44th Division faced the Belgians as well as the Germans on the eve of their withdrawal from the Escaut. They shot a Belgian liaison officer coming to see them. In my opinion it should be a principle that neighbouring formations of Allied armies, down to the brigade or even battalion level, should exchange liaison officers automatically without being told to do so. General Montgomery's division had taken no steps whatever, and not only was his rearguard facing the wrong way, but if I had not intervened personally with the commander of the Chasseurs Ardennais division, these neighbouring divisions would have withdrawn on diverging lines and created a gap of fifteen miles in the Allied front. Moreover the Belgian division commander had no idea that General Montgomery was going to withdraw at all, even when the British division was already on the move. The Belgians often tried to send liaison officers to our flank divisions, but they had some difficulty because GHQ either did not know or were reluctant to divulge the location of their divisional headquarters. Such information was most difficult to procure, and cipher telegrams asking for it remained unanswered. Staff officers at GHQ appeared not to know.'

t   p. 245 Not all the incidents were as serious as that on the River Dendre. Indeed the following comments from a member of the Needham Mission illustrate the kind of misunderstanding which arose due to the differences of motivation, language and temperament between the two nations, with which the Mission had to contend:

> May 17th: General Van Overstraeten and another Belgian General came in, very irritated because a British officer has blown the bridge at Vilvorde (in the Belgian zone) under threat of his revolver, obliging the Belgians to retire . . . it also appears that one of the bridges blown up by the British is only half destroyed.
> May 21: The Belgian Major Defraiteur made urgent representations to the British Mission not to blow up the Sweveghem power-station, as there appeared to be no point in it. This scorched earth policy of the British caused grave friction, as it did not appear to take into account the fact that the Belgians would have to continue to live in their country.

u   p. 302 In his review of the English translation of Paul Reynaud's memoirs, A. J. P. Taylor wrote of the six weeks' campaign in 1940:

'Every French politician and every French general has recorded his experiences of these dramatic weeks. But their record would have been more useful . . . if they had stuck to narration and not sought in every case to shift the blame on to others . . . every French testimony of 1940 is part of a gigantic litigation, not experiences recollected in tranquillity. The memoirs of the Prime Minister . . . are naturally the most litigious, the most controversial of all. Everyone blamed Paul Reynaud, and he flung the blame back on to everyone else.

'Soon after the war he published two fat volumes with the dramatic but misleading title 'France Saved Europe'; to which the reader was supposed to add: and Paul Reynaud saved France. Then . . . he crammed it into a still more bloated work . . . The narrative is interrupted to get in further telling points . . . footnotes spring up like mushrooms after rain. Conversations in anterooms, in lifts, in taxis, epigrams late at night, grumbles in the early morning, all go in; until the book resembles a suitcase that will never shut, however many men sit on it.

'Clear sighted as ever, he was the first to realize that the battle of France was lost . . . he concealed from them [his Cabinet colleagues] that the British would agree to an armistice for France on certain conditions. The result was to make the worst of both worlds. France might have obtained an armistice on more favourable terms if it had been made earlier . . .'

v p. 341 The wording of this signal was clearly inspired by Spaak, who had obtained a lift from London to Paris in Reynaud's aircraft on the previous day, since its phraseology is similar to that used by Spaak in his subsequent references to this matter. In fact the Belgian Ambassador, Baron Cartier de Marchienne, strongly denied that he, or anyone at the Belgian Embassy, had ever assumed or declared that King Leopold 'regarded the war as lost' and contemplated a 'separate peace'. Indeed, as Hans Roger Madol, a Luxembourgeois historian, diplomat and old friend of King Albert, who was in London throughout the war, wrote in his book, *The League of London*: 'Baron de Cartier, who had known King Leopold since early manhood, never for a single moment believed a word of M. Reynaud's imputations against King Leopold's loyalty. In fact, Baron de Cartier and the staff of his Embassy, together with the Belgian Colony in Great Britain, headed by Professor Cammaerts, stoutly took up the cause of their King which Admiral of the Fleet Sir Roger Keyes so ably defended during that tragic period and afterwards.' (*The League of London*, Hutchinson)

w p. 366 In his book, *Publish and be Damned*, Hugh (now Lord), Cudlipp, chronicles the following facts about the wartime role of the *Daily Mirror*, of which he was the features editor:

On March 20th 1942 the Labour Party Home Secretary, Herbert Morrison, informed Parliament that he had warned those responsible for the publication of the *Daily Mirror* (and the *Sunday Pictorial*) that it would be suppressed, as the Communist *Daily Worker* had been, under Regulation 2D, which covered 'a newspaper which systematically published matter calculated to foment opposition to the successful prosecution of the war', if it continued with its present line.

The newspaper, Morrison declared, 'intent on exploiting an appetite for sensation and with reckless indifference to the national interest, and to the prejudicial effect on the war effort, has repeatedly published scurrilous misrepresentations, distorted and exaggerated statements and irresponsible generalizations . . . Reasonable criticism on specific points and persons is one thing; general, violent denunciation, manifestly tending to undermine the Army and depress the whole population is another.'

Eighteen months earlier, in the House, the tone of the *Daily Mirror* and its sister paper, the *Sunday Pictorial*, was described by the Prime Minister, Winston Churchill, as 'so vicious and malignant' that it would be almost indecent if applied to the enemy. A few days later Clement Attlee, the Labour Party Deputy Prime Minister, summoned Cecil King, a director, and H. G. Bartholomew, the *Daily Mirror*'s Editor, to Whitehall and accused it of showing 'a subversive influence, which might at a critical time like this endanger the nation's war effort'. In January 1941 Churchill returned to the charge and in a letter to Cecil King wrote 'there is a spirit of hatred and malice against the Government . . . which surpasses anything I have ever seen in English journalism. One would have thought in these hard times that some hatred might be kept for the enemy.' Churchill then declared that the two newspapers' activities and methods were those of a Fifth Column. Despite an intensive investigation, however, the Government failed to discover the identity of the *Daily Mirror*'s financial backers and controllers.

x p. 372 In a letter to the President of the National Association of Belgian Reserve Officers, dated April 22nd 1949, General Weygand wrote:
'I cannot deny that the decision of the Belgian Command to withdraw from the fight, aroused in me a feeling of violent reprobation. I knew the Belgian Army was fighting, under difficult conditions, a very offensive enemy but it was not alone in this tragic situation.

'Five years later I returned from German prisons. My examination of the facts, and reading of the correspondence of Admiral Keyes have informed me. On that date (May 27th) the Belgian Army was in a critical situation . . . Its right wing, threatened with encirclement, could no longer be supported by the BEF which had already started the retreat towards Dunkirk. No French force was then in a state to give substantial support. The Belgian Command, no doubt, considered itself abandoned by its allies. This is how its decision is explained.'

y p. 389 *The Black Baroness* was first published at the end of 1940, by which time King Leopold had been publicly exonerated and praised by, amongst others, the Belgian Government-in-exile, and was reissued as much as ten years after the war.

In the climactic scene, set at Belgian GQG on May 27th, Wheatley describes how Gregory Sallust and the beautiful Erika, 'Leopold's new girl-friend', who is working for the Allies, try to stop the King signing the deed of surrender, which, along with a letter from Hitler, has been brought to him by 'two German emissaries'. Sallust then begs Leopold, who is 'terrified' by the bombs falling nearby, to come with him to England. ' "I can't – *I can't!*" cried the distraught King . . . "No – no, *no!* The German emissaries are waiting upstairs . . . I'm going to make an end before they kill us all." ' Erika then declares: 'Sire, if you once put your signature to that paper you will go down in history as a traitor and a coward. You mustn't do it . . .' She tries to prevent him from signing the fatal document, but is shot by the Black Baroness, who emerges from behind a curtain. 'The King now stood with her limp form in his arms. "You've killed her! You've killed her!" he screamed hysterically at the Baroness. "I'll have you shot for this." '

After slipping her smoking automatic back into the pocket of her silk coat, the Baroness 'curtsied as calmly as though Leopold had offered to take her out to dinner. "As it please Your Majesty," she said in her soft, musical voice . . .' When another stick of bombs falls outside, 'the King scrawled his signature, flung the pen down and shouted above the din: "There! Take it! And for God's sake stop this ghastly bombing!" "At once, Sir." The German bowed stiffly as he picked up the paper. "We can get a message through to our headquarters in about ten minutes."'

z p. 403 Scandal and disgrace soon overtook Paul Reynaud. On June 16th 1940 he tendered his resignation to President Lebrun, and advised him to call upon Marshal Pétain to form a new government, in the certain knowledge that Pétain would thereupon ask the Germans for an Armistice – on which advice the President immediately acted. Although Reynaud spent the rest of his life denying that he had so advised Lebrun – he even did so under oath when questioned by a Parliamentary Investigating Committee in 1950 – he had given himself the lie in the letter he wrote to Pétain on May 18th 1941: 'A year ago I took the responsibility . . . of advising the President of the Republic to designate you as my successor . . .' After handing over his office he obtained from the new Premier the offer of the post of French Ambassador in Washington. He therefore accepted the role of representing the collaborationist Vichy Government (to which he later maintained he had always been opposed) in the United States. But Pétain withdrew his offer when he learned that two of Reynaud's Chefs de Cabinet had been arrested in Spain while *en route* to America and that their baggage had been impounded by the Spanish authorities. This was a great embarrassment for Reynaud, because the cases contained secret State and private documents, gold bars, bearer bonds and eighteen million francs in cash, which Reynaud had withdrawn from secret government funds, together with the jewellery and valuables of his mistress, the Comtesse de Portes.

But Reynaud was 'utterly discredited', as one leading British newspaper put it, when the car in which he was travelling crashed and his mistress was killed. This brought his association with this notorious woman into the headlines of the world press, and the same newspapers which had accepted his slanderous broadcast about King Leopold as true, now turned on him and flayed his reputation. The scandals in his public and private life were avidly seized upon and lurid stories were published about the sinister influence the Comtesse was said to have exercised over Reynaud during the last weeks of his regime, and about her relationship with Otto Abetz, who had played a Fifth-Column role in Paris up to May 10th and became German Ambassador to France after the fall of that country.

On August 3rd 1945, Hanson Baldwin wrote in the *New York Times* that the efforts of Reynaud and the other French leaders who were trying to rid themselves of blame for the fall of France, 'to justify and rationalize their actions in their published memoirs and at Marshal Henri-Philippe Pétain's trial, are historically incomplete, judicially biased, and emotionally sickening'.

List of Sources

1 Pierre Daye, *Léopold II*, Arthème Fayard, Paris, 1934.
2 Emile Cammaerts, *The Keystone of Europe*, Peter Davies, 1939.
3 B. H. Liddell Hart, *History of the World War*, Faber & Faber, 1924.
4 General Baratier, *Le Temps*.
5 General Brécard, *En Belgique Auprès du Roi Albert*, Calmann-Lévy, Paris, 1934.
6 General Azan, *Les Belges sur l'Yser*, Berger-Levrault, Paris, 1929.
7 *Les Carnets de Guerre d'Albert I, Roi des Belges*, Charles Dessart, Brussels, 1953.
8 G. H. Dumont, *Léopold III, Roi des Belges*, Charles Dessart, 1944.
9 Comte Capelle, *Au Service du Roi 1940–45*, Charles Dessart,
10 *Daily Telegraph*. H. D. Ziman's review of *Mr Europe*, by J. H. Huizinga.
11 Henri De Man, *Cavalier Seul*, Editions du Cheval, Ailé, Geneva, 1948.
12 Alfred Fabre-Luce, *Une Tragédie Royale. L'Affaire Léopold III*, Flammarion, Paris, 1948.
13 Paul Henri Spaak, *Combats Inachevés*, Vol. I, Fayard, Paris, 1969.
14 Hubert Pierlot, *Pages d'Histoire*, Le Soir, July 5th to 19th, 1947.
15 Winston S. Churchill, *The Gathering Storm. The Second World War*, Vol. I, Cassell, 1948.
16 Major L. F. Ellis, *The War in France and Flanders, 1939–1940. The Official History*, HMSO, 1953.
17 William L. Shirer, *Berlin Diary 1934–41*, Hamish Hamilton, 1941.
18 Dr Paul Schmidt, *Hitler's Interpreter*, Heinemann, 1951.
19 *Documents diplomatiques français, 1932–1939*.
20 Keith Feiling, *Life of Neville Chamberlain*, Macmillan, 1946.
22 *Chief of Staff*. The Diaries of Lieutenant-General Sir Henry Pownall. Vol. I, 1933–1940, Edited by Brian Bond, Leo Cooper, 1972.
23 Ellis, op. cit.
24 J. K. Miller, *Belgian Foreign Policy Between Two World Wars, 1919–1940*, Bookman Associates, New York, 1951.
25 *Documents on British Foreign Policy, 1919–39. Second Series*, Vol. XVIII, HMSO.
26 C.P. 296 (37), December 3rd, 1937.
27 Paul Reynaud, *La France a sauvé l'Europe*, 1947. *Au coeur de la mêlée*, 1951, Flammarion, Paris.
28 Miller, op. cit.
29 *The Belgian Campaign and the Surrender of the Belgian Army*. Published by the Belgian-American Education Foundation, Inc., New York, 1940.
30 *The Diaries of Sir Alexander Cadogan, 1938–1945*, Cassell, 1971.
31 Ibid.
32 Schmidt, op. cit.
33 Shirer, op. cit.

34 Feiling, op. cit.
35 Schmidt, op. cit.
36 Feiling, op. cit.
37 *Ciano's Diaries, 1939–1943*, Heinemann, 1947.
38 Winston S. Churchill, *Their Finest Hour. The Second World War*, Vol. II.
39 Churchill, Vol. I, op. cit.
40 Major-General Sir Edward Spears, *Assignment to Catastrophe*, Vol. I, Heinemann, 1954.
41 *The Belgian Campaign*, op. cit.
42 *Recueil de Documents établi par le Secrétariat du Roi concernant la période 1936–1949*.
43 Harold Deutsch, *The Conspiracy against Hitler in the Twilight War*, Minnesota University Press, 1968.
44 Ibid.
45 Ibid.
46 Ibid.
47 Telford Taylor, *The March of Conquest*, Simon & Schuster, New York, 1958.
48 *The Memoirs of Ernst von Weizsäcker*, Head of the Foreign Office, 1938–1943, Gollancz, 1951.
49 *The von Hassell Diaries, 1938–1944*, Hamish Hamilton, 1948.
50 Telford Taylor, op. cit.
51 Benoist-Méchin, *Soixante Jours Qui Ebranlèrent l'Occident*, Albin Michel, Paris, 1956.
52 Major-General J. F. C. Fuller, *The Second World War*, Eyre & Spottiswoode, 1947.
53 John de Courcy, *Behind the Battle*, Eyre & Spottiswoode, 1942.
54 Gordon Waterfield (Reuter's War Correspondent with the French Army), *What Happened in France*, John Murray, 1940.
55 Shirer, op. cit.
56 Von Weizsäcker, op. cit.
57 *The Daily Telegraph*, August 25th 1939. Letter to the Editor.
58 *Le Figaro*, June 19th 1945.
59 Paul Baudouin, *Private Diaries* (March 1940 to January 1941), Eyre & Spottiswoode, 1948.
60 Ellis, op. cit.
61 Ibid.
62 *The Memoirs of Field Marshal Viscount Montgomery*, Collins, 1958.
63 Arthur Bryant, *The Turn of the Tide*. Based on the War Diaries of Field Marshal Viscount Alanbrooke, Collins, 1957.
64 J. R. Colville, *Man of Valour*. The Life of Field Marshal Viscount Gort, VC, Collins, 1972.
65 Robert Jackson, *The Air War over France*, Ian Allan, 1974.
66 Brian Bond, *France and Belgium, 1939–1940*, Davis-Poynter, 1975.
67 Ellis, op. cit.
68 Ibid.
69 Ibid.
70 Bond, op. cit.
71 *Chief of Staff*, op. cit.
72 Bond, op. cit.
73 Ellis, op. cit.
74 Bond, op. cit.

75 *Les Relations Militaires Franco-Belges, de Mars 1936 au 10 Mai, 1940.* Editions du Centre Nationale de la Recherche Scientifique, Paris, 1968.
76 Bond, op. cit.
77 Bryant, op. cit.
78 Von Hassell, op. cit.
79 Spears, Vol. I, op. cit.
80 *Daily Telegraph*, March 31st 1973, Review of Pownall's Diaries: *Taking the Lid off the War Office.*
81 *The Liddell Hart Memoirs*, Vol. II, Cassell, 1965.
82 Ellis, op. cit.
83 Von Hassell, op. cit.
84 Spaak, Vol. II, op. cit.
85 Paul Reynaud, *Au coeur de la mêlée*, op. cit.
86 Field Marshal Ironside, *The Ironside Diaries*, Constable, 1962.
87 Churchill, Vol. I, op. cit.
88 B. H. Liddell Hart, *History of the Second World War*, Cassell, 1970.
89 Baudouin, op. cit.
90 Von Weizsäcker, op. cit.
91 *The Times*, June 21st 1940.
92 *Cadogan Diaries*, op. cit.
93 Churchill, Vol. I, op. cit.
94 Ibid.
95 Benoist-Méchin, op. cit.
96 Ibid.
97 Baudouin, op. cit.
98 William L. Shirer, *The Collapse of the Third Republic.* (M. Lazareff's account of this episode is quoted therein.) Secker & Warburg, 1970.
99 Spears, Vol. I, op. cit.
100 General Gamelin, *Servir*, Plon, Paris, 1946–7.
101 Churchill, Vol. II, op. cit.
102 Bond, op. cit.
103 Deutsch, op. cit.
104 Jackson, op. cit.
105 Emile Cammaerts, *The Prisoner at Laeken. King Leopold, Legend and Fact.* With a Preface by Admiral of the Fleet Sir Roger Keyes, Bt. GCB KCVO CMG DSO, Cresset Press, 1941.
106 General Van Overstraeten, *Albert I, Léopold III. Vingt Ans de Politique Militaire Belge, 1920–1940.* Desclée de Brouwer, Bruges, 1946.
107 Telford Taylor, op. cit.
108 Von Weizsäcker, op. cit.
109 Spaak, op. cit.
110 Harold Nicolson, *Diaries and Letters, 1939–45*, Collins, 1967.
111 Keith Feiling, op. cit.
112 Spears, Vol. I.
113 Baudouin, op. cit.
114 *Belgium. The Official Account of What Happened, 1939–1940.* Published for the Belgian Ministry of Foreign Affairs by Evans Bros, 1941.
115 Anon. *The Diary of a Staff Officer* (Air Intelligence Liaison Officer) at Advanced Headquarters North BAFF, 1940, Methuen, 1941.
116 Pownall, op. cit.
117 Colville, op. cit.
118 Pownall's Diaries, op. cit.

119 Peter Hadley, *Third Class to Dunkirk*, Hollis & Carter, 1944. See also Nicholas Harman's *Dunkirk. The Necessary Myth*, Hodder & Stoughton, 1980.
120 Shirer, *Berlin Diary*, op. cit.
121 *Royal United Services Institution Journal*, February, 1954.
122 Montgomery, op. cit.
123 Ibid.
124 Colville, op. cit.
125 Bryant, op. cit.
126 Montgomery, op. cit.
127 Nigel Hamilton, *Monty. The Making of a General, 1887–1942*, Hamish Hamilton, 1981.
128 General Charles de Gaulle, *War Memoirs*, Vol. I, Collins, 1955.
129 Brigadier L. A. Hawes, *The Story of the 'W' Plan. The Army Quarterly*.
130 Pownall's Diaries, op. cit.
131 Spears, op. cit.
132 Montgomery, op. cit.
133 Bryant, op. cit.
134 Telford Taylor, op. cit.
135 Colville, op. cit.
136 Pownall, op. cit.
137 Telford Taylor, op. cit.
138 HRH Princess Wilhelmina of the Netherlands, *Lonely But Not Alone*, Hutchinson, 1959.
139 Sir John Wheeler-Bennett, *King George VI. His Life and Reign*, Macmillan, 1959.
140 *The White House Papers of Harry L. Hopkins*, Editor: Robert E. Sherwood, Eyre & Spottiswoode, 1948–9.
141 Princess Wilhelmina, op. cit.
142 B. H. Liddell Hart, *The Other Side of the Hill*, Cassell, 1948.
143 *Sunday Pictorial*, March 22nd 1959.
144 Spears, op. cit.
145 Montgomery, op. cit.
146 Van Overstraeten, op. cit.
147 Jackson, op. cit.
148 Heinz Guderian, *Panzer Leader*, Michael Joseph, 1952.
149 Alistair Horne, *To Lose a Battle*, Macmillan, 1969.
150 Guenther Blumentritt, *Von Rundstedt. The Soldier and the Man*, Odhams, 1952.
151 Colonel de Bardies, *La Campagne de 1939–1940*, Arthème Fayard, Paris, 1947.
152 Ibid.
153 Major Jacques Minart, *P. C. Vincennes*, Berger-Levrault, Paris, 1945.
154 Liddell Hart, *The Other Side of the Hill*, op. cit.
155 André Beaufre, *1940: The Fall of France*, Cassell, 1967.
156 Gamelin, op. cit.
157 *The Diary of a Staff Officer*, op. cit.
158 Albert Kammerer, *The Truth About the Armistice*, Médius, Paris, 1944.
159 Minart, op. cit.
160 Reynaud, op. cit.
161 Baudouin, op. cit.
162 Feiling, op. cit.

163 Churchill, Vol. II, op. cit.
164 Colville, op. cit.
165 Marc Bloch, *Strange Defeat*, Norton Library, New York, 1968.
166 *Recueil*, op. cit.
167 Ibid.
168 Pownall, op. cit.
169 *Recueil*, op. cit.
170 Kammerer, op. cit.
171 *The Diary of a Staff Officer*, op. cit.
172 Ironside, op. cit.
173 Lieutenant-General Sir Douglas Brownrigg, *Unexpected. A Book of Memories*, Hutchinson, 1942.
174 Brigadier George Davy, unpublished Memoirs.
175 Ellis, op. cit.
176 Colville, op. cit.
177 Bond, op. cit.
178 Lord Gort's *Despatches*. Supplement to *The London Gazette*, October 17th 1941.
179 Brownrigg, op. cit.
180 William L. Langer, *Our Vichy Gamble*, Alfred A. Knopf, New York, 1947.
181 Baudouin, op. cit.
182 Commandant J. Weygand, *The Role of General Weygand*. Conversations with his Son, Eyre & Spottiswoode, 1948.
183 Baudouin, op. cit.
184 General Maxime Weygand, *Recalled to Service*, Heinemann, 1952.
185 Baudouin, op. cit.
186 Churchill, Vol. II, op. cit.
187 Air Marshal Sir John Slessor, *The Central Blue*, Cassell, 1956.
188 Churchill, Vol. II, op. cit.
189 *The Memoirs of General the Lord Ismay*, Heinemann, 1960.
190 Pownall, op. cit.
191 Ironside, op. cit.
192 Ellis, op. cit.
193 Slessor, op. cit.
194 Churchill, Vol. II, op. cit.
195 Ironside, op. cit.
196 Ellis, op. cit.
197 Churchill, Vol. II, op. cit.
198 Ironside, op. cit.
199 Bryant, op. cit.
200 General Weygand, op. cit.
201 Van Overstraeten, op. cit.
202 *Rapport de la Commission d'Information instituée par S. M. le Roi Léopold III, le 14 Juillet 1946*.
203 Weygand, op. cit.
204 Van Overstraeten, op. cit.
205 Weygand, op. cit.
206 Ibid.
207 Commandant Weygand, op. cit.
208 General Weygand, op. cit.
209 Commandant Weygand, op. cit.
210 Spears, Vol. I, op. cit.

211 General Weygand, op. cit.
212 Commandant Weygand, op. cit.
213 Pierlot, op. cit.
214 Bryant, op. cit.
215 Ellis, op. cit.
216 Bond, op. cit.
217 Commandant Weygand, op. cit.
218 Ibid.
219 Spears, op. cit.
220 Wheeler-Bennett, op. cit.
221 General Weygand, op. cit.
222 Baudouin, op. cit.
223 Spears, op. cit.
224 Baudouin, op. cit.
225 Reynaud, op. cit.
226 Spears, op. cit.
227 Ibid.
228 Feiling, op. cit.
229 Cadogan, op. cit.
230 Spears, op. cit.
231 Bond, op. cit.
232 Ibid.
233 Pownall, op. cit.
234 Van Overstraeten, op. cit.
235 Bond, op. cit.
236 Van Overstraeten, op. cit.
237 De Man, op. cit.
238 *Rapport*, op. cit.
239 Spaak, op. cit.
240 Henri-François Van Aal, *Télé-Mémoires de De Vleeschauwer, Gutt, Spaak, Crisp*, Brussels, 1971.
241 Spaak, op. cit.
242 J. H. Huizinga, *Mr Europe. A Political Biography of Paul Henri Spaak*, Weidenfeld & Nicolson, 1961.
243 Van Overstraeten, op. cit.
244 De Man, op. cit.
245 Bond, op. cit.
246 Pownall, op. cit.
247 Ellis, op. cit.
248 Churchill, Vol. II, op. cit.
249 Anthony Eden, *The Eden Memoirs*, Vol. II, *The Reckoning*, Cassell, 1965.
250 Ellis, op. cit.
251 Van Overstraeten, *Albert I–Léopold III* 1946, and *Dans l'Etau*, Plon, Paris, 1960.
252 Ellis, op. cit.
253 Colville, op. cit.
254 Gort's *Despatches*, op. cit.
255 Pownall, op. cit.
256 Van Overstraeten, *Albert I–Léopold III*, op. cit.
257 Van Overstraeten, *Dans l'Etau*, op. cit.
258 Kennedy and Landis, *The Surrender of King Leopold*, Joseph P. Kennedy Memorial Foundation, 1950.

259 Robert Delmarcelle, *La Libre Belgique*, a series of articles recording his interviews with Colonel Werner Kiewitz, December 22–26th, 1948.
260 Colonel Rémy, *Le 18e Jour. La Tragédie de Léopold III, Roi des Belges*, Editions France Empire, Paris, 1976.
261 Delmarcelle, op. cit.
262 *Recueil*, op. cit.
263 Ibid.
264 *The Belgian Campaign*, op. cit.
265 Commandant Weygand, op. cit.
266 General Weygand, op. cit.
267 Baudouin, op. cit.
268 Spears, op. cit.
269 Ibid.
270 Baudouin, op. cit.
271 Huizinga, op. cit.
272 Ibid.
273 Rémy, op. cit.
274 Telford Taylor, op. cit.
275 David Fraser, *Alanbrooke*, Collins, 1982.
276 Pownall, op. cit.
277 Paul Struye, *L'Evolution de Sentiment Public en Belgique sous L'Occupation Allemande*, Lumière, Brussels, 1945.
278 *Télé-Mémoires*, op. cit.
279 Jean Stengers, *Léopold III et le Gouvernement. Les Deux Politiques Belges de 1940*, Duculot, Paris, 1980.
280 Cudahy, op. cit.
281 Huizinga, op. cit.
282 Alexander Werth, *The Last Days of Paris*, Hamish Hamilton, 1940.
283 Comte Capelle, *Dix-huit Ans Auprès du Roi Léopold*, Fayard, Paris, 1970.
284 *Recueil*, op. cit.
285 Huizinga, op. cit.
286 Ibid.
287 Ibid.
288 *Contribution à l'Etude de la Question Royale*, Groupe Nationale Belge.
289 *Recueil*, op. cit.
290 Huizinga, op. cit.
291 Davy, op. cit.
292 Bond, op. cit.
293 CP 65/7, May 28th, DC No. 10 and CP 65/7, May 27th 1940.
294 Prime Minister's Personal Minute, M. 689/4, May 27th 1941. 369A.
295 Camille Gutt, *La Belgique au Carrefour, 1940–44*, Fayard, Paris, 1971.
296 Cadogan, op. cit.
297 Churchill, Vol. II, op. cit.
298 Archduke Otto Hapsburg, *Naissance d'un continent*, Bernard Grasset, Paris, 1975.
299 Hopkins (*The White House Papers*), op. cit.
300 Wheeler Bennett, op. cit.
301 Sir Harold Nicolson, *King George V. His Life and Reign*, Constable, 1952.
302 *Evening Standard*, September 27th 1940.
303 Stengers, op. cit.
304 Spaak, op. cit.
305 Stengers, op. cit.

306 *Ambassade à Londres*. The secret archives of the Belgian Embassy in London May–October 1940, prepared for limited circulation by the Foreign Ministry.
307 *Foreign Office Archives*. Public Records Office, Kew.
308 *Télé-Mémoires*, op. cit.
309 Huizinga, op. cit.
310 *Recueil*, op. cit.
311 Léon Degrelle, *La Cohue de 1940*, Robert Crausaz, Lausanne.
312 Huizinga, op. cit.
313 Stengers, op. cit.
314 Pierlot, op. cit.
315 PRO FO.
316 Ibid.
317 Ibid.
318 *United States National Archives*.
319 PRO FO.
320 *Recueil*, op. cit.
321 Ibid.
322 *Télé-Mémoires*, op. cit.
323 PRO FO.
324 *Télé-Mémoires*, op. cit.
325 Ibid and *Recueil*, op. cit.
326 *Recueil*, op. cit.
327 *Télé-Mémoires*, op. cit.
328 Ibid.
329 *Recueil*, op. cit.
330 Ibid.
331 Ibid.
332 Ibid.
333 *Supplément au Recueil de Documents*.
334 *Rapport Pierlot*. Confidential report on relations between the King and the Government in 1940–1941, drawn up by Pierlot. An English translation of a copy obtained by the OSS (the US secret service) is in the National Archives Washington.
335 *Ambassade à Londres*, op. cit.
336 Ibid.
337 *Recueil*, op. cit.
338 *Supplément au Recueil*, op. cit.
339 *Recueil*, op. cit.
340 Ibid.
341 Ibid.
342 *Supplément au Recueil*, op. cit.
343 PRO FO.
344 PRO FO.
345 PRO FO.
346 *Recueil*, op. cit.
347 Cadogan, op. cit.
348 PRO FO.
349 PRO FO.
350 PRO Cabinet 1941, No. 10.
351 US National Archives 855.001.
352 Cecil Aspinall-Oglander, *Roger Keyes*, The Biography of Admiral of the

Fleet Lord Keyes of Zeebrugge and Dover, GCB, KCVO, CMG, DSO, The Hogarth Press, 1951.
353 Ibid.
354 Colville, op. cit.
355 Cammaerts, op. cit.
356 *Belgium*, op. cit.

Other publications studied include the following:
King Leopold III, *Albert Ier, Mon Père*, Revue Générale, Brussels, October, 1975.
Gilbert Kirschen, *Entretiens avec le Roi Léopold. Réflections sur l'éducation d'un prince*, Revue Générale, Brussels, January, 1984.
Jean Vanwelkenhuyzen, *Le Problème Belge vu par Charles de Gaulle*, Revue Générale, Brussels.
Baron Pierre van Zuylen, *Les Mains Libres*, Desclée de Brouwer, Paris, 1950.
J. Wullus-Rudiger, *Les Origines International du Drame Belges*, Vanderlinden, Brussels, 1950.
Princess Marie-José, *Albert et Elisabeth de Belgique, Mes Parents*, Plon, 1971.
S. Cunliffe-Owen, *Elisabeth, Queen of the Belgians*, Herbert Jenkins, 1954.
Jacques Pirenne, *Mémoires et Notes Politiques*, André Gérard, 1975.
Robert Goffin, *Was Leopold a Traitor?* Hamish Hamilton, 1941.
J. Wullus-Rudiger, *Defense de la Belgique, 1940,* Alfred Bador, 1940,
De Fabribeckers, *La Campagne de l'Armée Belge en 1940*, Rossel, Brussels.
William L. Shirer, *The Rise and Fall of the Third Reich*, Secker & Warburg, 1959.
Roger Motz, *Belgium Unvanquished*, Lindsay Drummond, 1942.
David Devine, *The Nine Days of Dunkirk*, Faber & Faber, 1959.
The Goebbels Diaries, Hamish Hamilton, 1948.
The Ribbentrop Memoirs, Weidenfeld & Nicolson, 1954.
Ciano's Diary, 1937–38, Methuen, 1952.
Piers Brendon, *Winston Churchill, A Brief Life*, Secker & Warburg, 1984.
Ronald Lewin, *Churchill as Warlord*, Batsford, 1973..
Martin Gilbert, *Finest Hour, Winston S. Churchill, 1939–1941*, Heinemann, 1983.

This recently published work, while disappointingly sparse and sometimes inaccurate with regard to what was actually happening on the Continental battlefields in 1940, presents a disturbing picture of the climate of ignorance, misconception and confusion prevailing in Whitehall – in which Churchill issued his often ill-judged and potentially disastrous orders, as self-appointed overlord.

Books bearing on the career of Admiral of the Fleet Lord Keyes:
Cecil Aspinall-Oglander, *Roger Keyes*, The Hogarth Press, 1951.
Peter Fleming, *The Siege at Pekin*, Rupert Hart-Davis, 1960.
Alan Moorehead, *Gallipoli*, Hamish Hamilton, 1956.
Sir Roger Keyes, *Adventures Ashore and Afloat*, with a Foreword by Winston S. Churchill, Harrap, 1939.
Sir Roger Keyes, *Naval Memoirs, 1910–1915* and *1916–1918*, Thornton Butterworth, 1933 and 1935.
Hilary St George Saunders, *Green Beret, The Story of the Commandos*, with a Foreword by Earl Mountbatten, Michael Joseph, 1949.
Professor Paul G. Halpern (Editor), *The Keyes Papers*, Volumes I, II and III, The Navy Records Society, 1972, 1980 and 1981.

Index